AF559557

# SOCIO-ECONOMIC PROFILE OF RURAL INDIA (SERIES II)

**Volume Four**

**EASTERN INDIA**

## ABOUT THE CENTRE FOR RURAL STUDIES

The Centre for Rural Studies (formerly Land Reforms Unit) of the Lal Bahadur Shastri National Academy of Administration was set up in the year 1989 by the Ministry of Rural Development, Government of India, with a multifaceted agenda that included among others, the concurrent evaluation of the ever-unfolding ground realities pertaining to the implementation of the Land Reforms and Poverty Alleviation Programmes in India. Sensitizing the officer trainees of the Indian Administrative Service in the process of evaluating of land reforms and poverty alleviation programmes by exposing them to the ground realities; setting up a forum for regular exchange of views on land reforms and poverty alleviation between academicians, administrators, activists and concerned citizens and creating awareness amongst the public about the various programmes initiated by the Government of India through non-governmental organisations are also important objectives of the Centre for Rural Studies. A large number of books, reports related to land reforms, poverty alleviation programmes, rural socio-economic problems etc. published both externally and internally bear testimony to the excellent research quality of the Centre.

---

## ABOUT THE EDITORS

**Dr. C. Ashokvardhan** is an IAS Officer of 1980 Batch and belongs to Bihar cadre. During his career as Indian Administrative Officer, he has been posted in several important Government Departments. Prior to joining Indian Administrative Service, he was teaching in Colleges as a Lecturer in Political Science. He is the author of many books and articles pertaining to issues on Land Reforms, Police Reforms, Agriculture, Rural Development etc. At present he is the Director, Consolidation (Bihar), Government of Bihar.

**Ashish Vachhani:** He completed M.Phil (International Organizations) School of International Studies, Jawaharlal Nehru University, New Delhi, before joining the Indian Administrative Service. He joined as Sub-Collector, Sivakasi, Virudhunagar District, in 1999 before moving over to the Finance Department in Government of Tamil Nadu as Under Secretary/Deputy Secretary (Budget)/ Joint Secretary. While in Finance Department as the State Budget Officer, he was responsible for preparing the Annual Budget of the State Government, piloting it through the Legislature for approval and overseeing its implementation. He was closely associated with revenue collection, Plan formulation, scheme expenditure, preparation and posing of development projects for external funding from multilateral institutions etc. He has worked as District Collector of Dharmapuri District and Tiruchirappalli District. He joined the Academy in March 2008 and has keen interest in riding and hiking.

# SOCIO-ECONOMIC PROFILE OF RURAL INDIA (SERIES II)

## VOLUME FOUR

## EASTERN INDIA

(Orissa, Jharkhand, West Bengal, Bihar and Uttar Pradesh)

*Edited by*

C. ASHOKVARDHAN, *I.A.S.*

ASHISH VACHHANI, *I.A.S.*

*Published for*

Centre for Rural Studies

L.B.S. National Academy of Administration, Mussoorie

*By*

**CONCEPT PUBLISHING COMPANY PVT. LTD.**

**NEW DELHI-110059**

**ISBN-13: 978-81-8069-721-0 (Series)**
**ISBN-13: 978-81-8069-723-4 (Vol. 4)**

First Published 2011

*Published and Printed by*

**Concept Publishing Company Pvt. Ltd.**
**Regd. Office:**
A/15-16, Commercial Block, Mohan Garden
New Delhi-110059 (India)
*Phones* : 25351460, 25351794, *Fax* : 091-11-25357109
*Email* : publishing@conceptpub.com
*Website*: www.conceptpub.com

**Editorial Office:**
H-13, Bali Nagar, New Delhi-110 015, India.

Cataloging in Publication Data--*Courtesy:* D.K. Agencies (P) Ltd. <docinfo@dkagencies.com>

**Socio-economic profile of rural India (series II).**
v. 4 cm.
Contributed articles.
Includes bibliographical references and index.
Contents: v. 4. Eastern India (Orissa, Jharkhand, West Bengal, Bihar and Uttar Pradesh) / edited by C. Ashokvardhan, Ashish Vachhani.
ISBN 9788180697210 (set)
ISBN 9788180697234 (v. 4)

1. India--Rural conditions. 2. India--Economic conditions. I. Lal Bahadur Shastri National Academy of Administration. Centre for Rural Studies.

DDC 307.720954 22

Lal Bahadur Shastri
National Academy of Administration
Mussoorie - 248179 (Uttarakhand) INDIA

**Padamvir Singh,** IAS
Director & Chairman
Centre for Rural Studies

# Foreword

This publication of the Centre for Rural Studies, Lal Bahadur Shastri National Academy of Administration, is a new addition to the series being brought out on Socio-Economic Profile of Rural India. This volume covers the profile of people from Orissa, Jharkhand, West Bengal, Bihar and Uttar Pradesh. It is based on data collected by Indian Administrative Service Officer Trainees during their 52 weeks District Training, interpreted and consolidated by experts in the field of development administration.

I am confident that this volume would be of utility to administrators, academics and planners.

**Padamvir Singh, *IAS***

Tel. : (0135) 2632727 (O)
EPABX : (0135) 26332374, 2632489, 2632405, 2632236, 2632367 Fax: (0135) 2632350, 2632720
Website : www.lbsnaa.ernet.in

**Socio-Economic Profile of Rural India (Series - I)**

**Vol. I** : SOUTH INDIA
(Andhra Pradesh, Karnataka, Kerala, Tamil Nadu)
*Edited by* **V.K. Agnihotri** IAS

**Vol. II** : NORTH-EAST INDIA
(Assam, Manipur, Tripura, Nagaland)
*Edited by* **C. Ashokvardhan** IAS

**Vol. III** : NORTH-CENTRAL & WESTERN INDIA
(Himachal Pradesh, Punjab, Haryana, Gujarat, Maharashtra) *Edited by* **Rajendra Vora**

**Vol. IV** : EASTERN INDIA
(Bihar, West Bengal, Orissa and Uttar Pradesh)
*Edited by* **C. Ashokvardhan** IAS

**Socio-Economic Profile of Rural India (Series - II)**

**Vol. I** : SOUTH INDIA
(Andhra Pradesh, Karnataka, Kerala, Tamil Nadu)

**Vol. II** : NORTH-EAST INDIA
(Assam, Manipur, Tripura, Nagaland)
*Edited by* **S.C. Patra & Ashish Vachhani** IAS

**Vol. III** : WESTERN INDIA
(Gujarat, Maharashtra, Rajasthan)

**Vol. IV** : EASTERN INDIA
(Orissa, Jharkhand, West Bengal, Bihar and Uttar Pradesh) *Edited by* **C. Ashokvardhan,** IAS & **Ashish Vachhani** IAS

**Vol. V** : NORTH & CENTRAL INDIA
(Punjab, Haryana, Himachal Pradesh and Madhya Pradesh *Edited by* **Raj Mohini Sethi**

# Preface

## Core Issues and the Setting

The foundation stone for this volume has been laid down by a group of Officer Trainees of the Indian Administrative Service, who despite being young and inexperienced, were, indeed, endowed with the propensity of reviewing the ongoing development programmes rather dispassionately. Their studies are marked by an inquisitiveness that is mostly associated with youth bereft of layers and layers of knowledge often contaminated by biases and preconceived notions. The insights developed, however, pertain to a few years ago and the times and the settings have since undergone a sea change. While core issues remain unaltered, the paradigm shift must be taken due notice of.

We review and supplement the field researches carried out by the IAS officers on training, at a time when the country has been severely impacted by the global, financial and economic crisis leading to significant slowdown in industrial and services sectors, demand, recession in export and domestic markets, and mounting job losses. The slowdown is much more painful for the poor and weaker sections in the absence of any safety net.

While the challenge is to initiate urgent measures to stem the downturn and put the economy back on the growth track, a still greater challenge would be to ensure that the growth process in the coming days becomes more equitable.

Unfortunately, the fruits of relatively high growth of the economy in recent years have bypassed the poor.

In the Indian context, the core agenda for inclusive growth must include: a new deal for agriculture, a greater thrust to manufacturing by strengthening physical and social infrastructure and a significant improvement in governance and delivery.

## Governance and Delivery

Poor governance has now become a major cause for worry. There are huge leakages and rampant corruption in the plethora of anti-poverty schemes launched over the years and more often the benefits fail to reach the targeted people below the poverty line. Even after spending over Rs. 300,000 crores of the tax payers' money over the last five years on poverty alleviation schemes—both old and new—there have been major slippages on goals. The previous Government's flagship programme, Bharat Nirman, launched in 2005 for creating rural infrastructure, for instance, could not achieve even a third of its target.

The inordinate delays in the Central sector projects have been costing thousands of crores of rupees every year. Public Accounts Committee reports have revealed huge misuse of funds in the Prime Minister's rural road scheme.

The Public Distribution System (PDS) has failed to provide food security to millions of poor.[1]

The juicy mix-reforms plus handouts, kind of please-all concoction has two dangerous presumptions—one, reforms are identical to disinvestment and privatization, and two, India's poor deserve condescending dollops of sympathy and money.

For the most critical needs of the people, shockingly unmet even 60 years after Independence, reforms cannot be equated with privatisation. Market fundamentalism and an indiscriminate advocacy of privatisation so dominate our discourse today that certain basic tenets of economic theory and the experience of most capitalist countries bear reiteration. This is not some form of subversive, closet socialism.

Markets fail when there are no profits to be made for capitalists or when the private rate of return on investment is significantly lower than the social rate of return. This is why thousands of Africans continue to die from sleeping sickness, even though the cure has been known since the early 1990s. There are no profits to be made from producing a drug that people who need it cannot afford to buy. Similar reasons explain why the proportion of malnourished children in India refuses to fall below 45-50 per cent even after 2 decades of economic reform. Or, why we have the largest proportion of pregnant anaemic women in the world.

If a sop like the farm loan waiver were to become policy, it could irretrievably compromise the integrity of India's banking system, whose robustness has been a lifeline for the rural poor, especially since the nationalization of banks in 1969. Similarly, in the absence of a far-reaching governance reform, NREGA is nothing but a handout. And it will do little to dent rural poverty. On the other hand, if it fulfils its promise of overthrowing the contractor *raj*, it could provide the big push for a new vision of sustainable development that grows organically from the soil, both literally and metaphorically.

Ever since the Great Depression of the 1930s, capitalist democracies have seen major investments by the State in the fundamental rights of its citizenry. The difference is that in the U.S., Europe, South-East and East Asia, the State has invariably delivered. In India, it has failed—both in the magnitude of its effort and in its quality. Thus, the suffering of our people is not just a tale of market failure. It is also a failure of governance. Which is where reforms for the poor must focus.

## Neglect of Rural India

A fundamental reason for this neglect of rural India is what may be termed as the 'urban telos'. It has been assumed that the salvation of people lies in urbanization and industrialization. Those who need Government support in the rural areas have received only second rate treatment. The condition of schools and hospitals in large tracts of village India is a testimony to this neglect. There are shortages of rooms, teachers and doctors.

One look at the ecological nightmare our cities have already become should be enough to convince us that a fresh view has to be taken of the possibility of any further movement from country to city. Let us work towards making our villages dynamic centres of growth and first rate habitats. That will give us breathing space to improve our cities as well. Our health sector is already overwhelmingly private. And it has failed miserably in delivering to the most vulnerable sections, especially in rural areas. How can reform here be achieved by more privatisation?

Our challenge is to improve the functioning of the public sector in rural development.[2] The need of the hour is the awareness of the recent trends that distort the very concept of sustainable development, essentially through blind aping of everything that defines lifestyles in the developing countries. The unregulated growth of shopping malls, each guzzling several megawatts of electricity; the unsustainable exploitation of our groundwater resources, driven essentially by heavy subsidies on the price of electricity for farmers; and incursions into tribal areas and agricultural or forest lands for setting up industrial projects—all of these violate the very fundamentals of sustainable development.

The country can ill-afford a continuation of these trends and their implications for distributive justice. Whatever may be the political forces behind the growth of Naxalite activity across the country, one major factor behind this is the growing disparity between the rich and the poor, symbolized by the insensitive and vulgar display of wealth by the rich in our society. In this respect, it is for the civil society and the intellectual class to establish some norms with relation to what would constitute socially acceptable behaviour.

Mahatma Gandhi rightly emphasised that development in India must have at its core rural development. The Government must intensify its efforts in this direction, but that would require a strengthening of the delivery system with a sense of urgency and purpose.[3] Even today, around 70 per cent of the countryside is left behind in the nations' march towards prosperity. And this could be attributed largely to lacklustre Government spending in rural areas. The combined total investment in the rural areas by both the Centre and States has remained more or less stagnant around 1 per cent of GDP since the 1990s.

The fact that rural development remains largely neglected becomes evident when the analysis is extended to the States. Available figures show that investment by the State Governments in the countryside—including public expenditure in agriculture, rural electrification, roads, housing, sanitation, schools, medical centres, ancillary units has declined for a majority of States since the nineties. In fact, the cumulative expenditure of the States in rural development as a percentage of total expenditure has dropped from almost 7 per cent in 1992-93 to 4 per cent at present. Most States spend as little as 1.5 per cent of their total expenditure on rural development. The exceptions are Madhya Pradesh (8%), Chhattisgarh (8%) and Bihar (7%).

No doubt, there are cases where there is apparently no close correspondence between fund allocation and rural prosperity. For example, rural Bihar suffers from economic deprivation despite higher State allocation. In contrast, Punjab is a front ranker. Perhaps, this could be attributed to the preponderance of non-farm rural employment (60%), greater urbanization, high minimum support price paid to farmers and well established rural infrastructure.

In Bihar, a higher proportion of the State Government funds have not made a visible impact in terms of rural uplift. This is because around 80 per cent of population continues to depend on low productivity agriculture for its livelihood. Nearly 40 per cent of the gross cropped area is still unirrigated and rural infrastructure is in a deplorable condition.[4]

## Inclusive Growth Remains Elusive

The Indian economy in recent years has emerged as one of the fastest growing economies of the world. GDP growth during the Tenth Plan period (2002-07) averaged 7.6 per cent with the growth rate accelerating to 9 per cent in 2005-06 and 9.4 per cent in 2006-07. What is more important, this higher growth rate has been achieved along with a significant improvement in macro-economic stability.

However, it remains a matter of grave concern that the recent acceleration in GDP growth has not been accompanied by an equitable distribution of wealth and well-being. In other words, the higher growth in recent years has not been inclusive.

While the percentage of people living below the poverty line did come down over the past two decades, the incidence of poverty as measured by the head count ratio (HCR) declined at a slower rate of 0.7 percentage point per annum during 1994-2005, compared with 0.85 percentage points per annum during 1983-94.

Again, while India now has the second highest growth rate in the world, its rank in terms of human development index (a composite measure of life expectancy, adult literacy and standard of living), has slipped to 128 among 177 countries in 2007 from 126 in 2006 even as incomes of middle-class people have surged and the country's dollar billionaire ranking rose to No. 4 in 2007 from 8 in 2006.

While the percentage of population below the poverty line has fallen from 36 per cent in 1993-94 to 27 per cent in 2004-05, the absolute number of total poor stood at 302 million in 2004-05—accounting for a quarter of the poor in the world.

The obstacles that need to be addressed if a real dent is to be made on poverty include widespread malnutrition and illiteracy. For example, in 2004-05, about 40 per cent of adults suffered from chronic energy deficiency, 35 per cent of workers were illiterate, and 20 per cent of workers were in the households below the poverty line, leading to low productivity of labour.

It may be noted here that India's record in poverty reduction pales before the achievements of China. The incidence of poverty in China declined by a staggering 45 percentage points in two decades from 53 per cent in 1981 to 8 per cent in 2001. In contrast, India could reduce poverty by a mere 17 percentage points in two decades.

The provision of gainful employment for all in the labour force is essential for reducing poverty and achieving inclusive growth. Accelerating productive employment is important because wage income is the main source of income for the poor.

While there has been no slowdown in employment growth since 1993-94; employment growth did not accelerate in consonance with GDP growth. Also, the quality of employment has deteriorated significantly with growing casualisation and underemployment.

The barriers to accelerating employment growth lie in labour laws and regulations which call for reform. In this context, the problem of low wage rates, particularly in laggard States, lack of employment opportunities in agriculture, increasing casualisation of employment, gender disparities in wage rates, and high levels of underemployment among those employed, continue to remain formidable issues that need to be addressed.

The rural-urban divide has widened significantly in the post-reform period. During the 1990s and beyond, inter-State inequalities in per capita State Domestic Product (SDP) worsened, and the laggard States, **Bihar, Jharkhand, Orissa** and **Uttar Pradesh** recorded low growth rates. If these States continue to grow slow, the overall GDP growth rate will be pushed down.

The most formidable constraint in making the growth process equitable and inclusive, however, is the crisis in agriculture and rural distress in post-reform India. The present crisis in agriculture could be traced back to the complacency and benign neglect of agriculture since the mid-1980s.

Apart from the big decline in public investment in the sector, the crisis was aggravated by the decline in the flow of the much-needed credit from the banking sector. The credit flow to agriculture, small-scale industries and other small borrowers was sluggish in the 1990s and thereafter till 2003.[5]

The present buzzword for India's development strategy is inclusive growth. Inclusive growth means an emphasis towards more equitable distribution of income and building capabilities in terms of attainment of better health and education.

## Unequal Payoffs

However, such an outcome is not surprising. Reforms entail unequal payoffs to economic agents. People with more skill stand to gain more compared to those with less skill sets. In the present context, the contribution of the services sector to the national income (GDP) is around 55 per cent, followed by manufacturing (26.4 per cent of GDP) and agriculture sector (18 per cent of GDP).

A more equitable income distribution would require a scenario with more people earning their livelihood from the agricultural sector and less people earning their livelihood from the services sector.

The present situation, however, is quite the opposite. Around 58.6 per cent of the Indian population earns its livelihood from agricultural and agriculture-related allied activities (such as cooperatives, fishing, dairies, etc.) compared to less than 10 per cent, dependent on organised services sector.

What is more worrying is that this inequality is going to increase as the agricultural sector is now growing at an annual rate of 2.6 per cent (from a lower base of 18 per cent growth) compared to services growing at 11 per cent (from a higher base of 55 per cent growth). There are too many people locked into the farm sector (with lower productivity and hence lower income) and there is an urgent need to absorb them either into the manufacturing or into services (with higher productivity and hence higher income).[6]

The recent report of the official Sengupta Committee to look into the status of the unorganised sector has assessed that in 2004-05, 77 per cent of the population, that is 836 million people, had an income of less than 20 rupees a day.[7]

While growth is extremely important, it cannot be the only goal and objective of all planning processes. Growth imperatives will have to be reconciled with a large number of other concerns. One such is inter-regional disparity with some States continuing to lag far behind others in terms of economic and social indicators and which, if left unattended, can do incalculable harm to the cohesion of the polity. The urban-rural disparity is another, and it is partly explained by the relative failure of agriculture. Thirdly, high growth rates have not made enough of a dent on poverty. In trying to address such equity concerns the Eleventh Plan has reoriented the priorities substantially by stepping up the allocations for education, agriculture, health care, and infrastructure. These sectors now account for almost 75 per cent of the total expenditure compared to 55 per cent in the Tenth Plan. Attention is also to shift to improving the delivery mechanisms at the ground level and ensuring that the plan targets are carefully monitored.[8]

## Agriculture: Strategic Concerns

The main strategic concerns include, one, promotion of high-value activities to diversify smallholder farming away from land-intensive staples to cater to rising urban incomes and dietary changes; two, extension and adaptation of technologies to enhance land productivity in less favoured areas with a large concentration of extremely poor; three, provision of infrastructural support to facilitate diversification of agriculture and of rural economies; four, expansion of rural non-farm activities to absorb a rapidly growing labour force, and finally, a massive increase in investment makes it easier for people to migrate to areas/sectors with greater potential for labour absorption.

The high-value revolution is led by the private sector, with the State facilitating it. Scale economies in processing and marketing are achievable with fragmenting and shrinking farm size. Contract farming has considerable potential in reducing transaction costs and risks of small-holders. However, the distribution of gains along the value chain depends on the bargaining power of various players. So producer groups could help small-holders achieve scale in marketing and negotiate better prices.

Both the high-value revolution and the extension of new technologies to less favoured areas require better water management in order to check mounting scarcity and deteriorating quality.[9]

To the extent that India imported food, it also imported higher inflation. Commodity prices are now trending low and food stocks in India are more than comfortable with warehouses overflowing with wheat and rice for public distribution. So why are prices high? A massive increase in minimum support prices, part of the Government attempt at putting purchasing power in farmers' hands, keeps prices from falling. In effect then, a well-intentioned policy of benefiting a productive option for the landholder costs the consumer dearly. Is it any surprise then that the average household per capita expenditure on food is increasing?

The policy of increasing the purchasing power of the farm sector tilts the terms of trade in favour of the farmer in the short run but it does so by setting domestic food prices 15 per cent higher than international prices, an anomaly that hurts the consumer and farm exports. A more sustainable strategy would aim to turn agriculture into a business proposition and there was no evidence of that in the past five years.[10]

## NREGA

The National Rural Employment Guarantee Act (NREGA) was supposed to bring about a radical change in this state of affairs. Under NREGA, rural labourers have a legal entitlement not only to work on demand but also to minimum wages. To prevent corruption, a wide range of transparency safeguards has been built into the Act. For instance, muster rolls are supposed to be kept at the worksite, displayed at the Panchayat Bhawan, and read out in public at the time of wage payments. Employment and wage details also have to be entered in the labourers' "Job Cards" to enable them to verify the records for themselves, contractors are banned.

In some States, there is evidence of substantial progress in this transition towards a transparent and accountable system. In Rajasthan, for instance, contractors have virtually disappeared from NREGA and mass fudging of muster rolls is a thing of the past. Andhra Pradesh is also making rapid strides in this direction through strict record keeping, institutionalized through post offices. In a recent survey of

Surguja and Koriya districts (Chhattisgarh), it was found that in gram panchayat works, 95 per cent of the wages paid according to the muster rolls had actually reached the labourers concerned.

However, the same transition is proving quite slow in some other States. A recent survey of NREGA in Western Orissa, for instance, suggests that the "contractor raj" is alive (if not well) in this region. This survey, initiated by the G.B. Pant Social Science Institute at Allahabad University, was conducted from 3-12 October, 2007 by students of the Delhi University in collaboration with local volunteers. Thirty randomly selected gram panchayats, spread over three districts (Bolangir, Boudh and Kalahandi) were studied. The survey included careful verification of "muster rolls" for one randomly-selected NREGA work in each of these gram panchayats.

The survey points to a quiet sabotage of the transparency safeguards aimed at perpetuating the traditional system of extortion in rural employment programmes. Before elaborating, a few words about how NREGA works in Orissa may be useful. To keep things simple, the main focus here is on works implemented by the gram panchayats (these account for the bulk of NREGA funds in Orissa). At the gram panchayat level, the main responsibility for implementing NREGA works lies with the Panchayat Executive Officer (PEO). In some panchayats, the PEOs are assisted by the Gram Rozgar Sevaks, but they are yet to be appointed in most cases. Another key actor is the Village Labour Leader (VLL), who is supposed to be selected by the gram sabha for the purpose of the "supervision" of a specific worksite.

The role of the VLL is actually in transition. The VLL concept goes back to the Sampoorna Grameen Rozgar Yojana (SGRY), where a VLL was a *de facto* contractor. He or she received the work orders, spent the funds, arranged the works, and filled the muster rolls. Under NREGA, funds are routed through the panchayat and the VLL is supposed to be a mere worksite supervisor, who earns wages at the same rate as other labourers. In practice, however, the post of VLL continues to act as a convenient foothold for the contractor. In about half of the 30 sample worksites, the survey team found evidence that a contractor was involved.[11]

The NREGS has many attractive features. First, it envisages wages for work, not doles. Wages confer dignity on our poorest fellow citizens. Second, the wage rates are not set too high. If alternative productive private sector employment were to come up, applicants will auomatically go in their search. Third and most important, it has the capacity to create social assets: lakes, check-dams, reclaimed waste lands with trees, toilets for schools, etc. By being gender neutral, it is conducive to the liberation of the enormous reservoir of human capital in our female workforce currently condemned to undervalued underpaid drudgery.[12]

Public pressure for transparency and regular monitoring by civil society has helped push the Rajasthan Government to look for innovative ways by streamlining measurement and payment processes. One such experiment took place when the Government collaborated with the Rozgar Evam Suchna Ka Adhikar Abhiyaan a coalition of civil society organizations in Rajasthan to develop a decentralized worksite management system. Over 165 activists from the abhiyaan participated in a monthlong campaign to create a pool of trained worksite managers—an innovation on the traditional mate who takes daily measurements of worksites and determines daily output. The activists worked closely with the local officials to develop model worksites and identify management practices that ensure transparency in measurement processes and through that overcome the free rider problem. The key emphasis was transparency. All labourers were kept informed of the total quantum of work that needed to be completed for them to access the minimum wage. Moreover, labourers were divided into groups of 5 each and the worksite manager was responsible for assigning specific tasks to each group at the start of the work day.

The results have been truly fantastic. In Jalore district as many as 3000 mates were trained to become full-fledged worksite managers. Each mate was given a calculator, a measuring tape and taught simple formulae for converting measurements into wages. Moreover, 2,000 of these trained mates were women. This could dramatically improve work conditions for women—who are the major participants in NREGA in the State. At the end of the training, most labourers in the model Panchayats were able to access Rs. 73 per day.

It would be naïve to suggest these experiments represent a magic bullet solution to our greatest problem—the failure of accountability in public services. But they have unleashed hopeful momentum. These experiments demonstrate the potential strength of collaboration between civil society and the Government in strengthening transparency and accountability. If these innovations are encouraged and allowed to flourish, the NREGA will offer us more than guaranteed employment. It may well guarantee us good governance.[13]

## Rural Health Care

Rural India consists of approximately 638,000 villages inhabited by more than 740 million individuals. A network of government owned and operated sub-centres, primary health centres (PHCs) and community health centres (CHCs) is designed to deliver primary health care to rural folks. Sub-centre is the first contact point between the community and the primary health care system. It employs one male and one female health worker, with the latter being an auxiliary nurse and midwife (ANM). They are responsible for tasks relating to maternal and child health, nutrition, immunization, diarrhoea control and communicable diseases.

Despite an elaborate network of facilities, only 20 per cent of those seeking outpatient services and 45 per cent of those seeking indoor treatment avail of public services. While the dilapidated state of infrastructure and poor supply of drugs and equipment are partly to blame, the primary culprit is the rampant employee absenteeism. Nation-wide average absentee rate is 40 per cent. The employees are paid by the State, with the local officials having no authority over them. Not surprisingly, many medical officers visit the PHCs infrequently, unavailable for childbirths even if the mother is willing to come to the PHC. Though PHCs are supposed to be free, most of them informally charge a fee.[14]

## Literacy, Basic Education and Community Values

Literacy and basic education are required for people to manage their daily lives and participate in democratic processes; vocational skills enable participation in the economy; and higher education enables citizens to play a more effective role in the globle knowledge, economy and international affairs. However, there is another need which runs through all forms of education. It is the need to inculcate the right values to develop responsible citizens of society.

Changing societal values is a recurring theme across the world. The erosion of 'family values' has been concerning leaders in the

USA where both Republican and Democratic political leaders regularly call for their restoration. The decay of 'community life' also bothers the Americans. Social studies reveal that family and community values contribute greatly to happiness, and their depletion in economically advanced countries is a significant reason why people in these countries are not happier even when they are richer.

Though children brought up in the education systems of these countries learn to stand on their feet, and be politically and economically independent, often they end up "Bowing Alone" (in sociologist Robert Putnam's memorable phrase) and unhappy. Therefore, as we strive to improve India's education systems to enable our children to become economically independent, they should also imbibe better family and community values in them if we want a more harmonious happy society.

At the heart of family and community values is the value of inclusion, of considering not only one's own needs, but also the needs of others. Some suggest that good values are built at home, in the family and the community, rather than in school. However, when good values are disappearing from families and communities themselves, schools must become the places where they are strengthened, and from which the required values will be reinserted into society. In India, citizens must think and act more inclusively than in any other country of the world perhaps, because we are very diverse a democracy with many iniquities. Values cannot be taught like texts, nor tested in written examinations. They are learned by living.[15]

Navodaya Vidyalayas provide good quality education to talented rural children irrespective of social and economic backgrounds. Most of these children would not even have continued their education otherwise. Entry to these schools also begins with a written test. But the test is professionally well designed and rural children are not put to any disadvantage because of their background or previous learning environment. The Central Government looks after the selected children from each district, and takes care of their educational expenses. The products of these schools are doing very well in the CBSE examinations. The Government of India intends to open more such schools. This is a welcome step.

The Navodaya Vidyalayas can develop into a model education system that brings out the best in the learner. This may be possible only when the Navodaya Vidyalaya Samiti gets the autonomy to conduct its own examination. Within the CBSE constraints, innovations are just impossible. It is all marks and marks.

The young talent pool is a measure of national cognitive capital and it alone determines the pace of progress. The final outcome depends on how the system continuously identifies and nurtures fresh talent and how far the political system accepts the inputs coming from teachers, scholar and academics. It is crucial to maintain the desired levels of dynamism in the system and make it alert and responsive to the emerging demands of the changing times. One of the most critical responsibilities of the education system is to identify special interests of every individual learner. In each case, these can be encouraged to blossom further by providing necessary motivation and environment. The process of talent identification and nurturance is most critical at the school stage. Schemes at the national and state levels exist to identify talent. Selected children are generally given scholarships. In some cases, selected children are also called to seminars, given book grants or taken on tours etc. The process of identification is, once again, a written test open to all. It is followed by an interview in some cases before the final selection. The continuance of the scholarship is subject to attainment of certain levels of marks each year.[16]

Sixty years after Independence, with 40 per cent of its population under 18, India is now confronting the perils of its failure to educate its citizens, notably the poor. More Indian children are in school than ever before, but the quality of public schools has sunk to spectacularly low levels, as Government schools have become reserves of children at the very bottom of India's social ladder.

India has long had a legacy of weak schooling for its young, even as it has promoted high quality Government financed universities. But if in the past a largely poor and agrarian nation could afford to leave millions of its people illiterate, that is no longer the case. Not only has the roaring economy run into a shortage of skilled labour but also the nation's many new roads, phones and television sets have fuelled new ambitions for economic advancement among its people—and new expectations for schools to help them achieve it.[17]

The UNDP releases values of HDI for roughly 175 countries. It is depressing to see that year after year, India figures somewhere near the bottom of the ladder. What is worse is that the low level of human development in India is not due simply to the fact that per capita GDP is relatively low. Even if countries were ranked simply in terms of health and education indicators, India would fare rather badly.[18]

## Infrastructure Constraints

We need to expand investment in infrastructure from 5 per cent of GDP in 2006-07 to 9 per cent of GDP in the final year of the Eleventh Plan, a four-percentage point of GDP increase in infrastructure investment. In terms of money, we estimate this at $500 billion in the five-year period.

Some of the additional investment will have to come from the public sector but a lot has to come from the private sector also. That is why we are emphasizing public-private partnership. The world sees India as on the cusp of a take-off. They recognize that infrastructure is a critical constraint and if we have the right policies which make infrastructure investment financially sustainable and create an attractive investment environment, capital is available. Getting $150 billion extra into India's infrastructure over five years is not impossible.

## Whether Private Investment in Infrastructure is Really Feasible

Investment in infrastructure is taking place already. Recently three ultra mega power projects have been bid out to the private sector amounting to 12,000 MW capacity. In the entire Tenth Plan period, the total additional capacity was only 21,000 MW.

Investment is taking place in airports, ports, roads and the railways too. However, there is no doubt that we need much more if we are to achieve our targets. This is where additional efforts are needed.[19]

## Roads for Rural Prosperity

Economist Robert Chambers had said back in the 1970s, "If I had money, I would use it to build roads. If I had more money, I would build more roads. If I had still more money, I would build still more roads."

Roads are not, of course, the only thing that matter—other rural projects and policies matter a great deal too. But connectivity enhances the value of every other rural investment, since it empowers people through improved mobility and access. People can more easily buy agricultural inputs and sell their produce. Children can go more easily to schools, cattle can more easily get veterinary help, and the sick can get to health centres. Remote areas have, by definition, the worst connectivity. They are among the poorest and slowest growing, but accelerate when given connectivity.

Roads can incubate a thousand small businesses, and can convert villages into towns. Government staff is much more willing to be posted to places with good connectivity, so roads improve administration. Rural productivity cannot be high without roads, but can be very high with them.

This was first demonstrated in India in Punjab and Haryana, which historically had the most dynamic rural economies and lowest poverty rates. Economist Ashok Gulati relates a conversation with M.S. Gill, who was Agriculture Secretary to Government of India and Development Commissioner in Punjab before becoming Election Commissioner. Gill said that in developing Punjab, he concentrated on a one-point agenda; build all weather (*pucca*) roads, and the people will take care of the rest. Revolution in Punjab hinged not only on R&D but roads too. Indeed, the returns to road investment were even higher than today.

Gulati says that studies by IFPRI (International Food Policy Research Institute) in China, Vietnam and some African countries point to the same conclusion—rural roads do more for growth and poverty mitigation than virtually anything else.[20]

Numbers benumb; the magnitude of funds required for the entire spectrum of services—from roads to drinking water—blinds the policymaker to its chances and challenges. Instead of worrying about the sources of funds, the Government of India in concert with the States, should be peering into the dense thicket of the constrictive regulatory framework and the multiple legislations that are hopelessly archaic.

All over the developing world, and in China, funds are eager to flow into the infrastructure so long as the policy environment for the deployment of funds is right. In India, it is terribly wrong.

With the States equally sharing the responsibility for infrastructure development, the legislative framework is more complex than it needs to be. The lack of financial devolution of powers below the State level to cities makes the task of urban renewal even more cumbersome.

No policymaker ever dreamt of as a problem despite the evidence, and that is land acquisition. For decades the public sector driven dams and power plants faced resistance from the displaced. But when the Special Economic Zones Act was passed in 2005 and the idea of large townships and industrial hubs took root in fund-rich investors, every policymaker assumed the transfer of agricultural lands as a routine matter.[21]

## Financial Inclusion

In the last decade, record growth in financial services has widened the gap between urban and rural India. Since 1999 bank deposits have grown 3.75 times to Rs. 29.29 trillion, but it is the cities where bank deposits have been piling up. Top 10 cities which accounted for only 50 per cent of bank deposits in 1999 today account for over 60 per cent. Metros have emerged as the largest beneficiaries of the high economic growth in India, as corporate posted robust performances resulting in higher corporate savings.

The change in the ideological profile of Indian banks, post-liberalisation, has also diluted the focus of the State-owned banks on rural credit. After losing their creamy layer to private banks, the State-owned banks have also begun to structure themselves in the form of new private banks. Many of them increased their minimum balance requirements, prompting the central bank to come out with a diktat asking banks to open 'no-frill' accounts with minimum or zero balance. Most private banks have introduced such 'no-frills' accounts only to fulfil statutory requirement and have made no effort to publicise the availability of such a product. As a result, there is a move to build a business providing financial services to those who are at present financially excluded.

On the lending side, there has been some progress towards financial inclusion with microfinance institutions (MFIs) becoming active in rural pockets and private and foreign banks lending in the urban subprime sector. But there have been setbacks as well. Private and foreign banks have pulled out of the subprime segment after facing flak for deploying recovery agents. Besides, microfinance institutions are facing increased regulatory scrutiny and a possible cap on interest rates.

The country's largest bank—State Bank of India—is planning to triple its ATM network by 2010, taking the total number of machines to over 25,000. A large number of these will be in the non-urban areas and be more user-friendly. The bank has targeted to issue around 10 million biometric cards by 2009.

The building blocks for improving financial inclusions are already in place. It is for the players now to grab the moment. Including even half of these excluded households provides an opportunity to bring in some 60 million households into the mainstream. The positive economic, not to mention social, impact of this, is huge.[22]

## Planning for the Unbanked

Against a national average of 59 per cent of the adult population, only 39 per cent of the adult rural population had a savings account, with the proportion of unbanked population being higher in the North-East. Of the 89 million farmer households in the country, 73 per cent had no access to the formal credit market. But the credit market is also regionally skewed, with the undeveloped States and the North-East suffering the worst consequences of under-banking.

For policymakers, the need of the hour is to innovate; the formal banking system has made little headway in reaching out to the poorer areas, despite all the efforts since bank nationalization in 1969. Co-opting the moneylender or using such intermediaries as the extensive postal services to reach farm households needs to be looked at to deepen the credit market; with just 2.6 per cent share in September 2007, the regional rural banks are clearly not enough.[23]

## Micro Enterprises in Rural Areas

The National Commission for Enterprises in the Unorganized Sector (NCEUS) has recently deliberated on the constraints plaguing the unorganized sector enterprises in terms of credit and developmental support including marketing. Based on projections using the National

Sample Survey (NSS) and Economic Census data, the Commission assessed the number of unorganised non-farm enterprises at 58 million in 2007.

## Potent Tool for Job Creation

Given the gigantic size and high growth potential of the unorganised sector, its innumerable enterprises need to be bolstered to a higher growth level, so that additional employment opportunities in the sector creates more income, which could add directly more than one per cent to GDP growth, the Commission pointed out. It feels that, if properly nurtured and strengthened, the unorganised non-farm sector would emerge as a potent tool for employment creation, poverty reduction and faster inclusive growth during the current Plan. The rationale for focusing on this much neglected sector flows from the incontrovertible fact that the contribution of the total unorganised sector as defined by NCEUS to total value added in 2004-05 (at 1999-2000 prices) is estimated at 50.6 per cent. Non-agricultural unorganised sector enterprises contribute as much as 62 per cent to total unorganised sector GDP and 31.5 per cent to total GDP.

## Definition Changed

The Government has defined the smallest segment of industries as micro enterprises (earlier tiny enterprises) covering the manufacturing sector and selected services. Till October 2, 2006, tiny units were defined as a segment of small-scale units, with investment in plant and machinery upto Rs. 25 lakh.

The Micro, Small and Medium Enterprises Act, 2006, which has come into force from October 2, 2006 has redefined micro enterprises as a separate segment of small industries, which in the case of manufacturing enterprises, has an investment in plant and machinery upto Rs. 25 lakh and in the case of service, an investment limit of Rs. 10 lakh in plant and machinery.

Even with this definition of micro enterprises, they barely received about three per cent of gross bank credit from 2002-03 to 2004-05. Against the RBI priority sector stipulation that micro enterprises should get 60 per cent of total credit to small scale industry, they have been getting just about 40 per cent and even this had skidded to 34 per cent in 2004-05.

What is more galling is that even within the non-farm unorganised sector, the most vulnerable group is the smaller size micro enterprises with investment upto Rs. 5 lakh. According to the Commission, this segment of unorganised enterprises, it is just about 2.2 per cent of gross bank credit from scheduled commercial banks, regional rural banks and urban cooperative banks. Even this was estimated to remain stagnant at that lamentably low level for the years 2004-05 to 2006-07.

Shockingly, only 4.2 per cent of such units (or an estimated 2.4 million of the 58 million in 2006-07) availed of institutional credit. This is notwithstanding a banking network of more than 75,000 branches of commercial banks across the country.

In a clear case of adding salt to the wounds of this segment that bleeds for want of requisite modest credit to overcome a host of other constraints they are facing in a high cost economy, is the substantial piggy-banking of the loans at the lower segment of the unorganised sector enterprises with investment of less than Rs. 5 lakh on the credit-*cum*-subsidy linked self-employment schemes, the numbers of which are legion.

Incidentally, in the latter scheme implemented by the Government, the banks are confident that a part of the loans is in the form of subsidy for margin money.[24]

## Women's Liberation in the Countryside

Amartya Sen defines "development as providing each person with access to capability, assets and opportunity". Providing women with opportunity by reducing time and energy spent in drudgery, and offering them dignity through ownership of the land on which they toil may be the path to development for all.

There are two pillars on which women's liberation in the countryside can stand: appropriate technology on the one hand, and gender-just-land reforms on the other, both of which will lead to increased agricultural production as well as all-round economic and social development.

Agriculture is rapidly becoming "feminised", with the continuing migration of men to towns and cities or into non-agricultural work and women are doing 60-70 per cent of the agricultural work.

Yet, their contribution is little recognized. One reason may be that there is a tendency to recognize only paid work as work and, as many of these women in agriculture work on their family land and so do not get a "wage" but are engaged in what is known as "unpaid family labour", their work becomes "invisible". This is true not only with regard to agriculture and horticulture, but with most of the traditional rural occupations, ranging from rearing of animals, to artisanal production and crafts like weaving, reflecting an earlier phase of the economy. As a result, census data reflects only work which has visible return, making the Labour Force Participating Rate for women as low as 32 per cent (Census 2001). Much of this work is monotonous, repetitive and physically tiresome—in other words, drudgery. Here is a major area where women's liberation from drudgery—is needed, not only to give women much needed rest, relief from fatigue and pain, leisure, and freedom from poor health and disease, but also to release their energy and creative and productive potential.

Here is a challenge to our science and technology institutions—to develop low-cost appropriate technology to specifically address the issue of reduction of drudgery and burdensome labour in the so-called "domestic" domain based on local resources, and combining traditional skills with environmental and health concerns.

The second area relates to liberating women farmers from their constraints and releasing their productive potential for agriculture, in the light of its feminization. For, breaking work, and their traditional knowledge and skills, the productivity of women farmers is low. There may be several reasons for this state of affairs. For one, extension services do not focus on reaching women farmers, though things have improved over the last 30 years. Also, women farmers, with their heavy workload, may have little time to attend meetings and workshops. But undoubtedly, one of the most significant reasons is women's lack of resources to access the necessary inputs even if they have the knowledge and skills. This is because most women do not own assets like land or houses in their own names, to put forward as collateral for loans. In the absence or lack of cooperation of their menfolk, it would become difficult or impossible for women to get credit from banks, which is the key to obtaining resources. Women headed rural families are the worst affected.

## Gender-Just Land Reforms

A major step forward to empower women in this area would be joint pattas for both agricultural land and houses. Many State Governments have already passed legislation to make this possible, but the progress in most States is minimal or slow because of general ignorance about laws, unwillingness to move away from traditional practices, burdensome and time consuming procedures, and corruption. But a Government that is serious about achieving it can break many of these constraints. One way would be to offer incentives to men who convert their agricultural holdings and/or houses to joint ownership.

The expected boost in agricultural and horticultural production should be stressed, since releasing women from their present status as bonded labour on their own farms, and giving them the opportunity to access resources would unlock their energies and lead to revolutionary progress in development.[25]

## Good Governance

Governance plays a critical role in addressing social and economic problems of people. Many of the poor countries, typically, have too much Government and too little governance. Good governance reflects transparency in decision-making and implementation, accountability and protection of rights. Fiscal policies (tax regime) are important for ensuring a more equitable distribution of income and wealth without compromising growth opportunities. Similarly, sound macro-economic policies as also trade policies encourage growth, while helping reduce the skew in income distribution.

These are broad policy parameters that need attention. But the policy design itself will have to vary depending on the facts and circumstances of each country. Numerous projects are going on around the world aimed at poverty alleviation. These projects are most desirable and necessary. But their impact is largely regional, and circumscribed by limitations of financial and human resources. So, while projects are important *per se*, they can seldom substitute strong governance and local initiatives.[26]

## NOTES

1. Naik, S.D., "New deal for inclusive growth", *The Business Line* (New Delhi: 3.6.2009), p. 7.
2. Shah, Mihir, "UPA's challenge: rural governance reform", *The Hindu* (New Delhi: 28-5-2009), p. 10.
3. Pachauri, R.K., "Growth for all", *The Times of India* (Patna-Ranchi: 5.6.2009), p. 14.
4. Ahuja, Shobha, "Declining rural funding by states", *The Economic Times* (Kolkata: 25.5.2009), p. 6.
5. Naik, S.D., "The India Story: Growth", *The Business Line* (New Delhi: 8.2.2008), p. 8.
6. Banik, Nilanjan, "Inclusive growth: an unfinished story", *The Business Line* (New Delhi: 7.2.2008), p. 8.
7. Karat, Brinda, "India grows but poor stagnate", *The Asian Age* (New Delhi: 30.12.2007), p. III.
8. Editorial, "Planning for equitable growth", *The Hindu* (New Delhi: 21.12.2007), p. 12.
9. Gaiha, Raghav, "Beyond agriculture", *The Indian Express* (New Delhi: 20.12.2007), p. 11.
10. Editorial, "Farm Health and Food Prices", *The Business Line* (New Delhi: 14.3.2009), p. 6.
11. Dreze, Jean, "NREGA: Dismantling the contractor raj", *The Hindu* (New Delhi: 20.11.2007) p. 10.
12. Rao, Jaithirth, "Best of bad choices", *The Indian Express* (New Delhi: 31.1.2008), p. 12.
13. Aiyar, Yamini, "A happy tale from two states", *The Indian Express* (New Delhi: 27.12.2007), p. 11.
14. Panagariya, Arvind, "The crisis in rural health care", *The Economic Times* (Kolkata: 24.1.2008), p. 8.
15. Maira, Arun, "Catch them young", *The Times of India* (Patna: Ranchi: 28.10.2007) p. 10.
16. Rajput, J.S., "Government must do its bit to nurture talent", *The Asian Age* (New Delhi: 19.12.2007), p. 6.
17. Sengupta, Somini, "Push for education yields little for India's poor", *The Asian Age* (New Delhi: 22.1.2008), p. 14.
18. Dutta, Bhaskar, "Get cracking on education", *The Times of India* (Patna: Ranchi: 24.1.2008), p. 10.
19. Srinivasan, G., "Setting store by faster and more inclusive growth", *The Business Line* (New Delhi: 19.12.2007), p. 8.

20. Aiyar, Swaminathan, "Roads will lead to rural prosperity", *The S. Anklesaria Times of India* (Patna: Ranchi: 3.2.2008), p. 10.
21. Upadhyay, Ashok, "Infrastructure's burden", *The Business Line* (New Delhi: 14.12.2007), p. 8.
22. Ikraman, Shaji, "Next big opportunities lie in rural areas", *The Economic Times* (Kolkata: 31.12.2007), p. 12.
23. Editorial, "Workable plan for the unbanked", *The Business Line* (New Delhi: 17.1.2008), p. 8.
24. Srinivasan, G., "Micro enterprises in rural areas need credit oxygen," *The Business Line* (New Delhi: 16.11.2007), p. 8.
25. Swaminathan, Mina, "She needs your help", *The Business Line* (New Delhi: 30.11.2007), p. 1.
26. Chandrashekhar, G., "Good Governance, key to fighting poverty", *The Hindu* (New Delhi: 6.11.2007), p. 11.

# Contents

*Foreword by* ***Mr. Padamvir Singh,*** *IAS* v
*Preface* vii
*List of Tables* xxxiii
*List of the Contributors* xl

**Introduction** **1**

**1. Orissa** **68**
*Ashish Vachhani , S. Tripathy* and *Varunendra Vikram Singh*
The State at a Glance / 68
Demographic Features / 80
Rural Infrastructure and Basic Amenities / 85
Education and Literacy / 91
Health and Sanitation / 96
Agriculture and Agrarian Relationships in Orissa / 100
Land Use Pattern of Various Villages / 104
Land Reforms—Agrarian Relationship, Land Ownership, Land Size, etc. / 117
Unemployment and Poverty / 136
Conclusion / 171

**2. Jharkhand** **176**
*Dr. C. Ashokvardhan, IAS*
Social Organization / 177
The Sub-National Movement in Jharkhand / 178
Tribal Economy in Jharkhand / 179
Study by the IAS Probationers / 181
Social System and Cultural Practices / 182
Impact of the Ram Krishna Mission / 183
Demography / 185
Land Use Pattern / 189
Livestock / 205
Village Industries / 208
Education / 209
Health and Sanitation / 210

Credit Facilities and Household Income / 211
Migration / 214
Status of Women / 215
Rural Development Programmes / 216
Land Reforms / 223
Conclusion / 225

**3. West Bengal** **231**
*S.K. Bhaumik*

Introduction / 231
Purpose of the Study / 233
Information Base for the Study / 233
Economic Activities / 233
Rural Infrastructure / 259
Rural Health / 270
Education / 281
Panchayati Raj System / 305
Agrarian Relations / 331
Anti-Poverty and Rural Development Schemes / 352
Social Structure / 360
Gender Empowerment / 365
Summary and Conclusions / 367

**4. Bihar** **395**
*Praveen Jha and Atul K. Singh*

Introduction / 395
An Evaluation Based on Field Reports / 399
A Brief Exploration into Political Economy of Bihar's Backwardness / 409
A Concluding Remark / 413

**5. Uttar Pradesh** **418**
*Bimal Kumar*

Introduction / 419
Conditions in Social Development / 423
Resource Base of Villages / 446
Sources of Livelihood / 465
Impact of Land Reforms / 474
Impact of Poverty Alleviation Programmes / 489
Panchayati Raj and People's Participation / 509
Conclusion / 518

**Summing Up** **533**

*Index* 551

# List of Tables


| | | |
|---|---|---|
| 1 | Agro-climatic Zones of Orissa | 3 |
| 2 | Health Status of Orissa vis-à-vis India | 5 |
| 3 | Status of Woman Development in Orissa | 7 |
| 4 | Status of Agricultural Production | 8 |
| 5 | Population (Census 2001) in Lakhs | 13 |
| 6 | Population Mix (In percentage) | 13 |
| 7 | Economic Activities | 14 |
| 8 | Per Capita Income (At Current Prices) | 14 |
| 9 | Gross State Domestic Product of Jharkhand | 14 |
| 10 | Gross State Domestic Product at Current Prices | 14 |
| 11 | Crop Production and Productivity | 15 |
| 12 | Animal Profile | 17 |
| 13 | Health Indicators | 21 |
| 14 | Health Care Infrastructure | 21 |
| 15 | Area and Production of Major Crops in Bihar (2000-2008) | 37 |
| 16 | Credit Flow to Agricultural Sector in Bihar (2003-04 to 2008-09) | 41 |
| 17 | Area and Production of Vegetable and Fruits in Bihar (2006-07) | 45 |
| 18 | Poverty Ratios in Bihar and India | 50 |
| 19 | Overview of IAY upto 2007-08 | 52 |
| 20 | Zone-wise Food Grain Production | 54 |
| 21 | Zone-wise Production of Pulses | 55 |
| 22 | Zone-wise Production of Oil Seeds | 55 |
| 23 | Crop Loan-Target, Distribution and gap of Previous Years | 56 |
| 24 | Trend of Land Holdings | 57 |
| 25 | Area under Various Land Holding Groups | 57 |
| 26 | Details of Land use Pettern | 58 |
| 27 | State-wise Consumption of Fertilizers in 2004-05 | 59 |
| 28 | Source-wise Irrigation Status | 60 |
| 29 | Expenditure and Benefits of Major and Medium Projects | 62 |
| 30 | Eleventh Plan Targets | 64 |

1.1 Introduction to the Villages 78
1.2 Population (2001 Census) 82
1.3 Basic Amenity—Drinking water facility (2001 Census) 86
1.4 Households by Source of Light (2001 Census) 86
1.5 Rural Infrastructure and Basic Amenities (All Orissa) (As per 2001 Census) 87
1.6 Basic Amenities in the Villages 88
1.7 Education (2001 Census) 92
1.8 Literate Population (Rural-Urban and Total) 92
1.9 Number of Primary Schools (Formal) with Teachers and Students in Orissa 93
1.10 Educational Status 93
1.11 Literacy Rate in Villages 94
1.12 Enrollments in the Village 95
1.13 Dropouts in the Village 95
1.14 Health Indicators (1998-99) 97
1.16 Broad Classification of Soil Types of Orissa 101
1.17 Land Classification in Brahmani Village of Bolangir District 102
1.18 Land Utilisation Pattern of Orissa 103
1.20 Land Use in Village: Kupudmaha, District: Kandhmal Land Details of the Village 104
1.21 Land use Pattern in village Seledi, District Sonepur 105
1.22 Land Use Pattern in Dumerpani 106
1.23 Agriculture Production Indices (Base 1981-82=100) 107
1.24 Cost of production of rice in 0.50 acre of Bahal land 110
1.25 Area Irrigated by Different Irrigation Sources in Orissa 113
1.27 Regression Statistics 115
1.26 Regression Result 116
1.28 Agrarian Structure (Operational Holding) (Year 1995-96) 121
1.29 Agrarian Relationship (Operational Holdings), 1985-86 122
1.30 Distribution of Landownership and Operational Holdings 123
1.31 Distribution of Land Ownership in the Village Patrabasa 124
1.32 Distribution of Land Ownership (Householdwise)—Village Sapmundi 125
1.33 Distribution of Land Ownership—Village Dumerpani 125
1.34 Land Distribution in the village Banspal 126
1.35 Distribution of Land Ownership (Household-wise) in Kupudmaha Village 126
1.36 Distribution of Land Ownership in the Village Taljhiri 127
1.37 Changes in Percentage Distribution of Leased-in Area by Terms of Lease 128
1.38 Distribution of Ceiling Surplus Land in Village Salebidi 135

1.39 Classification of Beneficiaries Who Got Ceiling Surplus Land 136
1.40 Work Participation Rate (1991 Census Data) 138
1.41 Classification of Workers and their Percentage in Different Districts of Orissa, 1991 Census 139
1.42 Number of Persons Engaged Occupation-wise 142
1.43 Per Capita Income of Orissa and India at Constant and Current Prices in Different Years (in rupees) 144
1.44 Per Capita Monthly Consumption Expenditure 145
1.45 Extent, Depth and Severity of Poverty in Orissa in Different Years 146
1.46 Poverty by Social Groups in Orissa 147
1.47 Financial and Physical Performances of Poverty Alleviation Schemes as on March 2004 152
1.48 Financial and Physical Performances of PAP Schemes in Cuttack District (2003-04) 154
1.49 Financial and Physical Achievement under Different Schemes during the Year 2003-04 upto End of March, 2004 155
1.50 Details of Economic Condition of five Beneficiaries 170
1.51 Profile of 7 SHGs of Village Dumerpani 171

2.1 Population Classification (1991 Census)—Religion-wise 185
2.2 Population Caste-wise 185
2.3 Occupation-wise 186
2.4 Population Characteristics 186
2.5 Caste-wise Break up of Population 186
2.6 Demography of Village Mahil 187
2.7 Distribution of households Caste-wise 188
2.8 Population of Malhan Bhuiadih, 1991 189
2.9 Land Use Pattern of Village Nichitpur, District Dhanbad 190
2.10 Land Use Pattern of Village Nichitpur 190
2.11 Distribution of Land Ownership (Household-wise) 191
2.12 Distribution of Operational Holding 191
2.13 Cultivation Seasons and Crops Cultivated 192
2.14 Cropping Pattern of Major Crops 192
2.15 Production of Food Grains in Nichitpur Village 193
2.16 Land Use Pattern of Village Charai (Block Chaibasa), District West Singhbhum 194
2.17 Distribution of Land Caste-wise 194
2.18 Crops and Source of Irrigation 195
2.19 Number of Households 196
2.20 Land use and landholding patterns of village Pratap Pur (Block Jamua), District Giridih 198

2.21 Distribution of Landholding 199
2.22 Distribution of government Land put under various uses 199
2.23 Input Market of Agricultural Produce 203
2.24 Non-Farm Activities 204
2.25 Education-wise Population 209
2.26 Income level of the households 212
2.27 Identified Sections Below Poverty Line and their population 216
2.28 Number of Beneficiaries, Occupation and Items of Benefits 217
2.29 Number and Types of Beneficiaries 218
2.30 Credit Disbursement Caste-wise 218

3.1 Worker-Population Ratio in Rural West Bengal by Districts 235
3.2 Percentage of Marginal Workers to Total Workers in Rural West Bengal by Districts 240
3.3 Percentage Distribution of Rural Workers (Main + Marginal) into Different Sectors in West Bengal by Districts 241
3.4 Cropping Intensity in West Bengal by Districts 246
3.5 Cropping Pattern in West Bengal by Districts in 1999-2000 248
3.6 Some Indicators of Adoption of Agricultural Inputs and Technology in West Bengal 250
3.7 Yield of Major Crops in West Bengal by Districts in 1999-2000 253
3.8 Share in Paddy Production and Yield Levels by Major Paddy Producing States in India in 1999-2000 254
3.9 Annual Growth Rates of Agricultural Production in West Bengal by Districts During 1980-81 to 1999-2000 256
3.10 Costs and Returns from Kharif (Aman) Paddy in Major States (Average of 1997-98 and 1998-99) 258
3.11 Road Connectivity in Rural West Bengal by Districts in 2001 260
3.12 Percentage of Villages Electrified in West Bengal 261
3.13A Rural Population per Rural Bank Office in West Bengal by Districts 263
3.13B Rural Population per Bank Office of Gramin Banks in West Bengal 264
3.14A Credit-Deposit Ratio for Commercial Banks and Co-operative Banks (Central+State) in West Bengal by Districts 265
3.14B Credit-Deposit Ratio for Gramin Banks in West Bengal 266
3.15 Finance to Agriculture by Commercial Banks in West Bengal 267
3.16 Some indicators of Rural Households' Access to Infrastructure Facilities in West Bengal and All India 270
3.17 Availability of Health Facilities in Rural West Bengal by Districts as on 31.3.1999 271

3.18 Some Health Indicators for Rural Areas—NHFS-2 (1998-99) 273
3.19A Morbidity for All Rural Population in West Bengal and All-India 274
3.19B Ailment Among Rural Persons (During Last 15 Days from the Date of Survey) 274
3.20 Nutritional Status of Rural Children under Age 3 Years 275
3.21 Ailment of Rural Children Under Age 3 Years 276
3.22A Childhood Vaccination in Rural Areas (% of Children Age 12-23 Months Who Received Vaccinations at any Time before Interview) 277
3.22B Vitamin A Supplementation for Children (12-35 Months) 277
3.23 Vaccinations of Rural Children (1-4 years): NSS 52nd Round Data (1995-96) 278
3.24 Health Care of Ever-married Rural Women [NHFS-2, 1998-99 Data] 278
3.25 Some Indicators of Health Care of Pregnant Women (15-49 years): NSS 52nd Round Data (1995-96) 279
3.26A Percentage of Rural Households Reporting Awareness of Need for Specific Health Precautions: NSS 52nd Round Data (1995-96) 280
3.26B Major source of Drinking Water for Rural Households: NSS 52nd Round Data (1995-96) 280
3.27 Rural Literacy Rates in West Bengal and All India (for Population Aged More than 6 years) 281
3.28 Rural Literacy Rates in West Bengal by Districts (for Population Aged More than 6 years) 283
3.29A Percentage Distribution of Rural Population (Aged 7 and Above) by Level of Education and Social Groups in West Bengal in 1999-2000 285
3.29B Percentage Distribution of Rural Population (Aged 7 and Above) by Level of Education and Size Class of Land Possessed in West Bengal in 1999-2000 287
3.30 Number of Educational Institutions in Rural West Bengal by Districts in 1999-2000 288
3.31 Student-Teacher Ratio in Educational Institutions in Rural West Bengal in 1999-2000 292
3.32 Sex Ratio of Students in Educational Institutions in West Bengal in 1999-2000 294
3.33 Progress of Sishu Siksha Karmasuchi (SSK) in West Bengal (as on September 2002) 296
3.34 Some Other Indicators of Educational Facilities in Rural West Bengal and All India as on 30.9.1993 298

3.35A Rate of Attendance in Educational Institutions by Rural Persons (age 5-24 years) in West Bengal and All India in 1995-96 299
3.35B Reasons Behind Non-enrolment in Educational Institutions by Never Enrolled Rural Persons (age 5-24 years) in West Bengal and All India in 1995-96 300
3.36A Percentage of Dropouts among Rural Persons (Age 5-24 Years) and the Educational Level at which Dropped-out in West Bengal and All India in 1995-96 303
3.36B Reasons for Dropouts from Educational Institutions among Rural Persons (Age 5-24 years) in West Bengal and All India in 1995-96 304
3.37 Incentives for Pursuing General Education by Rural Persons (Age 5-24 Years) in West Bengal and All India in 1995-96 305
3.38 Percentage Distribution of Zilla Parishad Seats under Different Political Parties 312
3.39 Percentage Distribution of Panchayat Samiti Seats under Different Political Parties 315
3.40 Percentage Distribution of Gram Panchayat Seats under Different Political Parties 318
3.41 Occupation (Main/Marginal) of the Gram Panchayat Members 320
3.42 Caste and Education of Gram Panchayat Members 322
3.43 Sex of Gram Panchayat Members 323
3.44 Occupation (Main/Marginal) of the Panchayat Samiti Members 325
3.45 Caste and Education of Panchayat Samiti Members 327
3.46 Sex of Panchayat Samiti Members 328
3.47 Distribution of Operational Holdings in West Bengal by Districts 329
3.48 Average Size of Operational Holdings 334
3.49 Incidence of Tenancy in West Bengal by Districts in 1995-96 337
3.50 Forms/Terms of Tenancy in West Bengal by Districts in 1995-96 [% of Leased in Area] 339
3.51 Recording of Bargadars in West Bengal (as on 30.9.2002) 343
3.52 Distribution of Vested Land and Number of Beneficiaries in West Bengal by Districts (as on 30.9.2002) 345
3.53A Money and Real Wages of Agricultural Labourers in West Bengal 347
3.53B Ratio of Female Labourers' Wages (Money/Real) to Male Labourers' Wages 351

| | | |
|---|---|---|
| 3.54 | Performance under Self-Employment Schemes in Rural West Bengal (IRDP/SGSY) | 357 |
| 3.55 | Performance under Rural Wage Employment Schemes in West Bengal | 358 |
| 3.56 | Number and Percentage of Population Below Poverty Line in West Bengal and All-India [Rural Areas only] | 360 |
| 3.57 | Poverty in West Bengal by Districts According to BPL Survey (as on 30.10.02) | 361 |
| 3.58 | Distribution of Rural Population by Caste in West Bengal in 1991 | 362 |
| 3.59 | Distribution of Rural Population by Religion in West Bengal in 1991 | 364 |
| 3.60 | Some Indicators of Autonomy of Ever-married Women in Rural Areas | 368 |
| 4.1 | Gross State Domestic Product (GSDP) at 1993-94 Prices (%) | 397 |
| 4.2 | Employment Structure (% of UPSS Workforce) | 397 |
| 4.3 | Per cent Distribution of Households and Area Owned over Five Major Classes in Bihar | 400 |
| 4.4 | Basic Infrastructure in the Villages surveyed by the Officer Trainees of LBSNAA | 407 |
| 5.1 | Mid-day Meal Scheme was Operational in the Village and had helped in reducing Dropout rates | 429 |
| 5.2 | Required Health Centres and Shortfall | 432 |
| 5.3 | Health Manpower Required and Shortfall | 432 |
| 5.4 | Basic Amenities in the Village | 444 |
| 5.5 | Basic Amenities in the Village | 445 |
| 5.6 | Land-Use Classification of Selected Villages | 450 |
| 5.7 | Landholdings and Occupational Distribution | 469 |
| 5.8 | Category of Land Operated (hectares) out of Total Land Operated Area | 485 |
| 5.9 | Socio-Economic Status of Tenants | 485 |
| 5.10 | Educational Status of Tenants | 486 |
| 5.11 | Residential Status of Tenants | 486 |
| 5.12 | Main Occupation of Tenant | 486 |
| 5.13 | Distribution of Beneficiaries by Income from IRDP | 498 |
| 5.14 | Distribution of IRDP Beneficiaries by Total Annual Income | 498 |
| 5.15 | Distribution of IRDP Beneficiaries by their performance | 499 |
| 5.16 | Beneficiary's Perception | 499 |
| 5.17 | Process of Selection of Beneficiary and Acquisition of Assets | 499 |

# List of the Contributors

**Dr. Praveen Jha,** Associate Professor of the Centre for Economic Studies and Planning, J.N.U., New Delhi.

**Atul K. Singh,** Research Scholar of the Centre for Economic Studies and Planning, J.N.U., New Delhi.

**Dr. C. Ashokvardhan, IAS,** Principal Secretary, Department of Revenue and Land Reforms, Government of Bihar, Main Secretariat, Patna.

**Ashish Vachhani, IAS,** Deputy Director and Coordinator, Centre for Rural Studies, Lal Bahadur Shastri National Academy of Administration, Mussoorie, Uttarakhand.

**Dr. S. Tripathy,** Associate Professor in Entrepreneurship Development Institute of India, Ahmedabad, Gujarat.

**Dr. Varunendra Vikram Singh,** Faculty, Centre for Rural Studies, Lal Bahadur Shastri National Academy of Administration, Mussoorie, Uttarakhand.

**S.K. Bhaumik,** Professor and Head, Department of Economics, Calcutta University, Kolkata, West Bengal.

**Shri Bimal Kumar,** Associate Professor in Govind Ballabh Pant Social Science Institute, Jhusi, Allahabad, Uttar Pradesh.

# Introduction

The study of Eastern India carried out by the IAS Probationers is basically empirical. Village visits have been an integral part of the officers' training where a live exposure to ground realities is provided to the trainee officers. Even though structured questionnaires and schedules are given to them to carry out the studies on a format, it does not debar them from holding interactions with officials and the people at large on the issues involved. The Probationers are required to stay in the rural environment where they get a comprehensive picture of various facets of rural life and ongoing schemes. The concept and operational modalities pertaining to a given Government programme come out in bold relief. Constraints, whatsoever, also come to the fore. It is expected of the trainees to conjure up a picture of the village under study and come out with broad-based generalizations.

Broadly, the studies have the following components:

1. Demographic and social profile
2. Occupational patterns, labour and employment
3. Patterns of agricultural holdings
4. Concept and operational modalities of Government programmes
5. Agriculture and allied activities
6. Animal husbandry and dairy development
7. Micro-Finance

8. Education
9. Health and sanitation
10. Irrigation
11. Rural development and employment
12. Regional disparities
13. Strategies and planning for future development
14. Panchayati Raj Institutions
15. Governance Issues

As mentioned earlier, there has been, since the village data were collected and compiled a veritable paradigm shift in our approach to and stratagem for the alleviation of rural deprivation. Hence, while introducing the universe under study, it will be our endeavour to present a State-wise to-date socio-economic profile of the concerned States. What follows is also a statement of priorities and the short and long term goals and objectives set out by the respective State Governments and the strategies adopted to meet the same.

## ORISSA

The State can be broadly divided into ten agro-climatic zones based on various factors like land, climate, elevation, water availability and other variables. Ten agro-climatic zones of the State with their distinguishing characteristics are listed in the following Table 1.

### Constraints and Concerns

There are some development constraints and concerns that deserve close attention while drawing up development strategies for Orissa. The important ones among the same are the recurring natural calamities, present regional and social disparities in development, high debt burden and extremist problems.

### Human Development

The Human Development Index (HDI) of the State has increased from 0.267 in 1981 to 0.404 in 2001, i.e., a rise of around 51 per cent. Orissa's relative position is 11th among major States. Life

**Table 1:** Agro-climatic Zones of Orissa

| *Sl. No.* | *Agro-climatic Zones* | *Climate* | *Mean Annual Rainfall (in mm)* | *Soil Type* |
|---|---|---|---|---|
| 1. | North western plateau | Hot and moist | 1,648 | Red and yellow |
| 2. | North central plateau | Hot and moist | 1,535 | Red loamy |
| 3. | North eastern coastal plateau | Hot and moist Sub-humid | 1,568 | Alluvial |
| 4. | East and south eastern plateau | Hot and moist | 1,449 | Coastal alluvial saline (near the coast line) |
| 5. | North eastern ghat | Hot and moist Sub-humid | 1,597 | Laterite and brown forest |
| 6. | Eastern ghat high land | Warm and humid | 1,522 | Red, brown |
| 7. | South eastern ghat | Warm and humid | 1,522 | Red, mixed red and yellow |
| 8. | Western undulating | Warm and humid | 1,527 | Black, mixed red and black |
| 9. | West central table land | Hot and moist | 1,527 | Red, heavy textured colourous |
| 10. | Mid-central table land | Hot and moist Sub-humid | 1,421 | Red loamy, laterite, mixed red and black |

expectancy at birth has increased from 51.93 years during 1971-81 to 60.05 years during 2001-06 in case of male and from 49.59 years in 1971-81 to 59.71 years in 2001-06 for female. While the corresponding increase at the all India level during the same period was from 50.90 years to 63.87 years for male and 50.00 years to 66.91 years for female.

## Human Resource Utilisation

The population of the State according to the 2001 Census is 368.05 lakh, which is about 3.58 per cent of India's population. The decennial growth rate of population at 16.25 per cent in the State during the decade 1991-2001 was lower than the national decadal growth rate, and the decadal growth rate of 20.06 per cent during the previous decade (1981-91). The sex ratio of 971 females per 1000 males in 1991 marginally increased to 972 in 2001, which is much higher than the corresponding all-India figures of 927 and 933 respectively. The total literacy rate in the State, which was 49.09 per cent during 1991, has increased to 63.08 per cent in 2001 Census. The female literacy rate has also increased remarkably from 34.68 per cent to 50.51 per cent during the same period.

The Census data reveal that, while the percentage of total workers to total population in the State has increased from 37.53 per cent in 1991 to 38.79 per cent in 2001, the percentage of main workers to total workers has declined from 87.33 per cent to 67.17 per cent. This indicates prevalence of under-employment in the State. The proportion of male workers to male population and female workers to female population in the State, as per the 2001 Census stood at 52.5 per cent and 24.7 per cent respectively while corresponding proportions at all-India level were 51.7 per cent and 25.6 per cent respectively.

## Health and Nutrition

Improved health is desirable not only in itself, but also because it leads to enhanced capacity to work and participate in the economic activities. A comparative picture of health status of Orissa *vis-à-vis* India in respect of key health indicators and health infrastructure is summarized in the following Table 2.

**Table 2:** Health Status of Orissa vis-à-vis India

| *Sl. No.* | *Indicator* | *Reference Year* | *Orissa* | *India* |
|---|---|---|---|---|
| 1 | Life expectancy at birth (in years) | 1981-85<br>1992-96 | 53.0<br>56.9 | 55.5<br>60.7 |
| 2 | Life expectancy at birth (in years):<br>(i) Male<br>(ii) Female | <br>2001-06<br>2001-06 | <br>60.05<br>59.71 | <br>63.87<br>66.91 |
| 3 | Crude birth rate per 1000 population | 2003<br>2005<br>2007 | 23.0<br>22.3<br>21.5 | 24.8<br>23.8<br>23.1 |
| 4 | Crude death rate per 1000 population | 2003<br>2005<br>2007 | 9.7<br>9.5<br>9.2 | 8.0<br>7.6<br>7.4 |
| 5 | Infant Mortality Rate (per 1000 live births) | 1981<br>1991<br>2001<br>2004<br>2007 | 125<br>124<br>91<br>77<br>71 | 77<br>80<br>66<br>55 |
| 6 | Maternity Mortality Rate (per lakh births) | 2001-03<br>2007-12 | 358<br>119 | 301<br>100 |
| 7 | Total fertility rate (number of children per couple) | 2004<br>2005 | 2.6<br>2.1 | 3.0<br>2.9 |
| 8 | No. of Government Medical Institution/100,000 people | 2004-05<br>2007-08 | 4.48<br>4.29 | 4.00<br>– |
| 9 | Hospital beds per lakh population | 1997<br>2004<br>2007 | –<br>38<br>36 | 93<br>–<br>– |
| 10 | Doctor-population ratio | 1999<br>2002 | 1:7440<br>1:7560 | 1:1923<br>– |
| 11 | Fully vaccinated children aged 12-13 months (in per cent) | 1992-93<br>1998-99 | 36.8<br>43.7 | 35.4<br>42.0 |

## Education

The literacy rate for Orissa has increased by 14 percentage points from 49.09 per cent in 1991 to 63.08 per cent in 2001. However, there are substantial social and regional disparities in literacy rate. The female tribal literacy in Orissa is very low. By the end of 2006-07, there were 46,722 primary schools with enrolment of 44.85 lakh students in the State, while the number of upper primary schools was 16,403 with enrolment of 18.17 lakh students. Like-wise, the number of high schools has gone upto 7,408 with total enrolment of 13.52 lakh students. The gross enrolment of students in relevant age groups has gone upto 93.49 per cent at primary school level and 100.31 per cent at upper primary level in 2006-07.

## Woman Development

The female literacy rate in the State has increased from 4.5 per cent in 1951 to 50.51 per cent in 2001. The proportion of women to the total employees in the organized sector has increased from 8.7 per cent in 1990 to 14.8 per cent in 2007. One of the reasons for such increase is the reservation of 1/3rd vacancies in all categories of posts under the Government for women since 1992. Half of the Old Age Pension beneficiaries are women, their number being 3.43 lakh in 2006-07. Similarly, under the National Old Age Pension Scheme, 2.51 lakh women (51.0%) were benefited during the same year. The State Government have launched "Mission Shakti" with effect from 8th March, 2001 with a view to ensuring active participation of women in the development process and making them self-reliant through the formation of Self Help Groups (SHGs). During 2006-07, 25767 women SHGs have been formed with 3.13 lakh members and Rs. 79.71 crore have been advanced till the end of March 2007. These groups have generated savings amounting to about Rs. 72.46 crore. The status of woman development in the State in terms of some indicators is summarized in Table 3.

## Irrigation

The net irrigation potential created by the end of 2007-08 from all sources was 28.34 lakh hectares, which is 56.79 per cent of the estimated irrigable area of the State. Out of this, 44.49 per cent was covered through major and medium irrigation, 18.67 per cent through minor (flow) irrigation, 14.91 per cent by minor (lift) irrigation and balance 21.93 per cent through other sources. The total cultivated area covered under irrigation till the end of 2006-07 was 45.63 per cent.

**Table 3:** Status of Woman Development in Orissa

| *Sl. No.* | *Indicator* | *Reference year* | *Orissa* | *India* |
|---|---|---|---|---|
| 1. | Sex ratio (Number of female per 1000 males) | 1991 | 971 | 927 |
| | | 2001 | 972 | 933 |
| 2. | Female literacy rate (in per cent) | 1991 | 34.68 | 39.29 |
| | | 2001 | 50.51 | 54.05 |
| 3. | Percentage of Gross enrolment of girls at Primary School level | 2003-04 | 107.44 | 95.67 |
| | | 2004-05 | 127.37 | 105.48 |
| 4. | Percentage of Gross enrolment of girls at Upper Primary School level | 2003-04 | 49.69 | 57.69 |
| | | 2004-05 | 69.21 | 65.76 |
| 5. | Life expectancy of girls at birth (year) | 2001-06 | 59.71 | 66.91 |
| 6. | Percentage of women in organized sector employment | 2003 | — | 18.4 |
| | | 2007 | 14.80 | — |
| 7. | Death rate | 2002 | 9.8 | 8.1 |
| | | 2005 | 9.5 | 7.8 |

Participatory Irrigation Management in the form of Pani Panchayats has been adopted as a policy for development of water resource sector. 17,067 Pani Panchayats have been formed as on December 2008 covering an area of 16.32 lakh ha, of which, 11.75 lakh ha has been handed over to 15,974 Pani Panchayats.

## Agricultural Production

Agricultural sector continues to be the backbone of the State's economy contributing about a quarter of total NSDP. While the contribution of the agriculture sector to NSDP has come down to about 26 per cent now from a level of 67 per cent in 1951 there has not been appreciable decrease in the workforce engaged in the sector. About 65 per cent of the total workforce is dependent on agriculture. This also suggests lower labour productivity in this sector.

The production of food grains in the State has increased from 51.04 lakh tonne in 1970-71 to 81.44 lakh tonne in 2007-08, but the increase in yield rate of food grain from 847 kg/ha in 1970-71 to 903.28 kg/ha in 2007-08 is not very significant as compared to the national average yield rate of 1,562 kg/ha in 2004-05. A comparative picture of agricultural development in the State *vis-à-vis* India is given in Table 4.

**Table 4:** Status of Agricultural Production

| *Sl. No.* | *Indicator* | *Reference Year* | *Orissa* | *India* |
|---|---|---|---|---|
| 1. | Average operational holding size (ha) | 1990-91 | 1.34 | 1.57 |
| 2. | Per capita net area sown (ha) | 2004-05 | 0.15 | 0.14 |
| | | 2007-08 | 0.13 | – |
| 3. | Per capita food grain production (kg) | 2005-06 | 190 | 185 |
| | | 2007-08 | 200 | – |
| 4. | Yield rate of food grain (kg/ha) | 2004-05 | 1,154 | 1,562* |
| | | 2007-08 | 903.28 | – |
| 5. | Fertiliser consumption per unit gross cropped area (kg/ha) | 2004-05 | 43 | 95.60 |
| | | 2006-07 | 47 | 104.5 |
| | | 2007-08 | 52 | – |

* This relates to the year 2002-03.

Over-dependence on paddy cultivation even in rainfed condition is a limiting factor to agricultural growth because of the State's proneness to natural calamities and drought condition. In terms of area, the share of paddy out of the net sown area has reduced from 64.36 per cent in 1950-51 to 57.18 per cent in 2002-03, which is still quite high. Other major constraints to the adoption of modern agricultural practices in the State are low levels of capital formation and the small size of operational holdings. The Orissa Agriculture Policy, 1996 addressed these issues and the overall agriculture production in the State has improved during the Tenth Plan. However, keeping in view the past experiences and changed scenario, the State Government has announced a new Agricultural Policy-2008 which is futuristic, flexible enough to anticipate and address emerging trends, to identify potential areas for development and to chalk out a clear agenda for agricultural development for at least next 10 years.

## Livestock Production

During 2007-08, total milk production in the State was 16.20 lakh tonne. Egg production was 1,549.488 million and meat production was 58.82 thousand tonne. There were 540 veterinary hospitals and dispensaries and 2,939 livestock aid centres in the State by the end of 2007-08.

## Fish Production

The total fish production in the State was 3.49 lakh tonne in 2007-08, of which the marine fish accounted for 1.31 lakh tonne, brackish water fish 0.23 lakh tonne and fresh water fish 1.95 lakh tonne. However, this production level is not commensurate with the available potential and there is scope for stepping up fish production substantially. Export of fish to other States and countries during 2006-07 was estimated at 89.02 TMT. The per capita consumption of fish in the State has increased from 7.71 kg in 2000-01 to 8.74 kg in 2007-08.

## Thrust Areas and Strategies

There are certain core issues that have shaped the broad development strategy that the State has been pursuing. These core issues emanate from the State's physiogeographic and socio-economic conditions and its development scenario *vis-à-vis* other progressive States and the national average. An outline of these development imperatives is given below.

## Bridging the Overall Development Gap

The Gross State Domestic Product of Orissa at current price was 3.49 per cent of GDP during 1951-52, which has come down to a level of 2.42 per cent by 2006-07. Likewise, the per capita income of the State as a percentage of national per capita income has declined from 75.38 per cent in 1951-52 to 68.28 per cent in 2006-07. This clearly shows that over the 56 years, both in terms of the size of the economy and level of development, the State has lagged behind the national average. This calls for achieving a faster economic growth to catch up with the nation.

## Need for Higher Agricultural Growth

Agricultural and Allied activities sector continues to be the mainstay of the Orissa economy contributing about a quarter of total NSDP and employing about 65 per cent of the workforce. But the sector, to a large extent continues to be traditional, and undiversified with low level of productivity. Therefore, any development strategy for the State needs to focus on accelerating development in this sector.

## Insulating the Economy against Natural Calamities

The performance of the State economy has been adversely affected by frequent natural calamities. Drought, flood and cyclone affect the production process. This calls for two-pronged strategies. First, to put in place effective means to reduce the physical impact of natural calamities and second, to reduce the economy's susceptibility to natural calamities.

## Diversification of the Economy

Over-dependence of the State economy on less productive agriculture and allied activities sector, which is prone to natural calamities, has prevented the State from achieving faster economic growth. Engagement of a large section of workforce in the farm sector has contributed to under-employment and low income among farm workers. The obvious solution to this is diversification of the economy making effective use of available natural and human resources and other growth potentials.

## Special Attention to Depressed Sections

Socio-economic development of the Scheduled Tribes and Scheduled Castes, constituting about 22.13 per cent and 16.53 per cent of State's population, has been much lower than that of the rest of the population. In case of the Scheduled Tribes, even the process of their mainstreaming is an issue till date. This apart, women across all communities in the State are yet to share the same level of development and empowerment compared to their male counterparts. This calls for sustained efforts to mainstream, develop and empower these depressed sections of the population.

## Focus on Unemployment and Under-employment

Unemployment and under-employment of the labour force both educated and uneducated, has been a feature of State's economic backwardness. Apart from contributing to poverty, this has also generated social tension. In order to address this, special effects are required to generate large scale employment and self-employment avenues and improve the employable skills of both educated and uneducated.

## Need for Infrastructure Upgradation

The State has embarked upon a massive industrialization process. In the coming years a large number of big and medium industrial units are expected to come up in different parts of the State. In order to support this industrialization process and also to stimulate the rural economy to grow faster, it is necessary to upgrade the physical infrastructure base of the State.

## Urgency of Poverty Reduction

Over the years, incidence of poverty in the State continues to be at a high level. While the overall development process is expected to reduce poverty, the extent and intensity of poverty in the State require urgent and special efforts to address the same.

Rural people depend mostly on agriculture and forest resources to eke out their subsistence. However, Orissa's agriculture generally remained stagnant. It has only recently started showing higher growth. Agricultural productivity is roughly half that of the national average. Use of improved inputs (e.g., better seeds and fertilizers) is also far below the national average. Want of adequate and assured irrigation facilities (except in certain pockets) is another limiting factor that keeps agriculture undeveloped.

It is not only that growth rate is low in Orissa, but annual fluctuations in GSDP have also been large mainly due to frequent natural calamities and other reasons. As a result, the State income growth has been very much unstable compared to India as a whole. However, in recent years, Orissa has registered a higher growth rate. During the Tenth Plan period the State has achieved an annual average growth rate of 8.59 per cent at 1999-2000 prices as against the target of 6.2 per cent. Moreover, the agriculture sector in the State has also registered a higher growth rate than that of the country. This positive trend, if maintained, will help in poverty reduction in Orissa. The State Government is making concerted efforts to continue with the same tempo during the Eleventh Plan period and to achieve an overall higher growth rate both in the agriculture and allied sector and in the entire economy.

Though extensive forest resources are an important source of sustenance to a majority of rural poor, they are highly degraded and lack desired financial and managerial inputs. Large forest areas are devoid of regeneration and, therefore, cannot provide livelihood support on a sustained basis unless substantial investments are made in them.

Orissa is also deficient in infrastructure (e.g., railways, paved roads, ports and telecommunication). A large number of the rural poor, particularly in hilly and interior areas, suffer from physical exclusion and are unable to access educational opportunities, health services and safe drinking water facilities. Optimal exploitation of Orissa's vast natural resources also demand heavy investments in infrastructure development.

## Special Area Development Programmes

Removal of regional disparities has been one of the important development strategies adopted by the State Government during successive Five Year Plans. However, due to several economic, social and institutional obstacles, all regions in Orissa have not shared the gains of development in an equitable manner. Some regions continue to languish in abject poverty. The undivided districts of Koraput, Bolangir and Kalahandi (popularly known as KBK districts) form one such region where incidence of poverty is the highest in the State. In fact, this region, with about 72 per cent of its rural people below poverty line, is perhaps the poorest region in the country. Several other pockets of southern and western Orissa are also socially and economically depressed. These regions are also frequently visited by natural calamities including severe drought and floods. Persistence of heavy incidence of poverty in these regions has been a cause of concern for the State Government as well as the Government of India. However, *adhoc* approaches adopted in the past to develop these regions did not yield desired results. Therefore, in consultation with the Government of India, the State Government have adopted a special area development approach for these regions with a view to focusing attention on them for accelerated development.

## Strategies for the Development of KBK Districts

The Special Plan for KBK districts under SCA and the new initiative, called the "Biju KBK Plan" launched by the State Government under State Plan (State's own resource), will effectively maintain and strengthen the momentum gained by the Revised Long Term Action Plan (RLTAP). The Special Plan for KBK districts and the Biju KBK

Plan aim at: (i) drought proofing, (ii) poverty alleviation, and (iii) improved quality of life in KBK districts. In order to achieve these objectives, the following strategies seem appropriate:

- Building rural productive infrastructure (e.g., roads, bridges, irrigation projects, tanks, watershed development, markets, storage godowns) and conserving natural resources (e.g., forests, soils and water).
- Developing programmes for income generation on sustainable basis (e.g., productive rural infrastructure, SGSY, SGRY, NREGP, agriculture development, and micro-credit support).
- Mobilising and empowering the rural poor (e.g., Self Help Groups (SHG), Vana Samrakshana Samitis (VSS), Pani Panchayats, and Bhumi Panchayats).
- Restructuring and enhancing the social security system (e.g., emergency feeding programme, special nutrition programme, mobile health units, promotion of education among ST/SC girls).

## JHARKHAND

### Social Composition

**Table 5:** Population (Census 2001) in Lakhs

| | *Male* | *Female* | *Total* |
|---|---|---|---|
| State | 138.85 | 130.60 | 269.45 |
| Urban | 32.06 | 27.88 | 59.94 |
| Rural | 108.79 | 102.73 | 209.52 |
| ST | 35.66 | 35.21 | 70.87 |
| SC | 16.40 | 15.48 | 31.88 |
| Population (0-6 yrs.) | 25.22 | 24.34 | 49.56 |

*Note*: Population density per sq. km-338 (National Average—324)

**Table 6:** Population Mix (In percentage)

| | *Jharkhand* | *National Average* |
|---|---|---|
| Urban | 22.24 | 27.8 |
| Rural | 77.76 | 75.2 |
| ST | 26.3 | 8.1 |
| SC | 11.8 | 16.2 |
| Population (0-6 yrs.) | 18.4 | 15.9 |

## Economic Features

**Table 7:** *Economic Activities*

| | *Jharkhand* | | *India* |
|---|---|---|---|
| | *(in lakhs)* | *% age* | *% age* |
| No. of Workers | 101.09 | 37.5 | 39.10 |
| Male | 66.60 | 24.70 | 26.75 |
| Female | 34.49 | 12.80 | 12.35 |
| Main Workers | 64.47 | 23.92 | 30.43 |
| Marginal Workers | 36.62 | 13.59 | 8.67 |
| Cultivators | 38.90 | 38.5 | 31.6 |
| Agricultural Labourers | 28.51 | 28.2 | 26.6 |
| Workers in Household Industries | 4.81 | 4.3 | 4.2 |
| Other Workers | 29.37 | 29 | 37.6 |

**Table 8:** Per Capita Income (At Current Prices)

| *2001-02* | *2002-03* | *2003-04* | *2004-05* | *2005-06 (P)* | *2006-07 (Q)* | *2007-08(A)* |
|---|---|---|---|---|---|---|
| 12859 | 13688 | 15050 | 17905 | 18901 | 21198 | 23162 |

**Table 9:** Gross State Domestic Product of Jharkhand

| *Sector* | *GSDP at current prices (Rs. In lakhs)* | | | | | | |
|---|---|---|---|---|---|---|---|
| | 2001-02 | 2002-03 | 2003-04 | 2004-05 | 2005-06 (P) | 2006-07 (Q) | 2007-08 (A) |
| *1* | *2* | *3* | *4* | *5* | *6* | *7* | *8* |
| Primary | 1181118 | 1167821 | 1226769 | 1430794 | 1357258 | 1453890 | 1554385 |
| Secondary | 878726 | 1180907 | 1388885 | 1728240 | 2024066 | 2481811 | 2861791 |
| Tertiary | 1447029 | 1448007 | 1629268 | 1973298 | 2121773 | 2331931 | 2534165 |
| Total GSDP | 3506873 | 3796735 | 4244922 | 5132332 | 5503097 | 6267632 | 6950340 |
| Per Capita GSDP | 12859 | 13688 | 15050 | 17905 | 18901 | 21198 | 23162 |

**Table 10:** Gross State Domestic Product at Current Prices

| *Sector* | *GSDP at Current Prices (in % age)* | | | | | | |
|---|---|---|---|---|---|---|---|
| | 2001-02 | 2002-03 | 2003-04 | 2004-05 | 2005-06 *(P)* | 2006-07 *(Q)* | 2007-08 *(A)* |
| *1* | *2* | *3* | *4* | *5* | *6* | *7* | *8* |
| Primary | 33.68 | 30.76 | 28.90 | 27.88 | 24.66 | 23.20 | 22.36 |
| Secondary | 25.06 | 31.10 | 32.72 | 33.67 | 36.78 | 39.60 | 41.17 |
| Tertiary | 41.26 | 38.14 | 38.38 | 38.45 | 38.56 | 37.21 | 36.46 |
| Total GSDP | 100 | 100 | 100 | 100 | 100 | 100 | 100 |

## Agriculture

| *Total Geographical Area* | *79.70 lakh ha (2.42% of Country's Area)* |
|---|---|
| Forest area | 22.39 lakh ha (28.10%) |
| Land put to Non-Agricultural use | 7.57 lakh ha (9.50%) |
| Barren and Unculturable land | 5.74 lakh ha (7.08%) |
| Permanent pasture and other grazing land | 1.10 lakh ha (1.38%) |
| Cultivable waste land | 3.34 lakh ha (4.19%) |
| Land under miscellaneous trees | 0.93 lakh ha (1.17%) |
| Other than current fallow (2-5 yr.) | 9.35 lakh ha (11.74%) |
| Current fallow | 13.18 lakh ha (16.54%) |
| Net Sown Area | 16.18 lakh ha (20.31%) |

### *Crop Pattern*

Approximately 85 per cent of cultivable area is under different food crops as against 65 per cent area at the national level. Rice is the major food grain crop of the State covering approximately 80 per cent of the total cropped area. Other important crops grown are wheat, oilseeds and minor millets. Vegetable production is high in certain pockets of the State placing it at a comfortable position compared to its neighbouring States.

The State is in deficit in all major crops except pulses in comparison to the national average. Out of an estimated 37 per cent of the total cultivable area only 20.31 per cent is used for cultivation and 3.5 per cent area is used for cash crops. This indicates that major portion of the cultivable land of the State is not profitable for agricultural productivity.

**Table 11:** Crop Production and Productivity

| *Year* | | *Crop Productivity (kg./ha)* | | | | |
|---|---|---|---|---|---|---|
| | | *Paddy* | *Wheat* | *Maize* | *Pulses* | *Oilseed* |
| 2002-03 | Jharkhand | 1338 | 1429 | 1203 | 1079 | 781 |
| | India | 1804 | 2619 | 1642 | 556 | 710 |
| 2003-04 | Jharkhand | 1324 | 1362 | 1389 | 1169 | 804 |
| | India | 2051 | 2707 | 1983 | 623 | 1072 |
| 2004-05 | Jharkhand | 1174 | 1278 | 1367 | 982 | 901 |
| | India | 2026 | 2718 | 1907 | 595 | 967 |
| 2005-06 | Jharkhand | 790 | 1024 | 1040 | 831 | 666 |
| | India | 2102 | 2619 | 1938 | 598 | 1004 |
| 2006-07 | Jharkhand | 1466 | 1338 | 1532 | 934 | 666 |
| 2007-08 | Jharkhand | 1635 | 1485 | 1230 | 666 | 835 |

### Land Holdings

72 per cent of the land holdings belong to small and marginal farmers. Less than 1 per cent of holdings are above 10 hectares, which covers 9 per cent of cultivable area. Agricultural operations are primarily of subsistence type due to the adverse land-man ratio.

### Challenges

- There is predominance of cereal crops in the State. About 85 per cent cropped area is covered under food grains and hardly 3-5 per cent area is under cash crops. 40 per cent of the total cropped area remains largely mono-cropped under rice. Lack of diversity in the cropping pattern makes the farmers more vulnerable against any downward deviation in rainfall.
- Agricultural operations are not profitable because they are primarily of subsistence type due to large number of fragmented holdings.
- Large tracts of land are left uncultivated by poor farmers due to lack of capital. They have little or no resources of their own to provide for high cost inputs needed to increase the agricultural productivity. The institutional credit flow to the agriculture sector is negligible and agricultural extension activities are minimal.
- 49 per cent of the soils have high concentration of toxicity. Therefore, the productivity of soil is very low.
- The agriculture is largely rain dependent because the irrigation coverage is only 23.95 per cent of the available arable land as against the national coverage of 70 per cent.
- The State does not have perennial river system. All rivers in the State are seasonal. They receive water during monsoon. 80 per cent of the rainfall is received during four monsoon months (June-September). Due to undulating topography, the water run off rate is very high.
- Inadequate or non-existent post-harvest management infrastructure at farm level, lack of price incentives, low access to credit and high transaction cost involved in institutional credit are some of the reasons, which have affected the productivity.

- All these factors converge into a vicious circle of low agricultural productivity, low farm income, low investment, low capital formation and subsequently stagnant rural economy. Contribution of agriculture to GSDP is less than 8 per cent while huge population (70-80%) depend on it for livelihood support.

## Animal Husbandry and Dairy

**Table 12:** Animal Profile

| *Species* | *Census 1982* | *Census 2003* | *Growth % Over 1982* |
|---|---|---|---|
| Cattle | 70.00 | 76.59 | 5.19 |
| Buffalo | 10.74 | 13.43 | 5.95 |
| Sheep | 11.68 | 6.80 | (-)2.77 |
| Goat | 44.49 | 50.31 | 5.38 |
| Pig | 7.80 | 11.08 | 6.76 |

### *Dairy Profile*

Total Milk Production : 14.00 lakh tonne/annum

Total requirement of milk : 23.36 lakh tonne/annum

Milk deficit : 9.36 lakh tonne/annum

| | |
|---|---|
| Breedable population of milch cattle (In million) | 1.90 |
| Breedable buffalo population (In million) | 0.39 |
| Productivity (kg./day/animal) | 1.59 |
| Per capita availability of milk (in gms.) | 152 |
| Milk production (million tonne per annum) (2006-07) | 1.40 |
| Total Nos. of milk producers Co-op. Societies | 1490 |
| Total producer members (in thousands) | 48.75 |
| Average milk collection per day through societies (in thousand litres) | 20.65 |
| Milk chilling capacity (in thousand litres) | 69.00 |
| Milk imported from other states through Comfed dairies (in thousand litres) | 185.00 |

- Recognized breeds of cattle represent a small fraction of the total cattle population in Jharkhand. The local indigenous breeds are mostly draft purpose breed. The local breeds do not produce adequate milk due to poor nutrition, poor management, tropical heat and diseases.

- Per cattle productivity is 1.59 kg. per cattle per day against the national average of 3 kg. per cattle per day.
- Per capita availability of milk is just 152 gm as against the national average of 240 gm per capita. We are deficit in milk production.

## Fisheries

### *Water Area*

- Private Ponds—24752 ha.
- Government Ponds—15843 ha.
- Reservoirs—94000 ha.
- Rivers—1800 km.
- Fish Seed Hatcheries
- Government Seed Hatcheries
- Government sector—6 hatcheries (Ranchi, Palamu, Gumla, Hazaribagh, Deoghar and Latehar)
- Private sector—3 hatcheries (Lohardaga, Ranchi and Hazaribagh)

### *Fish Production*

- Fish production in Jharkhand is 1435 kg./ha./year which is lower than the national average of 2150 kg./ha./year.
- The low fish production is because of most of the tanks are old and unsuitable for fish culture due to heavy siltation and weed infestation.

## Water Resources

### *Rainfall*

Jharkhand has an average yearly rainfall of 1000-1200 mm against the national average of 1000 mm. The rainfall is generally uniform with little variation.

### *Rivers and River Basins*

The State has the following main rivers and river basins.

| | | |
|---|---|---|
| Rivers | : | Subernarekha, Damodar, Barakar, South Koel, North Koel, Shankh, Ajay, Mauyrakshi, Gumani, Kharkai. |
| River Basins | : | Subernarekha, Damodar, Barakar, North Koel, South Koel, Mayurakshi, Gumani, Ajay, Bilasi, Chandan Chir. |

### *Ground/Surface Water*

Surface water availability in Jharkhand is 25877.53 MCM and Ground water availability in Jharkhand is 6870.95 MCM.

### *Water Availability*

| | | |
|---|---|---|
| Total availability of water | : | 32748.48 MCM |
| Ground Water | : | 6870.95 MCM |
| Surface Water | : | 25877.53 MCM |

### Use of Water

| | *Surface Water* | *Ground Water* |
|---|---|---|
| Irrigation purpose | 41% | 65% |
| Industry and drinking | 5249.69MCM | 1176.99 MCM |
| Municipal use | 6% | 17% |
| Industrial use | 15% | Nil |

### *Irrigation Potential*

| | | |
|---|---|---|
| Total irrigation potential created | : | 7.123 lakh ha |
| Major and Medium irrigation | : | 2.33 lakh ha |
| Minor irrigation | : | 4.78 lakh ha |

### *Challenges*

- The existing irrigation coverage is only 23.95 per cent against the national the coverage of 70 per cent. The agriculture is largely rain dependent.
- The State does not have perennial river system. All rivers in the State are seasonal. They receive water during the monsoon. 80 per cent of the rainfall is received during four monsoon months (June-September). Due to undulating topography, the water run off rate is very high.

- Only 50-60 per cent of created irrigation potential is being utilized. More than 50 per cent of the irrigation potential generated over the years has got eroded and would require massive resources and time to restore.
- Ponds and wells irrigate one fourth of the fields and the rest are irrigated by other sources.

## Human Resource

| Literacy Rate (%age) | Male | Female | Total |
|---|---|---|---|
| State | 67.3 | 38.9 | 53.6* |
| ST | 54.0 | 27.2 | 40.7 |
| SC | 51.6 | 22.5 | 29.1 |

* National average is 64.8 per cent

### *Primary and Secondary Education*

| | | |
|---|---|---|
| Primary Schools | : | 30,041 |
| Middle Schools | : | 10,259 |
| High Schools | : | 1,235 |
| Model Clusters | : | 2,975 (under NPEGEL) |
| No. of Para Teachers | : | 70,965 |

### *Drop-out Rate*

| Class | 2007-08 | 2008-09 |
|---|---|---|
| I—V | 15.85% | 8.27% |
| VI—VIII | 62.24% | 52.91% |

### *Areas of Concern*

- Weak monitoring system.
- Very high rate of teacher's absenteeism.
- Low female literacy rate.
- High drop-out rate in elementary sector.
- Poor infrastructure for elementary, secondary and higher education sector.

- Lack of quality teachers' training institutions.
- Lack of proper teacher recruitment agency.
- Low community participation.

## Health Care and Sanitation

**Table 13:** Health Indicators

| | |
|---|---|
| Decadal Growth Rate | 23.1 |
| Birth rate | 26.8 per 1000 population |
| Death rate | 7.9 per 1000 population |
| IMR | 69 per 1000 live births (National Avg.: 58 per 1000 live births) |
| MMR | 371 per 1 lakh live births (National Avg.: 301 per 1 lakh live births) |
| Sex Ratio | 941 females per 1000 males |
| Total Fertility rate | 3.30 (National Avg.: 2.68) |
| Safe Delivery | 28.70% |
| Couple protection rate | 36% |
| Complete ANC checkup | 38% |
| Institutional delivery | 19% |
| Rate of Blindness | 1.40% |
| Leprosy Prevalence Rate | 1.36 per 10000 population |
| TB Detection Rate (As per CDR) | 124 per 1 lakh population |
| ***Malaria*** | |
| SFR | 2.29 |
| SPR | 9.62 |
| PF | 23.82% |

*Source*: DHLS RCH-3 & UNICEF.

**Table 14:** Health Care Infrastructure

| | *Existing* | *Shortage* |
|---|---|---|
| Sub-Centre | 3958 | 3130 |
| Additional PHC | 330 | 796 |
| CHC | – | 168 |
| Referral Hospitals | 32 | |

### Challenges

- Unsafe Delivery
- Lack of Neonatal care
- Lack of immunization
- Lack of infrastructural facilities including equipment and drugs
- Shortage of trained manpower including Medical Officers and Paramedics
- Lack of knowledge about various diseases
- Lack of safe potable drinking water
- Lack of hygienic environment
- Poor nutrition

## WEST BENGAL

### Agriculture

West Bengal has tremendous natural resources and an advantage of six agro-climatic regions, fertile soil of vast biodiversity and consistent irrigation facilities. The importance of agriculture in the State's economy is reflected by its contribution of about 20 per cent to the total SDP (at constant price) and by its support to employment of nearly 58 per cent of its rural workforce.

For the Eleventh Five Year Plan, the growth rate of the agriculture and allied sector has been projected around 4 per cent per annum. This is a challenging task though the annual average growth rate in food grain production in the State during 1993-94 to 2003-2004 was 2.22 per cent as against all India growth rates of 0.83 per cent, 2.74 per cent in Haryana and 1.98 per cent in Punjab. Considering erratic weather conditions natural vagaries and other constraints, all efforts are being made for the full realization of the agricultural production potential in order to keep agricultural production in tandem with the demand for food grains etc. Out of the 335 agricultural blocks in the State, 172 blocks spread over from Teesta Terai flood prone zone in the north to the coastal area in the south and undulated lateritic area in the west, are low in productivity. Apart from that, the area and productivity of pulse and oilseed crops are low and there is scope to improve upon. Greater thrust will also be given to commercial crops like cotton, jute and other fibre crops. The extension and advisory service making use of IT will be made available to the farmers. For supporting farmers in natural calamities proper work plan has been envisaged. Emphasis is being laid on capacity building of the SCs, STs, minorities and women. Decentralised planning process will be followed. Guidelines regarding women's empowerment, minorities and skill development will be followed. Almost all the schemes are beneficiary-oriented.

The State's agriculture sector has been successful to meet the foodgrains demand of a growing population, and its production is likely to reach 182.92 lakh tonnes by the end of the Eleventh Plan Period.

West Bengal is deficient in pulses, oilseeds and wheat. All these crops are grown under less irrigated or non-irrigated conditions. Most farmers in the State tend to give priority to a rice-based cropping system. This is due to concerns for food security, low risk and easy market access. But this production system is not congenial for higher income generation. This has resulted in the shortage of commodities like pulses, wheat, oilseeds, timber and some other items for which there is demand in the market. Among foodgrains, West Bengal now occupies the first position in the case of rice, jute and allied fibre production among all the States of the country. This has also encouraged monoculture and unsustainable utilisation of natural resources in some areas. Greater thrust is needed on high value market-driven remunerative diversified crop. Emphasis will also be laid on flowers, fruits and other new horticultural crops having demand in the market along with extending the area of wheat, pulses and oilseeds and those varieties of potato, which are suitable for processing, and production of value added items, which has already been started during the Tenth Plan. Bamboo cultivation in a planned manner with support from the Bamboo Mission and Jatropha cultivation in wastelands would also be promoted. To encourage such activities, support would be provided for requisite market infrastructure, post-harvest handling, storage, and marketing.

### *Strategy for Achieving 4 per cent Agricultural Growth*

- Projection of 4.5 per cent production growth rate of food grains during the Eleventh Plan period.

- By the end of the Plan period the projected food grain production is 200.57 lakh tonnes.
- The target of the cropping intensity has been fixed at 195 per cent by the end of the Plan period.
- Ensure food security for the people of the State.
- Emphasis to be laid on production and availability of the quality seeds (hybrid and high yielding) and other agricultural inputs.
- Greater emphasis on overall increase in production and productivity in the hilly, terai, coastal and lateritic zones. More importance to be laid on demonstration centres, farmers' training, availability of agriculture inputs and infrastructure development.
- Crop Diversification, Integrated Crop Management, Integrated Pest Management will be given high priority.
- Expansion of area and production of cotton and other commercial fibre crops will be given high priority.
- Programming and implementation of watershed the development and construction of water harvesting structures to promote the area expansion and enhanced production in non-irrigated/rain fed areas.
- Government Seed Farms, Research Stations, Meteorological Observatories, Seeds, Fertilizers and Soil Testing Laboratories will be revitalized.
- Research extension linkage and extension reforms will be given due importance.
- Special emphasis will be on e-Governance in agriculture and capacity building of farm women, farmers belonging to the Scheduled Castes, Scheduled Tribes, minorities and other weaker sections, employment generation and disaster management.

Credit flow and irrigation facilities are proposed to be increased.

## Horticulture

The horticulture sector in West Bengal offers a wide variety of crops suitable for cultivation under different agro-climatic conditions and hills and terrain with possibility of multi-tier cropping systems, thus enhancing the returns per unit area of land and time, generating employment potential and providing food and nutritional security.

Development of horticulture will give rise to direct and indirect employment generation by way of maintaining nurseries, land development, orchard management, harvesting, storing, transportation, packing house operation, processing and marketing.

### *Objectives of the Eleventh Five-Year Plan*

- To provide holistic growth of the horticulture sector based on strategies which include research and development, technology promotion, extension, pre- and post-harvest management, processing and marketing;
- To enhance horticulture production, improve nutritional security and income support to the small and marginal farmers;
- To promote, develop and disseminate technologies, through an effective blend of traditional wisdom and modern scientific technology;
- To encourage joint projects for the production of quality hybrid seeds, medicinal plants and flowers;
- To promote capacity building and Human Resource Development;
- To create opportunities for employment generation, especially for focus groups like women, the Scheduled Castes and Scheduled Tribes.

### *Production and Productivity*

The Eleventh Five Year Plan will specially focus on increasing both production and productivity through adoption of improved technologies for ensuring quality, including genetic upgradation of all horticultural crops. The following strategies may be adopted:

- Distribution of vegetable seeds as minikits to the small and marginal farmers including SC and ST farmers;
- To increase the area, production and productivity of fruits in the State;
- Orchard subsidy scheme implemented during the Tenth Plan period is renamed as area expansion of fruit plants;

- To set up more number of seed production centres in the horticulture farms;
- Scheme for the distribution of coconut seedlings will be taken up among the small and marginal farmers including the SC and ST farmers;
- Schemes for floriculture like area expansion of flowers, setting up of poly green house, training of farmers.

## Animal Husbandry

The livestock sector plays a vital and crucial role in the West Bengal economy. The livestock sector contributes 4.41 per cent of the total SDP and 18.6 per cent of the agricultural SDP (year 2002-03). It plays an important role in employment generation and augmentation of rural income. The gross value of output of the State in the sector is about Rs. 11,500 crore at current prices (year 2004-05). The State held first position in meat production, 5th in egg production, and 11th position in milk production during 2003-04.

### *Goals and Objectives*

The long-term objective of the Government is to produce the required amount of milk, meat and eggs, which will be achieved through:

(i) Upgradation of different livestock and poultry products.

(ii) Extension of animal health coverage in the rural area.

(iii) Production of quality feed and fodder, milk procurement and processing through milk cooperatives and dairies.

(iv) Reduction of income inequality through transfer of resources to poorer people.

(v) Other related activities include:

  (a) Improvement in the standard of education and training in animal sciences,

  (b) Production of vaccines and facilities for referral diagnostic services,

  (c) Programmes for farmers' training, and

  (d) Animal welfare.

### *Animal Resources and Animal Health*

This sector is taking care of overall animal resources development, veterinary health care and manpower development. Along with these activities, the Government is providing opportunity for the generation of employment and creation of additional income.

### *Activities*

(i) Upgradation of different live stocks and poultry.

(ii) Extension of animal health coverage—both preventive and curative, upto the Gram Panchayats level in each block.

(iii) Production of vaccine and facilities for referral diagnostic services.

(iv) Production of quality feed and fodder.

(v) Formation of self-help groups and livestock co-operative.

(vi) Community Development like SCP for SC and TASP for the tribal community.

(vii) Additional income generation to the poorest people through animal husbandry practices.

(viii) Employment generation through livestock and poultry farming.

(ix) Farmers' training, publicity and awareness programme in respect of animal resources development programme.

(x) Adoption and enhancement of modern technology in the animal husbandry sector and disseminating the same to the field level.

(xi) Co-ordination with the Panchayats functionaries and line departments.

(xii) Distribution of animals and birds through family based programmes.

## Co-operative Credit Structure

### *(a) Revamping and Strengthening*

The West Bengal State Co-operative Bank Ltd. (WBSCB) is at the apex of the three tiers of short-term cooperative credit structure in the State. With its three regional offices and 17 District Central Co-operative Banks (DCCB) and 5162 numbers of PACS with 33.7 lakh members, it disburses short term credit in the agriculture sector.

### *(b) Kisan Credit Card (KCC)*

12,97,397 KCCs have been issued in the State till 31st March, 2007. Approximately Rs. 2800 crore have been disbursed through the KCC system in the State during the first four years of the Tenth Plan.

The effort of the State Government shall be to universalize the issuance of the Kisan Credit Cards, so that each and every farmer with land is given KCC during this period. Appropriate steps shall also be taken for issuing KCCs to women farmers by eliminating the existing lacuna. There is an anomaly with regard to the distribution of KCC, which is done by the central co-operative banks, while the credit is disbursed by the PACS. Effort shall be taken for the removal of this anomaly for ensuring effective functioning of the three tier credit set up.

### *(c) Self Help Groups (SHGs)*

The un-bankable group in rural areas mainly consists of small farmers, marginal farmers, landless poor and weaker sections like the Scheduled Tribes and Scheduled Castes whose financial exclusion is conspicuous. In view of the presence of a sizeable population of the weaker sections, there is a need to have special focus on the development of this lot. Organizing them into Self Help Groups was one significant step undertaken by the Government during the Tenth Plan.

The SHG model of accessing credit for the poorest of the poor has made certain dents. 132,292 SHGs have been formed in the State with 1,075,251 members. The deposit mobilised by these SHGs is Rs. 765 crores and loan disbursed by them is approximately Rs. 1521 crore. Experience shows that SHGs have enabled increase in the assets of the rural households, improved saving patterns, enhanced employment rates besides pecuniary benefits, have significantly contributed in improving self-confidence; inculcated a feeling of self-worth and improved communication levels as also their ability to resist social evils. Thus, the implementation of more credit instruments to reach the un-reached through SHGs would continue during the Eleventh Plan period. Linkage of SHG with the credit-dispensing agency already exists in the State. Efforts shall be made to make their operation more hassle-free and to diversify the activities taken up by SHGs further. For this purpose, it is under the active consideration of the Department to see that room for participation of the representative of the SHG in the Board of the PACS is made. Self-Help Groups are proposed to be developed as a sub-system of the primary co-operative movement.

## Rural Development

### *Special Programmes for Rural Development*

In West Bengal, the impact of land reforms and taking up a pro-poor strategy for rural development implemented by the Panchayats has made visible impact on the rural society. The same may be guessed by the fact that rural poverty, which was very high in the State thirty years back, declined faster as compared to other States. In 1973-74, when all-India rural poverty was at 56.4 per cent, as much as 73.2 per cent of West Bengal's rural people lived below the poverty line. Analysis of the data of the 61st round (2004-05) of the NSS (as made available by the Press Information Bureau of the Government of India in March 2007) shows that while rural poverty in the entire country has declined from 56.4 per cent in 1973-74 to 28.3 per cent in 2004-05, that in West Bengal declined from 73.2 per cent to 28.6 per cent. This achievement has also been recognized in the draft Eleventh Five Year Plan Document which recognizes West Bengal among States that have succeeded in reducing the absolute number of the poor in rural areas over the three decades from 1973 to 2004-05. The target at the end of the Eleventh Five Year Plan would be to reduce the percentage of rural population below the poverty line to less than 10 per cent.

During the Eleventh Plan period it would be the responsibility of the Panchayat bodies to take care of the basic needs of the deprived segment of the rural population through a decentralised planning, implementation and monitoring process.

## Rural Employment

### *NREGS, SGRY and REGP*

Eighteen districts of the State are already covered under the National Rural Employment Guarantee Act. This will be the major programme for providing income to the people in search of wage employment. However, given the rainfall pattern, cropping intensity and availability of public land, the scope to provide one hundred days employment under the Act will remain limited. The programme will be more useful in areas with low productivity and low cropping intensity. Efforts will be made to develop land, particularly those belonging to land reforms beneficiaries and bring micro-irrigation to those lands for growing at least two crops. Water conservation including recharging of water in appropriate places and soil conservation will be given priority in general for sustainability of agricultural operation. Assistance of the Science and Technology Department for the use of information available from satellite images will be taken to make the approach technically sound and effective. Priority will also be given on social forestry and rural connectivity out of the programme. The programme will be utilized to improve the productive resources of the poor, particularly the beneficiaries of land reforms and those belonging to the SC and ST families by developing their land, providing micro-irrigation sources like dug wells, tank excavation etc. However, because of the limited opportunities in providing employment during the period after sowing till harvesting of Aman paddy there will be need to have other interventions for the alleviation of poverty.

### Promotion of Self-employment

The limited access to land resources in the State has resulted in continuous increase in the number of agricultural labourers. Even districts with high cropping intensity face high incidence of poverty because of very adverse land-man ratio and too many people are chasing the job related to agricultural operation. Shifting large number of population, particularly the landless agricultural labourers to non-agricultural activities is urgently required for gainful employment of the rural population. Augmentation of livelihood opportunities will be a major intervention in the Eleventh Five Year Plan for alleviating rural poverty. The opportunities in agriculture and allied sectors have to be improved through better adoption of technology, appropriate diversification and arranging supply of good quality seeds and other inputs like irrigation, training them to manufacture compost fertilizer and channelising institutional credit for the poorer sections. For those who do not own any land, the interventions have to be based on non-agricultural activities or such activities, which can be taken up in their homestead itself. This will be possible only if the poor are organized and other supports are provided at the grassroots level, which the Government extension mechanism has not been able to deliver to the desired extent so far.

## Institutional Development of the Panchayats

In order to achieve all the tasks narrated above it will be necessary to improve the quality of governance by strengthening the local bodies and devolution of power to those bodies. So far, the Panchayats have mostly acted as an agent of the State. Devolution of fund, function and functionaries and improvement of capabilities of the Panchayats to discharge responsibilities devolved on them will be essential for that purpose. Clearer devolution of powers to the Panchayats, with associated earmarking of funds through budgetary process and development of own cadre of employees along with those deputed by the State Government, will be worked out during the Plan period. Each administrative department, having programme in rural areas, should come out with clear order, to be backed by legislation wherever necessary, on the devolution of functions to the Panchayat bodies and earmark fund by creating separate budget head, which will give clear indication to the Panchayats about availability of fund for the responsibilities devolved on them. In fact, there should be separation of budget head (Panchayat window) for all district sector schemes, which every department may work out in the first year of the Plan period so that it becomes easier to know the budgetary resources for the District Plan. State Government officials entrusted with the implementation of devolved functions will be suitably deputed to the Panchayat bodies and there should be enough control on such employees so that their services could be effectively utilized by the Panchayats. Funds for their establishment cost should be routed through the Panchayat bodies for better ownership of the related programmes by the Panchayats. Steps will be taken on building up capacities of the Panchayat functionaries and the officials for improving the efficiency of the Panchayats. Such capacity building will be linked to better delivery of the basic services related to both economic and social sectors. Enabling environment will be built up for more focus on the citizen, particularly the poorer and the weaker sections, as well as the quality of services being provided to them through better dissemination of information by enforcing the Right To Information Act. Arrangement for training of the members and functionaries will be boosted up for this purpose. The State Institute of Panchayats and Rural Development and the Extension Training Centres will be strengthened and each district and block will be provided with appropriate training facilities. Along with conventional classroom training and training to be conducted using distance learning facilities being developed with the help of the ISRO, more efforts will be made on sharing of good practices, exposure visits. Development of institutional aspects of functioning of the Panchayats related to better transparency, accountability, participation of the poor and organizational efficiency will be given more attention.

Steps will also be taken to improve revenue mobilization by the Panchayats, both tax and non-tax, during the Plan period.

With proper devolution of function, fund and functionaries, it will be easier to take up village-based planning exercise, with more active participation of the poor, the women and other weaker sections of the community so that resources available are best utilized to cater to the needs of the people. Such planning exercise will start from the Gram Samsad level, which will be facilitated by the Gram Unnayan Samitis. These plans will be integrated to form the GP plan, the PS plan and the ZP plan and eventually the District plan. There will be need for more manpower resources at the grassroots level and part of the need will be met by training the available local people, Panchayat functionaries on various aspects of decentralized planning including few relevant PRA (Participatory Rural Appraisal) techniques. Model for the same is being developed under the SRD (Strengthening Rural Decentralisation) Programme, being supported by the DFID and the same will be replicated in all the districts.

## Special Area Programmes

### *Hill Areas*

The Hill Affairs Department acts as the nodal Department of Darjeeling Gorkha Hill Council, established under the provision of Darjeeling Gorkha Hill Council Act, 1988 with the objective of total social, economic, cultural and educational upliftment of the hill people of the Darjeeling district under the jurisdiction of Darjeeling Gorkha Hill Council. The jurisdiction of the Hill Council covers an area of 2476 sq. km covering 3 Revenue Sub-divisions of Kalimpong, Kurseong and Darjeeling and 13 Mouzas of Siliguri Revenue Sub-division. Under the provision of Darjeeling Gorkha Hill Council Act, 1988 the executive powers of about 27 departments have been transferred to the Hill Council. The management and control of the programmes and schemes as well as the organizational set up of these departments have been transferred to the Darjeeling Gorkha Hill Council.

The Sundarban Affairs Department implements its activities through the Sundarban Development Board in the operational area of the department, which consists of 19 blocks spread in the North and South 24-Parganas districts. The land area measures about 9630 sq. km of which 4444 sq. km is inhabited and the rest is Reserve Forest. The present aggregate population of Sundarban is over 41 lakh. The density of population is 989.78 persons per square kilometre, which is higher than the State average. The level of literacy varies from 53 to 79 per cent.

The economy of the region is almost dependent on agriculture and allied activities. Total cultivable land area extends over 3.05 lakh hectare. The average landholding per household is around 0.55 hectare. The agricultural crop is aman rice grown in rainfed condition. Only 15 to 17 per cent of the cultivable land can be brought under a second crop like oilseed, pulses and vegetables with limited irrigation facilities so far created.

The Sunderbans Affairs Department with its Plan outlay has been trying to address the major problems like poor drainage and irrigation, lack of transport and communication, especially in the island areas, poor status of social services, conservation of sensitive biodiversity, underdeveloped agriculture and allied sectors, unemployment and under-employment etc.

## Irrigation

There are 7 major irrigation projects and 34 medium irrigation schemes in operation. Out of these, the work of barrage and irrigation system of the Damodar Valley Project, the Mayurakshi Reservoir project, The Kangsabati Reservoir Project, the Hinglow Reservoir Project and the Midnapor Canals are taken up. The Teesta Barrage Project and Subarnarekha Barrage Project are the two major on-going schemes. In addition to the above two irrigation schemes, namely Darakeshwar-Gandheswari Reservoir Project with ultimate irrigation potential of 51,200 ha and Siddheswari-Noonbeel Reservoir Project with irrigation potential of 25,000 ha have been proposed to be taken up during the Eleventh Five Year Plan.

## Minor Irrigation

According to the criteria laid down by the Planning Commission, the irrigation schemes having Cultivable Command Area (CCA) of 2000 hectares or less are classified as 'Minor Irrigation Schemes'. The Panchayat Bodies are involved at all stages in the implementation of the minor irrigation schemes. The sites of the schemes are selected as per the requirements of the local farmers particularly small and marginal farmers and also in consultation with the local Panchayat Bodies. Considering serious condition of Ground Water aquifer, emphasis has been given to the districts of North Bengal in formulating the schemes for execution. Proper attention has also been given to cover areas inhabited by persons of the scheduled castes, tribal and other backward classes. Schemes of water resources through regular monitoring of water level and water quality are also taken up. Work of assessment of Ground Water and Surface Water, augmentation of Ground Water Resources through artificial recharge and delineation of aquifer with saline, arsenic and fluoride contamination are also done. All these activities will be taken up during the Eleventh Five Year Plan period.

In terms of the 73rd Constitutional Amendment and in conformity with the provision of the West Bengal Panchayat Act, the Panchayat bodies are involved right from the preparation of the minor irrigation schemes. Sites of the schemes are selected in consultation with the local panchayat bodies taking due care of the requirements of the small and marginal farmers.

## Cottage and Small Scale Industries

The cottage and small-scale industries play a very important role in industrialization. At present over 90 per cent of the industrial units in the State are in micro and small-scale industries sector. This sector provides highest employment opportunities to the people only after the agriculture sector. Nearly 60 per cent of the industrial output in the State is from the cottage and small-scale industries sector, which also accounts for 50 per cent of the State's overall exports.

The Micro Enterprises have a direct impact on the generation of self-employment, particularly in the rural areas. This sub-sector has more social relevance than the enterprises in the small, medium and large sectors. This sector also provides for the new generation first entrepreneurs the first exposure to the entrepreneurship and industrial activities. At present, most of the enterprises/units in this sector are in the unorganized mould.

The Cottage and Small Scale Industries Department since renamed as the Department of Micro and Small Scale Enterprises and Textiles also monitors the activities and programmes for the development of handlooms and textiles in the State. The textiles sector includes the powerlooms, hosiery and readymade garments enterprises. There are nearly 6.67 lakh people, majority of them in rural areas, who are directly or indirectly associated with handloom activities. Out of these only 10 per cent are in the co-operative fold, while the remaining are outside of it—mostly in the unorganized sector. Besides, there are nearly 2.5 lakh people directly or indirectly associated with powerloom, hosiery, readymade garments and other textiles related activities.

The Department of Micro and Small Scale Enterprises and Textiles also administers the activities and programmes for the development of sericulture and silk weaving activities in the State. All the three varieties of sericulture, viz. mulberry, tassar and muga, are grown in the State with a combined area coverage of nearly 53000 acres. The number of sericulture farmers in the State is nearly 130000. The total silk production in the State is approximately 1585 M.T., while the silk waste production totals nearly 527 M.T. The total employment generation in the sericulture sector in the State is 3.07 lakh.

## People's Participation in Delivery of Public Health Services

The P&RD Department in collaboration with the H&FW Department is working for building capacities of the Panchayats so that they take the responsibility of improving better delivery of preventive and promotive health care services to the people. The Panchayats have been already given the responsibility of maintaining the physical infrastructure of the Sub-centres and the PHCs. Infrastructure of the BPHCs, PHCs and Sub-centres entrusted with the Panchayats will be improved to facilitate the delivery of better service, particularly to the mothers and the children. Panchayats with the support of the SHGs will help to promote IEC (Information, Education and Communication) activities related to prevention of disease and promotion of good health and accessing available services from the Government outlets. Effort will be made to provide some of the curative services (outdoor treatment) in all the Sub-centres located in the Gram Panchayat (head quarter sub-centre), where no PHC/BPHC is located so that access to such services to the poor people is substantially improved. The process entails capacity building of all the stakeholders involved and a small fund available with the village level functionaries and Panchayat bodies for community level preventive and promotive activities. Functional Committees of the Gram Unnayan Samiti have been formed at the Gram Sansad level under the overall control of the Gram Panchayats to take up this responsibility and capacity building initiatives have already been launched. The funding for this initiative is mostly being made by the Health and Family Welfare Department of the State Government under the National Rural Health Mission through the Panchayat and R & D Department.

## BIHAR

Bihar's economy is now set on a development path, which would ensure that it reaches its targets under the Eleventh Five Plan period (2007-12). Essentially, these targets include an accelerated growth, which is inclusive as well, implying higher levels of development in the social sector and improved delivery of social services. In 2008-09, the population of Bihar is estimated to be 99.0 million, implying a population density of 951 persons per sq. km. But, fortunately, in spite of such high demographic pressure on land, the present Bihar has abundant natural resourccs in the form of its fertile land and plentiful water to pursue its development goals.

Although a number of crucial steps have been taken to accelerate the growth process in Bihar, it has had to face a major challenge in the form of unprecedented floods, devastating a large part of its population in the north-eastern region. For rescue operations alone, the State Government has to spend a huge amount. This, however, has not deterred the State Government from continuing its efforts to strengthen the economy through higher levels of expenditure in infrastructure and social sectors.

## Production and Productivity

Because of its rich bio-diversity, the farmers in Bihar are able to produce a large number of crops: cereals, pulses, oilseeds, fibre crops, fruits and vegetables. The following table presents the area and production of major crops in Bihar in the last eight years—2000-01 to 2007-08. The average levels of the production of major crops in Bihar are—43.7 lakh tonnes (rice), 36.0 lakh tonnes (wheat), and 14.9 lakh tonnes (maize). Adding to this, the production of other cereals (which are all considered as coarse cereals), the total production of cereals is 95.4 lakh tonnes. Further, taking into consideration the total production of pulses at 4.9 lakh tonnes, the total production of food grains is 100.3 lakh tonnes, for a population of about 99.0 million. In addition to food grains, the major crops also include oilseeds and fibres and the average levels of their production are 1.3 lakh tonnes (oilseeds) and 13.1 lakh bales of (fibre crops).

**Table 15:** Area and Production of Major Crops in Bihar (2000-2008)

| *Crops* | *Percentage of Area* | | | | | | | |
|---|---|---|---|---|---|---|---|---|
| | 2000-01 | 2001-02 | 2002-03 | 2003-04 | 2004-05 | 2005-06 | 206-07 | 2007-08 (2nd Adv. Esti.) |
| Food grains | 95.98 | 96.01 | 96.09 | 96.12 | 53.34 | 62.96 | 49.99 | 46.84 |
| Cereals | 87.21 | 87.79 | 87.81 | 89.79 | 34.13 | 39.64 | 31.60 | 28.64 |
| Pulses | 8.77 | 8.22 | 8.28 | 6.33 | 19.21 | 23.32 | 18.38 | 18.20 |
| Oilseeds | 1.85 | 1.91 | 1.95 | 1.80 | 12.69 | 14.67 | 12.14 | 12.37 |
| Fibres | 2.17 | 2.07 | 1.97 | 2.09 | 33.97 | 22.38 | 37.87 | 40.78 |
| **Total** | **100.00** | **100.00** | **100.00** | **100.00** | **100.00** | **100.00** | **100.00** | **100.00** |

Since the agricultural economy of Bihar is still basically oriented towards subsistence, the foodgrains account for a very large part of the area under major crops. It is observed that nearly 95 per cent of the area under major crops is devoted to foodgrains. Within that category, the share of cereals production has been increasing: it was 87.21 per cent in 2000-01, but has reached 94.20 per cent in 2007-08. Consequently, the share of area under pulses has decreased from 8.77 per cent in 2000-01 to only 1.42 per cent in 2006-07. There is also a small increase in the share of area under oilseeds; from 1.85

per cent in 2000-01 it has increased to 2.03 per cent in 2007-08. For fibres, the share of area has remained nearly unaltered around 2.23 per cent.

For rice, the average productivity is 1287 kg/hectare, although for *aghani* rice (the most important among three rice varieties), the productivity is a little higher at 1327 kg/hectare. The productivity of wheat is higher and stands at 1749 kg/hectare. The most satisfactory levels of productivity is attained by maize (2367kg/hectare) and here again rabi maize (the most important among the three varieties of maize) has an even higher productivity at 3030 kg/hectare. For the pulses, the rabi season is more important as it accounts for more than 80 per cent pulse production; but the productivity of kharif pulses (929 kg/hectare) is found be higher than the productivity of rabi pulses (738 kg/hectare).

Bio-diversity is very wide in Bihar and, therefore, the farmers in Bihar produce a large number of fruits and vegetables, besides the major crops. Vegetables in 2006-07 were—11.8 lakh tonnes (potato), 10.1 lakh tonnes (cauliflower), 9.2 lakh tonnes (tomato) and 11.2 lakh tonnes (brinjal). The category of fruits also includes a number of species, but the four most important ones are—mango, litchi, guava and banana. The production levels of these fruits in 2006-07 were—13.1 lakh tonnes (mango), 2.1 lakh tonnes (litchi), 2.5 lakh tonnes (guava) and 11.3 lakh tonnes (banana).

## Irrigation

To free agriculture from the uncertainties of monsoon, it is extremely important to provide assured irrigation facilities to the sector. Not only does it provide stability of agricultural production, assured irrigation is also a necessary prerequisite for the adoption of high yielding variety (HYV) seeds. In view of the abundant water resources in the State, the provision of adequate irrigation facilities should not be a major challenge in Bihar, but unfortunately, only about 60 per cent of the cultivated area is endowed with some irrigation facility in the State.

As regards the contribution of different sources towards irrigation facilities, it is observed that tube well irrigation is the most important source, accounting for 83.8 per cent of the irrigated area in 2007-08. Over the years, this share has increased from 81.9 per cent in 2000-01 to its present level of 83.8 per cent. The share of other sources of irrigation (canal, tanks, wells and other sources) has either remained unaltered or decreased marginally.

The Road Map for Agriculture for Bihar, prepared by the State Government visualises the creation of additional irrigation capacity through a number of projects. Among these projects are included Western Kosi Canal, Durgawati Waterbody, Sone Canal Modernisation, Barnar Waterbody, Bateswarnath Ganga Pump Canal (Phase-I), Jamania Pump Canal, North Koel Waterbody, Punpun Barrage, Batane Waterbody, Underasthan Barrage and Bagmati Multipurpose Plans. The State Government is also planning the interlinking of rivers in the State as a step towards integrated water management of the State. Apart from generating additional irrigation capacity, the project will also alleviate the problems of flood and drought. For this, a river basin will be taken up as a unit and an integrated plan will be made for irrigation, flood control and water drainage.

## Seeds

For realising the full potential of land and irrigation inputs, availability of quality seeds is extremely important for raising the productivity of cultivation. For various reasons, the Seed Replacement Rate (SRR) is one of the lowest in Bihar among the major States in India and the State Government has made substantial efforts in recent years to improve the situation.

Among the kharif crops, the SRR for paddy in 2008-09 was 19.0 per cent, compared to only 12.0 per cent in 2006-07. In case of kharif maize, there has been a modest increase in SRR from 50.0 per cent in 2006-07 to 57.0 per cent in 2008-09. However, in case of *arhar*, *urad* and *moong*, the increase in SRR is only marginal. Among the rabi crops, the SRR is available only for 2006-07 and 2007-08. Between these two years, the SRR for two crops has gone up substantially—maize (from 60.0 to 74.0 per cent) and rape/mustard (from 40.0 to 73.0 per cent). For other crops (wheat, gram and *masoor*), the increase in SRR is moderate, while the same for peas has recorded a small decrease.

Realising the importance of the supply of quality seeds, the State Government has taken several steps to improve seed management.

While the Bihar State Seed Corporation was revived from a state of liquidation in 2006-07, all the seed multiplication farms were operationalised in 2007-08.

## Fertiliser

The consumption of chemical fertilisers in Bihar has been rising steadily in recent years. The consumption levels were—2250.19 thousand tonnes (2004-05), 2772.79 thousand tonnes (2005-06), 3225.31 thousand tonnes (2006-07) and, finally, 3649.32 thousand tonnes (2007-08). Thus, over a four-year period, the consumption has increased by 62.2 per cent, which shows the eagerness of the farmers in Bihar to utilize this valuable input. The per hectare consumption of fertiliser stood at 155.60 kg. in 2007-08. Between the two important crop seasons, the use of fertiliser is higher in rabi season (195.80 kg/ha). Among the different types of fertilisers, the use of urea is the widest, as it alone accounts for about half the fertilizer consumption.

## Agricultural Credit

As modern and scientific methods of production take root in agriculture, cultivation comes to be directly connected with market, both for its input and output. While production for market is not yet the predominant characteristic of agriculture in Bihar, its dependence on the market for inputs is quite large.

The relevant information on credit flow to the agricultural sector in Bihar is presented in Table 16. Since the figures for 2008-09 related to the first six months of the year, the low achievement rates for 2008-09 are not surprising. For previous years, one may first note that the achievement rate for the disbursement of credit from all banks has shown a declining trend since 2003-04, except for a single year in 2004-05. This is an extremely serious phenomenon, especially when one bears in mind that the targets themselves are much lower than the actual requirement of the farmers. Starting from an achievement rate of 82.01 per cent in 2003-04, it stands at 76.96 per cent in 2007-08.

Among the three principal sources of credit, the commercial banks are most important, which account for about 65 per cent of the total credit disbursement; the shares of regional rural banks and central co-operative banks are about 25 and 10 per cent respectively. Since the commercial banks are the most important source of credit, it is a matter of concern that the achievement rates for these banks have also shown a declining trend. In 2007-08, the achievement rate for the three types of banks were—81.47 per cent (commercial banks), 75.80 per cent (regional rural banks) and 57.42 per cent (central commercial banks).

**Table 16:** Credit Flow to Agricultural Sector in Bihar (2003-04 to 2008-09)

| Bank Groups | | 2003-04 | 2004-05 | 2005-06 | 2006-07 | 2007-08 | 2008-09 |
|---|---|---|---|---|---|---|---|
| Commercial Bank | Target | 1220.15 | 1386.39 | 1645.57 | 2274.36 | 3003.58 | 4355.35 |
| | Achievement | 792.44 | 1325.06 | 1489.33 | 1915.93 | 2447.04 | 1388.80 |
| | Percentage | 64.95 | 95.58 | 90.51 | 84.24 | 81.47 | 31.89 |
| RRBs | Target | 376.98 | 550.86 | 644.26 | 938.67 | 1256.34 | 1821.69 |
| | Achievement | 204.87 | 431.30 | 450.09 | 797.07 | 952.36 | 552.13 |
| | Percentage | 54.35 | 78.30 | 69.86 | 84.91 | 75.80 | 30.31 |
| CCB | Target | 303.21 | 402.71 | 407.65 | 509.34 | 619.75 | 898.69 |
| | Achievement | 561.11 | 273.75 | 234.61 | 272.04 | 355.85 | 97.02 |
| | Percentage | 185.06 | 67.98 | 57.55 | 53.41 | 57.42 | 10.80 |
| All Banks | Target | 1900.34 | 2339.96 | 2697.48 | 3722.37 | 4879.67 | 7075.73 |
| | Achievement | 1558.42 | 2030.11 | 2174.03 | 2985.04 | 3755.25 | 2037.95 |
| | Percentage | 82.01 | 86.76 | 80.59 | 80.19 | 76.96 | 28.80 |

Since the commercial banks and even regional rural banks are often reluctant to expand agricultural credit, the co-operative banks are often regarded as an ideal source of credit for the farmers. Unfortunately, co-operative banks presently account for only 10 per cent of the agricultural credit in Bihar. One of the main reasons for such limited reach of the co-operative banks is that such banks are absent in no less than 16 districts of Bihar. Among the 22 districts where they exist, the achievement rate is often less than 40 per cent. For six districts, the achievement rates are less than 10 per cent.

## Animal Husbandry

To strengthen the animal husbandry sector in Bihar, the Government provides a number of useful services like breeding, sterilisation, immunization and free distribution of fodder seeds. If one compares the extent of these services in 2006-07 and 2007-08, it is observed that breeding and immunisation services have increased, but the services have been lower for other two components of sterilisation and free distribution of fodder seeds. While a total of 24.96 lakh animals were treated in 2006-07, their number has gone upto 29.09 lakh in 2007-08. For sterilisation, the figures are—2.21 lakh (2006-07) and 1.74 lakh (2007-08). The improvement in immunisation services was extremely high—compared to 4.41 lakh animals in 2006-07, it was 61.95 lakh animals in 2007-08. Finally, there was a drop of about 18 per cent in the free distribution of fodder seeds, from 177.45 quintals in 2006-07, it fell to 146.09 quintals in 2007-08.

## Agriculture

The programmes for agricultural sector fall into four major groups—(a) input, access, supply and quality, (b) transfer of technology and extension, (c) income generation schemes, and (d) marketing. The specific programmes for agricultural development have been divided into the following 12 heads:

(i) *Seed Plan*: Achievement of ideal Seed Replacement Rate (SRR) for major crops through strengthening of seed infrastructure in the State—Bihar Rajya Beej Nigam (BRBN), Bihar State Seed Certification Agency (BSSCA), Seed Multiplication Farms (SMF) and, finally, fully Mechanised Agricultural Farms (MAF).

(ii) *Horticulture*: Provision of quality planting materials and establishment of a Tissue Culture Laboratory.

(iii) *Soil Health Management*: Improvement of soil health through the use of balanced nutrients (N, P and K), promotion of bio-fertilisers, and use of gypsum/pyrites in 24 districts where the soil has alkaline reaction.

(iv) *Crop Protection*: Prevention of crop losses by promoting Integrated Pest Management, Operationalisation of Plant Protection Centres and Bio-Control Laboratory.

(v) *Farm Mechanisation*: Promotion of mechanised farming through provision of financial subsidy for modern agricultural implements.

(vi) *Transfer of Technology*: Undertaking measures like Farmer's Field School, Field Demonstration, Farmers' Training and Exposure Visits, Awards to Progressive Farmers and Training of Officers at the Rajendra Agricultural University.

(vii) *Agricultural Extension*: Rejuvenation of the Department of Agriculture through appointment of officials at district, block and panchayat levels for extension work.

(viii) *Integrated Farming Model*: Promotion of integrated farming based on the model of the Indian Council of Agricultural Research (ICAR) through financial support to farmers.

(ix) *Soil and Water Conservations*: Promotion of soil and water conservation through the construction of Water Harvesting Structures, Silt Detention Dams, Earthen Check Dam and also promotion of dryland horticulture and agro-forestry.

(x) *Mini Weather Station*: Establishment of Mini Weather Stations, which could supply useful weather-related information to the farmers.

(xi) *Micro-Irrigation Projects*: Promotion of micro-irrigation through drip and sprinkling methods to about 2 lakh hectares of agricultural land, spread over all the 38 districts.

(xii) *Agricultural Marketing*: Establishment of a wide agricultural marketing infrastructure having three levels. At the top will be Model Terminal Markets (MTM), followed by Agri-Business Centres (ABC) and Rural Hats (RH). There will be 5 MTMs (at Patna, Muzaffarpur, Purnea, Bhagalpur and Gaya), 40 ABCs and 1500 RHs.

## Animal Husbandry

The scheme-wise programmes for the development of animal husbandry sector includes—(i) Doorstep Veterinary Service, (ii) Door-to-Door Vaccination and Drenching, (iii) Strengthening of Animal Husbandry offices, (iv) Extension services for animal husbandry, (v) Goat Breeding and Rearing Farm, (vi) Disposal of Carcass, (vii) Buffalo development, and (viii) Development of Rural Poultry.

## Dairy Development

With a share of about 5.6 per cent of the total livestock population of the country, the dairy sector is very important in the State's economy.

However, its potential is not fully utilised for several constraints. The Road Map visualizes the removal of these constraints throng several measures like animal input programmes (breeding facility, animal health care and animal nutrition), building of specialised infrastructure (dairy plants, chilling centres and bulk coolers) and arrangements for efficient marketing.

## Fisheries Development

Aquaculture and culture-based fisheries are valuable options for enhancing rural income. Overall, the proposed road map envisages the development of fisheries sector through (a) construction of water bodies like ponds and tanks, (b) intensive and semi-intensive fish culture in ponds, and (c) construction of inlet and outlet for easier passage in *mauns* (oxbow lakes) for culture-based fisheries. The specific programmes for the sector includes arrangement of fingerlings as seed, development of fisheries in water-logged areas, feed production, marketing infrastructure, training and extension services, and establishment of Fisheries Research Centre.

## Agro-based Industries

Based on the industrial units covered by Annual Survey of Industries (ASI), the agro-based industries in Bihar accounted for nearly half of the gross value added. If the remaining smaller units are also taken into account, the share of agro-based industries will be still higher. However, the potential of agro-based industries is not fully utilised. The development of agro-based industries is largely dependent on the importance assigned to fruits and vegetables *vis-à-vis* other crops. In 2006-07, the area under fruits and vegetables was 2.79 lakh hectares and 8.24 lakh hectares respectively, with their total production being 34.26 lakh tonne and 136.08 lakh tonne respectively.

The increase in the area and production of vegetables and fruits has not been satisfactory in recent years. In order to increase the volume of agro-based industries, it would be worthwhile to push both area and production much ahead of the present level so as to add to both income and employment to a large number of farmers. In honey, the State's average yield is 60 kg per box, which is three times more than the national average of 20 kg. Over one-lakh families are directly engaged in the honey sector.

**Table 17:** Area and Production of Vegetable and Fruits in Bihar (2006-07)

| *Vegetables* | *Area (hect.)* | *Production (tonne)* | *Fruits* | *Area (hect.)* | *Production (tonne)* |
|---|---|---|---|---|---|
| Cauliflower | 60135 | 1008975 | Mango | 140786 | 1306944 |
| Cabbage | 37003 | 623463 | Guava | 27994 | 247960 |
| Onion | 50472 | 962705 | Litchi | 28758 | 211905 |
| Tomato | 46461 | 916769 | Lemon | 17122 | 121601 |
| Potato | 322840 | 5741290 | Banana | 29013 | 1125099 |
| Brinjal | 54072 | 1120579 | Pineapple | 4454 | 121057 |
| Others | 253174 | 3234683 | Others | 31284 | 291919 |
| **Total** | **824157** | **13608464** | **Total** | **279411** | **3426485** |

*Source*: Department of Agriculture, GOB.

## Food Processing

The food processing industry has a great potential in the state. If developed properly, it may generate additional employment to at least 5 lakh persons. Besides processing of cereals, great potential remains to be tapped in fruits and vegetables. The processing of mango, litchi, banana, etc. will also take care of seasonal gluts, storage and retention of their nutritive value, apart from providing income and employment. *Makhana* is another leading crop that may help to enhance the income and employment of rural people. *Makhana* cultivation is spread over an area of 16.90 thousand hectares in about 10 districts in the north and north-eastern part of the State. Already a *Makhana* Processing Plant is successfully functioning at Patna. In view of huge potential for development of food processing industry in Bihar, the Industries Department has planned a Rs. 1760 crore project for the development of food processing infrastructure and other facilities in the State. Under the project, Rs. 500 crore would be spent on 100 rural commercial and primary processing centres. Another Rs. 250 crore is earmarked for the creation of two integrated food zones. For fish industry, there is a provision of Rs. 200 crore. In order to help the food processing units, a food park is being established at Hajipur by the Central Government with State's contribution in the form of land.

As a step towards promoting agro-industries, Kishanganj area has been identified as an ideal zone for tea plantation. The State Government welcomes private investment for comprehensive development of tea industry. Capital subsidy is available for setting up tea processing units in the area. Further, the potential for the development of farming and processing of medicinal, herbal and aromatic plants in the State is abundant because of its natural environment. The active participation of private sector and non-government organisations is encouraged and incentives are provided under the new industrial policy.

## Sugar

In view of favourable agro-climatic conditions for growing sugarcane in the State, there exists vast potential to increase the farm as well as the non-farm incomes. The objectives during the Eleventh Plan are to enhance the sugarcane production by augmenting the area under cultivation as also its productivity. The long-term goal is to gradually increase its area to 4.6 lakh hectares. The Sugarcane Research Institute, Pusa and the Rajendra Agriculture University are engaged in research in developing appropriate varieties for different agro-climatic conditions in the State and also to improve the quality of its yield. The State Government has also announced incentives like rebates for co-generation of power and manufacture of ethanol from molasses and waivers on administrative charges on molasses consumption by distilleries. The State Government has already come out with a Sugarcane Policy to help the sugar mills. Some reputed companies have been given the responsibility of the operation of 11 closed sugar mills in the State. The new Policy for Sugar Industry also grants the following incentives:

(i) To reimburse central excise duty on sugar for 5 years.
(ii) To exempt purchase tax on sugarcane for five crushing years.
(iii) To exempt stamp and registration fees for land transfer.
(iv) To grant 10 per cent subsidy on capital investment or a maximum of Rs. 10 crore, whichever is less, on machinery, after completion of the first year of commercial production.

## Non-Agro-Based Industries

*Handloom:* The handloom industry assumes great significance in the context of Bihar, because of a large number of weavers in the State. They are primarily concentrated in the districts of Patna, Gaya, Bhagalpur, Banka, Darbhanga, Arwal, Jehanabad, Aurangabad, Nawada, Nalanda, Bhabhua, Khagaria, Madhubani and Siwan. There are around 1071 weavers' cooperative societies in the State, with 10,817 handlooms. Besides, 23,503 handlooms are outside the co-operative sector. Around 1.33 lakh weavers are engaged in this sector, of which nearly a lakh are outside the co-operative sector. The State Government has introduced welfare schemes for weavers in the form of marketing assistance, modernization of training centres and repair of shed-*cum*-housing. Under the debt waiver scheme, the State Government has approved waiving of loans worth Rs. 12.24 crore.

If proper training, designing and marketing facilities are extended, this sector, including the power loom sector, has great potential of providing employment and enhanced income to an appreciable number of families.

*Textile:* For the development of textile and handloom sectors, the State Government has planned to establish a Textile Park with public-private partnership. Of the total cost of this plan, 40 per cent or a maximum of Rs. 40 crore will be invested by the Central Government as share money and 9 per cent by the State Government as subsidy and share money. Again, a Handloom Park at Bhagalpur is also being planned wherein all the necessary basic infrastructure and other facilities like raw material bank, pre- and post-processing facilities, artisan village, R & D Centre, testing laboratory, information and training centre, etc. will be made available for the weavers.

*Handloom Cluster Scheme:* For the integrated development of weavers in seven districts of Bhagalpur, Patna, Gaya, Darbhanga, Madhubani, Siwan and Nalanda, a diagnostic study and business plan has been prepared by IL&FS, New Delhi. It recommended the project cost of Rs. 68.65 crore, of which a sum of Rs. 24.00 crore is to be borne by the State Government and the remaining by the beneficiaries. Under this scheme, the looms of the weavers within the cluster will be modernized and a handloom park with all its amenities and facilities will be established.

*Sericulture:* The tussar and silk units are located mainly in and around Bhagalpur. The silk weaving and printing works are carried out here. There is a plan for physical infrastructure development during the Eleventh Plan, under which 5 pilot project centres and one marketing centre for tassar will be developed. In order to increase production, this will provide tassar silk cocoons to the persons engaged in this industry and also help in its marketing. With training facilities for the technical personnel through the Central Silk Board, there is also a provision of rewarding the best three cocoon rearers and silk producers, besides consolation prizes.

## Literacy

In all the districts of Bihar, the gender gap in literacy among SCs is lower than it is for the overall population. Historically, the SC population has been more concentrated in south Bihar. In the four districts of south Bihar where SC population is more than 20 per cent of the total, the gender gap in literacy is much lower than the average for the district. The gender gap among the SC population is 11 per cent in Nawada, 9 per cent in Gaya and 6 per cent in Aurangabad. In Darbhanga in north Bihar, the gender gap is also significantly low at 8 per cent. The overall gender gap is the highest in Bhojpur (the district with the highest proportion of literate males) at 32.5 per cent and the lowest in Bhagalpur at 21.2 per cent. Thus, an overall emphasis on female literacy at the district level to close the gender gap is warranted.

## Primary and Secondary Education

The overall enrolment at the primary and upper primary level has increased by 34.5 per cent in the period between 2003-04 and 2006-07. There has been a 41.5 per cent increase in enrolment of children from SC communities and 80.7 per cent increase for ST communities. The enrolment has significantly improved in upper primary level with an overall increase of 72.8 per cent. For SCs, the enrolment in upper primary has increased by 97.4 per cent while, for STs, it has increased by 126.0 per cent. Araria, Samsastipur, Purnea, Bhojpur and Begusari have seen more than 50 per cent overall increase in enrolment. All the districts, except Begusarai, have also seen more than 100 per cent increase in SC enrolment in the corresponding period.

## Interventions in Primary and Secondary Education

- For the enrolment of 6-14 year olds among Mahadalit children and to ensure their regular attendance, UTHAN KENDRA scheme has been implemented in their hamlets.
- *Talimi Markaj* scheme has been started to ensure primary education for disadvantaged sections in the minority community with targeted teaching facilities in their hamlets/villages.

- *Unnayan* scheme has been commenced to start residential centres for primary education of 50 children rescued from child labour in each block.
- Free textbooks have been distributed among children of Class I to VIII from most backward castes and minority communities.
- Free vocational training for girls between 10-16 years from minority background under *Hunar* to attract them to education.
- *Mukhya Mantri Balika Cycle Yojana* has been extended to aided schools including minority schools. 1.63 lakh girls came under the scheme in 2007-08.

## Health

Vaccination coverage increased in Bihar between 1998-99 and 2004-05, from 12 per cent to 33 per cent while there was only a 2 per cent increase in the national average in the same period. Infant mortality in Bihar decreased from 72 to 68 per 1000 live births in the same period. This was mainly attributable to rise in institutional deliveries from 15 to 22 per cent in the same period.

## Health Infrastructure

There are 11,107 health centres of all types in Bihar. Of these, 415 are rural Primary Health Centres (PHCs), 69 urban PHCs, 9588 sub-centres and 1035 Additional PHCs. For every lakh of population, there are 13 health centres. There are wide variations in coverage at the district level. While Khagaria has 153 health centres and Gopalganj has 89 centres for every lakh of population, Nawada has only 8. Apart from Goplaganj and Khagaria, no district has more than 19 centres for every lakh of population. While 28 districts have at least one rural referral hospital, the remaining 10 have none. The total number of referral hospitals in the state is 70.

## Labour, Employment and Poverty

Incidence of poverty has been very high in Bihar compared to the national average for decades. Estimates of poverty by the NSSO surveys, also established this point. The incidence of rural poverty in Bihar has come down from a level of 64.4 per cent in 1983-84 to 45.7 per cent in 2004-05. Urban poverty has declined from 47.3 per cent to 34.6 per cent during the same period. Nevertheless, the poverty ratio for 2004-05 is still quite high compared to the corresponding ratios at the national level—rural (28.3 per cent) and urban (25.7 per cent).

**Table 18:** Poverty Ratios in Bihar and India

| *Sector* | *Year* | *Bihar* | *India* |
|---|---|---|---|
| | 1983-84 | 64.4 | 45.7 |
| | 1987-88 | 52.6 | 39.1 |
| *Rural* | 1993-94 | 58.2 | 37.3 |
| | 1999-2000 | 44.3 | 27.1 |
| | 2004-05 | 42.1 | 28.3 |
| | 1983-84 | 47.3 | 40.8 |
| | 1987-88 | 48.7 | 38.2 |
| *Urban* | 1993-94 | 34.5 | 32.4 |
| | 1999-2000 | 32.9 | 23.6 |
| | 2004-05 | 34.6 | 25.7 |
| | 1983-84 | 62.2 | 44.5 |
| | 1987-88 | 52.1 | 38.9 |
| *Combined* | 1993-94 | 55.0 | 36.0 |
| | 1999-2000 | 42.6 | 26.1 |
| | 2004-05 | 41.4 | 27.5 |

Poverty as a basic deprivation of basic human needs is related to lives and livelihood issues in many ways. The employment pattern of different social groups is an indicator of the link between livelihood issues and poverty. The Work Participation Ratio (WPR) is the highest among ST (45.2 per cent), followed by SC (39.7 per cent) while the overall WPR for the state is 33.7 per cent.

The proportion of cultivators among various social groups is also further indicative of economic status. It is well known that less than 5 per cent of the State's cultivators own more than 10 acres of land each. Most cultivators are small or marginal farmers. But even within this, the proportion of cultivators is very low for SC (7.9 per cent) compared to the State average of 29.3 per cent. For ST, the corresponding figure is 21.3 per cent. Thus, landlessness is directly associated with SC status.

## Self-Help Groups (SHGs) and Swarnajayanti Grameen Swarozgar Yojana (SGSY)

SGSY is a scheme to promote self-employment among the communities through SHGs as well as individual self-employment programmes. A total of 14,036 SHGs were formed in 2007-08 under SGSY compared to 8,324 in the pervious year. Of these new SHGs, 8,120 were women SHGs (57.9 per cent). Upto the month of December 2008, 47 per cent of the funds available for SGSY has been utilised at the State level, compared to 52 per cent in the same period in the previous year.

A wide inter-district variation is seen in the performance of SGSY, both in terms of financial utilisation and physical achievements. While the recently created Arwal district has utilised 12.9 per cent of the funds available to it in 2007-08 compared to 7.5 per cent last year, Patna saw a high utilisation of 95.4 per cent of funds. The highest number of SHGs were formed in Muzaffarpur (2149), followed by Araria (830), East Champaran (784) and Saharsa (782). At the other end, there are two districts where no SHG has been formed—Bhagalpur and Lakhisarai, repeating the pattern from last year with a fund utilisation of 48 and 30 per cent respectively.

In 2007-08, a total of 85,355 *swarojgari* members of SHGs and 18,205 individual *swarojgaris* were given assistance for economic activities under SGSY. Similarly, 1,00,003 *swarojgari* members of SHGs and 10,036 individual *swarojgaris* were trained under the programme. The women *swarojgari* members of SHGs accounted for 51 per cent of total *swarojgari* members of SHGs who got economic assistance and 60 per cent of those who got training. The corresponding figures for individual women *swarojgaris* were 22 and 27 per cent. Thus, SHGs are seen to offer a better instrument for women's access to self-employment, as opposed to individual self-employment efforts. The SC *swarojgari* members of SHGs accounted for 38 per cent of total *swarojgari* members of SHGs who got economic assistance and 35 per cent of those who got training. The corresponding figures for individual SC *swarojgaris* were 42 and 41 per cent. Thus, for SCs again, the access through SHGs has not been a better option for women's self-employment.

## National Rural Employment Guarantee Scheme (NREGS)

The NREGS is a demand based guaranteed employment programme.

Any applicant is entitled as a right to 100 days of employment under the programme. The job cards were issued to 81,24,997 households in 2007-08 for this programme. Out of these, 45.1 per cent were SC households. Among the card-holding households, 48.3 per cent had demanded employment in 2007-08, and 39,25,748 of them (48.3 per cent) were provided employment. Only 1.3 per cent (49,945 households) of the total number of households were provided with 100 days of employment in 2007-08, as stipulated in the NREG Act.

## Indira Awas Yojana (IAY)

The Indira Awas Yojana is an important intervention for affordable housing for people below the poverty line. It is mandatory under the scheme to provide housing to a minimum of 60 per cent of SC and ST, 15 per cent of minorities and 3 per cent of the handicapped.

In 2007-08, the State Government completed 73 per cent of the physical target with a fund utilization of 72 per cent. The share of SCs and STs in the total houses completed was 55 per cent which was below the stipulated of at least 60 per cent. Similarly, the share of minorities was 8.5 per cent, against the stipulation of 15 per cent.

**Table 19:** Overview of IAY upto 2007-08

| *IAY Components* | *IAY New* | *IAY Upgraded* | *IAY Credit-cum-Subsidy* | *Total* | *Percentage share of Different Population Categories in the Scheme* |
|---|---|---|---|---|---|
| Total target | – | – | – | 567171 | – |
| Houses Completed | 377453 | 24740 | 2414 | 404607 | – |
| Houses Completed (SC) | 198417 | 12642 | 1129 | 212188 | 51.5 |
| Houses Completed (ST) | 12640 | 917 | 186 | 13743 | 3.3 |
| Houses Completed (Minorities) | 34251 | 928 | 19 | 35198 | 8.5 |
| Houses Completed (Others) | 132145 | 10253 | 1080 | 143478 | 34.8 |
| Total funds Available (Rs. lakhs) | 196448.107 | 7303.708 | 771.594 | 204523.409 | |
| Total Funds Utilized (Rs. lakhs) | 141790.12 | 3598.70 | 326.28 | 145715.09 | |
| Percentage of Utilization | 72.2 | 49.3 | 42.3 | 71.2 | |

## Interventions for Marginalised Sections

### Mahadalit

The State Government formed the State Mahadalit Commission for the development of the most deprived amongst the Scheduled Castes. The Commission observed that out of the 22 Scheduled Castes in Bihar, 20 castes are acutely deprived in terms of educational, economic, socio-cultural and political status. The Commission identified these 20 castes primarily on the basis of their literacy rate. While the total literacy rate of Bihar is 47 per cent, and that for all Scheduled Castes is 28.5 per cent, it is only 16.7 per cent in case of Mahadalits. It noted that populations belonging to these castes had not benefited from affirmative action meant exclusively for the Scheduled Castes.

## Economic Empowerment of Women

1. *Organising, nurturing and capacity building of women SHGs*: This programme will be implemented in all the districts to enable women to access services and schemes available, raise their awareness levels and help women to undertake various income generating activities. The objective is to help develop collective strength and leadership qualities among women so that they can manage and own their institutions, i.e. SHGs and Federations.
2. *Training in the service sector*: Through this programme, women and adolescent girls will be trained so that they can earn a livelihood in the service sector such as housekeeping, computer operation, etc.
3. *Initial capitalization of fund*: Grant support be extended to women federations amounting to Rs. 20,000 per SHG which will help them in on-lending to groups until bank loan is accessed.
4. *Infrastructure development and livelihood promotion*: Turn key projects will be supported for the economic empowerment of women through training and setting up of production centres.
5. *Preparation of project proposals, workshop and seminars/ monitoring*: Various action researches will be undertaken for the purpose of economic empowerment of women and presented in workshop and seminars for replication and scaling up. Monitoring activities will also be undertaken under this sub-component.

# UTTAR PRADESH

## Agriculture

Agriculture is the most crucial sector for economic development of the State. It contributes the highest share of about 33 per cent to the total income of the State. A vast majority of the population in the State virtually relies on agriculture for its livelihood. As high as 66 per cent of the workforce in the State depends on agriculture. A higher growth in the State's total economy cannot be achieved or sustained on a long-term basis, without good growth in agriculture nor any significant reduction could take place in poverty and employment without such growth. A higher growth in other sectors, howsoever desirable, can also not be sustained without sound growth in agriculture nor can it change the complexion of the economy, from backwardness to prosperity or compensate for lower growth in agriculture.

## Cereals

The average productivity of food grains is 20.77 q/ha and in case of cereals, it is 22.90 q/ha in the state. The food grains productivity varies in different agro-climatic zones from 10.51 q/ha (in Bundelkhand zone) to 30.49 q/ha (in western plain zone). Similarly, in case of cereals it varies from 16.19 q/ha (in Bundelkhand zone) to 31.40 q/ha (in western plain zone). The zone-wise details are presented below:

**Table 20:** Zone-wise Food Grain Production

*(q/ha)*

| Sl. No. | Zones | Food Grains | Total Cereals | Rice | Wheat | Jowar | Bajra | Maize (Kh) |
|---|---|---|---|---|---|---|---|---|
| 1. | Tarai and Bhabhar | 23.76 | 24.82 | 20.82 | 30.12 | 10.87 | 11.06 | 10.02 |
| 2. | Western Plain | 30.49 | 31.40 | 22.36 | 35.61 | 8.08 | 12.43 | 18.58 |
| 3. | Mid-Western Plain | 23.73 | 24.65 | 19.98 | 30.26 | 10.73 | 13.44 | 14.97 |
| 4. | South West Semi-Dry | 23.54 | 24.30 | 22.98 | 28.57 | 11.37 | 15.70 | 19.10 |
| 5. | Mid-Plain/Central | 22.23 | 24.00 | 19.52 | 29.10 | 12.08 | 14.92 | 13.03 |
| 6. | Bundelkhand | 10.51 | 16.19 | 8.20 | 19.11 | 8.41 | 13.61 | 9.19 |
| 7. | North Eastern Plain | 22.20 | 21.09 | 17.42 | 25.87 | 11.94 | 16.48 | 9.77 |
| 8. | Eastern Plain | 20.37 | 21.41 | 17.82 | 25.91 | — | 12.02 | 11.73 |
| 9. | Vindhyan | 16.22 | 17.64 | 18.27 | 19.94 | 11.71 | 9.30 | 6.30 |
| 10. | Uttar Pradesh | 20.77 | 22.90 | 18.78 | 27.66 | 10.29 | 14.55 | 13.26 |

## Pulses

The average productivity of pulses is 7.25 q/ha in the State. It varies in different agro-climatic zones from 6.57q/ha (in Bundelkhand zone) to 8.09 q/ha (in mid-central plain). The zone-wise details are presented below:

**Table 21:** Zone-wise Production of Pulses

*(q/ha)*

| *Sl. No.* | *Zones* | *Total Pulses* | *Arhar* | *Gram* | *Pea* | *Ma-soor* | *Urd (Kh)* |
|---|---|---|---|---|---|---|---|
| 1. | Tarai and Bhabhar | 7.18 | 6.70 | 7.44 | 9.67 | 7.22 | 7.38 |
| 2. | Western Plain | 7.91 | 9.55 | 7.30 | 9.67 | 5.66 | 5.61 |
| 3. | Mid-Western Plain | 7.61 | 6.92 | 7.30 | 9.67 | 7.68 | 6.63 |
| 4. | South West/Semi-Dry | 7.45 | 8.31 | 8.31 | 9.67 | 9.05 | 5.61 |
| 5. | Mid-Plain/Central | 8.09 | 8.22 | 10.66 | 12.13 | 7.68 | 5.17 |
| 6. | Bundelkhand | 6.57 | 6.40 | 6.22 | 9.36 | 5.52 | 5.40 |
| 7. | North Eastern Plain | 7.98 | 6.20 | 7.39 | 9.67 | 8.68 | 5.47 |
| 8. | Eastern Plain | 8.02 | 7.66 | 8.62 | 9.95 | 8.47 | 5.61 |
| 9. | Vindhyan | 7.94 | 6.90 | 9.59 | 10.38 | 6.88 | 4.89 |
| 10. | Uttar Pradesh | 7.25 | 7.49 | 7.42 | 9.67 | 7.05 | 5.61 |

## Oilseeds

The average productivity of oil seeds is 8.36Q/Ha in the State. It varies in different agro-climatic zones from 3.74Q/Ha (in Bundelkhand zone) to 13.03 Q/Ha (in south-western semi-dry zone). The zone-wise details are presented below:

**Table 22:** Zone-wise Production of Oil Seeds

*(Q/Ha)*

| *Sl. No.* | *Zones* | *Total Oilseeds* | *Rapeseed/Mustard* |
|---|---|---|---|
| 1. | Tarai and Bhabhar | 8.13 | 8.67 |
| 2. | Western Plain | 9.69 | 9.78 |
| 3. | Mid-Western Plain | 9.26 | 10.04 |
| 4. | South West/Semi-Dry | 13.03 | 13.17 |
| 5. | Mid-Plain/Central | 8.02 | 9.28 |
| 6. | Bundelkhand | 3.74 | 4.49 |
| 7. | North Eastern Plain | 8.26 | 8.42 |
| 8. | Eastern Plain | 10.39 | 11.68 |
| 9. | Vindhyan | 5.05 | 5.46 |
| 10. | Uttar Pradesh | 8.36 | 10.22 |

An analysis of the above table shows that the outlay for agriculture and allied sectors, which stood at 24.69 per cent in the First Plan, increased to 28.89 per cent in the Second Plan, but thereafter, it is continuously declining. During the Eleventh Five Year Plan it is expected to be 10.6 per cent.

## Institutional Credit

### *Crop Loan*

Ninety per cent of the farmers in the State are small and marginal and their purchasing capacity is also marginal. Credit is an important factor to the farmers for performing their farm activities. Non-institutional credit is always painful for the farmers because of high rate of interest.

Target, distribution and gap of the previous years in crop loan are shown as under:

**Table 23:** Crop Loan-Target, Distribution and gap of Previous Years

*(Rs. in crores)*

| *Sl. No* | *Year* | *Target* | *Distribution* | *Gap* |
|---|---|---|---|---|
| 1. | 2001-02 | 4867.64 | 3446.88 | –1420.76 |
| 2. | 2002-03 | 4513.22 | 3880.40 | –632.78 |
| 3. | 2003-04 | 4675.59 | 4110.84 | –564.75 |
| 4. | 2004-05 | 5375.48 | 5295.51 | –79.97 |
| 5. | 2005-06 | 7023.00 | 7464.00 | +441.00 |
| 6. | 2006-07 | 8640.00 | 8704.98 | +64.98 |
| 7. | 2007-08 (Kharif) | 3330.46 | 3518.39 | +187.93 |

## Kisan Credit Card (KCC)

In order to ensure hassle free and timely credit to the farmers, the Kisan Credit Card Scheme was introduced in the State since December 1999. Under the scheme Kisan Credit Card holders are allowed to take loan within their credit limit as many times as they want and repay their loans as per their convenience. As per the policy of the Government of India all the farmers are to be covered under the KCC Scheme. 195.01 lakh cards were distributed among the farmers till Kharif, 2007. Further Kisan Credit Card holders are also provided insurance cover upto Rs. 50,000 under the Janata Personal Accident Insurance Scheme at a nominal premium of Rs. 9.40 per year. For meeting the consumption needs of the farmers the KCC holders are also allowed to avail 10 per cent of their crop loan credit limits as consumption loan.

## Holdings

As per the 2000-01 Agriculture Census there is a predominance of marginal and small farmers in the State. Small farmers and marginal farmers account for 76.9 per cent and 14.6 per cent of the total holdings respectively. However, this group of small and marginal farmers own only 61.2 per cent of the total land area. Average size of holding is only 0.83 ha per farmer. However, the average size of holdings of marginal farmers is only 0.04 ha.

The trend of number of holdings in Uttar Pradesh from 1970-71 to 2000-01 is given in Table 24.

**Table 24:** Trend of Land Holdings

*(In thousands)*

| *Year* | *Marginal (below 1 ha)* | *Small (1-2 ha)* | *Semi Medium (2-4 ha)* | *Medium (4-10 ha)* | *Large Holding (10 ha & above)* |
|---|---|---|---|---|---|
| 1970-71 | 10453 | 2689 | 1652 | 733 | 112 |
| 1980-81 | 12582 | 2898 | 1614 | 661 | 72 |
| 1985-86 | 13702 | 2964 | 1582 | 602 | 55 |
| 1990-91 | 14819 | 3118 | 1543 | 549 | 45 |
| 1995-96 | 16237 | 3136 | 1585 | 532 | 39 |
| 2000-01 | 16659 | 3087 | 1427 | 463 | 32 |

**Table 25:** Area under Various Land Holding Groups

*(In percentage)*

| *Category* | *1970-71* | *1980-81* | *1985-86* | *1990-91* | *1995-96* | *2000-01* |
|---|---|---|---|---|---|---|
| Marginal | 21.1 | 25.7 | 28.29 | 31.43 | 33.75 | 36.97 |
| Small | 20.8 | 22.6 | 23.32 | 24.41 | 23.85 | 24.28 |
| Semi-Medium | 25.0 | 24.6 | 24.44 | 23.38 | 23.27 | 21.71 |
| Medium | 23.2 | 21.0 | 19.14 | 16.92 | 15.87 | 14.35 |
| Large | 9.9 | 6.1 | 4.81 | 3.86 | 3.26 | 2.69 |

As a matter of fact, there is an increase in the number of marginal farmers by 59 per cent during the above period. Incidentally, the percentage of marginal holdings in the State is 76.9 which is highest in the country.

The total reported area of the State for the purpose of land utilization is 242.01 lakh ha. Around 79 per cent is being irrigated against, the net area sown (166.83 lakh ha). Details of land use are given in Table 26.

**Table 26:** Details of Land use Pettern

| *Sl. No.* | *Item* | *2005-06* |
|---|---|---|
| 1. | Total Cropped Area (000 ha) | |
| | (a) Kharif | 11857 |
| | (b) Rabi | 12839 |
| | (c) Zaid | 791 |
| | Total | 25524 |
| 2. | Cropping Intensity % | 153.03 |

## Seed Replacement Rate

Seed is one of the most vital inputs responsible for higher production under specific agro-climatic conditions and can contribute 10 to 15 per cent increase in production. The seed scenario in U.P. during Tenth Five Year Plan period has been highly encouraging in the case of cereal seeds especially paddy and wheat.

Another remarkable aspect of the seed sector is the enhanced participation of the private sector in the entrepreneurial development programme. The private sector is now contributing around 25 per cent of the total certified seeds distributed in the State. The State Seed Certification Agency is now devoting more time in the certification of seeds grown by the private producers.

Despite all these efforts the State is still facing the problem of shortage of seeds of various crops, which are grown in drought prone areas. The availability of good quality seeds of pulses, groundnut and sunflower has also been a chronic problem, which needs greater attention.

## Fertilizer

At an all-India level, fertilizers are used by 76 per cent farmer households during Kharif and by 54 per cent farmer households during the Rabi season. 27 per cent household use fertilizers available within the village. In the case of U.P., fertilizers are used by 78 per cent farmer households during Kharif and 88 per cent during Rabi season and 23 per cent households use fertilizers available within the village. Pesticides are used by 39 per cent farmer households during Kharif and 35 per cent during Rabi whereas at an all-India level, pesticides are used by 46 per cent farmer households during Kharif and 31 per cent during Rabi season.

Consumption of N, P, K in Uttar Pradesh as compared to other major States is given in Table 27.

**Table 27:** State-wise Consumption of Fertilizers in 2004-05

*(In kg. per hectare)*

| *Sl. No.* | *Item* | *India* | *U.P.* | *Punjab* | *Haryana* | *Maharashtra* | *Tamil Nadu* |
|---|---|---|---|---|---|---|---|
| 1. | N | 61.00 | 92.60 | 150.60 | 124.90 | 42.60 | 77.50 |
| 2. | P | 24.30 | 28.60 | 39.70 | 38.10 | 23.50 | 33.90 |
| 3. | K | 10.80 | 7.00 | 5.40 | 3.10 | 11.50 | 41.40 |
| | **Total** | **96.70** | **128.20** | **195.70** | **166.20** | **77.70** | **152.90** |

Data from the above table show that the consumption of nitrogen in the State is much more in comparison to the use of phosphatic and potassic fertilizers, and the imbalance is seriously affecting soil fertility. The reason behind this is the enormous cost of phosphatic and potassic fertilizers. During the period 2002-05, per hectare consumption of chemical fertilizers has marginally increased from 126.72 kg to 128.20 kg.

## Irrigation

The irrigation potential created in the State is approximately 324.26 lakh ha. A major portion of the potential (241.84 lakh ha) has been created through minor irrigation projects and only 82.42 lakh ha of area is irrigated through large and medium irrigation projects. However, only 64.55 per cent of the gross irrigated potential is being utilized, 60.72 per cent during the Kharif and 85.08 per cent during the Rabi.

## Net Irrigated Area *versus* Net Area Sown

The total irrigated area of the State is 131.19 lakh hectares. The source-wise irrigation status, as indicated in Table 28, shows that canal irrigation is 20.52 per cent, irrigation through the State tube wells is 2.92 per cent and private tube wells have the maximum share of irrigation that is 68.57 per cent.

**Table 28:** Source-wise Irrigation Status

*(In th. ha.)*

| Sl. No. | Irrigation Source | Area | Percentage (NAS) | Percentage (Irrigated) |
|---|---|---|---|---|
| | Net Area Sown | 16683 | | |
| 1. | Canal | 2692 | 16.13 | 20.52 |
| 2. | State Tube-wells | 383 | 2.30 | 2.92 |
| 3. | Private Tube-wells | 8996 | 53.92 | 68.57 |
| 4. | Other Sources | 1048 | 6.28 | 7.99 |
| | Net Irrigated Area | 13119 | 78.63 | |

## Horticulture

During the Eleventh Five Year Plan period (2007-12), the growth rate of this sector has been fixed at 10 per cent. To achieve this growth rate the Government is implementing various developmental schemes, i.e. production of new varieties of fruits, adoption of hybrid varieties of vegetables and spices of high quality and production, adoption of new horticultural techniques, production of European vegetables, adoption of new techniques to increase production of flowers and medicinal plants, establishment of high-tech model nurseries, apiculture, mushroom cultivation, establishment of distillation units for flowers and medicinal and aromatic plants, onion storage units and the establishment of semi-processing and processing units in the State.

Horticulture sector may prove to be an important sector of the State's economy, with its highest shares both in terms of State income as well as employment. Its share in total work force is higher than its share in State income. Cultivation of vegetables and fruits creates two to three times more employment than cultivation of cereal crops. Employment in this sector can be increased by improving cropping intensity. Horticultural crops create 860 mandays per hectare.

## Dairy Development

The main thrust in the area of dairy development is to supplement the income of small and marginal farmers and landless labourers to bring about socio-economic transformation of the rural people through strengthening of co-operative structure and promoting private investment in the dairy sector. U.P. is the largest milk producing State in the country. With an annual milk production of 11.7 million MT the State accounts for around 16 per cent of the milk production of the country. Uttar Pradesh State Co-operative Milk Producers' Federation at the State level, milk unions at the district level and milk producers, co-operative societies at the village level, carry out milk procurement and marketing activities in the State. The milk procured of PCDF/Co-operative is marketed as liquid milk in Lucknow and the district towns. Butter, ghee, skimmed milk powder and other products are produced and marketed under the brand name PARAG.

It is proposed to further strengthen the existing dairy co-operative societies and to organize new societies to ensure timely supply of required inputs to the producers. For raising the income of farmers, it is essential to provide them remunerative prices by eliminating the middlemen. The value addition in this sector would also require capacity building in milk processing and storing for its subsequent marketing in the rural areas at remunerative prices.

## Co-operation

Initially, the co-operative system was oriented only towards the supply and provision of credit. Gradually, it has diversified its activities to include banking, input distribution, agro-processing, storage, warehousing etc. Supply of agricultural inputs such as chemical fertilizers, high yielding seeds and pesticides was also started by co-operatives and it proved a the success. Co-operatives have played a vital and commendable role in bringing about green revolution in the State. Consumer movement in India through co-operatives was introduced in the days of the scarcity of essential commodities in the Sixties. Today it also encompasses housing, dairy, handloom, fisheries, cold storage, processing, labour etc. The co-operative movement aims at serving the rural poor, small and marginal farmers, agricultural labourers and artisans.

## Irrigation

The growth in irrigation potential and investment made under major and medium schemes upto the end of the Tenth Five Year Plan (2002-07) is given in Table 29.

**Table 29:** Expenditure and Benefits of Major and Medium Projects

| Sl. No. | Period | Expenditure Incurred (Rs. In crores) | | Potential Created (Lakh Ha.) | | % of Potential Creation against Ultimate Potential |
|---|---|---|---|---|---|---|
| | | During | Cumulative up to | During | Cumulative | |
| 1. | Eighth Plan (1992-97) (Actual) | 1738.00 | 5423.45 | 2.54 | 69.10 | 56.85 |
| 2. | Ninth Plan (1997-2002) (Actual) | 3014.58 | 8438.03 | 8.78 | 77.88 | 64.08 |
| 3. | Tenth Plan (2002-2007) (Actual) | 4866.70 | 13304.73 | 5.31 | 83.19 | 68.45 |

Concrete steps need to be taken to increase the profitability of agricultural operations in a significant manner. As stated above, a large number of holdings are of less than half hectare. Through the traditional crop mix of food crops, it is difficult to make agriculture very profitable. Cultivation of cash crops, vegetables, medicinal plants etc. may be more profitable for marginal farmers. Similarly, cultivation of bio-diesel plants like jetropha on wastelands should be promoted. It is proposed to bring 10 lakh hectares of wastelands under jetropha cultivation in the State during the Eleventh Plan. The strategy should be to maximize the income of the farmers from his meagre land holding. The State Government proposes to significantly raise investment in Animal Husbandry, Dairy, Horticulture and Food Processing sectors during the Eleventh Plan. Detailed schemes have been prepared for each of the nine agro-climatic zones in the State and various farm models are proposed to be made available to farmers keeping in view their size of holdings, ability to make investment so as to maximize their returns from land.

In order to enable poor households to come out of poverty trap on sustainable basis, it is essential that the avenues of self-employment are opened up for them. *Swarnajayanti Grameen Swarojgar Yojana* (SGSY) is designed to achieve this goal by providing assistance to Self Help Groups. In Uttar Pradesh, over four lakh Self Help Groups have been constituted under the SGSY, NABARD funded schemes, UPDASP and Sodic Land Reclamation Project. These groups need to be made the focal points for anti-poverty intervention in the villages.

Experience suggests that the poverty alleviation strategy can be effective only if measures are simultaneously taken on several fronts with a view to increasing the income of the poor families. This cannot be achieved through a single scheme or intervention. This approach would require provision of wage employment to members of a BPL household, inclusion of a member in the Self Help Group so as to promote self-employment and assistance under other schemes of different departments in order to increase their incomes. This could involve help for rural backyard poultry, improvement in nutritional status/supplementary income through the production of vegetables in kitchen garden, cultivation of jetropha, developing bamboo groves (in eastern UP and Terai regions) as insurance for meeting urgent social, consumption or health needs, animal husbandry etc.

The State Government proposes to adopt a cafeteria approach in poverty alleviation strategy. This would mean listing out the options for different groups of poor people such as the landless labourers, those with land holdings of half acre or less, those with land holdings of one acre, two acres, two and a half acres or more. The options will include wage employment, self-employment, crop-mix for maximizing income from agriculture holdings, ways and means to improve/add on to the asset base of the poor etc. Together with a vibrant Self Help Group system wherein the poor people can take loan for meeting urgent social, consumption and health needs at reasonable rates of interest and a judicious mix of activities sufficient to generate an income of Rs. 2000 per month for the household and effective implementation of safety net programmes such as PDS, mid-day meal etc., it should be possible to bring poor people over the poverty line on a sustainable basis.

## Human Development in Uttar Pradesh

Universalization of the Elementary Education (Class 1 to 8) by 2012

- To bring the teacher-pupil ratio to 1:40.
- Provision of 5 rooms and 5 teachers/Shiksha Mitras in each primary school.

- Provision of 4 rooms, 5 teachers and one laboratory in the upper primary school.
- Focus on quality improvement.
- Provision of one additional hand pump in every primary school.
- To achieve the 85 per cent literacy level in the State.
- To reduce the present gender gap in literacy from 26.40 per cent to 10 per cent.
- To bring down the drop-out rate in primary level to 5 per cent.

## Medical and Public Health

Health care in UP can be summarized as a composite challenge of access, quality and demand. The large public sector does not have adequate access and there is a need to improve the quality of care at the cutting edge end (PHCs and Sub-centres). The private sector has access but poses a challenge on account of serious lack of quality to the extent that it often becomes a threat to the health of people. Thus, re-orientation of health strategies is being initiated where the focus would be on functionalizing existing infrastructure by saving synergy through public-private-partnership particularly for reaching the poor and the marginalized.

**Table 30:** Eleventh Plan Targets

| *Sl. No.* | *Index* | *Unit* | *Present Position* | *Target* |
|---|---|---|---|---|
| 1. | I.M.R. (S.R.S.) October 2007 | Per 1000 birth | 71 | 35 |
| 2. | M.M.R. (2001-03 RHIME) | Per 100000 live births | 517 | 100 |
| 3. | Total fertility rate (SRS 2002) | Per Productive Couple | 4.4 | 2.8 |
| 4. | Malnutrition, (0-3 years) Children (N.F.H.S. 1998-99) | According to age | 51.7 | 23.5 |
| 5. | Anaemia in Mothers (15-49 years) (NFHS 1998-99) | Percentage | 48.7 | 20 |
| 6. | Sex Ratio (0-6 year) (Census-2001) | Per 1000 Population | 916 | 924 |

Uttar Pradesh has great potential in the handicraft sector and the State enjoys a distinguished place in the handicraft industry in the country especially for its Banaras Silk and Brocade, Bhadohi and Mirzapur Carpet, Lucknow Chikan, marble products of Agra, wood carving items of Saharanpur etc. These items have good demand in overseas markets. Handicraft items such as hand knotted carpets, brassware, woodware, gift items, chikan works, zari-zardosi, marble inlay work, handlooms and other products constitute around 60 per cent of the exports of the State. In addition, there is tremendous potential for exporting non-traditional, high technology products such as electronics and computer software items. While there has been steady growth in handicrafts exports, yet there is additional latent potential, which could be exploited.

# *Appendix I*

## LIST OF TRAINESS WHOSE STUDIES ARE INCLUDED IN THIS VOLUME

### Orissa

| *Sl. No.* | *Author* | *Village* | *District* | *Year* |
|---|---|---|---|---|
| 1. | Bishnu Pada Sethi | Parapanga | Kandhmal | 1995 |
| 2. | Hemant Sharma | Kiralaga | Sundergarh | 1995 |
| 3. | Arabinda Kumar Padhee | Patrabasa | Kalahandi | 1996 |
| 4. | Pramod K. Meherda | Salebidi | Nabarangpur | 1997 |
| 5. | Sanjeev Kumar Misra | Chhamunda | Sundargarh | 1997 |
| 6. | Suresh Kumar Vashishth | Kupudamaha | Kandhmal | 1998 |
| 7. | Munish Moudgil | Sapmundi | Kalahandi | 1998 |
| 8. | Bhaskar J. Sharma | Banspal | Keonjhar | 1999 |
| 9. | Shubha Misra Sarma | Bishnupur | Keonjhar | 1999 |
| 10. | Manish Kumar Verma | Talijhiri | Raygada | 2000 |
| 11. | Sujata Rout | Brahmani | Bolangir | 2000 |
| 12. | Temjenwapang | Dumerpani | Naupada | 2000 |
| 13. | V. Karthikeya Pandian | Seledi | Sonepur | 2000 |

## Jharkhand

| Sl. No. | Author | Village | District | Year |
|---|---|---|---|---|
| 1. | Neerja | Malhan Bhuiadih | Ranchi | 1993 |
| 2. | N. Vijaya Lakshmi | Mahil | Ranchi | 1995 |
| 3. | Rahul Singh | Birkera | Gumla | 1996 |
| 4. | K. Senthil Kumar | Charai | West Singhbhum | 1996 |
| 5. | M.R. Meena | Nichitpur | Dhanbad | 1996 |
| 6. | Sunil Kumar Barnwal | Barwatoli and Rangamati | Ranchi | 1997 |
| 7. | Santosh Kumar Mall | Pratap Pur | Giridih | 1997 |
| 8. | Pankaj Kumar | Nakti | Dumka | 1997 |
| 9. | Narmdeshwar Lall | — | Dhanbad | 1998 |
| 10. | Kamal Kishore Soan | — | East Singhbhum | — |

## West Bengal

| Sl. No. | Author | Village | District | Year |
|---|---|---|---|---|
| 1. | Roshni Sen | Palasan | Burdwan | 1995 |
| 2. | Anoop Kumar Agarwal | Chandrapur | Birbhum | 1995 |
| 3. | Manish Jain | Lanka Bore | Cooch Behar | 1996 |
| 4. | Binod Kumar | Telota | Burdwan | 1998 |
| 5. | Onkar Singh Meena | Satghara | Hooghly | 1999 |
| 6. | Narayan Swaroop Nigam | Walipur | Midnapore | 2000 |
| 7. | Neelam Meena | Dharmadeb, Kharia-Berubari, Khaeya-2 & Araji-Marija-Kamala-Pukari | Jalpaiguri | 2000 |
| 8. | Parwez Ahmed Siddiqui | Bajuara | Midnapore | 2001 |
| 9. | Santanu Basu | Koimari | Cooch Behar | 2001 |
| 10. | Alakananda Dayal | Gotu | Hooghly | 2002 |
| 11. | Puneet Yadav | Silakota | Burdwan | 1999 |
| 12. | Ravinder Singh | Kharija-Berubari | Jalpaiguri | 1994 |
| 13. | Vandana Yadav | Shyamsunder | Burdwan | 1998 |

## Bihar

| Sl. No. | Author | Village | District | Year |
|---|---|---|---|---|
| 1. | Deepti Guar | Lodhipur | Gaya | 1993 |
| 2. | Avinash Kumar | Dharampur | Nalanda | 1993 |
| 3. | Dharmendra Kr. Singhal | Lanka | Palamu | 1995 |
| 4. | Arvind K. Chaudhary | Dewaria | Gaya | 1995 |
| 5. | Vandana Dadel | Kusmauth | Begusarai | 1996 |
| 6. | Sanjeev Hans | Sakarwara Sawik | Muzaffarpur | 1997 |
| 7. | B. Rajender | Saradhi | Munger | 1999 |
| 8. | Anshu Sinha | Sonaru | Patna | 1999 |
| 9. | Vinay Kumar | Gidha | Sahabad | 1999 |
| 10. | Kumar Rahul | Siswa | Begusarai | 2000 |
| 11. | N. Saravana Kumar | Sahmora | Saharsa | 2000 |
| 12. | Jitendra Srivastava | Mungauli | Muzaffarpur | 2000 |
| 13. | Prem Singh Meena | Eraura | Bhojpur | 2000 |
| 14. | Rajesh Kumar | Bealur | Bhojpur | 2001 |

## Uttar Pradesh

| Sl. No. | Author | Village | District | Year |
|---|---|---|---|---|
| 1. | Md. Mustafa | Parikhra | Ballia | 1995 |
| 2. | Bhuvnesh Kumar | Tikamau | Mahoba | 1995 |
| 3. | Mamta Verma | Aloonagar Diguria | Lucknow | 1996 |
| 4. | Subhash Chand Sharma | Himmatnagar Bhajera | Etah | 1996 |
| 5. | M. Devaraj | Khiroramohan | Gonda | 1996 |
| 6. | V. Hekalizhimomi | Jaffarpur | Barabanki | 1996 |
| 7. | Ramesh Kumar Sudhanshu | Koyala Alipur | Mathura | 1997 |
| 8. | Rita singh | Shahpur Kalan | Bulandshahr | 1997 |
| 9. | Aradhana Patnaik | Gulariha | Gorakhpur | 1998 |
| 10. | Anil Kumar | Jessukhpur | Etah | 1998 |
| 11. | P. Guruprasad | Ranipur | Azamgarh | 1999 |
| 12. | Navdeep Rinwa | Jiraunia | Pilibhit | 1999 |
| 13. | Maneesh Chauhan | Avarata | Allahabad | 2000 |
| 14. | Amit Gupta | Chirodi | Meerut | 2000 |

# 1

# Orissa

ASHISH VACHHANI[1], S. TRIPATHY[2] and
VARUNENDRA VIKRAM SINGH[3]

## THE STATE AT A GLANCE

The state of Orissa, blessed with a long coastline of the Bay of Bengal, is situated in the eastern coast of India. Orissa is bounded in the north by Jharkhand, in the north-east by West Bengal, in the south by Andhra Pradesh and in the west by Chhattisgarh. Most of the landmass of the state is watered by the rivers Mahanadi, Brahmani, and Baitarani flowing in the south-easterly direction before merging in the Bay of Bengal. These rivers and their tributaries provide the state with rich alluvial tracts. Orissa is possessed of an extensive plateau in the interior with sprawling coastal plains in the foreground. This plateau, an undulating upland, gently slopes down towards the Bay of Bengal. Its extensive palm fringed coast-line running to 482 km., serene holiday beaches, pronounced rural environs, charming blue hills rising here and there abruptly from the plains and the plateau, green wood-lands, rock caves, so fascinatingly sculptured temples and other monuments, picturesque mud villages set in greens, modern industrial townships and so rich and varied handicrafts make Orissa a miniature India.

1. IAS, Deputy Director and Coordinator, Centre for Rural Studies, LBSNAA, Mussoorie.
2. Associate Professor in Entrepreneurship Development Institute of India, Ahmedabad and he also worked as a Assistant Professor in Centre for Rural Studies, LBSNAA, Mussoorie for six years.
3. Faculty in Centre for Rural Studies, LBSNAA, Mussoorie.

According to 2001 census figure Orissa has a population of more than 36 million with approximately 38 per cent of the total population is of scheduled tribes and scheduled castes. The growth rate in Orissa has been abysmally poor in comparison with the national average, for instance; in the 1990 Orissa's growth rate was 4.3 per cent in comparison to the national average of 6.7 per cent. The agricultural sector accounts for 32 per cent of the GSDP and 62 per cent of the total employment; there is stagnation in per capita income in the past two decades. According to Planning Commission nearly 48.6 per cent of the people of the State live below the Poverty Line. And, the per capita income of the State is the lowest among the States except for Bihar, the gap between the per capita income of the State and the National average has risen from Rs. 316 in 1980-81 to Rs. 648 in 1991-92 and to Rs. 1292 in 1996-97 (White Paper on State Finances, Finance Department, Governmet of Orissa, 1999-2000). Around 17.5 million people live below the poverty line. Poverty is significantly worse in the western and southern districts of the state. The literacy rate is 50 per cent and the rate of literacy is even worse in case of Adivasis (Tribals) and Dalits.

Though Orissa is endowed with rich natural resources, like mineral deposits, forest covers, river basins, coastline, adequate water resources and fertile lands, the state is one of the backward states, because of under-utilization of potential resources. The state with splendid sculptures, temples, sea beaches, mangroves, tribal cultures, etc. can be one of the most attractive states for the tourists. With the availability of cheap labourers and mineral ores in addition to water resources, there are ample avenues for the investors. Major cities of the state are well connected as National Highway (N.H.-5) is covering the state from south to north. With huge deposits of coal and presence of number of hydel power projects in this state and in the nearby Jharkhand and West Bengal, the fuel or power supply is not a big problem for taking up industrial activities. This is surprise to note that the state, which is endowed with a long coastline, mineral deposits, fertile lands, forest covers and adequate rainfall is one of the poorest states of India. This clearly implies that either there is lack of incentives for growth-oriented activities or some structural problems within the system. On the other hand there are opinions that the natural resources are being degraded over the time. Forests, land and surface water resources are undergoing severe degradation, ground water, minerals and air are under serious threat of degradation. Not only the different patterns of development in the state have led to the degradation of these natural resources but also other factors like the growth of population and the unsustainable activities adopted by them have become crucial for the degradation of valuable natural resources in the state. The adoption of unsustainable activities is, however, driven by the market and institutional failure. It provides incentives to the poor to have short time preferences and to the rich to exploit the resource base at unsustainable rate. The degradation of natural resources has not only corroded the economic base of the state but has also adversely affected the environment. The adverse impacts like change in climatic condition, increased flooding, productivity drop, water shortage, increased infant mortality and morbidity rate etc. are some of the outcomes of continuing degradation. In the absence of proper measures to reduce the degradation of natural resources the problem will be aggravated. So at this juncture, one can conclude that natural resources depletions have not significantly contributed towards development of the state. So there may be a big question mark on the issue that whether the state is suffering from sheer exploitation or there is a problem of optimal resource allocation. In order to examine the causes of backwardness of the state, one should not forget to analyse the revenue generation potentialities.

## The History

The history of Orissa is unique and has a special place in the Indian historical documents. From the ancient historical period till medieval period the state of Orissa was known by different names such as the Kalinga, Utkal and Odra, the state was ruled over by many famous and powerful dynasties and its boundary was extended far beyond the present one. By the time of the *Mahabharata*, Kalinga, Utkal and Odra had entered into Aryan polity as powerful kingdoms. In the great epic the *Mahabharata*, the Kalinga as a province has been mentioned frequently. During 6th and 7th century B.C., i.e. flourishing time of Buddhism and Jainism, the state of Orissa was confined to Kalinga-Utkal region on the entire east coast of India acquired recognition and fame. Till the medieval period and during the Moghul period, Orissa was famous as Kalinga. The Sun temple at Konark and the Lord Jagannath temple at Puri are the two famous historical temples of the State. During British rule there were many regional rulers and revolutionaries against the British rule within different parts of Orissa.

Orissa was separated from Bihar and came into existence on 1 April, 1936. Initially the capital was established at the historic city of Cuttack. More regions were under the provisional rulers. After the attainment of Independence the princely states merged with the major unit in 1948 and the new State of Orissa was formed. An administrative reorganization of the State was taken in hand and thirteen districts were formed. Out of the former princely states the districts of Mayurbhanj, Sundergarh, Keonjhar, Dhenkanal, Phulbani, Bolangir and Kalahandi were carved out. The administration of the two princely states, viz. Saraikela and Kharswan was transferred to the state administration of Bihar in May 1948. The other princely state Mayurbhanj was merged completely with Orissa on 19th August, 1949 by the State Merger (Governor's Provinces) Order, 1949.

The princely states of Saraikela and Kharswan were merged with Bihar on the basis of Reorganization of States Committee Order. Earlier, they were parts of the Mayurbhanj district. The administrative divisions of Orissa contain 13 districts, 56 sub-divisions, and 301 police stations. On the ground of administrative simplicity, the 13 districts were further subdivided and there are now 30 districts in Orissa. In 2001 there were 51569 villages, out of which 4647 were uninhabited. There were 81 towns of all categories in the State.

## Geographical Features

On the basis of geographical homogeneity, the state of Orissa can be divided into the following divisions: (1) Coastal plains, (2) Middle Mountainous and Highlands Region, and (3) Central Plateaus.

## The Orissa Coastal Plains

The Orissa Coastal Plains comprising districts of Balasore, Bhadrak, Cuttack, Puri, Ganjam, etc. are the depositional landmass of recent origin and geologically belong to the Post-Tertiary Period. This region stretches from the West Bengal border, i.e. from the River Subarnarekha in the north to the River Rushikulya in the south. The 75 metre contour line delimits their western boundary and differentiates them from the Middle Mountainous Region.

This region is the combination of several deltas of varied sizes and shapes formed by the major rivers of Orissa, such as the Subarnarekha, the Budhabalanga, the Baitarani, the Brahmani, the Mahanadi, and the Rushikulya. Therefore, the coastal plain of Orissa is called the "Hexadeltaic region" or the "Gift of Six Rivers". It stretches along the coast of the Bay of Bengal having the maximum width in the Middle Coastal Plain (the Mahanadi Delta), narrow in the Northern Coastal Plain (Balasore Plain) and narrowest in the Southern Coastal Plain (Ganjam Plain). The North Coastal Plain comprises the deltas of the Subarnarekha and the Budhabalanga rivers and bears evidences of marine transgressions. The Middle Coastal Plain comprises the compound deltas of the Baitarani, Brahmani and Mahanadi rivers and bears evidences of past 'back bays' and present lakes. The South Coastal Plain comprises the laccustrine plain of Chilika Lake and the smaller delta of the Rushikulya River. The Middle Coastal Plain forms a "Pan plane". The process of delta formation is quite active here and very fast along the northern part of the coast, covering the Balasore Plain. The whole region is made up of older and recent alluvium.

This region has also well-defined morphological units parallel to the shoreline with relation to its configuration (a) the salt tract along the coast, (b) the arable tract on the middle, and (c) the submontane tract on the western foothills of the Eastern Ghats. This region has a remarkably straight shoreline with well-defined beaches of sand and shingles. Here the beach ridges indicate the emergence of the coast. There are also several sand bars and sand dune ridges parallel to the coastline with the height between 16 to 27 metres and length between 1 to 4 km. These have originated owing to the recent coastal uplift.

Three types of shorelines have developed along the coast: (a) the rocky shoreline between the deltas, (b) the sandy shoreline, and (c) the alluvial and silty deltaic shoreline. The spurs of the Eastern Ghats entered into this plain at some places forming several small hillocks on the plains and islands in the Bay of Bengal and inside the Chilika Lake.

## The Middle Mountainous and Highland Region

This region covers about three-fourth of the entire State. Geographically, it is a part of the Indian Peninsula, which was a part of the ancient landmass of the Gondwanaland. The major rivers of Orissa with their tributaries have cut deep and narrow valleys. This region mostly comprises the hills and mountains of the Eastern Ghats, which rise abruptly and steeply in the east and slope gently to a dissected plateau in the west running from north-east (Mayurbhanj) to north-west (Malkangiri). This region is well marked by a number of interfluves or watersheds. The Eastern Ghats is interrupted by a number of broad and narrow river valleys and flood plains. The average height of this region is about 900 metres above the mean sea level. There are five interfluves (The region of higher land between two rivers that are in the same drainage system):

- The Subarnarekha-Budhabalanga-Baitarani interfluve comprises the major mountain ranges like the Similipal (915 metres) and the Meghasan (1165 metres).
- The Baitarani-Brahmani interfluve comprises mountain ranges like Badampahar (1,075 metres), Kunaratir (1,064 metres), Malayagiri (1277 metres) and other mountains of Keonjhar, Palalahara and Dhenkanal.
- The Brahmani-Mahanadi interfluve comprises the discontinuous mountains of low heights stretching from Sambalpur to Cuttack such as: Nrusinghanath (986 metres), Panchdhar (915 metres), Tikarapara (901 metres), Bonai hill (769 metres), Bamra hill (761 metres), Kapilas hill (636 metres) etc.
- The Mahanadi-Rushikulya-Vansadhara interfluve comprises the mountain ranges of Nayagarh, Khandapara, Khondhmals, Phulbani and Ganjam. The important mountains are: Mahendragiri (1525 metres), Singra See hill (1313 metres), etc.
- The Nagavali-Sabari-Tel interfluve comprises the Chandragiri-Pottangi mountains with Deomali (1672 metres), the tallest peak of Orissa. The other peaks are—Sinkaram (1620 metres), Golikoda (1617 metres), Yendrika (1582 metres) etc.

## The Central Plateaus

The plateaus are mostly eroded plateaus forming the western slopes of the Eastern Ghats with elevation varying from 305-610 metres. There are two broad plateaus in Orissa: (i) the Panposh-Keonjhar-Pallahara plateau comprises the Upper Baitarani catchments basin and (ii) the Nabrangpur-Jeypore plateau comprises the Sabari basin.

*The Western Rolling Uplands:* These are lower in elevation than the plateaus having heights varying from 153 metres to 305 metres. There are seven distinct uplands in Orissa. These are:

- The Rairangpur rolling upland, a part of the Subarnarekha basin, comprises the northern part of the Mayurbhanj district and slopes towards the north.
- The Keonjhar rolling upland, a part of the Baitarani Basin, lies at the fringe of the Keonjhar Plateau.
- The Rourkela rolling upland lies on the Upper Brahmani basin.
- The Bolangir-Bargarh-Rairkhol rolling upland lies on the Ib-Jira-Jhaun-Suk-Tel-Tel basin (the Upper Mahanadi basin).
- The Aska rolling upland lies on the Upper Rushikulya basin.
- The Rayagada rolling upland lies on the Vansadhara and the Nagavali basins.
- The Malkangiri rolling upland lies on the Sabari-Machhkund basins of the Dandakaranya Region located on the southern tip of Orissa.

The long-term average rainfall in the state of Orissa is around 1500 mm, which is adequate for the monsoon dependent crops. Southwest monsoon is mainly causes the rainfall in the state. However, moderately high variability in the rainfall many times causes crop failure. The variability is due to the fact that rainfall is associated with depressions from the Bay of Bengal, which are often erratic. Areas of somewhat low variability lie in the coastal plains of Ganjam and Puri.

The whole coastal plain is prone to cyclones and during the post monsoon and early part of the Northeast monsoon, storms and depressions originating in the Bay of Bengal many times causes loss to human lives and resources. The recent super cyclone, which smashed into the coastal belt of Orissa on 29th October, 1999 was responsible for a loss of resources worth $2.5 billion, destruction of 774000 houses and loss of one million of animal lives. The most dangerous cyclone squalls giving heavy rainfall to the region and disrupting communication and causing loss to property and standing crops.

In most of the fertile plain land of coastal belt, in spite of having potentialities for growing multiple crops, only one crop grown that is paddy. There is no crop diversification in this region in the recent past. The main reasons for the prevalence of mono-cropping in this region are lack of investments in agriculture, non-availability of adequate irrigation facilities and the farmers are not in favour of taking risks attached with other types of crops except paddy. In case of many parts of coastal region black *mung* (*Urad*) cereal is grown as a mix crop along with the paddy cultivation. Lack of market availability and processing units along with poor infrastructure leave very little scope for the farmers to grow pulses, oil seeds, etc. There are three types of paddy that are usually grown—*Sarada* (Kharif) which is best suited for the low lands subject to flooding, *Biali* (Autumn) thrives best in *Sarada* lands which are slightly elevated and free from frequent flooding and *Dalua* (Summer paddy) grows well in marshy lands reclaimed by suitable drainage methods in areas subject to flooding and harvested before the onset of the monsoon. However, in the parts of Mahanadi-Luna and Devi Prachi doabs two crop combination covers.

Though paddy provides almost a monoculture landscape in several parts, it is grown in a two-crop combination with pulses, oilseeds or jute and also in three and four crop combinations with the same crops. The monoculture region lies in the northern and southeastern quarters and the central coastal belt. The two-crop combination covers an extensive tract of the middle delta. The four-crop combination region is concentrated in the Mahanadi-Luna and Devi-Prachi doabs.

On the basis of climatic and soil characteristics the whole State is divided into ten agro-climatic zones with varied characteristics. Its land can be classified into categories, low (25.6%), medium (33.6%) and up-lands (40.8%) with various types of soil like red yellow, red-loamy, alluvial, coastal alluvial, laterite and black soil etc. with low and medium texture.

The inter-regional disparities are more prominent between the coastal region and main southern parts (mainly highland) of Orissa. Because of its geography, the coastal region forged well ahead of the highland region in infrastructural development. Certain natural advantages (such as superior quality of soil) coupled with irrigation facilities in the coastal deltas made possible a certain degree of agrarian dynamism. In the post-Independence period the unevenness of development has persisted and perpetuated—particularly in respect of infrastructural development. In a poor and backward state like Orissa when the development positions of the districts are compared at the intra-state level, the districts in the coastal region and some of the districts of highland region having a few large industries such as Sambalpur, Jharsuguda, Bargarh and Sundargarh are found to be developed than the other districts predominantly resided by the depressed category of population.

## Introduction to the Villages

This report is prepared on the basis of fourteen village study Assignments of villages, namely Sapmundi, Patrabasa (Kalahandi), Kiralaga, Chhamunda (Sundargarh), Banspal, Bishnupur (Keonjhar), Mohandi, Salebidi (Nabarangpur), Kupudmaha, Parapanga (Kandhmal), Dumerpani (Nuapada), Taljhiri (Rayagada), Seledi (Sonepur), Brahmani (Bolangir) submitted by Indian Administrative Service Officer trainees to the Centre for Rural Studies. *All the above mentioned villages are located in the southern and western part of the state. So, socio-economic conditions of the sample of fourteen villages cannot represent the overall view of the state as a whole. However, attempts are made to make the report balance one by incorporating information from secondary materials.*

Out of these villages, two villages Mohandi and Salebidi are located in the district of Nabarangpur. Villages such as Sapmundi, Patrabasa and Dendaguda belong to Kalahandi District. The study also includes survey report of village Chhamunda and Kiralaga of Sundargarh district and survey report of another village named as Serapalli from Malkangiri. The two villages .Mohandi, Salebidi of Nabarangpur district, erstwhile part of undivided Koraput district have similar features of backwardness. Both the villages are located in the tribal dominated region of the district. The nearest town of both the villages is the tehsil headquarter Umerkote. The village Mohandi is well connected to the main road where as village Salebidi is connected through a *kutcha* road. The nearest bus stop Chandahandi is 2 km far from the village Salebidi and only two vehicles are runing everyday between Nabarangpur and Chandahandi. Similarly, out of the three villages of Kalahandi districts two villages are well connected through all weather approach road.

The southern part of Orissa is least urbanized as compare to the coastal region. Hardly 10 per cent of population of districts of south Orissa is living in urban areas. So for most of the villages block headquarters are the nearest town and serves as main trading centre. Exceptionally, for a few villages where local *hats* generally periodical markets serve the purpose of selling and purchasing basic goods. In the recent past it is observed that many small shops are coming up in the villages and this is happening due to the improvement in road connectivity. The importance of rural infrastructure with respect to rise in the non-farm employments is of immense. There are high externalities in case of provision of basic infrastructural facilities like an all weather approach road, electricity connectivity and transport facilities along with other agro-based marketing infrastructure. The deplorable condition of rural infrastructure is evidenced by non-availability of some or many facilities like all weather approach road, electricity, post office, public telephone booths, primary schools or middle/high schools, Panchayat bhawan, ICDS centre, adult literacy centre, drinking water sources, public health centres, co-operative societies or banks etc. Improvement in quality of life of rural people at least needs the development of infrastructures pertaining to health, communication and education. The socio-institutional factors in combination with the infrastructural problems have produced unequal access to basic needs of people, considering whole village mass. The widened gap between the villages and towns also arises due to the infrastructural problems found in the villages. The underdevelopment of non-farm activities in many villages also owes its origin to the underdeveloped infrastructure. The management and maintenance of rural infrastructures created under different employment generation schemes is very poor. Community involvement in management and maintenance of infrastructure assets created in the villages must be ensured. A detail villagewise analysis is presented in Table 1.1.

All the selected villages belong to districts of Southern part of Orissa, however, the analyses of the report broadly cover whole the State. Another important point is that most of the villages are located in the Kalahandi-Bolangir-Koraput (KBK). In the year 1992-93 the KBK districts were divided into eight districts such as: Koraput, Kalahandi, Malkangiri, Nabarangpur, Rayagada, Bolangiri, Sonepur and Nuapada. In our selected 14 villages, 11 villages are located in the KBK districts. Therefore, it becomes imperative to discuss briefly about the KBK project, which is a special project operative in the eight above-mentioned districts. The whole KBK region is underdeveloped due to (1) tribal backwardness, (2) hill area backwardness, (3) prone to natural calamities like flood and drought.

**Table 1.1:** Introduction to the Villages

| | |
|---|---|
| **Mohandi** | This is a typical small tribal village and is located at a distance of 74 km from the district headquarters and 6 kms from block headquarters. It is situated on the main road connecting the district headquarters with the block headquarters. The nearest town is Umerkote, which is at a distance of 35 km from the village. Umerkote is also the tehsil headquarters of this village. Umerkote is very well connected with Raipur (Chhattisgarh), Jagdalpur (Chhattisgarh), Vijainagaram (A.P.) etc. The nearest railway station, i.e. Rayagada is almost at a distance of 250 km from the village. |
| **Salebidi** | The village, with a total population of 310 (152 males and 158 females), is located in one of the most interior tribal-dominated areas of Orissa, i.e. the erstwhile-undivided district of Koraput and at present in the district of Nabarangpur. The village Salebidi itself is dominated by the other castes (205 OC, 83 ST and 17 SC) according to 1991 census. |
| **Chhamunda** | The village under study is located in Bargaon Block (Fulbari Gram Panchayat) of Sundargarh District of Orissa. Sundargarh is a tribal district of Orissa. Tribals represent more than 50 per cent of the population. Tribes predominantly inhabit the village Chhamunda. There are four hamlets in this revenue village. |
| **Patrabasa** | Village is situated at a distance of 66 and 6 kilometre from the district (Kalahandi) and block headquarters respectively. All weather roads are connected to it. The road connecting the village from the block headquarters has been constructed under the EAS (Employment Assurance Scheme) in the current year. |
| **Bishnupur** | The village is located around 8 km from the Jhumpura block headquarters. It is a medium sized village with tribal population. There are 3 hamlets (called *sahi* in local parlance) in Bishnupur and all of them are spread over an area of around 200 acres. The village is located adjacent to National highway number 215. |
| **Sapmundi** | The village is entirely a tribal village except one non-ST (that of an SC) family. All the tribals are from a single tribe—Kando. The village is located in the block Thaumul Rampur of district Kalahandi. The district head quarter is 30 km far from the village. The village comprises five *padas* (*tolas*) each tola is situated 2 km far from each other. The remoteness of the village is clearly visible as the village is far from the urban areas and markets. |
| **Dumerpani** | This Village falls under Darlipada Gram Panchayat of Komna block. There are three hamlets in the village, namely Dumerpani proper, Janbahali and Rengabahal. Even though the area of habitation is on the plains, cultivation is done on the nearby hill area. The village is about 27 km from Naupada and 25 km from Komna block headquarters. |

(*Contd.*)

**Table 1.1** (*Contd.*)

| | |
|---|---|
| **Banspal** | The village is located in the district of Keonjhar and the district headquarter is 25 km far from the village. This village comprises five *tolas*. The village is a remote village as the market is far from the village. The village is inhabited by a number of communities. |
| **Seledi** | This village is located at 30 kms from Sonepur on the northwestern side of Sonepur-Binka Road. The village is connected to the main road by a tar road. The block headquarter is Binka, which is 7 km away from the village. The nearest bus stop is 2.5 km on the Sonepur-Binka Road. The nearest Railway station is Barapali, which is 38 km away from the village. The nearest town is Binka, which is also a NAC area. The main market is located there. There is a post office in the village. The nearest CHC is in Binka. The grain storage facility is available in Mahadevpali, which is 3 km from Seledi. The cooperative society and bank branches, both are located in Mahadevpali. |
| **Brahmani** | The village is 92 km away from the district HQ (Bolangir) and 8 km from the block HQ. There is an approach road connecting the village to the block HQ from where all weather roads connect it to the district HQ. However, people mostly depend on rail communication as the block HQ has a railhead and there are daily passenger trains to Titilagarh, Bolangir, Sambalpur, Kesinga, Kantabanji and Ripur. |
| **Taljhiri** | The village is under Kashipur Panchayat, which is one of the seventeen Panchayats of Kashipur block. It is locate at about four km northwest of Kashipur, on the road connecting Kashipur to Mandibishi Panchayat. The district headquarters Raygada is about 70 km from Kashipur. Taljhiri is also surrounded by small hills on all the four sides. The village is about 50 metres from the main road. There are four Sahis in the village, two Adibashi Sahis, one Harijan Sahi and one Sahi for other caste people. Generally, people of one community stay together in one Sahi. There is one cluster of 18 IAY houses about 50 metres from the village, where 18 tribal families are residing on one side of the village. |
| **Kupudamaha** | The village comes under Ora Gram Panchayat of Kotagarh block. The village is inhabited by only tribals. The tribal of the village belongs to Kandha tribes. The village is 26 km from block headquarter and 162 from district headquarters. |

The KBK districts accounts for around 20 per cent of state population and spread over 30.59 per cent of geographical area of the state. The population density (152) is quite low as compare to the population density (236) of the state. It is observed that more than 80 per cent of the people in this area live in rural areas.

## DEMOGRAPHIC FEATURES

Demography profile generally refers to the features of population from the point view of age structure, density, caste composition, religion composition, sex ratio, etc. A high population growth has multiple effects on the development of a region, not only due to the fact that a rise in population growth leads to more pressure and exploitation of natural resources but also the quality of population resources deteriorated. In an agrarian economy, where the scope of service sector and other non-farm sector is very limited in terms of absorption of labour force, the rise in the population growth will certainly result in the fall in the productivity per head and low per capita income.

In Orissa, about 64 per cent of population depends on agriculture, a higher proportion of population growth ultimately will result rise in the magnitude of disguised unemployment. The state covering total area of 155,782 sq. km is 4.74 per cent of India's landmass supports a population as per 2001 census, 36,706,920, which is 3.75 per cent of the total population of the country. Scheduled Castes and Scheduled Tribes as per the 2001 Census constitute 16.20 per cent and 22.21 per cent respectively of the total population of the State. The scheduled areas cover nearly 45 per cent of the total geographical area. According to 2001 census figure, 85.03 per cent of the total population is living in rural areas and around 64 per cent of the total population depends on agriculture for their livelihood. The backwardness of the state clearly visible as 85.01 per cent of its population lives in rural areas and the rural area is primarily agricultural. In fact that agriculture sector is underdeveloped. The decennial growth rate of population of Orissa during 1991-2001 was 16.25 per cent. It is also important to point out that the decadal urban population growth (30.28%) during the same decade is almost twice of the population growth of the rural area (14.08%) during 1991-2001. This implies that lack of employment opportunities in rural areas is resulting in rural-urban migration. The decadal population growth during 1991-2001 is 16.25 per cent, which remained stagnant during 1971-81 and 1981-91. The stagnant growth rate attributed to the rise in literacy rate, effective dissemination of the message about benefits of small family and the drive launched by the State Government to provide access to family planning measures. The sex ratio in the State, i.e. number of females per 1000 males decreased from 981 in 1981 to 971 in 1991 as compared to the all-India average which decreased from 934 to 927. Another feature of sex ratio in Orissa is that urban sex ratio (866 as per 1991 census) is lower than the sex ratio (988) in rural areas. This is possibly due to the fact that migration of rural males to urban areas for work or the fact that economic activities in rural areas is in favour of a favourable sex ratio in rural areas. According to a village study assignment "It is found that the females have out-numbered males in all the three censuses. This is true of Ganjam district as a whole. The main reason for this trend is that quite a few people of Ganjam (over 2 lakh) work in textile industry in Surat and in Collieries of Chotanagpur and they are away from home for long period or a stretch." The population density of the state by the year 1991 is 203 per sq. km and it has increased to 236 by the Census year 2001.

According to the figures given in the growth rates of population in the last two decades 1981-1991 and 1991-2001 in the urban area are 36.1 per cent and 30 per cent respectively and in the rural areas the population growth rates are 17.9 per cent and 14 per cent during 1981-1991 and 1991-2001 respectively. In both the decades, the population growth in urban areas has remained substantially high as compare to the same in rural areas. However, the growth rate in urban areas has declined by 6.1 per cent and in rural areas growth rate has declined only by 3.9 per cent. This means either there has been a fall in the rural-urban migration or family planning concept is gaining momentum in rural areas. From the number of household data it is observed that during last 10 years (1991-2001) total number of households has increased from 5999447 to 7870127. The average household size of the state is 4.67 (Approximately 5).

The dependency ratios are used to analyse the implications of age structure with respect to potentiality of earning capacities of the people. The dependency ratios are calculated as young-number of persons of age 0-14 per 1000 persons aged 15-59, old-number of

**Table 1.2:** Population (2001 Census)

| | Number of households | Population | | Population Density (per sq. km) | Decadal Variation 1991-2001 (%) | Urban Population (%) |
|---|---|---|---|---|---|---|
| | | Persons | Sex Ratio | | | |
| Total | 78,70,127 | 36,804,660 | 953 | 236 | 16 | |
| Rural | 67,82,879 | 18,660,750 | 955 | 205 | 14 | 15 |
| Urban | 10,87,248 | 18,144,090 | 895 | 1975 | 30 | |

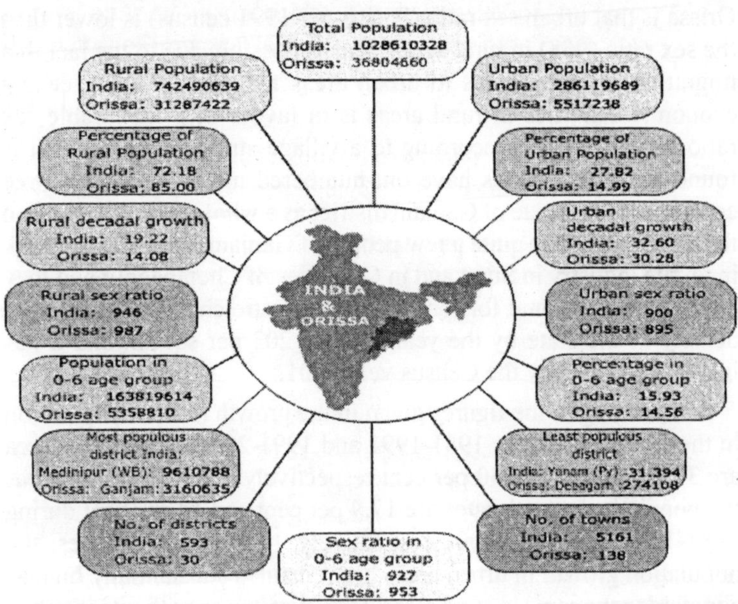


persons of age above 60 years per 1000 persons aged 15-59 and the total dependency ratio is calculated by adding up the dependency ratios of young and old.

Dependency Ratio, according to 1991 census data, of Orissa is 13 and for the country as a whole the dependency ratio is 12. However, taking only rural area into consideration, it was observed that the dependency ratio for the state is equal to the dependency ratio of the country. This simple means from the point view of population age composition there is hardly any difference between the state and country as a whole. So, demographic factor is not very much responsible for the backwardness of the state.

The percentages of population in the age groups of 15-45 years and 45-59 years are 45.2 and 11.4 respectively. In combine these two figures comes to be 56.6 per cent. So 56.6 per cent of total population is in the economically productive age group. There is a sharp rural-urban difference with respect to the percentages of population in the age groups of 15-44 years and 15-59 years. In urban area for the above mentioned two age groups taking together the percentage of male population is higher in urban areas as compare to rural areas. This implies a higher percentage of economically productive population is in urban area as compare to rural areas. This could be an outcome of low agricultural productivity and lack of practices of intensive cultivation. Hence seasonal unemployment is a major problem in rural Orissa.

It is mentioned that the population growth rate during 1991-2001 has declined to 16 per cent from 20 per cent during 1981-1991. Similarly the death rate of the state during the same period 1989-1993 also followed a marginally declining trend. So the overall gap between the death rate and birth rate has remained constant during the tenure of five years (1989-1993). However, the gap between birth rate and death rate is 17 to 18 per thousand. The birth rate (28.8) is marginally lower than the birth rate (29.5) of the country as a whole; whereas the death rate (12.7) of the state is marginally higher than the all-India death rate (9.8) by the year 1991. This has an important impact on the rate of growth of population.

The efforts of Family planning need an assessment keeping in view that a marginal fall in the birth rate has contributed to the some extent in keeping the population growth rate stagnant.

## Village Level Analysis

The demography profile of the selected villages explains that sex ratio except in case of two villages is quite higher than the same of the state. Most of the villages are dominated by SCs and STs. The data and analysis of demography at village level presented corresponds to the census years 1981, 1991 and 2001. The villages are located in the districts of southern part of Orissa such as Kandhamal, Kalahandi, Malkangiri, Nabarangpur, Nuapada, Sundargarh, Keonjhar and Rayagada. It is generally found that sex ratio is in favour of females in tribal areas. In case of all the districts to which the villages belong, except one, sex ratio is found to be higher than the same of the state. This implies that the status of women is high, but taking literacy level into consider, it can be inferred that high women status does not coincide with a high literacy level among the women. This is a proved fact that in the tribal dominated areas, economic activities are mostly carried out by women, so their status irrespective of educational level is quite high. Another reason for a favourable sex ratio may be large scale migration of male members from the villages to Rayapur, Surat and other cities.

As per findings mentioned in the village study report of village Taljhiri, Rayagada the reasons for high sex ratio is as follows: 'It is apparent from the table that the number of females are more than the number in each caste groups. This is a characteristic feature of tribal societies. This can be attributed to the egalitarian nature of gender relationship in tribal societies. Further men are very much prone to drinking habits, which decrease their life expectancy.'

The population of one of the villages (Saledi, Sonepur) is as high as 1800 and the total population is lowest (305) in case of the village Salebidi of Nabarangpur district. Presence of tribes in all the villages is another feature and in case of few villages the total population comprises tribes. Generally, the tribal dominated villages are smaller as compare to the non-tribal dominated areas. The size of population varies across the villages. The sample of 15 villages consist of large, medium and small sizes of population. So over all it can be inferred that the symptoms of underdevelopment of the villages will be found in all the village study assignments, which are used to prepare the report.

The adverse impact of high population growth is clearly mentioned in the village study report of village Dumerpani, Nuapada District. As per the report a high population growth creates demand for more homestead land. There is very little space for homestead purposes in the main village area. Out of the total 1943.10 acres of village land, 7.51 acres are homestead land. This area has expanded over the cultivable portions also. About 24 families have constructed houses outside the village.

According to another village Taljhiri of Rayagada District study report, the large population growth has put additional pressure over the natural resources like forest. The forest has been degraded at a very fast rate. The usual cycle of jhum used to be 7-8 years. Now it has been reduced to 4-5 years. As a result, the land could not get its original fertility. The soil erosion has taken place at a fast pace and base rock had come out over the hill slopes. This has reduced the land available for agriculture.

Similarly in another Village report of village Brahmani of Bolangir district it is mentioned that "As productive resources are few, even a slight growth of population puts tremendous pressure on them. In this village, there emerges the trend of increase in the area of cultivation, especially *att* land. More and more *gochar* and common lands are being occupied by the farmers. Another prominent instance of change in land use is reflected in the large scale encroachment in the bushy forest patches (Commonly referred to as *patra* jungle). These were originally earmarked out of reserve forest for the use of villagers and in many places have now been denuded and converted into *att* lands. In Brahmani, as much as 60 acres of land covered by *Patra* Jungle have been converted into agricultural land over the last ten years. Besides, no less than a quarter of the total of *gochar* land of the village has been encroached upon by cultivation."

## RURAL INFRASTRUCTURE AND BASIC AMENITIES

A developed rural infrastructure is a necessary condition for the development of rural areas. The externalities of rural infrastructure are of immense. Various economic activities in rural areas cannot be taken up without the presence of minimum basic infrastructure facilities like all weather approach road and electricity. Similarly, unavailability of primary schools, drinking water sources, health centres, etc. has lots of negative effects on the human resources, capability and quality of life also. The human resources remain under developed, so problems in capacity building also arise. So the basic amenities like drinking water, public health centre, housing, schools, sanitation facilities, etc. are closely associated with the rural poverty.

In Table 1.3 household-wise figures of basic amenities like drinking water facility, sources of lighting and toilet facility, etc. as per 2001 census survey are presented. From the table it is clear that more than 50 per cent of rural households are not having access to drinking water sources like tap or hand pump. So it can be said that safe drinking water is not available for more than a half rural population and they are depending on water sources like well, tank, pond, lake, river, canal, spring, etc. for drinking water. These sources are generally unsafe on health ground.

**Table 1.3:** Basic Amenity—Drinking water facility (2001 Census)

| *Source of Drinking Water* | *No. of Households (Rural)* | *% of Total Rural Households* |
|---|---|---|
| Tap | 1,88,170 | 2.77 |
| Hand pump | 21,22,822 | 31.30 |
| Tube well | 19,54,280 | 28.81 |
| Well | 19,37,084 | 29.09 |
| Tank, Pond, Lake | 1,41,038 | 2.08 |
| River, Canal | 1,99,816 | 2.95 |
| Spring | 1,67,921 | 2.48 |
| Any other | 35,748 | 0.53 |

In the following table, 2001 census data on household-wise availability of different sources of light are given. These figures reveal that only 26.91 percentage of households of the state are having electricity connections, in rural areas it is only 19.35 per cent only. So around 80 per cent households are not having electricity connections in rural areas, so in many cases it is not possible for the traditional skilled households (artisans) to mechanise their economic activities. Similarly, agriculture and other non-farm activities are underdeveloped due to lack of electricity facilities in many villages.

**Table 1.4:** Households by Source of Light (2001 Census)

| *Source of Lighting* | *Total No. of Households* | *In Percentage* | *Rural Households* | *In Percentage* |
|---|---|---|---|---|
| Electricity | 2118195 | 26.91 | 1312744 | 19.35 |
| Kerosene | 5674090 | 72.10 | 5409973 | 79.76 |
| Solar energy | 27208 | 0.35 | 22438 | 0.33 |
| Other oils | 4680 | 0.06 | 4019 | 0.06 |
| Any other | 9976 | 0.13 | 8317 | 0.12 |
| No lighting | 35978 | 0.46 | 25388 | 0.37 |

Again from above table, it can be observed that around 0.37 per cent of rural households are not having any type of lighting sources. This is peculiar to note that in most of the villages, where there is no electricity connection in Orissa, the villagers used to go to bed very early. So any type of economic activities are not generally taken up in the night.

In Orissa by the end of year 1990-91, only 15 per cent of total number of villages were connected by all weather approach roads, whereas at all India level, 41 per cent of six lakh total villages were connected by all weather approach roads. In the developed states like Punjab, Kerala, Haryana etc. more than 90 per cent of villages were connected by all weather approach roads by end of the year 1990-91. The census figures 2001 reveal that 26.9 per cent of households are having electricity connections and 64.2 per cent households are collecting drinking water from sources like water tap, tube wells and hand pumps. The rural-urban disparities in terms of availability of basic amenities starkly visible, more than 70 per cent of urban households are in the possession of electricity connections and drinking water facilities, whereas in rural areas only 19.4 per cent households are electrified. Similarly around 92 percentage of rural households according to 2001 census data are not having any type of latrine, where as in urban areas around 60 per cent households are having toilets.

**Table 1.5:** Rural Infrastructure and Basic Amenities (All Orissa) (As per 2001 Census)

(*In percentage*)

| *Basic Amenities* | *Electricity* | *Safe Drinking Water* | *No Toilet* |
|---|---|---|---|
| Total | 26.9 | 64.2 | 85.1 |
| Rural | 19.4 | 62.9 | 92.3 |
| Urban | 74.1 | 72.4 | 40.3 |

*Source*: Census 1991.

The socio-institutional factors, poor infrastructural facilities and lack of basic amenities in rural households are basically adversely affecting quality of life in rural Orissa. Because of infrastructural problems the non-farm activities are not able to flourish properly, in spite of having huge potentiality to grow. The management and maintenance of rural infrastructures created under different employment generation schemes is very poor. Participatory actions of stakeholders and government are essential for management and maintenances of community assets.

## Village Level Analysis

On the basis of the information given in the Village Study Assignments of 15 villages, the following table has been generated to show various kinds of infrastructure facilities such as all weather approach road, electricity connectivity, primary school, health centre, ICDS, drinking water facility and public distribution systems available in different villages.

**Table 1.6:** Basic Amenities in the Villages

| *Villages/District* | *Road* | *Electricity* | *Primary School* | *Health Centre* | *ICDS* | *Drinking Water* | *PDS* |
|---|---|---|---|---|---|---|---|
| Sapmundi (Kalahandi) | 2 | 2 | 1 | 2 | 2 | 1 | 1 |
| Dumerpani (Nuapada) | 1 | 2 | 1 | 2 | 2 | 2 | 2 |
| Patrabasa (Kalahandi) | 1 | 1 | 1 | 2 | 1 | 1 | 1 |
| Salebidi (Nabrangpur) | 1 | 2 | 1 | NA | 1 | 1 | 1 |
| Chhamunda (Sundar-garh) | 1 | 1 | 1 | 2 | 1 | 1 | NA |
| Kupudamaha (Kandhamal) | 1 | 1 | 1 | NA | 1 | 1 | 1 |
| Taljhiri (Rayagada) | 1 | 1 | 1 | 2 | 1 | 1 | 2 |
| Brahmani (Bolangir) | 1 | 1 | 1 | 2 | 1 | 1 | 1 |
| Seledi (Sonepur) | 1 | 1 | 1 | 2 | 1 | 1 | 1 |
| Banspal (Keonjhar) | 1 | 1 | 1 | 2 | 1 | 1 | 1 |
| Parapanga (Kandhamal) | 1 | 1 | 1 | 2 | 1 | 1 | 2 |
| Kiralaga (Sundargarh) | 1 | NA | 2 | 2 | NA | 1 | 1 |
| Mohandi (Nabarangpur) | 1 | 1 | 1 | 2 | NA | 1 | NA |
| Bishnupur (Keonjhar) | 1 | 1 | 1 | 2 | 2 | 1 | 1 |
| Total available in Per-centage | 93 | 77 | 93 | 0 | 75 | 93 | 75 |

This is already mentioned that most of the villages are located in the southern parts of the state and almost all the villages selected for the study are dominated by tribal people. The infrastructural facilities available in different villages as per the data compiled are presented in the above table clearly show the villages are better equipped with the basic infrastructure facilities as compare to the basic infrastructure available in the state in general. More than 90 per cent villages are provided with three basic infrastructure facilities like drinking water, primary school, all weather approach road and electricity connections are there in more than 75 percentages of villages. The most disgusting fact is that none of the villages is provided with any health centre. The health related services probably catered to the village people by the ICDS centres to certain extent. There are ICDS centers in 75 per cent of villages. Food security is a major challenge in tribal areas, so in around 9 villages out of total 12 villages there are Public Distribution Systems or fair price shops. All the figures presented in table 1.6 give an idea about the physical presence of basic infrastructure facilities, however, it cannot be inferred anything from the table regarding the actual status of the rural infrastructure. The following paragraph gives in detail about the status of existing infrastructure facilities.

According to the information provided in the assignment the status of village infrastructure in Chhamunda village of Sundergarh district is as follows: 'As regards basic amenities in the village there is an all weather approach road. Generally the people travel with cycles. There is electricity connection in the village. But not all the people/households have taken connection. Still, around a quarter households use kerosene lamps. Regarding the education, the village has a primary, middle and high school run by the Government. Regarding the medical facilities, it is quite poor as there is no primary health sub-centre. The nearest PHC is at Bargaon. But there is an ANM who visits the village and gives guidance on health matters. There is no Adult Literacy Centre. The children go to ICDS and it is working well. Mostly people live with agriculture and by doing labour work. There is no PACCS, Kisan Sewa Kendra, Public Telephone Service etc.' Though there are primary schools in most of the villages. The conditions of the primary schools are not good at all. In case of the village Salebidi of Nabarangpur district as mentioned in the report reads as 'Much need to be done to improve the condition of basic amenities in the school. There is no source of drinking water, no electricity (for that matter, the village itself is not electrified), no facility for toilet and no playground added to the fact that there are only 2 rooms for five classes—3 classes sitting in one room and 2 in the other room with their backs to each other and students in each class reading something on top of their voice causing total chaos.'

The absence of a health centres in many of the villages really creates a lot of hardships for the poor villagers. This is lucidly explained in one of the assignments pertaining to village Dumerpani, District Nuapada. 'The number of deaths due to malaria and dysentery is high. This year alone 3 deaths have occurred in the village. For availing medical help, the villagers have no choice but to travel 27 km to the nearest PHC. There is no ayurveda centre that, if established, could help avert such deaths. Visits by health officials are rare. Villagers mostly depend on local treatment like use of medicinal herbs and plants.'

Regarding the status of drinking water facility in the village it is important to quote from the village study assignment of village Taljhiri of Rayagada district. It is quoted that 'The drinking water facility is very poor in the village. The two hand pumps in the village are inadequate to meet the drinking water requirement of 600 people. There are two streams near the village, which supplement the tube wells as drinking water source.'

Similarly, though there is electricity connection in the village Seledi of Sonepur district, the facility is hardly contributing towards development of the village, because of the following reasons as mentioned in the assignment. 'The village is electrified and 90 per cent of the houses have electricity connection. But power cuts are a major problem. Especially in summer the power cuts are more acute. In Orissa power sector is privatized but the staff are the same, who were previously with the OSEB. There are huge transmission losses and to reduce/cover up this, illegal power cuts are done in addition to the legalized power cuts. Many a times these kinds of continuous power cuts leads to agitation, *Rasta rokko* and Law and Order problems. When I was doing survey in this village power was hardly there for 3-4 hours on an average per day. Sometimes when there is a breakdown power supply was not restored for three days.'

The concept of provision of community latrine is absolutely unknown to the villagers. So in the absence of community latrine, many sanitation problems are not uncommon in the village. In one of the village assignments the problems are clearly documented as, 'There are no community toilets in the village. Even in public places like schools, RI office, Panchayat Bhavan, there are no toilets. Private toilets are there in 12 houses in the village. Others follow open defecation and it is a big problem in this village as in most parts of Orissa. Because most of the fields are agricultural fields and water stagnation is there, people use the roadsides for open defecation. Men use the village approach road and women and small children use the village backside road. There is caste discrimination in this, i.e. the SC people are not allowed to use this road. They have to go to the fields. During rainy season, open defecation is a major problem. Drainage system is non-existent in the village.'

Most of the villagers are unable to avail the facilities of basic infrastructure due to the reason that they are poor and don't have purchasing power to meet the minimum expenditure required to avail the benefits of infrastructure. For example, though there is electricity connection in the village, only a few households are able to pay the electricity bills and able to purchase electricity accessories like bulbs, wires, etc.

## EDUCATION AND LITERACY

Education is an indispensable input for development of human resources. During 1951 census survey the overall literacy rate was 15.8 per cent, it was only 4.5 per cent among females. The total literacy rate in Orissa has increased to 64 per cent by the census survey 2001 from 49.1 per cent in 1991. The male literacy rate increased to 76 per cent and that for females to 51 per cent as per 2001 census from 63.1 and 34 percentages for males and females respectively in the Census Survey 1991. Literacy rate among the age group 15-19 is 61.0 per cent, whereas the literacy rate among 0-6 years age group is 66.2 as per 2001 census. This implies there is high incidence of dropouts in the state and the dropout rate is higher among the females as the figures suggest. Around 54 per cent of population in the age group of 6-10 years are attending school and the percentage of population in the age group 11-13 years is marginally higher than that. This is probably due to the fact that the same in the age group 15-19 is 61.0, which implies that there are dropouts at the higher-level education. A major factor responsible for low educational level among females and persons belonging to Scheduled Castes and Scheduled Tribes is the high dropout rate at primary level especially in the tribal and inaccessible areas. The literacy rate of Scheduled Caste and Scheduled Tribe populations was 36.78 per cent and 22.31 per cent respectively according to 1991 census. The literacy gap was as high as 28.4 per cent. The literacy rate of the state increased from 49.1 to 63.61 per cent between census years 1991 and 2001. This implies the rate of growth of literacy rate in the state is more than 1 per cent per annum.

Male literacy rate of the state has increased from 63.1 per cent by 1991 census year to 75.95 per cent by the 2001 census. Annual growth rate of male literacy in the last decade is around 1.28 per cent, whereas the growth rate of female literacy per annum during

1991-2001 is 1.627. This is a good sign that the rate of growth of female literacy has remained higher than the rate of growth of male literacy in the state during 1991-2001.

**Table 1.7:** Education (2001 Census)

| | *Literacy Rate* | *Literacy Rate among 0-6 Years Age Group* | *Literacy Rate among 15-19 Years Age Group* | *Per cent of Population Attending School in the Age Group* | |
|---|---|---|---|---|---|
| | | | | *6-10 years* | *11-13 years* |
| Persons | 64 | 66.2 | 61.0 | 54.3 | 59.4 |
| Males | 76 | 75.5 | 72.5 | 60.6 | 69.2 |
| Females | 51 | 56.9 | 50.1 | 48.0 | 49.5 |

In following table literacy rate on the basis of rural-urban classification has been presented. The literacy gap between the rural and urban areas of the state has remained very high during last 30 years.

**Table 1.8:** Literate Population (Rural-Urban and Total)

| | | *% of Population* | | | |
|---|---|---|---|---|---|
| | | 1971 | 1981 | 1991 | 2001 |
| *Urban:* | Total | 57.02 | 62.19 | 71.99 | 80.95 |
| | Male | 68.06 | 73.30 | 81.21 | 88.32 |
| | Female | 42.53 | 49.01 | 61.18 | 72.68 |
| *Rural:* | Total | 24.09 | 35.70 | 45.46 | 60.44 |
| | Male | 42.03 | 50.45 | 60.00 | 73.57 |
| | Female | 14.10 | 20.93 | 30.79 | 47.22 |
| *Total:* | | 80.53 | 38.83 | 49.09 | 63.61 |
| | Male | 44.50 | 53.34 | 63.09 | 75.95 |
| | Female | 16.29 | 23.99 | 34.68 | 50.97 |

The literacy gap between male and female according to 2001 census data is around 25 per cent in rural areas the gender gap with respect to literacy rate is 26.35 per cent, whereas in urban area the literacy gap between male and female as per the same census data is 15.64. So the literacy rates differences on the basis of male-female classification is high in rural areas as compare to urban areas. But it is seen earlier that sex ratio is more favourable in rural Orissa as compare to the urban areas. Hence any inference like a favourable sex ratio implies a better status of women cannot be asserted.

In Table 1.9 number of formal schools along with the strength of teachers and students are given.

**Table 1.9:** Number of Primary Schools (Formal) with Teachers and Students in Orissa

| *Year* | *No. of Primary Schools* | *No. of Teachers* | *No. of Students (in '000 No.)* | *Student-Teacher Ratio* |
|---|---|---|---|---|
| 1989-90 | 39593 | 103540 | 3580 | 35 |
| 1990-91 | 41204 | 104940 | 3600 | 34 |
| 1991-92 | 41204 | 104940 | 3680 | 35 |
| 1992-93 | 41204 | 104940 | 3780 | 36 |

In Orissa out of 46989 inhabited villages, around 15000 villages, there is no primary schools and more than 20 per cent people in rural areas does not have access to a primary school. The student-teacher ratio (36) is fairly good as compare to the acceptable limit of student-teacher ratio (40). The student-teacher ratio has almost remained around 34-36 in spite of the fact that there has been a rise in the number of teachers, student enrollments as given in the above table have not increased significantly. However, the data provided by Directorate of Economics and Statistics for the year 1998-99 suggest that the student teacher ratio has exceeded 40 by the year 1998-99. It can again be seen from the above table that the fall in the enrollment ratio between primary and middle school is very high, i.e. 3583000, whereas the enrolment ratio has increased between middle and secondary schools by 36000. The high enrollments at the primary and secondary level is mainly possibly because of the age-groupwise differentials in composition of population.

**Table 1.10:** Educational Status

| *Primary Schools (1998-99)* | | | *Middle Schools (1998-99)* | | | *Secondary Schools (1998-99)* | | |
|---|---|---|---|---|---|---|---|---|
| No. | Enrollment | Teachers | No. | Enrollment | Teachers | No. | Enrollment | Teachers |
| 42104 | 4578000 | 109448 | 11510 | 995000 | 109448 | 6160 | 1031000 | 51436 |
| Student Teacher Ratio | | | Dropouts between Primary and Middle schools | | | Dropouts between Middle and Secondary | | |
| 41.82 | | | 3583000 | | | -36000 | | |

## Village Level Analysis

As already depicted, the literacy rate in rural areas of the state is low as compare to urban areas of the state and the gender gap of literacy is also higher in rural areas. Data from different assignments have been compiled to look at the literacy scenario from a micro perspective.

**Table 1.11:** Literacy Rate in Villages

| *Village with District* | *Male* | *Female* | *Total* |
|---|---|---|---|
| Dumerpani (Nuapada) | 44.7 | 14 | 31 |
| Salebidi (Nabrangpur) | NA | NA | 29 |
| Taljhiri (Rayagada) | 42 | 5 | NA |
| Seledi (Sonepur) | 69 | 40.7 | 55 |
| Banspal (Keonjhar) | NA | 8 | 20 |
| Bishnupur (Keonjhar) | 49 (48.8) | 33 (8) | 44 |

From the above table, it can be observed that literacy rate is as low as 20 per cent in Banspal village of Keonjhar district and it is as high as 55 per cent in Seledi village of Sonepur district. Literacy rate in general of the selected villages is lower than the literacy rate of the state as a whole. However one should not ignore the fact that all the villages as mentioned earlier are located in the comparatively under-developed districts of Orissa and moreover the villages are more or less dominated by tribal people. The more depressing fact is that female literacy rate is only 5 per cent in case of the village Taljhiri of district Rayagada. The gender gap pertaining to literacy rate is more pronounced in all the villages. Here again the same fact comes out that though the literacy rate in a tribal dominated area among the females is low as compare to their counterparts, but the socio-economic status of tribal women is not worse as it is found among the non-tribals. In the following paragraph, the actual educational and literacy status as documented in the village study assignment of the village Dumerpani of one of the poorest districts of Orissa Nuapada is presented.

There is no doubt incentives provided by the government for enrolling children in schools are helping the increase in the enrollments. However, these incentives like free education, mid-day meal scheme and others are not successful in curbing upon dropout rates specifically dropout rates among girls. The picture is more clear when the real situations prevailing in village Dumerpani of district Nuapada is apprehended from the assignment. At present, mid-day meals are provided to the children. This has partially helped reduce the number of dropouts in the schools. About 2 quintals of rice, 2 litres of mustard oil and 20 kilos of *dal* are received every month from the MI. The teachers themselves purchase items like salt and vegetables, for which expense they are reimbursed at the end of every month. Free textbooks and uniforms are supposed to be provided to each student, but often these are not supplied in adequate numbers. Till now no scholarship has been given to any of the students even though applications have been sent to the Inspector of Schools.

The following table shows the male-female enrolment in the schools:

**Table 1.12:** Enrollments in the Village

| *Sex* | *SC* | *ST* | *OBC* | *Total* |
|---|---|---|---|---|
| Boys | 18 | 35 | 27 | 80 |
| Girls | 10 | 28 | 26 | 64 |
| Total | 28 | 63 | 53 | 144 |

During the academic year, there have been 35 dropouts, of which 26 were girls. The following table shows the respective breakups:

**Table 1.13:** Dropouts in the Village

| *Sex* | *SC* | *ST* | *OBC* | *Total* |
|---|---|---|---|---|
| Boys | 2 | 5 | 2 | 9 |
| Girls | 5 | 12 | 9 | 26 |
| Total | 7 | 17 | 11 | 35 |

Even though the sex ratio in the village is almost equal, enrolment of girls is lower than boys. Further, girls outnumber boys in the number of dropouts. Parents give little importance to female education. The place of a girl is considered to be in the house, helping her mother in domestic chores. There seems to be no urgent requirement for female education beyond the capability to read and write. Also, beyond primary level most girls from the village do not attend school due to factors of mobility, as higher level schools are located outside the village. The only remedy lies in setting up a high school within the village. Parents also need to be motivated to send their children to school.

However after the implementation of Total Literacy Campaigning, the educational status of women has increased in village area. According to a village study assignment of village Bishnupur of Keonjhar district, the following factuality is presented here. 'It is seen that there has been a remarkable improvement in the literacy rates, especially of women. There has been a four-fold increase in the number of literate women in Bishnupur village. The main reason behind this has been the success of the total literacy campaign in Keonjhar district wherein women were encouraged to learn how to read and write. It was observed that a number of tribal women were signing in the PDS register at the time of taking the delivery of PDS goods.'

## HEALTH AND SANITATION

As most of the villagers depend on their manual labour or physical capacity to earn their bread, they are more prone to loss of calorie. In rural areas it is generally found that the family size is large, so low wage rate and large family size are two basic reasons for which malnutrition is very common among the villagers. In addition to malnutrition, poor sanitation, lack of safe drinking water are responsible for many diseases in rural areas. The poor health infrastructures, poverty and lack of sanitation have caused a rise in the number of chronic patients in rural areas. In Orissa calorie intake on the average is very low. As around 48 per cent people are poor, as per the definition these, 48 per cent of people are not able to manage 2200-2400 calorie per day. So malnutrition is widespread in the state. This is again more acute in rural area.

The poor health infrastructure and less effectiveness of the existing facilities *vis-à-vis* the national level may be assessed from the comparative analysis of different health indicators. By the year 1993, Orissa had one health centre for every 19050 persons as against 13143 persons at all-India level. The number of people served per health centre of the state was found to be relatively much higher

**Table 1.14:** Health Indicators (1998-99)

| | |
|---|---|
| No. of Medical college/Dist. Hqrs. Hospitals | 34 |
| No. of Sub-divisional Hospitals | 136 |
| No. of PHCs | 1167 |
| No. of Additional PHCs | 644 |
| No. of Community Health Centres | 157 |
| No. of Mobile Health Units | 198 |
| No. of Subsidiary Health Centres | 172 |
| No. of Hospital Beds | 13786 |
| Doctor Population Ratio (1993) | 1 : 2794 |

than the national average. Similarly, the number of persons served per bed (2167) in different medical institutions of the state was in no way better than the all-India level (1362). At the all-India level the percentage of total expenditure incurred on medical and public health services including water supply and sanitation in 1991-92 was 7.25 per cent of the total government expenditure, whereas this was 6.85 per cent in Orissa. Also the per capita health related expenditure in 1991-92 was Rs. 35.01 at the all-India level as compared to Rs. 29.17 in Orissa. This shows that the provision of health infrastructure in Orissa was lower than the all-India level. The infant mortality rate in 1993 was 74 at the all-India level, which is far below than the same (110) in the case of Orissa. The infant mortality rate in the state is the highest among major states of the country. The death rate per 1000 population was 10.1 at the all-India level in 1992 as against 11.7 in the case of Orissa. The prevalence of major diseases like malaria, tuberculosis, leprosy and blindness per lakh population in Orissa was equally higher than the all-India level. Needless to say, rampant prevalence of anaemia and malnutrition among the small children and the women in the reproductive age group are a matter of serious concern as they cause increasing morbidity and reduce life expectancy rate of population. This shows that in the state not only the status of health infrastructure is poor, but also the incidences of many diseases are also high. The poverty in addition to lack of health facilities in the backward state like Orissa is affecting the quality of life to a great extent. There is fairly higher concentration of depressed category population and higher incidence of rural poverty in the state. There are also many less accessible pockets resided by the tribal population. So a rigorous public intervention with respect to provide health facilities in less accessible areas is required.

## Village Level Analysis

From the basic amenities Table 1.6 it can be found that there are no PHCs or sub-PHCs in any village. The health related services are mostly provided by ICDS centres, ANM and MPHW workers. Most of the health centres are located far from the selected villages. However, as reported in the assignments the health infrastructure of these villages is found to be at a reasonable level of locational spread from the human settlements. But, it is unfortunate that many of the health centres in the remote areas exist without any doctor and other supporting staff. In many villages the presence of ANM at the time of emergency becomes a problem, because the villagers many times are not able to differentiate between a doctor and ANM, so even at the time of serious illness also they approach the ANM. People in the tribal villages mostly depend upon their traditional medicine and a quack as consulting a doctor at the time of need is a luxury, which they cannot afford.

Ignorance in addition to non-existence of PHCs in the nearby area of the village has been responsible for making quacks/local traditional medicine practitioners as the first contact persons for many villagers in case of any illness. This is clearly mentioned in village study assignment of Taljhiri village. 'Though many villagers are literate, but superstition still has grip over the minds of the people, people believe in ghosts and super natural powers. If somebody fell ill, the Ojha of the village is the first man to be consulted for the cure. Generally some puja is offered to the village deity and sacrifice of cock is offered. If the disease is a minor one, it gets cured itself but in case of serious illness, they have to go to the community health centre Kashipur, located about 4 km from the village. According to the norms, this CHC serves about one lakh population.' The community hospital, where the people of Taljhiri are entitled to visit is located at block head quarter Kashipur. The status of CHC and other PHCs and additional PHC as reported in the Taljhiri village report is as follows. The situation of CHC, Kashipur is very pathetic. There is no specialist in the hospital. When the news of starvation death broke out, there was only one doctor in the CHC. All the posts of specialist have been lying vacant for last 7 years. The only doctor, Mr. Sethi, has been working there for the last 6 years. Even some doctors had been posted there but they did not join. The situation is very dismal in case of other six additional PHCs. Doctor is present only in one of the additional PHCs. In other PHCs, attendants are prescribing medicines. Kashipur is considered to be punishment posting by doctors and therefore, no doctor likes to join here. Sanitation problems in the villages selected for the report and spread of forest areas nearby these villages have been responsible for increasing instances of people suffering from Malaria and cerebral malaria. This is elaborated in the village study assignment of village of Dumerpani, Nuapada district as—'Malaria is rampant in the village. Every year 6-7 persons among those affected succumb to cerebral malaria. As a preventive measure, the ANM worker provides chloroquinine tablets to the villagers. Dysentery and cholera are endemic occurrences that mostly affect children. About 5 persons are undergoing treatment for TB. Besides, there are many hidden and suspected cases of TB among the villagers. A major cause for these entire ailments is the total absence of sanitation in the village. There is no drainage system and it is not hard to spot stagnant pools of wastewater in and around the village. There is no community latrine in the village. Defecation is done in the nearby fields, which has provided another cause for health problems in the village.'

Besides providing medical services for illness, it is also important for health department personnel to organise immunization programmes and provide mother and child care services. In most of the villages the immunization programmes were found to be successful as reported in various village study assignments. In case of Taljhiri village as reported by the probationer the child-maternity care services are very poor and most of the deliveries were conducted by untrained local *Dhai*. The local untrained *dhai* used to adopt traditional methods for conducting delivery, so mortality rate is very high in the village. Similarly, it has been reported in another assignment of village Dumerpani of Nuapada District. '*There have been 32 births in the last one year out of which 30 were home deliveries and 2 were institutional deliveries. 21 of these births were males while 11 were females. People still depend on the traditional system of engaging dais for deliveries. There have been no maternal or infant deaths in the last year. However, in the year before last year 2 maternal deaths occurred due to excessive bleeding. Both were local delivery cases.*'

In general after going through all the assignments mentioned else where, the following conclusions are drawn:

- More than half of married women in rural Orissa have chronic energy deficiency, close to 80 per cent are anemic.
- Seventy five per cent of children under three are severely and chronically malnourished.
- Only 42 per cent of children between the age of 12 and 14 months have completed their immunization schedule; a massive 14.4 per cent have not received a single vaccine.
- Only 20 per cent of the rural population have access to potable water supply and only 0.5 per cent enjoys basic sanitation.
- Babies continue to die everyday of treatable respiratory infections, diarrhoea and other illnesses either preventable through clean water, nutritious food and cheap vaccines, or treatable with basic drugs.
- There is no community participation in building up the health services.
- Various National Health Programmes function almost independently of each other. This has been sought to be redressed by the formation of the Zila Swasthya Samities at the district level.
- Public health experts in Orissa have suggested that allocation for disease control programmes is driven more by donor organisations than the state's epidemiological realities.
- Universal, comprehensive, primary health care services are still a distant dream.

## AGRICULTURE AND AGRARIAN RELATIONSHIPS IN ORISSA

The base of Village economy in Orissa is Agriculture. Agriculture is mainly subsistence oriented and rainfed in a scenario of intensive use of primitive and traditional technology. The state receives annual rainfall of about 1500 mm, 80 per cent of which is received during the monsoon period lasting from June to September. The distribution of rainfall quite often is erratic and uneven causing drought, floods and cyclone. There are good number of rain shadow pockets, especially in the inland districts of the state. So agriculture sector is badly affected. Single crop paddy is grown in the best quality land and pulses and oil seeds like gram, *arhar, til*, mustard, groundnut etc.

are grown in the upland. Agriculture sector alone by the year 1999-2000 was contributing Rs. 658094 lakh to the State's income, which is around 34 per cent of NSDP during 2000-01. Due to Population pressure, it is found that most of the cultivators in Orissa are marginal farmers (around 80%) owning less than 2 acres of land. The per capita availability of cultivated land, which was 0.39 hectare in 1950-51, has declined to 0.18 hectare in 1998-99. The yield rate of paddy is invariably low except some developed pockets of irrigated area in Puri, Cuttack, Sambalpur, Bargarh and Sonepur districts.

## Land Resource

For the state Orissa information on land resource by soil type is available for an area 15.48 million hectares. Out of this, net sown area of the state was 5.06 million hectares in 1990-91. So around one-third land resources are being used for cultivation. The Red loam soil constitutes 45.54 per cent of total landmass in Orissa. This type of soil is not suitable for cultivation. Because the red soils are light textured, shallow to medium in depth and usually underlain by compact subsoil, fairly porous and low water holding capacity. Soils are prone to erosion and surface crusting.

**Table 1.16:** Broad Classification of Soil Types of Orissa

| *Sl. No.* | *Types of Soil* | *Approximate Area ('000 Ha)* | *Percentage Distribution* |
|---|---|---|---|
| 1. | Red loam and red sandy soils | 7050 | 45.54 |
| 2. | Mixed red and yellow soils | 5440 | 35.14 |
| 3. | Black soils | 960 | 6.20 |
| 4. | Laterite and lateritic soils | 700 | 4.52 |
| 5. | Deltaic alluvial soils | 670 | 4.33 |
| 6. | Coastal saline and sandy soils | 390 | 2.52 |
| 7. | Brown forest soils | 170 | 1.10 |
| 8. | Mixed red and black soils | 100 | 0.65 |
| | Total Area | 15480 | 100.00 |

*Source*: Agriculture in Orissa, Directorate of Agriculture and Food Production, Orissa, Bhubaneswar.

Another 35 per cent is of mixed red and yellow variety and this type of soil is also not fertile. Thus there is a predominance of light textured red soil in the state. Fertile alluvial soil accounts for only a little more than 4 per cent of the area. The quality of soil, in general, is rather low, except in the coastal districts, which contains highly fertile alluvial soil and the soils of the river valleys. This is a natural weakness of the state's economy as agriculture is its mainstay.

Land resources of Orissa have both low and high agricultural production potential. The state has, however, scarcity of land. Due to increasing population, the average size of land decreased from 1.89 hectares in 1970-71 to 1.34 hectares in 1990-91. Not only is the per capita availability of land in the state low but also the degradation of land is severe. The degradation of land was due to various factors like soil erosion, shifting cultivation and degraded forest. At the same time, quarry and mine waste and water logging have emerged as potential threat to the land degradation. In the following table figures pertaining to Land Utilisation pattern for a period of five years beginning from 1988-89 to 1992-93 are given. Optimal utilization of Land resources forms the basis of the economic development of a region. From the table given below it can be seen that there are fluctuations in area under forest cover, grazing land, net area sown, etc. the increase in the net area sown over the five year (1988-89 to 1992-93) has been at the cost of depletion of grazing land. Point to be noted that grazing land as well as land under cultivation are important in increasing the prospects of agriculture and allied activities. The cultivable wasteland has remained almost over 500,000 hectares during whole five-year span. The cultivable waste generally not used for agricultural purposes due to the lack of irrigational facilities and land degradation.

The land many times classified by the local people on the basis of fertility and water availability. In this context it is worth to mention types of land available in the village Brahmani of Bolangir District.

**Table 1.17:** Land Classification in Brahmani Village of Bolangir District

| *Quality* | *Category* | *Area* | *Descriptions* |
|---|---|---|---|
| Good | Bahal | 25% | Lowlands with high water holding capacity more than one crop. Crop resistant to fluctuations in rainfall. |
| Medium | Berna | 12.5% | |
| | Mal | 12.5% | |
| Inferior | Att | 50% | Very low water holding capacity, uplands crop failure common |

It can be observed from the table given below that around 50 per cent land is hardly used for cultivation. Only 25 to 50 per cent land is cultivated every year. As there are no assured irrigation facilities, the land under cultivation in the year of scanty rainfall decreases. It can be infer that only 25 per cent land is brought under cultivation. The state has a cultivated area (net area sown + current fallow) of 6.4 m. hect. as against Geographical area of 15.5 m. hect. out of which 2.9 m.hect. are high land 1.9 m.hect medium land and 1.6 m.hect. low lands. The gross cropped area is 8.4 million ha. And the cropping intensity is 139 per cent. The land use pattern given in the table below shows that the net area shown in the state is 39 per cent. Fallow land constitutes around 4 per cent of total. The main reasons behind the land lying fallow are lack of irrigation facility, scarcity of funds with the marginal farmers, low productivity, etc. the most important point to note down that in spite of scarcity of cultivable land around 3 per cent land is under the category of cultivable waste.

**Table 1.18:** Land Utilisation Pattern of Orissa

| *Area Type* | *Area in Million hects.* | *Percentage* |
|---|---|---|
| Forest area | 5.6 | 36 |
| Net sown area | 6.0 | 39 |
| Miscellaneous Trees and Groves | 0.8 | 5 |
| Permanent Pasture | 0.5 | 3 |
| Culturable waste | 0.4 | 3 |
| Land put to non-agri uses | 0.9 | 6 |
| Barren and unculturable waste | 0.6 | 4 |
| Current fallow | 0.4 | 2 |
| Other fallow | 0.3 | 2 |

By the year 1998-99 as per data released by agricultural Department, Government of Orissa, the state has a cultivable area (net sown area and current fallow) of 6.41 million hectares. Total cultivable area of the state is 41 per cent of the total geographical area of the state. The gross cropped area is 8.4 million hectares, so the cropping intensity of the state is 139 per cent. Land use pattern as per the village study assignment of the village Salebidi is *'The whole village economy rests on agriculture. Out of the total land area of 92.62 ha, as reported by the Revenue Inspector (RI), 82.76 ha is under cultivation and that is exactly the net sown area as well.*

*Rest of the land, i.e. 8.81 ha is not available for cultivation whereas 0.64 ha is under notified forest cover and 0.40 ha under pastures. Thus as much as 89 per cent of land is under cultivation, clearly indicating the role of agriculture in the village economy.'*

## LAND USE PATTERN OF VARIOUS VILLAGES

From the following table it can be observed that only 41.13 acres of land out of total area of village, i.e. 645.47 acres are used for cultivation. It is surprise to learn that agriculture is the mainstay of the village. Lack of availability of agricultural land has given rise to the existence of large number of landless families in the village. However, shifting cultivation in large patches of forest land is supporting many families in terms of managing their daily food requirements.

**Table 1.20:** Land Use in Village: Kupudmaha, District: Kandhmal
Land Details of the Village

*(in acres)*

| | |
|---|---|
| Total area | 645.47 |
| Land cultivation | 41.13 |
| Land under forest cover | 520.84 |
| Fallow land | 32.51 |
| Pasture and grazing land | 3.99 |
| Waste land | 30.15 |
| Land for homestead | 2.89 |
| Net sown area | 30.44 |
| Community land | 10.22 |

Forestland of the village Kupudmaha constitutes around 80 per cent of total geographical area of the village. There are 32.51 acres of fallow land, for an optimal utilization of land resources available; these lands could be converted into forest land or agricultural land.

Similarly, the land use pattern of village Patrabasa of Kalahandi district as mentioned in the assignment is as follows. Total area of the village at present is 546.19 acres, out of which areas under cultivation is 434.98 acres (79%). Community lands constitute 4 per cent of the village area (20.62 acres). Land area under ownership cultivation is 331.13 acres (60%). Land area declared, as under forest cover is 10.52 acres. The land utilization situations of another village Seledi of Sonepur district is documented in a tabular form and it can be found that cultivable land is divided into high, medium and low lands. Each land is suitable for growing a particular type of crop, but here paddy is grown in all the lands. There is a forest area of about 19 ha and the vegetation in the forest is not thick. The pasture and grazing land also called as the gochar land is a common property resource and utilized by all the people in the village without any discriminations.

**Table 1.21:** Land use Pattern in village Seledi, District Sonepur

| *Type of Land* | *Area in ha.* |
|---|---|
| Geographical area | 520.635 |
| Cultivable land | 379.33 |
| High | 113 |
| Medium | 183 |
| Low | 82 |
| Paddy area | 338 |
| Non-paddy area | 41 |
| Cultivable waste land | 93.746 |
| Pasture and grazing land | 20.528 |
| Land put to non-agricultural use | 4.577 |
| Old fallow | 2.796 |
| Forest area | 19.151 |
| Miscellaneous trees and grooves | 0.804 |

All the cultivable lands are used for agricultural purposes. Out of the 338 ha of paddy area, forty per cent of the land is medium land, twenty-five per cent is low land and thirty-five per cent is high land area. Even though it is recommended not to grow paddy in the high land areas, farmers grow paddy as it is their traditional crop and they know the production system well.

The quantum of fallow lands in the village very less and these are kept fallow because of personal reasons. Non-availability of resources to do agriculture and the non-remunerative nature of the paddy crop also forces the farmers to leave the lands fallow. One more important reason for keeping land fallow is that the village is situated in the tail end of the catchments area and these fields are not able to get irrigation water.

In the village Dumerpani the areas under different types of land (in acres) is as follows:

**Table 1.22:** Land Use Pattern in Dumerpani

| *Types of Land Utilization* | *Area under Different Types* |
|---|---|
| Land for cultivation | 795.46 |
| Land under forest cover | 100.78 |
| Fallow land | 87.92 |
| Pasture and grazing land | 52.72 |
| Waste land | 165.11 |
| Land for homestead | – |
| Net sown area | 716.00 |
| Community land | 31.92 |
| Miscellaneous | – |

Population growth in the rural areas has significantly affected the land use pattern. Depletion of forest area due to population pressure is quite common. This is more clear from the in the village study assignment of village Dumerpani. It says 'Forest cover has drastically reduced over the last decade. Records show that it was as much as 256 acres. Due to increase in population of both men and cattle, forested areas have been under tremendous pressure. As can be made out from the figures, there has been a disproportionate increase in the area under cultivation. Even pasture land that was as much as 102 acres has been brought down to half its earlier size. Total area under use is 817.23 acres, including homestead, cultivated and leased land.'

## Food Grain Production and Agricultural Productivity

Production of food grains has fluctuated over the last five years. During 1990-91, the production of food grains declined to a low level of 5.41 lakh MT from 5.89-lakh tonnes production in the year 1988-89. In the food grain basket rice only accounts for near about 90 per cent of total food grains. Only 10 per cent food grains comprise wheat and other coarse grains. Coarse grains are more abundantly produced as compare to the production of wheat. Coarse grains are generally grown in up land southern region of Orissa. Similarly the area under more crops and cash crops accounted for 1.36 per cent and 1.92 per cent respectively of the gross cropped area under principal crops. Rice is the main agricultural product as 53 per cent of gross cropped area is under the cultivation of paddy and it contributes around 69 per cent of food grain.

Agricultural productivity is directly linked to methods of cultivation, irrigation facilities, and soil fertility. The types of soil availability in the state have already been discussed. The coastal plain area soil is alluvial in nature, so undoubtedly fertility is not low, but alluvial soil is around 4 per cent of the total land resources of the state. Similarly, the black soil is good for cash crops, however, cash crop has hardly cultivated in the region, where black soil is of dominant type. From the following table, it can be concluded that during the five years (1988-89 to 1992-93), the production index of rice (major crop) is following a discontinued trend. As most of the agriculturist in Orissa adopts mono cropping (Paddy), the variations in the production index of rice must be coinciding with fluctuations in rain fall and miseries of the farmers. The reason for variations in production index of rice cannot be attributed to diversification of cropping pattern. Because as per the table given above, rice constitutes nearly 90 per cent of total food grain production.

**Table 1.23:** Agriculture Production Indices (Base 1981-82=100)

| *Sl. No.* | *Commodity* | *1988-89* | *1989-90* | *1990-91* | *1991-92* | *1992-93* |
|---|---|---|---|---|---|---|
| 1. | Rice | 143.5 | 170.3 | 142.9 | 180.5 | 146 |
| 2. | Total Cereals | 140.8 | 165.5 | 140.1<br>(135.7) | 174.2<br>(170.8) | 141.7<br>(138.5) |
| 3. | Pulses | 134.2 | 135.6 | 142.3 | 136.9 | 127.6 |
| 4. | Foodgrains | 139.7 | 160.7 | 140.5<br>(136.8) | 168.1<br>(165.2) | 139.4<br>(138.9) |
| 5. | Oil-seeds | 193.7 | 193.1 | 218.00<br>(33.2) | 192.3<br>(42.7) | 173.3<br>(37.2) |
| 6. | Fibres | 98.5 | 98.00 | 131.00<br>(86.7) | 117.7<br>(94.1) | 88.1<br>(59.6) |
| 7. | Non-foodgrains | 153.5 | 157.2 | 172.6<br>(115.3) | 160.5<br>(133.1) | 140.6<br>(109.1) |
| 8. | All Commodities | 142.1 | 160.1 | 146.1<br>(133.0) | 166.8<br>(159.6) | 139.6<br>(133.7) |

Similarly it can be observed from the above table that index of food grain is also showing variability to a large extent. The index of food grain production was as high as 160.5 in the year 1989-90 and had reduced to a low level in the year 1990-91 (140.5). However, it was increased to 168.1 by the year 1991-92. Production index of all agricultural commodities follows a similar type of trend as shown by production trend food grains. The Agricultural productivity in case of Paddy crop was only 12.4 quintal per hectare and by the year 1991-92 it reached at 14.6 quintal per hectare. As compare to National average paddy productivity it is too low. Low agricultural productivity mainly attributed to adoption of traditional methods of cultivation and use of low quality seeds. Increase in the population has reduced the per capita availability of cultivated land in Orissa from 0.39 ha in the year 1950-51 to 0.14 ha in 1991. Despite the fact that there is some growth in the production of food grains over the year in the State, it is essential that the yield rate should be given substantial boost in view of reduction in the per capita availability of cultivated land by using more and more agriculture inputs. In case of village Patrabasa of Kalahandi district it is noted that 'the villagers are entirely dependent on rainfed agriculture. Paddy is the main crop grown in this village. Other crops that are grown in small patches are *mung*, *biri*, *arhar* and groundnut. The cultivation starts around July and harvesting is done around November/December. People get a return of about 15 quintals of unprocessed paddy per acre.' Low productivity, mono cropping and poor agricultural input use are mainly responsible for the poor conditions of farmers of Orissa. In Dumerpani village paddy is the main crop covering around 398 acres. Some farmers also grow black gram, groundnut, millet, hoarse gram, maize and *mung*. These are sown during June-September, while harvesting is done during the winter. Yield per acre is low for all these crops; about one and half quintals for paddy. Very few cultivators use fertilizers or hybrid seeds because they cannot afford them. They mostly depend on natural manure like cow dung and fermented *gigua* leaves. Mechanized farming has never been done, as tractors are not available in the area. There is no natural source of irrigation like rivers or streams. As already mentioned, the Sunder Irrigation Project does not cover Dumerpani. There are 4 tanks but they remain dry for most part of the year. The villagers mostly depend on rainwater to irrigate their fields. Only paddy and black gram are sold in the open market or to dealers. Last season, the villagers were able to sell 850 quintals or rice and 720 quintals of black gram. The returns were Rs. 2,97,500 for rice and Rs. 1,07,250 for black gram. The nearest grain market is located at Tarbod, which is 5 kms away from Dumerpani. There are few villages where paddy is not a dominant crop, however due to lack of marketing support the produce are not sold at remunerative prices. This is very clear from village study assignment of village Salebidi. 'In Salebidi village eighty (80) per cent of the soil is Black while 10 per cent is red and the rest does not fall into any common types of soil categories. The Black soil is rich in nitrogen, is water retentive and thus well suited for growing cotton and groundnut. However, the farmers in the village practice mainly a subsistence of type of agriculture and therefore, grow mainly paddy though some of which is finally sold, too. During Kharif-98, paddy was grown on about 41 ha of land, yielding 410 quintals (10 quintals per ha). The rest of the cultivable area was used in growing vegetables, groundnut, wheat, maize etc. The main crop during Rabi season is groundnut followed by pulses, ragi, sweet potato and vegetables. Groundnut is a major crop in the area although the farmers never get remunerative prices for their crop due to lack of proper marketing structure and facilities. Mostly traders, mainly from Rajasthan and nearby M.P. areas, would visit the village at the time of harvest and buy all groundnuts directly from individual farmers—at an estimated price, which is generally the last year's price with some change. It, thus, seems that there is an immense scope for forming a Groundnut Farmer's Co-operative in the village and nearby areas. But, when told about forming such a co-operative, there were few takers for this suggestion. Perhaps they were happy in whatever price they get with minimum effort on their part. Maybe this is one of the reasons of why there were no co-operatives in the village and the surrounding areas.' In case of village Chhamunda it is observed that 'Due to lack of irrigation facilities, land in Chhamunda gives only some amount of paddy. The yield per acre is just 5 quintals, which is extremely low. The return is negative if labour cost and other input cost is added to it. There are only about 40 ha of land, which are irrigated by private pumping sets. Due to lack of irrigation most people remain idle for major part of the year. Therefore, they go for labour work in nearby areas.' The villages located in the southern part of Orissa are generally having a plateau type topography. So small hills are found in many parts. There are different categories of land in the plateau area depending on different degree of fertility and water holding capacity. The cropping pattern and land use pattern of Taljhiri village according to different classes of land is very clearly mentioned in the village assignment as 'Three types of land are found in the village—the low land, the upland, the hill slopes. Stream water is flowing round the year through the low land. It is also the most fertile land of the village.

Only paddy can be grown over this area. The other two types of land are completely rainfed. A special type of paddy is grown over the upland, which is of short duration, and needs less water. It is called *dangar dhan*. Niger is also grown over the upland as cash crop. Mixed cropping is practiced over the hill slopes which includes millets like *ragi, suan, jana*, pulses like *kandul* etc. basically, shifting cultivation is practiced over the hill slopes which is called *podu* in local language. All these hill slopes have been categorized as government waste land.'

In order to investigate into the profitability of farmers cost of cultivation of paddy per 0.5 acre of good quality land as reported in Village study assignment of Brahmani village has been presented in the following table.

**Table 1.24:** Cost of production of rice in 0.50 acre of Bahal land

| *Cost Heads* | *Cost* |
|---|---|
| Ploughing 4 ploughs @ Rs. 50 each | 200 |
| Seeds | 100 |
| Seeds plantation: 1 labour day @ Rs. 25 | 25 |
| Weeding: 6 labour days @ Rs. 25 | 150 |
| Cutting of rice: 5 labour days @ Rs. 25 | 125 |
| Carriage from field: 3 labour days @ Rs. 25 | 75 |
| Threshing: 2 labour days @ Rs. 25 | 50 |
| Cost of production | 725 |
| Price of paddy produced: 7 bags @ Rs. 300 each | 2100 |
| Net Income | 1375 |

From the table it is clear the farmer, who is a land owner, roughly earns Rs. 1,375 per 0.5 acre of land. But as most of the land remains uncultivated round the year except kharif crop, it can be considered that the above shown income is annual income of a farmer from 0.5 acre of very good quality land. So on the average a farmer in the possession of 3-5 acres of land will get around annual agricultural income of Rs. 8,000 and this amount is short of the amount defined to demarcate poor from non-poor. So it can be inferred that most of the small and medium farmers must be below poverty line. Instance of low agricultural productivity is also reported in Seledi village study assignment as 'Productivity of paddy is 1.2t/ha, which is less than the national average. This will be one of the lowest productivity in an area with assured irrigation'. In the same assignment the reasons for poor productivity in paddy mentioned are as follows:

## Technological Factors

- Farmers follow traditional agricultural practices and they grow traditional varieties of paddy, which are basically of long duration and highly susceptible to pest and diseases.
- Use of high yielding varieties (HYV) is almost nil and this is because the seeds are not available on time and farmers are of the opinion that HYV give poor quality rice.
- Most of the farmers do not transplant and they practice direct sowing of paddy, this leads to reduction in the population and more weed growth, finally leading to yield loss.
- Farmers do not use bio-fertilizers and the interesting fact is that most of the farmers do not know about bio-fertilizers.
- Ploughing is not done properly by the farmers. They do shallow ploughing resulting in formation of hard pan in the soil. This inhibits the proliferation of roots and results in stunted growth. There is only one tractor in the whole village and maximum farmers use bullock drawn ploughs.
- Weeding is an important operation for paddy, but the farmers neither do manual weeding nor do they spray pesticides. During the peak growth period of the crop, the weed growth is also maximum leading to yield loss.
- Poor farmers apply only nitrogenous fertilizers are very costly. This affects the yield in two ways. It increases the vegetative growth of paddy and makes the crop more susceptible for pest and diseases. The other effect is that due to more vegetative growth, the grain number is decreased and size is reduced leading to reduced yields.
- The concept of pest management is non-existent and only the rich farmers follow it. Poor and marginal farmers do not apply pesticides or they apply the same pesticide for all pests. In addition to this as paddy is grown year after year, the pest build up is very high. This is the same case for diseases also. Growing paddy in every season makes the crop more susceptible to diseases. When weeding and bund cleaning are not done, they act as alternative hosts for pests and diseases.

- Farmers grow paddy even in lands unfavourable for paddy, e.g. in uplands. This also leads to reduction in yield.

## Institutional Factors

- All the above-mentioned factors show, that the agricultural extension has failed to make any impact on the agricultural practices. Interactions with the village community also showed that farmers do not know about the programme of the agricultural extension workers.
- Farmers face problems in getting credit for agriculture. They do not get timely and adequate amount of credit. Even after relaxing and simplifying the procedures, an illiterate farmer faces lot of harassment and hardships in availing credit facilities from both banks and co-operative institutions. This in turn encourages the farmers to get credit from moneylenders on a higher rate of interest.
- Input support mechanism is lacking, e.g. even when farmers want to grow HYV seeds are not available on time.

Training and exposure related to agriculture and allied activities may be proposed for improving the efficiency of farmers to manage matters on their own. Demonstration, experimentation and extension of improved and customized farming techniques have been undertaken at the block level. Irrigation development combined with soil and moisture conservation would be the main focus of attention along with complementary technologies to raise the productivity of the farmland. To sustain the practice at community level the farmer's societies are to be formed to address the farming related problems.

## Irrigation

In the absence of adequate irrigation facilities, agriculture is pathetically dependent upon the monsoons. As a result of the erratic behaviour of the monsoon, agricultural production fluctuates widely from year to year. The net irrigation potential created by the end of 1991-92 from all sources was 29,92,000 hectares, which is 42.71 per cent of the total irrigable area of the State. Out of 25.20 lakh hectares of irrigated area, 11.76 lakh hectares of land are irrigated through major and medium irrigation projects, 4.50 lakh through minor (flow), 3.63 lakh through minor (lift), and 5.58 lakh through other sources which include private tanks, ponds, dug wells, water harvesting structures and the like. However, assured irrigation available through major and medium irrigation projects accounts 46.52 per cent of the total area under irrigation and as a whole the irrigated area under kharif crop comes to be around 30 per cent. This underscores the need for stepping up the assured irrigation potential in order to insulate agriculture from the vagaries of monsoon.

**Table 1.25:** Area Irrigated by Different Irrigation Sources in Orissa

*(Area in '000 Hect.)*

| *Year* | *Major and Medium Irrigation Projects* | | *Minor Irrigation Projects (Flow)* | | *Lift Irrigation Projects* | |
|---|---|---|---|---|---|---|
| | *Kharif* | *Rabi* | *Kharif* | *Rabi* | *Kharif* | *Rabi* |
| 1988-89 | 891 | 403 | 369 | 60 | 239 | 143 |
| 1989-90 | 927 | 432 | 376 | 61 | 265 | 218 |
| 1990-91 | 937 | 434 | 378 | 61 | 264 | 159 |
| 1991-92 | 953 | 440 | 381 | 61 | 275 | 165 |
| 1992-93 | 967 | 443 | 386 | 62 | 280 | 168 |

As per data released by Department of Agriculture, Orissa, irrigation potential by the year 1998-99 for kharif crop was 2.41 million hectares (24,10,000 hectares), which is around 37.6 per cent of total cultivated area. Kharif crops are mainly grown during the rainy season and normally rainfall in Orissa during rainy season is sufficient to prevent water shortages for crops. However, floods and low rainfall during exceptional years give rise to floods and draughts. Water management specifically in southern parts of Orissa is a necessity to prevent acute water crisis during summer season. Lack of assured irrigation is mainly responsible for growing a mono-crop (paddy) in most parts of Orissa. Rabi crops are grown in those parts of Orissa, where there are some sort of irrigation facilities are available.

The real situation of irrigation facility can be very well gauged by going through the following portion of the village study assignment of village Banspal village. 'There is no government irrigation scheme functioning in the village. A few families have put pump sets and arranged irrigation in their land. There are around 30 acres of land in the village under private irrigation. One lift irrigation point was built in the eighties in the village by the Government. The cultivators did not pay the water cess and the lift irrigation department had discontinued supply of water. The electric wires for power supply were stolen subsequently.'

Total area of the village Patrabasa is 546.19 acres, out of which areas under cultivation is 434.98 acres (79%). Community lands constitute 4 per cent of the village area (20.62 acres). Land area under ownership cultivation is 331.13 acres (60%). Land area declared, as under forest cover is 10.52 acres. The village does not have any area under irrigation.

## Surplus Agricultural Produce and Marketing

Small and marginal farmers don't have marketable surplus, but the medium and rich farmers have marketable surplus. Paddy is sold through the *mandis* run by the RMC in Binka. Sonepur is a procurement district and it produces about one lakh bags of paddy in the Kharif season and forty thousand bags of paddy in Rabi season.

- There are four mills in the district and they can mill only 20 per cent of the marketable surplus of the district. Thus the district is dependent on millers from outside the district for selling paddy. The Collector, Sonepur does not have much control over the millers from outside the district. This leads to a situation wherein the millers come for procurement at their own will. They delay procuring paddy from Sonepur farmers, which leads to a panic situation resulting in distress sale of paddy.
- In addition to this the Food and Civil Supplies Department sometimes delays releasing procurement quotas to the millers. This also leads to distress sale of paddy.
- When farmers take credit from moneylenders they are forced to sell paddy at a cheaper price to the moneylenders most of whom are also middlemen in the paddy procurement system.

- Farmers also sell their produce before harvest or right in the field itself to middlemen. This they do to meet their urgent credit needs. Here also distress sale happens.

These are the factors that lead to distress sale of paddy. The District Collector is vested with the responsibility of ensuring minimum support price but there are many factors, which are beyond the control of the Collector, e.g. the release of procurement quotas to the millers. In addition to this the Collector does not have control over the millers from outside the district. In this setup the RDC can play a pivotal role in co-ordinating and monitoring the activities of millers in different districts under the division.

## Factors Affecting Agricultural Production

In order, find the real reasons behind the fact that agricultural productivity is low, a simple linear regression analysis using yield rate of food grains of undivided 13 districts as dependent variable and area under food grain production, fertilizer consumption per hectare, average rain fall and proportion of cropped area irrigated as independent variables has been done. All the figures of the parameters of the districts are for the year 1998-99. So the regression analysis is a cross-sectional one. The specification of yield rate function in the forms of regression model is as follows:

Yield rate = f (Area under food grain production, fertilizer consumption/hectare, average rain fall and proportion of cropped area irrigated)

**Table 1.27:** Regression Statistics

| | |
|---|---|
| Multiple R | 0.827586 |
| R Square | 0.684898 |
| Adjusted R Square | 0.527347 |
| Standard Error | 158.0962 |
| Observations | 13 |

$$Y = a + b_1X_1 + b_2X_2 + b_3X_3 + b_4X_4 + U$$

**Table 1.26: Regression Result**

| | *Coefficients* | *Standard Error* | *t Stat* | *P-value* | *Lower 95%* | *Upper 95%* | *Lower 95.0%* | *Upper 95.0%* |
|---|---|---|---|---|---|---|---|---|
| Intercept | 491.6795 | 452.7982 | 1.085869 | 0.30917 | –552.476 | 1535.835 | –552.476 | 1535.835 |
| X Variable 1 | 0.48355 | 0.315734 | 1.53151 | 0.164178 | –0.24453 | 1.211635 | –0.24453 | 1.211635 |
| X Variable 2 | 1.131799 | 2.609712 | 0.433688 | 0.675973 | –4.88621 | 7.149809 | –4.88621 | 7.149809 |
| X Variable 3 | –0.18329 | 0.501258 | –0.36567 | 0.724094 | –1.3392 | 0.97261 | –1.3392 | 0.97261 |
| X Variable 4 | 9.42667 | 5.086984 | 1.853096 | 0.100996 | –2.30394 | 21.15728 | –2.30394 | 21.15728 |

Where, Y = yield rate per hectare food grain, $X_1$ = Area under food grain production, $X_2$ = Fertiliser consumption/hectare in kg., $X_3$ = Averagerain fall in mm, $X_4$ = Proportion of cropped area irrigated.

Using the estimated coefficients given in the regression Table 1.26 the yield rate of regression can be represented as:

$$\text{Yield rate food grains (Y)} = 491.68 + 0.48\, X_1 + 1.13\, X_2 - 0.18\, X_3 + 9.42\, X_4$$

According to the regression results average rainfall has a marginally negative impact on the yield rate of food grains. The main reason for negative impact of rainfall on yield rate is that scanty rainfall during the cropping season causes draught and heavy rainfall causes loss to productivity because of floods. In Orissa, the rainfall is mostly erratic due to the influences of pressures built in the Bay of Bengal. The unpredictable and uncertain nature of monsoon rainfall as a result suggests that it must have some negative impact on crop productivity. The value regression coefficient in case of irrigation variable is 9.42 and it is the highest, this implies that irrigation variable is the most important variable among all the variables considered for estimating the yield rate function. The coefficient of irrigation variable indicates that 1 percentage increase in the proportion of cropped area irrigated leads to rise in the yield rate by 9.41 percentage. Similarly, increase in the fertilizer consumption per hectare in kg. by 1 per cent leads to rise in the yield rate of food grains by 1.13 percentage. Increase in area under cultivation does not have that much positive impact on yield rate as compare to the impacts of other variables like fertilizer consumption and proportion of cropped area irrigated. Over all the values of estimates of different variables implies that increase in irrigation potentialities has the largest impact on agricultural productivity. The values of $R_1$ and $R_2$ are 0.68 and 0.52 respectively. These values clearly show that the explanatory variables explain the variability in the yield rate.

## LAND REFORMS—AGRARIAN RELATIONSHIP, LAND OWNERSHIP, LAND SIZE, ETC.

The basic objectives of Land Reforms Policies generally confine to redistribution of land, abolition of intermediaries, tenancy reforms and consolidation of land holdings. However, the main motto behind all these objectives is to increase agricultural productivity and to initiate cooperative cultivation. The increase in population growth has been conducive for eliminating the concentration of lands in the hands of few, but the productivity of agriculture has not increased as expected. Land reforms in Orissa is a big failure from the point of views of tenancy reforms, consolidation of landholdings, increasing agricultural productivity, etc. The backwardness of agriculture sector clearly points out that Land Reforms in Orissa neither helped to increase agricultural productivity nor it has been successful in curbing tenancy. Tenancy practices are quite detrimental to private capital formation in agriculture sector. Various land reform legislations adopted in the state of Orissa are as follows:

*The Orissa Estates Abolition Act, 1951 (Orissa Act I of 1952)*— The Act provided for the abolition of all the rights, title and interest in land of intermediaries by whatever name known, including the mortgagees and lessees of such interest between the raiyat and the state of Orissa for vesting in the said rights, title and interest. In a nut-shell, the main purpose of the Act was to abolish all Zamindaris and proprietary estates and intermediary interests in the state of Orissa and to bring all raiyats or the actual tillers of the land in direct touch with the Government.

*The Orissa Tenants Protection Act, 1948*—The Act was enacted to give temporary protection to certain classes of tenants who were exploited by the big landowners. Provision of security to the tenants and fixation of fair rent to be paid by them were the two main objectives of this Act. The Act was extended to the whole of Orissa except the district of Sambalpur. In order to give the tenants temporary protection pending introduction of a comprehensive legislative measure on Land Reforms. *The Orissa Tenants Relief Act, 1955* was enacted to cover the whole State of Orissa.

*The Orissa Land Reforms Act, 1960*—The Orissa Land Reforms Act, 1960 was drastically recast in the O.L.R. Amendment Act (Act 13 of 1965), which received the President's assent on 11th August 1965. It was gazetted on 17th August 1965. The Preamble of the Act, which contains basic purposes runs as follows:

"*Whereas it is necessary to enact a progressive legislation relating to agrarian reforms and land tenures consequent on the gradual abolition of Intermediary interest, and whereas it is expedient to confer better rights on agriculturists to ensure increase in food production.*"

The preamble prefaced to the statute declares the basic objectives of the law. This intends to confer better tenurial rights on the actual tillers of the soil, to standardise the rates of rent and regulate its payment to the state, and to bring about social and economic justice in light of the provisions of Articles 38 and 39 under the Directive Principles of State Policy of our Constitution.

The law envisages a peaceful agrarian revolution preventing concentration of land in fewer hands. It empowers the state to acquire the ceiling surplus lands and distribute them among the landless and weaker sections of society. The law prohibits leasing out of lands on share-cropping basis in all cases excepting those who are persons under disability and are privileged raiyats. The Act also puts restriction on alienation of land by a member of the Scheduled Caste or Scheduled Tribe in favour of a person not belonging to S.C. or S.T.

Chapter II of the Act deals with Raiyats and Tenants. Section 4 of the Act has declared certain persons to be deemed as raiyats. They include various kinds of raiyats including those existing under tenancy law like M.E.L. Act, 1908, Orissa Tenancy Act, 1913, O.M.S.L. Act, 1950 and so on. The law grants every raiyat permanent, heritable and transferable rights on the land. Section 8 deals with the conditions under which a raiyat is liable to be evicted.

A tenant under the Act [Section 2 (31)] in relation to the landlord is a mere cultivator who has no right in the land he cultivates. He only pay to his landlord rent in the shape of the crop or the estimated value thereof.

Thus, the Orissa Land Reforms Act goes a long way to consolidate into one the various diversified tenancy laws existing and operating in the State. It also repeals the Orissa Tenants Relief Act, 1955.

Under Chapter III of the Act, provisions are made for resumption of land by the landlords for personal cultivation and for the tenants to acquire occupancy rights over tenanted lands.

Chapter IV of the Act dealing with ceiling and disposal of surplus lands is another important aspect of the law. Amendment in 1965, 1973, 1974, 1975 and 1976 hereby made substantial changes in the provisions of this chapter to make the law more dynamic and progressive and the society more egalitarian. The law determines the scope of a ceiling family and the limit of lands a ceiling family shall lawfully possess. The ceiling surplus lands which vest in the

Government are distributed among the landless and people belonging to the weaker section of the society. The salient features of the ceiling law are—

(i) An uniform ceiling on ten standard acres is applicable to all land owners throughout the state without any regional variation.

(ii) In addition to the ceiling area of ten standard acres, the landowner is allowed upto three acres more towards homestead and tanks.

(iii) Where ceiling is determined in respect of a family consisting of more than five members, the ceiling of ten standard acres is increased by two standard acres for each member in excess of five members, subject to a maximum of eighteen standard acres.

## Working of the Act

*Analysis of data on land records reveals that*, there had been concentration of land to a visible extent in the size-group of medium land holdings (4 hectares and above) during 1971-76. It is incorrect to say that land concentration has totally disappeared in respect of medium and large size classes of land holdings following the implementation of O.L.R. Act since 2nd October, 1973.

A downward variation of land concentration in case of the medium and large size class of the land holdings (4 hectares and above) had led to the corresponding substantial increase in the size-class of semi-medium land holders.

One of the reasons for downward variation in respect of holdings of hectare and above during 1971-1981 is the implementation of the land ceiling provisions of the O.L.R. Act which motivated the big land holders to resort to illegal devices like Benami and fictitious sub-divisions of land through wrongful and antedated family partitions till 26th September, 1970 and to escape from the statutory restrictions.

A review of the experience shows that much of the explanation for the unimpressive record of land reform is to be found primarily in the political factors at work, administrative failings, conflict of interests between the rural and urban units, passivity of the target group to assert because of socio-economic factors.

## Trends in Land Holdings

According to Agricultural Census division, Ministry of Agriculture, New Delhi, there were 39.66 lakh operational holdings in Orissa in 1995-96, of which small and marginal holdings accounted for 81.97 per cent while the remaining 18.03 per cent came under the category of semi-medium, medium and large holdings. As much as 50.27 per cent of the total operated area was owned by small and marginal farmers and the remaining 49.73 per cent by the semi-medium, medium and large farmers.

**Table 1.28:** Agrarian Structure (Operational Holding) (Year 1995-96)

| *Category of Land Holders* | *No. of Operational Holdings in '000* | *Area Operated by Different Size in '000 Hectares* | *Percentage of No. Operational Holdings* | *Percentage of Area Operated* |
|---|---|---|---|---|
| Marginal | 2145 | 1064 | 54.08 | 20.68 |
| Small | 1106 | 1522 | 27.88 | 29.58 |
| Semi-medium | 544 | 1451 | 13.71 | 28.20 |
| Medium | 156 | 864 | 3.93 | 16.79 |
| Large | 15 | 243 | 0.37 | 4.72 |
| Total | 3966 | 5144 | 100 | 100 |

*Source*: Agricultural Census, Ministry of Agriculture, New Delhi.

There are 15,000 large operational holdings in the state and these large farmers own 243,000 hectares of land. In terms of percentages 0.37 percentage of land holder are having 4.37 per cent of area operated. Though the number of small and marginal farmers is increasing, roughly 50 per cent of land is still owned by large, semi-medium and medium farmers in the state.

By incorporating another Table 1.29 similar to Table 1.28, attempts have been made to analyse the change in the operational holdings by different classes of farmers during tenure of 10 year (1985-86 to 1995-96). The number of operational holdings by the year 1985-86 was 3586,000 and it has increased to 3966,000 by the year 1995-96. So an increase of 380,000 operational holdings implies that during 10 years (1985-86 to 1995-96), the degree of fragmentations of holdings has increased and probably land redistribution is taking place in the state. This land redistribution

**Table 1.29:** Agrarian Relationship (Operational Holdings), 1985-86

| Size/Class of Holdings (in Hect.) | Number of Holdings (No. in '000) | Percentage to Total no. of Holdings | Area Operated (Area in '000 Hect.) | Percentage to Total Area Operated |
|---|---|---|---|---|
| Marginal Below 1.00 | 1868 | 52.09 | 919 | 17.47 |
| Small 1.00-1.99 | 910 | 25.38 | 1273 | 24.2 |
| Semi-Medium 2.00-3.99 | 583 | 12.26 | 1568 | 29.8 |
| Medium 4.00-9.99 | 204 | 5.69 | 1167 | 22.18 |
| Large 10.00 and above | 21 | 0.58 | 334 | 6.35 |
| All Sizes | 3586 | 100.00 | 5261 | 100.00 |

*Source*: Agriculture Census, Ministry of Agriculture, New Delhi

process in the state has taken place due to various factors like rise in population, number of households and due to the implementation of land reforms policies. But as it is reported by many studies, the impact of land reforms has helped in reducing inequality in land holding to a very limited extent during 1980s and 1990s. Surprisingly across the time the area operated by all the classes of farmers is gone down marginally from 5261,000 hectares in 1985-86 to 5144 thousand hectares in 1995-96 in the state. The most valid reason for such a fall in area operated may be the rise in demand for homestead land. However the inequality in land holdings has reduced as it is evidenced by the fact that the number of land holdings in the category of large size is gone down to 15 by the year 1995-96 from 21 in the year 1985-86. Similar trend also seen in case of area operated by large farmers (from 334,000 hectares in 1985-86 to 243,000 hectares in 1995-96). Obviously a fall in the number of operational land holdings by large farmers has given rise to a rise in the area operated by other categories. It can be seen by comparing the figures of Table 1.28 and Table 1.29 that the fall in the operational holdings and area operated in case of large farmers has resulted a rise in the land holdings both by area operated and number of holdings by all other classes of farmers, like medium, semi-medium, small and marginal. However, the highest rise in land operated has been seen in case of small farmers.

The land reforms laws have been enacted in the state in the year 1962. But the progress in this direction has been far from satisfactory. One of the important legislations, which affects the land holdings pattern, is the Orissa Scheduled Area (Restriction on Transfer of Immovable Property of SC/ST), 1956. According to which there can be no transfer of land owned by a tribal to a non-tribal person unless the same has been enquired properly by a competent authority who in this case is the local SDM. But it is rather unfortunate that there had been many cases of such transfers and the tribal has been dispossessed of his land. All such cases nobody has taken the pains to conduct the enquiry and see whether such transfer would adversely affect the tribal.

## Village Level Land Distribution

In the Village Chhamunda, average holding per household is very low. It can be seen that the size of operational holding shown in Table below is higher than the size of land owned, this is due to the fact the settlement records have not been updated. Land ownerships are mostly shown jointly in Khatas. The average land holding of household is around 80 to 90 decimals, i.e. less than one acre. Further, these lands are used for the cultivation of one crop only, in addition to this these are unirrigated lands and are classified as Class-III land, according to Orissa Land Reform Act, 1960. Three acres of such land make one standard acre of land classified as category-I. So the productivity of the land is very poor. Almost all the households own some amount of land.

**Table 1.30:** Distribution of Landownership and Operational Holdings

*(in Acres)*

| *Class size* | *No. of Land Holders* | *Land Owned* | *Area Operated* |
|---|---|---|---|
| 1 | 2 | 3 | 4 |
| <1 ha | 136 | 33.51 | 32.5 |
| 1-2 ha | 19 | 25.28 | 23.5 |
| 2-4 ha | 24 | 68.75 | 67.5 |
| 4-10 ha | 25 | 151.08 | 148.5 |
| 10+ ha | 3 | 51.16 | 50 |

From the above table it can be observed that highest concentration of land, i.e. 151.08 acres is among the medium farmers. Another notable thing is that numerically highest landholders are marginal and land owned by them is only 33.51 acres. This clearly implies there is high inequality in land holding pattern. Land reform policies in such situation hardly can help in redistributing land in favour of marginal framers, because most of the landowners belong to the landholder category of medium size (4-10 hectare).

Similarly in case of Village Salebidi, it was also found that the distribution of recorded landholding was unequal. Only two persons in the village had a recorded total land of 22.96 ha in their name, whereas 12 persons had a total land of just 5.97 ha, each owns less than 1 ha of land. This phenomenon of unequal distribution of land was continuous, which means as we move from the <1 ha category to the 10+ category, the land holding in acres increases. More clearly, whereas the number of land holders get reduced in a manner like 12 to 7, 7, 4 and 2, whereas the land owned gets progressively increased as 5.97, 10.04, 21.90, 21.86 and 22.96 per cent respectively. The total number of landless households is only 4, one being ST and the other three belonging to OC (Other Caste). The latter were migrants from Madhya Pradesh and are engaged in petty trade. It may be noted that the total number of land holders may not be equal the total number of households since many households have broken into nuclear families and practically possess separate lands, the same had not been updated in the existing the land records.

In the following table land distribution pattern in the village Patrabasa is compiled. The most important fact is that there are two land owners, who are in the possession of land more than 20 acres. The land owned by two families are more than the permitted size of land holding as per Ceiling Law of the state.

**Table 1.31:** Distribution of Land Ownership in the Village Patrabasa

| *Land Size* | *No. of Landholders* |
|---|---|
| <1 acre | 22 |
| 1-3 acres | 31 |
| 3-5 acres | 21 |
| 5-10 acres | 15 |
| 10-20 acres | Nil |
| > 20 acres | 2 |

It is also important to note that marginal and small farmers are numerically higher as compare to the medium and semi-medium farmers. By looking at the figures given in Table 1.31, it can be infer that more or less land holding pattern is unequal.

In case of village Sapmundi, it was observed that 150 acres of land is under ownership cultivation and only 15 acres are under tenancy cultivation. So tenancy is not practiced to a large extent. But the land holding pattern is not fair. From the given Table 1.32 it can be seen that there are 4 large farmers in the village, where as 40 households of the village are land less.

**Table 1.32:** Distribution of Land Ownership (Householdwise)—Village Sapmundi

| *Land Sizes* | *No. of Households* |
|---|---|
| Landless | 40 |
| < 1 acres | 11 |
| 1-3 acres | 7 |
| 3-5 acres | 9 |
| 5-10 acres | 11 |
| 10-20 acres | 3 |
| > 20 acres | 1 |

In the village *Dumerpani* as documented below, there are 15 large farmers and out of this 15 large farmers 4 framers own land more than 20 acres each. In contrast to this there are 54 landless families in the village. The following table shows the detail land ownership pattern of the village Dumerpani.

**Table 1.33:** Distribution of Land Ownership (Householdwise)—Village Dumerpani

| *Land size* | *No. of Families* |
|---|---|
| Landless | 54 |
| <1 acre | 49 |
| 1-3 acres | 36 |
| 3-5 acres | 32 |
| 5-10 acres | 43 |
| 10-20 acres | 11 |
| 20 acres | 4 |

From the above table it is observed that the land holding pattern is skewed in favour of large farmers. There is also a sizable households in the category of medium size land holding. The landless include those having homestead land but owning no land for cultivation. There are 39 such households and other 15 landless families live as tenants. There are 4 households having 20 or more acres of land under ownership. It is also worth to note that highest land is owned by the Other Backward Castes (277.13 Acres) and Scheduled Caste families own the least land (191.07 acres). Being a tribal dominated village, around 349 acres of land is owned by the tribal families.

In the village *Banspal* all cultivable land (183 hectares) is under ownership cultivation. There is no practice of tenancy in the village. The land distribution data will be able to explain the reasons of non-existence of practice of tenancy in the village.

**Table 1.34:** Land Distribution in the village Banspal

| *Types of Land size* | *No. of Households* |
|---|---|
| Landless | 13 |
| <1 acre | 135 |
| 1-3 acres | 144 |
| 3-5 acres | 34 |
| 5-10 acres | 12 |
| 10-20 acres | — |
| > 20 acres | — |

The reason for non-existence of tenancy in the village lies in the fact that there are no families in the categories of land ownership 10-20 acres and more than 20 acres. There are only 13 landless families in the village and as many as 135 families are marginal farmers. As a whole it can be inferred that inequality in land ownership is very less.

Land distribution pattern data in the forms of number of operational holdings owned by different families of the village Kupudmaha reveals that in the village largest land is owned by the families having land less than 1 acre of land. This means there are many marginal farmers in the village and land fragmentation is quite common.

**Table 1.35:** Distribution of Land Ownership (Household-wise) in Kupudmaha Village

| *Categories of Land size* | *No. of Operational Holdings* |
|---|---|
| Landless | — |
| <1 acres | 329 |
| 1-3 acres | 12 |
| 3-5 acres | 3 |
| 5-10 acres | 3 |
| 10-20 acres | 4 |
| 20 acres + | 13 |

But on the other hand there are 13 operational holdings in the category of 20 acres+ land size. The number of land holdings owned by medium and semi-medium farms is very less. Similarly, in case of the village *Taljhiri* it was observed that there are large number of marginal farmers in the village and 6 families are in the possession of land more than 4 hectares.

**Table 1.36:** Distribution of Land Ownership in the Village Taljhiri

| *Categories of Land Size* | *No. of Families* |
|---|---|
| Landless | 18 |
| <1 ha | 102 |
| 1-2 ha | 25 |
| 2-3 ha | 9 |
| 3-4 ha | 1 |
| 4-5 ha | 4 |
| > 5 ha | 2 |

Only 18 families out of 161 families of the village are not having any cultivable land. So the issue of inequality of land ownership is not an important one, however as there are six families in possession of land more than 10 acres each, it cannot be clearly inferred that land ownership pattern is not unfair.

## Tenancy

Incidence of tenancy is very high in Orissa. As per the Orissa Land Reforms Act tenancy is completely banned except under some special conditions. In most of cases tenancy is practiced verbally or on the basis of mutual unrecorded agreements. So the OLR Acts are helpless to put a check on practice of tenancy. As agriculture is not very remunerative in Orissa, even small and medium landholders, who are not having enough family labour to cultivate their land are leasing out their land. It is so because by utilizing hired labour to cultivate land, the above-mentioned families are not able to cover their cost of cultivation by selling the produce. According to the Planning Commission State Plan Report in 1991, the percentage of area leased-in to area operated in case of Orissa was 9.5 which were greater than the All-India average of 8.3 per cent. In Orissa, in 1991-92 there were numerically 6.9 lakh tenant holdings. They constituted 16.4 per cent of total operational holdings. They leased-in 4.5 lakh hectares of land, which was 9.5 per cent of total operational area. Average area leased-in per tenant holding was only 0.65 ha. But incidence of tenancy reveals a declining trend. The proportion of operated area leased-in has decreased from 13.5 per cent in 1970-71 to 9.5 per cent in 1991-92. This trend as noted by Planning Commission clearly shows tenancy is very common in rural Orissa. Another factor behind the practice of tenancy and arbitrary eviction of tenants is lack of awareness among the landowners and tenants regarding the provisions of OLR Act. Another fact is that most of time land is leased out for a single crop and for another crop during the same year; the land is cultivated by the landowner.

Share cropping type of terms of lease is mostly in practice in Orissa. Area leased in under fixed produce and fixed money tenancy is not very high. In 1991-92 about 50.9 per cent of leased-in area was under sharecropping. The coverage under fixed money and fixed produce was only 19.7 per cent and 4.7 per cent respectively. Proportion of area under share tenancy shows an increasing trend. In 1971-72, 41.8 per cent of leased-in area was under sharecropping which had increased to 50.9 per cent in 1991. It is to be noted that in agriculturally advanced states like Punjab, Haryana, Tamil Nadu fixed tenancy is more prominent than share tenancy. The following table contains data pertaining to different types of Terms of Lease in Orissa.

**Table 1.37:** Changes in Percentage Distribution of Leased-in Area by Terms of Lease

| *Terms of Lease* | *1971-72 (26th)* | *1981-82 (37th)* | *1991-92 (48th)* |
|---|---|---|---|
| Fixed Money | 7.6 | 5.1 | 19.7 |
| Fixed Produce | 13.6 | 8.1 | 4.7 |
| Share of Produce | 41.6 | 42.0 | 50.9 |
| Others | 37.2 | 44.8 | 24.7 |
| All terms | 100.0 | 100.0 | 100.0 |

*Source*: (a) N.S.S Report 17th Round (1961-62); (b) N.S.S. Report 26th Round (1971-72); (c) N.S.S. Report 37th Round (1981-82); (d) N.S.S. Report 48th Round (1991-92).

However, NSSO figures on tenancy are considered underestimates, as tenants are often hesitant to reveal their tenurial identity in fear of eviction. As lease contracts are mostly oral and informal, they remain in concealed form. Recently many micro-level studies undertaken by research scholars report that the share tenancy is quite pervasive in Orissa due to emigration of able adult male members of farm family to urban areas for employment, increase in wage cost and difficulty in labour supervision. In the absence of alternative job opportunities in the non-farm sector the land scarce and labour abundant households are leasing in land to earn their livelihood.

In Orissa mostly the marginal and small farmers lease-in land. The distribution of leased-in area according to size classes of operational holdings shows that in 1991-92 about 71 per cent of leased-in area was in the size classes of less than 2 hectares and only 5 per cent of leased-in area was in size classes above 4 hectares. In Orissa subsistence tenancy is more widespread than commercial or capitalist tenancy. There is a popular belief that the landlords or the big farmers lease out land to small peasants to wield economic power over them. An analysis of distribution of lessor households and leased-out area according to size classes of ownership holdings shows that in 1991-92, a significant proportion (90%) of lessor households belonged to category of 'less than 2 ha' and they also accounted for a major proportion (81%) of leased out area. Thus the lessor households were mainly marginal and small farmers. On the other hand, a very small percentage (3%) of lessors belonged to big farmer category owning more than 4.01 ha of land, which accounted for only 8 per cent of leased-out area. Thus, in Orissa mainly marginal and small farmers lease out land.

High incidence of share tenancy with high rents (50% of gross produce), absence of input cost sharing and no security of tenure adversely affects use of yield enhancing inputs and fixed investments in agriculture by the tenants and thus, acts as a barrier to agricultural development of Orissa.

Very little has been done on the land reforms front. The OLR Act has been bye-passed by transferring huge areas of land to Trusts operated through Charities, *Maths* and Temples. The Ex-Zamindar king of Athagadapatna who does not stay in the village controls the major trusts through his appointees. As a result the tenants of the village are cultivating large areas of the trusts, the land cannot be recorded in their name.

In tribal dominated area the practice of tenancy is not rampant. Because tribals are mutually exchange family labour among themselves for cultivation works. According to the village report of Bishnupur village— 'In the village Bishnupur of Keonjhar district there is no tenancy or share cropping. All the villagers are small and marginal farmers and there is hardly any family, which has surplus land that can be let out to some one else. There is, however, the practice of employing labour to work in the fields along with the members of the family. This labour is generally drawn from the people of the village itself. This is a close-knit tribal community. In most cases it is a mutual agreement. They work on each other's field and assist each other. However in some case, payment in cash is also made.'

## Land Ceiling

### *Briefly the Salient Features of Ceiling Acts in Orissa*

*Section 37*

According to Section 37 of OLR, the basic objective of imposing ceiling on agricultural holding and acquisition and distribution of the surplus land to landless and weaker sections of the society and is in substance and reality an enactment relating to agrarian reforms. The Statute has been intended to strike at vast concentration of land in the hands of a few and to act as a great equiliser by reducing inequality in holding of land between the haves and the have-nots. The purpose of the Act is to make "progressive legislation relating to agrarian reforms and land tenures" and with a view to implement the Directive Principles as laid down in Article 39 of the Constitution "that the operation of the economic system does not result in the concentration of wealth and means of production to the common detriment", the Act seeks to provide a scheme for fixing a ceiling for land to be possessed by a family and the surplus to vest in the State Government on payment of a small compensation for settlement of such land with persons belonging to the Scheduled Tribes or Scheduled Castes and failing them with people of economically backward classes.

In order to determine the ceiling area of person that counts is the land held by him as a "raiyat" or as a "Land holder", but in reckoning the extent of his holding, transfers of partitions of land made after the 26th day of September, 1970 are not recognized, but on suits for specific performance there is restriction.

In order to get entitlement for separate ceiling a son of an individual it must have been shown that he was separated from the father prior to 26.9.1970 and he must have been both major and married prior to that date.

### *Section 37B*

In the Section 37B of OLR, it is mentioned that Ceiling Area (Substituted by Act 9 of 1974)—The ceiling area in respect of a person shall be ten standard acres:

Provided that where the person is a family consisting of more than five members, the ceiling area in respect of such person shall be ten standard acres increased by two standard acres for each member in excess of five, so however, that the ceiling area shall not exceed eighteen standard acres.

Persons not entitled to hold land in excess of ceiling area—On and from the commencement of the Orissa Land Reforms (Amendment) Act, 1973 (President's Act 17 of 1973), no person shall, either as landholder or raiyat or as both, be entitled to hold any land in excess of the ceiling area.

### *Section 38*

(Substituted by Act 9 of 1974) [Exemption from Ceiling—Save as otherwise provided in this section the provisions of this Chapter shall not apply to—

(a) Land held by privileged raiyat. Provided that nothing in this clause shall apply to any land held by a raiyat under a privileged raiyat;

(b) Lands held by industrial or commercial undertaking or comprised in mills, factories or workshops, where such lands are necessary for the use, for any non agricultural purpose, of such undertakings, mills, factories or workshops:

Provided that where the said land are not actually used within a period of five years from the commencement of the Orissa Land Reforms (Amendment) Act, 1973 (President's Act 17 of 1973), for the purpose for which they had been set apart, the collector may, after giving notice to the persons concerned, by order, direct that the provisions of this Chapter shall apply to the said lands:

Provided further that the Collector may, on an application made to him in this behalf and on being satisfied that it is necessary or expedient so to do, extend the said period of five years by such further period or periods as he may deem fit, so however, that the total period of such extension shall not exceed in any case, eight years;

(c) Plantations:

*Explanation:* "Plantation" means any land used principally for cultivation of coffee, cocoa or tea (hereafter in this Explanation referred to as plantation crops) and includes lands used for any purpose ancillary to the cultivation of the plantation crops or for the preservation of the same for their marketing;

(d) Lands held by any agricultural university, agricultural school or college, or any institution conducting research in agriculture.]

*Section 3ъ*

(Substituted by Act 9 of 1974) [Principles for Determining the Ceiling Area—In determining the ceiling area in respect of a person, the following principles shall be followed, namely:]

(a) homestead lands, or tanks with their embankments, or both, to the extent of three acres in the aggregate shall not be taken into account;

(b) (Substituted by Act 29 of 1976) [the transfer of any land by sale, gift or otherwise or the partition thereof by a person during the period beginning with the 26th day of September 1970 and ending with the commencement of the Orissa Land Reforms (Amendment) Act, 1973 (President's Act 17 of 1973) shall, if such person was holding land on the said day in excess of the ceiling area, be deemed to be void, anything contained in any law or agreement or in any decree or order of any Court notwithstanding];

(c) [the lands so transferred or partitioned shall be taken into account as if the transfer or partition had not taken effect and the Revenue Officer may, at his discretion ignore the selection made by the person of lands to be retained in his possession];

(d) where the person is a member of a co-operative farming society, the extent of land which he would get as his share if the land held by such society is divided shall be taken into account;

(e) [lands in the possession of a tenant or a mortgages shall be deemed to be lands held by the person.]

## Section 45B

(Inserted by Act 44 of 1976) 45B. Lands escaping ceiling proceedings to vest along with surplus lands already vested—(1) If at any time within six years from the date of finalization of the statement under sub-section (3) of Section 44 relation to any person, holding land in excess of ceiling area, it is found that some more lands held by such person have escaped inclusion in the above statement due to any reason whatsoever, the Revenue Officer may, after giving the person an opportunity of being heard and after making such enquiry as he deems proper, declare in the prescribed manner, the whole or any part of such land as are found to be held by the person to be surplus land in relation to him.

(2) All lands declared to be surplus land under sub-section (1) shall be deemed to have vested in the Government free from all encumbrances along with the surplus lands mentioned in the aforesaid statement and the provisions of 45, 45A and 46 to 51 shall, so far as may be, apply to the lands so vested:

Provided that the amount payable in respect of the interest of the person to whom the surplus lands relate shall be subject to reduction at the following rate:

| | | Rate of Reduction |
|---|---|---|
| (i) | Where the land was in occupation of the person for a period not exceeding one year from the date of finalization of the statement under Sec. 44(3) | Fifty-five per centum |
| (ii) | Where the period of such occupation exceeds one year | Fifty-five per centum plus five per centum for each year or part thereof in excess of one year |

(3) Without prejudice to the provisions of Section 39, the transfer of any land declared to be surplus land under sub-section (1), by sale, gift or otherwise or the partition thereof, made of effected after the date of finalization of the statement under sub-section (3) of Section 44 shall be deemed to be void.]

*Section 51*

(Substituted by Act 9 of 1974) [Settlement of surplus lands—(1) Seventy per centum of the surplus land vested in the Government under Section 45 shall be settled with persons belonging to the Scheduled Tribes or Scheduled Castes in proportion to their respective populations in the villages in which the lands are situated and the remaining lands shall be settled with persons not belonging to the aforesaid categories]:

(Substituted by Act 44 of 1976) [Provided that where the population of the Scheduled Tribes and Scheduled Castes in a village exceeds seventy per cent of the total population of village, the percentage of lands to be reserved for persons of the said communities shall be equal to the percentage of their population:

Provided further that if sufficient number of persons belonging to the aforesaid categories are not available in the village in which the lands are situated or, being available, are not willing to accept settlement of land, so much of the lands reserved for the said persons as cannot be settled with them may be settled with other persons:

Provided also that the Collector of a district may, with the prior approval of the Government, set apart any of the said surplus lands for being utilized for any public purpose, other than the purpose of cultivation, and thereupon the remaining surplus lands shall be settled in accordance with the provisions of this section.]

(Substituted by Act 9 of 1974) [(2) Notwithstanding anything contained in Orissa Government Land Settlement Act, 1962, the procedure for the Settlement of lands under this section shall be such as may be prescribed, and the settlement shall be made in favour of the following categories of persons and in the following order of priority, namely—

(a) Co-operative farming societies formed by landless agricultural labourers;

(b) Any landless agricultural labourers of the village in which the land is situate or of any neighbouring village;

(c) Ex-servicemen or members of the Armed Forces of the Union, if they belong to the village in which the land is situate;

(d) Raiyats who personally cultivate not more than one standard acre of contiguous land; and

(e) In the absence of persons belonging to any of the foregoing categories; any other persons.]

## Village Level Analysis

In Salebidi village, no land was acquired as ceiling surplus land. However, 3 households of this village have been given ceiling surplus lands in the nearby villages. The following table shows the details of distribution of ceiling surplus land among three beneficiaries.

**Table 1.38:** Distribution of Ceiling Surplus Land in Village Salebidi

| *Sl. No.* | *Name of the Allottees* | *Caste* | *Area Allotted (in ha.)* | *No. of Plots Allotted* |
|---|---|---|---|---|
| 1. | Komulu Naik | ST | 0.88 | 1 |
| 2. | Dhaneshwar Kachin | SC | 1.23 | 2 |
| 3. | Tulsiram Kota | OC | 0.79 | 1 |

It was found that all the allotted plots fall in the upland category and are presently under self-cultivation of the allottees. While Komulu Naik is still growing paddy on his land, Dhaneshwar and Tulsiram are growing a variety of crops, mainly sweet potato and vegetables. None of them have been provided assistance of any kind after the allotment of surplus lands, except for a well under MWS to Komulu. When asked about the overall impact, the allotment of the said land has definitely helped these earlier landless households to meet the two ends. However, the quality of the land being poor, the returns from the land never exceed more than Rs. 2000 per annum.

In the Village Chhamunda Seventeen beneficiaries have received the ceiling surplus land. As per the provisions of Ceiling Act, 7.03 hectares of lands were declared as ceiling surplus land. Government through the Revenue Department has distributed all these lands and they are in possession of the beneficiaries. The detail castewise allotment of ceiling surplus land is given below.

**Table 1.39:** Classification of Beneficiaries Who Got Ceiling Surplus Land

| *ST* | | *SC* | | *Others* | |
|---|---|---|---|---|---|
| No. of beneficiaries | Land area under possession | No. of beneficiaries | Land area under possession | No. of beneficiaries | Land area under possession |
| 2 | 0.86 | 11 | 4.45 | 4 | 1.72 |

The ceiling land allottees are mostly the STs. At present only two households attract provision of Ceiling Act but they would claim partition and it won't come under ceiling law. There are no litigations in any state. The allottees were provided only monetary help. It was a big amount of money considering value of money 18-20 years back. No other facility in terms of seed, fertilizer, pesticides were provided. Rs. 400 per acre were provided. According to the locals, this money was not used to upgrade the land and use for cultivation. This was one of the wrong policies of the Government. Disposable money in hands of tribals gets either siphoned off or gets wasted. Instead of providing cash incentive, kind incentive should have been provided. Most of the land allotted is being used now but only during Kharif season. Land continues to be in their possession. The allotment of ceiling surplus land has improved the standard of livings of the allottees, as they were able to eat better and acquired immovable assets. In spite of the fact that the net return is negative to the land allottees. There are no share cropping done by allottees. To a certain extent the land ceiling provision have achieved the objective.

In *Dengaguda* village total land taken in possession was 22.42 acres. Most of this has gone to SC beneficiaries (67%), followed by STs (24%) and lastly OBCs (9%). The surplus land was claimed from only two landlords. Of the total ten cases initiated in the village eight were dropped.

## UNEMPLOYMENT AND POVERTY

According to the 2001 census data, in the state total workers are 38.9 per cent of total population and percentage of workers in the rural area is 40.3 per cent. The 1991 census data show that 73 per cent of the main workers of the state are directly dependent on agriculture either as cultivators (44.31%) or agricultural labourers (28.68%) as against 65 per cent directly dependent workers in this category at the all-India level. However, by the census year 2001, percentage of workers in the agriculture sector is 64.7, this implies during last decade there has been a decline in the percentage of population engaged in agriculture sector. But in rural area still more than 70 (72.3%) of population are working in the agriculture sector as per the 2001 census data. Apart from that it is found that 3.13 per cent of the workers according to 1991 census data are earning their bread in the household sector industry and the percentage of the workers engaged in non-agriculture sector is only around 35 per cent as per 2001 census data. In this set up of the economy agriculture in the state is highly underdeveloped and mostly subsistence oriented particularly in the highland region. The highest incidence of poverty is mainly due to the reason that industrialization in the state has helped generating employment only in few pockets of the state. In addition to this factor like distribution of the rural assets and underdevelopment of the agricultural economy with little linkage effects of the industry are not conducive for generating employment and alleviating poverty in the state. As the state has a sizeable portion of depressed category population (38.41%) such as 16.20 per cent Scheduled Castes and 22.21 per cent Scheduled Tribes as per 1991 Census in comparison to 16.48 per cent Scheduled Castes and 8.08 per cent Scheduled Tribe population at the national level, the process of socio-economic transformation in Orissa has been much slower than many other states of the country.

The following Table 1.40 contains data pertaining to workers of the state. From the table it is observed that percentage of female agricultural labourers is almost double of percentage of female cultivators. Livestock, fisheries, etc. allied activities play very limited role in providing employment to the people of Orissa. Only 1.9 per cent of workers as per 1991 Census data are engaged in allied activities.

Proportionate of female workers in agriculture sector is around 80 per cent, whereas percentage of male workers engaged in agriculture sector is around 70 per cent. Percentage of workforce in general is not enough to give the insights of economic development.

**Table 1.40:** Work Participation Rate (1991 Census Data)

| | *Per cent Main Worker Engaged in* | | |
|---|---|---|---|
| | *Cultivation* | *Agricultural Labour* | *Livestock, Forestry, etc.* |
| Persons | 29.75 | 26.55 | 1.9 |
| Males | 48.4 | 22.8 | 2.1 |
| Females | 25.8 | 55.1 | 0.8 |

In an agricultural dominating economy, seasonal unemployment is very common. So marginal workers percentage in the state is very high. In the state as per 2001 census data there are 29.7 per cent of the total workforce are cultivators, which is marginally lower than the same at all India level. This clearly proves the fact that percentage of agricultural labourers (64.77) is higher in Orissa as compare to the country as a whole.

It is found that in the old and undivided districts like Bolangir, Kalahandi, Keonjhar, Koraput, Mayurbhanj and Phulbani more than 80 per cent of the main workers were employed in primary sector occupations at the time of 1991 Census. Among the districts of the highland region only Sambalpur and Sundargarh had fairly higher percentage of workers engaged in non-farm sector occupations. It is observed that in between 1971 and 1991 only a few among the 13 old and undivided districts of Orissa such as Baleswar (83.79 to 78.33%), Cuttack (76.29 to 66.44%), Dhenkanal (83.81 to 75.15%), Puri (75.78 to 64.97%), and Sundargarh (65.60 to 61.59%) could register marked decline of their main workers' dependence on primary sector occupations. Among these, three are old and undivided coastal districts such as Baleswar, Cuttack and Puri. Dhenkanal forms a part of the central tableland region and Sundargarh is from the northern plateau region. At the state level, dependence of the main workers on primary sector occupations declined from 80.35 per cent to 75.83 per cent in 1991.

In Table 1.41 figures pertaining to the marginal and main workers of different districts of the state are given. The backward districts are found to be having generally higher percentage of main workers and the percentage of main workers to total population is lower in the coastal districts. For example, in the districts like Kalahandi, Nuapara, Nabarangpur, Phulbani, Koraput, etc. the main workers constitute more than 35 per cent of total population and it is more than 40 per cent in the Koraput district. Whereas in the districts like Balasore, Cuttack, Jagatsinghpur, Bhadrak, Puri, Khurda, etc. the percentage of main workers to total population is less than 30 per cent. So it can be concluded that higher percentage of main workers to the total population is not a symbol of economic prosperity. Per head earning.

**Table 1.41:** Classification of Workers and their Percentage in Different Districts of Orissa, 1991 Census

| *Sl. No.* | *Name of the Districts* | *Total Workers* | *Main Workers* | *Marginal Workers* | *Percentage of Main Workers to Total Population of the Districts* |
|---|---|---|---|---|---|
| 1. | Angul | 368107 | 315601 | 52506 | 32.84 |
| 2. | Balasore | 500758 | 473255 | 27503 | 27.89 |
| 3. | Bargarh | 534769 | 446935 | 87834 | 37.02 |
| 4. | Bhadrak | 294635 | 284167 | 10468 | 25.7 |
| 5. | Bolangir | 501516 | 425507 | 76009 | 34.57 |
| 6. | Boudh | 147856 | 120675 | 27181 | 37.99 |
| 7. | Cuttack | 585515 | 563792 | 21723 | 28.58 |
| 8. | Deogarh | 105096 | 85696 | 19400 | 36.59 |
| 9. | Dhenkanal | 311871 | 284289 | 27582 | 29.99 |
| 10. | Gajapati | 224136 | 190704 | 33432 | 41.94 |
| 11. | Ganjam | 1083903 | 947048 | 136855 | 35.02 |
| 12. | Jagastsinghpur | 279250 | 269022 | 10228 | 26.52 |
| 13. | Jajpur | 366453 | 353280 | 13173 | 25.49 |
| 14. | Jharsuguda | 174469 | 149756 | 24713 | 33.52 |
| 15. | Kalahandi | 509730 | 426175 | 83555 | 37.68 |
| 16. | Kendrapara | 288284 | 279392 | 8892 | 24.31 |
| 17. | Keonjhar | 519026 | 439953 | 79073 | 32.91 |
| 18. | Khurds | 449676 | 436036 | 13640 | 29.03 |
| 19. | Koraput | 514001 | 423115 | 90886 | 41.08 |
| 20. | Malkangiri | 197709 | 157765 | 39944 | 37.39 |
| 21. | Mayurbhanj | 863477 | 702511 | 160966 | 37.28 |
| 22. | Nawapara | 214314 | 173459 | 40855 | 36.95 |
| 23. | Nayagarh | 252682 | 236575 | 16087 | 30.23 |
| 24. | Nabarangpur | 415001 | 382300 | 86701 | 38.78 |
| 25. | Phulbani | 260876 | 212946 | 47930 | 38.98 |
| 26. | Puri | 383249 | 368044 | 15205 | 28.19 |
| 27. | Rayagada | 349079 | 294522 | 54557 | 41.25 |
| 28. | Sambalpur | 356630 | 308397 | 48233 | 38.12 |
| 29. | Sonepur | 210042 | 172579 | 37463 | 36.19 |
| 30. | Sundargarh | 620672 | 508139 | 112533 | 32.29 |
| | Orissa | 11882762 | 10377635 | 1505127 | 32.78 |

could be the major criteria for gauging the economic development. All the districts where percentage of main workers to total population is higher are dominated by tribal community. The poor earning capacity and poor economic base are the major factors for forcing the tribals to work round the year. Another possible reason is that in southern parts of Orissa, agriculture sector is not able to provide sufficient employment, so most of the workers are engaged in non-farm sector and migrating out in search of works.

## Village Level Analyses

In the village Patrabasa non-farm activities undertaken by some of the villagers include poultry and dairying. However, these activities are mostly confined to the well off sections of the village. Allied agricultural activities such as horticulture, fisheries, etc. are totally absent in the village. Rural industries in the form of traditional artisans are present in the village, like carpenters, blacksmith and a tailor. Otherwise, there are no other rural industries in the village. The demand of the villagers for the services/products of the artisans (carpenter, blacksmith or tailor) is not high and therefore, so these artisans mostly depend on agriculture for their livelihood.

As the village Seledi is just located 2 km away from the Mahanadi river bank, so fishing is an important allied activity carried out by the villagers. Many villagers from the SC community are involved in fishing and they go at night to catch prawns. They use lanterns to attract and catch fish. Generally two persons form a team and go out for fishing. On an average the team can catch about 2.5 to 4.0 kgs. The net returns for a person will be around Rs. 60 per night for ordinary fish and about Rs. 150 for prawns. Under SGSRY scheme some of the villagers have got loans to purchase fishing nets and boats. The market for selling fish is in Binka. Another allied activity in this village is rearing of cattle especially milch animals, bullocks, poultry and goats. The milch animals are of local breed and the milk production is about 1 to 1.5 litre per day. Generally, the milk is used for self-consumption. Out of the 80 houses surveyed, only 10 houses sell milk. There is no co-operative arrangement for milk marketing. So private individuals sell milk. It is interesting to notice that some of the rich people in the village purchase milk for their domestic need on a contract basis and they pay in kind like paddy, after harvest. Bullocks are used as drought animals and there is high demand for drought animal during the agricultural season. They are used for ploughing, levelling and pudding operations. A person earns about Rs. 65 per day (6 hrs) for ploughing. Animals are fed paddy straw and grass. They are also taken to the hills for grazing.

Goat is reared for meat purposes and on an average a person has about 6 to 8 goats. They are Bolangir breed of goat and the meat is very popular in this side of the state. Meat is sold for Rs. 100 per kg. There is a lot of demand for meat in the market but the supply is very less. During festivals advance booking happens for meat and the rates go upto Rs. 150 per kg. There are two small poultry farms in the village and they grow both white leghorn and broiler chicken. It is interesting to note that the rates of both chicken and mutton are same and it is Rs. 100 per kg. This is also observed that the demand for chicken and mutton are high, whereas the supply is very less.

In addition to all these activities a small portion of the people are involved in brick making, small business etc. Migration is very minimal and it happens during the summer months. Out of the eighty households surveyed migration of labourers found in case of only three families. All three of them are landless labourers and they go to Cuttack for brick making. There is no exploitation or forced migration.

Three out of the eighty households surveyed are involved in *kendu* leaf collection. The forest department procures the *kendu* leaves from them. The payments for the *kendu* leaves are delayed by 10 to 15 days. But there were no complaints about less payment. Poverty alleviation programmes form a major form of livelihood for the landless poor people during the lean seasons. There are no factories or industries in the nearby areas, so employment opportunities in those are almost nil.

The villagers of the village Banspal get higher wages if they come to the Keonjhar town and its neighbouring areas. The wages here is 40 rupees whereas in the village it is 30 rupees only. The wages are still higher at 50 rupees a day in the coastal belt.

Fifty-seven of the 72 families in the village Bishnupur have self-cultivation as their main occupation. The rest of them are either working in a regular job (one family head is a peon in the sub-collector office while another is a primary school teacher) or are labourers. Even in the second category, there are the regular industrial labourers working in the Sponge Iron plant at Palaspanga or the mines of Joda and Barbil. There are also the irregular non-farm and farm sector labourers who work in EAS projects or in the fields of richer landlords.

**Table 1.42:** Number of Persons Engaged Occupation-wise

| Occupation | No. of Persons Engaged | Per cent |
|---|---|---|
| Agriculture/self cultivation | 95 | 20.34 |
| Self-employed | 7 | 1.47 |
| Domestic labour | 111 | 23.31 |
| Students | 45 | 9.45 |
| Casual labour (agriculture) | 26 | 5.46 |
| Casual labour (non-agricultural sector) | 11 | 2.3 |
| Industrial labour | 7 | 1.47 |
| Class IV employees | 5 | 1.05 |
| Disabled | 5 | 1.05 |
| Retired | 4 | 0.84 |
| Unemployed | 20 | 4.2 |
| Collection of fuel and fodder | 5 | 1.05 |
| Traditional occupations | 2 | 0.42 |
| Domestic servant | 1 | 0.21 |
| None | 123 | 25.83 |

In addition to this, some of the villagers have taken up occupations in the tertiary sector with the help of funding under SGSY. They have opened small shops in Jhumpura or on the adjacent National Highway. Apart from this, traditional activities like cattle rearing, goat and sheep rearing, poultry and duck keeping are popular. These do not yield much income but are mainly kept for consumption by the family.

## Poverty and Poverty Alleviation Programme

The concept of poverty according to the understandings of a very common man is the shortfall of expected income to meet the food requirements of a person from the income actual earned by the person.

Orissa is endowed with rich natural resources in the form of vast mineral deposits, forest, fertile land, plentiful surface and ground water resources, long coastline, and picturesque tourist potential. But, such resources have not been exploited adequately for income generation activities. As a result, Orissa ranks very low among the Indian states in terms of per capita income, and it has become one of the poorest states of the country. Large proportion of people in the state have very poor living conditions. As per an estimate, among the fifteen major states of India, the position of Orissa with regard to living conditions or standard of living is fourteenth. So, it becomes necessary to examine the poverty scenario and living condition of the people of Orissa. Per capita income is one of the most important indicators of economic development. A rise in per capita income has a positive impact on reduction of poverty. In the context of Orissa, it is observed that the state is a low income and slow growing state of the country. Because of low income, larger proportions of people are living below the poverty line in the state. The per capita income of Orissa, as measured by Net State Domestic Product per head of population, was about 23 per cent lower than the all India per capita income (Net National Product) in 1980. But, this difference widened during the period 1980-81 to 2000-01. In 2000-01, the per capita income of Orissa remained as much as 50 per cent below that of national average. This is also reflected in the trend of growth rate of per capita real income. During the period 1980-81 to 2000-01, the trend of growth rate of per capita real income of Orissa was 1.39 per cent per annum as against 3.37 per cent per annum at the national level.

The per capita income of the state as a percentage of per capita income of the country as a whole over the years as per the data given in the above table has declined. In the section on demography, it is already discussed that the population growth has almost remained stagnant, so it can be inferred that the state is becoming poor to poorer in the last decade taking all India average per capita income as the benchmark. The pace of growth of the state economy is rather slow as compare to the same of many other states. The comparison between figures of the per capita income at 1993-94 prices and at current prices shows that the inflation rate has negligible impact on earnings of the people.

**Table 1.43:** Per Capita Income of Orissa and India at Constant and Current Prices in Different Years (in rupees)

| Year | At 1993-94 Prices | | | At Current Prices | | |
|---|---|---|---|---|---|---|
| | Per Capita Income | | Orissa/ All-India | Per Capita Income | | Orissa/ All-India |
| | Orissa (NSDP) | All-India (NNP) | | Orissa (NSDP) | All-India (NNP) | |
| 1980-81 | 4085 | 5352 | 0.763 | 1352 | 1741 | 0.777 |
| 1981-82 | 4010 | 5555 | 0.722 | 1485 | 1985 | 0.748 |
| 1982-83 | 3703 | 5555 | 0.667 | 1544 | 2143 | 0.720 |
| 1983-84 | 4374 | 5854 | 0.747 | 1957 | 2464 | 0.794 |
| 1984-85 | 4091 | 5956 | 0.687 | 1899 | 2690 | 0.706 |
| 1985-86 | 4483 | 6082 | 0.737 | 2238 | 2932 | 0.763 |
| 1986-87 | 4464 | 6189 | 0.721 | 2382 | 3191 | 0.746 |
| 1987-88 | 4244 | 6260 | 0.678 | 2375 | 3546 | 0.670 |
| 1988-89 | 5046 | 6777 | 0.745 | 2954 | 4153 | 0.711 |
| 1989-90 | 5282 | 7087 | 0.745 | 3311 | 4693 | 0.706 |
| 1990-91 | 4300 | 7321 | 0.587 | 3166 | 5365 | 0.590 |
| 1991-92 | 4757 | 7212 | 0.660 | 4020 | 6012 | 0.669 |
| 1992-93 | 4589 | 7433 | 0.617 | 4233 | 6732 | 0.629 |
| 1993-94 | 4797 | 7690 | 0.624 | 4797 | 7690 | 0.624 |
| 1994-95 | 4913 | 8070 | 0.609 | 5638 | 8857 | 0.637 |
| 1995-96 | 5050 | 8489 | 0.595 | 6806 | 10149 | 0.671 |
| 1996-97 | 4652 | 9007 | 0.516 | 6401 | 11564 | 0.554 |
| 1997-98 | 5272 | 9242 | 0.570 | 7831 | 12707 | 0.616 |
| 1998-99 | 5165 | 9647 | 0.535 | 8324 | 14395 | 0.578 |
| 1999-00 | 5265 | 10067 | 0.523 | 8733 | 15562 | 0.561 |
| 2000-01 | 5187 | 10254 | 0.506 | 8547 | 16487 | 0.518 |

*Source*: Central Statistical Organisation (F. No. U-11017/2/2002-NAD-g).

In Table 1.44 per capita monthly consumption expenditures of important items of the consumption basket are presented to compare the changes in the consumption pattern over two points of 46th NSS survey. From the table given below it is clear that per capita monthly consumption expenditure is the highest in case of cereals (38%) and for the non-food items only Rs. 45 is the per capita monthly expenditure, which is around 29 per cent of the total consumption expenditure. When we compare the state's figures of consumption expenditure with the figures of the consumption expenditure of an individual of the country as a whole, it is found that cereals per capita consumption is higher in the state as compare to the national average. This is also many times considered as a symbol of backwardness.

**Table 1.44:** Per Capita Monthly Consumption Expenditure

| *Sl. No.* | *Important Items of Expenditure Group* | *1989-90* | | *1990-91* | |
|---|---|---|---|---|---|
| | | *July* | June | *July* | *June* |
| | | *Orissa* | *All-India* | *Orissa* | *All-India* |
| 1. | Total Cereals | 60.37 | 45.38 | 63.4 | 49.61 |
| 2. | Pulses and Pulse Products | 6.39 | 8.31 | 5.61 | 8.8 |
| 3. | Edible Oils | 5.62 | 9.1 | 7.52 | 12.09 |
| 4. | Milk and Milk Products | 3.67 | 18.35 | 3.7 | 19.04 |
| 5. | Meat, Egg and Fish | 6.41 | 6.84 | 9.25 | 7.08 |
| 6. | Vegetables | 12.44 | 10.25 | 14.27 | 12.75 |
| 7. | Sugar | 3.99 | 6.34 | 2.87 | 6.03 |
| 8. | Food Total | 108.93 | 121.78 | 120.37 | 133.34 |
| 9. | Fuel and Light | 11.61 | 14.44 | 14.35 | 15.62 |
| 10. | Clothing | 8.21 | 12.15 | 10.33 | 9.78 |
| 11. | Non-Food Total | 45.19 | 67.68 | 61.04 | 68.78 |
| 12. | Total Expenditure | 154.12 | 189.46 | 181.91 | 202.12 |

*Source*: 46th NSSO Round.

Similarly relatively higher proportion of consumption expenditure on cereals is an indicator of poor economic status. The concept of poverty generally defined in terms of consumption expenditure. If an individual is unable to meet a estimated consumption expenditure in rupee term, he is supposed to be identified as poor. However, there are individuals who can earn to cover 99 per cent of the estimated consumption expenditure and there are individuals also, who are not able to even earn to cover 50 per cent of the consumption expenditure taken as benchmark for Poverty line. So the depth and burden of poverty are vital for targeting the poor people. In Table 1.45 in addition to Head Count ratio, Poverty Gap Ratio, Squared Poverty Gap Ratio have been taken into account to find out the depth of poverty. The trends in the Head count ratio, Poverty gap and squared poverty ratio over the years from 1957-58 to 1973-74 continuously in the state and for different points of time. From the table it is found that from the year 1957-58 to 1973-74, fluctuations in the head count ratio are there. This implies there were many transitory below poverty line people in the state.

For example, in the year 1990-91 according to 46th NSS data, the head count ratio was 27.14 and this was increased to 36.57 by the year 1992 (NSS 48th). So one can safely on the basis of NSS data infer that a lot of people are in the vicinity of the consumption expenditure level, which defines Poverty line. Similar trends are also observed in cases of Poverty gap and squared poverty gap parameters. The extent of poverty reached the peak, i.e., 70.29 per cent in 1968-69 in rural Orissa. In the eighties and early part of nineties, the extent of poverty was found to be much less compared to the previous years in rural Orissa.

**Table 1.45:** Extent, Depth and Severity of Poverty in Orissa in Different Years

| *NSS Round* | *Year* | *Rural* | | | *Urban* | | |
|---|---|---|---|---|---|---|---|
| | | *HCR* | *PG* | *SPG* | *HCR* | *PG* | *SPG* |
| 13 | 1957-58 | 65.06 | 23.180 | 11.129 | 64.07 | 23.338 | 10.619 |
| 14 | 1958-59 | 56.09 | 18.967 | 8.474 | 46.79 | 20.991 | 12.646 |
| 15 | 1959-60 | 62.49 | 19.494 | 7.723 | 64.79 | 28.756 | 16.047 |
| 16 | 1960-61 | 61.72 | 20.129 | 8.287 | 69.12 | 25.752 | 12.081 |
| 17 | 1961-62 | 46.89 | 13.909 | 5.912 | 50.81 | 17.760 | 8.016 |
| 18 | 1963-64 | 58.04 | 17.954 | 7.468 | 54.88 | 18.437 | 8.258 |
| 19 | 1964-65 | 61.36 | 18.528 | 7.548 | 60.07 | 19.023 | 7.639 |
| 20 | 1965-66 | 59.98 | 18.280 | 7.806 | 64.84 | 23.051 | 10.676 |
| 21 | 1966-67 | 62.86 | 19.001 | 7.963 | 65.47 | 23.314 | 10.503 |
| 22 | 1967-68 | 63.40 | 19.980 | 8.449 | 59.11 | 21.315 | 10.125 |
| 23 | 1968-69 | 70.29 | 24.308 | 11.070 | 61.90 | 20.050 | 8.426 |
| 24 | 1969-70 | 66.20 | 22.902 | 10.637 | 49.19 | 16.567 | 7.473 |
| 25 | 1970-71 | 64.77 | 22.173 | 10.162 | 54.43 | 17.162 | 7.121 |
| 27 | 1972-73 | 67.03 | 23.693 | 10.952 | 55.53 | 18.133 | 7.853 |
| 28 | 1973-74 | 58.67 | 17.662 | 7.108 | 59.99 | 20.203 | 8.778 |
| 32 | 1977-78 | 62.52 | 20.443 | 8.955 | 57.26 | 19.743 | 9.057 |
| 38 | 1983 | 56.76 | 16.962 | 7.126 | 54.94 | 16.701 | 6.710 |
| 42 | 1986-87 | 44.95 | 11.950 | 4.462 | 49.81 | 14.793 | 5.789 |
| 43 | 1987-88 | 47.86 | 11.699 | 3.840 | 47.53 | 13.371 | 5.014 |
| 45 | 1989-90 | 39.48 | 8.454 | 2.403 | 41.09 | 11.599 | 4.385 |
| 46 | 1990-91 | 27.14 | 5.376 | 1.532 | 40.42 | 10.913 | 3.928 |
| 48 | 1992 | 36.57 | 8.195 | 2.530 | 48.74 | 17.120 | 7.366 |
| 50 | 1993-94 | 40.28 | 8.724 | 2.790 | 40.76 | 11.257 | 4.148 |

*Note*: 1. HCR =Head Count Ratio, 2. PG = Poverty Gap, 3. SPG = Squared Poverty Gap

*Source*: World Bank data set on Indian Poverty in internet.

As per the latest estimates of the Modified Expert Group of Planning Commission, Orissa has the highest proportion of population living below the poverty line. According to the Planning Commission state plan document in the year 1999-2000, the percentage of people living below the poverty line in the state was 47.15, whereas, it was 42.6 per cent in case of Bihar. On the other hand, the all-India average was found to be 26.1 per cent. The estimates of the Expert Group of Planning Commission, 1993 show that, in 1993-94, the poverty ratio was 48.6 per cent, which was second highest in the country. Bihar occupied the first position with 54.6 per cent population living below the poverty line.

## Distribution of Poverty

The burden of poverty is very high on marginal farmers, as marginal farmers are neither able to benefit from agricultural land in terms of high yield nor able to work in other's agricultural field as agricultural labourers due to family labour involvements in owned land. Low prevailing agricultural wage and lack of mobility due to engagement as a cultivator, generally makes the life of marginal farmers miserable. Next to marginal farmers, the incidence of poverty is very high among the agricultural labourers. This is because of low prevailing wage rates and seasonal nature of agricultural labour demand. Because of low productivity and marketing problems of agricultural.

**Table 1.46:** Poverty by Social Groups in Orissa

| Social Group | 1983 | | | 1993-94 | | |
|---|---|---|---|---|---|---|
| | Poverty Ratio (%) | Contribution to Poverty (%) | Population Share (%) | Poverty Ratio (%) | Contribution to Poverty (%) | Population Share (%) |
| Rural: | | | | | | |
| ST | 79.1 | 33.1 | 23.1 | 63.6 | 38.0 | 25.1 |
| SC | 62.6 | 18.9 | 16.6 | 40.5 | 17.8 | 18.5 |
| Others | 43.8 | 48.0 | 60.3 | 32.9 | 44.1 | 56.3 |
| All Groups | 55.1 | 100.0 | 100.0 | 42.0 | 100.0 | 100.0 |

*Note*: 1. ST = Scheduled Tribe
2. SC = Scheduled Caste

*Source*: As reported in Panda (2000).

As different studies suggest the incidence of poverty by social groups shows that there was higher concentration of poverty among the Scheduled Caste (SC) and Scheduled Tribe (ST) population in both rural and urban areas. The incidence of poverty among the ST population was near about two times more than that of the other castepopulation. The percentage of ST poor to total number of poor was 38.0 while the share of ST population to total population was 25 per cent in rural areas in 1993-94. Out of the total rural poor families in Orissa, 87.36 per cent of rural poor families were agricultural labourers, marginal farmers and small farmers. The rest 12.64 per cent of rural poor families were non-agricultural labourers, rural artisans and others. It can be seen from Table 1.45 that the percentage shares of rural poor families of the categories of small farmers, marginal farmers, agricultural labourers, non-agricultural labourers, rural artisans and others to total rural families were 12.64, 34.19, 21.91, 6.91, 2.05 and 0.91 respectively. Districts like Rayagada, Koraput, Phulbani and Ganjam had a little higher percentage of rural poor families of the category of non-agricultural labourers.

In Orissa, regions like the southern and northern are not well developed as compared to the coastal region. One of the important reasons for this is the higher concentration of ST population in the above two regions. The poverty ratio in the coastal region was estimated at 64.0 per cent as against 85.5 and 79.1 per cent in the southern and northern regions respectively. The incidence of poverty among SC population was more or less same in all the three regions, i.e., 61.64 per cent. But, in case of general caste population, the incidence of poverty was comparatively much less in the coastal region than that in the southern and northern regions. Thus, in all the cases, the poverty ratio was found to be less in the coastal region.

According to the Planning Commission's state plan report, out of 52.23 lakh of rural families in the state of Orissa in 1992, 78.70 per cent of rural families were living below the poverty line. Out of 78.70 per cent of rural poor families, the shares of destitute (in the income range Rs. 0-4000), very very poor (in the income range Rs. 4001-6000), very poor (in the income range Rs. 6001-8500), and poor (in the income range Rs. 8501-11000) families were 25.89, 30.01, 15.55 and 7.24 per cent respectively. This shows that the shares of destitute and very very poor families were much more than that of very poor and poor families, and the destitute and very very poor families constituted 71.03 per cent of the total number of rural poor families in the state. In other words, the severity and intensity of rural poverty was much higher in the state.

As per 1997 survey of Panchayati Raj Department, Government of Orissa, out of 67.87 lakh rural families, 66.37 per cent rural families were living below the poverty line, which indicates the decline of 12.33 percentage points over 1992 survey. District-wise analysis shows that, in almost all the districts, there were higher concentration of small farmers, marginal farmers and agricultural labourers, who were living below the poverty line. This 1997 survey data reveal almost similar picture. Agricultural labourers, marginal farmers and small farmers constituted 85.61 per cent of the total rural poor of Orissa. This is 1.75 percentage points less than the 1992 survey. Even than percentage share of agricultural labourers, marginal farmers and small farmers out of the total rural families are found to be higher. The percentage shares of BPL families of the categories of agricultural labourers, marginal farmers, small farmers and rural artisans to total rural families in the state were found to be 24.91 per cent, 20.90 per cent, 11.02 per cent and 3.24 per cent respectively.

### *Poverty Alleviation Programmes*

The Poverty alleviation programmes are implemented with multiple objectives like, (1) providing wage employments, (2) providing self-employments, and (3) to improve the rural infrastructure and other socio-economic capital base of rural areas. Besides these, many social assistance schemes are also implemented in the rural areas to take care of most down-trodden and vulnerable sections of the rural society. There are many poverty alleviation programmes, which are sponsored by Central Government and there are also some anti-poverty programmes, which are designed by the state governments and implemented by the state governments. However, the implementation of poverty alleviation programmes is moreover lies with the state governments. In this section our focus is on the issues related to the efficacy of state government in terms of implementation of various poverty alleviation programmes. In general an over all assessment of poverty alleviation programmes implemented in the state will be the matter. Broadly the self-employment programmes include Integrated Rural Development Programme (IRDP), Development of Women and Children in Rural Areas (DWCRA), Training of Rural Youth for Self-employment (TRYSEM), and Supply of Improved Tool-kit to Rural Artisans (SITRA). On the other hand, wage employment programmes cover schemes like Jawahar Rojgar Yojana (JRY), Employment

Assurance Scheme (EAS), Indira Awaas Yojana (IAY), and Million Wells Scheme (MWS).

Many of the centrally sponsored poverty alleviation schemes have been redesigned. At present, various centrally sponsored schemes like SGSY, SGRY, IAY, etc. are in operation. The basic concept is to provide financial support to poor village artisans as well as poor families in a village for self-employment. But basically, SGSY is aimed at poorest of the poor in the community.

*Swarnjayanti Gram Swarozgar Yojana* (SGSY) has come into operation since 1.4.1999. Before this, Integrated Rural Development Programme (IRDP), Development of Women and Children in Rural Areas (DWCRA), Training of Rural Youth for Self-Employment (TRYSEM), Supply of Improved Tool-kits to Rural Artisans (SITRA), Ganga Kalyan Yojana (GKY) and Million Wells Scheme (MWS) were in operation in rural areas. It was felt that this fragmented approach with a multiplicity of schemes was not able to focus on the needs of rural poor in a coherent manner. Hence, the above schemes were amalgamated by Government of India and merged into single new scheme called SGSY. It aims at establishing a large number of micro-enterprises in the rural areas, building upon the potential of the rural poor. Beneficiaries, known as *swarozgaris*, may be individual families or Self-Help Groups (SHG). During the year 2000-01, 87 per cent families out of the targeted number of 99094 families have been assisted in the State. The percentages of SC, ST and women *swarozgaris* work out to be 22, 23 and 25 per cent respectively. The average per family investment was Rs. 22004 with subsidy-credit ratio 35:65 (Government of Orissa, 2002). According to the Panchayati Raj Department, Government of Orissa, it is better to extend SGSY to middle class families, so that, they being themselves enterprising will act synthesiser and catalyst for development of enterprises in rural areas, which will result into sustainable development of the poor. *This is quite rational that in rural areas, if anybody becomes enterprising and take up any self-employment activities, it will definitely boost up the employment and other developmental activities.*

The Sampoorna Gramin Rozgar Yojana (SGRY) (integration of JGSY and EAS) has been introduced very recently in the State. Under SGRY, village infrastructures are being constructed and at the same time food security is ensured. But, the basic concept here is to provide food and employment. In Orissa, due to geo-political situation, there is less demand of food grains in coastal areas than the hilly areas. So, there should be flexibility in implementation of SGRY. Unless and until, complete freedom is given relating to utilisation of cash and food grains, over all goal cannot be achieved. Moreover, the village infrastructures need to be strengthened by large flow of funds under SGRY. There are large numbers of water resources, which are remaining defunct and unutilised because of paucity of funds. These could be renovated and put to better use. So for these maximum funds may be released.

As per the guidelines under IAY, and now it is termed as integrated Rural Housing Scheme, below poverty line families are being given grant of Rs. 20,000 per unit. But invariably, total cost of house now comes to Rs. 30,000 to Rs. 35,000 depending upon the geographical condition and availability of infrastructure facilities. Unless and until, the unit cost is enhanced from Rs. 20,000 to minimum Rs. 30,000, it may not be possible on the part of the BPL families to construct a house of their own.

Government of India, while releasing funds under SGRY, SGSY, and IAY, have prohibited inter-district diversion of funds. But, complete freedom should be given to State Government for diversion of funds in a particular year taking into account necessity of the area of a particular district. Unless flexibility is given, to the desired extent of development may not take place.

It is necessary to look into the physical and financial performances of anti-poverty programmes in a poverty trodden state like Orissa. It is generally found that the poorer states are not able to reap much benefit from the poverty alleviation programmes. There are problems in implementation, poor targeting and gap between the target and achievement is high. In addition to this, it is also argued that in order to reach at the target as prescribed by the government, the beneficiaries are not selected in a fair manner. Lack of flexibility in using funds and poor monitoring systems are also responsible for poor performances of anti-poverty eradication programmes. The political influences and other social and economic factors always created a biased atmosphere in favour of certain sections of rural society. Keeping all these in view, one cannot assess the efficacies of poverty alleviation programmes only by looking at macro level parameters like percentage of fund utilization or percentage of physical achievements. However, it is also obvious that the macro level indicators will give an over all picture of efforts made at the state level towards Poverty Alleviation.

**Table 1.47:** Financial and Physical Performances of Poverty Alleviation Schemes as on March 2004

| *Name of the Schemes* | *Financial* | | | | *Physical* | | | |
|---|---|---|---|---|---|---|---|---|
| | *O.B. as on 1.4.03 (in lakhs)* | *Total Funds Available (in lakhs)* | *Expen. (in lakhs)* | *% of exp.* | *Target* | *Achi.* | *% of ach.* | *Unit* |
| SGRY | 3889.44 | 40387.43 | 38608.74 | 96 | 639.23 | 618.57 | 97 | lakh mandays |
| IAY | | | | | | | | |
| a. IAY | 433.31 | 13524.62 | 12635.92 | 93 | 66026 | 58996 | 89 | no. of houses |
| b. IAY (Upgradation) | 35.36 | 300.36 | 313.66 | 104 | 2477 | 3196 | 129 | no. of houses |
| SUB-TOTAL | 468.67 | 13824.98 | 12949.58 | 94 | 68503 | 62192 | 91 | no. of houses |
| O.B.B. | 53.48 | 53.48 | 28.17 | 53 | 68 | 47 | 69 | no. of school bldg. |
| S.G.S.Y. | –77.62 | 6062.92 | 6699.2 | 110 | 54348 | 39289 | — | no. of swarozgaris |
| | 4333.97 | 60328.81 | 58285.69 | 97 | | | | |

A glance at Table 1.47 given reveals that highest percentage (104%) of utilization of funds as on March 2004 is in case of PAP upgradation of IAY houses. IAY scheme is found to be functioning well. In case of SGRY percentage of fund utilization is also quite impressive that is 96 per cent. The percentage of physical achievement is also quite impressive in case of SGRY, as out of targeted number of man-days 97 per cent have been created. Fund utilization is more than 90 per cent in case of all the wage employment schemes. Such a high percentage of fund utilization has hardly helped in reducing poverty, so it can be inferred that wage employments anti-poverty programmes are really not helping eradication of poverty on a long term basis. It gives temporary respite only. From Table 1.47 it can be found that there has been an over utilization of funds in case of Self-employment scheme SGSY (110%). Similarly, number of swarozagaris are around 39,289 out of targeted 54,348, as already mentioned the rosy picture at macro level never has any impact on poverty reduction. There are many other fundamental problems are there at the grassroots level, which are making the efforts of poverty eradication futile.

Studies undertaken on the impact of various anti-poverty programmes, namely, IRDP, DWCRA, TRYSEM, SITRA, JRY, EAS, IAY and MWS in tribal and backward districts of Orissa such as Mayurbhanj, Koraput and Nabarangpur by the State Government clearly indicate several weaknesses like improper identification of beneficiaries, inadequate and improper supply of assets to beneficiaries, untimely supply of subsidies by government and inadequate supply of loans by banks, inadequate generation of mandays of employment by contractors and their highhandedness in operating the programme, inadequate supervision, monitoring and follow up action either by block staff or bank staff to assess the end use of credit, poor marketing and training facilities available to the beneficiaries, etc. As the result of the weaknesses witnessed in the implementation of the schemes, the impact on generation of output, income and employment in the post-assistance period was marginal compared to pre-assistance period. Furthermore, the objective of assisting poor people to cross the poverty line through the benefits of the programmes was largely not materialised. The beneficiaries who were able to cross the poverty line were few in numbers. Qualitatively, the programmes did not have adequate impact on the poor as expected.

In order to investigate into inter-district variations in the financial and physical achievements of anti-poverty alleviation programmes, two tables (1.48 and 1.49) showing figures of financial and physical performances of two districts—Cuttack (developed) and Kalahandi (underdeveloped).

From Tables 1.48 and 1.49, it can be found that wage employment programmes are slightly better in Kalahandi district in terms of both mandays generated and total expenditure. However, number of *swarozgaris* is marginally higher in the developed Cuttack district as compare to the underdeveloped Kalahandi district. It is already mentioned that self-employments through SGSY are successful in relatively developed regions. So more developed districts are doing better so far as SGSY is concerned.

**Table 1.48:** Financial and Physical Performances of PAP Schemes in Cuttack District (2003-04)

| Sl. No. | Name of the Schemes | Financial and Physical | | | | | | | Unit |
|---|---|---|---|---|---|---|---|---|---|
| | | *Total Funds Available* | *Expen-diture* | *% of Exp.* | *Closing Balance* | *Target* | *Achi.* | *% of Achi.* | |
| (1) | (2) | (6) | (7) | (8) | (9) | (10) | (11) | (12) | (13) |
| 1. | SGRY | | | | | | | | |
| | a. SGRY (Steam-I) | 616.71 | 555.12 | 90 | 61.59 | 9.91 | 10.16 | 103 | Lakh Mandays |
| | b. SGRY (Steam-II) | 595.70 | 540.47 | 91 | 55.23 | 9.22 | 9.38 | 102 | Lakh Mandays |
| | Sub-Total | 1212.41 | 1095.59 | 90 | 116.82 | 19.13 | 19.54 | 102 | Lakh Mandays |
| 2. | AY | | | | | | | | |
| | a. IAY | 561.05 | 504.95 | 90 | 56.10 | 2423 | 2189 | 90 | No. of Houses |
| | b. IAY (Upgradation) | 0.00 | 0.00 | 0 | 0.00 | 0 | 0 | 0 | No. of Houses |
| | Sub-Total | 561.05 | 504.95 | 90 | 56.10 | 2423 | 2189 | 90 | No. of Houses |
| 3. | O.B.B. | 11.06 | 6.47 | | 4.59 | 15.00 | 11.00 | 73 | No. of School Bldg. |
| 4. | S.G.S.Y. | 221.96 | 228.46 | 103 | –6.50 | 2208 | 2215 | 100 | No. of Swarozgaris |
| | District Total | 2006.48 | 1835.47 | 91 | 171.01 | | | | |

**Table 1.49:** Financial and Physical Achievement under Different Schemes during the Year 2003-04 upto End of March, 2004

| | | District Name: KALAHANDI | | | | | | | | | | |
|---|---|---|---|---|---|---|---|---|---|---|---|---|
| Sl. No. | Name of the Schemes | Financial (Rs. In lakhs) | | | | | | | Physical | | | |
| | | O.B. As on 1.4.03 | Receipts | Other Receipts | Total Funds Available | Expen. | % of exp. | Closing Balance | Target | Achi. | % of achi. | Unit |
| 1 | 2 | 3 | 4 | 5 | 6 | 7 | 8 | 9 | 10 | 11 | 12 | 13 |
| 1 | SGRY | | | | | | | | | | | |
| | a. SGRY (Steam-I) | 94.58 | 838.94 | 4.95 | 938.47 | 892.75 | 95 | 45.72 | 14.06 | 15.52 | 110 | Lakh Mandays |
| | b. SGRY (Steam-II) | -7.44 | 852.22 | 0.00 | 844.78 | 826.99 | 98 | 17.79 | 11.98 | 13.74 | 115 | Lakh Mandays |
| | Sub-Total | 87.14 | 1691.16 | 4.95 | 1783.25 | 1719.74 | 96 | 63.51 | 26.04 | 29.26 | 112 | Lakh Mandays |
| 2 | IAY | | | | | | | | | | | |
| | a.IAY | 0.73 | 415.97 | 49.10 | 465.80 | 424.22 | 91 | 41.58 | 2377 | 2036 | 86 | No. of Houses |
| | b.IAY (Upgradation) | 0.00 | 0.00 | 0.00 | 0.00 | 0.00 | 0 | 0.00 | 0 | 0 | 0 | No. of Houses |
| | Sub-Total | 0.73 | 415.97 | 49.10 | 465.80 | 424.22 | 91 | 41.58 | 2377 | 2036 | 86 | No. of Houses |
| 3 | O.B.B. | 0.00 | 0.00 | | 0.00 | 0.00 | | 0.00 | 0 | 0.00 | 0 | No. of School bldg. |
| 4 | S.G.S.Y. | 22.69 | 277.20 | 2.89 | 302.78 | 276.38 | 91 | 26.40 | 1666 | 2045 | 123 | No. of Swarozgaris |
| | District Total | 110.56 | 2384.33 | 56.94 | 2551.83 | 2420.34 | 95 | 131.49 | | | | |

*Mission Danapani*: Self-targeting Wage Employment Programme is a state sponsored Anti-poverty programme. In Orissa lakhs of landless agricultural labourers (LAL) going without work for a period ranging 30 days and above. The analysis of this information speaks about massive gap between claims made by various wage-employment generation schemes under implementation in the state. This also highlights the necessity of launching of a self-targeting wage employment programme to meet this challenge. It should be possible to provide wage employment assurance for 20 days in a month for six months to many LAL to generate large number of mandays using 4.40 lakh MT of food grains available to tackle current drought. It is this section of society that moves out of Orissa as DADAN SHRAMIK and is subjected to all types of exploitation in the hands of labour contractors and anti-social elements. Since large numbers of them are unskilled women labourers belonging to SC/ST category and are likely to return home once the agricultural season starts, a need-based demand-driven, food security oriented wage employment appears to be an IDEAL solution to this human problem. Landless Agricultural Labourers (LAL) is the most vulnerable group in a drought situation and is likely to accept 100 per cent wages in kind.

## Project Identification

As and when a group of 20 or more un-skilled labourers want work and are willing to accept 100 per cent wages in kind, Collector will be duly bound to provide them work. The Project mandate is that only one of the labourers shall be the executant. No middleman is to be permitted. The work shall be stopped as soon as the monsoon breaks or the labourers are not willing to work. However, the incomplete work should be completed in the following working season. Care should be taken that the works should be completed as far as possible in the same working season. The monitoring of work shall be based on Muster roll basis. The reporting of non-existent and fake labourer shall be taken up seriously. Village having higher concentration of SC/ST population with drinking water problem shall be given preference.

During droughts it warrants focused intervention to provide landless agricultural labourers (LAL) wage employment and create permanent and durable drought proofing assets like water bodies, preferably by renovation, wherever feasible or by creating new water bodies.

## Project Implementation

Gram Panchayat is to implement this scheme through its executive officer, i.e. Village Level Worker (VAW/VLW). Sarpanch and Panchayat Samity member may supervise the payment of wages on weekly basis. CEOs Zilla Parishad and Collectors are to monitor the project and submit information in the MIS system developed by SRC for fortnightly review of Government.

## Project Advantages

More than 20 wage seekers in a village or in a group of village may be entitled for a work to be started irrespective of Shelf of Projects already prepared. The project aims at providing wage employment to able-bodied landless agricultural labourers who are willing to work and accept wages in kind. The creation of socially useful and productive water body as a community asset is secondary objective. This is not an expenditure driven programme that has its limitation. This is designed to provide assured wage employment for 100 days to all those who are going without work. You may ask District Labour Officer to open a Live Register of wage employment seekers in consultation with you and ask him to check up payment of minimum wages. This may prevent pilferage and may be an additional check. The projects taken up under this mission may be allowed to continue pre-monsoon. No use of Machine is to be ensured.

## Target Group

All un-skilled labourers willing to work and accept minimum wages in kind are the target group. No contractor and no middlemen are to be permitted. Self-targeting—if a GP has no such category of work or labourer no such work may be taken up. No cash hence no being schemes with huge material component. Proper utilisation of Food Grains has to be ensured.

## Project Objectives

Renovation of all village pond/tanks at the rate of one project per Gram Panchayat is the sole and measurable objective.

## Employment Assurance Scheme (EAS)

Realising the success of the Employment Guarantee Scheme (EGS) in Maharashtra, the Employment Assurance Scheme (EAS) was launched in the country in the year 1993-94 as a centrally sponsored scheme with a sharing pattern of 80:20 between the Centre and the State. It aims at providing assured employment of about 100 days to rural poor between 18-60 years of age during the lean agricultural season.

In Orissa, for generating wage employment opportunities for the rural poor, the scheme was introduced initially in 143 Revamped Public Distribution System (RPDS) blocks of 16 districts on 2nd October, 1993. Subsequently, the scheme was extended to all the 314 blocks of the State. Table 1.48 reveals the financial and physical targets and achievements of EAS in different years in Orissa. Out of the total funds available for the programme in the State, cent per cent fund was not spent in any of the years beginning from the launching of the programme till the year 2000-01. In 1993-94, only 28.79 per cent of the total fund was utilised for the purpose. This happened due to preparations and ground level modalities undertaken for the adoption of the programme. In subsequent years, the percentage of utilisation was more than 70 per cent. With regard to physical achievement, the performance was better in the recent years, i.e. 1999-2000 and 2000-2001. The percentages of physical achievements, i.e. mandays of employment generated during the above two years were 96.34 and 140.16 respectively.

## Public Distribution System (PDS)

Public Distribution System is an effective instrument for maintaining price stability as well as for equitable distribution of essential commodities to consumers particularly belonging to weaker sections. It has played an important role for ensuring food security and reducing poverty in the economy. The system operates through a network of fair price shops. In Orissa, OCSC (Orissa Civil Supply Corporation) has been entrusted with the responsibility of distributing rice, wheat, sugar, imported edible oil, which are allotted by Government of India. By the year 1999-2000, the above essential commodities were distributed to 81 lakh ration card holders (17.16 per cent in urban areas and 82.84 per cent in rural areas) through 24,782 fair price shops (Government of Orissa, 2001).

It is observed that the allotment and distribution of the essential commodities under PDS to the consumers are not adequate and proper in the State. The National Sample Survey, 42nd round has reported that at the all-India level rice purchased from PDS formed only 16.7 per cent of the total rice purchased by the households. In case of wheat, it was 12.6 per cent only. Further, a study by Kirit S. Parikh has shown that in states like U.P., Bihar and Orissa where bulk of the rural poor are concentrated, 98 per cent of the rural population did not make any purchase from PDS.

In Orissa, the problems identified in the PDS are: (a) all the essential commodities required by the poor are not supplied through PDS; (b) the quantities of different commodities supplied to the poor are not sufficient to maintain their livelihood, and even the quality of the ration is not good; (c) physical accessibility of the poor to the fair price shops is less and irregular due to the location of fair price shops at a distant place far away from the homes; and (d) the supply of kerosene oil, the much needed fuel for lighting purposes by the poor is much less compared to the demand for the product in rural areas. Sometimes, unscrupulous activities of dealers prevent the beneficiaries to receive their due share of kerosene quota.

For the successful implementation of PDS, the measures needed are: (a) revamping the Public Distribution System to include the poor persons only, and consumers above BPL are restricted to use PDS; (b) ghost cards be limited and abolished in order to enable only genuine card holders to approach the fair price shops; (c) the dealers need not be appointed on political lines, and unemployed youths having community approach and service mentality be assigned the job of manning the fair price shops; and (d) the fair price shops must provide all essential commodities to the poor like coarse cloths, baby food, matches and edible oils, etc.

## Integrated Child Development Scheme (ICDS)

The Integrated Child Development Scheme (ICDS) has been introduced in the state from the year 1975-76. Presently, the scheme is being implemented through 281 ICDS projects in 269 blocks of Orissa. It offers a package of health care services covering supplementary nutrition, immunisation, health check up, nutrition and health education, maternal care, and pre-school education to children in the age group of 0 to 6 years. The above services are being delivered to the beneficiaries through 28,612 Anganwadi workers. The total number of beneficiaries under different health care services of ICDS in Orissa from the year 1996-97 to 1999-2000 can be seen from Table 1.49. The table shows that except immunisation in almost all types of services the numbers of beneficiaries have increased in 1999-2000 compared to the year 1996-97.

In spite of the good coverage of ICDS in Orissa, micro studies made in several parts of the State indicate that the beneficiaries under the programme had not received adequate care. Besides, the Anganwadi workers being untrained and inadequate in strength could not administer the programme effectively. Furthermore, there was absence of co-ordination and co-operation among different government functionaries on the one hand and Anganwadi workers on the other at the grassroots level. This is noticed in almost all the blocks in the State.

## Mid-Day Meals Scheme (MDM)

In order to increase enrolment, attendance and retention among primary schools going children (6-11 yrs.) by reducing dropout rates, the Central Government launched Mid-day Meals programme on August 15, 1995. In Orissa the programme was started in the said year. The food basket under Mid-day Meal programme in Orissa consists of 100 grams of rice, 15 grams of *dal*. Rice is provided free of cost by the Central Government to State Governments. Even the cost of transportation of rice from FCI godown to the schools is borne by the Central Government at the rate of Rs. 25 per quintal for the benefit of the State. *Dal* and other provisions like vegetables, edible oil, firewood and spices etc. required for mid-day meals are the responsibility of the State Government.

The scheme was operating in 40,697 primary schools covering 45,03,045 number of students belonging to all the 30 districts of Orissa in 1998-99. The Mid-day Meals scheme is aimed at benefiting the poor and needy primary school going children in the State particularly in rural and backward areas. The total allotment made for Mid-day Meals scheme in 1995-96 was Rs. 65.71 crore, in 1996-97 it was Rs. 71.21 crore and in 1997-98 this declined to Rs. 42.51 crore. However, there is a gap between the allotment and the actual expenditure on Mid-day Meals scheme. In 1995-96 the total expenditure made was Rs. 65.66 crore in 1996-97 it was Rs. 67.21 crore and in 1997-98 it was only Rs. 37.94 crore. There is thus a mismatch between allocation and expenditure on Mid-day Meals programme. This mismatch is more pronounced in the year 1997-98 than earlier years. Taking into consideration the coverage of the programme both in terms of the number of schools and the students, the allocation appears to be inadequate for mid-day meals. At the same time, whatever is allotted, the actual expenditure seems to be lagging considerably.

The impact of Mid-day Meals scheme in Orissa reveals that the programme is more successful in educationally backward districts relatively to educationally advanced districts. In the educationally backward districts, enrolment, attendance and retention of children in schools have gone up considerably with reduction in the dropout of the children. In the educationally developed districts, on the other hand, enrolment of children has shown a declining trend due to (a) non-availability of children in the district in the age group of 6 to 11, (b) preference of parents to educate their children in English medium and public schools, etc. However, there has taken place a significant improvement in percentage of attendance and retention of children with sharp decline in dropout rates after the introduction of Mid-day Meals scheme. The impact of mid-day meals is, therefore, more felt in educationally backward and tribal dominated districts of Orissa than in educationally advanced districts.

However, the Mid-day Meals programme in Orissa is confronted with several problems. These problems are the following:

(a) Teacher is the sole manager and organiser of the programme. This has affected the teaching ability of the teachers and study atmosphere in the schools.

(b) Infrastructure in the form of utensils, kitchen room and cooking materials is inadequate and scarce affecting the implementation of the programme.

(c) There is corruption and pilferaging in the programme affecting the very objective of the programme for which it is meant, i.e. to provide nutritional food to school going children at the elementary level.

(d) Absence of a separate budgetary provision for the implementation of the programme. Presently, the programme is sustained by the allocation of funds by Department of Women and Child Development, which receives the budgetary grants for several welfare schemes. Mid-day Meals programme is looked upon as one of such programmes.

In order to make the programme sustainable for removing nutritional deficiency among poor children, the following measures be adopted. First, the teacher be relieved from the duty of managing and operating the Mid-day Meals programme. A separate staff, in the name of mid-day meal organiser as it exists in Tamil Nadu be engaged to look after the programme wholeheartedly. Second, better supervision and effective monitoring at all levels of administration would make the programme more viable. Finally, separate budgetary allocation with larger involvement of the State Government in the programme would make all the difference. Once these measures are adopted attacking poverty at the lower rung will be more beneficial.

## Village Level Analysis

In the village Banspal according to the BPL list for the year 2001, 315 families were BPL. Out of the total population of 1589 for the village as 1165 come under the BPL category. So around 73 per cent of population in the village are below poverty line and this is quite higher than the state average. It again gives a hint that poverty is very local specific.

Similarly in the village Brahmani the percentage of families below the poverty line is 80 per cent according to the survey carried out by the district authorities in 1998. The number of tribals and scheduled castes in the category of BPL are more in this than the OBCs. In earlier years there were some programmes like JRY but there has been no change in the poverty profile of the block. The anti-poverty schemes not had much impact on either increasing incomes or reducing household poverty. In the same village under the IAY scheme nearly 30 odd houses are built in the last seven years. So as already it is mentioned the success of IAY scheme is universal, this village is not an exception to it. However, there are many problems encountered under the scheme. The problems are:

- According to the guidelines, beneficiary selection should happen through the palli sabhas, but 90 per cent of the distribution was being decided jointly by the GP Secretary, the sarpanch and some influential ward members.
- There is no fixed date when the cheques are released. The application might have sanctioned months earlier, but the payments are not received in time due to sheer negligence. The beneficiary keeps running to the block office many times before he finally gets his due.
- The amount sanctioned is only Rs. 20,000. It is clearly impossible to build a slab roof dwelling with a toilet within this amount. Many houses are shown as completed but they almost never have toilets and sometimes do not have doors and windows. The amount (Rs. 500) that is withheld for the smokeless *chullah* is not released and neither is the *chullah* provided to the beneficiaries. The *chullah* is also not available at the block office. But this did not explain as to why then Rs. 500 was being cut from every beneficiary.
- Many IAY houses keep on pending at different stages of work. This problem mainly arises where the beneficiaries are extremely poor. Since money is released only after the work is done, they fail to get material or labour to work for them. Hence the contract system sometimes comes into play. The contractor who is usually close to the Junior Engineer agrees to do the work in return for the money being given to him. In Brahmani there were two such cases and the work was not of good quality.
- However, there seemed to be some kind of a consensus that there is very little cut in IAY projects as the money sanctioned is anyway less and the beneficiaries are more or less very

poor, except for those cases where the beneficiary selection was itself flawed.

In the village under the scheme SGSY, there were two individual beneficiaries and two groups that had received assistance in the village. The individual beneficiaries had got a goatery unit each at the cost of Rs. 25,000 and the groups were given loans for the following purposes:

- One onion storage godown.
- One tractor loan.

The SGSY was conceived as a holistic programme of micro enterprises covering all aspects of self-employment which includes organising rural poor into Self-Help Groups (SHGs). It integrates various agencies like—District Rural Development Agencies, banks, line departments, Panchayati Raj Institutions (PRIs), non-governmental oganisations, and other semi-government organisations. The objective of SGSY is to bring the existing poor families above the poverty line by providing them income generating assets through a mix of bank credit and government subsidy and to ensure that an assisted family has a monthly net income of at least Rs. 2000. Subsidy under SGSY is uniform at 30 per cent of the project cost subject to a maximum of Rs. 7500. In respect of SCs/STs, it is 50 per cent subject to a maximum of Rs. 10,000. For groups, the subsidy of 50 per cent subject to a ceiling of Rs. 1.25 lakh. SGSY is funded by the centre and states in the ratio of 75:25. The guidelines suggest that Gram Panchayats will play a crucial role in SGSY. The Gram Sabha will first approve the list of BPL families. Besides, at the beginning of each year, the potential Swarozgaris for taking up the designated key activities would be identified in each habitation by a 3-member committee including the Sarpanch. The list of Swarozgaris who are sanctioned the loan by the banks would be placed before the Gram Sabha. The Gram Panchayat would also be taking steps to provide from its funds under JGSY or any other programme or the common infrastructure necessary for the key activities. The Gram Panchayat would actively monitor the performance of the Swarozgaris and in particular whether they are replaying the loan regularly.

The Panchayat Samiti (block level) will approve the key activities that are identified for the blocks before the list is sent to the BDO through the District Level Technical Group. The Panchayat Samiti would review every month the reports sent by Block SGSY committee. In particular, the Panchayat Samiti would review the recovery performance. The Zilla Parishad will be reviewing the performance under SGSY in its general meetings. The Bankers play a very critical role in the implementation of Swarnajayanti Gram Swarozgar Yojana. SGSY is a credit-*cum*-subsidy programme. Credit is the key component and subsidy is only a minor and enabling component. SGSY envisages the close association of bankers at all stages of the programme implementation, right from the identification of key activities, clusters, self-help groups, identification of individual swarozgaris as well as planning for all the elements of the key activities. The bank has the final say in the selection of swarozgaris. An elaborate mechanism has been put in place to ensure post-credit monitoring as well as for loan recovery.

Since it would not be much beneficial to just study the programme in one village the Officer Trainee took the entire block as the base.

## Socio-Economic Condition of Beneficiaries of SGSY in the Block

Institutional factors had dominant role in the process of development. Out of 180 beneficiaries, 161 (89.4%) were male and 19 (10.6%) were female. 41 per cent beneficiaries were literate while the rest were not. Out of the literate population, 35.5 per cent had education below matriculation level, 21.6 per cent had qualification of matriculation and above but below graduation level. Only 3.9 per cent had qualification of graduation and above. Out of 180 beneficiaries 5.0 per cent were small farmers, 11.2 per cent were marginal farmers, 29.5 per cent were agricultural labourers, 7.2 per cent were non-agricultural casual labourers, 37.2 per cent were non-agricultural self-employed, 2.7 per cent were artisans, and 7.2 per cent were others. Agricultural labourers and non-agricultural self-employed had taken maximum benefit of the scheme. 70 (38.9%) beneficiaries belonged to Scheduled Castes and 100 (55.9%) belonged to OBCs. Only one (0.6%) beneficiary belonged to Scheduled Tribes and 9 (5.0%) belonged to other caste groups. Hence OBCs had taken maximum benefit of the SGSY followed by Scheduled Caste group. Priority under the scheme was to be given the freed bonded labourers and assignees of surplus land. But only 4 beneficiaries (2.2%) were freed bonded labourers and only 2 (1.1%) were assignees of surplus land. Remaining 174 (96.7%) belong to other categories. Only 11 (6.11%) beneficiaries had income below Rs. 6401. 31 (17.22%) beneficiaries had income in between Rs. 6401 to Rs. 11000. 56 (31.1%) beneficiaries had income in between Rs. 11001 to Rs. 16000. And 43 (23.88) in between Rs. 16001 to Rs. 21000. 22 (12.22%) beneficiaries had income above Rs. 21001.

The Village Seledi is a relatively rich village as it comes under the Hirakud Command Area and farmers are able to grow two crops of paddy in one year. Thirty per cent of the population lives below the poverty line. As per the observation of Officer Trainees, people who have five acres of double cropped irrigated land are also included in the BPL list. These kind of fraudulent entries distort the distribution pattern.

According to the village study report, the PDS system in the village Seledi is run totally by the GP and the GP secretary is responsible for running PDS in the GP. This system is found to be more effective than the system of private dealers. This is because the elected representatives are more accountable to the people. As PDS affects the day-to-day life of people, the elected representatives also take proper care in running the PDS. Funds are a major problem to run the PDS. As of now an amount of Rs. 50,000 is diverted from the JGSY funds to purchase the commodities for PDS. When the off take is less then the JGSY fund gets blocked in the PDS operations. This affects the developmental activities. Thus there is an urgent need to earmark some funds for PDS operations at GP level. Along with this if the storage facilities in GP office were increased, it would go a long way in strengthening the PDS system. In case of IAY scheme in the same village it was observed by the Officer Trainee that the main problem with scheme is the faulty selection of the beneficiaries. For example, in case of IAY houses the beneficiary's name has to be passed in Palli Sabha and then in Gram Sabha. But in practice the beneficiaries are selected without Palli Sabha and Gram Sabha. Out of the ten houses allotted for this village five were given to those people who were not selected by Gram Sabha. There are also problems in payment of dues after the work is completed. The JE and the block staff demand money and delay the payments. Eighteen IAY houses were pending for the last three years and a close look at each case showed that the non-completion is either because of wrong beneficiary selection or non-payment of running bill. It is also a fact that in 90 per cent of the completed IAY houses smokeless *chullahs* and toilets were never made. This is because the people are neither interested nor motivated to go for these things. There is a need to create awareness among the people about the uses and importance of toilets and smokeless *chullahs*. The system of giving advances is banned and that is also a reason for non-completion of IAY houses. The poor people do not have money for construction and claim it later on. There should be advances and the monitoring system should be strengthened. Similarly, in the same village Seledi as documented in the study report twelve houses under PMGAY are allotted to this village and the houses were pending for the last one year. After discussing with the District Collector advances were given to the beneficiaries through the VLW of the village and he was asked to monitor the work closely and report on day-to-day basis. The work went on very fast and all the houses were completed within 120 days. After this, the Collector has extended advances to all the PMGAY houses in the district through the VLWs.

Under the scheme SGSY in the village Seledi the key activities identified are goatery, sheep rearing, dairy and fishing (Net and Boat). Under this scheme three Self Help Groups (SHGs) have been formed and it is in the revolving fund stage. Activities are yet to be taken up by the group. The SHGs have 12 to 15 members belonging to BPL families and were started in 2001. They have been registered and the government has contributed Rs. 10,000 as a revolving fund and with that the group is functioning. Meetings of the groups are held in one month frequency. Two of the groups (Maheswar and Bhagabati) have exclusively SC members and one group is women's group (Jai Durga). Interaction with the group members made me realize that the members are not aware of the concept of SHGs and they see it as one more way of getting government aid. Even though the objective of the SHGs is to encourage credit and thrift, members are just interested in getting loans and aid. They are unaware of the benefits of the SHG concept. So far no training has been given to the leaders and members.

Sixteen individual families have been covered under this scheme out of which 12 are SC, 1 ST, and five are women. A major component of the scheme is follow up action and training. But in the field this is the weakest link. After the groups are formed, individual beneficiaries have been identified and the loan disbursed to them, there is practically no interaction between the block level SGSY committee and the beneficiary. They are remembered only when loan payments are long overdue but by then it is too late. Another problem lies in the process of beneficiary selection. According to the guidelines they are supposed to be selected by the GP, but in practice it is the block level officer, the VLW and the bank field officer who have full discrefion.

In the village study report of Dumerpani village it is mentioned that the government has initiated numerous programmes for upliftment of the poor. For families below poverty line, BPL cards are issued with which they can avail PDS services. From the GP storeroom items like rice, sugar and kerosene oil can be purchased at subsidized rates. Every month, each BPL cardholder is entitled to 18 kg of rice, 2 kg of sugar and 4 litres of kerosene oil. The respective minimum rates are Rs. 4.75 and Rs. 13.25 per kg of rice and sugar and Rs. 9.75 per litre of kerosene. Annapurna and Antyodaya benefits are also given to identified beneficiaries. While 10 kg of free rice grains are given to the beneficiaries under Annapurna, 25 kg of rice grains are provided at a rate of Rs. 3 per kg every month to Antyodaya beneficiaries. Pension benefits like Old Age Handicap and Widow pensions are available for identified individuals at a sum of Rs. 100 per month.

Four construction of houses under IAY, materials like cement, iron windows and doors worth Rs. 5000 are supplied to every identified BPL beneficiary. The remaining Rs. 15000 is given to the beneficiary, with which he can purchase bricks, nuria tiles, stones, sand, smokeless *chullah*, wooden beams and reefs. At present, there are 5 IAY beneficiaries in the village, 2 belonging to SC and 3 to ST category. About 1000 man-days of employment was generated during the construction period. There is no Gramin Awas beneficiary in the village.

The Jawahar Gram Samriddhi Yojana aims at creating demand driven community village infrastructure, and durable assets that would enable the rural poor to increase the opportunities for sustained employed. Wage employment under the programme is given to Below Poverty Line families. At Dumerpani, this programme was initiated in 1998-99. Total funds allotted to Darlipada GP during 2000-01 was Rs. 5,47,700. The amount earmarked for SC/ST welfare was Rs. 1,23,000. All the works have been undertaken by the GP. One irrigation tank worth Rs. 1,09,747.97 was constructed during 2000-01. Total workforce was 92, including 46 women. About 55 ST workers also benefited from this work. Total man-days generated was 2744 hours. Another tank was constructed at a cost of Rs. 36,000 where 24 villagers, including 10 women were engaged. Total man-days generated were 360 hours. About 2 hectares of land has been developed at a cost of Rs. 10,000 where two ST persons were engaged and man-days generated were 250 hours.

Other asset-creations included construction of 20 km of road and one school building. This involved a total of 518 workers, including 259 women. About 7770 man-days of employment were generated in these works. All men and women were given daily wages at a rate of Rs. 50. Total expenditure on wages of unskilled labourers was Rs. 4,89,947, while expenditure on non-wage component was Rs. 92,800.

The primary objective of the Employment Assurance Scheme is creation of additional wage employment opportunities during the period of acute shortage of wage employment through manual work for the rural poor living below poverty line. It aims at creating durable community, social and economic assets for sustained employment and development. Priority is given to works for soil and moisture conservation, minor irrigation, rejuvenation of drinking water sources and augmentation of groundwater, traditional water harvesting structures, drainage, forestry and formation of rural roads linking villages. During the year one tank was constructed under EAS at a cost of Rs. 55,000.

Both JGSY and EAS are components of SGRY since 2000. All works are undertaken after Gram Sabha resolution and due sanction from the DRDA. No NGO has so far been involved in the implementation of any of the above programmes. The Panchayat looks after the maintenance of all these assets as well as the records pertaining to each. All records, including accounts and muster rolls, are properly maintained in the Darlipada GP under which Dumerpani falls.

There are 5 beneficiaries of Swarnajayanti Gram Swarozgary Yojana in the village Dumerpani. Under this loan and subsidy scheme, the bank provided money after approval from the DRDA. The Gram Sabha selected one member and the VLW identified the other four. Subsidy has not been given to them. This shall be provided only after repayment of loans in full. This scheme has made significant contribution towards improving the economic condition of all 5 beneficiaries. The following table shows the details for each of these beneficiaries.

**Table 1.50:** Details of Economic Condition of five Beneficiaries

| *Name* | *Loan Rs.* | *Subsidy Rs.* | *Asset* | *Cost Rs.* | *Insu-rance* | *Wor-king Capital Rs.* | *Income Before** | *Income Now** | *Training* |
|---|---|---|---|---|---|---|---|---|---|
| Yadram Sahu | 12500 | 7500 | Shop | 20000 | None | None | 12000 | 14000 | No |
| Biharilal Sahu | 14000 | 6000 | Tailoring | 11000 | None | 9000 | 12000 | 15000 | Yes |
| Bhukau Sahu | 23000 | 7000 | Holler | 36000 | None | 6000 | 12000 | 17000 | No |
| Bhuk Singh | 6667 | 3333 | Cycle shop | 9000 | None | 1000 | 12000 | 14000 | No |
| Kapil Majhi | 14000 | 6000 | Cycle shop | 9000 | None | 9000 | 12000 | 16000 | No |

*Per annum

## Loan Details

| *Name* | *Month of Loaning* | *Amount* | *Inte-rest* | *Periodi-city of Instal.* | *Amount per Instal.* | *Amount Retur-ned* | *Month of Last Instal.* | *Outstan-ding* |
|---|---|---|---|---|---|---|---|---|
| Yadram Sahu | Aug. 2001 | Rs. 20000 | 18% | 76 months | Rs. 239 | Rs. 22000 | Sep. 01 | Nil |
| Biharilal Sahu | Dec. 2000 | Rs. 14000 | 18% | 60 months | Rs. 235 | Rs. 4735 | April 02 | Rs. 16840 |
| Bhukau Sahu | Dec. 2000 | Rs. 23000 | 18% | 5 years | Rs. 7000 | Rs. 12000 | Dec. 01 | Rs. 18000 |
| Bhuk Singh | Dec. 1999 | Rs. 6667 | 18% | 12 months | Rs. 835 | Rs. 8400 | Dec. 01 | Rs. 1600 |
| Kapil Majhi | Dec. 2000 | Rs. 14000 | 18% | 60 months | Rs. 235 | Rs. 5000 | April 02 | Rs. 16620 |

All the beneficiaries have been able to pay the installments in time. However, the interest rate at 18 per cent is a bit steep. Ideally, this should be brought down to 12-13 per cent so that cost recovery could be faster. Also, the beneficiaries are left on their own after disbursement of loan. Proper training and guidance should be arranged for them for better management of their business. To ensure sustainability, there must be diversification of activity among the beneficiaries. For this, orientation programmes should be held in the village for interested individuals. Potential areas for investment could be identified with the help of higher-level authorities at the block.

There are 7 SHGs formed under the SGSY in the same village Dumerpani. None of the SHGs is registered and all are exclusive women groups. Each member makes a monthly contribution of Rs. 10. None of the groups has been graded as yet, nor has any revolving fund been availed of by any. The details of each are as follows:

**Table 1.51:** Profile of 7 SHGs of Village Dumerpani

| *Name of Group* | *Member-ship* | *SC/ST Members* | *Opening of Bank Account* | *Frequency of Meeting* | *Bank Credit Availed* |
|---|---|---|---|---|---|
| Jai Maa Laxmi | 17 | 12 | 18.6.01 | Monthly | No |
| Jai Maa Saraswati | 16 | 6 | 9.8.01 | Monthly | No |
| Maa Mangala MSS | 11 | 11 | 22.3.99 | Monthly | Yes |
| Brundabati MSS | 13 | 13 | 29.11.95 | Monthly | Yes |
| Pardesan MSS | 19 | 19 | 13.12.98 | Monthly | Yes |
| Thakur Thakurani MSS | 35 | 35 | 14.10.98 | Monthly | Yes |
| Gouri MSS | 20 | 20 | 20.5.99 | Monthly | Yes |

**Table 1.52:** Financial Position of 7 SHGs

(*In rupees*)

| *Name of Group* | *Savings* | *Total funds* | *Amount Lent to Members* | *Recovery %* |
|---|---|---|---|---|
| Jai Maa Laxmi | 2040 | 2040 | — | — |
| Jai Maa Saraswati | 1600 | 1600 | — | — |
| Maa Mangala MSS | 7920 | 7920 | 2000 | 50 |
| Brundabati MSS | 10920 | 10920 | 5000 | 50 |
| Pardesan MSS | 9120 | 9120 | 4000 | 60 |
| Thakur Thakurani MSS | 12600 | 12600 | 5000 | 70 |
| Gouri MSS | 6000 | 6000 | — | — |

Two NGOs, namely Mahila Vikash and FARR are involved in formation of SHGs. The rest have been formed under Mission Shakti (AWW) and Watershed Mission. Only the members of Maa Mangala Mahila Sanjoy Samiti and Brundabati Mahila Sanjoy Samiti have undergone training so far.

## CONCLUSION

Orissa is not only to be one of the poorest states of the country but also one of the mineral resource rich states of the country. The socio-cultural pattern is more ethnic in nature. The festivals and other family related functions are very extravagant affairs. People are peace loving and social conflicts are not at all serious. Orissa is also famous for traditional skill based handicrafts and beautiful tourist places. Lack of entrepreneurship and dearth of funds are two main constraints for the Orissa people to develop further. Poor infrastructure facilities and lack of incentives for diversification of agriculture are also responsible for poor performances of agriculture sector. Demand driven forces are too weak to initiate any enterprise. People are poor because they are poor perfectly suits here. Implementational problems along with corruption from top to bottom in almost all the government departments has helped to increase inefficiencies.

The inter-regional disparities pertaining to various parameters are large. Incidence of poverty was more in northern and southern regions of Orissa compared to coastal region. Caste-wise, among the Scheduled Tribe population, the incidence of poverty was higher than that among Scheduled Caste and other caste population. Further, the percentage of rural families living below the poverty line was found to be much higher in the State. As a result of higher incidence of poverty in the State, the living condition of the people in terms of the development indicators like literacy rate, infant mortality rate, per capita income, per capita food grain production, etc. was much below the national average. Even within the State, composite indices of the socio-economic indicators show that there was greater inter-district variation in the living condition of the people. Moreover, the performances of the welfare activities like EAS, PDS, ICDS and MDM are observed to be not satisfactory in the State, and these factors are mainly responsible for the poor living condition of the people.

In the light of the above findings, it is suggested that efforts should be made to reduce the incidence of poverty among the people of the State at least to the national average through appropriate policy measures. To improve the living conditions of the people, increase in economic growth is necessary. As the economy grows, poverty diminishes faster when growth is strong, slower when it is not. For this, the values of the development indicators like literacy rate, per capita income, infant survival rate, per capita foodgrain production, per capita net value added by manufacture, etc. have to be improved through appropriate and adequate investment in the sectors like education, agriculture, health, industry and transport and communication. An integrated approach in all these sectors is very much necessary for the all-round development of the State. To reduce the higher concentration of rural poverty in the State, adequate funds should be diverted to the rural sector in the form of poverty alleviation programmes and other rural developmental programmes and at the same time, efforts should be made to rectify the present loopholes and problems in the rural developmental programmes. Administration should see that the funds are utilised properly. For better levels of living of the rural poor, increase in agricultural production and stability in foodgrain prices are highly necessary. With regard to climatic crises like flood, drought, cyclone, etc., the government should take necessary steps to control all these crises, so that, the conjunctural poverty causing mass structural poverty (headcount index) in the State can be reduced. To improve the living conditions of the people of the State, inter-district disparity in the levels of living of the people should be reduced to the minimum level and for this the government should give more emphasis for the development of backward districts. Finally, the government should take necessary and appropriate steps for the better performance of the welfare activities like EAS, PDS, ICDS and MDM, so that the living conditions of the people can be improved.

It is to be noted that attacking poverty requires actions beyond the economic domain. For this, the World Bank in its latest *World Development Report* (2000/2001) has suggested three pronged measures for attacking poverty in developing countries including India and her poverty centred regions. These measures seek to achieve the following:

(a) *Promoting opportunity*: This seeks to expand economic opportunities for poor people by stimulating overall growth and by building up their assets and increasing the returns on these assets, through a combination of market and non-market actions;

(b) *Facilitating empowerment*: Under this, the governments of the poor countries are to make state institutions more accountable and responsible to poor people by strengthening the participation of poor people in political process and local decision making. This can be achieved only by removing the social barriers that result from distinctions of gender, ethnicity, race and social status; and

(c) *Enhancing security*: This can be achieved by reducing poor people's vulnerability to ill health, economic shocks, policy-induced dislocations, natural disasters, crime and violence as well as helping them to cope with adverse shocks when they occur.

For removing poverty and improving standard of living of poor in the State, the policy prescriptions as suggested by World Bank appear to have greater relevance today than what were discussed in yesteryears.

## REFERENCES


Allaoua, Z., *et al.* (1997). *India—Achievements and Challenges in Reducing Poverty*, The World Bank, Washington, D.C.

Behera, M. and A.K. Mitra (1996). 'The Standard of Living in India: An Attempt towards Inter-Regional Study', *Indian Journal of Regional Science*, Vol. XXXVIII, No. 2.

*Economic Survey 2000-2001.* Directorate of Economics and Statistics, Planning and Co-ordination Department, Government of Orissa (2001).

*Economic Survey 2001-2002.* Directorate of Economics and Statistics, Planning and Co-ordination Department, Government of Orissa (2002).

EPW Research Foundation (1993). 'Poverty Levels in India: Norms, Estimates and Trends', *Economic and Political Weekly*, Vol. XXVIII, No. 34, August 21.

Kar, G.C. and R.K. Meher (2001). *An Evaluation of Anti-poverty Programmes in Koraput District of Orissa (Mimeo)*, Nabakrushna Choudhury Centre for Development Studies, Bhubaneswar.

Kar, G.C. and R.K. Meher (2001). *An Evaluation of Anti-poverty Programmes in Nawarangpur District of Orissa (Mimeo)*, Nabakrushna Choudhury Centre for Development Studies, Bhubaneswar.

Kar, G.C. *Poverty and Human Development: An Enquiry into the Causes of Rural Poverty in Orissa*, Deptt. of A. and A. Economics, Utkal University, Bhubaneswar *(Mimeo)*.

Khan, M.H. (2001). *Rural Poverty in Developing Countries—Implications for Public Policy*, International Monetary Fund, Washington D.C., March.

Lal, D. (1999). *Unfinished Business: India in the World Economy*, Oxford University Press, Oxford.

Lal, D. and H. Myint (1996). *The Political Economy of Poverty, Equity and Growth—A Comparative Study*, Clarendon Press, Oxford.

Misra, S.N. and M. Behera (2000). *A Comparative Study of Nutritional Support to Primary Education (Mid-day Meals Scheme) in Orissa and*

*Tamil Nadu*, Nabakrushna Choudhury Centre for Development Studies, Bhubaneswar.

Misra, S.N. and M. Behera (2000). *An Evaluation of Anti-poverty Programmes in Mayurbhanj District of Orissa (Mimeo)*, Nabakrushna Choudhury Centre for Development Studies, Bhubaneswar.

Misra, S.N. and S. Meher (1997). *Freedom from Hunger: A Study of Begunia Block in Khurda District, Orissa (Mimeo)*, Nabakrushna Choudhury Centre for Development Studies, Bhubaneswar.

Panda, M. (2000). 'Changing Poverty Scenario in Orissa', *Paper presented in the Seminar on 'Social Development Research in Orissa'*, Nabakrushna Choudhury Centre for Development Studies, Bhubaneswar, March.

Reddy, P.H. (1977). 'Educational Development in India: Comparison by Taxonomic Method', *Social Change*, 7/1, March.

Samal, K.C. and D. Jena (1998). *Freedom from Hunger: A Study of Laikera Block (Mimeo)*, Nabakrushna Choudhury Centre for Development Studies, Bhubaneswar.

Shankar, K. (1997). 'Revamped Public Distribution System—Who Benefits and How Much?' *Economic and Political Weekly*, Vol. XXXII, No. 13.

Tendulkar, S.D. and L.R. Jain (1995). 'Economic Growth and Equity: India 1970-71 to 1988-89', *Indian Economic Review*, Vol. XXX, No. 1.

Vaidyanathan, A. (2001). 'Poverty and Development Policy', *Economic and Political Weekly*, Vol. XXXVI, No. 21, May 26-June 1.

World Development Report (2000/2001), *Attacking Poverty,* Oxford University Press, Delhi. In this chapter in-detail analyses of causes, nature and types of poverty by using poverty related indicators have been done.

# 2

# Jharkhand

DR. C. ASHOKVARDHAN, *IAS*

The process of development is multidimensional. It connotes economic growth, social change and the transformation of society. It involves a measure of ends and means sustained by a social philosophy and economic programmes. It has been characterized as 'modernization by design'.

Development administration in the tribal context of the country is an exceedingly complex enterprise involving correct diagnosis of problems, setting right priorities, planning action programmes, mobilizing adequate resources, creating new organizations and improving the capacity of the existing ones. It further involves implementing programmes and projects within a definite time-frame through requisite administrative infrastructure. The tribal population, has, by and large, been characterized by its ecological and social isolation. For centuries the tribal people have been confined to hills, to forests and to villages and hamlets more or less untouched by the wheels of modernization. All this, in turn, has accorded to them, in spite of wide cultural variations, a common destiny in the Indian society. The biggest question mark has been their integration into the wider social, economic and political systems.

The tribal economy is largely self-sufficient, unstructured and non-specialized. The situation, nonetheless, has undergone some change with the onset of new developments in the tribal region. Industrial and mining initiatives in some tribal regions aim primarily at tapping immense natural resources. Intensive development programmes have been taken up almost universally, with varied results. Hence, the level of tribal economy is quite uneven. On the one extreme, there are tribal communities which are at the food-gathering and hunting stage whereas on the other extreme, they have become rather indistinguishable from the modern agricultural and industrial societies. Similarly, varying levels of educational status have come to the fore. Some of these communities, particularly in the North-East India are at par with the general educational levels in the country, but on the other end, there are communities which are still at a pre-literate stage.[1]

There are in all 427 tribal communities all over India. These communities live in ecologically marginal areas of the country and belong to different races, languages and levels of socio-economic and cultural integration. Considering the general features of their eco-system, traditional economy, supernatural beliefs and practices and recent influences, the tribes of India may be classified into six cultural types. These are: (1) forest-hunting type, (2) primitive hill cultivation type, (3) plain agriculture type, (4) simple artisan type, (5) cattle-herder type, and (6) industrial-urban worker type. Each type of tribes has developed a distinct style of life which could be best understood in the context of nature-man-spirit complex.[2]

Indigenous human populations in most parts of the world have been subjected to various kinds of threat, sometimes even endangering their very existence. They are being constantly pushed out of their resources as well as livelihood. On the plea of integration and extension of welfare measures such programmes are implemented that appear to lead to their cultural disintegration, often threatening their biological survival.[3]

## SOCIAL ORGANIZATION

The traditional three-tier hierarchy applies only to the caste society. It does not apply to the tribal society in the tribal regions of middle India. The model is much less applicable to the tribes of north-east India which remain outside the *Varna-Jati* based hierarchic Hinduism. Some of them appear to be closer to another great tradition, namely, the Buddhist, which does not subscribe to the notion of 'purity and pollution' in this part of the country.[4]

The tribals have their own notions of hierarchy and perception of status in relation to themselves and others. Generally they consider themselves as the authocthones, superior to all those who came later. Thus the Santal view themselves (*hor*) as superior to outsiders (*dikus*). The Munda consider themselves superior to the Oraon in Chotanagpur. In Madhya Pradesh, the Gond, especially the Raj Gond consider themselves superior to other sections of Gonds and to the other tribes of the region. In Manipur, the Meitei (including the Brahman and Kshatriya) occupy a higher position, with the Loi coming in the middle followed by Thanga and Yaithibi. The hill tribes are considered lower than the Meitei. In Meghalaya, the Garo, Khasi and Jaintia considered themselves the best people. The Angami, Ao and Sema in Nagaland perceive themselves as superior to the rest of the Naga tribes. In Arunachal Pradesh, the typical relationship between the Sulung community and the Bangi (as well as the Nishi, Aka and Miji) had once been termed as a 'slave-master' relationship. In Sikkim, the Bhotia being the community of the erstwhile rulers, consider themselves superior to the Lepcha and the immigrant Nepalis.[5]

There is now the rise of hierarchy and differentiation in tribal societies which used to be relatively egalitarian. The hierarchy among artisan groups like weavers, oil pressers, fishermen etc. is based on the control of technology and resources. Those divisions which consist of manufacturers and producers are placed lower than those who control the resources and sell the products.

## THE SUB-NATIONAL MOVEMENT IN JHARKHAND

Historically, the tribals of Jharkhand have remained backward mainly on account of two reasons—their long isolation from the mainstream society and their persistent exploitation by the non-tribals especially the Zamindars, the moneylenders, contractors and others who have been grabbing their lands. Some of the noteworthy tribal uprisings of the eighteenth and nineteenth centuries are the Mal Paharia uprising in 1772, the mutiny of the Hos of Singhbhum in 1831, the Khond uprisings in 1846 and the Santal rebellion of 1855. These uprisings were ruthlessly crushed by the British Government. The local Zamindars who acted as the agents of the British Government also helped the Government in crushing those uprisings.

When India attained Independence and the Constitution of India was enforced, special care was taken to ameliorate the conditions of the tribals and other backward communities. To help the proper and smooth implementation of the Directive Principles of State Policy contained in Article 46, suitable provisions have been made in the fifth and sixth schedules to the Constitution.[6]

The sub-national movement in Jharkhand is a good example where the ascriptive features of tribal heritage and culture have combined with the poor development profile of the region, with a view to forging a politically significant ethnic identity. The movement began with the desire for the betterment of the tribal people and had a significant anti-non-tribal component. However, the demographic reality of the region (only about a quarter of the total population today is of tribal origin) forced the leaders to modify the rules of exclusion. Consequently, all people settled in the region came to be included within the definition of a Jharkhandi.[7]

The socio-economic condition of most of the tribals in Jharkhand is poor, with low literacy rates and employment levels. Most tribal agriculturists have been engaged in subsistence agriculture. Since the colonial period, therefore, there has been a tradition of seasonal economic migration of tribals as unskilled labourers to the tea gardens of Assam and to fields and construction projects in other parts of India. In the last few decades, growing industrialization in the Jharkhand region has led them to unskilled jobs in the industries and mines of the region.[8]

## TRIBAL ECONOMY IN JHARKHAND

**Forest Correlates:** The bulk of the tribal communities in the country were forest dwellers. They evolved a way of life which on the one hand is woven around the forest ecology and on the other, ensured that the forest was protected against the depredations of man and nature. The symbiotic relationship suffered a setback during the British rule when the forest was looked upon only as a source of maximization of profit and not a vital link between human habitat and the larger environment.

In Jharkhand, the tribals dig out a variety of roots varying in depths from 1 to 7 feet. The roots include—Haser, Kulu, Bawala, Kundari, Pathal, Kohara, etc. The varieties of Haser are: Kukuch, Bapta, Dura, Jaranga, Archota Petai, Sanga, Bariyang, Hasses, etc. The tribals also collect a variety of edible shoots like the stalk of Kanda, Karami Sag, Gandhari Sag, Bathua Sag, etc. The tribals also eat leaves of different plants available in and around the forest. Leaves eaten by them are Saoura, Maltha, Birlak, Chuchi, Purlak, Pinder, Muchara, Dhai, Janaru, Hisa, Pathan, Chhata, etc. The edible flowers which tribals in Jharkhand collect are Dhawai, Murup, Koinar, Kehanar, Yarm, Nayor and Sidha. The edible fruits which the tribals collect from the forest are Jamun, Mahua, Bair, Katahal, Khekhasa, Kạhua, Sarai, Udra, Tiril, Piyar, Pithor, Amla, Imali, Marleth, Janu, Karundh, Sajom, Kunda, etc. The tribals collect various types of mushroom too which are Morang, Simdali, Kanar, Badho, Talros, Sarjan, Lawa, Moth, Mochi, Paltera Phulkhel, etc. Minor forest produce, which are collected for sale in the local markets or for using as folk medicine, include, seeds of Imali, Babul, Jamun, Mahua, Harre, Bahera, Kahua, Kendu, Siris, Lac, honey and wax.[9]

**Rope-Making:** Rope-making is an important economic activity of the tribals in Jharkhand. During off-season they prepare rope with different types of barks of trees, creepers and plants. While collecting food materials and other minor forest produce, they also collect rope fibres like Mahulain, Sisir, Udal, Chelnet, Larparagi, Bari, Dandekheshara, Hisa, Telhal, etc. They also prepare different kinds of baskets, brooms and mats from bamboo, khajur and tar.

**Domestication of Animals:** The tribals domesticate animals for agricultural purposes and for eating flesh and taking milk. They also rear animals for getting cash by selling them in the market. This way they rear goat. They also rear hen, cocks, ducks, etc.

**Land Uses in Jharkhand:** Each family has got some *bari land* in front of the house. In the bari land, vegetables are grown. The vegetables grown in the bari land are gourd, pumpkin, gongara, jhingi, ladies finger, brinjal, chilly, potato, tomato, garlic, coriander, etc. Coarse variety of grains are sown along *hilly slopes*. The grains like kodo and kurathi are sown in such plots. The *tanr lands* have less capacity to preserve water, for a longer period. The surface of such lands becomes dry soon. The crops sown in tanr lands are kodo, kurathi, til, marua, bajara, seraha, sathe, maize, etc. The *Don land* is considered as the best variety of land. This land has greater capacity of preserving water. Good varieties of paddy are sown in such fields. Rabi crops like khesari, gram, masuri are cultivated in some plots of the Don land. Wheat too is sown in some plots where water for irrigation is easily available.

**Means of Irrigation:** There are no assured means of irrigation. The villagers depend upon rainfall for the purpose. Rain water is stored in Don land. Ponds and Nalas are also used for irrigation purposes.

**Implements of Cultivation:** The implements used for cultivation in Jharkhand are Hal, Juath, Lagana, Haris, Henga, Kudal, Khanti, Hansua, Barketa, etc. which are prepared from the woods available in the forest. Iron implements like karvar, phar, kudal, khanti, hansua, etc. are also used in cultivation.

**Elementary Education in Jharkhand:** For a tribal family, sending their children to a school is essentially a matter of economics and entails dislocation in the traditional pattern of division of labour. Girls render help to their mothers at home. During the agricultural season, boys work in the fields with their parents. In other seasons, they are busy in collecting minor forest produce and firewood, grazing goats and cattle, watching the crops, bringing water, hunting and fishing. Obviously many parents cannot afford to send their children to school.[10]

In the tribal belt of Jharkhand, the credit for the progress of education goes mainly to the missionaries. The early history of educational movement in Chotanagpur and Santal Parganas is the movement launched by the Christian missionaries. The question of educating the people of this area attracted the early attention of the British Government of India, because the Government felt that the tribals were much oppressed by the landlords, the moneylenders and the non-tribals and they wanted someone to help them out of their difficulties.[11]

## STUDY BY THE IAS PROBATIONERS

The present socio-economic profile of Jharkhand is based upon the following socio-economic studies made by IAS probationers from time to time. The probationers were given village assignments and their reports are based upon data generated by structured schedules as well as upon interactions and observations. The study encompasses both the social system and the process and levels of economic development. The reports also carry case studies in their fold.

**List of Trainees and Area Studied**

| Sl. No. | Name of the Officer Trainee | Batch | Village | Block | District |
|---|---|---|---|---|---|
| 1. | Neerja | 1993 | Malhan Bhuiadih | Tamar | Ranchi |
| 2. | N. Vijaya Lakshmi | 1995 | Mahil | Murhu | Ranchi |
| 3. | Rahul Singh | 1996 | Birkera | – | Gumla |
| 4. | K. Senthil Kumar | 1996 | Charai | Chaibasa | West Singh-bhum |
| 5. | M.R. Meena | 1996 | Nichitpur | Baghmara | Dhanbad |
| 6. | Sunil Kumar Barnwal | 1997 | Barwatoli and Rangamati | – | Ranchi |
| 7. | Santosh Kumar Mall | 1997 | Pratap Pur | Jamua | Giridih |
| 8. | Pankaj Kumar | 1997 | Nakti | Dumka | Dumka |
| 9. | Narmdeshwar Lall | 1998 | – | Nirsa | Dhanbad |
| 10. | Kamal Kishore Soan | – | – | Dumariya | East Singhbhum |

## SOCIAL SYSTEM AND CULTURAL PRACTICES

In village Mahil (Block Murhu), District Ranchi though the tribal and non-tribal cultures are quite different, due to long years of co-existence, there seems to be an overlapping between these two cultures. The difference between the tribal and non-tribal cultures was very thin and all the festivals of the tribals were observed by the non-tribals also, and *vice versa*. But there is a difference in their respective attitudes towards life. Tribal people generally do not plan for the future. Whatever they get today, they spend it and keep happy and the day ends with drinking *hadia* (rice beer). Addiction to *hadia* is found to be a major problem in the entire tribal belt. Non-tribals especially OBCs like Mahtos are hard workers and they are the cultivating class. The OBCs prayed to their own gods which were the traditional Hindu gods. The tribals had their own gods. They had a place called '*Sarna*' which was the place of tribal worship.

The marriage rites of the tribals were quite different from that of the non-tribals but then the tribals had adopted many practices of the non-tribal marriage. Music and dances are also different but the tribals have adopted the non-tribal ways of dance. The traditional dance is seen only during auspicious occasions and on other days a mixed type of tribal and non-tribal dance is resorted. There is no untouchability in the village and that everybody is treated on equal terms. When these questions were asked directly to the *dalits* in the group, they said that they were suffering due to unemployment and landlessness, rather than due to their social position in the society. It was noticed that opportunities while providing wage employment and agricultural labour were not denied just because they belonged to the Scheduled Castes.

In village Rangamati (Tolas: Barwatoli and Rangamati), District Ranchi, the social system and cultural practices in the two tolas—Rangamati and Barwatoli, are quite different. This is mainly due to the reason that castes in the two tolas are different. Barwatoli is purely a Bedia tribe tola while Rangamati has mixed Munda and Anyaks (Scheduled Caste). Therefore, the religion in Barwatoli is only 'Sarna' while in Rangamati both 'Sarna' and 'Hindu' religions are being followed. Again, the festivals of Sarna and Hindu religions are different. Scheduled Tribes in both tolas follow 'Sarna' religion and celebrate festivals like Karma Manda, Sarhul, etc. But now tribals also celebrate the Hindu festivals like Holi. Scheduled Castes in Rangamati celebrate all Hindu festivals. There is no case of Christianity in any of the tolas.

Tribals in all their festivals, normally, consume alcohol. This was accepted by most of the villagers in Rangamati. Even some were found drunk during the present survey when there was no festival. But this is no longer true to Barwatoli. In normal days, it is difficult to find anyone drunk. Sometimes if any guest (*Mehman*) comes to the village, *hadia* is consumed to celebrate. In festivals, the incidence of alcohol has reduced drastically and people do not consume it publicly. This change is attributed solely to the Ram Krishna Mission.

## IMPACT OF THE RAM KRISHNA MISSION

The impact of the NGO, the R.K. Mission, on the social system and cultural practices has been conspicuous. In Barwatoli, the society is very homogenous and no social tension due to the caste system existed. But the society did not work together for development. The NGO had been able to inculcate cooperation among the people. The bad habit of alcohol has been almost removed. Even the up-keep of houses and places had changed. Almost every house had a poster of maintaining cleanliness, keeping water covered etc. in their language 'Kurmali-Nagpuria'. The food habits have changed drastically. They started eating '*Roti*' only after persuasion by the R.K. Mission. Wheat was not grown earlier. Rice was the only food. Earlier they did not know cooking. In fact, they saw milk for the first time only five years back. Now there are cows in the village and villagers, besides consuming milk, sell it to the Ranchi Dairy. Earlier only oxen and male buffaloes use to be domesticated mainly for the purpose of agriculture. Now villagers are doing horticulture also. In part of their raiyati land they are growing mango, litchi, guava, etc. These are being done on the direction of the R.K. Mission and good quality seeds are being provided by them. Earlier piggery was the only source of additional income. But now, besides piggery, goatery and poultry pursuits too, have increased.

Distinct impact can be seen on the awareness of the villagers about development and education. Non-formal education in the form of night school has been a success. This is unique to the R.K. Mission, in which as it gets dark the kids from different hamlets of Barwatoli come in groups shouting slogans like '*Anpadh rahna pap hai*' (it is sin to be illiterate) and '*Bachchon ko school bhejo, school bhejo-school bhejo*' (send the children to school). Then in the night school, they will put '*dari*' themselves and take slate and pencil from the wardrobe. The teachers are from the village who are themselves in class IX and X and live in the community centre itself where the night school is run.

The effect can also be seen on the women folk but not to the extent expected. The Mahila Mandal, which was started at the initiative of the R.K. Mission, worked well. All women pooled one fist of rice everyday and thus pooled enough revolving fund. Earlier, they used to meet weekly but now-a-days due to internal bickering the Mandal is not meeting regularly. But still the conditions of women in Barwatoli are much better than that in Rangamati. Due to the absence of alcohol in Barwatoli, the family tension has reduced. Crime against women is almost nil. This is not due to the presence of the R.K. Mission, but due to inherent homogeneity of the tribal society.

Society in Rangamati is very different. Here the women take up all responsibility of work in the village while men go to Ranchi for daily wage labour. Gender discrimination is visible. When men come from Ranchi after a day's hard work, they are very tired and resort to alcohol for relaxation. Many a time they return home drunk. This habit leads to family tension and also crime against women. Women are beaten up sometimes. Awareness in society about education and development is very less. Only a sarpanch, who is graduate of his own time, takes interest in education as well as development. But he does not get support from anyone else.

The village Nakti (District Dumka) has a mixed population of tribal Hindus, tribal Christians, Scheduled Castes and Backward Castes. The Christian tribals get married in the church and subsequently they celebrate the marriage as per the tribal culture since most of their relatives were not converted into Christianity. The most important festival of the tribals is 'Bandhana', which is celebrated in February. They consume local '*Hadia*' and dance with their traditional bows and arrows, dhol etc. Females also take part in dancing. Hunting is no longer resorted to. Besides being fond of music and dance the tribals also have a good aesthetic sense. Their houses are clean and artistically designed with prominent colour patterns. They speak their own language called Santhali. The village was highly influenced by missionary activities. Out of 195 tribals, 69 were converted into Christianity. They were more educated and well off than the Hindu tribals. They were quite active in taking advantage of the Government sponsored schemes. They have almost given up alcohol. Many tribal girls were seen unmarried even at the age of 30 years.

## DEMOGRAPHY

In village Nichitpur (Block Baghmara), District Dhanbad the population has increased steadily from 1710 in 1981 to 2189 in 1991.

**Table 2.1:** Population Classification (1991 Census)—Religion-wise

| *Sl. No.* | *Religion* | *Number* | *Per cent* |
|---|---|---|---|
| 1. | Hindu | 1963 | 90 |
| 2. | Muslim | 226 | 10 |
| 3. | Christian | – | – |
| 4. | Sikh | – | – |
| 5. | Others | – | – |
| | **Total** | **2189** | **100** |

**Table 2.2:** Population Caste-wise

| *Sl No.* | *Caste* | *Number* | *Per cent* |
|---|---|---|---|
| 1. | SC | 679 | 31.01 |
| 2. | ST | 109 | 4.98 |
| 3. | OBC | 1377 | 62.90 |
| 4. | Others | 24 | 1.10 |
| | Total | 2189 | 99.99 |

**Table 2.3:** Occupation-wise

| Sl. No. | Occupation | Number | Per cent |
|---|---|---|---|
| 1. | Agriculture | 640 | 29.23 |
| 2. | Service | 225 | 10.28 |
| 3. | Wage Employment | 950 | 43.40 |
| 4. | Rural Artisan | 185 | 8.45 |
| 5. | Others | 189 | 8.65 |
| | **Total** | **2189** | |

**Table 2.4:** Population Characteristics

| | | |
|---|---|---|
| 1. | Population | 2189 |
| 2. | Area | 567.39 Acres |
| 3. | No. of occupied residential houses | 334 |
| 4. | No. of households | 334 |
| 5. | Population | Male: 1118; Female: 1071 |
| 6. | SC | 679 |
| 7. | ST | 109 |
| 8. | Literates | Male: 559; Female: 428 |

There has been a steady rise in the population of Nichitpur between the last two censuses. Between 1981 and 1991 the population increased by 21.88 per cent. Therefore, there has also been an increase in the rate of population growth. The absence of an effective family planning programme in the area is responsible for the upsurge. Most people in Nichitpur seemed wary of family planning. Primarily because even today there is no certainty that children will survive to be adults. Several stories were narrated to this effect. Most of the people speak Khortha and Hindi.

The total population of village Charai (Block Chaibasa), District West Singhbhum is 395, according to the 1991 census. Male counts 203 and female counts 192. This indicates the poor sex ratio (946 per thousand male) of the village. This is one of the non-tribal predominant areas. The backward class constitutes 80 per cent of the population. The following table shows the caste-wise break up:

**Table 2.5:** Caste-wise Break up of Population

| Caste | Number | Per cent |
|---|---|---|
| SC | 57 | 14 |
| ST | 27 | 06 |
| OBC and others | 311 | 80 |
| **Total** | **395** | **100** |

As far as the head of the family is concerned, the male partner heads almost all families. Out of the 40 households surveyed, a female headed a house, since her husband had expired. Even though these areas do not sense the smell of urbanization, most of the families are nuclear in nature. As per survey it is 77.5 per cent, whereas the joint family constitutes only 22.5 per cent. The main reason for the larger number of nuclear families could be derived from the tribal culture. In tribal families, it is mandatory that once a person attains marriageable age he/she should get married and set up a separate house. The elder people of the tribal community encourage nuclear rather than joint families.

People do not adopt any temporary/permanent birth control methods. This could be corroborated by the following information. About 45 per cent of the households have 5-7 members per family. So we end up with the vicious circle involving high birth rate, higher population and less productive groups. This greatly affects the overall development of the society.

In village Mahil (Block Murhu), District Ranchi, the following demographic figures are worth noting:

**Table 2.6:** Demography of Village Mahil

| *Year* | *Male* | *Female* | *Total* | *Increase* |
|---|---|---|---|---|
| 1991 | 534 | 531 | 1085 | 9.8% |
| 1981 | 512 | 476 | 988 | |

From the figures above it is quite evident that there has been a shift in the male-female ratio and that the per cent of increase in the population has remained constant. From a male/female ratio of 51.82 : 48.1 it has gone to 51 : 48.9. The change in ratio has been very small but the change in ratio may indicate change in social values or change in the health standards of the girl child. The increase in the population being so marginal also points out the fact that the level of awareness of a planned family has increased and that the pressure on the natural resources of the village has not changed since the last 10 years.

The distribution of the age of male and female is almost the same. The distribution of age in the age group 25-29, 30-34 is almost the same, male being 12.82 per cent, 6.41 per cent and female being 13.11 per cent and 8.2 per cent respectively.

An interesting point to note regarding the life span is that there are no women above the age of 60 whereas there are 2 men in the sample in the age group of 60. It shows that the life expectancy of men is greater than that of women.

The distribution of households, across the village and their caste composition is as below:

**Table 2.7:** Distribution of households Caste-wise

| Sl. No. | Name of the Hamlet | No. of Households | Main Caste |
|---|---|---|---|
| 1. | Mahit Khas | 27 | Manjih/Teli/Mahat/Uraon/Munda |
| 2. | Usawr Toli | 18 | Uraon/Munda |
| 3. | Tangara Toli | 15 | Paike/Lohar/Hazam |
| 4. | Sake Toli | 20 | Munda |
| 5. | Jam Toli | 15 | Munda/Teli/Mahto |
| 6. | Manjih Toli | 27 | Manjih |
| 7. | Lauw Toli | 25 | Munda/Lohar/Hazam |
| 8. | Harijan Toli | 10 | Ghasi |
| | **Total** | **157** | |

Village Malhan Bhuiadih (Block Tamar), District Ranchi is a Khunt-Katti village of Baburamdih Panchayat of the Tamar Block of Ranchi District. This village is located aside the National Highway No. 33 at a distance of 14 km from the block headquarters. The distance from the district headquarter of Ranchi is 70 km. Jamshedpur is further 60 km east.

Malhan Bhuiadih village consists of 10 scattered hamlets, namely:

1. Malhan Bhuiadih
2. Gathar Tanp
3. Gokul Nagar
4. Sinduwardih
5. Baburamdih
6. Nawagarh
7. Dwarsini
8. Sarna Toli
9. Jaidbera
10. Bhussudih

According to the 1991 census, the total population of Malhan Bhuiadih village is 2262 comprising 1179 males and 1083 females. The sex ratio of the village is 919. The sex ratio among the Scheduled Tribes is 864 and 1500 among Scheduled Castes. Among other castes of the village, it is 925.

**Table 2.8:** Population of Malhan Bhuiadih, 1991

| *Caste/Tribe* | *Males* | *Females* | *Total* | *Sex Ratio* | *No. of Families* |
|---|---|---|---|---|---|
| Scheduled Tribe | 154 | 133 | 287 | 864 | 40 |
| Scheduled Caste | 4 | 6 | 10 | 1500 | 2 |
| Others | 1021 | 944 | 1965 | 925 | 325 |
| **Total** | **1179** | **1083** | **2262** | **919** | **367** |

*Source*: Census of India, 1991, NIC NET.

A multiplicity of castes inhabit the village with the Kurmis being the dominant caste. The castes and tribes like Kurmi, Oraon (ST), Ahir, Bhogata, Munda (ST), Lohra (ST), Nai, Bania, Swansi (SC), Machhua (SC), Shrawak Manjhi, Brahmin, Muslim (Ansari), reside here.

The population of the village Pratap Pur (Block Jamua), District Giridih as on the survey date, was 1122; males being 553 and females 569. In 1991, the total population was 901, with 441 males and 460 females. The number of the households in the village was 155 and there were four tolas in all. The SCs had a separate tola. Even among them, the released bonded labourers were living in a separate colony. There were tribals, too, in the village.

The village Nakti is located at a distance of 6 km from the Dumka town (District Dumka) and 3 km from the Dumka block on the Dumka-Pakur road. The village has a predominant SC/ST population. The population of the village as on the day of survey stood at 550. The village is divided into 4 tolas earmarked on the basis of caste.

## LAND USE PATTERN

The following is the Land Use Pattern of village Nichitpur (Block Baghmara), District Dhanbad:

The total area of the village is 567.39 acres. The soil is sandy loam. The following are the statistics regarding the nature and classification of land and its area.

**Table 2.9:** Land Use Pattern of Village Nichitpur, District Dhanbad

| *Sl. No.* | *Land Details* | *Area (in acres)* |
|---|---|---|
| A. | Land Type | |
| | 1. Land for cultivation | 164.5 |
| | 2. Land under forest cover | 0.0 |
| | 3. Fallow land | 103.0 |
| | 4. Pasture and grazing land | 66.8 |
| | 5. Waste land | 201.0 |
| | 6. Land for Homestead | 31.7 |
| | 7. Net sown area | 164.5 |
| | 8. Community land | 0.0 |
| | 9. Miscellaneous | 0.0 |
| B. | Total land area irrigated | 12.4 |
| C. | Land Area (under) | |
| | 1. Ownership cultivation | 153.2 |
| | 2. Tenancy | 11 |
| D. | Area under cultivation | |
| | 1. One crop | 164.5 |
| | 2. Two crops | > 8 |
| | 3. Multi-crops | > 4.4 |

There is no source of irrigation in Nichitpur village except a few shallow wells and a pond. There is no deep tube well in the village. Because of coal bearing area the water table is very high. The success and failure of crops depend on rainfall. Land adjacent to the coal bearing area is going for more than Rs. 2 lakh per acre.

The following is a table of the area under various crops:

**Table 2.10:** Land Use Pattern of Village Nichitpur

| *Sl. No.* | *Landholdings (Crops)* | *Area (Acre)* |
|---|---|---|
| A. | Kharif crops | |
| | 1. Paddy (Rice) | 150.0 |
| | 2. Maize | 5.0 |
| | 3. Vegetables | 10.0 |
| B. | Rabi crops | |
| | 1. Wheat | 5.0 |
| | 2. Vegetables | 8.0 |

There was no data with reference to crops at Block and Circle Office. Therefore, a comprehensive study was not possible.

**Table 2.11:** Distribution of Land Ownership (Household-wise)

| *Sl. No.* | *Area* | *No. of Landowners* |
|---|---|---|
| 1. | Landless | Nil |
| 2. | < 1 acre | 15 |
| 3. | 1-3 acres | 108 |
| 4. | 3-5 acres | 129 |
| 5. | 5-10 acres | 45 |
| 6. | 10-20 acres | 9 |
| 7. | > 20 acres | Nil |

**Table 2.12:** Distribution of Operational Holding

| *Sl. No.* | *Area (Acre)* | *Holdings* |
|---|---|---|
| 1. | < 1 acre | 5 |
| 2. | 1-3 acres | 52 |
| 3. | 3-5 acres | 66 |
| 4. | 5-10 acres | 29 |
| 5. | 10-20 acres | 4 |
| 6. | > 20 acres | 0 |

It is clear from the above tables that the vast majority of lardholdings are varying in between 3-5 acres in area. But the numbers inthe larger acreage categories decline sharply. In the last category of more than 20 acres, not even a single farmer was available. It is not surprising, therefore, that the instance of sharecropping is negligible. The number of settlement cases recorded in Nichitpur tolas is 12. All settlees are cultivating land.

In this area the average rainfall is 1063.79 mm/year. Monsoon, late May to September, is the main rainy season. Some showers are also experienced in December and January. During the monsoon, winter and early spring the water table is high. But it shrinks rapidly with the onset of summer. The ponds that were overflowing their banks in November are half empty by March and dry by May.

Almost 90 per cent of the cultivable land bears one crop in a year whereas some lands also bear two crops. Table 2.13 shows the cultivation seasons and the crops cultivated therein.

**Table 2.13:** Cultivation Seasons and Crops Cultivated

| *Sl. No.* | *Crops* | | *Month of Sowing* | *Month of Harvesting* |
|---|---|---|---|---|
| 1. | Paddy | | May-June | November-December |
| 2. | Maize | | June-July | September-October |
| 3. | Vegetables | (a) | May-June | September-October |
| | | (b) | January-February | April-May |

**Table 2.14:** Cropping Pattern of Major Crops

| *Sl. No.* | *Crops* | *Area under Cultivation* | *Area under Irrigation* | *Source of Irrigation* |
|---|---|---|---|---|
| *Kharif Crops* | | | | |
| 1. | Paddy | 150 acres | Rainfed | — |
| 2. | Maize | 15-20 acres | Rainfed | — |
| 3. | Vegetable | 5-10 acres | Rainfed | — |
| *Rabi Crops* | | | | |
| 1. | Vegetables | 5-8 acres | All | Wells, ponds |
| 2. | Wheat | 8-10 acres | All | Wells, ponds |

There is no major change in agricultural practices in Nichitpur village. Most of the farmers are traditional. They are growing paddy and maize. Moreover, there is good scope of vegetable crops. There is lack of irrigation facility.

The traditional plough is still widely used. Renting it for the day costs Rs. 50 and about half an acre can be ploughed in one day. The bullocks are not of very good quality; though hybrid breeds have made an appearance. There are no tractors and power tillers in the village.

Some other implements used by the farmers are sprayers and dusters. There are 40 animal carts and 10 diesel pumpsets in the village. Diesel pumpsets have proliferated because the village does not have electric pumpsets.

Cattle dung is collected in heaps near the house, next to which the cattle are tied. Small children are entrusted with the task of collecting dung from the fields. Only about 45 per cent of the dung is used as manure while the rest is used as fuel for plastering the mud walls and so on. Cattle dung comprises no more than 20 per cent of the total fertilizer used. The villagers seem to be unaware of the potential of green manure. They also fear the failure of the second crop.

Among the chemical fertilizers the farmers hardly use any fertilizers except urea. They obtain it from the open market. Fertilizer is generally used in paddy and vegetable crops. The HYV seeds that the farmers of Nichitpur use are those supplied only by the National Seeds Corporation through dealers.

As noted earlier, most of the farmers are traditional and they are growing local varieties. Hardly they use NSC seeds. However, the scope for development is considerable and depends on vigorous extension work lacking at present. The villagers are very willing to adopt new techniques if their superiority over traditional methods is potentially explained and clearly demonstrated.

Common crop pests are rice hispa, stem borer and leaf curling. Insecticides are widely used by almost everyone. For rice and vegetables, insecticides are used according to need.

**Table 2.15:** Production of Food Grains in Nichitpur Village

| *Sl. No.* | *Crop* | *Average Yield (per acre) Qt.* | *Average Cost (per acre)* | *Average Return (per acre)* |
|---|---|---|---|---|
| 1. | Paddy (HYV) | 30-35 | 3000 | 4000-4500 |
| 2. | Paddy local | 20-22 | 2000-2500 | 3000-3500 |
| 3. | Maize | 25-30 | 2000 | 3000 |
| 4. | Wheat | 30-32 | 2500 | 8000 |

A farmer with a family of five can grow enough paddy to feed it if he raises crops in two acres of land. Most of the farmers grow enough paddy for themselves. Many of them also grow some vegetables. The quantity of pulses and oilseeds produced in the village is certainly not sufficient. No cash crop is grown in Nichitpur village.

Irrigation in Nichitpur is provided mainly by shallow tube-wells, wells and ponds. Most of the crops are grown in Kharif seasons. All the crops are rainfed in nature. Shallow tube-wells and wells have proliferated in the last few years and are a dependable source of irrigation water. There are 5-6 shallow tube-wells and wells in Nichitpur. They are run by diesel pumpsets. Although there are 3 ponds in the village, they are not considered as an irrigation source. They are rainfed and provide water in the winter months for brief periods. By March, most ponds are half empty, by May, they are dry.

The following table shows the land use pattern of village Charai (Block Chaibasa), District West Singhbhum:

**Table 2.16:** Land Use Pattern of Village Charai (Block Chaibasa), District West Singhbhum

| *Sl. No.* | *Land Usage* | *Area (acres)* |
|---|---|---|
| 1. | Land for cultivation | 387.40 |
| 2. | Land under forest cover | Nil |
| 3. | Fallow land | Nil |
| 4. | Pasture and grazing land | 3.45 |
| 5. | Waste land | 133.25 |
| 6. | Land of homestead | 22.56 |
| 7. | Net sown area | 387.40 |
| 8. | Community land | 7.98 |
| 9. | Miscellaneous | 52.12 |

Among the surveyed forty households, nine households do not possess any land to cultivate. However, they have own houses. Like any other part of India in this village also the land has been fragmented into pieces. Out of 40 households, twenty-three households have less than one acre. From this we could imagine the level of poverty and the importance of land which is the main source of livelihood in the rural areas. Since this village is being dominated by OBCs, they top in poverty, landlessness, etc.

**Table 2.17:** Distribution of Land Caste-wise

| *Sl. No.* | *Land (in acres)* | *SC/ST* | *OBC* | *Others* | *Total* |
|---|---|---|---|---|---|
| 1. | No land | 2 | 5 | 2 | 9 |
| 2. | 1 | 3 | 9 | 2 | 14 |
| 3. | 1-3 | 2 | 7 | 4 | 13 |
| 4. | 3-5 | 1 | 0 | 1 | 2 |
| 5. | 5-10 | 0 | 1 | 1 | 2 |

From this data we infer that about 22.5 per cent of the surveyed households are landless. It clearly shows that the degree of land reforms is at a very low level. Even though lot of surplus land is available, the government machinery is quite indifferent towards the distribution of land to the landless people. As far as the distribution of land to the landless is concerned merely two households have been vested with some amount of land. This in fact creates lot of resentment among the masses.

There is hardly any surplus produce for the market. Most of the produce is being used for the growers' own consumption. Only 2 persons out of 40 households told that they were selling their produce in the nearby weekly market in Chaibasa, the H.Q. of the district. Out of these two, one person said that the produce would be sold immediately after the harvest in order to repay the loan taken from the bank and other persons. Another person told that the produce would be sold after a gap of six months during the lean season.

However, in the winter season, near the riverbed, some people take up vegetable cultivation. This brings to them some amount of profit from the town areas like Chaibasa and Jamshedpur.

**Table 2.18:** Crops and Source of Irrigation

| *Sl. No.* | *Crop* | *Area under Cultivation* | *Area under Irrigation* | *Source of Irrigation* |
|---|---|---|---|---|
| 1. | Paddy | 348.660 | Nil | Rainfall |
| 2. | Vegetables and oil seeds | 18.740 | Nil | Rainfall |

The following land use patterns of village Mahil (Block Murhu), District Ranchi, are coming out of the survey.

Since most of the people have less amount of land, they cultivate on their own. According to the survey only three households have leased their land among which two are from the forward caste. The main reason for this is that the forward caste people are involved in some other activities, like priesthood of temples etc. The most pathetic situation in this village is that even though the land is fertile for want of irrigation facility and credit, people are not able to develop their land to the optimum level. As far as loaning by banks is concerned the fault lies with the people also. For example, some people who availed of the loan facilities have not repaid their loans so far, hence the banks are unwilling to disburse the credit facilities.

The return from the land is very poor since there is no application of scientific methods and tools and lack of irrigation adds a lot to this problem. The productivity of the land is meagre.

As far as agriculture is concerned, single cropping is done during the rainy season, under the southwest monsoon. Paddy is the only crop cultivated in this area and cultivation is solely dependent on raingod alone. Even though there is a perennial river, due to the difficulties in the topography of the land and the poor financial status of the people the technology used for agriculture is primitive. They do not even use any hybrid seed varieties, fertilizers etc. for want of credit. We may define this as 'Subsistence Agriculture'.

**Table 2.19:** Number of Households

| | |
|---|---|
| 1. Landless | Nil |
| 2. 1 acre | Nil |
| 3. 1-3 acres | 33 |
| 4. 3-5 acres | 40 |
| 5. 5-10 acres | 50 |
| 6. 10-20 acres | 25 |
| 7. 20 + | 9 |
| **Total** | **157** |

The common resources as recorded in the survey are the grazing land, community ponds and community forest. The accessibility of the villagers to these lands is common irrespective of caste and tribe. The grazing lands have become so depleted that they no longer constitute common resources. The community ponds have also become so silted that they no longer serve the common objective.

The following land use patterns of village Rangamati (Tolas Barwatoli and Rangamati), District Ranchi appear through the survey. The total area of Rangamati (137.90 hectare) is higher than that of Barwatoli (117.97 hectare). But land for cultivation is much lower in Rangamati (44.41 hectare) than in Barwatoli (65.05 hectare). Similarly, the net sown area is also lower in Rangamati (40.00 hectare) than in Barwatoli (61.16 hectare). This shows that people in Rangamati do not use the land fully. The reason pointed out was that they do not have irrigation facility. Forest cover in Rangamati (50.53 hectare) is much higher than Barwatoli (14.17 hectare) which shows that land use for agriculture is quite high in Barwatoli. In fact, the villagers in Barwatoli said that earlier there was a lot of forest cutting. It is only when the villagers decided to save the forests themselves, the forest cover has improved. Now even villagers do not cut trees and do policing of forest. Most of the forest cover is of teak trees whose leaves are used to make *Dona* and *Pattal* and sold in the market of Getalsud and Ranchi. The business of making *Dona* and *Pattal* is much more prevalent in Rangamati than in Barwatoli and mostly the women folk are involved.

Total area under irrigation in Barwatoli (27.52 hectare) is much higher as compared to Rangamati (only 0.42 hectare). The irrigation is mainly done by tanks/wells. The relatively new source of irrigation in Barwatoli is pond as it has been constructed recently. Some people use pumping sets given under the IRDP. In Rangamati, tanks/wells are the only source of irrigation. Thus it is true that Rangamati has been neglected in the process of the development of the irrigation potential.

Regarding the distribution of operational landholdings, most of the landholders in both tolas have land less than one hectare. Also, none of the landholders has land above ten hectares in Barwatoli and above 4 hectares in Rangamati.

In Barwatoli, two families which are basically outsider to the village and staying for some job, do not hold any land of their own. They are also not given any government schemes. Hence, there is only one landless household. But in Rangamati there is no landless household. Here the landless means those who do not have any land.

Soil condition of both the tolas is similar and is alluvial. But soil in Barwatoli is also *pathrili* due to lot of rock. In fact, Barwatoli is situated on the bank of the Swarnarekha river. Average rainfall is 1752.8 mm.

The whole revenue village (including both tolas) does not have a single case of land ceiling. In both the tolas, every household owns land. There is presence of tenancy in both Rangamati and Barwatoli. But the main form of tenancy is share cropping. The land under tenancy is much less compared to land under self-cultivation. The number of tenants in Barwatoli is twelve leasing in 11.87 hectare while the area under self-cultivation is 74.35 hectare. Comparatively, the number of tenants in Rangamati is only three leasing in only 0.54 hectare while the area under self-cultivation is 24.06 hectare. So there is no case of land reform. Only some government land has been settled to landless persons.

Government land as on the day of survey was 17.51 hectare being the same as in 1971. Government land has been allotted to 11 STs before 1971 totalling 0.33 hectare. Presently, most of the government land is barren. In Rangamati, the government land on the day of survey was 13.08 hectare which is less than that in 1971 (13.36 hectare). Till date, the government land has been allotted to three SCs and three STs totalling 3.89 hectare. Part of land allotment has been done before 1971.

Number of tribal households in Barwatoli is 76 and the total area of tribal land is 74.35 hectare. In the past 0.67 hectare land was alienated from the tribals by fraudulent sale in which restoration order was passed and even physical possession was given. In Rangamati, the number of tribal households is only 13 and the total area of tribal land is 16.13 hectare. Here there is no case of alienation of tribal land. There is no land consolidation in either of the tolas.

In common property resources (CPR), the main CPR is forest under the forest department and is maintained by the community and by the government. There is no encroachment on any of CPRs. Grazing/pasture land in Barwatoli is used by all and is not maintained by anyone. It is maintained only by nature. Other CPRs like water tank, fishing ponds, community centre, village deity and Kisan Seva Kendra in Barwatoli are maintained by the community and used exclusively by the village community. In Rangamati, CPRs are only forest and Vachanalaya.

Land use and landholding patterns of village Pratap Pur (Block Jamua), District Giridih are as follows:

**Table 2.20:** Land use and landholding patterns of village Pratap Pur (Block Jamua), District Giridih

| *Usage* | *Area* |
|---|---|
| Total area of the village | 170.55 |
| Land for cultivation | 100.46 |
| Land under forest cover | 21.91 |
| Fallow land | 44.74 |
| Pasture land | 1.60 |
| Cultivable wasteland | 0.78 |
| Land under miscellaneous tree and groves | 0.86 |
| Net sown area | 85.87 |

Due to the terrain of the Chotanagpur plateau, canal irrigation on a large scale is not possible here. Most of the villagers rely on monsoon for their paddy crop and almost nobody grows crops in other seasons with irrigation. Only two households use pump sets (area irrigated 2.51 hectares). They grow some wheat. The area irrigated by *Ahars* is about 3.29 hectares.

**Table 2.21:** Distribution of Landholding

| *Class Size* | *No. of Landholders* | *Land Owned* | *Area Operated* |
|---|---|---|---|
| < 1 hectare | 105 | 44.50 | 29.03 |
| 1-2 hectares | 40 | 64.74 | 42.26 |
| 2-4 hectares | 08 | 29.43 | 16.57 |
| > 4 hectares | Nil | Nil | Nil |

There is no tube-well in the area. Three wells are put into good use for growing vegetables by the industrious villagers who were selling out in the Jamua market.

The area (hectare) of government land put under various uses is as follows:

**Table 2.22:** Distribution of government Land put under various uses

| *Wasteland* | *Barren land* | *Homestead* | *Cultivation* | *Pasture* | *Others* |
|---|---|---|---|---|---|
| 4.35 | 4.35 | 0.29 | 20.24 | 1.78 | 2.88 |

As per the revenue records, there is no encroachment of the government land in the village. There was only a small piece of land where the villagers used to rest their cattle, but that too only sometimes in summers. After the cadastral survey of 1911, there has been no survey and settlement operation here. Land records have not been computerized and it has not started as yet in Giridih.

The prominent few among these are pasture (1.78 ha), forest under forest department (21.9 ha), panchayat ghar and a temple. There is one fishing pond, jointly held by a group of three. There is one *ahar* and 15 households have their rights of its use. Temple is open for use by all, though the SCs do not frequent there. The pasture and the forest are under mild encroachment and the people are not bothered about the maintenance of the CPRs except for the temple, '*chanda*' for which is collected at the time of major festivals.

The people of village Malhan Bhuiadih (Block Tamar), District Ranchi are dependent on agriculture. The area of the village is 974.12

acres. All land area is cultivable, there is no wasteland, as the whole area has come under the Khunt-katti raiyats. Usually single cropping is practised but sometimes more than one crop are also grown. This area is also one of the most fertile lands of South Chotanagpur. Cropping pattern is usually paddy-vegetable, maize-potato, paddy-gram.

There is no permanent facility of irrigation—agriculture being rainfed. Only surface water is being used. Ground water is still not tapped. Most of the villagers grow a single crop in rainy season as paddy. Majority of the land is self-cultivated and all members of the family, men, women and children are involved in farming. Some people cultivate others' land on *Adh-Batai* or *Sajha*. The produce is divided into equal shares between the owner of the land and the farmer who cultivated the land. However, heavy rainfall sometimes destroys the crop, as it happened in 1994.

Main crops of this village are paddy, *arhar*, *khesari*, *tisi* (oil seeds), tomato, brinjal, lady finger, etc. Tomato is the main cash crop of this area. The soil is suitable for tomato production. The whole life of this village revolves around tomato production. They get net cash income by selling tomato in the local market.

They are engaged for about six months in the year in plain land cultivation. After this, they also engage as day labourers in the village itself or in neighbouring villages.

For any requirement of cash, credit can be taken from the co-villagers at a very high rate of interest.

Local tomato and other vegetables are collected at a centre which is situated near the village on NH-33 Ranchi-Jamshedpur road. Traders come from distant places to make purchases. The produce goes to Jamshedpur, Kolkata and places in Orissa with only a little being sold in the local market of Ranchi. The market system of this area is simple. It should be developed in a proper way.

Seeds are generally produced by the farmers themselves in their fields.

Fertilizers are not used much in the village. However, fertilizers are available at the roadside local shops in sufficient supply but are not taken by the villagers.

Agricultural implements used by the villagers are traditional and locally produced, that is plough, sickle, spade, etc. The terrain of the village also does not allow large scale use of tractors in the fields. Modern technology has not yet touched the village as far as such implements are concerned.

The local people do not have knowledge regarding the diseases of the crop resulting in large scale destruction of the tomato and other crops.

Horticulture has a good prospect in Ranchi due to favourable climatic conditions and if better irrigation facilities are made available, this will add to the income of the cultivators, besides making nutritious food available for the masses.

The government is giving stress on fruit cultivation. The Agriculture Department has appointed a horticulturist to look after the development of fruit trees and vegetables. The research work on fruits is also done by horticulturists at the Agricultural Research Institute, Kanke through the Agriculture Department. The registered cultivators are given better type of seeds for multiplying them.

The village is situated on the National Highway 33 km. equi-distant from Ranchi and Jamshedpur. Ever since the highway has been built, since 1965, the village has emerged as a local vegetable collection centre and caters to the surrounding villages. After 1965, it came as a boom and lot of trading activity started here. Before that it was like any other sleepy village in the interiors of Khunti sub-division, untouched by the facilities of modern life. The highway brought it in direct contact with the district headquarters at Ranchi, 70 km away. Now there are buyers from Jamshedpur, Kolkata and Rourkela. Truckloads of vegetables are taken to all these markets. Transaction with outsiders is done on a commercial basis, in cash. Locally, they exchange it even in kind.

Ever since the tomato boom, the production of other items too has been taken up. More and more village land has been put into use and now all agricultural land is producing crops around the year. However, the winter season has only vegetables and Kharif has paddy cultivation. Because of this ready market as the surrounding villages too abound in vegetable production, a small market has started developing on the highway. This has benefited the local villagers only to an extent as most of the farmers, who are also from other villages, sell their produce to middlemen, who further sell the crops to traders at far off places. In the process, these middlemen are taking away a major portion of the profit.

A survey was made to compare the prices at which certain crops are available at a given point of time in the village market where the farmers are selling themselves and in Ranchi city, where the produce is sold by the middlemen. Agriculture is the main activity of village Rangamati (Ranchi) and is the main source of income for the people. Mostly, they grow paddy and wheat. Rice is the main food item and mostly paddy is grown for self-consumption. This is sown in Kharif season and normally harvested in the month of October-November. The production of paddy in this area very much depends upon rain due to lack of adequate irrigation facilities. Almost, all cultivable land is used for paddy cultivation. In Barwatoli, the area under cultivation of paddy is 60.70 hectare while that in Rangamati only 20.31 hectare. Again, the paddy production in Barwatoli is about 300 quintals while only 900 quintals in Rangamati. In '*Don*' (low land) areas even paddy is grown in *Jait* which also called '*Jethua Dhan*' or '*Garma Dhan*'. This paddy is not of good quality but breweries (*Hadia*) are made out of it.

Wheat is another important crop in the village which is sown in the Rabi season. Earlier in this tribal village, people used to eat only rice but due to contact with outsiders, they started eating wheat. Sometimes they grow wheat to sell and buy rice. Wheat is grown in only 3.24 hectare land in Barwatoli and production is 136 quintals while this figure is 1.21 hectare and 55 quintals in Rangamati.

Pulse is also an important crop for both Barwatoli and Rangamati. Only '*Arhar*' and '*Urad*' variety of pulses are grown in both tolas, as villagers eat these varieties. This is only for self-consumption. In Barwatoli 2.02 hectare land is used for pulse cultivation and production is about 15 quintals while in Rangamati only 0.70 hectare land is used for the production of 5 quintals of pulse.

Besides these, vegetable is produced in large quantity in Barwatoli, not in Rangamati. Due to high quality seeds provided by the R.K. Mission, people in Barwatoli produced large quantity of tomato, cauliflower, brinjals, etc. and sold the same in the nearby market. In Rangamati, vegetable production is very less and is only for self-consumption.

Maize is also grown in the village in summer. In horticulture, Rangamati and Barwatoli both are underdeveloped. Only now it is picking up in Barwatoli due to the efforts of the R.K. Mission. Guava, jackfruit and papaya are grown. Mango has just started in Barwatoli.

Forward and backward linkage of agriculture and horticulture is not well developed. Inputs like fertilizers, seeds, pesticides are mainly supplied through large area multipurpose cooperative society (LAMPS which is in loss), block and open market (Getalsud). Outputs are marketed only in the block market.

Paddy is the main crop for the people of Pratap Pur village (Block Jamua), District Giridih and the whole area in general. There being no irrigation, other crops do not yield much and paddy is grown during the monsoon. Paddy is estimated to be grown on 26.19 hectare and the produce is 652.2 quintals whereas wheat (sown in winter by the two families which have pumping sets) is grown on barely 2.49 hectare and the produce is 48.83 quintals (*halka karmachari's* figures). No body grows pulses, sugarcane, maize or tobacco.

Litchi, grapes, cashew nut, coconut, etc. are not grown in this area. Among the fruits we have mango but there is no orchard as such and nobody is growing them on a commercial basis and within the village there are only two trees. The owners roughly estimated the production at about 6 quintals.

A few enterprising villagers grow vegetables in their backyards and sell them within the village and in the block market.

**Table 2.23:** Input Market of Agricultural Produce

| *Input* | *Source of Procurement* | *Current Price (Rs. per kg)* |
|---|---|---|
| Urea | Open Market | 3.86 |
| DAP | Open Market | 8.84 |
| Seed of Wheat | Open Market | 11.00 |
| Seed of Paddy | Open Market | 11.00 |
| Pesticides | Open Market | 180.00 |

'Rogar' is the most commonly used pesticide here, which is sold at the rate of Rs. 180 per 1000 ml.

Whatever produce is left after self-consumption is sold in the block market.

Though there are non-farm activities in the village, most of the households claimed that these activities were not their mainstay as far as 'earning' was concerned. They were basically in the nature of 'side business'. Only two households are actually dependent on the non-farm activities—(1) Auraini Mis—Poultry, (2) Indrajit Rai—Hotel (wayside *dhaba*).

**Table 2.24:** Non-Farm Activities

| *Nature of Activities* | *Dependent Households* | *Source of Technology* | *Financial Assistance* | *Place of Marketing* |
|---|---|---|---|---|
| Vending | – | Traditional | Self | Block |
| Petty trade | – | Traditional | Bank, Government, Self | Village, Block |
| Traditional trade and craft | – | Traditional | Bank, Government, Self | Village, Block |
| Food processing | – | Market | Bank, Self | Village |
| Poultry | 1 | Government | Bank, Government | Village, Block |
| Fishery | – | Traditional | Self | Village, Block |
| Horticulture | – | Traditional | Bank, Government, Self | Village, Block |
| Hotel | 1 | Traditional | Bank, Self | Block |
| Brick making | – | Traditional | Bank, Government, Self | Village, Block |

The one activity of food processing is a flour mill which is located in the village itself. Among the traditional trades and crafts, shoe making and carpentry, have been taken up. There are two carpenters and one shoe maker in the village. One of the carpenters has been an IRDP beneficiary in the past.

Fishery is taken up as an activity, twice or thrice in the year by families from the pond they own, but they do not take any special care of the pond and no serious business orientation was found.

In village Nakti (District Dumka), despite the fact that majority of agricultural land belongs to the tribals, the land use patterns were far from being satisfactory. There was hardly any irrigation facility available. Four irrigation wells and two major tanks, constructed by the Government, were not being properly used. The soil too is infertile. In the red soil the yield is very low and water requirement is very high. A small watershed programme is being implemented by a

Christian missionary in the village. A total of 35 hectares of land will be benefited by this scheme. The Scheduled Caste farmers were found more associated with agricultural activity. There was no horticultural activity in the village. There are around 20 landless households belonging to the Scheduled Castes.

Majority of the people of village Nakti (District Dumka) are dependent on agriculture. Paddy is the main crop, which is rainfed. In case of the failure of the monsoon, tanks and irrigation wells rescue 50 per cent of the paddy crop by providing the last few rounds of irrigation. Other major crop is wheat, which is being sown in only 25 per cent of the cultivable area, especially near the wells by the farmers having pumpsets. The yield of both the crops is low. On upland, pulses and maize are sown as rabi crop. Perhaps yield of these crops is better than any other crop. *Arhar* and *Urad* are the main pulse variety and RR-8, Bhadai are the traditional variety having reasonable yield. The "*Jal Hai Jahan Hai*" is most successful programme in this district as vegetable is being grown in huge quantity. Nakti village has an advantage of using wells for a third crop, i.e. vegetable. Tomato, cauliflower, bins, potato, etc. are being produced in huge quantity and sold in local market. Horticultural activity is just picking. No major breakthrough has been seen.

As far as backward and forward linkage is concerned there is a Large Area Multi Purpose Society which caters to the need of crop loan, seeds etc. but there is no co-operative society for ensuring remunerative prices of grain to the poor. However, the Krishi Utpadan Bazar Samiti is giving marketing facility to the villagers. Local moneylenders have full control over the area and buy most of the grain. Again due to poverty, farmers sell grain as per need in small quantity in emergency. Agriculture and allied activities do not give them sufficient income for survival. However, vegetable growing remains the hope for their livelihood.

## LIVESTOCK

The exact data could not be available in the Baghmara block office on the livestock. But in Nichitpur cattle, goats, pigs and hens are commonly reared by the people. There is one chunk of pasture and grazing land of 66.81 acres.

Villagers both breed cattle as well as buy some from outside, the first more often than the second. Ranikhet and toxicosis are the main poultry diseases. Among the cattle, foot and mouth diseases, and worms in the stomach are found to be common. The nearest veterinary doctor and veterinary centre is at block headquarters at Baghmara.

There is a large potential for poultry farming in the area, because there is very good market for the same. However, no schemes are available. Instead of wasting money on other impracticable projects, in the area, poultry farms could be started. The potential for dairy is also ample but the farmers do not have the money or other resources for rearing high quality-hybrid cattle.

Most of the households in village Charai (Block Chaibasa), District West Singhbhum possess cattle or goat or fowl as per survey. Even though these are not meant for commercial exploitation they consume fowls etc. on their own. Most of the draught animals (bullocks) provided under the IRDP vanished from the beneficiaries' houses. The reason is very simple. In order to meet the needs of daily consumption or family function like marriage, generally people sell their assets. They do not see the rearing of goat or fowl as a source of income generation. Moreover, since there are no proper medical facilities for the animals, the people are not ready for taking any adventure. Actually, the lack of infrastructure has driven the people into the vicious circle of poverty.

In village Mahil (Block Murhu), District Ranchi, draught animals were with 20 families, milch animals with 14 families, sheep with 5 and goat with 5 families. The families that held these animals were in the land-holding group of 1-3 acres. This goes to show that only marginal farmers and small farmers had livestocks. The big farmers had only draught and milch cattle. They did not have the smaller livestocks like sheep or goat.

The cattle of the Ranchi District are very small and undersized, and this is largely due to the lack of good pasturage and fodder. In the remote forest parts there is still ample pasturage, but owing to the extension of cultivated parts, cattle are grazed on the waste lands of the village, or on the fields after the crops have been harvested but in the hot weather they are in a wretched condition. In the rains, when grass grows rapidly, they pick up and become somewhat fat. Paddy straw is stored for use as fodder. Cows are not kept for milk. The

Mundas, in fact, think it almost a crime to drink the milk of a cow which they consider should be left entirely to the calf. Cows are usually yoked to the plough and are known as *gundri* or plough cows. This yoking affects the breed of the cattle. Buffaloes are not bred in the district, but are imported from North and South Bihar and also from Palamau. They are used for ploughing the heavier "*don*" lands. Cattle and goat are exported to Kolkata and Jamshedpur.

Not much has been done so far as sheep and goat breeding is concerned. The indigenous population of the district, both tribals and non-tribals, keep goat as a matter of routine. A few high breed bucks have been distributed, but little improvement is noticed. There is a class of shepherds (*gareris*) who rear sheep and move with their flock from place to place. Their wool is in demand, particularly in the Central Jail at Hazaribagh and a few other centres where carpets and coarse blankets (*Kambals*) are made. Among the non-farm activities, dairy and poultry are the main activities in Barwatoli (Ranchi) while traditional craft (making "*Patta-Dona*" and fishing set) and poultry are the main activities in Rangamati. In dairy, the Government is the main source of technology and financial assistance. Milk is being sold through the Barwatoli Milk Producing Co-operative Society to the Ranchi Dairy. A separate case study has been made of dairy in Barwatoli. Poultry is also due to the effort of the R.K. Mission. High breed of poultry is provided by the R.K. Mission. But poultry is mainly for self-consumption. Few families are dependent on small business like hotels, cycle repair shop etc. Bee-keeping was earlier a very important income generating activity. But now it has declined as the Italian variety of bee needs more care which villagers could not give due to increase in other activities of the villagers. Bee-keeping of the Italian variety was started by the R.K. Mission only by giving training to a few young people. This seems the only area where the R.K. Mission has not been able to sustain the activity and it is declining. Now, the R.K. Mission is planning to train women in the village itself for bee-keeping which is happening in another R.K. Mission village "Dimra". In Dimra groups of five women do bee-keeping in twenty boxes.

In Rangamati, fishery is the traditional non-farm activity of the "Naik" caste families. But due to lack of water storage facilities, the activity is declining. In the village, people fish even in drains (*Nalas*). Piggery and goats have also developed in Barwatoli due to the effort of a Milk Co-operative formed recently. This is the only successful co-operative formed due to proper forward linkage. Backward linkage is still not very good. This is for the first time that the people have done dairy in the village. Right now there are 18 members in this Co-operative. It is expanding. Another co-operative is "Getalsud" LAMPS which is almost non-performing. This was basically a Government supported co-operative. Presently, it is under heavy loss due to bad loans.

There are 64 cows and 21 buffaloes in the whole village. In the calculation for milk production, the average yield per cow is taken as 405 litres per annum and for buffaloes—765 litres.

The size of the cows here is very small as compared to those in the other parts of the country. In fact the size of a few grown up cows was found to be barely more than a large size goat. The cows are not put to any special care as well. There are no green pastures and the quality of grass available is bad. Approximately 60 per cent of the milk is self-consumed. There is no milk cooperative. The sale pertains to local households only.

## VILLAGE INDUSTRIES

In village Nichitpur (Block Baghmara), District Dhanbad, the only industry that is taken up by 5 of the families is muri-making. *Muri* is tuffed rice and a very common and affordable food form in the region, especially among the poorer sections. *Muri*-making is an enterprise that employs the entire family. The women prepare the rice (soak and dry it) and then roast it in large *Karahis* over *chullhas* in the courtyard. The art is in roasting them over slightly in the locally available black sand, and then brushing the rice puff out of the *Karahi*. If the labour for *muri* making comes from women, men look after the task of management: purchase of rice, fuel, transportation and marketing. Moreover, it is the men who take charge of the cash.

Marketing *muri* has one problem. Whole-sellers are not to pay immediately which causes hardships to *muri*-makers. This shortage of working capital is a constant problem. Here is where DRDA loans could be useful.

On an average the daily earnings of one family are Rs. 25-40. They are employed for about 25 days in every month.

However, Nichitpur is surrounded by coal mineral resources. It provides employment to a number of villagers.

There exists no electricity in village Malhan Bhuiadih (Block Tamar), District Ranchi. No industry has been able to develop. One case of a village flour mill was found but it is run with the help of a diesel motor.

## EDUCATION

There are two schools in Nichitpur (Block Baghmara), District Dhanbad: one is a Government Primary School and another one is a middle school. Both are housed in a *pucca* structure. But the middle school is much better in all respects. In this school, 100 girls were studying in different classes. This is a well furnished school. The classrooms are crowded. 185 children attended the primary school out of which there were 25 girls. Of these 84 belong to the Scheduled Castes.

**Table 2.25:** Education-wise Population

| *Sl. No.* | *Education Level* | *Number* | *Percentage* |
|---|---|---|---|
| 1. | Up to VII | 320 | 48.4 |
| 2. | Upto Matric | 240 | 36.3 |
| 3. | Upto H.S. (10+2) | 65 | 9.8 |
| 4. | Graduate | 35 | 5.3 |
| 5. | Post-graduate | Nil | 0.0 |

The only positive aspect in village Charai (Block Chaibasa), District West Singhbhum is that 75 per cent of the surveyed male population is literate. Out of 100 male population only 24 persons were illiterate. Most of them are above 25 years. However, the literacy rate of the female population is below 25 per cent which shows the attitude of the society towards females. This tiny village has produced two graduates so far. The village has one primary school with two teachers. The school building was constructed in 1995 under the employment assurance scheme. The general complaint from the villagers is that the teachers usually come late to the school. Normally the teachers will come to the school by 11.00 A.M. and leave by 3.00 P.M. Since the village people understand the importance of the education they send their children to the school regularly.

In village Malhan Bhuiadih (Block Tamar), District Ranchi, increasing number of students coming to the schools has led to shortage of space due to which classes have to be held in the verandah.

There are three primary schools in the village one of which has been adopted by the Bihar Education Project. The enrolment percentage of the school is very high as all the villagers are eager to get their children, both boys and girls educated.

There has been no discrimination against the girls' education. There are almost the equal number of boys and girls in the schools. The villages also formed an education committee in which they constantly review the working of the school.

## HEALTH AND SANITATION

Ponds do a disservice to the people in village Nichitpur (Block Baghmara), District Dhanbad by acting as breeding grounds for mosquitoes. Malaria is an annual feature of the village. Even though drinking water is drawn from hand pumps, it is not boiled or otherwise treated to remove impurities. Therefore, stomach ailments are a common ailment especially in the wake of monsoon. Gastroenteritis and in some cases even cholera spreads.

The nearest Public Health Centre is in Baghmara, 5 km away. Otherwise, the villagers of Nichitpur have to depend upon private practitioners.

In case of emergencies the villagers have to rush to the BCCL hospital. There is one Health sub-centre in the village. But hardly any doctor visits. Traditional midwives are the only experts available in case of a delivery. A programme of mass education on personal hygiene and sanitation would prevent the eruption of several diseases. The need for better medical facilities is self-evident.

In village Charai (Block Chaibasa), District West Singhbhum, since most of the people are leading subsistence life, they do not take care of their health problems. In fact, they are living with all kinds of ailments like malnutrition, skin diseases, TB etc. Most of the children and elder people are underweight. Even though the district hospital is located at a reachable distance they are indifferent towards their own health. If at all they go there they won't get medicines. The most pathetic situation is that the doctors in the nearby Primary Health Centre (15 km at Rajnagar) take Rs. 20-25 per patient in the PHC itself. The root cause of this problem is that people drink the river water directly even though hand pumps have been provided.

The people address their problem to the local quack. Only when the problem becomes serious, they will go to the town for consulting the doctors. The main reason is that the doctors charge unreasonable fees from the people. Even though Chaibasa is a small town and the people are very poor, the doctor's minimum charge is Rs. 50. Because of this situation most of the pregnant women deliver their child under the supervision of "*Dai*" who are untrained for this purpose. And if a person falls ill, the relatives will do some kind of *puja* in order to get him well. This shows the height of superstition. The maternity coverage in the village is very poor. Only one household responded that they received a minimum 3 ANC checkups and full TT doses. And only 4 households availed the facility of immunization to some extent. The other families are not aware of such programmes.

In village Malhan Bhuiadih (Block Tamar), District Ranchi, in general, the health of the people is normal. During sickness, they use local treatment in the village, which is not adequate. In special cases, they go to Bundu (30 km), Tamar (14 km) and Ranchi (70 km) for better treatment. There is a sub-health centre in this village which again has inadequate medical facilities.

In fact, the health sub-centre has not been provided with any facilities. It remain closed. There is great resentment in the village.

## CREDIT FACILITIES AND HOUSEHOLD INCOME

In village Charai (Block Chaibasa), District West Singhbhum, the village people are deprived of credit facilities in general. Out of 40 households only 5 persons received loans from banks. Since the people do not have any enterprising attitude they do not bother about any credit facilities. Moreover, since the returns from the land are very poor the farmers also do not want to take any risk. The crux of the problem is that whenever some farmer gets crop loan from the bank, first he repays the loan amount taken from money lenders and the remaining amount will be spent on consumable items, liquor and also on family functions. Since the loan amount is not being utilized for productive purposes the farmer ultimately is not able to repay the bank loans. Because of this, the recovery rate of the banks is very poor. All over the district it is somewhere near 15 per cent to 20 per cent. The poor repayment rate discourages the banks from providing credit facilities. This always creates differences between the District Collector and the banks, because the Collector emphasizing only the targets to be achieved.

As far as the income of the household is concerned 80 per cent of the families get less than Rs. 3,500 per annum. Only one household is earning Rs. 8,000-10,000 per annum. However, the figures given by the villagers do not reflect exact figures. The people want to suppress the information knowingly or unknowingly.

The following table shows the income level of the households:

**Table 2.26:** Income level of the households

| Sl. No. | Income Level | Households | SC/ST | OBC | Others |
|---|---|---|---|---|---|
| 1. | 3,500 | 27 | 5 | 15 | 7 |
| 2. | 3,500-4,800 | 5 | 1 | 3 | 1 |
| 3. | 4,800-6,400 | 7 | 2 | 3 | 2 |
| 4. | 6,400-8,000 | 0 | 0 | 0 | 0 |
| 5. | 8,000-10,000 | 1 | 0 | 1 | 0 |

From the study it is found that about 50 per cent of the households, which possess no land and less than 3 acres earn less than Rs. 3,500 per annum. This group is generally of agricultural labourers.

In village Charai (Block Chaibasa), District West Singhbhum, the main occupation is agriculture. Most of the people do cultivation on their own land. Those who do not possess any land, work in others' land in the same or outside the village as casual labourers on daily wage basis. The most disheartening feature of this is that the agricultural labourers get only Rs. 16 per day as wages. Even though the government has decided that the minimum wage is Rs. 39.75, it is not practiced in the field. Only under the rural development programmes the people get the prescribed minimum wages.

Since the agricultural season ranges only for 90-100 days, most of the people are idle for the remaining period. During agricultural lean season some people migrate to nearby towns like Jamshedpur and Chaibasa for some work, where they will get Rs. 25-30 a day. Since the availability of unskilled force is more than the demand, the daily wages reach such a low level. This is nothing but exploitation of the poor people who do not have any bargaining capacity. And there is no organized set up for unorganised workers to take up the cause of the poor workers. Besides this, some people work in local brick kilns, where they will get Rs. 25 a day for which they have to work hard throughout the day. As far as migration is concerned it is limited upto Jamshedpur only. Otherwise nobody migrates permanently to other areas of the state or out of the state even though Kolkata is situated only at a distance of four-hour train journey.

In village Malhan Bhuiadih (Block Tamar), District Ranchi, agriculture is the main occupation. All activities are woven around it throughout the year. Paddy is the staple crop, but some crops as brinjal, are grown on a commercial scale. In winter, the main source of their income is tomato cultivation. They sell it in the local daily market from November to March to local and outside traders and also exchange their goods with others.

Another source of livelihood is casual labour for wage. They work as agricultural labourers in the fields of rich persons. Unemployed and even educated youths, who have no permanent work also work in others' fields. They get a wage of about Rs. 20.00 per day and one meal at noon. This wage is equal for both men and women. The relationship between employer and employee is good as no reports of any exploitation have been going around.

The forest products are also associated with their economic life. They purchase fuel wood locally and some of them also get it from the nearby forest.

In this village, the Loharas (Scheduled Tribe) also reside. Ironsmithy (Blacksmithy) is the main occupation of the Loharas. They sharpen the plough-edges, sickles and axes of the villagers. For this they get Rs. 2 per item. They also work as agricultural labourers in others' fields, when they are not preoccupied. For this they get one *paila* paddy (750 grams) per day and sometimes Rs. 12 in cash in addition to one meal (*murhi*: a rice preparation) at noon. Their economic condition is weak.

The *banias* run shops in the village on the National High Way and in other tolas. All the things of daily requirement are available in these shops, which are obtained by the villagers on cash payment or by exchanging paddy.

Farmers of the village carry heavy loads of articles either in "*Sika* and *Bahinga*" or on their heads. The bullock carts are used by them on payment for carrying articles from one place to another. They try to cover distant places on foot. Modern means of transportation are also used.

Blacksmithy is the main occupation of this community. They manufacture sickle, axe, iron-head of the arrow and plough after obtaining the iron materials from the local markets. Through stone cutting and agriculture also they supplement their living. The Lohara women also attend delivery cases in the village and thus earn a little.

The incidence of drink is heavy among them. They have no *akharas* of their own, but go to the village *akhara* occasionally and dance and sing there along with other tribals.

## MIGRATION

The impact of poor agriculture, non-existence of industry and lack of development of trade and commerce in village Birkera (District Gumla) has led to migration on a large scale. We generally find that the locals move out to tea plantations in Assam as casual labourers, to Nagaland and Jamshedpur or as workers in the brick kilns of eastern U.P. Most of the migrants remain in the places where they have gone to. An important issue in this context would be to harness their abilities for the betterment of their lot and thus to create sufficient opportunities there itself. Migration is an important ingredient of the socio-economic milieu of this village. Another factor which weighs heavy with the tribals here is the fact that in the close by areas of Madhya Pradesh, the levels of development are much higher. Those areas have good electricity supplies and telecommunication facilities, while these tribals are yet to see electricity or the phone.

In village Rangamati (Tolas Barwatoli and Rangamati), District Ranchi, the cases of migration are very less. In Barwatoli, there is no case of emigration. In fact, three persons are staying in the tola who are outsiders. But in Rangamati, twelve have migrated to other districts for employment.

But another form of migration, which we can say daily migration, is very high in Rangamati. Many people migrate every morning for daily wages to Ranchi. They mostly pull rickshaws and work in some shops. Some sell "*Patta-Dona*" and fishing net in Ranchi. They come back everyday around 8.00 p.m. and again leave at 7.00 a.m. next day. This routine is very tiring and is one of the main causes of resorting to alcohol.

Earlier, daily migration for daily wage was prevalent in Barwatoli also. But now the activities in the village itself are many and all villagers are employed. Credit for this also goes to the R.K. Mission as it provides training of "Raj Mistri" or "Hand-pump repair". The persons get employment almost daily in nearby villages.

## STATUS OF WOMEN

Irrespective of caste, all women in village Mahil (Block Murhu), District Ranchi are hard-working primarily because of their economic condition. Women start their day very early and go in search of firewood and come back by 8 O'clock and cook food, take care of the menfolk and children and then go to the field to work as agricultural labourers. Men generally are lazy as compared to women. When asked about the problems of women, men replied that since they are "women" they have to face it. Even though it is believed that there is no discrimination against women in the tribal societies, women are not equal to their menfolk. Tribal men drink *hadia*. Women do all the work both in the field and at home. Malnutrition, lack of awareness about family planning and reproductive health were observed as major problems. Men also do not take much care about women's problems as they also are not aware. The women were not aware of any government programmes specifically designed for women. They did not know that special attention was being paid to them by the government.

In village Malhan Bhuiadih (Block Tamar), District Ranchi according to the 1991 census, women constitute 47.88 per cent of the village population. The sex ratio in this village is 919 (1991 census). The status of women is lower in comparison to males due to patrilocal, patrilineal and patriarchal family pattern. The literacy rate among the women of this village is negligible. They assist the men in all economic activities. The tribal women of this village are emancipated in comparison to the non-tribal women. Due to the tribal customary law tribal women are not successors of their parental property, but they have a right to living and marriage cost from their parents before marriage. Bride price is paid for acquiring unmarried tribal girls as wives. The position of widows and separated women in the village is comparatively low. The Hindu women of the village can perform religious rituals but the position of tribal women is low in comparison to males in the performance of religious rituals. In the tribal community, mainly the male priests perform all religious activities. The entrance of tribal women in sarna place is forbidden and they cannot even worship the household deities on the occasion of different festivals. Tribal women mainly participate in folk dance and merry making. Tribal women neither have membership of the tribal traditional panchayat nor they can participate in the traditional panchayat meeting. Widow re-marriage is practised among the tribal communities of the village. The divorce among the tribals of the village is taken by both the husband and wife on the ground of barrenness, idleness, objectionable sex relationship, and disagreement to live together etc.

The status of the Muslim women of the village is inferior in comparison to the Muslim males due to illiteracy. They generally work in houses. Some Muslim women of the village are engaged in tailoring in their homes.

The Hindu women of the village participate in all economic activities but their position is not equal to males due to illiteracy and traditional practices.

## RURAL DEVELOPMENT PROGRAMMES

From no angle Nichitpur (Block Baghmara), District Dhanbad, could be viewed as the model village for rural development. However, investment in this village has increased. The below poverty line population survey was conducted in 1997. According to the latest survey there are 220 families below the poverty line. Identified sections below the poverty line and their population are as follows:

**Table 2.27:** Identified Sections Below Poverty Line and their population

| | |
|---|---|
| Kurmi Mahto | 67 |
| Kumhar | 26 |
| Mohli | 11 |
| Rajwar | 18 |
| Ravidas | 16 |
| Muslims | 14 |
| Others | 68 |

The last household survey for the identification of beneficiaries was conducted in 1992. Till now, there were 87 families benefited by different kinds of inputs like generator, diesel pumpsets, agricultural seeds, cattle, etc. The beneficiaries were selected from different categories: SC (29), ST (4), Women (8), Others (46). In the year 1996-97, the credit disbursement is Rs. 7,35,000. The assets which have been given in the financial year are milch animals—18, bullock pairs—12, pumpset—3, generator—3, goat—12, *tokri* making—11 etc.

Under the TRYSEM system, 12 persons have been covered. Out of the 12 persons, at present, 11 are self-employed in different activities like making of *tokris*. The Baghmara block has not been covered under the DWCRA scheme.

Under the JRY, the village had been covered in 1989-90. Allocation of fund to the Panchayat during 1996-97 is Rs. 3,56,000. But the budget is generally not utilised regularly. Under the JRY since 1989 to 1996-97, eight schemes have been taken up in the Nichitpur village. But none of the schemes is complete except one brick soling and two road culverts and one 1.5 km *pucca* road stretch.

**Table 2.28:** Number of Beneficiaries, Occupation and Items of Benefits

| *Sl. No.* | *Items of Benefits* | *No. of Beneficiaries Coming from* | | | | | |
|---|---|---|---|---|---|---|---|
| | | *Marginal Farmer* | *Small Farmer* | *Agri. Labour* | *Non-Agri. Labour* | *Rural Artisan* | *Others* |
| 1. | Milch animal | 3 | – | 6 | 2 | 5 | 2 |
| 2. | Bullock pair | 8 | – | 4 | – | – | – |
| 3. | Pumpset | 3 | – | – | – | – | – |
| 4. | Poultry | 10 | – | 3 | 3 | 4 | – |
| 5. | Small business | 2 | – | 2 | 8 | – | 6 |
| 6. | Gen. Set | – | – | – | 3 | – | – |
| 7. | Goatry | – | – | 4 | 5 | 3 | – |
| 8. | *Tokri* | – | – | 7 | – | 4 | – |
| 9. | Others | – | – | 2 | – | 3 | 4 |

Village Charahi (Block Chaibasa), District West Singhbhum is getting poverty alleviation programmes like the JRY, EAS, IRDP loans etc.

First, we will analyse the status of the IRDP loans. The selection procedure for the loan itself is very much wrong. Generally, the block level officials impose it on the people in order to achieve the target. The most common things provided under this loan are bullocks and goats. But what is the use of giving such things to the areas where the animal wealth is too high. Moreover, people are also not interested in such things. In order to achieve the target the bank and block officials purchase everything on paper and take their share with the connivance of the beneficiary. These officials also encourage the beneficiaries not to repay the loan amount. All these lead to a very poor recovery rate.

In general, the beneficiaries who actually purchased some cattle, sell them after some time to meet the house needs at a very low price. Moreover, the beneficiaries are not in a position to assess the value of the cattle due to ignorance.

The following table shows the number of beneficiaries for 1996-97.

**Table 2.29:** Number and Types of Beneficiaries

| Total No. of Beneficiaries | SC | ST | Women | Assignees of Surplus Land | Freed Bonded Labour | Handicapped Person | Others |
|---|---|---|---|---|---|---|---|
| 22 | 09 | 01 | 03 | Nil | Nil | Nil | 12 |

The credit disbursement among the various sections of the people:

**Table 2.30:** Credit Disbursement Caste-wise

| Total Disbursement | SC | ST | Women | Others |
|---|---|---|---|---|
| 1,30,400 | 49,600 | 10,900 | 18,700 | 69,900 |

Normally the JRY schemes will be taken up just before the rainy season and measurements will be taken after the rain, so that the officers can blame nature for washing off the unlaid roads. Even though the JRY is meant for and supposed to be implemented through the panchayats, the panchayat sevak and the BDO will select and implement the schemes due to the absence of the panchayat structure. This, in fact, makes the block level officials more powerful and arrogant and finally, they end up as indiscreet officials.

This village was covered under the JRY in the year 1989-90. During 1996-97, only one scheme, hume pipe culvert, for Rs. 25,000 was implemented. Under this work the labourers got Rs. 39.70 per day, which is the minimum wage under the state Act. Even though there is a provision to provide rice and wheat for the labourers against wages, they want nothing but hard cash. The women labourers received wages equal to men. However, the wages were paid normally once in a week.

In 1995-96, the village was given 36 units of the Indira Awas Yojana, out of which 32 were given to OBCs and 4 were given to STs. Almost 90 per cent of the houses were completed.

The main reason is, there are no cuts in the amount given to the people and ISI cement is supplied through the block at very low prices (wholesale rate) compared to the market price. In Chaibasa, the open market price of one bag of cement is about Rs. 160, but the block rate is just Rs. 97. Apart from this, people's ownership also gives motivation for them to complete the schemes.

Under the TRYSEM only one person received benefit. There is no million well scheme and social forestry in the village. DWCRA group also does not exist.

Most of the villagers in village Mahil (Ranchi) do not have any idea about various government schemes meant for rural development. When asked about the JRY, EAS etc. some of them said that roads and school buildings constructed were quite useful. But regarding wage employment they had many complaints against the engineer and the contractor. They do not get their wages in time. They were of the view that the government money was always misutilized and all the money sanctioned for the projects were not used.

Regarding the IRDP, the beneficiaries are not aware of the availability of various assets that were given under IRDP. Most of the times, the Panchayat Sevaks and VLWS go to the village, fill in some names in the application forms and the beneficiary does not even know that he is taking a loan and has to repay it. He is happy that he is getting money (in terms of an asset) now, and is not bothered about repaying the loan. The cows given under the IRDP were often sold away by the beneficiary or the cows died due to malnutrition.

There is nobody trained under the TRYSEM in this village. Nor there were any DWCRA groups.

The beneficiaries of the IRDP complained that the loan amount given was lesser than the market price and hence quality assets could not be assured with that amount.

A number of projects have been taken up under the Jawahar Rozgar Yojana in village Malhan Bhuiadih (Block Tamar), District Ranchi in recent years. The general assets created have been roads, school and a community centre. An Indira Awas has been made for a dalit family. The village is spread over ten hamlets. Most of the hamlets are connected with each other through the JRY *Kutcha* roads. Since only earthwork has been done during rains it gets filled with water and is thus difficult to use. After completion of the work, no maintenance has yet been done on these roads, particularly when they are so frequently used. The village school has been the most utilised asset created under the JRY. Now with more and more children coming in, there is a demand and need to upgrade the school. A community hall was also constructed and is used for village meetings, celebrating festivals etc. Along with the hall, it is the vacant land around it which is put to use for various gatherings. Foodgrain was also a component in wages and that the prevalent wage rate was paid to everyone. At present there is no JRY scheme going on.

Under the Million Wells Scheme, no irrigation well has been taken up in the village at all. All agricultural production is based on rainfall or water from the village *nala*. There is good demand for such wells even though the water level is low because of the terrain.

The Employment Assurance Scheme is being implemented in the Block and a number of projects have been started. But as yet no such work has been taken up in this village.

There is a demand to construct water conservation works in the village so that the rain water can be fully utilised.

A number of works have been completed under the JRY in these hamlets. Ever since the construction of roads, communication between the hamlets and from the hamlets to the main road has become fast and very easy.

During the last one year no IRDP credit was given in Rangamati (District Ranchi). But infrastructures were created both in Barwatoli and Rangamati. A village road (Muram road) from one corner to another was constructed in Barwatoli while a Vachanalaya was constructed in Rangamati. In both the schemes the amounts earmarked were spent and the schemes have been completed.

The IRDP survey was conducted to identify the beneficiaries below the poverty line. This survey includes every household of the village which is below the poverty line.

Twenty-one S.T. beneficiaries were given credit. Among them 11 beneficiaries were given milch cattle, a group of five beneficiaries were given a trekker, three were given sewing machines and two small shops. Thus among 21 units, 11 are in the primary sector, 5 in the secondary sector (sewing machines and shops) and 5 in the tertiary sector (trekker). The total amount of credit disbursed was Rs. 8,81,000 in which Rs. 1,05,000 was the subsidy component. In Rangamati, the credit demand is there but most of the households have taken loan and have not returned yet. So, banks are averse to giving loans in Rangamati.

Under the JRY during the last one year a rural road and a village pond were taken up in Barwatoli and one Vachanalaya in Rangamati. Except the village pond other schemes are complete. Normally in the JRY, schemes are formulated and selected at village level through general meeting (*Aam Sabha*). Also the schemes are executed and maintained by the local people. At different stages of schemes, measurement is taken by the Junior Engineer. Muster Roll verification is also done by the JE, the Supervisor and the BDO. The JRY schemes are very useful in terms of employment generation.

Only 24 households were benefited under the Indira Awas Yojana in Barwatoli and none in Rangamati during the last one year. Out of 24 Indira Awas units, all have been given to ST category households. 23 houses have been completed and one is in progress.

As on the day of the survey, there were 60 functioning wells, irrigation sources and 4 defunct in Barwatoli while these figures are very low respectively 14 and 5, in Rangamati. Thus the irrigation facilities are rather poorly developed in Rangamati compared to Barwatoli.

In village Pratap Pur (Block Jamua), District Giridih, the BPL survey was conducted last year for the years 1998-2003. A team of primary school teachers, VLWs and panchayat *sewaks* did it. The approval of the Gram Sabha was taken through collecting individual signatures and no actual gram sabha was conducted. The list of the BPL families is generally as per the norms but the people were complaining that some were deliberately missed out and the names of a few better off have been included.

Since the panchayats do not function, the BDO, Panchayat Sewak and the respective supervisor for the panchayat select the schemes under the JRY (65%). The gram sabhas are always a farce.

The wages paid in the JRY schemes were Rs. 39.70 per day whereas the latest rate was Rs. 51.01. Actually the new rate had not been implemented in the whole district. In two blocks Bagodar and Birni, which are dominated by the Left, these rates have come into practice.

There is no discrimination in the wages paid to the female labourers. The wages are usually given within a week. It is all in cash. The executing agents had a marked tendency to prefer outside tribal labour from the adjacent blocks in the district, for they are more obedient and sincere.

One very important thing to be noted here is that the beneficiaries of wage employment category are SCs and those in the executing agent class are all non SCs.

About the leakage in the schemes, it is the same old nexus between the executing agent, supervisor, the JE, the AE and the BDO. This village is definitely no exception.

There are a total number of 7 completed Indira Awas schemes in the village, out of which—

- 4 beneficiaries are Muslims (BC) (one is a widow headed household)
- 2 beneficiaries are thakurs (BC)
- 1 beneficiary is a SC widow headed household

These were taken up during November 1996 to May 1997. The estimated cost of each unit has been Rs. 14,500. The beneficiaries themselves have constructed the houses on their own lands and they have put in their labour also. They are supposed to follow a particular design pattern.

Besides, there are 12 houses in progress which have an estimated cost of Rs. 20,000. These beneficiaries are all released bonded labourers.

In this village, 10 wells were taken up under MWS, out of which 5 wells have been completed, 4 are in progress and one well-digging has struck hard rock and so it is almost abandoned.

In this scheme, the beneficiary is given Rs. 26,765 (in stages) to complete the digging as well as building of the well of 10′ inner diameter and 35′ depth with brick work and plaster. The land should be his own and he should be BPL. This is a popular scheme and it has the potential for future earnings of the beneficiary.

As far as the implementation of the Integrated Rural Development Programme in village Nakti (District Dumka) is concerned, milch cattle, tractor, buffalo, pumping set and ration shops have been given to the beneficiaries. There is great demand for pumping sets in the village as an irrigation well constructed under the Jaldhara has not been used properly.

## LAND REFORMS

The ceiling limit for this area is 45 acres of land per family and in the survey nobody in village Pratap Pur (Block Jamua), District Giridih, was found to possess this much of land. Also no land consolidation exercise has taken place.

There has been distribution of Government land (*bandobasti*) in favour of released bonded labourers, the landless ones, at the rate of 1 acre each about 0.75 km from the village. But actually the lands are almost barren and no efforts have been made for the reclamation of the same by the developmental agencies under the JRY etc. Thus these people are not cultivating their own land and act as labourers only. The same has been the story of the beneficiaries of the *bhoodan* movement.

Land records have not been computerised and the exercise has not begun in Giridih. The last Survey operation took place only in the year 1911 and thereafter the updating of records has taken place in the form of mutation only.

Only six men in village Pratap Pur are doing tenancy and it is in the form of *bataaidaari*. They are all marginal or small farmers. Only two have had some education. All reside in the same village. They have leased in very small pieces of land, no body more than 2 acres. The land leased-in is unirrigated. Except for one, all others have leased-in from one single man—Sudhi Rai who is a school teacher from the same village serving in an adjoining district. The other man has leased land from two persons, who hail from an adjoining village and he is the only one to grow wheat whereas all others grow paddy only. All the tenants belong to the backward classes and the landlords are all from the forward castes. The lease period is more than a year in all the cases.

The form of tenancy can be understood through the share of the tenant as follows:

- 50 per cent in fertilizer
- 50 per cent in produce
- 100 per cent in labour
- Nil in seeds' input
- 100 per cent in byproducts—hay etc.

Two of the tenants are marginally indebted to the commercial banks from where they had taken crop loans. None of the tenants provides any free service to the landowners and the terms of tenancy have been customary. The fear of loosing land is the main reason why a landowner changes tenants. The tenants were generally not very unsatisfied with their relation with the landlord.

The prevalence of tenancy is low in this region and the reason lies in the very low productivity of agriculture where they earn more as labourer than as a cultivator.

In village Nakti (District Dumka) *satta* and mortgage are used to exploit the tribals. In *satta*, farmers give Rs. 2000 to Rs. 3000 per acre and cultivate land for a period of 5-6 years. In mortgage, tribals take the money from the moneylender and give them their land in lieu of interest. The principal remains till they pay and get back their land. Due to this, many tribals have virtually lost their lands. In this village, as many as 15 persons belong to the service class, who live away from the village and give their land for sharecropping. They get Rs. 1000-2000 as net return from the land. The quality of life has not improved because of the fragmentation of holdings and infertility of soil, but status has improved, as rural culture is deeply associated with land. A person having more land is treated with respect. Health status has increased due to more availability of food within the family. Their immovable property has also increased. Due to lack of education they do not use new technology for land development. There are as many as 10 tenants in the village, five cultivate land on the basis of sharecropping, 3 on fixed cash and 2 on fixed produce for a period of 1 to 2 years. Most of the tenants are indebted. They get loan from landowner, moneylender, relatives, etc. They have hardly access to PACS and commercial banks. They pay interest from 18-40 per cent to moneylender and landowner. Few of them also provide free service to the landowner by cattle grazing and time-to-time household work. There is no role of the panchayat or any institution in the fixation of tenancy. It is just an understanding between the landowner and the tenants. Conflict arises between the tenant and landowner in case of crop failure, rate of interest, duration of tenancy, terms and conditions of tenancy and other matters at the time of sharing produce after harvesting. There is also the fear of losing land. Hence, the landowner changes a tenant every 2-3 years.

Land record is in a very bad shape in village Nakti (District Dumka). No steps have been taken to improve the land record. Over a period of time, many changes have taken place in the real field situation but no change has been done in the records. There are also cases of illegal change in the records leading to litigation in courts. However, a project of the computerisation of land records has started.

## CONCLUSION

As the majority of the tribal agriculturists in Jharkhand are not able to produce enough for their subsistence, they have been in the practice of going out to seek employment in the four months' slack agricultural season soon after the paddy harvest in December. They go to the tea gardens of Assam and North Bengal, to the jute mills and brick kilns round about Kolkata and elsewhere. When these people come back, they carry with them not only their earnings, but also the rich experience of the world outside, new ways of life and alternative patterns of behaviour.

Most of the land in the tribal areas in Jharkhand have been reclaimed from the forest and made fit for cultivation by them and their forefathers. Land is not just a means of subsistence for them, it is a spiritual bond between them and their ancestors. Incidentally the process of land alienation has been in operation in the tribal pockets of Jharkhand for a long time. The recurrent needs of cash, frequent famines and addiction to drinks have forced the tribals into the clutches of moneylenders who, in course of time, get tribal lands transferred to them.[12]

In the case of industrialisation, large-scale acquisition of tribal land took place in Ranchi, Hatia, Bokaro, Sindri etc. The tribals were uprooted from their hearth and homes. In the matter of employment, however, the claims of the local tribals have been skipped over. Although they had to give up their home and means of subsistence for the industry, a viable alternative employment was not provided to them.[13] Nor could they be imparted technical education to cope with new demands.

It has come out of the studies carried out by the IAS probationers that inadequate credit facilities have led to the exploitation of the tribals by unscrupulous moneylenders. Loans were advanced to them in cash and kind at exorbitant rates of interest. Sometimes in lieu of interest, the moneylender used to cultivate the land of the debtor and claimed its produce.

It has come out clearly in the IAS probationer's study that tribal agriculture cannot look up unless adequate irrigation facilities are made available.

There is the imperative need for evolving an integrated policy and programme for the economic development within the protective framework of agrarian legislation, which in turn, should be reviewed and strengthened from time-to-time. Land alienation, indebtedness, slow growth of the tribal economy, growing unemployment among the tribal youths are symptoms of the much larger problems of economic backwardness in Jharkhand. It is only with the diversification of the tribal economy and the development of agriculture based on the new technology that a solution to agrarian problems of alienation and indebtedness could be found. The agrarian question in Jharkhand poses essentially an issue of modernization of the existing agrarian structure and technique.[14]

As the experience shows, the path to development in the tribal areas is strewn with innumerable difficulties. In fact, methods of development that ordinarily work well enough do not make any dent here. It is, therefore, important that we devise a strategy of development suited specifically to the tribal needs and potentialities. But this presupposes a thorough knowledge of the local situation.

The kernel of the study by the IAS probationers in a cross-mix of the Jharkhand villages lies in the fact that unless the administrators are willing to develop a measure of sympathy and understanding for the tribal way of life, they perhaps will not find work in the tribal areas a rewarding experience. Therefore, both to develop tribal areas and to find satisfaction in this work, the administrators must try and learn about the life style of the tribal people whom they are supposed to serve. This understanding must consciously be fostered among officers responsible for the development of the tribal people and areas.

Tribal development is a difficult task, mainly because tribal people have long been living in far-flung hilly and forest habitations virtually cut off from the mainstream of the Indian society. The task of development today is both to accelerate economic development in these areas as well as to see that in the process these people do not lose their identity.

The 'environment', the 'organisation' and the long-term 'goals and objectives' of a programme are the three variables which influence organisational performances according to the strategic management approach. The term 'environment' is used for the conglomeration of technological, regulatory, social, economic and competitive forces external to a development programme. 'Organisation' refers to the durable arrangements within a programme to perform the given tasks and to the systems of information, planning and monitoring. The latter includes coordination, training and evaluation of the programme and personnel, in particular, leadership and its influence on the process of management. The goals and objectives of a programme, or its 'strategy' are a third major determinant of the programme's performance.

Decisions of strategic management combine the three variables in order to achieve the objectives of the programme. The argument is that when choices of organisation and 'strategy' are consistent with the characteristics of the 'external environment', they are likely to lead to superior performances.[15]

The advocates of the sociological-anthropological view of the development projects do not deny the importance of proper management procedures. But they perceive the relation between the project and the 'environment' differently. In their opinion, projects and their results reflect the socio-economic conditions and express the dominant structural and cultural characteristics of the society in which they take place. The structural variables comprise social divisions like caste and class, the contradictions between the rich and the poor and between the 'centre' and the 'periphery'.[16]

## NOTES

1. L.P. Gupta, *Tribal Development Administration* (Classical Publishing Company, 28, Shopping Centre, Karampura, New Delhi: 1998), pp. 7-8.
2. L.P. Vidyarthi, "Strategy for Tribal Development in India" in Hari Mohan Mathur (ed.) *Development Administration in Tribal Areas* (The HCM Institute of Public Administration, Jaipur: 1976), p. 10.
3. P. Pal, "Tribes of Andaman and Nicobar Islands" in S.N. Tripathy (ed.) *Glimpses of Tribal Development* (Discovery Publishing Company, New Delhi: 2000), p. 1.
4. K.S. Singh, *People of India: An Introduction* (Anthropological Survey of India, Calcutta: 1992). pp. 80.
5. *Ibid.*
6. *Ibid.*, p. 81.
7. Amit Prakash, *Jharkhand: Politics of Development and Identity* (Orient Longman: 2001), p. 20.
8. *Ibid.*, p. 21.
9. A.K. Singh, G. Pandey and P.K. Singh, *Forest and Tribals in India* (Classical Publishing Company, New Delhi: 1998), pp. 48-49.
10. Sita Toppo, *Dynamics of Educational Development in Tribal India* (Classical Publications, C-4A/30-C, Janakpuri, New Delhi-110 058: 1979), p. 6.
11. *Ibid.*, p. 84.
12. Sachchidananda, "The Tribal Situation in Bihar" in K. Suresh Singh (ed.) *Tribal Situation in India* (Indian Institute of Advanced Study, Simla: 1972), p. 177.
13. *Ibid.*, p. 178.
14. K. Suresh Singh, "Agrarian Issues in Chotanagpur" in K. Suresh Singh (ed.) *Tribal Situation in India* (*op. cit.*) p. 385.
15. Klass W. van der veen, "Introduction: Management and the Socio-cultural context" in Hein Streefkerk and T.K. Moulik, *Managing Rural Development: Health and Energy Programmes in India* (Sage Publications, M-32, Greater Kailash Market-I, New Delhi: 1997).
16. *Ibid.*, p. 14.

## BIBLIOGRAPHY

Ahmed, Ehtisham, Jean Dreze, John Hills and Amartya Sen (eds.), *Social Security in Developing Countries*, Clarendon Press, Oxford: 1991.

Beattie, JHM and R.G. Lienhardt (eds), *Studies in Social Anthropology*, Oxford University Press, Ely House, London: 1975.

Cotlow, Lewis, *In Search of the Primitive*, Robert Hale Ltd., London: 1967.

Ghosh, Abhik, *History and Culture of the Oraon Tribe*, Mohit Publications, 4675/21 Ansari Road, Daryaganj, New Delhi-110002: 2003.

Gupta, Lala P., *Tribal Development Administration*, Classical Publication Company, 28, Shopping Centre, Karampura, New Delhi, 1998.

Mathur, Hari Mohan (ed.), *Development Administration in Tribal Areas*, The HCM State Institute of Public Administration, Jaipur: 1976.

Oraon, Dr. Prakash Chandra, *Land and People of Jharkhand*, Jharkhand Tribal Welfare Research Institute, Morabadi, Ranchi: 2003.

Prakash, Amit, *Jharkhand: Politics of Development and Identity*, Orient Longman; 3-6-272, Himayat Nagar, Hyderabad: 2001.

Roy, S.B. and A.K. Ghosh (eds.), *People of India: Bio-Cultural Dimensions*, Inter-India Publications, D-17, Raja Garden, New Delhi-110 015: 1993

Sahay, Sarita, *Tribal Women in the New Profile*, Anmol Publications Pvt. Ltd., 4374/4B Ansari Road, Daryaganj, New Delhi: 2002.

Singh, A.K. and M.K. Jabbi (eds.), *Tribals in India*, Har-Anand Publications, 364-A, Chirag Delhi, New Delhi: 1995.

Singh, A.K., G. Pandey and P.K. Singh, *Forest and Tribals in India*, Classical Publishing Company, 28, Shopping Centre, Karampura, New Delhi: 1998.

Singh, B. and J.S. Bhandari, *The Tribal World and its Transformation*, Concept Publishing Company, H-13, Bali Nagar, New Delhi: 1980.

Singh, K. Suresh (ed.), *Tribal Situation in India*, Indian Institute of Advanced Study, Simla: 1972.

Singh, K.S., *People of India: An Introduction*, Anthropological Survey of India, Calcutta: 1992.

Streefkerk, Hein and T.K. Moulik, *Managing Rural Development*, Sage Publications, M-32, Greater Kailash Market-1, New Delhi-110048: 1997.

Thakur, Devendra and D.N. Thakur (eds.), *Tribal Development and Planning*, Deep and Deep Publications, F-159, Rajouri Garden, New Delhi-110027: 1997.

Toppo, Sita, *Dynamics of Educational Development in Tribal India*, Classical Publications, C-4-A 30/C, Janakpuri, New Delhi-110058: 1979.

Tripathy, S.N., *Tribal Women in India*, Mohit Publications, 4675/21, Ansari Road, Daryaganj, New Delhi-110002: 2002.

——, *Glimpses of Tribal Development*, Discovery Publishing House, 4831/24, Ansari Road, Daryaganj, New Delhi-110002: 2000.

# 3

# West Bengal

S.K. BHAUMIK*

## INTRODUCTION

West Bengal has been one of the 28 states of the Indian Union. According to Census 2001, West Bengal accounted for 7.81 per cent of total population of the country while its share in land (geographical) area has been 2.70 per cent only. The high concentration of population in the state becomes further clear from the fact that while for all-India the population density (population per sq. km) in 2001 has been only 312, the same for West Bengal is found to be as high as 904. This unusually high concentration of population is sure to have profound impact on the economic and social life of its population. As regards the concentration of population in rural areas, it is found that nearly 72 per cent of the state's populations resided in rural areas in 2001. In other words, the state continues to be predominantly rural although there are some indications of percentage of rural population declining in the state, albeit slowly, in recent years.

Another important feature about the state of West Bengal is that the same Left Front Government (LFG) has been governing continuously since 1977. Apart from the stability in governance that the state enjoys, the developmental policies formulated and implemented by the LFG have significantly altered the economic and

* Head, Department of Economics, Calcutta University, Kolkata-700050; E-mail: bhaumiksk@yahoo.co.in

social life of the people over 29 years or so. As is well known, on assuming power in 1977, the LFG adopted a rurally oriented developmental policy whereby the main thrust has been serious implementation of land reforms provisions and laws and also revival of the panchayati raj system so as to establish a system of decentralized governance. There is a vast literature now available to show that rural West Bengal underwent serious transformation, consequent upon the implementation of its policies, in terms of attainment of significantly high growth of agricultural production (particularly that of food grains) since early 1980s and also establishing a more egalitarian agrarian system (see, for example, Lieten, 1992, 1996; Webster, 1992; Chadha and Bhaumik, 1992; Bhaumik, 1993; Saha and Swaminathan, 1994; Sen and Sengupta, 1995; Sengupta and Gazdar, 1997; Rawal and Swaminathan, 1998; Banerjee *et al.*, 2002c; Ramchandran and Swaminathan, 2002; Khasnabis, 2003). The positive declines in rural poverty in West Bengal, particularly since mid-1980s are also in evidence (see Deaton and Dreze, 2002; Sundaram and Tendulkar; 2003). Such positive developments notwithstanding, there have been a lot of hue and cry in recent years over the fact that the development strategies which have been pursued vigorously by the LFG for so long years (to which land reforms have been a significant component), have perhaps reached to a saturation point. While the growth rate of agricultural production itself has reached a plateau towards the end of 1990s, agricultural employment has not been growing any more to any significant extent. It is also pointed out by the critics that, while over-emphasizing the programmes of land reforms and the development of agricultural sector, the LFG has ignored the other vital sectors of the economy, particularly industries. In West Bengal, the rural industrial sector is reported to be in complete doldrums and the urban industries have been registering continuous decay under the LFG regime (see Chadha, 2001; Banerjee *et al.*, 2002a, 2002b). As a consequence of these developments, unemployment in the state, particularly in rural areas, has now assumed a serious dimension (see Bhaumik, 2002, 2003). There are other areas as well where the state has performed rather unsatisfactorily, which are education and health. The public health delivery system in the state is reported have almost collapsed while in the sphere of education the state is being cited as a failure when compared with many other states of India (e.g. Kerala, Himachal Pradesh, Karnataka etc.).

## PURPOSE OF THE STUDY

Against the above backdrop, the present study seeks to build the social and economic profiles for rural West Bengal towards the end of 1990s. For doing this, our chosen indicators are: (1) Economic Activities; (2) Infrastructure; (3) Health; (4) Education; (5) Panchayati Raj System; (6) Agrarian Relations; (7) Anti-Poverty and Rural Development Schemes; (8) Social Structure; and (9) Gender Empowerment. Hopefully, our analysis of these aspects would provide some understanding of rural transformation that West Bengal has been undergoing and also to identify the problem areas that would possibly require active government intervention in the years to come.

## INFORMATION BASE FOR THE STUDY

It is necessary to spell out the information/data to be used for the purpose of our study. For building a reasonable account of the social and economic structure in the state and understanding the rural transformation processes that the state has been experiencing, we would use extensively district level secondary data, available from various sources on the above-identified aspects. We would also draw insights, wherever possible, from the village studies conducted recently by the researchers (the IAS trainees) at the Lal Bahadur Shastri National Academy of Administration, Mussoorie (hereafter called LBSNAA-VSs)[1]. These apart, we would use the findings from recently conducted studies by independent researchers covering some of the above-mentioned aspects. It is to be noted that the secondary data available from the published reports are of quantitative types, while the information available from LBSNAA-VSs are mostly qualitative in nature. The intermingling of quantitative and qualitative information would hopefully provide more satisfactory account of social and economic structures in rural West Bengal at the dawn of the new millennium.

## ECONOMIC ACTIVITIES

The main purpose of this section is looking the economic activities to which the rural people of West Bengal have been engaged. One way of doing this is to examine the distribution of working population into various activities. In other words, we might look into the sectoral distribution of rural workers. Before doing that, we would have a look into other indicators such as worker-population ratio and the extent of marginal workers. Since employment opportunities are determined by the performances of various sectors of the economy, in this very section, we would also discuss the present status of the most important sector of the rural economy of West Bengal, viz. agriculture.

## Worker-Population Ratio

In order to assess the employment situation in any region, the researchers usually begin by looking at worker-population ratio. We have compiled data on this aspect as available from the reports of Census of India for the years 1991 and 2001 for all districts of West Bengal. Table 3.1 gives data on worker-population ratio for rural areas only and by male-female division. Several points emerge here. (1) When we consider the main workers[2] only, the worker-population ratio for rural males in West Bengal appears to have declined sizeably between 1991 and 2001. While the worker-population ratio for rural males in the state was 51.18 in 1991, the same in 2001 is found to be as low as 46.0. There is clear indication of worsening of employment situation for rural male workers in West Bengal during the decade of 1990s[3]. (2) The employment opportunities for rural females have been much restricted in West Bengal as compared to their male counterparts. Considering main workers, the worker-population ratio for rural females is found to be only 8.74 in 1991, which increased marginally to 8.87 in 2001. (3) There is wide inter-district variation as regards worker-population ratios both for males and females. Considering main workers only, as regards males, the worker-population ratio in 2001 turns out to be the highest in Nadia, which is followed by Hooghly, Cooch Behar, Uttar and Dakshin Dinajpur, Burdwan, Howrah and Bankura. On the other hand, the worker-population ratio for male main workers has been on the lower side in Purulia, Darjiling, Midnapore, Malda, 24 Parganas (North & South), Murshidabad, Birbhum and Jalpaiguri. As regards females, the worker-population ratio (considering main workers only) in 2001 was the highest in Darjiling, which is followed by Malda, Jalpaiguri,

**Table 3.1:** Worker-Population Ratio in Rural West Bengal by Districts

| District | Male | | | Female | | | Person | | |
|---|---|---|---|---|---|---|---|---|---|
| | 1991 | 2001 | Change in 2001 over 1991 | 1991 | 2001 | Change in 2001 over 1991 | 1991 | 2001 | Change in 2001 over 1991 |
| **Main workers only** | | | | | | | | | |
| Bankura | 51.00 (8) | 46.35 (7) | –4.64 | 14.70 (3) | 11.98 (5) | –2.73 | 33.29 (4) | 29.58 (7) | –3.71 |
| Burdwan | 52.07 (5) | 47.22 (5) | –4.85 | 9.36 (8) | 9.11 (8) | –0.25 | 31.45 (7) | 28.73 (9) | –2.72 |
| Birbhum | 52.07 (6) | 46.11 (9) | –5.96 | 8.27 (9) | 7.76 (12) | –0.51 | 30.75 (11) | 27.44 (11) | –3.32 |
| Cooch Behar | 53.80 (2) | 50.52 (3) | –3.28 | 6.10 (12) | 9.19 (7) | 3.09 | 30.78 (9) | 30.42 (1) | –0.36 |
| Darjeeling | 46.39 (15) | 41.48 (14) | –4.91 | 23.93 (1) | 17.27 (1) | –6.66 | 35.54 (2) | 29.64 (6) | –5.90 |
| Hooghly | 53.35 (3) | 50.79 (2) | –2.56 | 8.14 (10) | 9.02 (9) | 0.89 | 31.38 (8) | 30.18 (4) | –1.20 |
| Howrah | 50.43 (11) | 46.83 (6) | –3.60 | 2.62 (15) | 5.11 (14) | 2.49 | 27.25 (14) | 26.42 (12) | –0.83 |
| Jalpaiguri | 49.59 (13) | 46.23 (8) | –3.36 | 13.02 (4) | 13.30 (3) | 0.28 | 31.97 (6) | 30.24 (3) | –1.73 |
| Malda | 50.90 (9) | 44.57 (12) | –6.32 | 11.86 (5) | 13.44 (2) | 1.58 | 31.99 (5) | 29.43 (8) | –2.56 |
| Midnapore | 50.60 (10) | 43.61 (13) | –6.99 | 9.88 (7) | 8.19 (11) | –1.69 | 30.77 (10) | 26.28 (13) | –4.49 |
| Murshidabad | 51.42 (7) | 45.85 (10) | –5.57 | 7.09 (11) | 8.47 (10) | 1.38 | 29.92 (12) | 27.64 (10) | –2.28 |
| Nadia | 52.65 (4) | 51.49 (1) | –1.16 | 3.52 (13) | 6.99 (13) | 3.47 | 28.99 (13) | 29.90 (5) | 0.92 |
| North & South 24 Parganas | 49.21 (14) | 44.62 (11) | –4.59 | 3.21 (14) | 5.06 (15) | 1.85 | 26.95 (15) | 25.42 (15) | –1.53 |
| Purulia | 49.89 (12) | 37.99 (15) | –11.90 | 22.08 (2) | 12.42 (4) | –9.66 | 36.33 (1) | 25.49 (14) | –10.84 |
| Uttar & Dakshin Dinajpur | 55.49 (10) | 48.16 (4) | –7.33 | 10.34 (6) | 11.35 (6) | 1.01 | 33.68 (3) | 30.27 (2) | –3.41 |
| West Bengal | 51.18 | 46.00 | –5.18 | 8.74 | 8.87 | 0.13 | 30.61 | 27.91 | –2.70 |
| All India* | 51.88 | 44.67 | –7.21 | 18.75 | 17.09 | –1.66 | 35.84 | 31.26 | –4.58 |
| **Main + Marginal workers** | | | | | | | | | |
| Bankura | 52.15 (8) | 57.17 (2) | 5.02 | 20.22 (3) | 33.46 (2) | 13.24 | 36.57 (2) | 45.60 (2) | 9.03 |
| Burdwan | 52.68 (6) | 56.78 (3) | 4.10 | 11.22 (9) | 19.69 (10) | 8.47 | 32.67 (9) | 38.79 (8) | 6.12 |
| Birbhum | 52.99 (4) | 54.68 (8) | 1.70 | 13.35 (8) | 20.17 (9) | 6.82 | 33.70 (8) | 37.88 (10) | 4.18 |
| Cooch Behar | 54.11 (2) | 55.28 (6) | 1.18 | 9.26 (12) | 23.13 (8) | 13.87 | 32.46 (10) | 39.64 (7) | 7.18 |
| Darjeeling | 46.77 (15) | 48.01 (15) | 1.25 | 24.82 (2) | 25.33 (6) | 0.51 | 36.17 (3) | 36.92 (11) | 0.76 |
| Hooghly | 53.69 (3) | 57.96 (1) | 4.27 | 9.32 (11) | 18.69 (11) | 9.37 | 32.13 (11) | 38.58 (9) | 6.46 |

*(Contd.)*

**Table 31.** *(Contd.)*

| District | Male | | | Female | | | Person | | |
|---|---|---|---|---|---|---|---|---|---|
| | 1991 | 2001 | Change in 2001 over 1991 | 1991 | 2001 | Change in 2001 over 1991 | 1991 | 2001 | Change in 2001 over 1991 |
| Howrah | 50.95 (12) | 55.81 (4) | 4.87 | 3.90 (15) | 10.01 (15) | 6.11 | 28.14 (15) | 33.41 (14) | 5.27 |
| Jalpaiguri | 50.79 (13) | 52.48 (13) | 1.70 | 17.24 (6) | 26.06 (4) | 8.81 | 34.63 (7) | 39.66 (6) | 5.03 |
| Malda | 51.88 (11) | 52.83 (12) | 0.95 | 17.56 (5) | 29.51 (3) | 11.95 | 35.26 (6) | 41.48 (3) | 6.22 |
| Midnapore | 52.40 (7) | 55.15 (7) | 2.75 | 18.53 (4) | 24.30 (7) | 5.77 | 35.91 (4) | 40.06 (5) | 4.15 |
| Murshidabad | 51.94 (9) | 51.45 (14) | –0.48 | 9.61 (10) | 14.43 (12) | 4.83 | 31.41 (12) | 33.43 (13) | 2.02 |
| Nadia | 52.93 (5) | 55.35 (5) | 2.42 | 4.24 (14) | 13.02 (13) | 8.78 | 29.48 (13) | 34.82 (12) | 5.34 |
| North & South 24 Parganas | 50.09 (14) | 52.87 (11) | 2.78 | 6.06 (13) | 11.96 (14) | 5.90 | 28.78 (14) | 33.01 (15) | 4.23 |
| Purulia | 51.88 (10) | 53.05 (10) | 1.17 | 37.44 (1) | 39.14 (1) | 1.70 | 44.84 (1) | 46.25 (1) | 1.41 |
| Uttar & Dakshin Dinajpur | 55.98 (1) | 53.99 (9) | –1.99 | 14.02 (7) | 25.91 (5) | 11.88 | 35.71 (5) | 40.34 (4) | 4.63 |
| West Bengal | 52.09 | 54.30 | 2.21 | 13.07 | 20.70 | 7.63 | 33.18 | 37.93 | 4.75 |
| All India* | 52.58 | 52.48 | –0.10 | 26.79 | 31.31 | 4.52 | 40.09 | 42.19 | 2.10 |

*Notes*: Figures in the brackets are ranks.

* All India excluding Assam and Jammu & Kashmir.

*Source*: Census of India reports for 1991 and 2001.

Purulia, Bankura, Uttar and Dakshin Dinajpur and Cooch Behar. The worker-population ratio for female workers has been low in 24-Parganas (North+South), Howrah, Nadia, Birbhum, Midnapore, Murshidabad, Hooghly and Burdwan. By and large, it appears that the rural males have been participating in main economic activities at a relatively higher rate in agriculturally progressive districts (Nadia, Hooghly, Burdwan, Howrah etc.). On the other hand, work participation rate for females has been relatively higher in the backward districts, which are also known to have greater concentration of tribal/scheduled caste population (Darjeeling, Jalpaiguri, Malda, Purulia, Bankura and Cooch Behar need specific mention here).

The above observations regarding work participation rate in rural West Bengal would change a bit if we consider the main and marginal workers together. Table 3.1 also provides data on worker-population ratio considering all workers together (main and marginal[4]) for West Bengal as a whole as well as districts. Our main observations here are: (1) Considering all workers, the worker-population ratio for rural males in West Bengal is found to have increased from 52.09 per cent in 1991 to 54.30 per cent in 2001. This trend is just reverse to what is observed above while considering only main workers among the rural males. Clearly, this increase in worker-population ratio, while considering all workers, is an indication of large number of male workers being pushed to marginal economic activity in the decade 1990s; (2) As regards females, the worker-population ratio, while considering all workers, in rural West Bengal turns out to be much higher as compared to worker-population ratio computed considering main workers only. Further, the worker-population ratio (considering all workers) for rural females increased significantly from 13.07 in 1991 to 20.70 in 2001. All these imply that a large proportion of workers among rural females have been engaged in marginal economic activities in West Bengal; (3) Among the districts of West Bengal, the worker-population ratio (considering all workers) for rural males in 2001 appears to be the highest in Hooghly, which is followed, in descending order of the value of worker-population ratio, by Bankura, Burdwan, Howrah, Nadia, Cooch Behar, Midnapore, Birbhum, Uttar and Dakshin Dinajpur, Purulia, 24 Parganas (North & South), Malda, Jalpaiguri, Murshidabad and Darjeeling. As regards rural females, the worker-population ratio (considering all workers) in 2001 is found to be the highest in Purulia, which is followed, in descending order of the value of worker-population ratio, by Bankura, Malda, Jalpaiguri, Uttar and Dakshin Dinajpur, Darjeeling, Midnapore, Cooch Behar, Birbhum, Burdwan, Hooghly, Murshidabad, Nadia, 24 Parganas (North & South) and Howrah; (4) It is clear that the worker-population ratio (considering all workers) for rural males has been relatively higher in agriculturally progressive districts of West Bengal while the same for rural females has been relatively higher in the backward districts; and (5) It is also observed that when we considered only the main workers, the worker-population ratio for rural males declined in all districts of West Bengal between 1991 and 2001 while in the case of rural females such a decline is observed in 6 out of 15 districts. This trend is almost completely reversed when we considered all workers for computation of worker-population ratios. In this case, only in 2 out of 15 districts, the rural males registered decline in worker-population ratio while in all districts the rural females experienced increase in worker-population ratio between 1991-2001. This finding reaffirms our previous observation that a sizeable section of rural workers (both males and females) had to be satisfied with marginal economic activities only in the decade of 1990s; whatever employment expansion has taken place in rural West Bengal and her districts has been by and large of marginal character.

## Extent of Marginal Workers

We have noted above the growing tendency of marginalisation of employment in rural West Bengal in recent years. This becomes further clear when we look into the percentage of marginal workers to total workers in rural areas (Table 3.2). It is clear that the marginalisation of employment has been very high during the decade of 1990s in rural West Bengal. While only 1.75 per cent of rural male workers in West Bengal have been in marginal employment in 1991, the same increased to 15.28 per cent in 2001. The rate of marginalisation of employment has been much higher for rural female workers as compared to the rural male workers. As regards rural female workers in West Bengal, the percentage of marginal workers to total workers was 33.12 per cent in 1991, which increased to as high as 57.13 per cent in 2001. Once again, there is wide variation among the districts of West Bengal as regards the marginalisation of employment in rural areas. However, taking a broad view, marginalisation of employment appears to be relatively greater in the districts that are agriculturally backward. In the year 2001, both for rural males and females, the percentage of marginal workers has been the highest in Purulia that is agriculturally backward while this has been the lowest in Nadia, which is known to be one of the agriculturally progressive districts in the state. It seems that because of lack of any stable employment opportunities and their very poor economic conditions, a large section of rural workers in backward areas of the state accepted, as part of their survival strategy, employment that were of marginal nature. In any case, this is indicative of the precarious conditions a large section of rural workers are subjected to in West Bengal in the decade of 1990s.

## Sectoral Distribution of Workers

Let us now look at the sectors to which rural workers have been engaged in West Bengal and its districts. For this purpose, we continue with the census data for the years 1991 and 2001. We consider distribution of all workers (main plus marginal) into four categories, viz. cultivators, agricultural labourers, household industry workers and other workers[5]. Table 3.3 gives data on distribution of rural workers into these categories. The main observations here are the following:

(1) Within the farm sector (comprising cultivators and agricultural labourers), there has been a clear tendency of percentage of workers as cultivators declining while that of agricultural labourers increasing during the decade of 1990s in West Bengal. This has happened with respect to the rural male workers. As of 2001, only about 29 per cent of rural male workers have worked as cultivators, the percentage of rural male workers as agricultural labourers being nearly 31 per cent. The decline in the percentage of cultivators among rural female workers is also visible during the period 1991-2001. However, the percentage agricultural labourers among rural females registered some decline during the same period. In the year 2001, nearly 42 per cent of rural female workers

**Table 3.2:** Percentage of Marginal Workers to Total Workers in Rural West Bengal by Districts

| District | Male | | Female | | Person | |
|---|---|---|---|---|---|---|
| | 1991 | 2001 | 1991 | 2001 | 1991 | 2001 |
| Bankura | 2.22 (4) | 18.92 (3) | 27.27 (8) | 64.20 (3) | 8.98 (4) | 35.13 (2) |
| Burdwan | 1.15 (8) | 16.83 (4) | 16.59 (13) | 53.75 (9) | 3.71 (11) | 25.92 (6) |
| Birbhum | 1.73 (7) | 15.68 (6) | 38.07 (4) | 61.52 (4) | 8.74 (5) | 27.57 (5) |
| Cooch Behar | 0.56 (14) | 8.61 (14) | 34.14 (5) | 60.25 (5) | 5.19 (9) | 23.27 (9) |
| Darjeeling | 0.81 (12) | 13.62 (9) | 3.56 (15) | 31.82 (15) | 1.72 (14) | 19.72 (13) |
| Hooghly | 0.62 (13) | 12.36 (10) | 12.68 (14) | 51.73 (10) | 2.32 (13) | 21.77 (11) |
| Howrah | 1.02 (9) | 16.10 (5) | 32.78 (6) | 48.98 (11) | 3.15 (12) | 20.92 (12) |
| Jalpaiguri | 2.36 (3) | 11.92 (11) | 24.49 (11) | 48.97 (12) | 7.67 (6) | 23.74 (8) |
| Malda | 1.90 (5) | 15.63 (7) | 32.46 (7) | 54.43 (8) | 9.27 (3) | 29.06 (4) |
| Midnapore | 3.43 (2) | 20.93 (2) | 46.68 (2) | 66.30 (2) | 14.30 (2) | 34.39 (3) |
| Murshidabad | 1.00 (10) | 10.90 (12) | 26.21 (10) | 41.35 (14) | 4.74 (10) | 17.30 (14) |
| Nadia | 0.52 (15) | 6.96 (15) | 16.96 (12) | 46.35 (13) | 1.66 (15) | 14.11 (15) |
| Purulia | 3.84 (1) | 28.39 (1) | 41.04 (3) | 68.28 (1) | 18.98 (1) | 44.89 (1) |
| North and South 24 Parganas | 1.76 (6) | 15.60 (8) | 47.07 (1) | 57.69 (6) | 6.37 (7) | 23.00 (10) |
| Uttar and Dakshin Dinajpur | 0.86 (11) | 10.79 (13) | 26.24 (9) | 56.18 (7) | 5.68 (8) | 24.95 (7) |
| West Bengal | 1.75 | 15.28 | 33.12 | 57.13 | 7.73 | 26.41 |
| All India* | 1.34 | 14.88 | 30.02 | 45.42 | 10.61 | 25.90 |

*Notes*: * All India excluding Assam and Jammu and Kashmir
Figures in brackets are ranks

*Source*: Census of India reports for 1991 and 2001.

**Table 3.3:** Percentage Distribution of Rural Workers (Main + Marginal) into Different Sectors in West Bengal by Districts

| District | Cultivators | | Agricultural Labourers | | All Farm Workers | | Household Industry Workers | | Other Workers | | All Nonfarm Workers | |
|---|---|---|---|---|---|---|---|---|---|---|---|---|
| | 1991 | 2001 | 1991 | 2001 | 1991 | 2001 | 1991 | 2001 | 1991 | 2001 | 1991 | 2001 |
| **RURAL MALE** | | | | | | | | | | | | |
| Bankura | 48.60 | 38.50 | 28.49 | 29.76 | **77.09** (3) | **68.26** (3) | 2.71 | 3.39 | 20.20 | 28.34 | **22.91** (13) | **31.74** (13) |
| Burdwan | 34.30 | 25.17 | 36.92 | 38.13 | **71.22** (10) | **63.30** (8) | 3.03 | 3.18 | 25.75 | 33.52 | **28.78** (6) | **36.70** (8) |
| Birbhum | 40.62 | 29.95 | 36.33 | 36.16 | **76.96** (4) | **66.11** (4) | 3.06 | 3.14 | 19.98 | 30.75 | **23.04** (12) | **33.89** (12) |
| Cooch Behar | 54.80 | 43.55 | 25.42 | 26.36 | **80.22** (2) | **69.91** (2) | 1.70 | 2.40 | 18.08 | 27.69 | **19.78** (14) | **30.09** (14) |
| Darjeeling | 34.15 | 20.74 | 16.38 | 13.36 | **50.53** (14) | **34.11** (14) | 0.53 | 2.45 | 48.94 | 63.44 | **49.47** (2) | **65.89** (2) |
| Hooghly | 32.97 | 24.09 | 31.38 | 30.63 | **64.35** (12) | **54.72** (11) | 3.25 | 3.76 | 32.40 | 41.52 | **35.65** (4) | **45.28** (5) |
| Howrah | 21.67 | 10.90 | 27.79 | 20.79 | **49.46** (15) | **31.69** (15) | 3.31 | 10.76 | 47.23 | 57.55 | **50.54** (1) | **68.31** (1) |
| Jalpaiguri | 38.67 | 26.36 | 18.80 | 16.92 | **57.47** (13) | **43.28** (13) | 0.87 | 1.27 | 41.66 | 55.44 | **42.53** (3) | **56.72** (3) |
| Malda | 41.96 | 29.60 | 34.69 | 32.78 | **76.64** (5) | **62.39** (9) | 2.66 | 4.80 | 20.70 | 32.81 | **23.36** (11) | **37.61** (7) |
| Midnapore | 48.94 | 34.21 | 22.88 | 30.90 | **71.82** (8) | **65.10** (6) | 3.84 | 3.93 | 24.34 | 30.97 | **28.18** (8) | **34.90** (10) |
| Murshidabad | 38.74 | 26.11 | 34.62 | 38.06 | **73.36** (7) | **64.17** (7) | 4.87 | 5.28 | 21.77 | 30.55 | **26.64** (9) | **35.83** (9) |
| Nadia | 38.38 | 27.71 | 33.41 | 32.39 | **71.79** (9) | **60.10** (10) | 4.36 | 5.44 | 23.85 | 34.46 | **28.21** (7) | **39.90** (6) |
| North and South 24 Parganas | 34.06 | 21.08 | 33.02 | 30.18 | **67.08** (11) | **51.25** (12) | 2.85 | 3.82 | 30.06 | 44.92 | **32.92** (5) | **48.75** (4) |
| Purulia | 53.86 | 37.54 | 22.48 | 27.71 | **76.34** (6) | **65.25** (5) | 2.60 | 6.02 | 21.06 | 28.73 | **23.66** (10) | **34.75** (11) |
| Uttar and Dakshin Dinajpur | 51.98 | 39.67 | 33.97 | 36.81 | **85.95** (1) | **76.48** (1) | 1.25 | 1.81 | 12.79 | 21.71 | **14.05** (15) | **23.52** (15) |
| West Bengal | 40.89 | 28.72 | 30.03 | 31.04 | **70.92** | **59.76** | 3.04 | 4.03 | 26.04 | 36.21 | **29.08** | **40.24** |
| All India* | 51.33 | 42.03 | 26.47 | 28.08 | **77.80** | **70.11** | 1.96 | 2.85 | 20.23 | 27.03 | **22.19** | **29.88** |
| **RURAL FEMALE** | | | | | | | | | | | | |
| Bankura | 28.73 | 22.06 | 58.19 | 50.27 | **86.93** (2) | **72.32** (4) | 6.07 | 9.26 | 7.00 | 18.41 | **13.07** (14) | **27.68** (12) |
| Burdwan | 8.94 | 5.97 | 69.72 | 53.58 | **78.65** (4) | **59.56** (7) | 7.33 | 12.21 | 14.02 | 28.24 | **21.35** (12) | **40.44** (9) |
| Birbhum | 19.07 | 10.25 | 59.15 | 49.75 | **78.22** (6) | **60.00** (6) | 8.85 | 16.53 | 12.93 | 23.46 | **21.78** (10) | **40.00** (10) |

*(Contd.)*

**Table 3.3:** (*Contd.*)

| *District* | *Cultivators* | | *Agricultural Labourers* | | *All Farm Workers* | | *Household Industry Workers* | | *Other Workers* | | *All Nonfarm Workers* | |
|---|---|---|---|---|---|---|---|---|---|---|---|---|
| | 1991 | 2001 | 1991 | 2001 | 1991 | 2001 | 1991 | 2001 | 1991 | 2001 | 1991 | 2001 |
| Cooch Behar | 32.67 | 32.57 | 45.41 | 45.51 | **78.08** (7) | **78.08** (2) | 6.71 | 7.68 | 15.21 | 14.24 | **21.92** (9) | **21.92** (14) |
| Darjeeling | 32.19 | 20.29 | 15.25 | 16.35 | **47.44** (11) | **36.65** (12) | 0.42 | 3.67 | 52.15 | 59.68 | **52.56** (5) | **63.35** (4) |
| Hooghly | 6.50 | 10.86 | 67.42 | 45.28 | **73.93** (8) | **56.14** (8) | 8.37 | 13.30 | 17.70 | 30.56 | **26.07** (8) | **43.86** (8) |
| Howrah | 20.60 | 3.96 | 26.76 | 12.93 | **47.36** (12) | **16.90** (14) | 15.41 | 33.55 | 37.22 | 49.55 | **52.64** (4) | **83.10** (2) |
| Jalpaiguri | 16.29 | 17.68 | 21.72 | 27.96 | **38.01** (13) | **45.64** (9) | 1.49 | 2.50 | 60.50 | 51.86 | **61.99** (3) | **54.36** (7) |
| Malda | 14.64 | 7.36 | 43.18 | 31.90 | **57.83** (10) | **39.27** (11) | 7.70 | 37.74 | 34.47 | 22.99 | **42.17** (6) | **60.73** (5) |
| Midnapore | 42.61 | 21.24 | 35.88 | 41.10 | **78.49** (5) | **62.33** (5) | 10.83 | 17.16 | 10.68 | 20.50 | **21.51** (11) | **37.67** (11) |
| Murshidabad | 5.81 | 3.43 | 13.45 | 10.53 | **19.26** (15) | **13.96** (15) | 64.19 | 61.43 | 16.54 | 24.61 | **80.74** (1) | **86.04** (1) |
| Nadia | 7.73 | 11.25 | 29.39 | 13.96 | **37.12** (14) | **25.21** (13) | 23.42 | 29.09 | 39.46 | 45.70 | **62.88** (2) | **74.79** (3) |
| North and South 24 Parganas | 29.12 | 13.25 | 30.37 | 26.84 | **59.48** (9) | **40.09** (10) | 11.71 | 17.22 | 28.80 | 42.69 | **40.52** (7) | **59.91** (6) |
| Purulia | 49.78 | 27.21 | 42.76 | 53.61 | **92.55** (1) | **80.82** (1) | 2.49 | 10.24 | 4.97 | 8.94 | **7.45** (15) | **19.18** (15) |
| Uttar and Dakshin Dinajpur | 17.94 | 19.23 | 65.79 | 54.30 | **83.73** (3) | **73.53** (3) | 5.57 | 8.63 | 10.69 | 17.84 | **16.27** (13) | **26.47** (13) |
| West Bengal | 27.82 | 16.07 | 41.76 | 38.56 | **69.58** | **54.63** | 11.18 | 18.20 | 19.24 | 27.17 | **30.42** | **45.37** |
| All India* | 42.07 | 36.10 | 47.37 | 44.33 | **89.44** | **80.43** | 2.72 | 5.35 | 7.84 | 14.21 | **10.56** | **19.56** |
| **RURAL PERSON** | | | | | | | | | | | | |
| Bankura | 43.24 | 32.61 | 36.50 | 37.10 | **79.74** (4) | **69.72** (4) | 3.62 | 5.50 | 16.64 | 24.79 | **20.26** (12) | **30.28** (12) |
| Burdwan | 30.10 | 20.44 | 42.36 | 41.94 | **72.45** (7) | **62.38** (7) | 3.74 | 5.40 | 23.81 | 32.22 | **27.55** (9) | **37.62** (9) |
| Birbhum | 36.47 | 24.85 | 40.73 | 39.68 | **77.20** (5) | **64.53** (5) | 4.18 | 6.61 | 18.62 | 28.86 | **22.80** (11) | **35.47** (11) |
| Cooch Behar | 51.75 | 40.43 | 28.18 | 31.79 | **79.92** (3) | **72.23** (2) | 2.39 | 3.90 | 17.68 | 23.87 | **20.08** (13) | **27.77** (14) |
| Darjeeling | 33.50 | 20.59 | 16.01 | 14.37 | **49.50** (14) | **34.96** (14) | 0.49 | 2.86 | 50.00 | 62.18 | **50.50** (2) | **65.04** (2) |
| Hooghly | 29.24 | 20.93 | 36.46 | 34.13 | **65.70** (11) | **55.06** (8) | 3.97 | 6.04 | 30.33 | 38.90 | **34.30** (5) | **44.94** (8) |
| Howrah | 21.60 | 9.89 | 27.72 | 19.64 | **49.32** (15) | **29.52** (15) | 4.12 | 14.10 | 46.56 | 56.38 | **50.68** (1) | **70.48** (1) |
| Jalpaiguri | 33.31 | 23.59 | 19.50 | 20.44 | **52.80** (13) | **44.04** (13) | 1.02 | 1.66 | 46.18 | 54.30 | **47.20** (3) | **55.96** (3) |

(*Contd*)

**Table 3.3:** (*Contd*)

| *District* | *Cultivators* | | *Agricultural Labourers* | | *All Farm Workers* | | *Household Industry Workers* | | *Other Workers* | | *All Non-farm Workers* | |
|---|---|---|---|---|---|---|---|---|---|---|---|---|
| | 1991 | 2001 | 1991 | 2001 | 1991 | 2001 | 1991 | 2001 | 1991 | 2001 | 1991 | 2001 |
| Malda | 35.37 | 21.91 | 36.74 | 32.48 | **72.10** (8) | **54.38** (9) | 3.87 | 16.20 | 24.02 | 29.41 | **27.90** (8) | **45.62** (7) |
| Midnapore | 47.35 | 30.36 | 26.14 | 33.92 | **73.49** (6) | **64.28** (6) | 5.60 | 7.86 | 20.91 | 27.86 | **26.51** (10) | **35.72** (10) |
| Murshidabad | 33.85 | 21.34 | 31.48 | 32.27 | **65.34** (12) | **53.61** (11) | 13.67 | 17.09 | 21.00 | 29.30 | **34.66** (4) | **46.39** (5) |
| Nadia | 36.26 | 24.72 | 33.14 | 29.05 | **69.39** (9) | **53.77** (10) | 5.68 | 9.73 | 24.93 | 36.50 | **30.61** (7) | **46.23** (6) |
| North and South 24 Parganas | 33.56 | 19.70 | 32.75 | 29.59 | **66.31** (10) | **49.29** (12) | 3.76 | 6.18 | 29.93 | 44.53 | **33.69** (6) | **50.71** (4) |
| Purulia | 52.20 | 33.27 | 30.74 | 38.43 | **82.94** (2) | **71.69** (3) | 2.56 | 7.77 | 14.51 | 20.54 | **17.06** (14) | **28.31** (13) |
| Uttar and Dakshin Dinajpur | 45.52 | 33.29 | 40.01 | 42.27 | **85.53** (1) | **75.56** (1) | 2.07 | 3.94 | 12.39 | 20.50 | **14.47** (15) | **24.44** (15) |
| West Bengal | 38.40 | 25.36 | 32.27 | 33.04 | **70.67** | **58.40** | 4.59 | 7.80 | 24.74 | 33.80 | **29.33** | **41.60** |
| All India* | 48.34 | 39.89 | 33.23 | 33.95 | **81.57** | **73.84** | 2.21 | 3.75 | 16.22 | 22.41 | **18.43** | **26.16** |

*Notes*: * All India excluding Assam and Jammu and Kashmir
Figures in brackets are ranks

*Source*: Census of India reports for 1991 and 2001.

in West Bengal have worked as cultivators while their percentage as agricultural labourers has been 39 per cent.

(2) In rural West Bengal, there has been a rather steep decline in the percentage of farm workers (cultivators + agricultural labourers) both among males and females during the decade of 1990s. As regards rural male workers, this declined from 70.92 per cent in 1991 to 59.76 per cent in 2001, while the corresponding percentages for female workers have been 69.58 and 54.63 for the two years respectively. In other words, as per census data, the decade of 1990s has been marked by a sharp shift of employment by the rural workers (both males and females) towards the non-farm sector in West Bengal[6]. In 2001, about 40 per cent of rural male workers and 45 per cent of rural female workers have been engaged in non-farm employment in West Bengal. However, it is quite possible that the bulk of increased employment within the non-farm sector is of 'marginal' type. This observation follows from the general tendency towards greater marginalisation of employment, in recent years, in rural areas of the state, as indicated previously.

(3) There exists wide variation as regards the degree of diversification of rural employment in the districts of West Bengal. Broadly speaking, rural male workers have been engaged relatively more in farm employment in the backward districts of the state. In the year 2001, as regards rural males, the percentage of farm workers to total workers has been the highest in Uttar and Dakshin Dinajpur, which is followed by Cooch Behar, Bankura, Birbhum, Purulia, Midnapore and Murshidabad. On the other hand, the percentage of farm workers to total workers for males has been the lowest in Howrah, which has been one of the advanced districts of the state. As regards female workers, the percentage of farm workers to total workers in 2001 is found to be the highest in Purulia, while the other districts reporting higher percentage of female farm workers to total workers have been Cooch Behar, Uttar and Dakshin Dinajpur, Bankura, Midnapore and Birbhum. The percentage of female farm workers to total workers has been the lowest in Murshidabad. This is possibly because there is high concentration of Muslim population in this district, which might restrict mobility of the female members to work in the fields. Barring

this district, once again, the percentage of female farm workers to total workers seems to be relatively low in the advanced districts of the state. Specific mention may be made here about Howrah and Nadia.

(4) The overall pattern obtained on the basis of 2001 census data seems to suggest that, for male workers, the incidence of rural non-farm employment has been relatively higher in the districts, which are advanced in terms of agricultural development[7]. This is particularly so if we exclude Darjeeling and Jalpaiguri from our comparison, which report very high incidence of non-farm workers possibly because of high concentration of tea gardens. Considering male and female workers together, it is observed that, in 2001, among the advanced districts of West Bengal having more diversified employment structure in rural areas (and hence higher incidence of non-farm employment) are Howrah, North and South 24 Parganas and Nadia. The two districts of sub-Himalayan region, Darjeeling and Jalpaiguri, join this list because of higher employment availability in tea gardens while Murshidabad too turns out to be fairly diversified primarily because of greater participation of female workers in various kinds of non-farm activities. On the other hand, less diversified districts have been Uttar and Dakshin Dinajpur, Cooch Behar, Purulia, Bankura and Birbhum all of them are known to be relatively backward in terms of level of agricultural development.

## Agricultural Performance

We have discussed above the participation of rural population into various economic activities in the districts as well as the state as a whole. We noticed a clear tendency towards diversification of rural employment, away from the farm to the non-farm sector, in the decade of 1990s. Nevertheless, we cannot lose sight of the fact that the farm/agricultural sector still enjoys the status of most dominant sector in rural areas of West Bengal. The predominance of the farm/agricultural sector in rural West Bengal is also borne out by the LBSNAA Village Surveys by the end of 1990s. Not only this sector currently absorbs nearly three-fifths of all rural workers of the state, but also it contributed nearly one-fourth of the Net State Domestic Products in

West Bengal in 1999-2000 (Government of West Bengal, 2002a, p. 417). Recognizing the importance of the agricultural sector in the state of West Bengal, we discuss below the performance of this sector particularly in the decade of 1990s.

## Cropping Intensity and Cropping Pattern

We begin by looking at the cropping intensity and cropping pattern in the districts as well as the state of West Bengal. The data on cropping intensities in the districts as well as states are presented in Table 3.4. It is observed that cropping intensity in the state of West Bengal increased from 1.59 in 1990-91 to 1.74 in 1990-2000. There exists wide inter-district variation in this regard. In the year 1999-2000, cropping intensity is found to be the highest in Nadia (2.49) and lowest in Purulia (1.10). Among other districts with high levels of cropping intensity in 1999-2000 are Hooghly (2.20), Murshidabad (2.10), North 24 Parganas (2.09), Howrah (2.06), Cooch Behar (2.03), Burdwan (1.91), North and South Dinajpur (1.73) and Midnapore (1.66). The districts with relatively low cropping intensities are Darjeeling (1.17), South 24 Parganas (1.48), Bankura (1.50), Jalpaiguri (1.53), Malda (1.56) and Birbhum (1.56).

**Table 3.4:** Cropping Intensity in West Bengal by Districts

| *District* | *1990-91* | *1999-00* |
|---|---|---|
| Bankura | 1.39 (12) | 1.50 (13) |
| Birbhum | 1.44 (11) | 1.56 (10) |
| Burdwan | 1.62 (8) | 1.91 (7) |
| Cooch Behar | 1.84 (5) | 2.03 (6) |
| Darjeeling | 1.25 (15) | 1.17 (15) |
| Hooghly | 2.03 (2) | 2.20 (2) |
| Howrah | 2.03 (3) | 2.06 (5) |
| Jalpaiguri | 1.36 (13) | 1.53 (12) |
| Maldah | 1.92 (4) | 1.56 (11) |
| Midnapore | 1.50 (10) | 1.66 (9) |
| Murshidabad | 1.83 (6) | 2.10 (3) |
| Nadia | 2.30 (1) | 2.49 (1) |
| North and South Dinajpur | 1.61 (9) | 1.73 (8) |
| North 24 Parganas | 1.63 (7) | 2.09 (4) |
| Purulia | 1.06 (16) | 1.10 (16) |
| South 24 Parganas | 1.28 (14) | 1.48 (14) |
| West Bengal | 1.59 | 1.74 |

*Source*: Governemint of West Bengal, *Statistical Abstract 2001-2002*, Bureau of Applied Economics and Statistics, Kolkata, 2002.

Table 3.5 presents data on the cropping pattern. It emerges that even in 1999-2000, the state agriculture is largely dominated by cultivation of foodgrains, which accounted for 71.11 per cent of gross cropped area. Within the group of foodgrains, Paddy has been the most important, capturing 64.43 per cent of gross cropped area. Further, Aman Paddy alone captured 44.51 per cent of gross cropped area while the corresponding percentages for Boro Paddy and Aus Paddy have been 15.45 and 4.48 respectively. To the extent that wheat and other food crops do not absorb much of cropped areas, agriculture in West Bengal is still dominated by Paddy cultivation. Of course, there have been cultivation of some commercial/cash crops, the most notable of which are Jute (covering 6.43 per cent of cropped area), Oilseeds (5.26 per cent of cropped area) and Potato (3.31 per cent of cropped area). Nevertheless, the data on cropping pattern for the state of West Bengal clearly shows the absence of a satisfactory level of agricultural diversification even by 1999-2000.

There is clear evidence of inter-district variations in cropping pattern in West Bengal. Table 3.5 shows that there are 6 districts (out of 17) where more than three-fourths of cropped areas are devoted for cultivation of Paddy alone. These are Purulia (83.05 per cent), South 24 Parganas (79.74 per cent), Bankura (78.77 per cent), Midnapore (77.99 per cent), Burdwan (77.72 per cent) and Birbhum (76.45 per cent). In districts such as Howrah, and South Dinajpur, more than 70 per cent of cropped area have been devoted to Paddy cultivation. It is also to be noted that Burdwan, Hooghly, Howrah, Midnapore and North 24 Parganas are also known for Boro Paddy cultivation inasmuch as more than one-fifth of cropped areas are devoted to cultivation of this crop in these districts. If we consider the percentage of cropped area under foodgrains, there are 9 districts, namely Bankura, Birbhum, Burdwan, Howrah, Maldah, Midnapore, Purulia, South 24 Parganas and South Dinajpur, where such a percentage exceeds 70 per cent.

Among the commercial/cash crops, oilseeds occupies more than one-tenth of cropped area only in Nadia (11.48 per cent). As regards Jute, more than one-tenth of cropped areas have been devoted in Cooch Behar, Murshidabad, Nadia, North 24 Parganas and North Dinajpur. The other important commercial crop, namely Potato, has been important in Hooghly (absorbing 14.88 per cent of cropped area), Howrah (5.28 per cent), Burdwan (5.18 per cent) and Midnapore (5.15 per cent).

**Table 3.5:** Cropping Pattern in West Bengal by Districts in 1999-2000

| District | % of Gross Cropped Area Under | | | | | | | | | | | | | |
|---|---|---|---|---|---|---|---|---|---|---|---|---|---|---|
| | Paddy | | | | Wheat | Cereals (total) | Pulses (Total) | Food-grains (Total) | Rape and Mustard | Oilseeds (Total) | Jute | Sugar-cane | Toba-cco | Potato |
| | Aus | Aman | Boro | Total | | | | | | | | | | |
| Bankura | 6.35 | 63.54 | 8.89 | 78.77 | 1.07 | 80.05 | 0.23 | 80.28 | 2.18 | 5.29 | 0.06 | 0.06 | 0.00 | 4.97 |
| Birbhum | 1.82 | 59.57 | 15.05 | 76.45 | 4.03 | 80.54 | 2.08 | 82.62 | 5.41 | 5.78 | 0.04 | 0.16 | 0.00 | 2.74 |
| Burdwan | 4.03 | 47.45 | 26.24 | 77.72 | 0.26 | 78.03 | 0.64 | 78.67 | 3.93 | 4.71 | 1.72 | 0.10 | 0.00 | 5.18 |
| Cooch Behar | 6.78 | 45.91 | 5.92 | 58.61 | 3.23 | 62.04 | 1.79 | 63.82 | 1.52 | 2.81 | 16.27 | 0.00 | 1.77 | 2.87 |
| Darjeeling | 2.99 | 17.33 | 0.23 | 20.56 | 1.67 | 39.90 | 1.04 | 41.05 | 0.06 | 0.17 | 1.32 | 0.00 | 0.00 | 4.09 |
| Hooghly | 1.73 | 38.56 | 22.59 | 62.88 | 0.16 | 63.06 | 0.26 | 63.32 | 1.23 | 5.32 | 6.37 | 0.00 | 0.00 | 14.88 |
| Howrah | 0.77 | 40.96 | 32.09 | 73.82 | 0.33 | 74.15 | 0.17 | 74.31 | 0.50 | 2.20 | 2.31 | 0.00 | 0.00 | 5.28 |
| Jalpaiguri | 12.27 | 36.89 | 1.29 | 50.46 | 4.93 | 56.02 | 1.19 | 57.21 | 1.45 | 2.23 | 9.34 | 0.06 | 0.31 | 2.84 |
| Maldah | 2.82 | 33.35 | 16.25 | 52.42 | 10.86 | 64.84 | 5.68 | 70.52 | 4.86 | 5.04 | 5.43 | 1.39 | 0.20 | 0.57 |
| Midnapore | 4.96 | 52.83 | 20.19 | 77.99 | 0.70 | 78.75 | 0.87 | 79.61 | 1.18 | 4.45 | 0.58 | 0.32 | 0.00 | 5.15 |
| Murshidabad | 5.86 | 26.90 | 11.39 | 44.15 | 14.16 | 58.62 | 4.85 | 63.47 | 6.38 | 7.01 | 16.11 | 0.77 | 0.00 | 0.99 |
| Nadia | 7.79 | 16.41 | 17.38 | 41.58 | 6.79 | 48.41 | 6.98 | 55.39 | 8.63 | 11.48 | 16.75 | 0.16 | 0.00 | 0.48 |
| North 24 Parganas | 4.71 | 35.19 | 20.53 | 60.43 | 1.39 | 61.81 | 1.73 | 63.55 | 6.55 | 7.68 | 10.42 | 0.18 | 0.00 | 1.37 |
| North Dinajpur | 0.21 | 39.10 | 19.16 | 58.47 | 6.95 | 65.66 | 1.62 | 67.29 | 6.06 | 8.08 | 11.86 | 0.06 | 0.00 | 1.13 |
| Purulia | 0.64 | 81.41 | 1.00 | 83.05 | 0.78 | 86.65 | 4.32 | 90.96 | 0.19 | 1.25 | 0.00 | 0.11 | 0.00 | 0.39 |
| South 24 Parganas | 0.93 | 65.35 | 13.47 | 79.74 | 0.37 | 80.11 | 1.33 | 81.44 | 0.54 | 1.03 | 0.09 | 0.00 | 0.00 | 0.94 |
| South Dinajpur | 3.05 | 57.67 | 12.17 | 72.89 | 3.08 | 75.97 | 1.34 | 77.32 | 6.84 | 6.91 | 4.56 | 0.07 | 0.00 | 1.14 |
| West Bengal | 4.48 | 44.51 | 15.45 | 64.43 | 3.82 | 68.87 | 2.24 | 71.11 | 3.62 | 5.26 | 6.43 | 0.24 | 0.12 | 3.31 |

*Source*: Governemnt of West Bengal, *Statistical Abstract 2001-2002*, Bureau of Applied Economics and Statistics, Kolkata, 2002.

It appears from the above discussion that although cropping intensity in the state increased quite significantly during the decade of 1990s, there exists wide inter-district variation in this regard. One of the crops that helped towards expansion of cropping intensity has been Boro Paddy, which is cultivated during Rabi/Boro season. Overall, the cropping pattern is still tilted in favour of foodgrains, particularly Paddy. The degree of diversification in cropping pattern has not yet been very high in a good number of districts in West Bengal; not many of the districts have been cultivating commercial/cash crops at a higher scale even in 1999-2000.

The picture of cropping pattern and cropping intensities obtained on the basis of secondary data is corroborated by the LBSNAA-VSs as well. Not only Paddy dominated the cropping pattern in 13 village studies, conducted between 1995-2002, but also the degree of crop-diversification has been generally low.

## *Agricultural Inputs and Technology*

Let us now look at the rate of adoption of some important agricultural inputs and technology in West Bengal and her districts by the end of 1990s. We concentrate on three indicators here: (1) percentage of net irrigated area to net sown area, (2) fertilizer consumption per hectare (kgs.), and (3) number of power tillers and tractors per thousand hectares of gross cropped area.

Table 3.6 shows that nearly one-half of net sown areas are irrigated in West Bengal in 1999-2000. In other words, there is a lot more to achieve in this regard. Among the districts, percentage of net sown area irrigated is the highest in Hooghly at 90.74 per cent and lowest in Darjeeling at 13.87 per cent. The districts where the percentage of net sown area irrigated is above the state average are Birbhum (84.19 per cent), Burdwan (75.10 per cent), Bankura (74.93 per cent), Midnapore (68.65 per cent), Nadia (67.27 per cent) and North 24 Parganas (55.47 per cent). On the other hand, apart from Darjeeling, the other districts with percentage of net sown area irrigated being below state average are South 24 Parganas (16.60 per cent), Jalpaiguri (22.08 per cent), North Dinajpur (23.59 per cent), Cooch Behar (24.50 per cent), Purulia (25.00 per cent), South Dinajpur (25.96 per cent), Murshidabad (32.89 per cent), Malda (39.62 per cent) and Howrah (41.83 per cent).

In the year 1999-2000, the fertilizer consumption in the state stood at 129.04 kgs. per hectare of gross cropped area, which is somewhat higher than the all-India average (95.33 kgs./hectare) although this is much lower than per hectare consumption in states such as Punjab (184.57 kgs), Tamil Nadu (162.91 kgs), Andhra Pradesh (155.50 kgs) and Haryana (148.47 kgs) (CMIE, 2000, p. 53). Among the districts of West Bengal, per hectare fertilizer consumption is extremely high in Howrah (346.25 kgs.) and Hooghly (223.48 kgs.). The other districts reporting per hectare consumption of fertilizer being higher than the state average are Darjeeling, Burdwan, Birbhum, North 24 Parganas, Purulia and Malda. On the other hand, in Cooch Behar, South 24 Parganas, Midnapore, Jalpaiguri, Bankura, Nadia, North Dinajpur, Murshidabad and South Dinajpur fertilizer consumption per hectare has been lower than the state average.

**Table 3.6:** Some Indicators of Adoption of Agricultural Inputs and Technology in West Bengal

| *District* | *% of Net Irrigated Area (1999-2000)* | | *Fertiliser consumption per hectare (Kgs.) (1999-2000)* | | *No. of Power Tiller and Tractor per 1000 hectares (1997)* | | *Overall rank* |
|---|---|---|---|---|---|---|---|
| Bankura | 74.93 | (4) | 106.56 | (13) | 3.26 | (6) | 7 |
| Birbhum | 84.19 | (2) | 143.96 | (5) | 2.18 | (9) | 4 |
| Burdwan | 75.10 | (3) | 152.22 | (4) | 7.52 | (3) | 2 |
| Cooch Behar | 24.50 | (13) | 123.27 | (9) | 1.22 | (10) | 10 |
| Darjeeling | 13.87 | (17) | 199.75 | (3) | 0.43 | (16) | 12 |
| Hooghly | 90.74 | (1) | 223.48 | (2) | 12.12 | (2) | 1 |
| Howrah | 41.83 | (8) | 346.25 | (1) | 12.48 | (1) | 3 |
| Jalpaiguri | 22.08 | (15) | 109.17 | (12) | 0.68 | (14) | 15 |
| Malda | 39.62 | (9) | 135.07 | (8) | 1.13 | (11) | 8 |
| Midnapore (East + West) | 68.65 | (5) | 114.04 | (11) | 3.46 | (5) | 6 |
| Murshidabad | 32.89 | (10) | 89.42 | (16) | 0.84 | (13) | 14 |
| Nadia | 67.27 | (6) | 102.35 | (14) | 2.79 | (8) | 9 |
| North 24 Parganas | 55.47 | (7) | 143.18 | (6) | 3.98 | (4) | 5 |
| North Dinajpur | 23.59 | (14) | 99.05 | (15) | 0.95 | (12) | 16 |
| Purulia | 25.00 | (12) | 142.12 | (7) | 0.22 | (17) | 13 |
| South 24 Parganas | 16.60 | (16) | 115.77 | (10) | 2.86 | (7) | 11 |
| South Dinajpur | 25.96 | (11) | 67.86 | (17) | 0.59 | (15) | 17 |
| West Bengal | 49.82 | | 129.04 | | 3.32 | | |

*Note:* Figures in brackets are ranks.

*Sources*: (i) Govt. of West Bengal, *Statistical Abstract 2001-2002*, BAES;
(ii) Govt. of West Bengal, *Distict Statistical Handbooks 1999-2000*, BAES.

Table 3.6 also presents data on number of power tillers and tractors (per thousand hectares) in West Bengal as well as her districts in 1997. This number is found to be 3.32 in 1997. Among the districts, these implements have been in great use in three districts in particular, which are Howrah (12.48), Hooghly (12.12) and Burdwan (7.52). Accordingly, a good number of households in the villages surveyed by the LBSNAA in these districts are reported to own these implements. In the districts of North 24 Parganas and Midnapore also the numbers of power tillers and tractors (per thousand hectares) exceeded the state average. However, in the remaining 12 districts, this has been lower than the state average.

If we consider these three items of new agricultural technology together and compute the 'combined rank'[8], it appears that in terms of adoption of modern inputs and technology, Hooghly comes first in West Bengal, which is followed by Burdwan, Howrah, Birbhum, North 24 Paraganas and Midnapore. In terms of adoption of modern inputs and technology, these 6 districts appear to be most progressive in the state. On the other hand, the most backward districts are South Dinajpur, North Dinajpur, Jalpaiguri, Murshidabad, Purulia, Darjeeling, South 24 Parganas and Cooch Behar. The remaining 3 districts (Nadia, Malda and Bankura) fall in the middle category as regards adoption of modern inputs and technology.

### *Yield of Major Crops*

We now look at the yield levels of various crops in West Bengal and her districts in 1999-2000 (Table 3.7). In case of Paddy, the most important crop of the State, the yield level is 2,237 kgs. per hectare, which is considerably high from its levels in 1980-81 (1,440 kgs./hectare) and 1990-91 (1,800 kgs./hectare) (CMIE, 2000, p. 74). Hence, there is no doubt that the yield of Paddy increased in West Bengal considerably all through the decades of 1980s and 1990s. However, it also needs to be noted that in comparison to major Paddy producing states of India, the yield level for Paddy in West Bengal still lagged behind rather substantially. As observed from Table 3.8, there are 12 states in the country that accounted for 95 per cent of total Paddy production in the year 1999-2000. Among these states, although West Bengal makes the largest contribution to the country's total Paddy production, its rank in terms of yield level has been sixth. Among the states of India, the yield of Paddy has been the highest in

Punjab at 3,346 kg/hectare which is much higher than West Bengal. Even the states of Tamil Nadu and Andhra Pradesh performed much better than West Bengal in this regard. In any case, the yield level of be Paddy in West Bengal has to be improved a lot in the years to come.

Table 3.7 also shows that there are wide variations among the districts in terms of yield of Paddy. In this regard, Burdwan comes first, followed by Birbhum, Nadia, North 24 Parganas, Hooghly and Bankura. In all these districts, the yield of Paddy has been much higher than the state average. On the other hand, the most lagging districts have been Darjeeling, Jalpaiguri, Cooch Behar, Purulia, South Dinajpur, North Dinajpur and South 24 Parganas. Even in Midnapore and Howrah, which are otherwise known to be agriculturally progressive districts (in terms of adoption of modern inputs and technology), the yield of Paddy has fallen behind the state average.

As regards the commercial crop Jute, the state average in 1999-2000 has been 2,227 kgs. per hectare, which is higher than its level in 1990-91 (1,980 kgs./hectare) (*Ibid.*, p. 210). Among the districts, the yield of Jute is the highest in Bankura (3,409 kgs./ hectare). This is also very high in the districts of Birbhum (3,409 kgs./hectare), Midnapore (3,263 kgs./hectare), Hooghly (3,179 kgs./ hectare), Howrah (3,098 kgs./hectare) and Burdwan (2,905 kgs./ hectare). The other districts where the yield the Jute exceeded the state average are South 24 Parganas, Nadia, North 24 Parganas and Murshidabad. The yield of Jute has been extremely low in Jalpaiguri, Cooch Behar, North Dinajpur, South Dinajpur, Darjeeling and Malda.

In recent years, Potato has been emerging as an important commercial crop in West Bengal. The yield of Potato in 1999-2000 has been 23,689 kgs./hectare that is marginally higher than its level in 1990-91 (23,040 kgs./hectare). Among the districts, the yield of Potato has been the highest in Burdwan, which is followed by Midnapore, Bankura, Cooch Behar and Hooghly. The yield level of Potato has been the lowest in Darjeeling. This has been very low also in Purulia, South Dinajpur and South 24 Parganas.

### Growth of Agricultural Production

In recent years, a great deal of discussion has taken place on the growth performance of agriculture in West Bengal, particularly during the period following the implementation of land reforms programmes in West Bengal since early 1980s. In almost all recent official

**Table 3.7:** Yield of Major Crops in West Bengal by Districts in 1999-2000

(*Kgs. Per Hectare*)

| District | Paddy | | | | | Wheat | Pulses (Total) | Food-Grains (Total) | | Rape and Mustard | Oilseeds (Total) | Jute | | Sugar-cane | Toba-cco | Potato | |
|---|---|---|---|---|---|---|---|---|---|---|---|---|---|---|---|---|---|
| | Aus | Aman | Boro | Total | | | | | | | | | | | | | |
| Bankura | 2298 | 2389 | 2724 | 2419 | (6) | 2147 | 572 | 2407 | (5) | 590 | 615 | 3409 | (1) | 9710 | 222 | 24537 | (3) |
| Birbhum | 2228 | 2550 | 3071 | 2645 | (2) | 2746 | 974 | 2607 | (2) | 964 | 930 | 3409 | (2) | 9710 | – | 23289 | (6) |
| Burdwan | 2413 | 2416 | 3378 | 2740 | (1) | 2247 | 731 | 2772 | (1) | 891 | 874 | 2905 | (6) | 6498 | – | 27485 | (1) |
| Cooch Behar | 1577 | 1334 | 2749 | 1505 | (15) | 2089 | 679 | 1510 | (16) | 819 | 654 | 1577 | (15) | 7753 | 500 | 23556 | (4) |
| Darjeeling | 1446 | 1426 | 2712 | 1443 | (17) | 1566 | 714 | 1589 | (15) | 712 | 521 | 1768 | (12) | – | – | 12747 | (17) |
| Hooghly | 2067 | 2366 | 2648 | 2459 | (5) | 1862 | 856 | 2451 | (3) | 698 | 611 | 3179 | (4) | – | – | 23385 | (5) |
| Howrah | 2016 | 1650 | 2919 | 2206 | (9) | 1103 | 605 | 2198 | (7) | 586 | 627 | 3098 | (5) | 5928 | – | 22796 | (7) |
| Jalpaiguri | 1621 | 1388 | 2419 | 1471 | (16) | 2054 | 566 | 1502 | (17) | 548 | 562 | 1521 | (16) | 7753 | 999 | 22718 | (8) |
| Maldah | 1687 | 1862 | 3148 | 2252 | (7) | 2437 | 453 | 2117 | (10) | 922 | 900 | 1804 | (11) | 7753 | 670 | 18040 | (12) |
| Midnapore | 2019 | 1964 | 2807 | 2186 | (10) | 1852 | 838 | 2168 | (8) | 707 | 888 | 3263 | (3) | 10928 | – | 25482 | (2) |
| Murshidabad | 1621 | 1906 | 3368 | 2245 | (8) | 2359 | 861 | 2158 | (9) | 849 | 837 | 2470 | (10) | 5758 | – | 20560 | (10) |
| Nadia | 2076 | 1885 | 3401 | 2554 | (3) | 2301 | 560 | 2271 | (6) | 795 | 897 | 2531 | (8) | 5928 | 570 | 17779 | (13) |
| North 24 Parganas | 2368 | 2197 | 3072 | 2507 | (4) | 2122 | 643 | 2448 | (4) | 854 | 899 | 2493 | (9) | 5928 | – | 21158 | (9) |
| North Dinajpur | 906 | 1541 | 2933 | 1995 | (12) | 2590 | 477 | 2018 | (12) | 578 | 561 | 1586 | (14) | 7753 | – | 18526 | (11) |
| Purulia | 1474 | 1821 | 2418 | 1826 | (14) | 2518 | 520 | 1756 | (14) | 783 | 495 | – | | 9710 | – | 13245 | (16) |
| South 24 Parganas | 2055 | 1888 | 2809 | 2046 | (11) | 1357 | 696 | 2020 | (11) | 889 | 935 | 2560 | (7) | 5928 | – | 17111 | (14) |
| South Dinajpur | 1720 | 1790 | 2748 | 1947 | (13) | 2423 | 643 | 1943 | (13) | 797 | 797 | 1649 | (13) | 7753 | – | 13863 | (15) |
| West Bengal | 1938 | 1902 | 3031 | 2237 | | 2336 | 661 | 2187 | | 805 | 808 | 2227 | | 7704 | 858 | 23689 | |

*Note*: Figures in brackets are ranks.

*Source*: Govt. of West Bengal, *Statistical Abstract 2001-2002*, BAES.

**Table 3.8:** Share in Paddy Production and Yield Levels by Major Paddy Producing States in India in 1999-2000

| State | % Share in Country's Total Produnction | Cumulative % in Total Production | Yield Level (kgs./Hectare) | |
|---|---|---|---|---|
| West Bengal | 15.59 | 15.59 | 2259 | (6) |
| Uttar Pradesh | 14.43 | 30.02 | 2176 | (7) |
| Andhra Pradesh | 11.72 | 41.74 | 2687 | (3) |
| Punjab | 9.75 | 51.49 | 3346 | (1) |
| Bihar | 8.65 | 60.14 | 1540 | (9) |
| Tamil Nadu | 8.08 | 68.22 | 3278 | (2) |
| Madhya Pradesh | 7.13 | 75.35 | 1191 | (11) |
| Orissa | 5.80 | 81.15 | 1128 | (12) |
| Assam | 4.31 | 85.46 | 1479 | (10) |
| Karnataka | 4.07 | 89.53 | 2512 | (4) |
| Haryana | 2.89 | 92.42 | 2386 | (5) |
| Maharastra | 2.84 | 95.26 | 1682 | (8) |

*Note*: Figures in parentheses are ranks.
*Source*: Govt. of India, Agricultural Statistics at a Glance 2001, Agrl. Statistics Division, Directorate of Economics and Statistics, Ministry of Agriculture, p. 32.

documents by the Government of West Bengal, it has been highlighted that the state has achieved the highest growth, among major states of India, with regard to foodgrains production since about mid-1980s. Several researchers have also confirmed this fact (see Saha and Swaminathan, 1994; Rawal and Swaminathan, 199?) and declared that West Bengal has of late been able to break away from the 'impasse' [this term has been used earlier by Boyce (1987)] that plagued its agriculture till about early 1980s. However, there has been some controversy as regards the explanatory factors towards impressive growth performance by West Bengal agriculture. There are some differences of opinion among the scholars in this regard. Scholars such as Harriss (1993) and Rawal (2001b) attributed this to greater utilization of modern inputs such as irrigation (through shallow tube wells) and HYV seeds of Paddy. While appreciating the contributions of institutional reforms, Sengupta and Gazdar (1997) and Gazdar and Sengupta (1999) identified better seeds, cheap fertilizers and irrigation as being important towards better agricultural performance in West Bengal since mid-1980s. On the other hand, Bhaumik (1993), Mukherjee and Mukhopadhyay (1996) and Banerjee *et al.* (2002c) assigned greater importance to institutional factors/ land reforms as compared to technological factors in explaining higher production growth in West Bengal agriculture.

Our purpose here is limited in that we seek to compare the growth rates of agricultural production in the state as well as districts between 1980s and 1990s. For this purpose, we have computed annual growth rates of production of foodgrains, non-foodgrains and foodgrains plus non-foodgrains for the periods 1980-81 to 1989-90 and 1990-91 to 1999-2000. Our computed growth rates are reported in Table 3.9. It is observed that the growth of foodgrains was really impressive in the decade of 1980s; this grew at a high rate of 6 per cent per annum in West Bengal. However, the rate of growth of foodgrains declined significantly to 2.30 per cent per annum during 1990s. This clearly shows that West Bengal has not been able to sustain high growth of foodgrains production in recent years in particular. The deceleration in production growth rate during 1990s is also observed with regard to non-foodgrains production as well (declining from 5.57 per cent per annum in 1980s to 3.72 per cent per annum in 1990s). Considering foodgrains and non-foodgrains together, the growth rates are found to be 5.84 per cent and 2.74 per cent for the decades of 1980s and 1990s respectively.

When we look at the production growth rates of foodgrains for the districts, several points emerge: (1) During the decade of 1980s, one-third of the districts recorded very impressive annual growth rates of foodgrains production. These were Nadia (8.06 per cent), Howrah (7.84 per cent), Bankura (7.65 per cent), Midnapore (7.20 per cent) and 24 Parganas (North and South) (6.38 per cent); (2) In the decade of 1990s, in all districts of West Bengal, the annual growth rates of foodgrains production are found to be much lower as compared to the same for 1980s. This implies that the deceleration in growth rates of foodgrains production in the state has been fairly widespread; and (3) Contrary to the situation in 1980s, the growth rates of foodgrains production have been negative in three districts during 1990s, which are Howrah, Cooch Behar and Darjeeling.

As regards non-foodgrains production in the districts, it is found that there are five districts, namely Cooch Behar, Uttar and Dakshin Dinajpur, Howrah, Malda and Jalpaiguri, where annual growth rates of the same during 1990s exceeded the rates of growth in 1980s. However, the remaining 10 districts suffered declines in growth rates of non-foodgrains production during 1990s.

**Table 3.9:** Annual Growth Rates of Agricultural Production in West Bengal by Districts During 1980-81 to 1999-2000

| *District* | *Foodgrains* | | *Non-food-grains* | | *Food-grains + Non-Food-grains* | |
|---|---|---|---|---|---|---|
| | 1980-81 to 1989-90 | 1990-91 to 1999-2000 | 1980-81 to 1989-90 | 1990-91 to 1999-2000 | 1980-81 to 1989-90 | 1990-91 to 1999-2000 |
| Bankura | 7.65 | 2.16 | 4.89 | 0.81 | 5.55 | 2.87 |
| Birbhum | 5.15 | 2.84 | 9.64 | –0.18 | 5.71 | 2.44 |
| Burdwan | 5.87 | 3.55 | 13.34 | 3.02 | 8.57 | 2.38 |
| Cooch Behar | 4.48 | –0.38 | 13.28 | 6.19 | 8.33 | 3.19 |
| Darjeeling | 5.83 | –3.82 | 4.66 | 6.23 | 7.19 | 0.73 |
| Hooghly | 4.35 | 2.78 | 7.68 | 1.94 | 6.15 | 2.44 |
| Howrah | 7.84 | –1.09 | 3.17 | 2.67 | 5.78 | 2.25 |
| Jalpaiguri | 2.09 | 1.15 | 5.90 | 2.36 | 7.25 | 1.83 |
| Malda | 5.94 | 1.49 | 6.04 | 5.05 | 5.35 | 4.19 |
| Midnapore | 7.20 | 1.96 | 1.38 | 6.14 | 4.23 | 4.06 |
| Murshidabad | 5.87 | 2.90 | 4.26 | 4.29 | 5.70 | 1.90 |
| Nadia | 8.06 | 1.59 | 1.55 | 2.33 | 1.67 | 2.02 |
| North and South 24-Parganas | 6.38 | 1.77 | 2.92 | –0.01 | 3.65 | –0.82 |
| Purulia | 5.96 | 1.17 | 1.11 | 9.44 | 3.29 | 3.30 |
| Uttar and Dakshin Dinajpur | 4.90 | 3.53 | 11.57 | –2.58 | 6.12 | 1.06 |
| West Bengal | 6.00 | 2.30 | 5.57 | 3.72 | 5.84 | 2.74 |

*Note*: The growth rates have been calculated by fitting kinked exponential function as devised by Boyce (1987).

It thus appears that West Bengal agriculture has again entered the phase of low production growth in the decade of 1990s[9]. This has been true for both foodgrains as well as non-foodgrains production, although the fall in production growth rate was much higher in the case of former as compared to the latter.

## Costs and Returns from Cultivation: Case of Aman (Kharif) Paddy

It may be of some interest to know the costs and returns from cultivation, as this would provide some idea about how agriculture has been faring as an economic activity[10]. We concentrate here on the main crop Aman (Kharif) Paddy, which alone accounts for nearly 45 per of cropped area in the state. We also provide a comparative picture with some other major Paddy growing states of India.

It appears from Table 3.10 that in terms of cost A1 (representing all actual expenses in cash and kind incurred in production) per hectare for Aman Paddy, West Bengal ranked third among 7 states considered. With such a cost standing at Rs. 9,716 per hectare, the state is far behind the state of Tamil Nadu (Rs. 15,301 per hectare), which topped in terms of value of output (main + by product) per hectare. When we look at some of the inputs used, it appears that in terms of fertilizers use, the state ranked fifth. This also has been highest in Tamil Nadu at 193 kgs. per hectare while in West Bengal it is reported to be only 95 kgs. per hectare. However, West Bengal produced Aman Paddy through the most labour intensive technique, as borne out by the fact that the state ranked first in terms of per hectare uses of both human and animal labour. While in West Bengal per hectare use of human labour has been 1,233 man-hours per hectatre, this has been the lowest in Punjab at 447 man-hours. Similarly, utilization of animal labour in West Bengal has been 155 man-hours per hectare in contrast to only 1 man-hour in Punjab and 36 man-hours in Uttar Pradesh.

In terms of net returns (profit) from Aman Paddy cultivation, West Bengal ranked third among the 7 states considered by us. This has been the highest in Tamil Nadu (Rs. 4,738 per hectare), followed by Punjab (Rs. 3,863 per hectare). In West Bengal, net income per hectare from Aman Paddy cultivation stands at Rs. 2,027 per hectare. This means that though the Paddy farmers in the state of West Bengal have not been incurring any loss, their margin of profit has been far less as compared to states such as Tamil Nadu and Punjab. Of course, this has been due to rather high application of human labour (put in by farmers' family members) towards paddy cultivation, which is accounted for while calculating net income. This becomes clear when we look at farm business income per hectare (which does not consider imputed value of family labour). On this count, the state ranks second while the first position is captured by Tamil Nadu. In a situation of excessive pressure of population on land (high man-land ratio) and lack of alternative employment opportunities, the farming families in West Bengal possibly put in additional human labour for cultivation of any crop, including Aman Paddy, which leads to low returns from cultivation. Clearly, for the sake of increasing average labour productivity as also net returns from cultivation, it is necessary to rationalize human labour utilization in West Bengal agriculture through adoption of more diversified cropping pattern, development of suitable technology for inter-cropping and creation of alternative employment opportunities in the rural non-farm sector simultaneously.

**Table 3.10:** Costs and Returns from Kharif (Aman) Paddy in Major States (Average of 1997-98 and 1998-99)

(*in Rs.*)

| *Item* | *West Bengal* | | *Uttar Pradesh* | | *Andhra Pradesh* | | *Punjab* | | *Bihar* | | *Tamil Nadu** | | *Madhya Pradesh* | |
|---|---|---|---|---|---|---|---|---|---|---|---|---|---|---|
| Cost of Cultivation (per hectare): Cost A1 | 9715.80 | (3) | 5540.91 | (6) | 11794.89 | (2) | 9060.34 | (4) | 4672.12 | (7) | 15301.36 | (1) | 5754.09 | (5) |
| Cost B2 | 16005.72 | (4) | 9421.84 | (5) | 19501.61 | (2) | 17808.61 | (3) | 8094.24 | (7) | 21542.88 | (1) | 9030.65 | (6) |
| Cost C2 | 19794.97 | (3) | 11792.40 | (5) | 21918.58 | (2) | 19059.59 | (4) | 9582.92 | (7) | 24174.01 | (1) | 10713.05 | (6) |
| Yield (Quintals/hectare) | 36.04 | (4) | 31.05 | (5) | 46.19 | (3) | 49.62 | (1) | 22.02 | (6) | 47.88 | (2) | 19.71 | (7) |
| Value of output (main + by-product)/ hectare | 21821.54 | (4) | 13574.92 | (5) | 23345.98 | (2) | 22922.11 | (3) | 10616.03 | (6) | 28911.66 | (1) | 6010.65 | (7) |
| Fertilizers (Kgs./hectare) | 95.48 | (5) | 104.49 | (4) | 187.07 | (2) | 172.56 | (3) | 76.22 | (6) | 192.83 | (1) | 71.18 | (7) |
| Human labour (man hours/hectare) | 1232.81 | (1) | 802.31 | (5) | 1023.86 | (4) | 447.44 | (7) | 865.11 | (4) | 1134.83 | (2) | 706.63 | (6) |
| Animal labour (pair hours/ hectare) | 155.40 | (1) | 36.55 | (6) | 61.01 | (3) | 1.03 | (7) | 103.53 | (3) | 59.77 | (5) | 133.46 | (2) |
| Farm business income/ hectare | 5815.83 | (2) | 4153.08 | (4) | 3844.37 | (5) | 5113.50 | (3) | 2521.80 | (6) | 7368.78 | (1) | –3020.01 | (7) |
| Net income/hectare | 2026.57 | (3) | 1782.52 | (4) | 1427.40 | (5) | 3862.52 | (2) | 1033.12 | (6) | 4737.65 | (1) | –4702.40 | (7) |

*Notes*: (1) Cost A1 = all actual expenses in cash and kind incurred in production; Cost B2 = Cost A1 + interest on value of owned capital assets (including land) + rent paid for leased in land; Cost C2 = Cost B2 + imputed value of family labour; (2) * represents data for 1998-99 only; and (3) Figures in brackets are ranks among 7 states.

*Source*: Reports of the Commission for Agricultural Costs and Prices for the Crops Sown During 2001-02 Season, Department of Agriculture and Co-operation, Ministry of Agriculture, Government of India, New Delhi, 2002.

## RURAL INFRASTRUCTURE

The fact that infrastructure development is a pre-condition to any process of economic development needs no great elaboration. Recognizing its importance in the context of rural development, the report prepared by the Planning Commission (2002d) entitled *India: Vision 2020* calls for strengthening rural infrastructure alongside urban infrastructure development.

In this section, we look at the status of rural infrastructure development in the state of West Bengal and its districts. We specifically concentrate on three key infrastructure indicators: (1) road connectivity in rural areas, (2) rural electrification, and (3) rural banking network. While we begin by looking at availability of these facilities, we also consider the accessibility of rural households to these facilities in the state.

### Road Connectivity

Among all rural infrastructures, road connectivity has been viewed as the most important. As noted by the *Tenth Five Year Plan* (Vol. I, pp. 14-15), prepared by the Planning Commission (2002b), "the rate of growth of rural incomes and reduction in rural poverty are strongly influenced by the provision of rural road connectivity. Other forms of rural infrastructure are also important, but the impact of rural roads has a dominant bearing on widening the opportunities and alternatives available to our people."

In rural West Bengal, the roads are maintained mostly by the Zilla Parishads although some limited portions are also looked after by the Public Works Department (Roads) [PWD]. We have computed length of rural roads (in km.) per 100 sq. km of geographical areas (rural only) in the year 2001 separately for Zilla Parishad roads and PWD roads as well as the total of these two[11]. The data on these are presented in Table 3.11. It is observed that while rural roads per 100 sq. km. of geographical areas (rural) under Zilla Parishad has been 49.71 km (87 per cent of total roads), the same for PWD roads stands at only 7.64 km (13 per cent). Combining these two, rural roads per 100 sq. km has been 57.35 km in West Bengal in 2001.

There is a very high inter-district variation in terms of road connectivity in rural West Bengal. While rural roads per 100 sq. km have been highest in Hooghly (241.30 km), the same has been lowest in Uttar Dinajpur (14.28 km). The two other districts with fairly high and impressive road connectivity have been Howrah and South 24 Parganas. In the districts of Darjeeling and Purulia also the length of rural roads (per 100 sq. km) has been higher than the state average, while in the remaining 10 districts (out of total seventeen), this has been lower than the state-average. This clearly implies that vast areas of the state are yet to climb upto the level of state-average in terms of rural road connectivity. The same story gets reflected from some of the LBSNAA-VSs (e.g. Bajura village in Midnapore). In any case, in rural areas of a good number of districts, a lot have to be done in the matter of improvement in road connectivity.[12]

## Rural Electrification

In order to obtain an idea about the extent of rural electrification, we have compiled data on percentage of villages electrified in Table 3.12.

**Table 3.11:** Road Connectivity in Rural West Bengal by Districts in 2001

| *District* | *Rural Roads (in km.) per 100 sq. km. of Rural Geographical Area in 2001 under* | | | | | |
|---|---|---|---|---|---|---|
| | *Zilla Parishad* | | *PWD (Roads)* | | *Total* | |
| Bankura | 15.90 | (14) | 4.44 | (13) | 20.35 | (15) |
| Birbhum | 37.11 | (7) | 10.03 | (8) | 47.14 | (9) |
| Burdwan | 35.83 | (8) | 11.83 | (7) | 47.66 | (8) |
| Cooch Behar | 34.22 | (9) | 15.51 | (3) | 49.74 | (7) |
| Dakshin Dinajpur | 18.33 | (13) | 13.24 | (5) | 31.57 | (12) |
| Darjeeling | 74.18 | (4) | 0.00 | (17) | 74.18 | (4) |
| Hooghly | 222.66 | (1) | 18.64 | (1) | 241.30 | (1) |
| Howrah | 116.00 | (3) | 18.59 | (2) | 134.59 | (2) |
| Jalpaiguri | 11.77 | (16) | 4.15 | (14) | 15.92 | (16) |
| Maldah | 22.90 | (12) | 7.93 | (10) | 30.83 | (13) |
| Midnapore | 29.07 | (11) | 3.82 | (15) | 32.89 | (11) |
| Murshidabad | 41.92 | (6) | 9.57 | (9) | 51.49 | (6) |
| Nadia | 29.91 | (10) | 12.00 | (6) | 41.91 | (10) |
| North 24-Parganas | 11.93 | (15) | 15.01 | (4) | 26.93 | (14) |
| Purulia | 63.60 | (5) | 3.12 | (16) | 66.72 | (5) |
| South 24-Parganas | 124.97 | (2) | 4.78 | (12) | 129.75 | (3) |
| Uttar Dinajpur | 6.91 | (17) | 7.37 | (11) | 14.28 | (17) |
| West Bengal | 49.71 | | 7.64 | | 57.35 | |

*Note*: Figures in brackets are ranks among 17 districts.

*Sources*: (i) Govt. of West Bengal, *Statistical Abstract 2001-02*;
(ii) Govt. of West Bengal, *District Statistical Hand Books 1999-2000*.

It needs to be noted here that we are very likely to have an over-estimate of rural electrification on the basis of this indicator primarily because a large number of villages in the state, though officially declared electrified, no longer possess such a facility because of several reasons (destruction of connection owing to theft of wares, uprooting of poles due to storms etc.).

**Table 3.12:** Percentage of Villages Electrified in West Bengal

| ###cistrict | 1990-91 | 1995-96 | 1999-2000 | |
|---|---|---|---|---|
| Bankura | 56.9 | 66.7 | 67.7 | (15) |
| Birbhum | 99.1 | 99.1 | 99.1 | (4) |
| Burdwan | 95.9 | 97.1 | 98.1 | (7) |
| Cooch Behar | 98.1 | 98.2 | 98.2 | (6) |
| Dakshin Dinajpur | }76.4 | }78.5 | 74.9 | (14) |
| Uttar Dinajpur | | | 82.5 | (13) |
| Darjeeling | 78.7 | 82.6 | 84.5 | (11) |
| Hooghly | 98.3 | 100.0 | 100.0 | (1) |
| Howrah | 100.0 | 100.0 | 100.0 | (2) |
| Jalpaiguri | 98.6 | 98.8 | 98.8 | (5) |
| Malda | 97.2 | 97.3 | 97.3 | (8) |
| Midnapore | 43.5 | 51.4 | 53.2 | (17) |
| Murshidabad | 91.8 | 93.3 | 93.5 | (10) |
| Nadia | 100.0 | 100.0 | 100.0 | (3) |
| North 24 Parganas | 92.4 | 93.9 | 95.5 | (9) |
| Purulia | 54.7 | 62.5 | 63.8 | (16) |
| South 24 Parganas | 80.1 | 82.0 | 84.3 | (12) |
| West Bengal | 72.8 | 77.0 | 78.0 | |

*Notes*: For the year 1985-86 the percentage has been calculated on the basis of number of villages as per 1981 Census and for rest of the years on the basis of number of villages as per 1991 Census. Figures in brackets are ranks among 17 districts.

*Source*: Govt. of West Bengal, Statistical Abstract, various years.

It is observed that in the year 1990-91, 72.8 per cent of villages in West Bengal were declared electrified, which increased to 77 per cent in 1995-96. However, since then nothing much has changed on this front in West Bengal in as much as 78 per cent of villages have been electrified till 1999-2000.

Currently, there are three districts in West Bengal where all the villages are reported to have electricity facility. These are Hooghly, Howrah and Nadia. There is another set of 7 districts, namely Birbhum, Jalpaiguri, Cooch Behar, Burdwan, Malda, North

24 Parganas and Murshdabad, where more than 90 per cent of villages have been electrified. There are only four districts where percentage of villages electrified has been lower than the state average, which are Midnapore (53.2 per cent), Purulia (63.8 per cent), Bankura (67.7 per cent) and Dakshin Dinajpur (74.9 per cent).

## Rural Banking Network

In this sub-section, we look into the banking network and flow of institutional credit in West Bengal in recent years. To begin with, we look into rural population (in thousand) per bank office separately for Commercial Banks, Co-operative Banks (Central + State), Primary Agricultural Credit Societies (PACS) and Gramin Banks. The data on these aspects, presented in Tables 3.13A and 3.13B, reveal the following:

(1) For all categories of banks, the rate of growth of bank offices has fallen short of rate of growth of rural population in West Bengal in the decade of 1990s. Consequently, for commercial banks, rural population per bank office increased from 20.78 thousand in 1990-91 to 25.37 in 2000-01; for Co-operative banks this increased from 232.36 thousand in 1990-91 to 235.36 in 1995-96; for PACS from 7.43 thousand in 1990-91 to 7.66 thousand in 2000-01; and for Gramin Banks from 57.15 thousand in 1990-91 to 64.74 thousand in 2000-01.

(2) Among all categories of institutional lending agencies, the reach of the PACS among the rural households has been far entrenched; in fact, in recent years, the PACS have emerged as the most important source of production credit to a vast majority of farmers in West Bengal.

(3) As regards concentration of institutional lending agencies in rural areas, there are clear inter-district variations. In 2000-01, the concentration of commercial banks (as measured by rural population per bank branch) have been higher than the state average in rural areas of the districts of Birbhum, Burdwan, Bankura, Howrah, Midnapore, Hooghly, Malda, Darjeeling and Purulia. On the other hands, PACS have concentration higher than state average in Midnapore, Hooghly, Burdwan, North and South Dinajpur and Birbhum. As regards the Gramin Banks, population per branch has been the lowest in the zone comprising Birbhum, which is followed

**Table 3.13A:** Rural Population per Rural Bank Office in West Bengal by Districts

| District | Rural Population ('000) per Bank Office | | | | | | | | | | | |
|---|---|---|---|---|---|---|---|---|---|---|---|---|
| | Commercial Banks | | | | Co-operative Banks (Central+State) | | | | Primary Agricultural Credit Societies (PACS) | | | |
| | 1990-91 | | 2000-01 | | 1990-91 | | 1995-96* | | 1990-91 | | 2000-01 | |
| Bankura | 18.01 | (2) | 20.70 | (3) | 202.01 | (7) | 184.07 | (5) | 5.79 | (4) | 8.64 | (6) |
| Birbhum | 17.38 | (1) | 20.43 | (1) | 155.29 | (4) | 168.97 | (4) | 6.64 | (6) | 7.73 | (5) |
| Burdwan | 17.79 | (3) | 20.43 | (2) | 113.94 | (3) | 118.16 | (3) | 6.45 | (5) | 6.97 | (3) |
| Cooch Behar | 25.05 | (13) | 28.54 | (10) | – | | – | | 9.82 | (14) | 10.22 | (10) |
| Darjeeling | 20.57 | (8) | 25.27 | (8) | 100.58 | (1) | 110.20 | (1) | 9.05 | (12) | 10.56 | (12) |
| Hooghly | 18.75 | (6) | 22.08 | (6) | 272.71 | (8) | 288.44 | (11) | 5.24 | (3) | 6.60 | (2) |
| Howrah | 17.59 | (2) | 21.02 | (4) | 188.24 | (5) | 199.89 | (6) | 8.56 | (10) | 10.59 | (13) |
| Jalpaiguri | 26.66 | (15) | 33.38 | (14) | 390.96 | (12) | 284.94 | (10) | 9.57 | (13) | 11.20 | (14) |
| Maldah | 18.46 | (5) | 25.25 | (7) | 306.87 | (9) | 273.85 | (8) | NA | | 17.79 | (15) |
| Midnapore | 18.75 | (7) | 21.76 | (5) | 110.99 | (2) | 113.51 | (2) | 4.01 | (1) | 3.95 | (1) |
| Murshidabad | 25.16 | (14) | 34.04 | (15) | 354.38 | (11) | 389.58 | (12) | 8.77 | (11) | 10.44 | (11) |
| Nadia | 24.07 | (12) | 31.03 | (13) | 189.53 | (6) | 205.76 | (7) | 8.11 | (7) | 9.67 | (8) |
| North and South 24 Parganas | 23.02 | (10) | 29.07 | (11) | – | | – | | 8.40 | (8) | 9.90 | (9) |
| Purulia | 22.41 | (9) | 25.36 | (9) | 672.22 | (13) | 715.13 | (13) | 8.47 | (9) | 8.77 | (7) |
| Uttar and Dakshin Dinajpur | 23.62 | (11) | 30.90 | (12) | 339.49 | (10) | 278.66 | (9) | 5.10 | (2) | 7.71 | (4) |
| West Bengal | 20.78 | | 25.37 | | 232.36 | | 235.50 | | 7.43 | | 7.66 | |

*Notes*: For co-operative banks, 1995-96 is the latest year for which data are available.
Figures in brackets are ranks.

*Sources*: (1) Reserve Bank of India, *Banking Statistics: Basic Statistical Returns* (Various years); (2) NABARD, Statistical Statements Relating to Co-operative Movement in India.

**Table 3.13B:** Rural Population per Bank Office of Gramin Banks in West Bengal

| *Banking Zone* | *Population ('000) per Bank Office* | | | |
|---|---|---|---|---|
| | 1990-91 | | 2000-01 | |
| Burdwan-Hooghly-Howrah | 59.15 | (5) | 63.83 | (5) |
| Maldah-Murshidabad-North and South Dinajpur | 51.49 | (4) | 60.39 | (4) |
| Bankura-Purulia-Midnapore | 68.82 | (6) | 75.85 | (6) |
| Birbhum | 35.84 | (1) | 41.16 | (1) |
| Nadia | 45.93 | (2) | 55.01 | (3) |
| North and South 24 Parganas | 74.06 | (7) | 84.01 | (7) |
| Cooch Behar-Darjeeling-Jalpaiguri | 46.92 | (3) | 54.87 | (2) |
| All zones | 57.15 | | 64.74 | |

*Note*: Figures in brackets are ranks.
*Source*: As in Table 3.13A.

by zones of North and South 24 Paraganas, Nadia, Malda-Murshidabad-North and South Dinajpur, Burdwan-Hooghly-Howrah, Bankura-Purulia-Midnapore and North and South 24 Parganas. On the whole, the concentration of institutional credit agencies seems to be better in the districts of Birbhum, Bankura, Burdwan, Hooghly, Howrah and Nadia most of which are known to be agriculturally progressive districts of the state.

It is to be admitted that the actual performance of the institutional credit agencies could not be understood fully from mere concentration levels of bank branches in rural areas. It is also necessary to look into other indicators such as rural credit-deposit ratio, proportion of agricultural credit to total bank credit and so on.

Table 3.14A presents data on rural credit-deposit ratio by the commercial banks and co-operative banks (Central + State) in the districts as well as the state. It is clearly observed that rural credit-deposit ratios have declined for both categories of banks in West Bengal in the decade of 1990s. However, the rate of decline in rural credit-deposit ratios was much higher in the case of commercial banks. The rural credit-deposit ratio for the commercial banks in West Bengal reduced from 44.11 in 1990-91 to 23.04 in 2000-01. In the case of Co-operative banks (Central + State), the corresponding figures have been 81.85 and 72.52 for the two years respectively.

**Table 3.14A:** Credit-Deposit Ratio for Commercial Banks and Co-operative Banks (Central+State) in West Bengal by Districts

| District | Commercial Banks | | | | Co-operative Banks (Central+State) | | | |
|---|---|---|---|---|---|---|---|---|
| | 1990-91 | | 2000-01 | | 1990-91 | | 1995-96 | |
| Bankura | 40.49 | (9) | 22.45 | (9) | 50.77 | (13) | 46.69 | (13) |
| Birbhum | 51.37 | (6) | 32.23 | (4) | 116 | (2) | 54.05 | (12) |
| Burdwan | 40.43 | (10) | 24.72 | (7) | 76.09 | (7) | 96.78 | (3) |
| Cooch Behar | 93.96 | (1) | 52.96 | (1) | – | | - | |
| Darjeeling | 46.09 | (7) | 20.38 | (10) | 67.96 | (10) | 103.45 | (2) |
| Hooghly | 37.47 | (12) | 19.27 | (11) | 76.66 | (6) | 82.12 | (4) |
| Howrah | 29.19 | (14) | 12.60 | (15) | 59.98 | (12) | 61.79 | (11) |
| Jalpaiguri | 28.52 | (15) | 15.75 | (14) | 77.18 | (5) | 68.86 | (8) |
| Maldah | 55.42 | (5) | 33.09 | (3) | 103.43 | (3) | 72.97 | (5) |
| Midnapore | 63.20 | (3) | 27.41 | (5) | 93.33 | (4) | 70.37 | (6) |
| Murshidabad | 60.19 | (4) | 26.84 | (6) | 73.22 | (8) | 68.95 | (7) |
| Nadia | 38.75 | (11) | 23.57 | (8) | 72.82 | (9) | 64.53 | (10) |
| North and South 24 Parganas | 35.48 | (13) | 18.09 | (13) | – | | - | |
| Purulia | 42.20 | (8) | 18.50 | (12) | 66.92 | (11) | 107.3 | (9) |
| Uttar and Dakshin Dinajpur | 89.22 | (2) | 44.48 | (2) | 198.42 | (1) | 107.3 | (1) |
| West Bengal | 44.11 | | 23.04 | | 81.85 | | 72.52 | |

*Notes*: For co-operative banks, 1995-96 is the latest year for which data are available.
Figures in brackets are ranks.

*Source*: As in Table 3.13A.

Surprisingly, in the year 2000-01, in the case of commercial banks, the credit-deposit ratio has been the highest in the backward district Cooch Behar, which is followed by other backward districts such as North and South Dinajpur, Malda and Birbhum. This is possibly because, these being agriculturally backward, there have not been much of deposits by the rural households, which resulted in higher credit-deposit ratios in them. Another noteworthy point here is that all districts of West Bengal suffered from declines in credit-deposit ratios by commercial banks during 1990-91 to 2000-01. As regards Co-operative banks (Central + State), a similar tendency is observed for all districts except Burdwan, Darjeeling, Hooghly, Howrah and North and South Dinajpur (Table 3.14A). The credit-deposit ratio for Gramin banks has been the highest in Cooch Behar-Darjeeling-Jalpaiguri zone (Table 3.14B). This has been above the state average in two other zones, which are Birbhum and Malda-Murshidabad-North and South Dinajpur.

**Table 3.14B:** Credit-Deposit Ratio for Gramin Banks in West Bengal

| *Banking Zone* | *1990-91* | | *2000-01* | |
|---|---|---|---|---|
| Burdwan-Hooghly-Howrah | 54.11 | (4) | 26.14 | (6) |
| Maldah-Murshidabad-North and South Dinajpur | 81.27 | (1) | 37.30 | (3) |
| Bankura-Purulia-Midnapore | 58.82 | (2) | 31.16 | (4) |
| Birbhum | 38.32 | (7) | 38.21 | (2) |
| Nadia | 54.82 | (3) | 27.86 | (5) |
| North and South 24 Parganas | 38.70 | (6) | 21.70 | (7) |
| Cooch Behar-Darjeeling-Jalpaiguri | 53.28 | (5) | 40.87 | (1) |
| All zones | 56.22 | | 31.39 | |

*Note*: Figures in brackets are ranks.
*Source*: As in Table 3.13A.

As regards the percentage of agricultural credit to total bank credit by the commercial banks, it is found that this has been only 6.12 per cent in West Bengal in 1990-91, which further declined to a low level of 4.47 per cent in 2000-01 (Table 3.15). This clearly indicates violation of the banking norm, which stipulated the commercial banks to direct 18 per cent of total credit to the agricultural sector alone. In the year 2000-01, in West Bengal, the districts where the commercial banks advanced more than 18 per cent of total bank credit to the agricultural sector are Hooghly, North and South 24 Parganas, Midnapore,

Murshidabad, Birbhum, Bankura, Nadia and Cooch Behar. In terms of advancement of agricultural credit by the commercial banks, the districts to perform rather poorly are Howrah, Darjeeling, Purulia, Burdwan, Jalpaiguri and North and South 24 Parganas.

**Table 3.15:** Finance to Agriculture by Commercial Banks in West Bengal

| *District* | *% of Agrl. Credit to Total Bank Credit* | | *Credit per Hectare of GCA (at 1981-82 Prices)* | |
|---|---|---|---|---|
| | 1990-91 | 2000-01 | 1990-91 | 2000-01 |
| Bankura | 26.54 (7) | 19.95 (6) | 137.77 (12) | 176.91 (9) |
| Birbhum | 33.26 (1) | 20.60 (5) | 247.94 (7) | 247.00 (6) |
| Burdwan | 18.16 (11) | 13.45 (12) | 393.42 (2) | 380.63 (2) |
| Cooch Behar | 21.12 (9) | 18.19 (8) | 109.74 (15) | 115.73 (13) |
| Darjeeling | 16.31 (14) | 5.72 (14) | 457.94 (1) | 259.02 (4) |
| Hooghly | 17.57 (12) | 23.12 (1) | 386.94 (3) | 568.18 (1) |
| Howrah | 6.84 (15) | 3.66 (15) | 373.86 (4) | 251.51 (5) |
| Jalpaiguri | 25.74 (8) | 13.59 (11) | 222.67 (8) | 118.79 (12) |
| Maldah | 28.76 (6) | 17.78 (9) | 169.36 (10) | 165.56 (11) |
| Midnapore | 29.82 (4) | 21.67 (3) | 255.63 (6) | 222.23 (7) |
| Murshidabad | 29.01 (5) | 21.19 (4) | 151.82 (11) | 173.98 (10) |
| Nadia | 30.49 (2) | 19.78 (7) | 193.99 (9) | 193.98 (8) |
| North and South 24 Parganas | 17.26 (13) | 14.40 (10) | 347.54 (5) | 343.38 (3) |
| Purulia | 20.78 (10) | 13.10 (13) | 126.78 (13) | 110.81 (15) |
| Uttar and Dakshin Dinajpur | 30.37 (3) | 22.63 (2) | 114.39 (14) | 115.52 (14) |
| West Bengal | 6.12 | 4.47 | 311.09 | 320.73 |

*Note*: Figures in brackets are ranks
*Source*: As in Table 3.13A.

However, if we consider commercial bank credit to the agricultural sector per hectare of gross cropped area, for the state as whole, this stands at Rs. 321 in 2000-01. The districts where this has been above the state-average are Hooghly (Rs. 568), Burdwan (Rs. 381) and North and South 24 Parganas (Rs. 343). On the other hand the districts to perform rather poorly are Purulia (Rs. 111), North and South Dinajpur (Rs. 116), Cooch Behar (Rs. 116), Jalpaiguri (Rs. 119), Malda (Rs. 166), Murshidabad (Rs. 174) and Bankura (Rs. 177).

The above analysis of institutional banking network and its performance in rural West Bengal leads to the conclusion that the relatively advanced districts of the state have better banking network and in terms of advancement of credit, the banks too have performed better in such districts. However, in overall terms, it clearly emerges that the institutional lending agencies, particularly the commercial banks, have not only supplied inadequate credit to the agricultural sector but also have been shrinking their business from this sector in recent years. In any case, extremely low proportion of total commercial bank credit (4.47 per cent in 2000-01) being supplied to the agricultural sector is a clear indication of discrimination this sector has been subjected to in West Bengal.

In the context of discussion of lending by the institutional agencies to the rural and agricultural sector in West Bengal, the LBSNAA-VSs and other micro studies throw useful insights. Almost all the village studies by the LBSNAA reported strong presence of the non-institutional lending agencies (including village moneylenders) consequent upon inadequate supply of credit from the institutional agencies. In a detailed study covering eight villages fron Burdwan and Bankura districts of West Bengal, Bhaumik and Rahim (1998) found that of the total amount borrowed by the rural households, nearly two-thrids have come from the non-institutional sources. Rajeev and Deb (1998) also make a similar observation from their study of some villages in Hooghly. These micro studies also reveal that the most important among the non-institutional lenders in rural West Bengal are 'village money-lenders', 'inputs sellers', 'friends and relatives', 'traders' and 'big cultivators'. Loans obtained from the non-institutional lenders have been both for the purposes of production and consumption. It is also to be noted that rural borrowers pay high interest charges while borrowing from the non-institutional agencies[13].

## Rural Households' Access to Infrastructure Facilities

We now look at the rural households' access to infrastructure facilities in West Bengal using data available from National Health and Family Welfare Survey-2 (NHFS-2) and NSSO survey on Travel and Use of Mass Media and Financial Services (1998, 54th Round). We provide a comparative picture between West Bengal and all-India in terms of accessibility of some of the infrastructure facilities by the rural households.

The data on accessibility of infrastructure facilities by rural households are compiled in Table 3.16. It is observed that only 19.2

per cent of rural households have accessed the facility of electricity in 1998-99, which is far lower than the figure for all-India (48.1 per cent). It is also found that during the same year, only 21 per cent of inhabited villages in West Bengal have banking facility (the figure for all-India is 20.7 per cent), 41.4 per cent of villages have Post Office (43.2 per cent in all-india), 7 per cent of the villages have telegraph office (for all-India, this is 13.7 per cent) and 8.2 per cent of the villages have STD telephone booth (13.7 per cent in all-india). As regards percentage of rural households having bank/post office savings account, the figure for West Bengal is 23.7 per cent that is lower than all-India figure of 28.3 per cent.

The situation in West Bengal is also no better in terms of availability/working of co-operative societies of different types. While only 28.6 per cent of the villages are reported to have agricultural co-operative society in West Bengal (27.2 per cent in all-India), only 16.7 per cent of the villages have credit co-operative society (25 per cent in all-india). For both West Bengal and all-India, only 5.5 per cent of the villages are found to have fishermen's co-operative society. The availability of milk co-operative society is far less in West Bengal (covering only 3.6 per cent of total villages) as compared to all-India (21.8 per cent of total villages).

Although West Bengal villages have better marketing facilities in as much as 31.3 per cent of inhabited villages have weekly market (for all-India, this is 23.1 per cent), in terms of availability of fair price/PDS shop, West Bengal is lagging behind all-India. It is found that while in West Bengal 56.4 per cent of the villages have fair price/PDS shop, the corresponding figure for all-India is 61.1 per cent.

It clearly emerges that on the basis of most indicators of accessibility of infrastructure facilities by the rural residents, West Bengal lagged behind all-India at the close of 1990s. This conclusion is easily confirmed from the village studies by the LBSNAA. Most of the village studies report non-avialability of electricity to a large proportion of households although there is presence of electricity in the villges. In the same way, as regards the presence of banks, post offices, telephone booths etc. the picture does not appear to be a happy one. The experience of the villagers with regard to the functioning of PDS has not been happy either in some of the villages.

**Table 3.16:** Some indicators of Rural Households' Access to Infrastructure Facilities in West Bengal and All India

| *Source of data* | *Item* | *West Bengal* | *All India* |
|---|---|---|---|
| NHFS-2 (1998-99) | % of rural households with electricity | 19.2 | 48.1 |
| NHFS-2 (1998-99) | % of rural residents living in villages that have: | | |
| | Bank | 21.0 | 20.7 |
| | Post Office | 41.4 | 43.2 |
| | Telegraph Office | 7.0 | 10.9 |
| | STD Telephone Booth | 8.2 | 13.7 |
| NSSO (54th Round 1998) | % of rural households having bank/post office savings account | 23.7 | 28.3 |
| NHFS-2 (1998-99) | % of rural residents living in villages that have: | | |
| | Credit cooperative society | 16.7 | 25.0 |
| | Agricultural cooperative society | 28.6 | 27.2 |
| | Fishermen's cooperative society | 5.5 | 5.5 |
| | Milk cooperative society | 3.6 | 21.8 |
| NHFS-2 (1998-99) | % of rural residents living in villages that have: | | |
| | Weekly Market | 31.3 | 23.1 |
| | Fair Price/PDS Shop | 56.4 | 61.1 |

*Source*: (i) NSSO, Travel and Use of Mass Media and Financial Services by Indian Households, 54th Round, Report No. 450;

(ii) National Health and Family Welfare Survey 2 (1998-99), Reports for All India and West Bengal.

## RURAL HEALTH

The main purpose of this section is to understand the availability of health care facilities in rural areas of West Bengal and its districts. We would also attempt to throw some idea about the health status of rural people. Some idea is also provided about the health care facilities extended to rural women and children in the state.

### Availability of Health Facilities

In order to gather some idea about availability of health care facilities for rural people in the state and the districts, we have compiled in

**Table 3.17:** Availability of Health Facilities in Rural West Bengal by Districts as on 31.3.1999

| *District* | *RH per lakh Population* | | *BPHC and PHC per 30,000 Population* | | *No. of health sub-centres per 5,000 Population* | | *Beds per 10,000 Population* | | | |
|---|---|---|---|---|---|---|---|---|---|---|
| | | | | | | | *RH* | *BPHC and PHC* | *Total* | |
| Bankura | 0.17 | (10) | 0.88 | (3) | 0.88 | (2) | 6.23 | 23.64 | 29.88 | (3) |
| Burdwan | 0.14 | (15) | 0.93 | (1) | 0.78 | (5) | 6.32 | 22.98 | 29.29 | (4) |
| Birbhum | 0.15 | (14) | 0.82 | (4) | 0.74 | (9) | 7.10 | 24.20 | 31.30 | (2) |
| Cooch Behar | 0.05 | (17) | 0.53 | (11) | 0.71 | (10) | 1.36 | 11.64 | 12.99 | (17) |
| Dakshin Dinajpur | 0.16 | (12) | 0.57 | (9) | 0.67 | (11) | 4.39 | 12.36 | 16.74 | (15) |
| Darjeeling | 0.29 | (1) | 0.77 | (5) | 0.76 | (7) | 10.45 | 23.28 | 33.73 | (1) |
| Hooghly | 0.24 | (2) | 0.63 | (8) | 0.90 | (1) | 9.57 | 15.38 | 24.95 | (7) |
| Howrah | 0.19 | (8) | 0.75 | (6) | 0.84 | (4) | 8.42 | 18.96 | 27.38 | (5) |
| Jalpaiguri | 0.22 | (4) | 0.51 | (13) | 0.62 | (16) | 9.75 | 11.37 | 21.12 | (8) |
| Malda | 0.20 | (6) | 0.46 | (15) | 0.63 | (15) | 8.10 | 12.04 | 20.14 | (10) |
| Midnapore | 0.15 | (13) | 0.64 | (7) | 0.76 | (6) | 5.63 | 15.47 | 21.10 | (9) |
| Murshidabad | 0.16 | (11) | 0.54 | (10) | 0.64 | (14) | 6.03 | 13.98 | 20.01 | (11) |
| Nadia | 0.20 | (7) | 0.49 | (14) | 0.53 | (17) | 6.84 | 12.37 | 19.21 | (13) |
| North 24 Parganas | 0.18 | (9) | 0.51 | (12) | 0.76 | (8) | 5.91 | 12.37 | 18.27 | (14) |
| Purulia | 0.22 | (3) | 0.91 | (2) | 0.86 | (3) | 6.72 | 19.57 | 26.28 | (6) |
| South 24 Parganas | 0.21 | (5) | 0.43 | (16) | 0.65 | (12) | 9.17 | 10.26 | 19.42 | (12) |
| Uttar Dinajpur | 0.10 | (16) | 0.41 | (17) | 0.64 | (13) | 4.12 | 9.12 | 13.24 | (16) |
| West Bengal | 0.18 | | 0.62 | | 0.72 | | 6.81 | 15.41 | 22.22 | |

*Notes*: (1) RH = rural hospital/community health centre; BPHC = block primary health centre; and PHC = primary health centre. (2) We have used projected population as on 31.3.99 to compute number of health centres per population unit. (3) Figures in brackets are ranks among 17 districts.

*Source*: Govt. of West Bengal, *Health on March, West Bengal, 1999*, Directorate of Health Services, 2000, p. 71.

| | Item | Norm |
|---|---|---|
| (1) | At least one trained *Dai* | For each village. |
| (2) | One trained village health guide | For each village/1000 population. |
| (3) | One health sub-centre | For 5,000 population in plain area and for 3,000 population in tribal, hilly and backward areas. |
| (4) | One primary health centre | For every 30,000 population in plain area and for 20,000 population in tribal, hilly and backward areas. |
| (5) | One community health centre/Rural hospital | For every 1 to 1.20 lakh population. |

Table 3.17 data on concentration of rural hospitals (RH), block primary health centres (BPHC) and primary health centres (PHC) and also health sub-centres (HSC). Our objective here is to examine whether the availability of these health institutions in rural areas is adequate in the sense of fulfilling the 'national norm'. The 'national norm' as regards primary health care facilities is as follows (Government of West Bengal, 2002c, p. 73).

### Rural Hospital

It emerges from Table 3.17 that West Bengal has been far away from fulfilling the above norm as regards provision of public health care facilities in rural areas. While there should have been at least one rural hospital per one lakh population, for rural West Bengal this figure stands at 0.18 only. Similarly, the number of BPHS/PHC in rural areas per 30,000 populations is 0.62, while HSC per 5,000 populations is 0.72. None of the districts of West Bengal fulfilled the national norm in terms of availability of these health care institutions in rural areas.[14]

It is also to be noted from Table 3.17 that there are inter-district variations in terms of availability of public health care facilities in rural areas. Out of 17 districts of West Bengal, there are 9 districts (Uttar Dinajpur, South 24 Parganas, Malda, Nadia, Jalpaiguri, North 24 Parganas, Cooch Behar, Murshidabad and Dakshin Dinajpur) that lagged behind the state-average in terms of concentration of BPHC/PHC (per 30,000 population) in rural areas. On the other hand, there are 8 districts (Nadia, Jalpaiguri, Malda, Murshidabad, Uttar Dinajpur, South 24 Parganas, Dakshin Dinajpur and Cooch Behar) where the concentration of HSC has fallen short of the state-average. It clearly emerges that both the state as well as the districts have been lagging in terms of availability of public health care institutions in rural areas. It is, therefore, no surprising that some of the villages surveyed by the LBSNAA reported absence of even a PHC or a sub-PHC at the village level although they deserved to have one (e.g. Satghara in Hooghly and Bajura in Midnapore). There is also complaining in some villages about unsatisfactory services provided by the health staff in the sub-PHCs (e.g. Walipur in Midnapore).

## Health Status of Rural Population

In order to gather some idea about health status of the rural population, we begin by looking at some health indicators (Table 3.18) and morbidity profile (Table 3.19). In spite of inadequate availability of health care institutions in West Bengal, the crude death rate (per 1000 population) for rural areas in 1990s has been low compared to all-India from whichever source we gather data. For example, data available from NHFS-2 show that crude death rate for rural West Bengal in 1998-99 is 8.7 which is lower than 10.4 for all-India (Table 3.18). The situation with regard to both infant and child mortality rates (per 1000 population) also appear to be better in rural West Bengal than for rural India as a whole. In 1998-99, while the infant mortality rate is 53.2 in rural West Bengal, the corresponding figure in all-India is 73.3. Similarly, the child mortality rate in rural West Bengal is 21.2, which is 32.8 for all-India.

**Table 3.18:** Some Health Indicators for Rural Areas—NHFS-2 (1998-99)

| *Item* | *West Bengal* | *All India* |
|---|---|---|
| Crude death rate (NFHS-1, 1992-93) | 10.2 | 10.4 |
| Crude death rate (SRS, 1991-92) | 8.9 | 10.8 |
| Crude death rate (NHFS-2, 1998-99) | 8.7 | 10.4 |
| Crude death rate (SRS, 1997) | 7.9 | 9.6 |
| Infant mortality rate (NHFS-2, 1998-99)* | 53.3 | 73.3 |
| Child mortality rate (NHFS-2, 1998-99)* | 21.2 | 32.8 |

*Note*: * For five year period preceding the survey.

*Source*: National Family Health Survey (NFHS-2, 1998-99)—West Bengal, International Institute of Population Sciences, Mumbai, October 2001; Sample Registration Systems, 1997.

Table 3.19A gives some idea about morbidity for population in rural West Bengal and all-India as drawn from NHFS-2. The situation appears to be a mixed one.[15] While the incidences of asthma and jaundice are found to be relatively high in West Bengal as compared to all-India, the same for tuberculosis and malaria are low. As per NHFS-2, the males are more prone to all these diseases as compared to females both in rural West Bengal and all-India. An alternative source of data on morbidity is the NSSO (Table 3.19B). According to the NSSO survey during 1995-96, 6.5 per cent of rural persons suffered from any ailment (during 15 days preceding the date of survey), which for all-India is 5.5 per cent. It is also found that the incidence of ailment is the highest among non-SC/ST persons and lowest among ST persons both in rural West Bengal and all-India.

**Table 3.19A:** Morbidity for All Rural Population in West Bengal and All-India

| *Region* | *Category* | *Per Thousand Persons Suffering from* | | | |
|---|---|---|---|---|---|
| | | *Asthma* | *Tuberculosis* | *Jaundice during Past 12 Months* | *Malaria during Past 3 Months* |
| West Bengal | Male | 28.75 | 9.84 | 31.51 | 18.56 |
| | Female | 24.22 | 7.45 | 19.06 | 14.73 |
| | Person | 26.54 | 8.67 | 25.44 | 16.69 |
| All India | Male | 27.84 | 12.48 | 16.75 | 43.20 |
| | Female | 25.08 | 8.98 | 11.34 | 41.84 |
| | Person | 26.49 | 10.76 | 14.10 | 42.54 |

*Source*: National Family Health Survey (NFHS-2, 1998-99), West Bengal, International Institute of Population Sciences, Mumbai, October 2001.

**Table 3.19B:** Ailment Among Rural Persons (During Last 15 Days from the Date of Survey)

| *Item* | *West Bengal* | | | *All India* | | |
|---|---|---|---|---|---|---|
| | *Male* | *Female* | *Person* | *Male* | *Female* | *Person* |
| % Reporting any kind of ailment: | | | | | | |
| (i) Scheduled Castes | 5.9 | 7.7 | 6.7 | 5.2 | 5.5 | 5.4 |
| (ii) Scheduled Tribes | 3.6 | 2.6 | 3.2 | 4.2 | 4.3 | 4.2 |
| (iii) Non-SC/STs | 6.6 | 7.1 | 6.9 | 5.6 | 6.0 | 5.8 |
| (iv) All | 6.1 | 7.0 | 6.5 | 5.4 | 5.7 | 5.5 |

*Source*: NSSO (1998), *Morbidity and Treatment of Ailments*, 52nd Round (July 1995-June 1996), Report No. 441, November.

## Health Status of Rural Children

We begin by looking at the nutritional status of rural children (under age 3 years) in West Bengal. Table 3.20 presents data on this aspect drawn from the NHFS-2. It is found that in 1998-99, among the rural children in West Bengal, 17.8 per cent were 'severely under-nourished' (19.9 per cent for all-India) and 52.8 per cent were 'under-nourished' (49.6 per cent in all-India). In the same year, 21.4 per cent children were 'severely stunted' in rural West Bengal (25.4 for all-India) while 'stunted' children being 45.1 per cent (48.5 per cent for all-India).

**Table 3.20:** Nutritional Status of Rural Children under Age 3 Years

| *Region* | *Weight-for-Age* | | *Height-for-Age* | |
|---|---|---|---|---|
| | % Below-3SD (Severely under-nourished) | % Below-2SD (under-nourished) | % below-3SD (Severely Stunted) | % Below-2SD (Stunted) |
| West Bengal | 17.8 | 52.6 | 21.4 | 45.1 |
| All India | 19.9 | 49.6 | 25.4 | 48.5 |

*Source*: National Family Health Survey (NFHS-2, 1998-99), West Bengal, International Institute of Population Sciences, Mumbai, October 2001.

The NHFS-2 also throws some data on ailment of rural children (Table 3.21). It is found that about 81.5 per cent of rural children (under age 3 years) in West Bengal had suffered from any anaemia during 6-35 months preceding the survey (1998-99); this for all-India has been 75.3 per cent. It is also found that 25.6 per cent of rural children suffered from cough and/or acute respiratory infection in West Bengal, in all-India this has been 20.3 per cent. Similarly, both in rural West Bengal and all-India, about 30 per cent of children had suffered from fever. However, the incidence of rural children suffering from diarrhoea has been relatively less in West Bengal than all-India.

## Child Health Care

In recent years, a lot of health care programmes have been initiated for children and women in particular. As regards children, important

**Table 3.21:** Ailment of Rural Children Under Age 3 Years

| Region | % of Children (6-35 Months) with any Anaemia | % of Children Suffering in Past two Weeks from | | |
|---|---|---|---|---|
| | | Cough+acute Respiratory Infection | Fever | Diarrhoea |
| West Bengal | 81.5 | 25.6 | 29.6 | 9.8 |
| All India | 75.3 | 20.3 | 29.7 | 21.9 |

*Source*: National Family Health Survey (NFHS-2, 1998-99), West Bengal, International Institute of Population Sciences, Mumbai, October 2001.

programmes are for vaccination, Vitamin A supplementation and so on. On both these counts, the performance is better in rural West Bengal compared to all-India, although there still exists a considerable gap in terms of attainment of complete vaccination/immunization of children (Tables 3.22A and 3.22B). As of 1998-99, although 75.3 per cent of rural children received first DTP, the percentages of those receiving second and third DTP are 66.3 and 53.6 respectively. Similarly, the percentages of children administered Polio doses reduce gradually from 81.7 (first dose) to 73.8 (second dose) and 58.1 (third dose). The percentage of children receiving BCG is 73.8. Nearly one-half of rural children are found to have received measles vaccine. However, it is to be noted that the percentage of fully vaccinated rural children (those who received BCG, all DTP, all Polio and measles vaccines) is about 41 per cent only in West Bengal in 1998-99, which is far short of the desired stage of 'universal immunization' for the children in rural West Bengal. This deficiency in vaccination of rural children is also corroborated by the NSS (52nd Round, 1995-96) data on vaccination of rural children (1-4 years) as presented in Table 3.23.

## Health Care for Women

We can also gather some idea about health care for all women in general and pregnant women in particular in rural areas by using NHFS-2 and NSS (52nd Round, 1995-96) data. The NHFS-2 data, presented in Table 3.24, reveal that the general health condition of rural women has been worse in West Bengal as compared to the same

**Table 3.22A:** Childhood Vaccination in Rural Areas (% of Children Age 12-23 Months Who Received Vaccinations at any Time before Interview)

| Region | Percentage Vaccinated | | | | | | | | | | |
|---|---|---|---|---|---|---|---|---|---|---|---|
| | | | DPT | | | Polio | | | | | |
| | BCG | Polio O | 1 | 2 | 3 | 1 | 2 | 3 | Measles | Fully Vacci-nated* | Not Recei-ved any Vacci-nations |
| West Bengal | 73.8 | 1.1 | 75.3 | 66.3 | 53.6 | 81.7 | 73.8 | 58.1 | 49.1 | 40.8 | 15.4 |
| All India | 67.1 | 10.1 | 67.1 | 60.1 | 49.8 | 81.1 | 75.0 | 58.3 | 45.3 | 36.6 | 16.7 |

*Note*: * Those who received BCG, all DPT, all Polio (except Polio O) and measles vaccines.

*Source*: National Family Health Survey (NFHS-2, 1998-99), West Bengal, International Institute of Population Sciences, Mumbai, October 2001.

for all-India. While about 64.2 per cent of ever-married rural women are reported to have anaemia in West Bengal, the corresponding figure for all-India has been 53.9 per cent. Similarly, as against 49.8 per cent of rural women being nutritionally deficient in West Bengal, the same for all-India has been 40.6 per cent.

**Table 3.22B:** Vitamin A Supplementation for Children (12-35 Months)

| Region | % of Children who Received Vitamin A | |
|---|---|---|
| | At Least 1 Dose | At least 1 Dose Within Past 6 Months |
| West Bengal | 40.2 | 22.5 |
| All India | 27.0 | 15.9 |

*Source*: National Family Health Survey (NFHS-2, 1998-99), West Bengal, International Institute of Population Sciences, Mumbai, October 2001.

However, as regards health care for pregnant women, the situation in rural West Bengal is found to be much better than all-India. Both in terms of receiving antenatal check-up and adoption of preventive measures (e.g. getting tetanus toxoid injections, iron and folic acid tablets and so on) the pregnant women are much better placed in

**Table 3.23:** Vaccinations of Rural Children (1-4 years): NSS 52nd Round Data (1995-96)

| *Item* | *Category* | *West Bengal* | *All India* |
|---|---|---|---|
| % of rural children who received BCG: | Boys | 72.9 | 67.9 |
| | Girls | 64.6 | 66.1 |
| | Boys+Girls | 68.8 | 67.0 |
| % of rural children who received DPT: | Boys | 64.4 | 46.5 |
| | Girls | 44.7 | 43.4 |
| | Boys+Girls | 49.3 | 45.0 |
| % of rural children who received OPV: | Boys | 62.0 | 56.7 |
| | Girls | 54.1 | 55.6 |
| | Boys+Girls | 57.8 | 56.1 |
| % of rural children who received MV: | Boys | 48.7 | 44.1 |
| | Girls | 40.3 | 42.9 |
| | Boys+Girls | 44.6 | 43.5 |

*Note*: BCG = vaccine given at birth for protection against tuberculosis; DPT = triple antigen (Diphtheria, Pertussis and Tetanus); OPV = oral polio vaccine; and MV = measles vaccine

*Source*: NSSO (1998), *Morbidity and Treatment of Ailments*, 52nd Round (July 1995-June 1996), Report No. 441, November.

**Table 3.24:** Health Care of Ever-married Rural Women [NHFS-2, 1998-99 Data]

| | *Indicator* | *West Bengal* | *India* |
|---|---|---|---|
| (1) | % of Ever-married Rural Women with any Anaemia | 64.2 | 53.9 |
| (2) | % of nutritionally deficient ever-married rural women (those with mean body mass index below 18.5 kg/m$^2$) | 49.8 | 40.6 |
| (3) | % of pregnant rural women receiving any antenatal check-up | 89.7 | 60.2 |
| (4) | % of rural women given tetanus toxoid injections during pregnancy | 91.9 | 71.8 |
| (5) | % of rural women given iron and folic acid tablets during pregnancy | 68.2 | 52.5 |

*Source*: National Family Health Survey (NFHS-2, 1998-99), West Bengal, International Institute of Population Sciences, Mumbai, October 2001.

**Table 3.25:** Some Indicators of Health Care of Pregnant Women (15-49 years): NSS 52nd Round Data (1995-96)

| | *Item* | *West Bengal* | *All India* |
|---|---|---|---|
| (1) | % of women registered for pre-natal care | 61.1 | 41.1 |
| (2) | % of women registered for pre-natal care under: | | |
| | (i) Public Hospital/Primary Health Centre | 66.4 | 65.0 |
| | (ii) Private Hospital/Nursing Home/Private Doctor | 27.8 | 28.5 |
| | (iii) Other | 5.8 | 6.5 |
| (3) | % of women taken anti-tetanus | 73.0 | 56.8 |
| (4) | % of women taken iron foloc acid tablets | 62.0 | 41.4 |
| (5) | % of women receiving medical attention at child birth | 85.5 | 64.2 |
| (6) | % of women reporting home as place of child birth | 74.4 | 77.9 |

*Source*: NSSO (1998), *Morbidity and Treatment of Ailments*, 52nd Round (July 1995-June 1996), Report No. 441, November.

rural West Bengal as compared to their sisters at the all-India level (Tables 3.24 and 3.25). It is also encouraging to note that nearly 86 per cent of rural women in West Bengal are reported to have received medical attention at the time of childbirth, which at the all-India level is only 64 per cent (Table 3.25). It is, however, to be noted that about three-fourths of rural women in West Bengal reported their residences, rather than hospitals, being the place of childbirth.

## Health Awareness

In the context of health management, it is often mentioned that a lot of diseases could be prevented through precaution only. For this purpose, it is necessary to build awareness among the people. We can have some idea about the level of health awareness among the rural people in West Bengal from NSS data for 52nd Round (1995-96). In Table 3.26A, we present data on some indicators of health awareness by the rural people in West Bengal and all-India. It clearly emerges that the level of health awareness has been generally high among rural population in West Bengal as compare to all-India. Thus, a much higher percentage of rural households are found to have gone in for immunization of children and pregnant women and also consumed ORT for severe diarrhoea. However, only 34.3 per cent of rural households in West Bengal are found to consume iodized salt, which at the all-India level is 45.1 per cent.

**Table 3.26A:** Percentage of Rural Households Reporting Awareness of Need for Specific Health Precautions: NSS 52nd Round Data (1995-96)

| *Item* | *West Bengal* | *All India* |
|---|---|---|
| Immunization of children | 83.6 | 75.9 |
| Immunization of pregnant women | 79.2 | 71.2 |
| Consuming iodized salt | 34.3 | 44.3 |
| ORT for severe diarrhoea | 61.8 | 45.1 |

*Source*: NSSO (1998), *Morbidity and Treatment of Ailments*, 52nd Round (July 1995-June 1996), Report No. 441, November.

However, a look into the sources of drinking water used by the rural households does not present a happy picture. The percentage of rural households using tap water for drinking (which is the safest) in West Bengal is only 3.9 per cent, which at the all-India level is 23.2 per cent in 1995-96 (Table 3.26B). On the other hand, an overwhelming majority of households (82.3 per cent) use water from tube well/hand pump for the purpose of drinking, most of which are presumably privately owned. These tube wells/hand pumps, if not sunk deep, are likely to lift contaminated water and raise the vulnerability of rural people to water-borne diseases.[16]

**Table 3.26B:** Major source of Drinking Water for Rural Households: NSS 52nd Round Data (1995-96)

(*Percentage*)

| *Source* | *West Bengal* | *All India* |
|---|---|---|
| Tap | 3.9 | 23.2 |
| Tubewell/hand pump | 82.3 | 49.0 |
| Pucca well | 11.3 | 21.8 |
| Other | 2.5 | 6.0 |

*Source*: NSSO (1998), *Morbidity and Treatment of Ailments*, 52nd Round (July 1995-June 1996), Report No. 441, November.

We also have some information on types of latrines used by rural households (Table 3.26C). In rural West Bengal, about 78 per cent of households do not use any latrine for defecation (at the all-India level, this is 84 per cent). Almost all the villages surveyed by the LBSNAA also categorically reported this lacuna. It is also found that nearly 84 per cent of rural households in the state do not have any drainage facility (63 per cent at the all-India level). Clearly, these are some of the possible means through which various kinds of diseases spread among rural population in the state.

**Table 3.27:** Rural Literacy Rates in West Bengal and All India (for Population Aged More than 6 years)

| *Source/Year* | *West Bengal* | | | *All India* | | |
|---|---|---|---|---|---|---|
| | *Male* | *Female* | *Person* | *Male* | *Female* | *Person* |
| Census of India, 1981 | 52.76 | 26.77 | 40.18 | 49.59 | 21.70 | 36.01 |
| Census of India, 1991 | 62.05 | 38.12 | 50.50 | 73.75 | 53.82 | 64.06 |
| NSS, 1993-94 (50th Rd.) | 68.00 | 47.00 | 58.00 | 63.00 | 36.00 | 50.00 |
| NSS, 1999-2000 (55th Rd.) | 71.00 | 52.00 | 62.00 | 68.00 | 43.00 | 56.00 |
| Census of India, 2001 | 73.75 | 53.82 | 64.06 | 71.18 | 46.58 | 59.21 |

*Source*: (1) Government of India, *National Human Development Report 2001*, Planning Commission, New Delhi, March 2002 and (2) NSSO, *Literacy and Levels of Education in India 1999-2000*, Report No. 473, September 2001.

## EDUCATION

This section is devoted towards understanding the status of education in rural West Bengal. To begin with, we look at the changes in literacy rates of population, the most widely used indicator of educational status. We look at literacy rates in the districts as well as the state as a whole. We then examine whether levels of education by the rural population varies in terms of their class/caste backgrounds. The discussion then moves towards understanding the educational infrastructure in rural areas of the state and the districts. The final sub-section discusses the issue of quality of education in the state.

### Literacy Rates

The data on rural literacy rates (for population aged more than 6 years) in West Bengal and all-India are presented in Table 3.27. It is observed that rural literacy rates have gradually progressed both in West Bengal and all-India over past twenty years or so. The rural literacy rates have been all along higher in West Bengal as compared to all-India both for males and females. In 2001, nearly 74 per cent of rural males (aged more than 6 years) and 54 per cent of rural females were literates; the corresponding figures for rural males and females at the all-India level have been 71 per cent and 47 per cent respectively. However, it also needs to be mentioned that even in 2001, among the rural persons, about 36 per cent in West Bengal and 41 per cent in all-India remained illiterate. It is also observable that the rate of illiteracy has been much higher among the rural females as compared to rural males both in West Bengal (46 per cent in 2001) and all-India (53 per cent in 2001).

The rates of literacy as well as the spread of it over the years have not been uniform across different districts of West Bengal. Table 3.28 presents district-wise data on rural literacy rates for males and females for the years 1991 and 2001. In 2001, among the districts of West Bengal, literacy rate for rural males was the highest in Midnapore (84.76 per cent) and lowest in Uttar Dinajpur (55.12 per cent). Some other districts having more than three-fourths of rural males being literate are Howrah (81.30 per cent), Hooghly (80.25 per cent), South 24 Parganas (78.68 per cent), Darjeeling (77.21 per cent), North 24 Parganas (77.20 per cent), Bankura (76.27 per cent), Burdwan (75.72 per cent) and Cooch Behar (75.32 per cent). On the other hand, the districts with relatively low male literacy rates are Malda (57.03 per cent), Murshidabad (59.23 per cent) and Nadia (68.70 per cent). As regards rural females, the highest literacy rate in 2001 is recorded for Howrah (65.13 per cent). The other districts where more than one-half of rural females have been literates are Midnapore (63.63 per cent), Hooghly (62.58 per cent), North 24 Parganas (61.71 per cent), Burdwan (57.08 per cent), South 24 Parganas (56.89 per cent), Darjeeling (56.14 per cent), Nadia (55.50 per cent), Cooch Behar (54.49 per cent), Dakshin Dinajpur (51.16 per cent) and Birbhum (50.35 per cent). The literacy rate for rural females has been the lowest in Uttar Dinajpur (31.43 per cent); the other districts with very low female literacy rates are Purulia (33.91 per cent), Malda (38.85 per cent), Murshidabad (46.37 per cent), Bankura (47.92 per cent) and Jalpaiguri (47.97 per cent).

Table 3.28 also shows that, as expected, the growth of literacy rates during the decade of 1990s have been relatively higher in the districts having low rates of literacy for both rural males and females. Considering rural males and females together, the progress of literacy was the highest in Cooch Behar; the other districts to perform impressively on this count are Dakshin Dinajpur, Jalpaiguri, Darjeeling, Murshidabad, North 24 Parganas, Nadia, South 24 Parganas,

**Table 3.28:** Rural Literacy Rates in West Bengal by Districts (for Population Aged More than 6 years)

| District | Census 1991 | | | Census 2001 | | | % point Change between 1991 and 2001 | | |
|---|---|---|---|---|---|---|---|---|---|
| | Male | Female | Person | Male | Female | Person | Male | Female | Person |
| Bankura | 65.17 (6) | 34.06 (10) | 50.01 (7) | 76.27 (7) | 47.92 (13) | 62.44 (9) | 11.10 (13) | 13.86 (14) | 12.43 (13) |
| Birbhum | 57.52 (10) | 35.00 (9) | 46.60 (9) | 70.18 (13) | 50.35 (11) | 60.55 (12) | 12.66 (11) | 15.35 (12) | 13.95 (11) |
| Burdwan | 66.91 (4) | 45.95 (4) | 56.83 (4) | 75.72 (8) | 57.08 (5) | 66.69 (7) | 8.81 (15) | 11.13 (16) | 9.86 (15) |
| Cooch Behar | 55.06 (11) | 29.74 (11) | 42.89 (11) | 75.32 (9) | 54.49 (9) | 65.21 (8) | 20.26 (1) | 24.75 (1) | 22.32 (1) |
| Dakshin Dinajpur | 52.08 (13) | 29.05 (12) | 40.96 (12) | 70.83 (11) | 51.16 (10) | 61.27 (11) | 18.75 (3) | 22.11 (2) | 20.31 (2) |
| Darjeeling | 59.96 (9) | 37.53 (7) | 49.17 (8) | 77.21 (5) | 56.14 (7) | 66.92 (6) | 17.25 (4) | 18.61 (7) | 17.75 (4) |
| Hooghly | 72.85 (2) | 51.08 (2) | 62.29 (2) | 80.25 (3) | 62.58 (3) | 71.52 (3) | 7.40 (16) | 11.50 (15) | 9.23 (16) |
| Howrah | 72.21 (3) | 49.61 (3) | 61.28 (3) | 81.30 (2) | 65.13 (1) | 73.39 (2) | 9.09 (14) | 15.52 (11) | 12.11 (14) |
| Jalpaiguri | 51.37 (14) | 26.99 (13) | 39.70 (14) | 70.75 (12) | 47.97 (12) | 59.73 (13) | 19.38 (2) | 20.98 (3) | 20.03 (3) |
| Maldah | 42.80 (16) | 21.60 (15) | 32.57 (16) | 57.03 (16) | 38.85 (15) | 48.21 (16) | 14.23 (8) | 17.25 (9) | 15.64 (10) |
| Midnapore | 80.73 (1) | 55.13 (1) | 68.27 (1) | 84.76 (1) | 63.63 (2) | 74.42 (1) | 4.03 (17) | 8.50 (17) | 6.15 (17) |
| Murshidabad | 43.68 (15) | 26.77 (14) | 35.52 (15) | 59.23 (15) | 46.37 (14) | 52.99 (15) | 15.55 (6) | 19.60 (5) | 17.47 (5) |
| Nadia | 53.84 (12) | 37.56 (6) | 46.06 (10) | 68.70 (14) | 55.50 (8) | 62.32 (10) | 14.86 (7) | 17.94 (8) | 16.26 (7) |
| North 24 Parganas | 63.78 (7) | 42.12 (5) | 53.36 (5) | 77.20 (6) | 61.71 (4) | 69.69 (4) | 13.42 (9) | 19.59 (6) | 16.33 (6) |
| Purulia | 59.98 (8) | 19.57 (16) | 40.32 (13) | 72.82 (10) | 33.91 (16) | 53.82 (14) | 12.84 (10) | 14.34 (13) | 13.50 (12) |
| South 24 Parganas | 66.60 (5) | 36.89 (8) | 52.20 (6) | 78.68 (4) | 56.89 (6) | 68.13 (5) | 12.08 (12) | 20.00 (4) | 15.93 (8) |
| Uttar Dinajpur | 39.13 (17) | 15.41 (17) | 27.78 (17) | 55.12 (17) | 31.43 (17) | 43.68 (17) | 15.99 (5) | 16.02 (10) | 15.90 (9) |
| West Bengal | 62.05 | 38.12 | 50.50 | 73.75 | 53.82 | 64.06 | 11.70 | 15.70 | 13.56 |

*Note*: Figures in brackets are ranks among 17 districts of West Bengal.
*Source*: Census of India 2001, *Provisional Population Totals: Distribution of Rural-Urban Population*, Series 20, West Bengal.

Uttar Dinajpur and Malda. However, it is to be noted that some of these districts are still plagued by low literacy rates, more specifically for rural females.

## Educational Status by Caste/Class Backgrounds of Rural Population

We now look at the relationship, if any between educational attainment and caste/class backgrounds of rural population in West Bengal. For this purpose, we utilize the NSSO data for the year 1999-2000 (55th Round). Table 3.29A presents data on level of education by various social groups in rural West Bengal. The main points emerging are: (1) Among all social groups, the rate of illiteracy in rural West Bengal is the highest among the Scheduled Tribes and lowest among other Backward Castes (OBCs). It is found that among the rural persons, the rate of illiteracy is 58.4 per cent for the Scheduled Tribes, 42.9 per cent for the Scheduled Castes, 35.3 per cent for general castes and 25.5 per cent among the OBCs. (2) The rate of illiteracy is very high among the females belonging to scheduled tribe category (70 per cent). It is also fairly high among Scheduled Caste women (56 per cent). For the females belonging to general castes, 43.4 per cent are found to be illiterate, the corresponding figure for the OBC females being 34.7 per cent. (3) Although the illiteracy rates for males of various caste categories are much lower as compared to females, there also exists inter-caste variation in this regard. For the rural males belong to Scheduled Tribes, 47.5 per cent are illiterate; the corresponding figures for scheduled castes, general castes and OBCs are 30.8 per cent, 28 per cent and 17 per cent respectively. (4) Table 3.29A also reveals that the rate of attainment of education beyond middle level is generally very low in rural West Bengal and this is more so among the females and also among Scheduled Castes and Tribes. Only 11 per cent of all rural males and 4.1 per cent of females could cross middle level education in the state. It is also found that only 5 per cent among the Scheduled Tribe males and 6.6 per cent among the Scheduled Caste males have crossed the middle level education. As regards Scheduled Tribe females, only 2 per cent have crossed middle level education, which for Scheduled Caste females is 2.7 per cent. These observations clearly show very weak educational base, particularly at the higher level by rural population in general and Scheduled Tribes/Castes in particular.

**Table 3.29A:** Percentage Distribution of Rural Population (Aged 7 and Above) by Level of Education and Social Groups in West Bengal in 1999-2000

| *Sex* | *Social Group* | *Level of Education* | | | | | | |
|---|---|---|---|---|---|---|---|---|
| | | *Illiterate* | *Up to Primary* | *Middle* | *Secondary* | *Higher Secondary* | *Graduate and Above* | *All* |
| Male | Scheduled Tribe | 47.5 | 39.5 | 8.0 | 3.2 | 0.8 | 1.0 | 100.0 |
| | Scheduled Caste | 30.8 | 49.7 | 12.9 | 3.8 | 1.6 | 1.2 | 100.0 |
| | Other backward castes | 17.0 | 46.1 | 21.8 | 8.3 | 2.5 | 4.3 | 100.0 |
| | General caste | 28.0 | 41.2 | 18.1 | 7.3 | 2.5 | 2.9 | 100.0 |
| | All | 29.3 | 43.6 | 16.3 | 6.2 | 2.2 | 2.4 | 100.0 |
| Female | Scheduled Tribe | 70.0 | 24.8 | 3.2 | 1.3 | 0.7 | 0.0 | 100.0 |
| | Scheduled Caste | 56.0 | 34.6 | 6.7 | 1.9 | 0.5 | 0.3 | 100.0 |
| | Other backward castes | 34.7 | 39.7 | 18.4 | 4.4 | 1.1 | 1.7 | 100.0 |
| | General caste | 43.4 | 38.3 | 13.6 | 3.2 | 0.8 | 0.7 | 100.0 |
| | All | 48.1 | 36.5 | 11.3 | 2.8 | 0.7 | 0.6 | 100.0 |
| Male + Female | Scheduled Tribe | 58.4 | 32.4 | 5.7 | 2.3 | 0.7 | 0.5 | 100.0 |
| | Scheduled Caste | 42.9 | 42.4 | 9.9 | 2.9 | 1.1 | 0.8 | 100.0 |
| | Other backward castes | 25.5 | 43.0 | 20.2 | 6.4 | 1.8 | 3.1 | 100.0 |
| | General caste | 35.3 | 39.7 | 16.0 | 5.4 | 1.7 | 1.9 | 100.0 |
| | All | 38.3 | 40.2 | 13.9 | 4.5 | 1.5 | 1.6 | 100.0 |

*Source*: NSSO, Literacy and Levels of Education in India: 1999-2000 (55th Round), Report No. 473, September 2001.

Table 3.29B provides some idea about the relationship between the class background of rural households and their educational attainments. It is observed that the rate of illiteracy is much higher among the 'landless' (possessing less than 0.01 hectare of land) and 'sub-marginal' landholders (possessing 0.01-0.40 hectare of land). It is as well clear that the rate of illiteracy is even greater among the females of these categories of households as compared to other categories. Thus, while 28.7 per cent males among the 'landless' are reported to be illiterate in rural West Bengal, the corresponding figure for females is 52.6 per cent. Table 3.29B also reveals that there exists a positive relationship between the size class of land possessed and the level of educational attainment in rural West Bengal. Not only the level of illiteracy being lower among the people belonging to higher size groups of land possessed, but also their attainment of higher education has been greater.

## Educational Infrastructure

### *Concentration of Educational Institutions*

We now focus our attention to the issue of educational infrastructure available currently in rural West Bengal. We look at the number of educational institutions available in rural areas. Table 3.30 presents data on various types of educational institutions being available in rural areas of the state of West Bengal and her districts in 1999-2000. The main points to be noted are the following:

(1) At present, the number of primary schools available per lakh rural population in West Bengal is 74.33, which per thousand students works out to be 5.82. However, there are wide inter-district variations in terms of availability of primary schools. While the number of primary schools per thousand students being the highest in Bankura (10.81), this has been lowest in Jalpaiguri (3.92). The other districts with relatively high (above state-average) concentration of primary schools are Purulia (10.19), Darjeeling (7.75), Midnapore (7.53), Hooghly (6.50), Birbhum (6.32) and Howrah (6.50). On the other hand, the districts to report relatively low (below state-average) concentration of primary schools are Murshidabad (4.25), North 24 Parganas (4.37), South 24 Parganas (4.38), Nadia (4.42), Malda (4.93), Uttar Dinajpur (5.23), Dakshin Dinajpur (5.42), Cooch Behar (5.42), and Burdwan (5.51).

**Table 3.29B:** Percentage Distribution of Rural Population (Aged 7 and Above) by Level of Education and Size Class of Land Possessed in West Bengal in 1999-2000

| Sex | Size Class of Land Possessed (in hectares) | Level of Education | | | | | | |
|---|---|---|---|---|---|---|---|---|
| | | Illiterate | Up to Primary | Middle | Secon-dary | Higher Secondary | Graduate and Above | All |
| Male | Less than 0.01 | 28.7 | 52.5 | 8.8 | 5.8 | 1.5 | 2.7 | 100.0 |
| | 0.01-0.40 | 34.3 | 45.2 | 13.5 | 4.1 | 1.6 | 1.3 | 100.0 |
| | 0.41-1.00 | 19.0 | 40.9 | 22.2 | 10.1 | 3.5 | 4.3 | 100.0 |
| | 1.01-2.00 | 16.3 | 37.3 | 25.7 | 11.9 | 2.8 | 6.0 | 100.0 |
| | 2.01-4.00 | 15.4 | 34.6 | 27.0 | 14.3 | 3.3 | 5.4 | 100.0 |
| | 4.01 and above | 3.6 | 38.9 | 24.8 | 14.4 | 11.4 | 6.9 | 100.0 |
| | All classes | 29.3 | 43.6 | 16.3 | 6.2 | 2.2 | 2.4 | 100.0 |
| Female | Less than 0.01 | 52.6 | 39.1 | 6.2 | 1.2 | 0.8 | 0.1 | 100.0 |
| | 0.01-0.40 | 52.8 | 35.2 | 8.9 | 2.0 | 0.6 | 0.5 | 100.0 |
| | 0.41-1.00 | 38.4 | 37.9 | 17.2 | 4.1 | 1.2 | 1.2 | 100.0 |
| | 1.01-2.00 | 34.8 | 39.6 | 18.8 | 5.2 | 1.1 | 0.5 | 100.0 |
| | 2.01-4.00 | 25.7 | 42.8 | 20.8 | 6.9 | 1.6 | 2.2 | 100.0 |
| | 4.01 and above | 17.3 | 53.9 | 19.8 | 6.5 | 1.4 | 1.1 | 100.0 |
| | All classes | 48.1 | 36.5 | 11.3 | 2.8 | 0.7 | 0.6 | 100.0 |
| Male+Female | Less than 0.01 | 40.0 | 46.2 | 7.5 | 3.6 | 1.2 | 1.5 | 100.0 |
| | 0.01-0.40 | 43.3 | 40.3 | 11.3 | 3.1 | 1.1 | 0.9 | 100.0 |
| | 0.41-1.00 | 28.1 | 39.5 | 19.8 | 7.3 | 2.4 | 2.9 | 100.0 |
| | 1.01-2.00 | 24.7 | 38.4 | 22.6 | 8.8 | 2.0 | 3.5 | 100.0 |
| | 2.01-4.00 | 20.5 | 38.7 | 23.9 | 10.6 | 2.5 | 3.8 | 100.0 |
| | 4.01 and above | 9.9 | 45.8 | 22.5 | 10.8 | 6.8 | 4.2 | 100.0 |
| | All classes | 38.3 | 40.2 | 13.9 | 4.5 | 1.5 | 1.6 | 100.0 |

*Source*: NSSO, Literacy and Levels of Education in India: 1999-2000 (55th Round), Report No. 473, September 2001.

**Table 3.30:** Number of Educational Institutions in Rural West Bengal by Districts in 1999-2000

| *District* | *Primary Schools* | | *Middle Schools* | | *High and Higher Secondary Schools* | | *Colleges/University* | |
|---|---|---|---|---|---|---|---|---|
| | *Number of Institution Per Lakh Population** | | | | | | | |
| Bankura | 113.39 | (2) | 4.17 | (6) | 9.90 | (5) | 0.34 | (4) |
| Birbhum | 83.38 | (6) | 3.64 | (8) | 9.33 | (6) | 0.22 | (9) |
| Burdwan | 74.49 | (9) | 3.17 | (9) | 10.66 | (2) | 0.19 | (11) |
| Cooch Behar | 72.04 | (10) | 2.57 | (14) | 7.27 | (11) | 0.14 | (15) |
| Dakshin Dinajpur | 85.10 | (5) | 2.99 | (10) | 7.41 | (9) | 0.08 | (16) |
| Darjeeling | 94.39 | (3) | 4.82 | (4) | 6.81 | (12) | 0.38 | (2) |
| Hooghly | 76.43 | (8) | 3.88 | (7) | 10.39 | (3) | 0.36 | (3) |
| Howrah | 78.67 | (7) | 4.46 | (5) | 10.79 | (1) | 0.43 | (1) |
| Jalpaiguri | 65.98 | (11) | 2.42 | (15) | 6.23 | (15) | 0.26 | (8) |
| Malda | 59.91 | (13) | 2.88 | (11) | 6.77 | (13) | 0.17 | (12) |
| Midnapore | 86.11 | (4) | 6.39 | (1) | 8.87 | (7) | 0.26 | (7) |
| Murshidabad | 56.01 | (16) | 2.70 | (12) | 5.57 | (16) | 0.20 | (10) |
| Nadia | 55.88 | (17) | 2.61 | (13) | 6.67 | (14) | 0.14 | (14) |
| North 24 Parganas | 58.85 | (14) | 1.75 | (17) | 10.05 | (4) | 0.15 | (13) |
| Purulia | 128.15 | (1) | 5.18 | (2) | 7.63 | (8) | 0.27 | (5) |
| South 24 Parganas | 56.70 | (15) | 4.87 | (3) | 7.40 | (10) | 0.26 | (6) |
| Uttar Dinajpur | 64.66 | (12) | 1.98 | (16) | 4.16 | (17) | — | — |
| West Bengal | 74.33 | | 3.80 | | 8.15 | | 0.23 | |
| | *Number of institutions per 1000 students* | | | | | | | |
| Bankura | 10.81 | (1) | 3.81 | (8) | 1.52 | (5) | 0.88 | (11) |
| Birbhum | 6.32 | (6) | 5.05 | (4) | 1.52 | (4) | 0.95 | (10) |
| Burdwan | 5.51 | (8) | 4.05 | (6) | 1.45 | (7) | 1.15 | (7) |

(*Contd.*)

**Table 3.30:** (*Contd.*)

| *District* | *Primary Schools* | | *Middle Schools* | | *High and Higher Secondary Schools* | | *Colleges/University* | |
|---|---|---|---|---|---|---|---|---|
| | | | *Number of Institution Per Lakh Population** | | | | | |
| Cooch Behar | 5.42 | (9) | 4.71 | (5) | 1.73 | (2) | 1.22 | (6) |
| Dakshin Dinajpur | 5.42 | (10) | 3.44 | (10) | 1.37 | (10) | 4.26 | (1) |
| Darjeeling | 7.75 | (3) | 6.90 | (1) | 1.73 | (1) | 2.14 | (2) |
| Hooghly | 6.50 | (5) | 2.02 | (17) | 1.37 | (11) | 0.44 | (16) |
| Howrah | 6.23 | (7) | 5.40 | (2) | 1.42 | (8) | 0.86 | (12) |
| Jalpaiguri | 3.92 | (17) | 2.53 | (14) | 0.90 | (17) | 1.73 | (3) |
| Malda | 4.93 | (12) | 2.37 | (15) | 1.40 | (9) | 1.24 | (5) |
| Midnapore | 7.53 | (4) | 3.99 | (7) | 1.16 | (14) | 0.99 | (9) |
| Murshidabad | 4.25 | (16) | 2.25 | (16) | 1.31 | (13) | 1.05 | (8) |
| Nadia | 4.42 | (13) | 2.87 | (13) | 0.95 | (16) | 0.50 | (15) |
| North 24 Parganas | 4.37 | (15) | 3.27 | (11) | 1.71 | (3) | 0.83 | (13) |
| Purulia | 10.19 | (2) | 5.09 | (3) | 1.34 | (12) | 1.59 | (4) |
| South 24 Parganas | 4.38 | (14) | 3.79 | (9) | 1.49 | (6) | 0.57 | (14) |
| Uttar Dinajpur | 5.23 | (11) | 2.90 | (12) | 1.16 | (15) | — | — |
| West Bengal | 5.82 | | 3.48 | | 1.34 | | 0.84 | |
| | | | *Number of students per institution* | | | | | |
| Bankura | 92.48 | (17) | 262.67 | (10) | 659.60 | (13) | 1321.83 | (11) |
| Birbhum | 158.30 | (12) | 198.09 | (14) | 656.25 | (14) | 1484.23 | (8) |
| Burdwan | 181.40 | (10) | 246.96 | (12) | 690.98 | (11) | 1469.14 | (9) |
| Cooch Behar | 184.37 | (9) | 212.14 | (13) | 577.48 | (16) | 1652.00 | (6) |
| Dakshin Dinajpur | 184.42 | (8) | 291.00 | (8) | 730.88 | (8) | 900.50 | (16) |
| Darjeeling | 129.11 | (15) | 144.82 | (17) | 577.33 | (17) | 772.67 | (17) |
| Hooghly | 153.75 | (13) | 495.18 | (1) | 731.60 | (7) | 1828.18 | (3) |
| Howrah | 160.51 | (11) | 185.11 | (16) | 702.56 | (10) | 2208.47 | (1) |

(*Contd.*)

**Table 3.30:** (*Contd.*)

| *District* | *Primary Schools* | | *Middle Schools* | | *High and Higher Secondary Schools* | | *Colleges/University* | |
|---|---|---|---|---|---|---|---|---|
| | *Number of Institution Per Lakh Population** | | | | | | | |
| Jalpaiguri | 255.02 | (1) | 395.20 | (4) | 1105.37 | (1) | 1198.45 | (13) |
| Malda | 202.72 | (6) | 421.21 | (3) | 714.38 | (9) | 1446.00 | (10) |
| Midnapore | 132.77 | (14) | 250.68 | (11) | 858.96 | (4) | 1117.50 | (14) |
| Murshidabad | 235.27 | (2) | 444.27 | (2) | 760.69 | (5) | 1248.94 | (12) |
| Nadia | 226.48 | (5) | 347.95 | (5) | 1048.54 | (2) | 1988.40 | (2) |
| North 24 Parganas | 228.75 | (3) | 305.96 | (7) | 586.05 | (15) | 1728.39 | (5) |
| Purulia | 98.13 | (16) | 196.54 | (15) | 744.13 | (6) | 907.56 | (15) |
| South 24 Parganas | 228.23 | (4) | 263.82 | (9) | 671.81 | (12) | 1787.86 | (4) |
| Uttar Dinajpur | 191.08 | (7) | 344.32 | (6) | 864.40 | (3) | 1520.75 | (7) |
| West Bengal | 171.86 | | 287.56 | | 746.24 | | 1504.54 | |

*Notes*: (1) * for computing this we have considered projected population at the mid-point of year 1999-2000, i.e. on 1.10.99; and
(2) figures in brackets are ranks among 17 districts of West Bengal.

*Source*: *District Statistical Hand Books 1999-00*, BAES, Government of West Bengal.

(2) As expected, the availability of schools of higher standard is much less as compared to the primary schools. The number of high and higher secondary schools per thousand students in rural areas of the state is only 1.34, which for primary schools were 5.82 (noted earlier). This lower availability of schools at the high and higher secondary levels partly explains the failure of a large section of rural population (both male and female) to attain education beyond middle level. There is also clear inter-district variation in terms of concentration of high and higher secondary schools. While the concentration of high and higher secondary schools in rural areas of the state has been the highest in Darjeeling (1.73 per thousand students), the same has been the lowest in Jalpaiguri (0.90 per thousand students). Some other districts to perform relatively better on this count are Cooch Behar, North 24 Parganas, Birbhum, Bankura, South 24 Parganas, Burdwan and Howrah; the lagging districts being Nadia, Uttar Dinajpur, Midnapore, Murshidabad and Purulia.

(3) The concentration of Colleges/University is further reduced in rural areas and there also exists clear inter-district variation in this regard. On the basis of number of Colleges/University per thousand students, some of the front-runners are Dakshin Dinajpur, Darjeeling, Jalpaiguri, Purulia, Malda, Cooch Behar and Burdwan while the laggards are Hooghly, Nadia, South 24 Parganas, North 24 Parganas and Howrah. These latter districts clearly have much greater pressures of students in the existing colleges in rural areas.

## Student-Teacher Ratio

We have worked out student-teacher ratios for educational institutions of various grades in rural areas of the state and her districts. Table 3.31 presents data on this aspect. It is to be noted that in respect to primary schools in rural areas, only one district (Bankura) out of a total of 17, has the student-teacher ratio that is close to the norm (Student:Teacher = 40 : 1) that is supposed to be followed.[17] For all other districts as well as the state as a whole, the student-teacher ratio is far away from the norm of 40 : 1. For rural West Bengal, this works out to be nearly 61. In as many as 10 districts (namely Jalpaiguri, South 24 Parganas, Nadia, Hooghly, Uttar Dinajpur, Murshidabad, Malda, North

**Table 3.31:** Student-Teacher Ratio in Educational Institutions in Rural West Bengal in 1999-2000

| *District* | *No. of Students per Teacher* | | | | | | | |
|---|---|---|---|---|---|---|---|---|
| | *Primary Schools* | | *Middle Schools* | | *High and Higher Secondary Schools* | | *Colleges/University* | |
| Bankura | 38.46 | (17) | 38.34 | (10) | 41.66 | (12) | 47.95 | (12) |
| Birbhum | 53.38 | (11) | 31.93 | (13) | 45.03 | (9) | 50.34 | (11) |
| Burdwan | 60.37 | (10) | 41.77 | (9) | 46.05 | (7) | 84.62 | (3) |
| Cooch Behar | 48.08 | (14) | 31.25 | (15) | 32.63 | (16) | 56.09 | (7) |
| Dakshin Dinajpur | 62.61 | (9) | 32.91 | (12) | 40.77 | (14) | 47.00 | (13) |
| Darjeeling | 40.00 | (16) | 28.41 | (17) | 41.32 | (13) | 7.98* | (16) |
| Hooghly | 73.61 | (4) | 72.85 | (1) | 40.21 | (15) | 55.57 | (8) |
| Howrah | 46.66 | (15) | 31.76 | (14) | 45.49 | (8) | 51.86 | (9) |
| Jalpaiguri | 88.92 | (1) | 65.87 | (4) | 72.75 | (1) | 59.60 | (6) |
| Malda | 67.38 | (7) | 67.55 | (3) | 51.06 | (5) | 103.72 | (2) |
| Midnapore | 50.69 | (12) | 42.62 | (8) | 53.51 | (4) | 44.25 | (14) |
| Murshidabad | 70.06 | (6) | 72.43 | (2) | 49.23 | (6) | 63.17 | (5) |
| Nadia | 78.52 | (3) | 50.73 | (6) | 59.45 | (2) | 761.77 | (1) |
| North 24 Parganas | 65.75 | (8) | 29.14 | (16) | 30.85 | (17) | 51.83 | (10) |
| Purulia | 49.36 | (13) | 34.34 | (11) | 44.52 | (10) | 29.23 | (15) |
| South 24 Parganas | 88.69 | (2) | 44.00 | (7) | 41.78 | (11) | 80.19 | (4) |
| Uttar Dinajpur | 73.04 | (5) | 56.92 | (5) | 58.03 | (3) | – | – |
| West Bengal | 61.17 | | 45.65 | | 45.97 | | 55.21 | |

*Notes*: * includes North Bengal University.
Figures in brackets are ranks among 17 districts of West Bengal.

*Source*: *District Statistical Hand Books 1999-2000*, BAES, Government of West Bengal.

24 Parganas, Dakshin Dinajpur and Burdwan) the student-teacher ratio at the primary school level is even greater than this rather high state average. The high student-teacher ratio is very likely to adversely affect the quality of teaching in the primary schools in rural areas of the state.

The student-teacher ratio gets somewhat better as we move on to the middle level schools and high and higher secondary schools. For rural West Bengal, the student-teacher ratio for both middle level schools and high and higher secondary schools works out to be nearly 46. For the colleges located in rural areas of the state, this is found to be 55. However, there are inter-district variations with regard to student-teacher ratios in institutions of higher level. For example, in high and higher secondary schools in rural areas, the student-teacher ratio is lower than the state-average in North 24 Parganas, Cooch Behar, Hooghly, Dakshin Dinajpur, Darjeeling, Bankura, South 24 Parganas, Puraulia, Birbhum and Howrah; for the remaining 7 districts, the student-teacher ratio for high and higher secondary schools being above the state-average.

All these observations clearly indicate wide discrepancy as regards provisioning of teaching staff in the rural schools of various grades in the districts. In any case, there is no uniformity among the districts as regards availability of teachers in the schools and hence inter-district variations emerging rather glaringly in terms of student-teacher ratios.

## *Sex Ratio of Students*

We may also look at the sex ratio (female : male) of the students in different types of educational institutions in rural areas of the state in terms of Table 3.32. The table presents clear evidence of sex bias in terms of enrolment of students in all types of educational institutions in rural West Bengal. At the primary level, the number girl students per 100 boy students for rural areas of the state as whole is about 91; this number goes down gradually as we move on to the educational institutions of higher level. As regards sex ratios of students in various educational institutions of the districts, there also exists a wide variation. In the primary schools, these ratios have been highly against the girl students and also lower than state-average in the districts of Darjeeling, Purulia, Burdwan, Birbhum, Uttar Dinajpur, Cooch Behar, Jalpaiguri, Bankura and Malda. The very poor admission of female

**Table 3.32:** Sex Ratio of Students in Educational Institutions in West Bengal in 1999-2000

| *District* | *No. of Female Students per 100 Male Students* | | | | | | | |
|---|---|---|---|---|---|---|---|---|
| | *Primary Schools* | | *Middle Schools* | | *High and Higher Secondary Schools* | | *Colleges/University* | |
| Bankura | 87.24 | (10) | 54.09 | (14) | 41.42 | (15) | 43.06 | (14) |
| Birbhum | 83.48 | (14) | 118.65 | (2) | 62.92 | (8) | 39.01 | (15) |
| Burdwan | 82.13 | (15) | 27.82 | (17) | 19.73 | (17) | 58.63 | (8) |
| Cooch Behar | 86.40 | (12) | 40.60 | (15) | 41.37 | (16) | 33.61 | (17) |
| Dakshin Dinajpur | 95.77 | (6) | 84.91 | (9) | 67.07 | (7) | 62.55 | (7) |
| Darjeeling | 71.01 | (17) | 63.32 | (13) | 59.20 | (11) | 49.40 | (11) |
| Hooghly | 97.20 | (5) | 93.68 | (7) | 93.35 | (2) | 73.81 | (2) |
| Howrah | 97.48 | (3) | 32.31 | (16) | 52.40 | (13) | 82.72 | (1) |
| Jalpaiguri | 86.82 | (11) | 127.87 | (1) | 73.88 | (6) | 66.92 | (4) |
| Malda | 88.48 | (9) | 63.43 | (12) | 59.30 | (10) | 63.02 | (6) |
| Midnapore | 94.35 | (7) | 110.67 | (3) | 55.20 | (12) | 44.97 | (13) |
| Murshidabad | 97.31 | (4) | 94.64 | (6) | 92.62 | (3) | 49.59 | (10) |
| Nadia | 98.04 | (2) | 88.12 | (8) | 81.26 | (4) | 56.42 | (9) |
| North 24 Parganas | 98.27 | (1) | 98.02 | (5) | 98.02 | (1) | 69.78 | (3) |
| Purulia | 76.48 | (16) | 75.97 | (11) | 46.15 | (14) | 38.94 | (16) |
| South 24 Parganas | 91.54 | (8) | 105.63 | (4) | 61.64 | (9) | 63.19 | (5) |
| Uttar Dinajpur | 84.43 | (13) | 83.11 | (10) | 74.82 | (5) | 45.49 | (12) |
| West Bengal | 90.65 | | 84.78 | | 61.59 | | 58.45 | |

*Note*: Figures in brackets are ranks among 17 districts of West Bengal.

*Source*: District Statistical Hand Books 1999-2000, BAES, Government of West Bengal.

students *vis-à-vis* male students in high and higher secondary schools is also glaring in Burdwan, Cooch Behar, Bankura, Purulia, and Birbhum where lass than 50 female students were admitted to the high and higher secondary schools per 100 male students. The same trend of poor attendance of girl students in Colleges/University is also observed in a large number of districts.

### *Sishu Siksha Karmasuchi*

An important attempt recently to promote the cause of universal elementary education in shortest possible time in West Bengal has been through establishment of Sishu Siksha Kendras (SSKs) [Child Education Centres]. The SSKs are supposed to rope in the children, particularly from underprivileged families, who remained outside the ambit of formal education centres/primary schools in the villages. The SSKs have started being established from the year 1999. The SSKs are put under the supervision of panchayats and direct management of village education committees with 75 per cent representation of guardians. In the SSKs, the lady teachers (called *sahayikas*) over the age of 40 years and having necessary qualification were to be appointed on contract basis, the monthly remuneration to each *sahayika* being Rs. 1000 only.

Table 3.33 presents data on the progress made so far in respect of SSKs in the state and also districts. It is reported that till September 2002, 14,699 SSKs have been established in the state and 33,670 *Sahayikas* recruited. The total number of students admitted in the SSKs has been 7,98,867.[18] As compared to the traditional primary schools, the SSKs are found to be in an advantageous position at least on two counts: (1) The number of students per SSK (54) is far less than number of students per primary schools (172); and (2) The student-*Sahayika* ratio (23.73) is also much lower than student-teacher ratio in the primary schools (61.17). The clear implication of these facts is that SSKs are more favourably placed to render better attention to their students.

However, it also need to be noted that the concentration of students as also student-*Sahayika* ratio in SSKs has not been uniform across the districts of West Bengal. The admission of students in the SSKs has been thiner in Darjeeling, Bankura, North 24 Parganas, Nadia, Midnapore, Cooch Behar, Dakshin Dinajpur and Jalpaiguri. In all these districts, the number of students per SSK has been less

**Table 3.33:** Progress of Sishu Siksha Karmasuchi (SSK) in West Bengal (as on September 2002)

| *District* | *No. of SSKs* | *No. of Sahayikas* | *No. of Students (Class I-IV)* | *No. of Sahayikas per SSK* | | *No. of Students per SSK* | | *Student-Sahayika Ratio* | |
|---|---|---|---|---|---|---|---|---|---|
| Bankura | 404 | 662 | 11309 | 1.64 | (16) | 27.99 | (16) | 17.08 | (16) |
| Birbhum | 581 | 1098 | 34840 | 1.89 | (15) | 59.97 | (6) | 31.73 | (5) |
| Burdwan | 976 | 2204 | 55485 | 2.26 | (6) | 56.85 | (8) | 25.17 | (8) |
| Cooch Behar | 900 | 1979 | 44316 | 2.20 | (8) | 49.24 | (12) | 22.39 | (12) |
| Dakshin Dinajpur | 459 | 1006 | 22788 | 2.19 | (9) | 49.65 | (11) | 22.65 | (10) |
| Darjeeling | 807 | 1749 | 17722 | 2.17 | (11) | 21.96 | (17) | 10.13 | (17) |
| Hooghly | 263 | 540 | 18529 | 2.05 | (14) | 70.45 | (4) | 34.31 | (4) |
| Howrah | 285 | 658 | 16977 | 2.31 | (5) | 59.57 | (7) | 25.80 | (7) |
| Jalpaiguri | 1121 | 3056 | 55851 | 2.73 | (2) | 49.82 | (10) | 18.28 | (14) |
| Maldah | 494 | 1043 | 48508 | 2.11 | (12) | 98.19 | (1) | 46.51 | (1) |
| Midnapore | 3249 | 7857 | 151860 | 2.42 | (3) | 46.74 | (13) | 19.33 | (13) |
| Murshidabad | 1540 | 4344 | 107155 | 2.82 | (1) | 69.58 | (5) | 24.67 | (9) |
| Nadia | 561 | 888 | 23060 | 1.58 | (17) | 41.11 | (14) | 25.97 | (6) |
| North 24 Parganas | 868 | 1888 | 32886 | 2.18 | (10) | 37.89 | (15) | 17.42 | (15) |
| Purulia | 220 | 512 | 11517 | 2.33 | (4) | 52.35 | (9) | 22.49 | (11) |
| South 24 Parganas | 1379 | 2853 | 98769 | 2.07 | (13) | 71.62 | (3) | 34.62 | (3) |
| Uttar Dinajpur | 592 | 1333 | 47295 | 2.25 | (7) | 79.89 | (2) | 35.48 | (2) |
| West Bengal | 14699 | 33670 | 798867 | 2.29 | | 54.35 | | 23.73 | |

*Note*: Figures in brackets are ranks among 17 districts of West Bengal.

*Source*: Government of West Bengal, *Economic Review 2002-2003*, Statistical Appendix, p. 200.

than 50. Consequently, in a good number of these and other districts, the student-*Sahayika* ratio turns out to be very low. This not only points to unplanned opening of SSKs in some of the districts, but also raises doubts about their viability and acceptability among the potential students (also their guardians) in some areas.

## *Educational Facilities in Rural West Bengal vis-à-vis All India*

We may look at the data available from the reports of *Sixth All India Educational Survey (1993)*, as published by the NCERT (1997), to get a view of educational facilities, as they are available in rural West Bengal *vis-à-vis* all-India. Although these data are now somewhat dated, they nevertheless offer some useful idea about the village-level availability of educational facilities by mid-1990s both in West Bengal and all-India. These data, presented in Table 3.34, show that nearly 71 per cent of the villages have been covered by primary schools both in West Bengal and all-India in mid-1990s. However, the availability of schools from middle level onwards has been few and far between in the villages both in West Bengal and all-India. Table 3.34 shows that only 8.89 per cent of the villages in West Bengal had secondary schools by mid-1990s, the corresponding figure for all-India was 8.76 per cent. The situation is worse as regards availability of higher secondary schools in as much as only 1.70 per cent of villages in West Bengal and 1.96 per cent of villages in all-India are reported to have such schools.

The educational survey data also point to very poor infrastructure facilities within school premises both in West Bengal and all-India. As regards West Bengal, it is found that in 58.39 per cent of rural schools there is facility of drinking water, which at the all-India level is 41.38 per cent. Further, only 15.20 per cent of rural schools in West Bengal have urinal, only 3.07 per cent have separate urinal for girls, 5.46 per cent have lavatory and 1.24 per cent have separate lavatory for girls.

Two other points that need mention from Table 3.34 are: (1) very poor representation of Scheduled Castes and Tribes and also females among the teachers in rural schools both in West Bengal and all-India; and (2) much lower 'gross enrolment ratio' among the girls as compared to boys in rural schools in West Bengal and all-India.

**Table 3.34:** Some Other Indicators of Educational Facilities in Rural West Bengal and All India as on 30.9.1993

| *Item* | | *West Bengal* | *All India* |
|---|---|---|---|
| % of villages having schools | Pre-primary (incl. Anganwadi) | 25.34 | 29.76 |
| | Primary (Class I-V) | 71.07 | 71.18 |
| | Middle (Class VI-VIII) | 13.68 | 23.32 |
| | Secondary (Class IX-X) | 8.89 | 8.76 |
| | Higher secondary (Class XI-XII) | 1.70 | 1.96 |
| % of rural schools having facilities for | Drinking water | 58.39 | 41.38 |
| | Urinal | 15.20 | 14.02 |
| | Separate urinal for girls | 3.07 | 5.54 |
| | Lavatory | 5.46 | 6.40 |
| | Separate lavatory for girls | 1.24 | 2.40 |
| % of teachers in rural areas who are | Scheduled Castes | 13.28 | 12.49 |
| | Scheduled Tribes | 2.95 | 9.01 |
| | Other backward castes (OBCs) | 0.90 | 28.20 |
| | Females | 13.98 | 23.50 |
| Gross enrolment ratio at primary and middle level* | Primary (Class I-V) —Boys | 96.91 | 92.76 |
| | Primary (Class I-V) —Girls | 83.80 | 71.82 |
| | Middle (Class VI-VIII) —Boys | 47.41 | 55.91 |
| | Middle (Class VI-VIII) —Girls | 33.24 | 35.82 |
| Sex ratio of students** | Primary (Class I-V) | 83.26 | 72.30 |
| | Middle (Class VI-VIII) | 66.24 | 57.31 |
| | Secondary (Class IX-X) | 54.38 | 47.57 |
| | Higher secondary (Class XI-XII) | 42.38 | 42.37 |
| Student-teacher ratio*** | Primary (Class I-V) | 45.28 | 40.94 |
| | Middle (Class VI-VIII) | 33.66 | 35.84 |
| | Secondary (Class IX-X) | 39.23 | 29.33 |
| | Higher secondary (Class XI-XII) | 39.51 | 33.57 |

*Notes*: * Gross enrolment ratio = (actual enrolment/estimated child population) per 100; ** Number of female students per 100 male students; and *** number of students per teacher.

*Source*: NCERT, Sixth All India Educational Survey, Vols. I-VI, October, 1997.

## Incentives/Disincentives for Education

The issue of incentives/disincentives for pursuing education becomes important in the context of any discussion on education by the persons. The Government to encourage specifically the primary education has introduced several incentive schemes (e.g. mid-day meal scheme, free text book scheme etc.). We could dwell upon the effectiveness of these incentives, though only in a limited manner, by using NSS data for 1995-96 (52nd Round). To begin with, we look at the rate of attendance of educational institutions among rural persons aged 5-24 years (Table 3.35A). It is found that among the rural males (age 5-24 years) in West Bengal, 51 per cent have not been attending any school/ educational institution currently, the corresponding figure among the females of same age group being 59.7 per cent. The rate of non-attendance of schools by rural males has been slightly greater in West Bengal as compared to all-India although the situation is just opposite in the case of rural females. However, considering rural males and females together, while 55.2 per cent in West Bengal have not been attending any school, the corresponding figure at the all-India level has been slightly lower at 53.6 per cent.

**Table 3.35A:** Rate of Attendance in Educational Institutions by Rural Persons (age 5-24 years) in West Bengal and All India in 1995-96

| *Item* | *Sex* | *West Bengal* | *All India* |
|---|---|---|---|
| (1) % of persons not attending school currently: | Male | 51.0 | 46.4 |
| | Female | 59.7 | 61.7 |
| | Male + Female | 55.2 | 53.6 |
| (2) % of persons attending pre-primary school currently: | Male | 1.1 | 1.3 |
| | Female | 1.1 | 1.1 |
| | Male + Female | 1.1 | 1.2 |
| (3) % of persons attending primary school currently: | Male | 28.4 | 28.0 |
| | Female | 25.6 | 23.1 |
| | Male + Female | 27.0 | 25.7 |
| (4) % of persons attending post-primary school currently: | Male | 19.1 | 23.9 |
| | Female | 13.6 | 13.9 |
| | Male + Female | 16.4 | 19.2 |

*Source*: NSSO, Attending an Educational Institution in India: Its Level, Nature and Cost, 52nd Round (July 1995-June 1996), Report No. 439, October 1998.

The NSS data also enable us to look into the causes behind non-enrolment in schools by the rural persons. These information are presented in Table 3.35B. The first point to note is that in West Bengal, 30.5 per cent of rural persons (age 5-24 years) have never enrolled in any educational institution, which for all-India is 31.5 per cent.

**Table 3.35B:** Reasons Behind Non-enrolment in Educational Institutions by Never Enrolled Rural Persons (age 5-24 years) in West Bengal and All India in 1995-96

*(Percentage)*

| *Item* | *Male* | *Female* | *Male+Female* |
|---|---|---|---|
| **West Bengal** | | | |
| (1) % of never enrolled | 26.3 | 35.0 | 30.5 |
| (2) Reasons behind non-enrolment (Percentage): | | | |
| (i) no tradition in the family | 1.1 | 3.6 | 2.5 |
| (ii) child not interested in studies | 21.7 | 18.9 | 20.1 |
| (iii) parents not interested in studies | 17.7 | 32.0 | 25.6 |
| (iv) education not considered useful | 4.0 | 2.4 | 3.1 |
| (v) schooling/higher educational facilities not available conveniently | 0.1 | 0.1 | 0.1 |
| (vi) has to work for wage/salary | 2.6 | 0.3 | 1.3 |
| (vii) has to participate in economic activities | 1.4 | 0.7 | 1.0 |
| (viii) has to look after younger siblings | 0.4 | 1.4 | 1.0 |
| (ix) has to attend to other domestic activities | 0.1 | 1.4 | 0.8 |
| (x) financial constraints | 27.3 | 17.1 | 21.7 |
| (xi) Others | 23.6 | 22.1 | 22.8 |
| **All India** | | | |
| (1) % of never enrolled | 23.5 | 40.6 | 31.5 |
| (2) Reasons behind non-enrolment (Percentage): | | | |
| (i) no tradition in the family | 1.5 | 5.4 | 3.9 |
| (ii) child not interested in studies | 20.5 | 15.1 | 17.3 |
| (iii) parents not interested in studies | 27.8 | 35.6 | 32.6 |
| (iv) education not considered useful | 2.7 | 2.9 | 2.8 |
| (v) schooling/higher educational facilities not available conveniently | 2.0 | 2.3 | 2.2 |

*(Contd.)*

**Table 3.35B** (*Contd.*)

| | *Item* | *Male* | *Female* | *Male+Female* |
|---|---|---|---|---|
| (vi) | has to work for wage/salary | 2.2 | 0.9 | 1.4 |
| (vii) | has to participate in economic activities | 4.6 | 3.0 | 3.6 |
| (viii) | has to look after younger siblings | 0.7 | 1.6 | 1.3 |
| (ix) | has to attend to other domestic activities | 0.7 | 4.0 | 2.7 |
| (x) | financial constraints | 16.3 | 13.6 | 14.6 |
| (xi) | Others | 21.0 | 15.6 | 17.6 |

*Source*: SSO, *Attending an Educational Institution in India: Its Level, Nature and Cost*, 52nd Round (July 1995-June 1996), Report No. 439, October 1998.

Further, as expected, the rate of non-enrolment is much higher among the females (35 per cent) in rural West Bengal as compared to their male counterparts (26.3 per cent). The main reasons behind non-enrolment in schools are: (1) financial constraints, (2) parents/child not interested in studies, (3) to attend domestic activities and so on.

The NSS data also show that among the rural persons aged 5-24 years, the percentage of dropouts from educational institutions is very high in West Bengal (Table 3.36A). For West Bengal, this is found to be 64.7 per cent, which for all-India is 58.1 per cent. It is also to be noted that the percentage of dropouts among the rural males has been greater than females both in West Bengal and all-India. Another important point to note in the context of West Bengal is that among the rural persons dropping out from educational institutions, nearly 85 per cent have done so at the primary/middle level, which for all-India is about 62 per cent. Clearly there is a tendency among the rural persons in West Bengal to drop out from educational institutions much earlier than the dropouts in all-India. Among the prominent reasons behind dropping out are: (1) Child being disinterested in studies, (2) Inability to cope with/failure in studies, (3) Financial constraints, (4) To participate in economic activities, (5) To work for wage/salary, (6) To attend to domestic activities etc. (Table 3.36B). The same set of reasons applies both in West Bengal and all-India.

The NSS survey also furnishes some data on incentives provided by the government/school authorities for pursuing education by the rural persons. Some such data are presented in Table 3.37. It is clearly observed that there have not been many incentives that are actually provided to the rural persons (age 5-24 years) who were pursuing education. In West Bengal, although nearly two-thirds of rural persons pursuing education have been provided with free/subsidized books and/or stationary, only 5.8 per cent of them received scholarships and a meagre 5.7 per cent were given mid-day meals. At the all-India level, nearly one-third of rural persons pursuing education received free/subsidized books and/or stationary, nearly 21 per cent were served with mid-day meals and about 8 per cent given scholarships.

## Quality of Education

Several scholars have commented upon the issue of quality of education in West Bengal particularly at the primary education level in recent years. Due to paucity of space, we briefly touch upon this

**Table 3.36A:** Percentage of Dropouts among Rural Persons (Age 5-24 Years) and the Educational Level at which Dropped-out in West Bengal and All India in 1995-96

| *Region* | *Item* | *Male* | *Female* | *Male + Female* |
|---|---|---|---|---|
| West Bengal | (1) % of dropouts | 67.40 | 61.70 | 64.70 |
| | (2) Educational level at which dropped out: | | | |
| | (i) Primary | 41.72 | 48.87 | 44.99 |
| | (ii) Middle | 44.72 | 35.60 | 40.56 |
| | (iii) Secondary | 10.97 | 13.58 | 12.18 |
| | (iv) Higher secondary | 1.55 | 1.34 | 1.44 |
| | (v) Above higher secondary | 1.04 | 0.62 | 0.83 |
| | (vi) Total | 100.00 | 100.00 | 100.00 |
| All India | (1) % of dropouts | 60.50 | 55.10 | 58.10 |
| | (2) Educational level at which dropped out: | | | |
| | (i) Primary | 31.34 | 38.72 | 34.48 |
| | (ii) Middle | 28.25 | 27.70 | 27.93 |
| | (iii) Secondary | 29.59 | 25.71 | 27.93 |
| | (iv) Higher secondary | 8.04 | 6.40 | 7.37 |
| | (v) Above higher secondary | 2.78 | 1.47 | 2.28 |
| | (vi) Total | 100.00 | 100.00 | 100.00 |

*Source*: NSSO, *Attending an Educational Institution in India: Its Level, Nature and Cost*, 52nd Round (July 1995-June 1996), Report No. 439, October 1998.

issue here taking recourse to the findings emanating from some of the micro studies conducted during 1990s. Studying the functioning of primary schools in rural West Bengal, Acharya (2002) concludes that "two decades of left rule in West Bengal was not all that bliss, particularly for primary education". He finds ample evidence of absenteeism among the teachers of primary schools apart from highly inadequate infrastructure that played havoc to satisfactory progress of primary education in the state[19]. There are two other studies conducted very recently by the Pratichi (India) Trust in some sample villages in six districts of West Bengal (Birbhum, Midnapore and Purulia in the first phase, and Burdwan, Murshidabad and Darjeeling in the second phase), which provide detailed account of the state of primary education in rural West Bengal (see Rana *et al.*, 2002, 2003). Among the deficiencies of primary schooling system in West Bengal as identified by the Pratichi (India) Trust studies are (1) Poor quality of teaching (including teacher absenteeism), (2) Poor education-quality

**Table 3.36B:** Reasons for Dropouts from Educational Institutions among Rural Persons (Age 5-24 years) in West Bengal and All India in 1995-96

*(Percentage)*

| Region | | Reasons | Male | Female | Male + Female |
|---|---|---|---|---|---|
| West Bengal | (i) | child not interested in studies | 35.8 | 20.9 | 29.0 |
| | (ii) | parents not interested in studies | 3.4 | 15.5 | 8.5 |
| | (iii) | inability to cope with/failure in studies | 12.5 | 12.0 | 12.3 |
| | (iv) | has to work for wage/salary | 6.8 | 0.4 | 3.8 |
| | (v) | has to participate in economic activities | 7.4 | 2.8 | 5.3 |
| | (vi) | has to look after younger siblings | 0.1 | 2.4 | 1.2 |
| | (vii) | has to attend to other domestic activities | 1.2 | 12.2 | 6.2 |
| | (viii) | financial constraints | 27.8 | 22.4 | 25.3 |
| | (ix) | others | 5.0 | 11.4 | 8.4 |
| All India | (i) | child not interested in studies | 28.5 | 21.0 | 25.3 |
| | (ii) | parents not interested in studies | 5.6 | 16.3 | 10.2 |
| | (iii) | inability to cope with/failure in studies | 24.1 | 18.0 | 21.5 |
| | (iv) | has to work for wage/salary | 6.1 | 1.4 | 4.1 |
| | (v) | has to participate in economic activities | 11.4 | 3.9 | 8.2 |
| | (vi) | has to look after younger siblings | 0.6 | 2.5 | 1.4 |
| | (vii) | has to attend to other domestic activities | 1.2 | 9.2 | 4.6 |
| | (viii) | financial constraints | 13.6 | 10.2 | 12.1 |
| | (ix) | others | 8.9 | 17.5 | 12.6 |

*Source*: As in Table 36A.

in primary schools fuelling the need for private tuition, (3) Discrimination against the students from inferior class/caste, (4) Lower rate of school-attendance by the girls as compared to boys, (5) Very high student-teacher ratio (54 : 1) and poor facilities in the schools, (6) Poor governance and supervision of the primary schools and so on. However, the Pratichi (India) Trust studies have some words of praise with regard the performance of SSKs *vis-à-vis* the usual primary schools, which is explained by greater accountability of SSKs to the local community and class affinity of their *Sahayikas* with the children's families. For improvement in the quality of primary education, the suggestions are: (1) Parents' participation in monitoring and governance of schools, (2) Enhancement of remuneration to

**Table 3.37:** Incentives for Pursuing General Education by Rural Persons (Age 5-24 Years) in West Bengal and All India in 1995-96

| | *Item* | *Sex* | *West Bengal* | *All India* |
|---|---|---|---|---|
| (1) | % of persons getting scholarship | Male | 7.8 | 8.1 |
| | | Female | 3.1 | 7.2 |
| | | Male + Female | 5.8 | 7.8 |
| (2) | % of persons getting free/subsidised books and/or stationary: | Male | 66.0 | 32.3 |
| | | Female | 72.0 | 37.2 |
| | | Male + Female | 68.6 | 34.2 |
| (3) | % of persons getting mid-day meals | Male | 6.4 | 19.5 |
| | | Female | 4.8 | 24.3 |
| | | Male + Female | 5.7 | 21.3 |

*Source*: As in Table 3.36A.

*Sahayikas* of SSKs and recognising them as '*Sikshak*' rather than '*Sahayika*', (3) Extending mid-day meals and other incentive schemes to all schools, including SSKs, and (4) Eradication of private tuition system. It is further urged "there has to be a qualitative improvement in the delivery of primary education, something that can be achieved through teachers' dedication, parents' co-operation and participation and proper inspection on part of the government" (Rana *et al.*, 2003, p. 2163).

## PANCHAYATI RAJ SYSTEM

In this section, we look into the workings of panchayati raj system in the state of West Bengal. Our main purpose is to understand the organizational structure of panchayati system, powers and functions of its different tiers and the socio-economic backgrounds of panchayat members. We would also briefly note the issues being raised by several scholars as regards the effectiveness of the panchayats in the state.

### The Background[20]

West Bengal has a long tradition of rural local self-government institutions. During the British era, in order to satisfy the popular demands, the Bengal Village Chowkidari Act (1870) was passed. The purpose of the Act was levying and collecting *chowkidar* tax for the maintenance of village watchman. However, at that time, the panchayats were not democratic as they were composed of persons nominated by the district collector or any subordinate officer chosen by him.

On 18 May 1882, Lord Rippon, the Viceroy of India, issued a resolution encouraging the setting up of local government, which culminated into putting up of Bengal Local Self-Government Act (1885). These were at best half-hearted attempts at establishing local self-government in rural Bengal. Subsequently, the Bengal Village Self-Government Act (1919) was passed which is viewed as the first attempt to introduce self-governing institutions for the rural people of the province. In fact, this Act had been passed based on the reports of the Royal Commission on Decentralization (1909) and the District Administrative Committee (1913). Following the passage of the Act (1919), a system of 'District Boards' and 'Union Boards' was introduced. Each 'Union Board' represented a group of villages. It was to be elected by all adult males having residence within the union and was given a variety of functions. Thus from 1919 onwards, undivided Bengal had a two-tier local government institutions—'District Boards' at the uppermost level and 'Union Boards' at the lowest. However, although each tier had a distinct corporate status and a separate statute delineating its powers, functions and obligations, there was no organic linkage between the two institutions. This system more or less continued till about mid-1950s.

Constitution of village panchayats replacing the 'Union Boards' was initiated in the fifties in West Bengal, which led to the passage of the West Bengal Panchayat Act (1957). This Act replaced the Bengal Village Self-Government Act (1919) and sought to restructure local self-government in villages by introducing two tiers—gram panchayats and *anchal* panchayats—in place of 'Union Boards'. Besides, a new concept called 'gram sabha' was introduced. Subsequently, the West Bengal Zilla Parishads Act was passed in 1963 to remodel local government to associate local authorities with development activities and bringing about democratic decentralization and people's participation in planning and development. Later on, an initiative was taken to frame a consolidated piece of legislation and the West Bengal Panchayat Act (1973) was passed, which introduced a three-tier system with Zilla Parishad at the district level, Panchayat Samitis at the block level and Gram Panchayat at the *anchal* (group of villages) level.

The Government of India had set up the Asoka Mehta Committee in 1978 to review the working of panchayats and to make recommendations for strengthening the existing system. The Committee found panchayats as most appropriate instruments of rural development and recommended introduction of two-tier panchayat system, open participation by the political parties in panchayat elections, direct involvement of elected bodies in development programmes and constitutional provision for further decentralization of power.

However, the first panchayat election in West Bengal was held under the West Bengal Panchayat Act (1973) in June 1978 and since then panchayat elections have been held in 1983, 1988, 1993, 1998 and 2003 strictly observing the five-year period. A three-tier panchayat system has been established with election contested on party lines.

Meanwhile, the Constitution (73rd Amendment) Act came into force in 1993. This Act prescribed a uniform three-tier structure in the local bodies (at the district, block and village levels) and made periodic elections mandatory; it also ensured representation of the most disadvantaged sections of society such as the scheduled castes/ tribes and women at all levels of local self-governance. West Bengal went ahead with this Act and reserved one-third of the seats for women and proportional seats for Scheduled Castes and Scheduled Tribes. Consequently, the participation of these sections is well established and many of them are holding positions of authority.

## The Organizational Structure and Functions

At present, the panchayati system in West Bengal is organized along the following structure:

| *The Organizational Linkage* | | |
|---|---|---|
| Gram Sansad | Generally consists of one village with about 3-5 'paras' or neighbourhood | 400-1000 voters per polling station |
| Gram Panchayat (GP) | Generally consists of 10-15 villages; population: approx. 20,000 | Gram Pradhan |
| Panchayat Samilty (PS) | Generally consists of 10-15 gram panchayats | Sabhapati |
| Zilla Parishad (ZP) | Size varies widely at the district | Sabhadhipati |

| *The Official Linkage* | | |
|---|---|---|
| | *Elected Head* | *Official* |
| Gram Panchayat (GP) | Gram Pradhan | Executive Officer: Panchayat Secretary |
| Panchayat Samity (PS) | Sabhapati | Executive Officer: Block Development Officer |
| Zilla Parishad (ZP) | Sabhadhipati | Executive Officer: District Magistrate |

It is also to be noted that all three tiers are organizationally interlinked inasmuch as the Gram Pradhans of Gram Panchayats are *ex officio* members of immediate superior body, i.e. Panchayat Samity and the Sabhapatis of the Panchayat Samitis are *ex officio* members of the Zilla Parishad. The law also empowers the bodies of higher tier to supervise the functions of the lower ones.

The powers and duties of the panchayat bodies of different tiers are elaborately set out in Chapters III, IX and XIV of the West Bengal Panchayat Act. The Act lays down the functional mechanism of ZPs and PSs through functional standing committees called 'Sthayee Samitis'. Each Sthayee Samiti is constituted of a mix of elected representatives of ZPs/PSs and officials concerned with the related programmes. One of the elected members of the ZP/PS becomes the Chairperson or 'karmadhyaksha' of the Sthayee Samiti. The karmadhyakshas are responsible for formulation and implementation of schemes and programmes entrusted upon the Sthayee Samitis and have been vested with necessary powers. As already mentioned, such karmadhyakshas are directly elected members of ZPs/PSs. One of the Officers appointed by the State Government in the Sthayee Samiti is selected to act as the Secretary of the Sthayee Samiti. Under the latest amendment, all ZPs and PSs have 10 Sthayee Samitis with distinctly separate areas of functions. These are:

1. Artha, Sanstha, Unnyan O Parikalpana Sthayee Samiti (Finance, Establishment, Development and Planning Standing Committee).
2. Jana Swasthya O Paribesh Sthayee Samiti (Public Health and Environment Standing Committee).

3. Purta Karya O Paribahan Sthayee Samiti (Public Works and Transport Standing Committee).
4. Krishi, Sech O Samabay Sthayee Samiti (Agriculture, Irrigation and Co-operation Standing Committee).
5. Siksha, Sanskriti, Tathya O Krira Sthayee Samiti (Education, Culture, Information and Sports Standing Committee).
6. Sishu O Nari Unnyan, Janakalyan O Tran Sthayee Samiti (Women and Child Development, Social Welfare and Relief Standing Committee).
7. Bon O Bhumi Sanskar Sthayee Samiti (Forest and Land Reforms Standing Committee).
8. Matsya O Prani Sampad Bikash Sthayee Samiti (Pisciculture and Animal Resource Development Standing Committee).
9. Khadya O Sarabaraha Sthayee Samiti (Food and Supplies Standing Committee).
10. Shudra Silpa, Bidyut O *Achiracharit* Sakti Sthayee Samiti (Small Industries, Power and Non-Conventional Energy Standing Committee).

In addition, there is a Standing Committee named 'Samanway Samiti' that co-ordinates between the above Sthayee Samitis and the main body and also between ZP and PS and its lower tier bodies. Each ZP also has District Council headed by the leader of the major opposition party in the ZP, a Vice-Chairperson and five members elected by the members of the ZP from among themselves. There are three government officers appointed as members by the State Government. The Additional Executive Officer acts as the Secretary of the Council. The Council is empowered to ensure that the Panchayat Bodies within the district maintains financial propriety and discipline and may examine, for this purpose, the records of accounts in the Panchayat.

As pointed out above, the District Magistrate of the district is the Executive Officer of the ZP. There is an Additional Executive Officer in the rank of Additional District Magistrate who is placed exclusively in the ZP. One senior member of State Civil Service functions as the Secretary of the ZP. The Deputy Secretary who is also a member of the State Civil Service assists the Secretary. There is an accounts wing in the ZP with an Accounts Officer. There are two Executive

Engineers and a number of Assistant Engineers and Sub-Assistant Engineers in the ZP. Further, there is a contingent of junior level officers to support the ZP.

Among the major functions of ZP are: (1) Drawing up a development plan for the five-year term and also annual plan of action for each year for the ZP, (2) Convergence of sectoral activities at the district level, (3) Implementation of major development programmes/ schemes with funds received from the State Government and Government of India, (4) Implementation of programmes for securing social justice for the people especially for the weaker section of the community, (5) Distributing funds as also monitoring and supervision of development activities taken up by PSs and GPs, (6) Collection of revenue and generation of fund for development work and so on.

As already mentioned, the block level tier of the Panchayati Raj Institution is the Panchayat Samiti (PS). The Sabhapati (Chairperson) heads the PS. There is also one Sahakari Sabhapati (Vice-Chairperson). The directly elected members from among them elect both. The PS also has ten standing committees in the name and style identical with the standing committees of ZPs. There is also a coordination committee at the PS level. As regards the functions, the PS is responsible for (1) Receiving fund from the ZP for various development programmes, (2) Preparation of block level plan of action, (3) Collection of revenue, (4) Convergence of sectoral activities at the block level, (5) Supervision of development activities taken up by the GPs and so on.

At the GP level, the executive authority is vested upon the Pradhan. Although no committee system of functioning was envisaged for GPs initially, the amendment of the Panchayat Act in 1992 empowers the GPs to delegate functional responsibilities to one or more members and this has been acted upon in a number of GPs to good effect.

Among the various functions of GP are (1) Drawing up perspective and annual action plan for the GP with the active participation of community for the all-round economic and social development of the villages within the GP utilizing whatever resources are available in the locality and allocations available from the Government, (2) Execution of various development schemes and creation and maintenance of assets and infrastructures at the village level, (3) Resolution of social conflict through mediation, (4) Imposition and collection of taxes etc.

## *Gram Sansad and Gram Sabha*

The Gram Sansad is the most vibrant constitutional institution at the village level. All the electors of the GP constituency are the members of the Gram Sansad for that constituency. Meeting of the Gram Sansad is held compulsorily twice a year. It is composed of all voters of each GP constituency with mandatory presence of at least one-tenth of the total number of members as quorum. In adjourned meetings, however, no quorum is required. The village level plan is initiated from the Gram Sansad. It is also used as a platform for prioritization of schemes and selection of beneficiaries for different programmes and for social audit of financial administration of the GP.[21]

Further, to strengthen participative structures at the grassroots level, it is mandatory for the GPs to call an annual and a half-yearly meeting of the Gram Sabha for each constituency of the GP. In the half-yearly meeting, the audited accounts of the GP is placed, while in the annual meeting the budget of the GP and the report on the work done during the previous year and the work proposed to be done in the following year is to be placed. It is also mandatory for the GPs to publish half-yearly reports showing amounts received by them from different sources and amounts actually spent on different items along with a list of beneficiaries for information of the general public.

## Representation of Various Political Parties in the Panchayats

We now look at the pattern of representation of various political parties in the three-tier panchayats representing ZP, PS and GP. As already mentioned, panchayat elections are fought among the political parties. Naturally the panchayat members elected in one body or the other are very likely to have some political affiliation (except those elected as independents). In the context of West Bengal, the left parties have had an overwhelming majority at each tier of panchayats all through the period 1978-2003. Among the left parties, the Communist Party of India (Marxist) alone captured the majority of the panchayat seats. In other words, it is the left parties, more specifically the CPI (M) that has dominated the rural scene in West Bengal from the point of view of controlling panchayat bodies over past 25 years or so.

Table 3.38 gives information on percentage distribution of ZP seats in the state as well as districts for the years 1998 and 2003. It is found that for the state as a whole, the left parties together have been

**Table 3.38:** Percentage Distribution of Zilla Parishad Seats under Different Political Parties

| *District* | *Year* | *Total Seat* | *C.P.I. (M)* | *C.P.I.* | *F.B.* | *R.S.P.* | *Other Left* | ***Left Front*** | *Congress* | *T.M.C.* | *B.J.P.* | *Others* |
|---|---|---|---|---|---|---|---|---|---|---|---|---|
| Coochbehar | 2003 | 26 | 69.23 | 0.00 | 26.92 | 0.00 | 0.00 | **96.15** | 0.00 | 0.00 | 0.00 | 3.85 |
| | 1998 | 27 | 66.67 | 0.00 | 7.41 | 0.00 | 0.00 | **74.07** | 14.81 | 0.00 | 0.00 | 11.11 |
| Jalpaiguri | 2003 | 30 | 83.33 | 0.00 | 0.00 | 10.00 | 0.00 | **93.33** | 6.67 | 0.00 | 0.00 | 0.00 |
| | 1998 | 32 | 90.63 | 0.00 | 0.00 | 6.25 | 0.00 | **96.88** | 3.13 | 0.00 | 0.00 | 0.00 |
| Uttar Dinajpur | 2003 | 21 | 61.90 | 0.00 | 4.76 | 4.76 | 0.00 | **71.43** | 28.57 | 0.00 | 0.00 | 0.00 |
| | 1998 | 23 | 52.17 | 0.00 | 4.35 | 8.70 | 0.00 | **65.22** | 34.78 | 0.00 | 0.00 | 0.00 |
| Dakshin Dinajpur | 2003 | 15 | 66.67 | 0.00 | 0.00 | 26.67 | 0.00 | **93.33** | 0.00 | 6.67 | 0.00 | 0.00 |
| | 1998 | 15 | 60.00 | 0.00 | 0.00 | 40.00 | 0.00 | **100.00** | 0.00 | 0.00 | 0.00 | 0.00 |
| Malda | 2003 | 33 | 42.42 | 3.03 | 3.03 | 0.00 | 0.00 | **48.48** | 45.45 | 3.03 | 3.03 | 0.00 |
| | 1998 | 33 | 75.76 | 0.00 | 3.03 | 0.00 | 0.00 | **78.79** | 21.21 | 0.00 | 0.00 | 0.00 |
| Murshidabad | 2003 | 60 | 38.33 | 0.00 | 1.67 | 5.00 | 0.00 | **45.00** | 55.00 | 0.00 | 0.00 | 0.00 |
| | 1998 | 60 | 75.00 | 1.67 | 1.67 | 6.67 | 1.67 | **86.67** | 13.33 | 0.00 | 0.00 | 0.00 |
| Nadia | 2003 | 41 | 87.80 | 2.44 | 0.00 | 0.00 | 2.44 | **92.68** | 2.44 | 2.44 | 0.00 | 2.44 |
| | 1998 | 41 | 92.68 | 2.44 | 0.00 | 0.00 | 2.44 | **97.56** | 0.00 | 2.44 | 0.00 | 0.00 |
| North 24 Parganas | 2003 | 50 | 82.00 | 4.00 | 4.00 | 0.00 | 0.00 | **90.00** | 6.00 | 4.00 | 0.00 | 0.00 |
| | 1998 | 50 | 72.00 | 4.00 | 4.00 | 0.00 | 0.00 | **80.00** | 0.00 | 20.00 | 0.00 | 0.00 |
| South 24 Parganas | 2003 | 66 | 86.36 | 0.00 | 0.00 | 6.06 | 0.00 | **92.42** | 0.00 | 4.55 | 0.00 | 3.03 |
| | 1998 | 67 | 71.64 | 0.00 | 0.00 | 8.96 | 0.00 | **80.60** | 0.00 | 11.94 | 0.00 | 7.46 |
| Howrah | 2003 | 36 | 80.56 | 5.56 | 11.11 | 0.00 | 0.00 | **97.22** | 0.00 | 2.78 | 0.00 | 0.00 |
| | 1998 | 34 | 70.59 | 5.88 | 11.76 | 0.00 | 0.00 | **88.24** | 0.00 | 11.76 | 0.00 | 0.00 |
| Hooghly | 2003 | 47 | 95.74 | 2.13 | 2.13 | 0.00 | 0.00 | **100.00** | 0.00 | 0.00 | 0.00 | 0.00 |
| | 1998 | 47 | 85.11 | 2.13 | 2.13 | 0.00 | 0.00 | **89.36** | 0.00 | 10.64 | 0.00 | 0.00 |
| Midnapore | 2003 | 114 | 88.60 | 5.26 | 0.00 | 0.00 | 1.75 | **95.61** | 0.00 | 1.75 | 0.00 | 2.63 |
| | 1998 | 108 | 82.41 | 4.63 | 0.00 | 0.00 | 1.85 | **88.89** | 0.00 | 6.48 | 0.93 | 3.70 |

(Contd.)

**Table 3.38** (*Contd.*)

| *District* | *Year* | *Total Seat* | *C.P.I. (M)* | *C.P.I.* | *F.B.* | *R.S.P.* | *Other Left* | ***Left Front*** | *Congress* | *T.M.C.* | *B.J.P.* | *Others* |
|---|---|---|---|---|---|---|---|---|---|---|---|---|
| Purulia | 2003 | 34 | 70.59 | 0.00 | 8.82 | 0.00 | 0.00 | **79.41** | 8.82 | 5.88 | 0.00 | 5.88 |
| | 1998 | 34 | 64.71 | 0.00 | 17.65 | 0.00 | 0.00 | **82.35** | 8.82 | 5.88 | 0.00 | 2.94 |
| Bankura | 2003 | 41 | 82.93 | 4.88 | 4.88 | 4.88 | 0.00 | **97.56** | 0.00 | 2.44 | 0.00 | 0.00 |
| | 1998 | 42 | 85.71 | 2.38 | 4.76 | 4.76 | 0.00 | **97.62** | 0.00 | 2.38 | 0.00 | 0.00 |
| Burdwan | 2003 | 65 | 81.54 | 4.62 | 4.62 | 4.62 | 1.54 | **96.92** | 0.00 | 1.54 | 1.54 | 0.00 |
| | 1998 | 68 | 83.82 | 4.41 | 4.41 | 4.41 | 1.47 | **98.53** | 1.47 | 0.00 | 0.00 | 0.00 |
| Birbhum | 2003 | 35 | 71.43 | 2.86 | 5.71 | 0.00 | 2.86 | **82.86** | 14.29 | 2.86 | 0.00 | 0.00 |
| | 1998 | 35 | 91.43 | 2.86 | 2.86 | 2.86 | 0.00 | **100.00** | 0.00 | 0.00 | 0.00 | 0.00 |
| Total | 2003 | 712 | 76.69 | 2.67 | 3.79 | 2.81 | 0.70 | **86.66** | 9.55 | 2.25 | 0.28 | 1.26 |
| | 1998 | 716 | 78.21 | 2.37 | 3.35 | 3.63 | 0.70 | **88.27** | 4.47 | 5.31 | 0.14 | 1.82 |

*Source*: Compiled from results published in Newspapers.

controlling nearly 87 per cent of ZP seats while the CPI (M) alone has a share of 77 per cent of all ZP seats in 2003. Among the major opposition parties, the Congress has under its control about 10 per cent of ZP seats in 2003. Its presence has been appreciable in the districts of Murshidabad (controlling 55 per cent of ZP seats), Malda (45 per cent) and Uttar Dinajpur (29 per cent). It is also to be noted that the Trinamul Congress (TMC) that had a share of 5.31 per cent of ZP seats in 1998 election, suffered a set back in 2003 election and its share dropped to only 2.25 per cent.

At the PS level, the dominance of left parties continues (Table 3.39). In 2003, nearly 74 per cent of PS seats are under the control of left parties; the CPI (M) alone having 67 per cent of the seats. Once again, among the opposition parties, Congress comes second with 12.29 per cent of seats in 2003, which is higher than its share in 1998 (9.76 per cent). The decline in the fortune of the other opposition parties, namely TMC, continues as its share of PS seats dropped from 16.90 per cent in 1998 to 9.61 per cent in 2003. Among the districts, the Congress has strong presence in Panchayat Samitis of Murshidabad, Malda and Uttar Dinajpur, while the TMC confronts somewhat better situation in Howrah, Nadia and South 24 Parganas (capturing nearly one-fifth of PS seats in these districts).

Although the dominance of left parties continues even at the GP level in the state, the opposition parties seem to display a better representation at this level. In 2003, the Left Front controlled nearly 66 per cent of GP seats; the CPI (M) alone having 59 per cent of seats in GP. The congress has a share of 13.64 per cent of total GP seats while the TMC has 13.30 per cent of seats. The increasing share of the Left parties [particularly CPI (M)] in GP seats during 1998 to 2003 and the concomitant decline in the fortunes of TMC is clearly visible. The same set of three districts, Murshidabad, Malda and Uttar Dinajpur, provides a better representation for Congress at the GP level. On the other hand, the TMC seems to have a better representation in North and South 24 Parganas, Nadia and Midnapore. Another opposition party, namely BJP, controls 9.16 per cent of GP seats in Nadia in 2003.

## Socio-Economic Background of the Panchayat Representatives

We now look at the socio-economic backgrounds of the elected panchayat representatives in West Bengal. For this purpose, we utilize

**Table 3.39:** Percentage Distribution of Panchayat Samiti Seats under Different Political Parties

| District | Year | Total Seat | C.P.I. (M) | C.P.I. | F.B. | R.S.P. | Other Left | Left Front | Cong-ress | T.M.C. | B.J.P. | Others |
|---|---|---|---|---|---|---|---|---|---|---|---|---|
| Coochbehar | 2003 | 338 | 65.38 | 0.59 | 15.98 | 0.00 | 0.89 | **82.84** | 8.28 | 2.66 | 2.07 | 4.14 |
| | 1998 | 339 | 58.70 | 0.29 | 5.90 | 0.00 | 0.00 | **64.90** | 12.68 | 7.08 | 5.60 | 9.73 |
| Jalpaiguri | 2003 | 374 | 66.31 | 0.00 | 0.27 | 12.30 | 0.00 | **78.88** | 14.17 | 4.55 | 2.14 | 0.27 |
| | 1998 | 388 | 64.18 | 0.00 | 0.26 | 11.08 | 0.00 | **75.52** | 9.28 | 11.08 | 3.61 | 0.52 |
| Uttar Dinajpur | 2003 | 263 | 53.99 | 0.76 | 3.42 | 3.42 | 1.14 | **62.74** | 33.08 | 3.42 | 0.38 | 0.38 |
| | 1998 | 272 | 48.90 | 0.00 | 5.88 | 2.57 | 0.00 | **57.35** | 38.24 | 3.68 | 0.37 | 0.37 |
| Dakshin Dinajpur | 2003 | 179 | 46.37 | 0.00 | 0.00 | 28.49 | 0.00 | **74.86** | 7.82 | 11.17 | 6.15 | 0.00 |
| | 1998 | 178 | 35.96 | 0.00 | 0.00 | 39.33 | 0.00 | **75.28** | 5.06 | 15.73 | 3.37 | 0.56 |
| Malda | 2003 | 388 | 49.23 | 1.55 | 0.26 | 0.00 | 0.00 | **51.03** | 41.75 | 1.80 | 5.15 | 0.26 |
| | 1998 | 385 | 54.03 | 1.30 | 0.26 | 0.00 | 0.00 | **55.58** | 39.48 | 1.56 | 3.38 | 0.00 |
| Murshidabad | 2003 | 697 | 44.19 | 0.29 | 0.72 | 4.45 | 0.14 | **49.78** | 49.07 | 0.57 | 0.43 | 0.14 |
| | 1998 | 700 | 55.00 | 0.71 | 0.86 | 8.14 | 0.14 | **64.86** | 27.14 | 4.29 | 3.00 | 0.71 |
| Nadia | 2003 | 512 | 56.05 | 0.59 | 0.00 | 0.20 | 0.00 | **56.84** | 14.06 | 20.70 | 7.03 | 1.37 |
| | 1998 | 504 | 59.52 | 0.79 | 0.40 | 0.40 | 0.00 | **61.11** | 12.90 | 18.45 | 7.14 | 0.40 |
| North 24 Parganas | 2003 | 555 | 66.85 | 2.34 | 2.34 | 0.00 | 0.00 | **71.53** | 10.99 | 13.51 | 3.24 | 0.72 |
| | 1998 | 549 | 53.01 | 2.00 | 1.64 | 0.73 | 0.00 | **57.38** | 6.38 | 29.69 | 5.65 | 0.91 |
| South 24 Parganas | 2003 | 845 | 62.96 | 0.24 | 0.12 | 6.15 | 0.00 | **69.47** | 4.97 | 19.41 | 0.59 | 5.56 |
| | 1998 | 843 | 54.57 | 0.24 | 0.24 | 5.34 | 0.00 | **60.38** | 3.32 | 28.00 | 1.07 | 7.24 |
| Howrah | 2003 | 426 | 63.62 | 0.94 | 6.34 | 0.00 | 0.00 | **70.89** | 6.57 | 20.89 | 0.94 | 0.70 |
| | 1998 | 433 | 57.74 | 1.15 | 3.93 | 0.00 | 0.00 | **62.82** | 6.00 | 27.71 | 2.08 | 1.39 |
| Hooghly | 2003 | 577 | 87.35 | 1.39 | 2.08 | 0.00 | 0.17 | **90.99** | 0.17 | 8.32 | 0.17 | 0.35 |
| | 1998 | 577 | 63.26 | 1.39 | 1.56 | 0.00 | 0.35 | **66.55** | 0.87 | 28.60 | 3.12 | 0.87 |

(Contd.)

**Table 3.39** (*Contd.*)

| District | Year | Total Seat | C.P.I. (M) | C.P.I. | F.B. | R.S.P. | Other Left | Left Front | Congress | T.M.C. | B.J.P. | Others |
|---|---|---|---|---|---|---|---|---|---|---|---|---|
| **Midnapore** | 2003 | 1337 | 76.36 | 3.96 | 0.00 | 0.00 | 0.97 | **81.30** | 2.17 | 11.29 | 0.75 | 4.49 |
| | 1998 | 1295 | 64.86 | 3.32 | 0.31 | 0.15 | 0.77 | **69.42** | 2.47 | 20.85 | 2.78 | 4.48 |
| **Purulia** | 2003 | 384 | 68.23 | 0.52 | 5.99 | 0.00 | 0.78 | **75.52** | 10.42 | 8.85 | 1.30 | 3.91 |
| | 1998 | 391 | 57.54 | 0.51 | 8.44 | 0.00 | 0.00 | **66.50** | 13.81 | 11.00 | 5.37 | 3.32 |
| **Bankura** | 2003 | 477 | 82.60 | 2.10 | 2.94 | 3.35 | 0.21 | **91.19** | 0.21 | 6.08 | 1.05 | 1.47 |
| | 1998 | 496 | 68.95 | 0.40 | 2.22 | 2.02 | 0.00 | 73.59 | 0.20 | 16.94 | 7.46 | 1.81 |
| **Burdwan** | 2003 | 734 | 81.20 | 2.32 | 3.00 | 1.77 | 1.50 | **89.78** | 3.81 | 4.09 | 2.04 | 0.27 |
| | 1998 | 743 | 73.76 | 2.02 | 2.69 | 2.15 | 1.35 | **81.97** | 3.10 | 10.50 | 4.17 | 0.27 |
| **Birbhum** | 2003 | 414 | 71.50 | 1.69 | 2.90 | 0.48 | 0.00 | **76.57** | 13.53 | 6.04 | 1.69 | 2.17 |
| | 1998 | 422 | 71.33 | 1.90 | 2.13 | 0.24 | 0.24 | **75.83** | 6.64 | 10.90 | 6.16 | 0.47 |
| **Total** | 2003 | 8498 | 67.39 | 1.54 | 2.28 | 2.60 | 0.42 | **74.24** | 12.29 | 9.61 | 1.84 | 2.02 |
| | 1998 | 8515 | 60.60 | 1.30 | 1.88 | 3.02 | 0.28 | **67.08** | 9.76 | 16.90 | 3.85 | 2.41 |

*Source*: As in Table 3.38.

data collected from 57 GPs of the state, which are spread over 45 Panchayat Samitis/blocks covering all districts of West Bengal.[22] Actually, we have at our disposal data, *inter alia*, on social and economic background of all elected gram panchayat members of 57 GPs. We also have data on these aspects for PS members who have been elected for Panchayat Samitis from the villages falling under our sampled GPs (Table 3.40).

To understand the socio-economic background of the panchayat members in West Bengal, we begin by looking at their occupational status. Table 3.41 gives data on this aspect for the elected GP members for the years 1978 through 1998. The main points to be noted here are: (1) In 1998, the majority of the elected GP members belonged to the category of farmers/cultivators. This has been true irrespective of the party affiliation of the elected GP representatives. Considering all political parties together, nearly 35 per cent of GP members in 1998 belonged to the category of farmers/cultivators. (2) Over the years, there has been a tendency of the share of farmers/cultivators among the elected GP members declining. Table 3.41 shows that while 53 per cent of elected GP members in 1978 belonged to the category of farmers/cultivators, the corresponding figure is reduced gradually to 35 per cent in 1998. (3) In the initial years, particularly in 1978, 1983 and 1988, a sizeable proportion of GP members were drawn from the school teachers (more than 15 per cent in each of these years). However, in recent years, their share has reduced considerably; in 1998, only about 5 per cent of GP members are found to have teaching as their occupation. (4) Although the share of agricultural labourers among the elected GP members has increased over time, this category has remained highly under-represented in the gram panchayats.[23] In 1998, only 8.61 per cent of GP members belonged to the category of agricultural labourers, which is far low than their share in the pool of rural workers in West Bengal.[24] Of course, among the political parties, the CPI(M) offered relatively higher representation to this category in the GPs in 1998. The marginal farmers are also somewhat under-represented as their share being about one-fifth of all GP members. (5) In recent years (1993 and 1998), there has been a tendency of good percentage of GP members getting elected who belong to the "others" category. In 1998, this category got elected to about 28 per cent of all GP seats. It is to be noted that the bulk of these people do not have any occupation at all, which imply that there have been an increasing tendency by all political parties to field their unemployed members as panchayat representatives.

**Table 3.40:** Percentage Distribution of Gram Panchayat Seats under Different Political Parties

| District | Year | Total Seat | C.P.I. (M) | C.P.I. | F.B. | R.S.P. | Other Left | Left Front | Congress | T.M.C. | B.J.P. | Others |
|---|---|---|---|---|---|---|---|---|---|---|---|---|
| Coochbehar | 2003 | 1903 | 56.75 | 0.37 | 12.66 | 0.16 | 0.00 | 69.94 | 8.62 | 5.47 | 3.21 | 12.77 |
| | 1998 | 1879 | 50.88 | 0.43 | 5.64 | 0.05 | 0.00 | 57.00 | 11.50 | 9.47 | 8.83 | 13.20 |
| Jalpaiguri | 2003 | 2241 | 51.32 | 0.76 | 0.76 | 13.83 | 0.00 | 66.67 | 16.15 | 8.75 | 4.55 | 3.88 |
| | 1998 | 2341 | 50.41 | 0.68 | 0.64 | 11.53 | 0.34 | 63.61 | 14.69 | 11.96 | 7.26 | 2.48 |
| Uttar Dinajpur | 2003 | 1528 | 44.31 | 1.37 | 6.02 | 2.68 | 0.00 | 54.38 | 34.95 | 3.08 | 2.23 | 5.37 |
| | 1998 | 1594 | 37.89 | 0.31 | 6.46 | 2.63 | 0.50 | 47.80 | 36.20 | 4.64 | 6.02 | 5.33 |
| Dakshin Dinajpur | 2003 | 991 | 45.21 | 0.71 | 0.91 | 23.31 | 0.00 | 70.13 | 8.68 | 14.83 | 5.65 | 0.71 |
| | 1998 | 1008 | 30.65 | 0.89 | 0.50 | 24.70 | 0.00 | 56.75 | 9.82 | 20.04 | 9.13 | 4.27 |
| Malda | 2003 | 2230 | 44.13 | 1.26 | 1.61 | 1.84 | 0.40 | 49.24 | 40.49 | 3.32 | 4.71 | 2.24 |
| | 1998 | 2195 | 42.23 | 0.87 | 0.91 | 1.55 | 0.00 | 45.56 | 39.64 | 3.74 | 9.07 | 2.00 |
| Murshidabad | 2003 | 4093 | 39.60 | 0.49 | 2.35 | 4.91 | 0.00 | 47.35 | 46.62 | 1.17 | 1.37 | 3.49 |
| | 1998 | 4158 | 40.69 | 0.89 | 2.36 | 7.91 | 0.96 | 52.81 | 32.13 | 6.37 | 6.52 | 2.16 |
| Nadia | 2003 | 3113 | 46.87 | 0.48 | 0.10 | 0.39 | 0.03 | 47.86 | 18.21 | 21.20 | 9.16 | 3.57 |
| | 1998 | 3052 | 46.00 | 0.46 | 0.23 | 0.66 | 0.13 | 47.48 | 18.25 | 20.48 | 11.83 | 1.97 |
| North 24 Parganas | 2003 | 3315 | 53.48 | 2.17 | 2.62 | 0.30 | 0.00 | 58.58 | 12.55 | 20.66 | 4.07 | 4.13 |
| | 1998 | 3233 | 43.18 | 2.13 | 1.73 | 0.84 | 0.00 | 47.88 | 10.30 | 30.68 | 8.54 | 2.60 |
| South 24 Parganas | 2003 | 4898 | 54.23 | 0.29 | 0.22 | 5.61 | 0.02 | 60.37 | 7.47 | 23.52 | 1.45 | 7.19 |
| | 1998 | 4879 | 47.12 | 0.23 | 0.31 | 4.78 | 0.00 | 52.43 | 6.37 | 30.21 | 2.99 | 7.99 |
| Howrah | 2003 | 2514 | 56.52 | 0.88 | 5.45 | 0.04 | 0.00 | 62.89 | 10.86 | 21.72 | 2.63 | 1.91 |
| | 1998 | 2576 | 46.78 | 0.62 | 3.49 | 0.04 | 0.00 | 50.93 | 9.94 | 31.83 | 5.05 | 2.25 |

(Contd.)

**Table 3.40** (*Contd.*)

| *District* | *Year* | *Total Seat* | *C.P.I. (M)* | *C.P.I.* | *F.B.* | *R.S.P.* | *Other Left* | *Left Front* | *Congress* | *T.M.C.* | *B.J.P.* | *Others* |
|---|---|---|---|---|---|---|---|---|---|---|---|---|
| Hooghly | 2003 | 3431 | 78.40 | 1.98 | 2.94 | 0.09 | 0.00 | 83.42 | 2.16 | 12.33 | 1.11 | 0.99 |
| | 1998 | 3418 | 57.81 | 1.26 | 1.70 | 0.00 | 0.15 | 60.91 | 2.52 | 28.64 | 6.55 | 1.38 |
| Midnapore | 2003 | 7551 | 66.03 | 4.65 | 0.15 | 0.21 | 0.79 | 71.83 | 3.19 | 17.35 | 1.68 | 5.95 |
| | 1998 | 7187 | 54.08 | 3.81 | 0.22 | 0.19 | 1.11 | 59.43 | 3.38 | 25.69 | 5.59 | 5.91 |
| Purulia | 2003 | 2067 | 57.86 | 0.24 | 7.01 | 0.00 | 0.00 | 65.12 | 11.85 | 14.71 | 1.21 | 7.11 |
| | 1998 | 2140 | 49.16 | 0.61 | 7.66 | 0.00 | 0.00 | 57.43 | 12.90 | 12.38 | 10.28 | 7.01 |
| Bankura | 2003 | 2632 | 73.06 | 1.25 | 2.51 | 2.28 | 0.84 | 79.94 | 0.87 | 11.93 | 3.31 | 3.95 |
| | 1998 | 2737 | 54.88 | 0.80 | 1.64 | 1.86 | 0.00 | 59.19 | 0.40 | 21.15 | 15.35 | 3.91 |
| Burdwan | 2003 | 4346 | 77.20 | 2.07 | 2.12 | 0.97 | 0.92 | 83.27 | 5.41 | 6.67 | 3.24 | 1.40 |
| | 1998 | 4460 | 63.00 | 1.75 | 1.32 | 0.58 | 1.01 | 67.67 | 4.91 | 17.65 | 8.14 | 1.64 |
| Birbhum | 2003 | 2256 | 59.84 | 1.33 | 5.19 | 0.93 | 1.29 | 68.57 | 13.39 | 10.20 | 4.48 | 3.37 |
| | 1998 | 2334 | 53.73 | 1.11 | 4.37 | 1.03 | 0.17 | 60.41 | 9.77 | 13.92 | 12.60 | 3.30 |
| Total | 2003 | 49109 | 58.58 | 1.63 | 2.57 | 2.58 | 0.33 | 65.69 | 13.64 | 13.30 | 3.03 | 4.34 |
| | 1998 | 49191 | 49.71 | 1.34 | 1.95 | 2.69 | 0.39 | 56.08 | 12.12 | 19.87 | 7.79 | 4.15 |

*Source*: As in Table 3.38.

**Table 3.41:** Occupation (Main/Marginal) of the Gram Panchayat Members

| Year | Party Affiliation | Total Members | % of Members with Principal Occupation as | | | | | | | | | | | |
|---|---|---|---|---|---|---|---|---|---|---|---|---|---|---|
| | | | Agrl. lab. | Non-Agrl lab. | All lab. | Farming | | | | | Teaching | Service (Other than Teaching) | Business | Others |
| | | | | | | Marginal (0.01-2.49 acres) | Small (2.50-4.99 acres) | Medium (5.00-7.49 acres) | Large (7.50 acres and above) | Total | | | | |
| (1) | (2) | (3) | (4) | (5) | (6) | (7) | (8) | (9) | (10) | (11) | (12) | (13) | (14) | (15) |
| 1978 | CPI (M) | 472 | 6.99 | 5.72 | 12.71 | 28.76 | 12.20 | 5.45 | 7.62 | 54.03 | 14.62 | 5.08 | 6.99 | 6.57 |
| | Congress (I) | 149 | 2.01 | 2.68 | 4.70 | 25.85 | 4.89 | 5.59 | 14.67 | 51.01 | 25.50 | 4.03 | 10.74 | 4.03 |
| | Other Left | 101 | 2.97 | 0.99 | 3.96 | 24.09 | 15.71 | 6.28 | 8.38 | 54.46 | 18.81 | 5.94 | 9.90 | 6.93 |
| | Others | 70 | 1.43 | 7.14 | 8.57 | 31.43 | 8.57 | 5.71 | 7.14 | 52.86 | 25.71 | 1.43 | 7.14 | 4.29 |
| | Total | 792 | 5.05 | 4.67 | 9.72 | 27.88 | 10.94 | 5.60 | 8.99 | 53.41 | 18.18 | 4.67 | 8.08 | 5.93 |
| 1983 | CPI (M) | 380 | 6.05 | 4.47 | 10.53 | 29.68 | 12.03 | 4.81 | 3.48 | 50.00 | 15.53 | 6.32 | 9.74 | 7.89 |
| | Congress (I) | 257 | 2.72 | 1.95 | 4.67 | 26.47 | 11.17 | 5.38 | 9.51 | 52.53 | 19.46 | 4.28 | 15.18 | 3.89 |
| | Other Left | 92 | 1.09 | 2.17 | 3.26 | 30.43 | 11.96 | 10.87 | 6.52 | 59.78 | 11.96 | 3.26 | 16.30 | 5.43 |
| | Others | 24 | 4.17 | 4.17 | 8.33 | 37.50 | 0.00 | 16.67 | 12.50 | 66.67 | 8.33 | 0.00 | 12.50 | 4.17 |
| | Total | 753 | 4.25 | 3.32 | 7.57 | 28.96 | 11.34 | 6.15 | 6.15 | 52.59 | 16.20 | 5.05 | 12.48 | 6.11 |
| 1988 | CPI (M) | 563 | 6.39 | 3.55 | 9.95 | 26.82 | 14.70 | 4.04 | 2.76 | 48.31 | 16.34 | 8.35 | 8.70 | 8.35 |
| | Congress (I) | 236 | 4.24 | 4.66 | 8.90 | 24.07 | 13.43 | 7.41 | 5.09 | 50.00 | 10.59 | 5.51 | 17.80 | 7.20 |
| | Other Left | 105 | 0.95 | 2.86 | 3.81 | 31.67 | 8.91 | 7.92 | 1.98 | 50.48 | 20.00 | 1.90 | 18.10 | 5.71 |
| | Others | 21 | 0.00 | 0.00 | 0.00 | 52.38 | 9.52 | 4.76 | 9.52 | 76.19 | 9.52 | 0.00 | 9.52 | 4.76 |
| | Total | 925 | 5.08 | 3.68 | 8.76 | 27.30 | 13.59 | 5.32 | 3.40 | 49.62 | 15.14 | 6.70 | 12.11 | 7.68 |

(Contd.)

**Table 3.41** *(Contd.)*

| (1) | (2) | (3) | (4) | (5) | (6) | (7) | (8) | (9) | (10) | (11) | (12) | (13) | (14) | (15) |
|---|---|---|---|---|---|---|---|---|---|---|---|---|---|---|
| 1993 | CPI (M) | 626 | 9.27 | 6.71 | 15.97 | 21.20 | 7.29 | 4.75 | 2.54 | 35.78 | 7.03 | 4.95 | 6.71 | 29.55 |
| | Congress (I) | 288 | 5.56 | 4.51 | 10.07 | 18.77 | 9.02 | 4.69 | 3.97 | 36.46 | 7.99 | 4.51 | 15.97 | 25.00 |
| | Other Left | 84 | 2.38 | 5.95 | 8.33 | 20.24 | 9.52 | 3.57 | 1.19 | 34.52 | 7.14 | 8.33 | 15.48 | 26.19 |
| | Others | 81 | 6.17 | 2.47 | 8.64 | 16.64 | 11.52 | 2.56 | 3.84 | 34.57 | 1.23 | 9.88 | 20.99 | 24.69 |
| | Total | 1079 | 7.51 | 5.75 | 13.25 | 20.12 | 8.26 | 4.47 | 2.92 | 35.77 | 6.86 | 5.47 | 10.94 | 27.71 |
| 1998 | CPI (M) | 414 | 12.56 | 6.76 | 19.32 | 17.27 | 11.65 | 2.41 | 3.21 | 34.54 | 6.52 | 3.14 | 11.11 | 25.36 |
| | Congress (I) | 101 | 3.96 | 4.95 | 8.91 | 14.58 | 9.72 | 6.48 | 4.86 | 35.64 | 2.97 | 3.96 | 21.78 | 26.73 |
| | Other Left | 70 | 4.29 | 12.86 | 17.14 | 20.30 | 12.18 | 4.06 | 2.03 | 38.57 | 5.71 | 2.86 | 14.29 | 21.43 |
| | Others | 298 | 5.70 | 5.03 | 10.74 | 24.66 | 3.02 | 4.53 | 3.02 | 35.23 | 3.02 | 4.70 | 13.76 | 32.55 |
| | Total | 883 | 8.61 | 6.46 | 15.06 | 19.85 | 8.40 | 3.75 | 3.22 | 35.22 | 4.87 | 3.74 | 13.48 | 27.63 |

*Source*: Field Survey on West Bengal Panchayats (2000).

The information on caste and educational background of elected GP members are presented in Table 3.42. It is found that the Scheduled Castes/Tribes had their due share in panchayats all through the period 1978 to 1998. In fact, in recent years, their share among the GP members increased further. In 1998, nearly 44 per cent of GP members in West Bengal belonged to Scheduled Castes/Tribes. It is also clear that there is a tendency among the left parties [particularly CPI (M)] to offer greater representation to these weaker sections in the panchayats. As regards educational backgrounds of panchayat members, there is no sign of improvement over the period 1978-1998. In 1998, average years of schooling for a gram panchayat representative stood at 7.62.

**Table 3.42:** Caste and Education of Gram Panchayat Members

| *Year* | *Party Affiliation* | *Total Members* | *Average years of Schooling of Members* | *% of Members with Caste as* | |
|---|---|---|---|---|---|
| | | | | *SC/ST* | *Others* |
| 1978 | CPI (M) | 472 | 7.86 | 31.14 | 68.86 |
| | Congress (I) | 149 | 7.95 | 14.09 | 85.91 |
| | Other Left | 101 | 8.76 | 33.66 | 66.34 |
| | Others | 70 | 8.37 | 10.00 | 90.00 |
| | Total | 792 | 8.04 | 26.39 | 73.61 |
| 1983 | CPI (M) | 380 | 8.36 | 31.58 | 68.42 |
| | Congress (I) | 257 | 9.45 | 13.62 | 86.38 |
| | Other Left | 92 | 8.72 | 28.26 | 71.74 |
| | Others | 24 | 9.54 | 4.17 | 95.83 |
| | Total | 753 | 8.81 | 24.17 | 75.83 |
| 1988 | CPI (M) | 563 | 8.74 | 30.73 | 69.27 |
| | Congress (I) | 236 | 9.29 | 18.22 | 81.78 |
| | Other Left | 105 | 9.30 | 29.52 | 70.48 |
| | Others | 21 | 9.57 | 9.52 | 90.48 |
| | Total | 925 | 8.97 | 26.92 | 73.08 |
| 1993 | CPI (M) | 626 | 7.82 | 44.57 | 55.43 |
| | Congress (I) | 288 | 8.56 | 32.29 | 67.71 |
| | Other Left | 84 | 8.49 | 42.86 | 57.14 |
| | Others | 81 | 7.25 | 38.27 | 61.73 |
| | Total | 1079 | 8.03 | 40.69 | 59.31 |
| 1998 | CPI (M) | 414 | 7.62 | 47.34 | 52.66 |
| | Congress (I) | 101 | 8.36 | 29.70 | 70.30 |
| | Other Left | 70 | 7.10 | 47.14 | 52.86 |
| | Others | 298 | 7.49 | 42.95 | 57.05 |
| | Total | 883 | 7.62 | 43.83 | 56.17 |

*Source*: Field Survey on West Bengal Panchayats (2000).

The issue of gender division of panchayat members is also important since the Government of West Bengal, following the 73rd Constitutional Amendment, went ahead with reservation of one-third seats in panchayats for women. Table 3.43 gives data on sex of GP members in West Bengal. It is clear that until the decade of 1990s, women did not find any appreciable representation in the GPs. For the years 1978, 1983 and 1988, less than 4 per cent of GP members have been drawn from the females. The situation is drastically changed since 1993 as one-third of the gram panchayat members in the state are now drawn from the rural females.

**Table 3.43:** Sex of Gram Panchayat Members

| *Year* | *Party Affiliation* | *Total Members* | *% of Members with sex as* | |
|---|---|---|---|---|
| | | | *Male* | *Female* |
| 1978 | CPI(M) | 472 | 96.19 | 3.81 |
| | Congress (I) | 149 | 95.97 | 4.03 |
| | Other Left | 101 | 96.04 | 3.96 |
| | Others | 70 | 95.71 | 4.29 |
| | Total | 792 | 96.09 | 3.91 |
| 1983 | CPI(M) | 380 | 94.47 | 5.53 |
| | Congress (I) | 257 | 98.83 | 1.17 |
| | Other Left | 92 | 94.57 | 5.43 |
| | Others | 24 | 100.00 | 0.00 |
| | Total | 753 | 96.15 | 3.85 |
| 1988 | CPI(M) | 563 | 95.74 | 4.26 |
| | Congress (I) | 236 | 99.15 | 0.85 |
| | Other Left | 105 | 97.14 | 2.86 |
| | Others | 21 | 100.00 | 0.00 |
| | Total | 925 | 96.86 | 3.14 |
| 1993 | CPI(M) | 626 | 69.49 | 30.51 |
| | Congress (I) | 288 | 69.10 | 30.90 |
| | Other Left | 84 | 63.10 | 36.90 |
| | Others | 81 | 65.43 | 34.57 |
| | Total | 1079 | 68.58 | 31.42 |
| 1998 | CPI(M) | 414 | 68.84 | 31.16 |
| | Congress (I) | 101 | 69.31 | 30.69 |
| | Other Left | 70 | 54.29 | 45.71 |
| | Others | 298 | 62.42 | 37.58 |
| | Total | 883 | 65.57 | 34.43 |

*Source*: Field Survey on West Bengal Panchayats (2000).

We also have data on the above aspects for the PS members who got elected from our sampled GPs. As regards occupational background of the PS members (Table 3.44), it is noted that prior to 1993, nearly one-third or more of them belonged to the teaching community, which is closely followed by the farmers/cultivators. On the other hand, the representation by the labouring class in PS bodies was very low. Since 1993, the share of teachers in PS bodied declined although they continued to occupy nearly 15 per cent of PS seats in 1998. There is also some evidence of increasing share of labouring class in PS bodies. In 1998, they held 7.64 per cent of PS seats. As regards the share of Scheduled Castes/Tribes in PS bodies (Table 3.45), it is found that these categories increased their representation significantly from 1993 onwards. In 1998, these categories shared nearly 45 per cent of PS seats in West Bengal. The PS members also appear to be better educated as compared to GP members. In 1998, the average schooling by a PS member is found to be 10.11 years (Table 3.45). Further, as in the case of GP, in case of PS also women got much better representation from 1993 onwards. In 1998, among our sampled PS members, 28.03 per cent were women (Table 3.46).

## Panchayats in West Bengal: Missing Links

It becomes abundantly clear from the above discussion that the Left Front Government in West Bengal has displayed sustained interest in decentralization through revival of the panchayati raj system and holding of panchayat elections at regular intervals since 1978. The panchayats have been the most effective forum through which the poorer sections (comprising agricultural labourers, marginal/small farmers, village craftsmen etc.) organized themselves to fight against the vested interests and exploiting classes in the villages (Dutta, 1992, 1997). The panchayats in West Bengal helped a great deal in the implementation of agrarian reforms programmes of which the main components have been the programmes of “Operation Barga” and “land redistribution” (Lieten, 1992). The panchayats also play an important role in implementation of various rural development schemes that include the schemes of employment generation, poverty alleviation and so on (*Ibid.*).

Nevertheless, it is being alleged by several scholars that the Panchayati Raj Institutions (PRIs) in West Bengal have not blossomed into full-fledge local government bodies. Not only that the panchayts are still far from being financially self-reliant,[25] but also they have not been effectively empowered in spite of official claim towards

**Table 3.44:** Occupation (Main/Marginal) of the Panchayat Samiti Members

| Year | Party Affiliation | Total Members | % of Members with Principal Occupation as | | | | | | | | | | | |
|---|---|---|---|---|---|---|---|---|---|---|---|---|---|---|
| | | | Agrl. lab. | Non-Agrl lab. | All lab. | Farming | | | | | Teaching | Service (Other than Teaching) | Business | Others |
| | | | | | | Marginal (0.01-2.49 Acres) | Small (2.50-4.99 Acres) | Medium (5.00-7.49 Acres) | Large (7.50 Acres and Above) | Total | | | | |
| (1) | (2) | (3) | (4) | (5) | (6) | (7) | (8) | (9) | (10) | (11) | (12) | (13) | (14) | (15) |
| 1978 | CPI (M) | 81 | 0.00 | 0.00 | 0.00 | 24.69 | 6.17 | 4.94 | 7.41 | 43.21 | 32.10 | 12.35 | 3.70 | 8.64 |
| | Congress (I) | 15 | 0.00 | 0.00 | 0.00 | 0.00 | 6.67 | 33.33 | 13.33 | 53.33 | 26.67 | 0.00 | 20.00 | 0.00 |
| | Other Left | 18 | 0.00 | 11.11 | 11.11 | 12.96 | 19.44 | 0.00 | 6.48 | 38.89 | 27.78 | 0.00 | 16.67 | 5.56 |
| | Others | 1 | 0.00 | 0.00 | 0.00 | 0.00 | 0.00 | 0.00 | 100.00 | 100.00 | 0.00 | 0.00 | 0.00 | 0.00 |
| | Total | 115 | 0.00 | 1.74 | 1.74 | 19.51 | 7.98 | 7.98 | 8.87 | 44.35 | 30.43 | 8.70 | 7.83 | 6.96 |
| 1983 | CPI (M) | 68 | 0.00 | 0.00 | 0.00 | 19.12 | 11.76 | 1.47 | 7.35 | 39.71 | 29.41 | 13.24 | 2.94 | 14.71 |
| | Congress (I) | 41 | 0.00 | 2.44 | 2.44 | 17.97 | 7.70 | 0.00 | 23.11 | 48.78 | 39.02 | 2.44 | 2.44 | 4.88 |
| | Other Left | 12 | 0.00 | 16.67 | 16.67 | 16.67 | 8.33 | 0.00 | 0.00 | 25.00 | 50.00 | 8.33 | 0.00 | 0.00 |
| | Others | 5 | 0.00 | 0.00 | 0.00 | 40.00 | 0.00 | 0.00 | 0.00 | 40.00 | 60.00 | 0.00 | 0.00 | 0.00 |
| | Total | 126 | 0.00 | 2.38 | 2.38 | 19.42 | 9.71 | 0.81 | 11.33 | 41.27 | 35.71 | 8.73 | 2.38 | 9.52 |
| 1988 | CPI (M) | 96 | 2.08 | 0.00 | 2.08 | 18.23 | 8.58 | 1.07 | 8.58 | 36.46 | 31.25 | 12.50 | 8.33 | 9.38 |
| | Congress (I) | 27 | 0.00 | 0.00 | 0.00 | 9.05 | 13.58 | 4.53 | 13.58 | 40.74 | 37.04 | 0.00 | 18.52 | 3.70 |
| | Other Left | 8 | 0.00 | 0.00 | 0.00 | 37.50 | 0.00 | 0.00 | 0.00 | 37.50 | 37.50 | 12.50 | 0.00 | 12.50 |
| | Others | 4 | 0.00 | 0.00 | 0.00 | 75.00 | 0.00 | 25.00 | 0.00 | 100.00 | 0.00 | 0.00 | 0.00 | 0.00 |
| | Total | 135 | 1.48 | 0.00 | 1.48 | 19.63 | 8.64 | 2.36 | 8.64 | 39.26 | 31.85 | 9.63 | 9.63 | 8.15 |
| 1993 | CPI (M) | 104 | 11.54 | 2.88 | 14.42 | 17.31 | 5.77 | 1.92 | 1.92 | 26.92 | 16.35 | 18.27 | 0.96 | 23.08 |
| | Congress (I) | 39 | 0.00 | 15.38 | 15.38 | 5.13 | 10.26 | 7.69 | 7.69 | 30.77 | 10.26 | 5.13 | 17.95 | 20.51 |
| | Other Left | 12 | 0.00 | 33.33 | 33.33 | 0.00 | 41.67 | 0.00 | 0.00 | 41.67 | 8.33 | 0.00 | 8.33 | 8.33 |
| | Others | 7 | 0.00 | 0.00 | 0.00 | 0.00 | 14.29 | 0.00 | 28.57 | 42.86 | 14.29 | 0.00 | 14.29 | 28.57 |
| | Total | 162 | 7.41 | 8.02 | 15.43 | 12.35 | 9.88 | 3.09 | 4.32 | 29.63 | 14.20 | 12.96 | 6.17 | 21.60 |

(Contd.)

**Table 3.44** (*Contd.*)

| (1) | (2) | (3) | (4) | (5) | (6) | (7) | (8) | (9) | (10) | (11) | (12) | (13) | (14) | (15) |
|---|---|---|---|---|---|---|---|---|---|---|---|---|---|---|
| 1998 | CPI (M) | 92 | 2.17 | 5.43 | 7.61 | 21.74 | 8.70 | 2.17 | 2.17 | 34.78 | 13.04 | 9.78 | 9.78 | 25.00 |
| | Cong(I) | 12 | 0.00 | 0.00 | 0.00 | 0.00 | 0.00 | 8.33 | 0.00 | 8.33 | 25.00 | 0.00 | 33.33 | 33.33 |
| | Other Left | 19 | 5.26 | 15.79 | 21.05 | 0.00 | 15.79 | 5.26 | 10.53 | 31.58 | 31.58 | 5.26 | 5.26 | 5.26 |
| | Others | 34 | 2.94 | 0.00 | 2.94 | 8.82 | 5.88 | 0.00 | 5.88 | 20.59 | 8.82 | 2.94 | 14.71 | 50.00 |
| | Total | 157 | 2.55 | 5.10 | 7.64 | 14.65 | 8.28 | 2.55 | 3.82 | 29.30 | 15.29 | 7.01 | 12.10 | 28.66 |

*Source*: Field Survey on West Bengal Panchayats (2000).

**Table 3.45:** Caste and Education of Panchayat Samiti Members

| Year | Party Affiliation | Total Members | Average years of Schooling of Members | % of Members with Caste as | |
|---|---|---|---|---|---|
| | | | | SC/ST | Others |
| 1978 | CPI(M) | 81 | 10.49 | 12.35 | 87.65 |
| | Congress (I) | 15 | 9.27 | 6.67 | 93.33 |
| | Other Left | 18 | 11.17 | 0.00 | 100.00 |
| | Others | 1 | 9.00 | 0.00 | 100.00 |
| | Total | 115 | 10.43 | 9.57 | 90.43 |
| 1983 | CPI(M) | 68 | 11.01 | 23.53 | 76.47 |
| | Congress (I) | 41 | 10.63 | 12.20 | 87.80 |
| | Other Left | 12 | 12.17 | 0.00 | 100.00 |
| | Others | 5 | 11.20 | 0.00 | 100.00 |
| | Total | 126 | 11.01 | 16.67 | 83.33 |
| 1988 | CPI(M) | 96 | 10.70 | 19.79 | 80.21 |
| | Congress (I) | 27 | 10.56 | 7.41 | 92.59 |
| | Other Left | 8 | 11.38 | 12.50 | 87.50 |
| | Others | 4 | 11.50 | 0.00 | 100.00 |
| | Total | 135 | 10.73 | 16.30 | 83.70 |
| 1993 | CPI(M) | 104 | 9.61 | 42.31 | 57.69 |
| | Congress (I) | 39 | 9.85 | 33.33 | 66.67 |
| | Other Left | 12 | 9.67 | 50.00 | 50.00 |
| | Others | 7 | 8.57 | 28.57 | 71.43 |
| | Total | 162 | 9.62 | 40.12 | 59.88 |
| 1998 | CPI(M) | 92 | 9.88 | 46.74 | 53.26 |
| | Congress (I) | 12 | 11.00 | 25.00 | 75.00 |
| | Other Left | 19 | 10.68 | 47.37 | 52.63 |
| | Others | 34 | 10.09 | 47.06 | 52.94 |
| | Total | 157 | 10.11 | 45.22 | 54.78 |

*Source*: Field Survey on West Bengal Panchayats (2000).

decentralization of power and functions.[26] As a recent study by the UNICEF (2000, p. 8) observes: "The biggest drawback of the PRIs in West Bengal is that its potential has never been fully explored. The PRIs have been reduced to being handy implementing agencies of state government policies and schemes, not agencies that make decisions, plan or control resources." Several other scholars had echoed an almost similar concern much earlier than the UNICEF study. For example, in an important study, Mukarji and Bandyopadhyay (1993) noted that the initial enthusiasm with which the panchayats in West Bengal started in 1978 has gradually faded away rendering them to a mere implementing agency of government-sponsored schemes. Further, Bhattacharjee (1993) and Mallick (1993) argued that downward devolution of power, which is expected with

**Table 3.46:** Sex of Panchayat Samiti Members

| *Year* | *Party Affiliation* | *Total Members* | *% of Members with Sex as* | |
|---|---|---|---|---|
| | | | *Male* | *Female* |
| 1978 | CPI(M) | 81 | 97.53 | 2.47 |
| | Congress (I) | 15 | 100.00 | 0.00 |
| | Other Left | 18 | 100.00 | 0.00 |
| | Others | 1 | 100.00 | 0.00 |
| | Total | 115 | 98.26 | 1.74 |
| 1983 | CPI(M) | 68 | 98.53 | 1.47 |
| | Congress (I) | 41 | 100.00 | 0.00 |
| | Other Left | 12 | 100.00 | 0.00 |
| | Others | 5 | 100.00 | 0.00 |
| | Total | 126 | 99.21 | 0.79 |
| 1988 | CPI(M) | 96 | 100.00 | 0.00 |
| | Congress (I) | 27 | 100.00 | 0.00 |
| | Other Left | 8 | 100.00 | 0.00 |
| | Others | 4 | 100.00 | 0.00 |
| | Total | 135 | 100.00 | 0.00 |
| 1993 | CPI(M) | 104 | 68.27 | 31.73 |
| | Congress (I) | 39 | 71.79 | 28.21 |
| | Other Left | 12 | 75.00 | 25.00 |
| | Others | 7 | 57.14 | 42.86 |
| | Total | 162 | 69.14 | 30.86 |
| 1998 | CPI(M) | 92 | 71.74 | 28.26 |
| | Congress (I) | 12 | 58.33 | 41.67 |
| | Other Left | 19 | 84.21 | 15.79 |
| | Others | 34 | 64.71 | 29.41 |
| | Total | 157 | 70.70 | 28.03 |

*Source*: Field Survey on West Bengal Panchayats (2000).

the revival of panchayati raj system, stood arrested and power, in actuality remained firmly entrenched in the hands of the rising middle sections of rural society. Scholars such as Webster (1992) and Kohli (1992) seem to explain this latter tendency as the fallout of the left front's gradual adoption of a policy that is of non-antagonistic nature and which purported "to sustain an alliance of the middle and lower strata and to avoid any further alienation of property-owning groups" (Kohli, 1992, p. 291). According to Ghatak and Ghatak (2002, p. 45), "despite its pioneering status in terms of reforms of the panchayat system West Bengal lags behind several other states today in terms of devolution of power, finances, and functions to the panchyats." Bandyopadhyay (2003b), another perceptive observer of West Bengal rural scene and the man playing a significant role in implementing the Operation Barga programme in late seventies/early eighties, opines that the

**Table 3.47:** Distribution of Operational Holdings in West Bengal by Districts

| District | *Percentage of holdings* | | | | | | *Percentage of Operated Area* | | | | | | Gini Inequality Coefficient | |
|---|---|---|---|---|---|---|---|---|---|---|---|---|---|---|
| | *Size Group (in hectares)* | | | | | | *Size Group (in hectares)* | | | | | | | |
| | *Below 1.0* | *1.0-2.0* | *2.0-4.0* | *4.0-10.0* | *10.0 and above* | *All sizes* | *Below 1.0* | *1.0-2.0* | *2.0-4.0* | *4.0-10.0* | *10.0 and above* | *All sizes* | | |
| **(1)** | (2) | (3) | (4) | (5) | (6) | (7) | (8) | (9) | (10) | (11) | (12) | (13) | (14) | (15) |
| **Year: 1990-91** | | | | | | | | | | | | | | |
| Bankura | 62.31 | 24.20 | 11.49 | 1.99 | 0.01 | 100.00 | 31.61 | 33.81 | 25.92 | 8.53 | 0.13 | 100.00 | 0.35 | (14) |
| Birbhum | 60.14 | 25.36 | 12.33 | 2.15 | 0.02 | 100.00 | 23.78 | 33.88 | 31.33 | 10.63 | 0.38 | 100.00 | 0.43 | (3) |
| Burdwan | 59.99 | 25.82 | 11.58 | 2.57 | 0.04 | 100.00 | 26.33 | 32.42 | 28.60 | 12.05 | 0.60 | 100.00 | 0.40 | (4) |
| Cooch Behar | 72.43 | 17.96 | 7.91 | 1.69 | 0.01 | 100.00 | 37.61 | 27.92 | 24.17 | 9.78 | 0.52 | 100.00 | 0.39 | (10) |
| Darjeeling | 59.76 | 22.98 | 13.52 | 3.46 | 0.29 | 100.00 | 15.84 | 15.83 | 16.90 | 9.23 | 42.20 | 100.00 | 0.65 | (1) |
| Hooghly | 81.79 | 13.35 | 4.25 | 0.61 | 0.00 | 100.00 | 47.28 | 29.83 | 18.02 | 4.84 | 0.03 | 100.00 | 0.36 | (13) |
| Howrah | 89.81 | 8.14 | 1.92 | 0.13 | 0.00 | 100.00 | 61.90 | 25.37 | 11.08 | 1.39 | 0.25 | 100.00 | 0.29 | (17) |
| Jalpaiguri | 69.34 | 20.03 | 8.57 | 1.95 | 0.11 | 100.00 | 22.58 | 19.42 | 15.90 | 6.94 | 35.16 | 100.00 | 0.60 | (2) |
| Malda | 75.53 | 16.15 | 6.57 | 1.71 | 0.03 | 100.00 | 39.16 | 27.84 | 21.25 | 11.22 | 0.54 | 100.00 | 0.40 | (5) |
| Midnapore (East) | 87.87 | 9.62 | 2.31 | 0.20 | 0.01 | 100.00 | 57.77 | 27.98 | 12.21 | 1.91 | 0.14 | 100.00 | 0.31 | (16) |
| Midnapore (West) | 75.48 | 17.04 | 6.52 | 0.96 | 0.01 | 100.00 | 42.49 | 32.29 | 19.86 | 5.16 | 0.20 | 100.00 | 0.35 | (15) |
| Murshidabad | 72.75 | 19.71 | 7.05 | 0.48 | 0.01 | 100.00 | 38.50 | 34.41 | 23.73 | 3.13 | 0.23 | 100.00 | 0.37 | (12) |
| Nadia | 67.11 | 22.21 | 8.94 | 1.72 | 0.03 | 100.00 | 32.29 | 33.38 | 24.71 | 9.18 | 0.43 | 100.00 | 0.39 | (7) |
| North 24 Parganas | 79.08 | 14.83 | 5.37 | 0.70 | 0.01 | 100.00 | 43.88 | 30.20 | 20.25 | 5.58 | 0.10 | 100.00 | 0.37 | (11) |
| Purulia | 63.30 | 21.84 | 12.86 | 1.98 | 0.02 | 100.00 | 28.74 | 31.07 | 30.33 | 9.57 | 0.29 | 100.00 | 0.39 | (6) |
| South 24 Parganas | 80.85 | 13.10 | 5.33 | 0.72 | 0.00 | 100.00 | 43.80 | 29.45 | 21.73 | 4.96 | 0.05 | 100.00 | 0.39 | (9) |
| Uttar and Dakshin Dinajpur | 69.46 | 19.71 | 8.70 | 2.11 | 0.02 | 100.00 | 34.40 | 30.13 | 24.01 | 11.08 | 0.39 | 100.00 | 0.39 | (8) |
| West Bengal | 73.83 | 17.62 | 7.28 | 1.26 | 0.02 | 100.00 | 36.50 | 29.95 | 22.44 | 7.52 | 3.58 | 100.00 | 0.41 | |
| **Year: 1995-96** | | | | | | | | | | | | | | |
| Bankura | 63.49 | 23.55 | 11.07 | 1.88 | 0.01 | 100.00 | 31.83 | 32.80 | 26.79 | 8.38 | 0.19 | 100.00 | 0.36 | (5) |
| Birbhum | 65.09 | 25.41 | 8.28 | 1.21 | 0.01 | 100.00 | 36.12 | 34.29 | 22.99 | 6.16 | 0.44 | 100.00 | 0.34 | (10) |

*(Contd.)*

**Table 3.47** *(Contd.)*

| District | Percentage of holdings | | | | | | Percentage of Operated Area | | | | | | Gini Inequality Coefficient | |
|---|---|---|---|---|---|---|---|---|---|---|---|---|---|---|
| | Size Group (in hectares) | | | | | | Size Group (in hectares) | | | | | | | |
| | Below 1.0 | 1.0-2.0 | 2.0-4.0 | 4.0-10.0 | 10.0 and above | All sizes | Below 1.0 | 1.0-2.0 | 2.0-4.0 | 4.0-10.0 | 10.0 and above | All sizes | | |
| (1) | (2) | (3) | (4) | (5) | (6) | (7) | (8) | (9) | (10) | (11) | (12) | (13) | (14) | (15) |
| Burdwan | 68.22 | 20.78 | 9.07 | 1.89 | 0.04 | 100.00 | 35.06 | 31.33 | 23.79 | 9.16 | 0.66 | 100.00 | 0.37 | (4) |
| Cooch Behar | 69.76 | 20.87 | 7.55 | 1.81 | 0.02 | 100.00 | 38.65 | 27.20 | 24.08 | 9.26 | 0.80 | 100.00 | 0.36 | (6) |
| Darjeeling | 68.87 | 20.24 | 9.28 | 1.39 | 0.22 | 100.00 | 21.37 | 17.45 | 14.42 | 4.29 | 42.48 | 100.00 | 0.63 | (1) |
| Hooghly | 81.52 | 14.73 | 3.24 | 0.51 | 0.00 | 100.00 | 51.09 | 29.74 | 14.81 | 4.29 | 0.08 | 100.00 | 0.32 | (13) |
| Howrah | 89.85 | 8.15 | 1.92 | 0.08 | 0.00 | 100.00 | 66.39 | 22.23 | 10.21 | 0.99 | 0.18 | 100.00 | 0.24 | (16) |
| Jalpaiguri | 73.69 | 17.70 | 7.12 | 1.39 | 0.09 | 100.00 | 27.79 | 19.62 | 13.59 | 5.12 | 33.88 | 100.00 | 0.57 | (2) |
| Malda | 75.63 | 16.16 | 6.55 | 1.64 | 0.03 | 100.00 | 39.81 | 28.39 | 20.95 | 10.49 | 0.37 | 100.00 | 0.39 | (3) |
| Midnapore (East) | 91.23 | 7.16 | 1.50 | 0.11 | 0.00 | 100.00 | 71.72 | 20.69 | 6.40 | 0.99 | 0.20 | 100.00 | 0.20 | (17) |
| Midnapore (West) | 79.58 | 15.39 | 4.27 | 0.75 | 0.01 | 100.00 | 49.90 | 30.91 | 14.23 | 4.63 | 0.33 | 100.00 | 0.31 | (14) |
| Murshidabad | 74.92 | 18.50 | 6.03 | 0.54 | 0.01 | 100.00 | 44.10 | 32.91 | 19.29 | 3.53 | 0.17 | 100.00 | 0.33 | (12) |
| Nadia | 71.37 | 22.67 | 5.08 | 0.87 | 0.01 | 100.00 | 47.31 | 33.93 | 13.94 | 4.54 | 0.29 | 100.00 | 0.26 | (15) |
| North 24 Parganas | 80.27 | 14.98 | 4.39 | 0.35 | 0.01 | 100.00 | 46.57 | 33.21 | 17.33 | 2.73 | 0.16 | 100.00 | 0.35 | (8) |
| Purulia | 68.72 | 22.40 | 7.67 | 1.18 | 0.02 | 100.00 | 36.61 | 34.17 | 22.02 | 6.88 | 0.32 | 100.00 | 0.36 | (7) |
| South 24 Parganas | 83.66 | 10.80 | 5.06 | 0.48 | 0.00 | 100.00 | 50.16 | 24.16 | 21.74 | 3.89 | 0.05 | 100.00 | 0.35 | (9) |
| Uttar and Dakshin Dinajpur | 69.07 | 21.28 | 8.28 | 1.35 | 0.02 | 100.00 | 39.67 | 30.12 | 22.76 | 7.12 | 0.32 | 100.00 | 0.33 | (11) |
| West Bengal | 76.42 | 16.81 | 5.83 | 0.92 | 0.02 | 100.00 | 42.93 | 29.06 | 18.73 | 5.66 | 3.62 | 100.00 | 0.37 | |

*Note*: Figures in brackets are ranks among 17 districts.

*Source*: *Agricultural Census 1990-91 and 1995-96* (Vol. 2), Directorate of Agriculture, Government of West Bengal.

government wilfully and consistently ignored the 'three-F formula' (functions, functionaries and finances) of devolution to make panchayats autonomous institutions of self-governance. According to him, the concept of autonomy is anathema to the culture of "control and command" of the dominant partner of the Left Front coalition [i.e. CPI (M)].

Since it is outside the purview of the present study to pass judgement on the validity or otherwise of above observations, we would round up this section simply by saying that the Government of West Bengal has been perhaps going through a process of experiment in so far as devolution of power and decentralization of rural governance (as through the panchayati raj system) are concerned. There has been no dearth of efforts from the side of the government to rectify the loopholes in the existing system and transform the panchayats into more vibrant institutions of self-governance. To this end, some experiments have been initiated also to draw up the 'village plan' involving the village people.[27] Further, the government has been amending the Panchayat Act from time to time to streamline further the process of decentralization/devolution.[28] The latest amendment with regard to the Panchayat Act has been in July 2003, which made provision for formation of Village Development Committees (VDCs) so as to further ensure "active participation of the people in implementation, maintenance and equitable distribution of benefits". However, it also needs to be noted that the Government's approach to amend the Act for formation of VDCs has also raised a fierce controversy.

## AGRARIAN RELATIONS

Agrarian relations in any region convey numerous facets of its agrarian realities (Sharma, 1995). For example, it may convey the structure of land distribution, levels and types/forms of tenancy, mode and level of wage payment, employer-employee relations in the labour market, class bias in the workings of local level institutions and so on.

In this section, we concentrate on four specific aspects of agrarian life to form some idea about the prevailing agrarian relations in West Bengal and its districts. These are: (1) The distribution of operational holdings, (2) The extent and forms of tenancy, (3) The land reforms programmes, and (4) The wages of agricultural labourers.

## Distribution of Operational Holdings

We have compiled the Agricultural Census data for the years 1990-91 and 1995-96 to gather some idea about the distribution pattern of operational holdings in the state of West Bengal and her districts. Table 3.47 presents data on percentage of operational holdings and area operated under five broad categories: (1) Below 1.0 hectare (Marginal), (2) 1.0-2.0 hectares (Small), (3) 2.0-4.0 hectares (Medium), (4) 4.0-10.0 hectares (Big), and (5) 10.0 hectares and above (Large). The main points to be noted in this context are the following:

(1) There is strong dominance of 'marginal' holdings (Operational) in rural West Bengal. The share of this category in total operational holdings is found to be 73.83 per cent in 1990-91, which increased to 76.42 per cent in 1995-96. In the year 1995-96, the share of 'small' holdings is 16.81 per cent while the same for 'middle' holdings being 5.83 per cent. On the other hand, the 'big' and 'large' holdings together accounted for less than 1 per cent of all operational holdings in West Bengal. Clearly, rural West Bengal has been overwhelmingly dominated by 'marginal and small' holdings. These two categories together represented nearly 93 per cent of all operational holdings in 1995-96.

(2) Although the 'marginal and small' holdings together controlled 93 per cent of holdings in 1995-96, their share in total operated are has been 73 per cent. On the other hand, the 'big and large' holdings had a share of nearly 9 per cent of operated area although they represented less than 1 per cent of all operational holdings. This implies that there exits some inequality in the distribution of operational holdings in West Bengal.

(3) In the year 1995-96, among the districts of West Bengal, more than 75 per cent of operational holdings belonged to the 'marginal' category in the districts of Midnapore (East), Howrah, South 24 Parganas, Hooghly, North 24 Parganas and Malda. Further, the 'marginal and small' holdings together accounted for 90 per cent or more of all operational holdings in all districts of West Bengal (except Bankura, Burdwan and Darjeeling).

(4) Over the years, there has been a tendency of equalization of distribution of operational holdings both in the state and most of the districts. For the state as a whole, the value of Gini inequality coefficient is found to be 0.41 for 1990-91, which got reduced to 0.37 in 1995-96. In each district of West Bengal (except Bankura), the value of Gini inequality coefficient declined between 1990-91 and 1995-96. This indicates that declining inequality in distribution of operational holdings in West Bengal has been largely widespread.

In the context of discussion on distribution of operational holdings, it may be worthwhile to look into the average size of operational holdings for various groups. Table 3.48 presents data on this aspect for the years 1990-91 and 1995-96. The important points to note here are: (1) The average size of operational holdings has been declining gradually in West Bengal. The average size of operational holdings in 1990-91 was 0.90 hectare, which reduced to 0.85 hectare in 1995-96; (2) The declining tendency of average size of operational holdings is also visible in most of the districts; the only exceptions being Cooch Behar and Murshidabad which registered slight increase in the average size of operational holdings between 1990-91 and 1995-96; (3) It is interesting to note that between the period 1990-91 to 1995-96, the average size of operational holdings for the 'marginal' category (operating less than 1 hectare) in West Bengal increased from 0.45 hectare to 0.48 hectare. Such a tendency is also discernible in 13 out of a total of 17 districts. This implies that the 'marginal' operators have been increasing their share of net leased in area (are leased in minus area leased out) and/or increasing own cultivated area;[29] and (4) The average size of operational holdings also increased in the state and most of the districts for the 'large' category as well. For all other categories, there has been a general tendency of average size of operational holdings declining during the period 1990-91 to 1995-96.

## Incidence of Tenancy

To understand the incidence and forms of tenancy, we continue with the agricultural census data.[30] As regards the incidence (extent) of tenancy, Table 3.49 reveals the following:

**Table 3.48:** Average Size of Operational Holdings

*(in hectare)*

| District | Below 1 hec (Marginal) | 1-2 hec (Small) | 2-4 hec (Medium) | 4-10 hec (Semi-medium) | 10 hec and Above (Large) | All sizes |
|---|---|---|---|---|---|---|
| **Year: 1990-91** | | | | | | |
| Bankura | 0.57 | 1.57 | 2.54 | 4.82 | 14.53 | 1.12 (4) |
| Birbhum | 0.44 | 1.49 | 2.84 | 5.51 | 22.22 | 1.12 (5) |
| Burdwan | 0.50 | 1.44 | 2.84 | 5.40 | 15.99 | 1.15 (3) |
| Cooch Behar | 0.50 | 1.50 | 2.95 | 5.59 | 37.89 | 0.97 (9) |
| Darjeeling | 0.55 | 1.43 | 2.60 | 5.55 | 306.62 | 2.08 (1) |
| Hooghly | 0.41 | 1.58 | 3.00 | 5.59 | 12.00 | 0.71 (14) |
| Howrah | 0.30 | 1.35 | 2.51 | 4.72 | 43.67 | 0.43 (17) |
| Jalpaiguri | 0.53 | 1.57 | 3.01 | 5.78 | 541.23 | 1.62 (2) |
| Malda | 0.45 | 1.50 | 2.82 | 5.71 | 15.63 | 0.87 (11) |
| Midnapore (East) | 0.38 | 1.66 | 3.02 | 5.49 | 15.20 | 0.57 (16) |
| Midnapore (West) | 0.57 | 1.92 | 3.09 | 5.48 | 35.22 | 1.02 (8) |
| Murshidabad | 0.40 | 1.31 | 2.53 | 4.86 | 13.07 | 0.75 (12) |
| Nadia | 0.46 | 1.44 | 2.65 | 5.12 | 15.77 | 0.96 (10) |
| North 24 Parganas | 0.38 | 1.41 | 2.61 | 5.48 | 11.19 | 0.69 (15) |
| Purulia | 0.48 | 1.49 | 2.47 | 5.06 | 13.33 | 1.05 (7) |
| South 24 Parganas | 0.38 | 1.59 | 2.89 | 4.91 | 12.11 | 0.71 (13) |
| Uttar and Dakshin Dinajpur | 0.53 | 1.65 | 2.98 | 5.67 | 18.43 | 1.08 (6) |
| West Bengal | 0.45 | 1.53 | 2.78 | 5.37 | 156.99 | 0.90 |
| **Year: 1995-96** | | | | | | |
| Bankura | 0.56 | 1.54 | 2.68 | 4.95 | 16.93 | 1.11 (5) |
| Birbhum | 0.62 | 1.50 | 3.09 | 5.69 | 48.54 | 1.11 (4) |

*(Contd.)*

**Table 3.48** *(Contd.)*

| District | Below 1 hec (Marginal) | 1-2 hec (Small) | 2-4 hec (Medium) | 4-10 hec (Semi-medium) | 10 hec and Above (Large) | All sizes | |
|---|---|---|---|---|---|---|---|
| Burdwan | 0.58 | 1.70 | 2.95 | 5.45 | 19.03 | 1.13 | (3) |
| Cooch Behar | 0.54 | 1.27 | 3.11 | 5.00 | 47.96 | 0.98 | (7) |
| Darjeeling | 0.53 | 1.48 | 2.67 | 5.29 | 339.22 | 1.72 | (1) |
| Hooghly | 0.41 | 1.34 | 3.02 | 5.54 | 13.83 | 0.66 | (14) |
| Howrah | 0.32 | 1.17 | 2.29 | 5.31 | 185.00 | 0.43 | (17) |
| Jalpaiguri | 0.55 | 1.61 | 2.77 | 5.33 | 532.30 | 1.45 | (2) |
| Malda | 0.45 | 1.50 | 2.74 | 5.48 | 11.27 | 0.86 | (11) |
| Midnapore (East) | 0.43 | 1.58 | 2.34 | 4.74 | 50.87 | 0.55 | (16) |
| Midnapore (West) | 0.55 | 1.75 | 2.91 | 5.37 | 48.06 | 0.87 | (10) |
| Murshidabad | 0.45 | 1.35 | 2.42 | 4.97 | 12.08 | 0.76 | (12) |
| Nadia | 0.62 | 1.40 | 2.57 | 4.88 | 36.96 | 0.94 | (8) |
| North 24 Parganas | 0.39 | 1.50 | 2.66 | 5.24 | 12.73 | 0.67 | (13) |
| Purulia | 0.47 | 1.35 | 2.55 | 5.15 | 11.91 | 0.89 | (9) |
| South 24 Parganas | 0.36 | 1.36 | 2.61 | 4.95 | 14.29 | 0.61 | (15) |
| Uttar and Dakshin Dinajpur | 0.59 | 1.45 | 2.83 | 5.43 | 18.49 | 1.03 | (6) |
| West Bengal | 0.48 | 1.48 | 2.74 | 5.25 | 175.83 | 0.85 | |
| **Change in Av. Size of Holdings in 1995-96 over 1990-91** | | | | | | | |
| Bankura | -0.01 | -0.03 | 0.15 | 0.13 | 2.40 | -0.02 | (5) |
| Birbhum | 0.18 | 0.01 | 0.25 | 0.18 | 26.32 | 0.00 | (4) |
| Burdwan | 0.07 | 0.25 | 0.11 | 0.05 | 3.04 | -0.02 | (9) |
| Cooch Behar | 0.04 | -0.23 | 0.16 | -0.58 | 10.06 | 0.01 | (1) |
| Darjeeling | -0.02 | 0.05 | 0.07 | -0.26 | 32.60 | -0.36 | (17) |
| Hooghly | 0.01 | -0.24 | 0.02 | -0.06 | 1.83 | -0.05 | (11) |
| Howrah | 0.02 | -0.18 | -0.22 | 0.59 | 141.33 | 0.00 | (3) |

*(Contd.)*

**Table 3.48** *(Contd.)*

| *District* | *Below 1 hec (Marginal)* | *1-2 hec (Small)* | *2-4 hec (Medium)* | *4-10 hec (Semi-medium)* | *10 hec and Above (Large)* | *All sizes* |
|---|---|---|---|---|---|---|
| Jalpaiguri | 0.02 | 0.04 | -0.24 | -0.45 | -8.93 | -0.17 (16) |
| Malda | 0.00 | 0.00 | -0.09 | -0.24 | -4.35 | -0.02 (7) |
| Midnapore (East) | 0.05 | -0.08 | -0.68 | -0.75 | 35.67 | -0.03 (10) |
| Midnapore (West) | -0.02 | -0.17 | -0.19 | -0.11 | 12.84 | -0.14 (14) |
| Murshidabad | 0.05 | 0.04 | -0.11 | 0.11 | -0.99 | 0.01 (2) |
| Nadia | 0.16 | -0.04 | -0.08 | -0.24 | 21.19 | -0.02 (8) |
| North 24 Parganas | 0.01 | 0.09 | 0.05 | -0.24 | 1.54 | -0.02 (6) |
| Purulia | 0.00 | -0.14 | 0.07 | 0.09 | -1.42 | -0.16 (15) |
| South 24 Parganas | -0.02 | -0.23 | -0.28 | 0.04 | 2.17 | -0.10 (13) |
| Uttar and Dakshin Dinajpur | 0.06 | -0.20 | -0.15 | -0.24 | 0.07 | -0.05 (12) |
| West Bengal | 0.03 | -0.06 | -0.03 | -0.12 | 18.84 | -0.05 |

*Note*: Figures in brackets are ranks among 17 districts.

*Source*: Agricultural Census 1990-91 and 1995-96 (Vol. 2), Directorate of Agriculture, Government of West Bengal.

**Table 3.49:** Incidence of Tenancy in West Bengal by Districts in 1995-96

| District | % distribution of total leased in area | | | | | | % of operated area leased in | | | | | |
|---|---|---|---|---|---|---|---|---|---|---|---|---|
| | Size Group (in hectares) | | | | | | Size Group (in hectares) | | | | | |
| | Below 1.0 | 1.0-2.0 | 2.0-4.0 | 4.0-10.0 | 10.0 and above | Total | Below 1.0 | 1.0-2.0 | 2.0-4.0 | 4.0-10.0 | 10.0 and above | All sizes |
| Bankura | 37.26 | 33.35 | 23.42 | 5.93 | 0.04 | 100.00 | 8.34 | 7.24 | 6.23 | 5.04 | 1.61 | 7.12 (10) |
| Birbhum | 29.04 | 46.39 | 21.70 | 2.78 | 0.07 | 100.00 | 10.05 | 16.91 | 11.80 | 5.65 | 2.13 | 12.50 (2) |
| Burdwan | 36.94 | 36.02 | 19.32 | 6.59 | 1.13 | 100.00 | 9.37 | 10.23 | 7.22 | 6.40 | 15.22 | 8.89 (8) |
| Cooch Behar | 36.29 | 28.30 | 21.50 | 13.79 | 0.12 | 100.00 | 10.40 | 11.52 | 9.89 | 16.49 | 1.63 | 11.07 (6) |
| Dakshin Dinajpur | 35.18 | 36.28 | 18.72 | 9.35 | 0.46 | 100.00 | 10.36 | 14.60 | 10.66 | 17.19 | 22.54 | 12.19 (3) |
| Darjeeling | 26.32 | 23.61 | 28.28 | 19.47 | 2.32 | 100.00 | 4.39 | 4.82 | 6.98 | 16.18 | 0.19 | 3.56 (17) |
| Hooghly | 61.48 | 25.98 | 9.40 | 3.14 | 0.00 | 100.00 | 12.24 | 8.88 | 6.45 | 7.45 | 0.00 | 10.17 (7) |
| Howrah | 47.39 | 33.08 | 15.69 | 2.86 | 0.98 | 100.00 | 10.28 | 21.42 | 22.12 | 41.59 | 80.00 | 14.40 (1) |
| Jalpaiguri | 28.67 | 27.23 | 22.44 | 20.77 | 0.89 | 100.00 | 11.52 | 15.50 | 18.45 | 45.36 | 0.29 | 11.17 (5) |
| Malda | 29.77 | 29.29 | 22.29 | 18.29 | 0.34 | 100.00 | 8.98 | 12.39 | 12.78 | 20.95 | 11.11 | 12.01 (4) |
| Midnapore (East) | 69.03 | 20.11 | 7.41 | 3.45 | 0.00 | 100.00 | 5.00 | 5.05 | 6.02 | 18.12 | 0.00 | 5.20 (14) |
| Midnapore (West) | 46.87 | 28.47 | 14.18 | 10.32 | 0.15 | 100.00 | 5.19 | 5.08 | 5.50 | 12.30 | 2.55 | 5.52 (13) |
| Murshidabad | 36.33 | 34.21 | 21.39 | 7.78 | 0.29 | 100.00 | 5.68 | 7.16 | 7.64 | 15.19 | 11.25 | 6.89 (11) |
| Nadia | 49.41 | 30.26 | 11.36 | 8.95 | 0.01 | 100.00 | 6.21 | 5.30 | 4.84 | 11.73 | 0.29 | 5.94 (12) |
| North 24 Parganas | 33.63 | 30.11 | 22.56 | 13.02 | 0.68 | 100.00 | 5.40 | 6.78 | 9.74 | 35.64 | 31.00 | 7.48 (9) |
| Purulia | 25.35 | 32.67 | 24.53 | 15.70 | 1.76 | 100.00 | 1.94 | 2.67 | 3.12 | 6.38 | 15.57 | 2.80 (18) |
| South 24 Parganas | 46.10 | 19.48 | 22.61 | 11.82 | 0.00 | 100.00 | 3.29 | 2.88 | 3.72 | 10.86 | 0.00 | 3.58 (16) |
| Uttar Dinajpur | 30.98 | 26.51 | 22.93 | 19.53 | 0.05 | 100.00 | 3.20 | 3.50 | 3.81 | 10.32 | 0.52 | 3.96 (15) |
| West Bengal | 38.63 | 31.42 | 19.28 | 10.24 | 0.42 | 100.00 | 6.94 | 8.33 | 7.94 | 13.93 | 0.90 | 7.71 |

*Note*: Figures in brackets are ranks among 18 districts.
*Source*: Agricultural Census 1995-96, Vol. 2, Directorate of Agriculture, Govenment of West Bengal.

(1) About 8 per cent of operated area in West Bengal has been under tenancy cultivation in 1995-96. The percentage of tenant-operated area has been above the state-average in the districts of Howrah (14.40 per cent), Birbhum (12.50 per cent), Dakshin Dinajpur (12.19 per cent), Malda (12.01 per cent), Jalpaiguri (11.17 per cent), Cooch Behar (11.07 per cent), Hooghly (10.17 per cent) and Burdwan (8.89 per cent).

(2) In West Bengal, among all size groups, the percentage of operated area leased in has been the highest (13.93 per cent) in the group representing 'Big', which is followed by 'Small' (8.33 per cent), 'Medium' (7.94 per cent), 'Marginal' (6.94 per cent) and 'Large' (0.90 per cent) holdings. There is clearly some evidence of better off holdings reporting some leased in area although the extent of the same has not been very high.

(3) There are six districts in West Bengal (namely North 24 Parganas, Jalpaiguri, Howrah, Dakshin Dinajpur, Malda and Murshidabad) where the better off holdings are reported to have rather high percentage of operated area leased-in.

(4) However, if we look into the distribution of total leased in area into various size groups, there appears to be only four districts (these are Jalpaiguri, Darjeeling, Uttar Dinajpur and Malda) where nearly one-fifth of total leased in area has been concentrated in 'Big and Large' holdings.

## Forms of Tenancy

Table 3.50 presents data on the forms of tenancy in West Bengal as well as the districts in 1995-96. Both for the state as well as districts, crop-sharing has been the predominant form of tenancy. In West Bengal, about 86 per cent of leased in area has been under crop-sharing arrangement in 1995-96. Among the districts, the percentage of leased in area under crop-sharing has been higher than the state-average in Darjeeling, Jalpaiguri, Cooch Behar, Malda, Hooghly, Burdwan, Birbhum, Purulia, Midnapore (East) and Midnapore (West). On the other hand, there is only one district, namely South 24 Parganas, where nearly one-fourth of leased in area has been under the fixed rent (produce/cash) contract. This apart, in six other districts (Murshidabad, Nadia, North 24 Paraganas, South 24 Paraganas, Howrah and Hooghly) more than one-tenth of leased in area is found to be under the fixed rent (produce/cash) contract.

**Table 3.50:** Forms/Terms of Tenancy in West Bengal by Districts in 1995-96 [% of Leased in Area]

| *District* | *Terms of Tenancy* | *Size Group (in Hectares)* | | | | | |
|---|---|---|---|---|---|---|---|
| | | *Below 1.0* | *1.0-2.0* | *2.0-4.0* | *4.0-10.0* | *10.0 and Above* | *All Sizes* |
| Darjeeling | Fixed rent (produce/cash) | 6.47 | 2.53 | 0.90 | 0.00 | 0.00 | 2.55 |
| | Crop-sharing | 79.22 | 84.19 | 96.60 | 100.00 | 100.00 | 89.84 |
| | Others (incl. Usufr. Mortgage) | 14.32 | 13.28 | 2.50 | 0.00 | 0.00 | 7.61 |
| Jalpaiguri | Fixed rent (produce/cash) | 5.38 | 7.77 | 4.51 | 1.60 | 0.00 | 5.00 |
| | Crop-sharing | 87.29 | 85.79 | 93.33 | 98.40 | 100.00 | 90.66 |
| | Others (incl. Usufr. Mortgage) | 7.34 | 6.44 | 2.16 | 0.00 | 0.00 | 4.34 |
| Cooch Behar | Fixed rent (produce/cash) | 4.52 | 1.92 | 3.71 | 0.09 | 16.67 | 3.01 |
| | Crop-sharing | 91.77 | 93.39 | 95.02 | 97.01 | 83.33 | 93.64 |
| | Others (incl. Usufr. Mortgage) | 3.72 | 4.69 | 1.26 | 2.90 | 0.00 | 3.35 |
| Uttar Dinajpur | Fixed rent (produce/cash) | 10.85 | 4.76 | 7.65 | 16.40 | 0.00 | 9.58 |
| | Crop-sharing | 74.55 | 87.14 | 84.09 | 82.90 | 100.00 | 81.72 |
| | Others (incl. Usufr. Mortgage) | 14.60 | 8.10 | 8.25 | 0.71 | 0.00 | 8.70 |
| Dakshin Dinajpur | Fixed rent (produce/cash) | 9.61 | 11.51 | 4.16 | 4.88 | 0.00 | 8.79 |
| | Crop-sharing | 74.12 | 65.63 | 90.68 | 92.73 | 100.00 | 76.00 |
| | Others (incl. Usufr. Mortgage) | 16.28 | 22.87 | 5.16 | 2.39 | 0.00 | 15.21 |
| Malda | Fixed rent (produce/cash) | 10.33 | 8.45 | 5.25 | 2.61 | 0.00 | 7.20 |
| | Crop-sharing | 81.35 | 87.08 | 92.12 | 97.06 | 100.00 | 88.37 |
| | Others (incl. Usufr. Mortgage) | 8.31 | 4.47 | 2.64 | 0.33 | 0.00 | 4.43 |
| Murshidabad | Fixed rent (produce/cash) | 24.14 | 19.27 | 7.25 | 2.66 | 0.00 | 17.12 |
| | Crop-sharing | 72.25 | 76.82 | 92.57 | 96.37 | 100.00 | 80.11 |
| | Others (incl. Usufr. Mortgage) | 3.62 | 3.91 | 0.18 | 0.97 | 0.00 | 2.77 |

(*Contd.*)

**Table 3.50** *(Contd.)*

| *District* | *Terms of Tenancy* | *Size Group (in Hectares)* | | | | | |
|---|---|---|---|---|---|---|---|
| | | *Below 1.0* | *1.0-2.0* | *2.0-4.0* | *4.0-10.0* | *10.0 and Above* | *All Sizes* |
| Nadia | Fixed rent (produce/cash) | 18.05 | 16.70 | 5.78 | 2.85 | 0.00 | 14.88 |
| | Crop-sharing | 71.81 | 74.86 | 91.60 | 93.09 | 100.00 | 76.89 |
| | Others (incl. Usufr. Mortgage) | 10.13 | 8.44 | 2.62 | 4.06 | 0.00 | 8.22 |
| North 24 Parganas | Fixed rent (produce/cash) | 17.23 | 12.49 | 7.24 | 0.00 | 63.01 | 11.61 |
| | Crop-sharing | 76.66 | 84.96 | 91.72 | 99.72 | 36.99 | 85.29 |
| | Others (incl. Usufr. Mortgage) | 6.11 | 2.55 | 1.05 | 0.28 | 0.00 | 3.09 |
| South 24 Parganas | Fixed rent (produce/cash) | 25.41 | 27.65 | 33.71 | 16.69 | – | 26.69 |
| | Crop-sharing | 55.79 | 49.67 | 52.16 | 72.34 | – | 55.73 |
| | Others (incl. Usufr. Mortgage) | 18.79 | 22.68 | 14.13 | 10.98 | – | 17.57 |
| Howrah | Fixed rent (produce/cash) | 25.65 | 2.82 | 0.00 | 0.00 | 0.00 | 13.09 |
| | Crop-sharing | 72.42 | 96.54 | 100.00 | 100.00 | 100.00 | 85.79 |
| | Others (incl. Usufr. Mortgage) | 1.92 | 0.64 | 0.00 | 0.00 | 0.00 | 1.12 |
| Hooghly | Fixed rent (produce/cash) | 10.48 | 9.62 | 14.20 | 32.10 | – | 11.29 |
| | Crop-sharing | 88.48 | 89.24 | 81.46 | 67.90 | – | 87.37 |
| | Others (incl. Usufr. Mortgage) | 1.03 | 1.14 | 4.34 | 0.00 | – | 1.34 |
| Burdwan | Fixed rent (produce/cash) | 7.96 | 10.13 | 3.27 | 1.88 | 0.00 | 7.35 |
| | Crop-sharing | 88.02 | 88.82 | 95.93 | 98.12 | 100.00 | 90.64 |
| | Others (incl. Usufr. Mortgage) | 4.02 | 1.04 | 0.80 | 0.00 | 0.00 | 2.02 |
| Birbhum | Fixed rent (produce/cash) | 5.71 | 3.95 | 6.05 | 8.08 | 65.52 | 5.08 |
| | Crop-sharing | 89.22 | 94.73 | 93.95 | 91.83 | 34.48 | 92.83 |
| | Others (incl. Usufr. Mortgage) | 5.07 | 1.32 | 0.00 | 0.09 | 0.00 | 2.09 |

*(Contd.)*

**Table 3.50** *(Contd.)*

| *District* | *Terms of Tenancy* | *Size Group (in Hectares)* | | | | | |
|---|---|---|---|---|---|---|---|
| | | *Below 1.0* | *1.0-2.0* | *2.0-4.0* | *4.0-10.0* | *10.0 and Above* | *All Sizes* |
| Bankura | Fixed rent (produce/cash) | 14.24 | 13.50 | 6.65 | 31.10 | 16.67 | 13.22 |
| | Crop-sharing | 76.41 | 82.09 | 86.10 | 68.35 | 83.33 | 80.10 |
| | Others (incl. Usufr. Mortgage) | 9.35 | 4.41 | 7.25 | 0.55 | 0.00 | 6.69 |
| Purulia | Fixed rent (produce/cash) | 9.48 | 4.25 | 7.95 | 7.52 | 5.47 | 7.02 |
| | Crop-sharing | 83.59 | 91.85 | 88.47 | 92.48 | 94.53 | 89.07 |
| | Others (incl. Usufr. Mortgage) | 6.93 | 3.91 | 3.58 | 0.00 | 0.00 | 3.91 |
| Midnapore (West) | Fixed rent (produce/cash) | 11.81 | 8.75 | 5.89 | 1.29 | 0.00 | 9.00 |
| | Crop-sharing | 84.59 | 89.95 | 92.80 | 98.71 | 100.00 | 88.76 |
| | Others (incl. Usufr. Mortgage) | 3.59 | 1.30 | 1.30 | 0.00 | 0.00 | 2.24 |
| Midnapore (East) | Fixed rent (produce/cash) | 8.40 | 4.83 | 6.44 | 1.91 | – | 7.31 |
| | Crop-sharing | 86.83 | 89.77 | 92.67 | 98.09 | – | 88.24 |
| | Others (incl. Usufr. Mortgage) | 4.77 | 5.41 | 0.89 | 0.00 | – | 4.45 |
| West Bengal | Fixed rent (produce/cash) | 12.12 | 9.45 | 6.48 | 4.83 | 6.90 | 9.42 |
| | Crop-sharing | 81.33 | 85.40 | 90.81 | 94.03 | 93.10 | 85.79 |
| | Others (incl. Usufr. Mortgage) | 6.54 | 5.15 | 2.71 | 1.14 | 0.00 | 4.79 |

*Source*: Agricultural Census 1995-96, Vol. 2, Directorate of Agriculture, Govenment of West Bengal.

## Land Reforms

There exits an extensive literature on the land reforms measures adopted and implemented so far by the Left Front Government (LFG) in West Bengal (see, for details, Lieten, 1992; Bhaumik, 1993; Sengupta and Gazdar, 1997; Mishra and Rawal, 2002). Therefore, instead of reviewing the past literature on this subject, we focus our attention here specifically on the progress made so far with regard to two important land reforms programmes by the LFG, which are: (1) Recording of bargadars—the programme known as 'Operation Barga'[31] and (2) Vesting of ceiling surplus land and distribution of the same among the landless and the marginal farmers (land re-distribution programme).

### *Recording of Bargadars*

Table 3.51 presents data on the number of bargadars recorded and area under barga recording till September 30, 2002 in West Bengal and her districts. It is observed that till that date, about 15.08 lakh bargadars have been recorded in the state and they involved 11.09 lakh acres of land. Our calculation shows that the recorded bargadars constituted 11.35 per cent of farm workers (cultivators plus agricultural labourers) of the state, which is sizeable by any means. Further, 7.61 per cent of cultivable area has been under barga in West Bengal. The area per bargadar stands at 0.74 acre. It is also to be noted that for the state as a whole, nearly 42 per cent of bargadars have been Scheduled Castes/Tribes.

We can gather some idea about the concentration of bargadars in the districts by looking at the percentage of bargadars to total farm workers. It is found that Howrah has the highest concentration of bargadars (22.13 per cent). The other districts where the percentage of bargadars to total farm workers has been higher than the state-average are South Dinajpur, Birbhum, Hooghly, Midnapore, Cooch Behar, South 24 Parganas, Burdwan, Jalpaiguri, Malda and Bankura. Table 3.51 also shows that there are inter-district variations with regard to the area per bargadar. While this has been the highest in Jalpaiguri (1.57 acre), it is the lowest in Midnapore (0.40 acre). Further, the districts also varied as regards the composition of the bargadars. While nearly 68 per cent of bargadars belonged to Scheduled Castes/Tribes in Jalpaiguri, the same in Murshidabad is only 19 per cent.

**Table 3.51:** Recording of Bargadars in West Bengal (as on 30.9.2002)

| District | Number of Recorded Bargadars | % of Bargadars to Total Cultivators and Agrl. Labs.* | | Area Under Barga Recording (in Acres) | % of Barga Area to Cultivable Area** | | % of Bargadars as | | | Area per bargadar (in acres) | | | All | |
|---|---|---|---|---|---|---|---|---|---|---|---|---|---|---|
| | | | | | | | Scheduled Castes | Scheduled Tribes | Others | Scheduled Castes | Scheduled Tribes | Others | | |
| Bankura | 116322 | 11.41 | (11) | 66841 | 6.50 | (11) | 27.23 | 10.73 | 62.04 | 0.58 | 0.66 | 0.56 | 0.57 | (15) |
| Birbhum | 112528 | 16.09 | (3) | 113740 | 13.10 | (1) | 41.08 | 15.36 | 43.56 | 1.07 | 1.15 | 0.90 | 1.01 | (3) |
| Burdwan | 132919 | 12.09 | (8) | 115355 | 9.32 | (8) | 33.96 | 13.05 | 52.99 | 0.89 | 1.01 | 0.82 | 0.87 | (7) |
| Cooch Behar | 84724 | 12.15 | (6) | 83387 | 12.16 | (2) | 59.41 | 1.12 | 39.48 | 0.97 | 1.31 | 1.00 | 0.98 | (4) |
| Dakshin Dinajpur | 71831 | 16.17 | (2) | 53406 | 11.23 | (5) | 28.17 | 22.38 | 49.45 | 0.78 | 0.87 | 0.67 | 0.74 | (10) |
| Darjeeling | 12879 | 9.68 | (13) | 17312 | 4.52 | (15) | 32.25 | 23.62 | 44.13 | 1.13 | 1.28 | 1.54 | 1.34 | (2) |
| Hooghly | 113649 | 15.29 | (4) | 62459 | 10.68 | (7) | 33.81 | 11.93 | 54.26 | 0.53 | 0.58 | 0.55 | 0.55 | (16) |
| Howrah | 42754 | 22.13 | (1) | 24845 | 10.70 | (6) | 23.49 | 1.01 | 75.50 | 0.65 | 0.19 | 0.57 | 0.58 | (14) |
| Jalpaiguri | 61314 | 11.96 | (9) | 96484 | 11.27 | (3) | 46.36 | 22.08 | 31.56 | 1.39 | 2.24 | 1.38 | 1.57 | (1) |
| Malda | 81434 | 11.43 | (10) | 78988 | 11.24 | (4) | 24.71 | 24.67 | 50.63 | 1.07 | 1.08 | 0.86 | 0.97 | (5) |
| Midnapore | 299856 | 12.96 | (5) | 119965 | 5.33 | (14) | 19.15 | 8.66 | 72.19 | 0.37 | 0.48 | 0.40 | 0.40 | (17) |
| Murshidabad | 85042 | 9.07 | (15) | 66383 | 6.47 | (12) | 16.73 | 2.72 | 80.55 | 0.83 | 1.28 | 0.75 | 0.78 | (8) |
| Nadia | 64213 | 9.11 | (14) | 46546 | 6.02 | (13) | 32.41 | 2.94 | 64.65 | 0.65 | 0.52 | 0.77 | 0.72 | (11) |
| North 24 Parganas | 74013 | 10.99 | (12) | 48130 | 6.99 | -10 | 28.09 | 14.14 | 57.77 | 0.71 | 0.57 | 0.64 | 0.65 | (13) |
| Purulia | 9141 | 1.21 | (17) | 8337 | 0.76 | (17) | 36.67 | 25.85 | 37.48 | 1.12 | 0.83 | 0.76 | 0.91 | (6) |
| South 24 Parganas | 113255 | 12.14 | (7) | 84607 | 8.52 | -9 | 36.53 | 3.02 | 60.45 | 0.69 | 1.02 | 0.77 | 0.75 | (9) |
| Uttar Dinajpur | 31928 | 4.54 | (16) | 22307 | 3.22 | (16) | 38.58 | 13.80 | 47.62 | 0.56 | 0.73 | 0.80 | 0.70 | (12) |
| West Bengal | 1507802 | 11.35 | | 1109095 | 7.61 | | 30.84 | 10.99 | 58.17 | 0.79 | 0.94 | 0.67 | 0.74 | |

*Notes*: * We have considered here projected numbers of cultivators and agricultural labourers as on 1.10.2002.

** cultivable area = net cropped area + current fallow + other fallow land + culturable waste + misc. tree crops and groves + permanent pastures and other grazing land

*Sources*: (1) *Economic Review 2002-03*, Govt. of West Bengal; (2) *Statistical Abstract 2001-02*, Govt. of West Bengal, BAES.

### *Distribution of Vested Land*

The land re-distribution programme (distribution of ceiling surplus land) in West Bengal has benefited nearly 26.7 lakh persons till September 30, 2002 (Table 3.52).[32] This represents about one-fifth of farm workers (cultivators plus agricultural labourers). Total land involved in this process has been nearly 10.7 lakh acres, which is 7.34 per cent of cultivable area in the state. Area of land distributed per beneficiary for the state stood at 0.40 acre. As in the case of 'Operation Barga' programme, a high percentage of beneficiaries under the land re-distribution programme too are drawn from the categories of Scheduled Castes and Scheduled Tribes (nearly 56 per cent).

There is, of course, wide inter-district variation in terms of achievements under land redistribution programme. Among the districts of West Bengal, the concentration of beneficiaries under this programme (as indicated by the percentage of beneficiaries to total farm workers) has been the highest in Darjeeling (39.06 per cent), while this has been the lowest in Hooghly (8.78 per cent). The other districts where the concentration of beneficiaries under the land re-distribution programme has been above the state-average are Midnapore, Jalpaiguri, Malda, Uttar Dinajpur and Birbhum. As regards the area of land distributed per beneficiary, Dakshin Dinajpur comes first (1.15 acre) while this has been the lowest in Howrah (0.18 acre).

It emerges that the programmes of 'Operation Barga' and land-redistribution of the LFG together involved nearly 4.17 million people (one-third of farm workers) and involved about 15 per cent of cultivable area in West Bengal.[33] Thus, not only these programmes affected a substantial proportion of population but also changed the balance of power in the countryside (Sengupta and Gazdar, 1996, p. 196). This also points to the massive support base of the Left parties in rural areas and explains uninterrupted continuance of the LFG for more than 26 years in West Bengal.

### Agricultural Wages

In this sub-section, we look into the movements of agricultural wages in the decade of 1990s. We also look at inter-district variations in this regard. It is to be noted that due to very active agricultural labourers'

**Table 3.52:** Distribution of Vested Land and Number of Beneficiaries in West Bengal by Districts (as on 30.9.2002)

| District | Total Number of Beneficiaries (Persons) | % of Beneficiaries to Total Cultivators and Agrl. Labs.* | | % of Beneficiaries as | | | Total Area of Land Distributed (in Acres) | Area of Land Distributed as % to Cultivable Area** (in Acres) | | Area of Land Distributed per Beneficiary (in Acres) | |
|---|---|---|---|---|---|---|---|---|---|---|---|
| | | | | Scheduled Castes | Scheduled Tribes | Others | | | | | |
| Bankura | 155559 | 15.27 | (13) | 51.88 | 21.14 | 26.98 | 57005 | 5.54 | (10) | 0.37 | (9) |
| Birbhum | 144067 | 20.60 | (6) | 48.01 | 23.58 | 28.42 | 44033 | 5.07 | (11) | 0.31 | (11) |
| Burdwan | 201639 | 18.34 | (7) | 41.81 | 20.68 | 37.50 | 57284 | 4.63 | (12) | 0.28 | (13) |
| Cooch Behar | 123139 | 17.66 | (8) | 66.45 | 4.08 | 29.46 | 62123 | 9.06 | (6) | 0.50 | (5) |
| Dakshin Dinajpur | 73809 | 16.62 | (11) | 24.95 | 63.19 | 11.86 | 85227 | 17.92 | (1) | 1.15 | (1) |
| Darjeeling | 51950 | 39.06 | (1) | 38.19 | 27.38 | 34.43 | 30853 | 8.06 | (7) | 0.59 | (4) |
| Hooghly | 65257 | 8.78 | (17) | 46.41 | 19.74 | 33.85 | 11938 | 2.04 | (16) | 0.18 | (16) |
| Howrah | 25223 | 13.06 | (14) | 23.36 | 2.14 | 74.50 | 4483 | 1.93 | (17) | 0.18 | (17) |
| Jalpaiguri | 128505 | 25.07 | (3) | 52.20 | 21.60 | 26.20 | 96952 | 11.32 | (2) | 0.75 | (3) |
| Malda | 151371 | 21.24 | (4) | 25.97 | 19.27 | 54.76 | 74920 | 10.66 | (4) | 0.49 | (6) |
| Midnapore | 801955 | 34.65 | (2) | 27.70 | 21.23 | 51.07 | 248507 | 11.04 | (3) | 0.31 | (10) |
| Murshidabad | 146797 | 15.66 | (12) | 21.04 | 5.63 | 73.32 | 42593 | 4.15 | (13) | 0.29 | (12) |
| Nadia | 91884 | 13.03 | (15) | 30.95 | 6.66 | 62.39 | 19955 | 2.58 | (15) | 0.22 | (14) |
| North 24 Parganas | 113782 | 16.89 | (9) | 36.78 | 17.31 | 45.91 | 22850 | 3.32 | (14) | 0.20 | (15) |
| Purulia | 89441 | 11.79 | (16) | 35.54 | 34.35 | 30.11 | 71087 | 6.47 | (9) | 0.79 | (2) |
| South 24 Parganas | 157035 | 16.83 | (10) | 39.86 | 8.24 | 51.89 | 69219 | 6.97 | (8) | 0.44 | (8) |
| Uttar Dinajpur | 144921 | 20.61 | (15) | 52.09 | 14.90 | 33.02 | 70652 | 10.18 | (5) | 0.49 | (7) |
| West Bengal | 2666334 | 20.08 | | 37.13 | 19.29 | 43.58 | 1069680 | 7.34 | | 0.40 | |

*Notes*: * We have considered here projected numbers of cultivators and agricultural labourers as on 1.10.2002.

** cultivable area = net cropped area + current fallow + other fallow land + culturable waste + misc. tree crops and groves + permanent pastures and other grazing land.

*Sources*: (1) *Economic Review 2002-03*, Govt. of West Bengal; (2) *Statistical Abstract 2001-02*, Govt. of West Bengal, BAES.

organization and the panchayati raj system, the revision of agricultural wages takes place even at the village level through consultation with all agencies (landowners, labourers, panchyats etc.) and keeping in view the minimum wages announced by the government. This leads to better enforcement of minimum wages for the agricultural labourers in West Bengal.

In Table 3.53, we present data on both money wages and real wages of agricultural labourers, separately for males and females, in West Bengal as well as the districts.[34] The data on money wages are drawn for the report entitled *Agricultural Wages in India* (various years), which have been deflated by consumer price index numbers for agricultural labourers for West Bengal (at 1960-61 prices) to arrive at the real wages. The important points emerging here are the following:

(1) The money wages for both male and female agricultural workers have increased continuously in West Bengal during the decade 1990s. The money wage (per day) for male workers was Rs. 21.79 in West Bengal in 1990-91 increased to Rs. 61.44 in 1999-2000. The corresponding figures of per day money wages for female workers for the two time points have been Rs. 18.36 and Rs. 49.45 respectively.

(2) There are inter-district variations in money wages of both male and female workers. For example, in 1999-2000, per day money wage of male workers was above the state-average in the districts of Burdwan, Darjeeling, Howrah, Hooghly, Midnapore, Nadia and North and South 24 Parganas most of which have been agriculturally developed. Likewise, in the same year, per day money wage of female workers was above state-average in the districts of Bankura, Burdwan, Darjeeling, Howrah, Hooghly, Jalpaiguri, Midnapore, Murshidabad, Nadia and North and South 24 Parganas.

(3) Over the years, there seems to be a tendency of inter-district variations in wages of agricultural workers (both male and female) declining. This becomes clear from the coefficients of variation in male and female wage computed for different years.

(4) It is found that money wages of male agricultural workers grew at an annual rate of 10.48 per cent during 1990s that is

**Table 3.53A:** Money and Real Wages of Agricultural Labourers in West Bengal

| District | 1990-91 | 1991-92 | 1992-93 | 1993-94 | 1994-95 | 1995-96 | 1996-97 | 1997-98 | 1998-99 | 1999-2000 | Annual Gr. Rate (%) | |
|---|---|---|---|---|---|---|---|---|---|---|---|---|
| **Money Wages: Male Labourers** | | | | | | | | | | | | |
| Bankura | 24.26 | 25.77 | 26.33 | 26.94 | 28.31 | 30.32 | 37.33 | 40.30 | 50.90 | 59.98 | 9.75 | (12) |
| Birbhum | 18.72 | 20.89 | 21.10 | 21.49 | 24.31 | 25.67 | 34.06 | 38.69 | 44.52 | 55.71 | 11.87 | (4) |
| Burdwan | 25.46 | 26.87 | 30.01 | 33.54 | 33.96 | 37.82 | 41.13 | 44.22 | 50.95 | 62.75 | 9.25 | (15) |
| Cooch Behar | 16.98 | 19.67 | 23.96 | 24.39 | 26.76 | 28.13 | 35.94 | 39.21 | 44.94 | 54.29 | 12.07 | (3) |
| Darjeeling | 16.50 | 20.00 | 28.34 | 36.68 | 37.75 | 39.67 | 48.10 | 49.20 | 60.48 | 69.79 | 14.76 | (1) |
| Howrah | 23.54 | 25.19 | 28.21 | 32.29 | 32.92 | 34.86 | 43.76 | 46.16 | 52.66 | 66.88 | 10.90 | (10) |
| Hooghly | 24.54 | 27.95 | 32.28 | 32.02 | 33.13 | 36.56 | 40.00 | 43.43 | 49.43 | 69.04 | 9.42 | (14) |
| Jalpaiguri | 20.00 | 23.73 | 25.93 | 28.13 | 29.00 | 34.70 | 40.41 | 46.11 | 50.57 | 59.21 | 11.64 | (6) |
| Malda | 19.84 | 23.27 | 23.73 | 24.15 | 25.94 | 27.77 | 36.32 | 38.83 | 44.56 | 58.63 | 10.94 | (9) |
| Midnapore | 23.34 | 24.77 | 26.53 | 27.63 | 28.67 | 27.44 | 34.25 | 41.72 | 48.72 | 62.46 | 9.97 | (11) |
| Murshidabad | 19.89 | 22.94 | 23.25 | 25.42 | 27.25 | 29.28 | 39.48 | 42.01 | 47.04 | 60.83 | 11.78 | (5) |
| Nadia | 21.79 | 24.14 | 25.23 | 25.74 | 27.52 | 31.04 | 38.80 | 42.64 | 47.54 | 63.42 | 11.11 | (8) |
| North and South 24 Parganas | 25.45 | 26.90 | 34.91 | 34.39 | 35.36 | 34.87 | 41.82 | 48.01 | 53.81 | 67.92 | 9.61 | (13) |
| Purulia | 16.73 | 20.04 | 21.02 | 22.00 | 22.33 | 23.38 | 31.50 | 33.16 | 38.66 | 54.04 | 11.25 | (7) |
| Uttar and Dakshin Dinajpur | 11.78 | 14.20 | 17.00 | 19.85 | 23.70 | 24.19 | 24.41 | 26.50 | 37.28 | 47.55 | 13.44 | (2) |
| West Bengal | 21.79 | 23.99 | 26.99 | 28.17 | 29.61 | 31.00 | 37.51 | 41.69 | 48.20 | 61.44 | 10.48 | |
| **Coefficient of Variation** | 19.31 | 15.65 | 17.68 | 18.48 | 15.59 | 16.42 | 14.75 | 14.06 | 12.09 | 10.28 | | |
| **Money Wages: Female Labourers** | | | | | | | | | | | | |
| Bankura | 21.49 | 22.50 | 20.67 | 21.18 | 22.21 | 23.93 | 30.44 | 34.44 | 40.92 | 49.94 | 9.39 | (11) |
| Birbhum | 16.49 | 18.26 | 19.61 | 19.60 | 20.50 | 22.00 | 29.13 | 34.78 | 37.69 | 47.78 | 11.38 | (6) |
| Burdwan | 23.42 | 22.79 | 24.05 | 23.62 | 24.33 | 27.70 | 32.33 | 36.18 | 42.15 | 53.46 | 9.00 | (14) |
| Cooch Behar | 13.38 | 15.84 | 17.06 | 17.53 | 20.06 | 22.40 | 29.12 | 31.72 | 36.38 | 44.97 | 13.01 | (3) |
| Darjeeling | 13.00 | 15.00 | 22.50 | 30.00 | 30.50 | 31.79 | 35.67 | 36.99 | 44.08 | 52.39 | 14.02 | (1) |
| Howrah | 15.90 | 17.00 | 20.00 | 22.38 | 25.00 | 27.59 | 33.63 | 36.30 | 41.54 | 51.89 | 12.85 | (4) |

*(Contd.)*

**Table 3.53A** *(Contd.)*

| *District* | *1990-91* | *1991-92* | *1992-93* | *1993-94* | *1994-95* | *1995-96* | *1996-97* | *1997-98* | *1998-99* | *1999-00* | *Annual Gr. Rate (%)* | |
|---|---|---|---|---|---|---|---|---|---|---|---|---|
| Hooghly | 21.35 | 24.33 | 25.89 | 24.48 | 25.94 | 28.96 | 31.97 | 34.99 | 40.38 | 58.29 | 9.09 | (13) |
| Jalpaiguri | 15.00 | 21.31 | 22.57 | 23.83 | 25.00 | 29.38 | 33.75 | 38.13 | 44.69 | 53.78 | 12.43 | (5) |
| Malda | 15.65 | 19.36 | 19.51 | 19.28 | 20.36 | 21.65 | 29.53 | 31.94 | 35.04 | 45.24 | 10.61 | (9) |
| Midnapore | 20.78 | 22.65 | 22.49 | 22.83 | 23.72 | 22.01 | 26.25 | 34.49 | 40.33 | 51.68 | 8.92 | (15) |
| Murshidabad | 17.11 | 19.56 | 22.00 | 22.39 | 21.44 | 23.24 | 30.19 | 32.58 | 38.64 | 51.57 | 10.69 | (8) |
| Nadia | 17.75 | 19.08 | 20.35 | 20.50 | 20.22 | 22.54 | 30.30 | 33.49 | 38.04 | 50.79 | 10.95 | (7) |
| North and South 24 Parganas | 19.28 | 21.61 | 26.71 | 25.89 | 25.42 | 27.24 | 32.92 | 37.67 | 41.46 | 52.78 | 9.78 | (10) |
| Purulia | 16.53 | 20.01 | 18.51 | 17.00 | 16.76 | 19.67 | 22.50 | 25.89 | 30.72 | 46.64 | 9.10 | (12) |
| Uttar and Dakshin Dinajpur | 9.74 | 11.23 | 12.59 | 14.74 | 16.64 | 17.51 | 20.08 | 20.85 | 29.53 | 39.16 | 13.81 | (2) |
| West Bengal | 18.36 | 20.38 | 20.97 | 21.06 | 21.90 | 23.38 | 28.24 | 32.49 | 38.02 | 49.45 | 9.95 | |
| **Coefficient of Variation** | 21.48 | 18.04 | 16.71 | 17.63 | 16.34 | 16.43 | 14.09 | 13.78 | 11.34 | 9.25 | | |
| **Real Wages (at 1960-61 Prices): Male Labourers** | | | | | | | | | | | | |
| Bankura | 2.88 | 2.63 | 2.65 | 2.43 | 2.38 | 2.30 | 2.64 | 2.72 | 2.96 | 3.45 | 1.69 | (12) |
| Birbhum | 2.22 | 2.14 | 2.12 | 1.94 | 2.04 | 1.95 | 2.41 | 2.61 | 2.59 | 3.21 | 3.81 | (4) |
| Burdwan | 3.02 | 2.75 | 3.02 | 3.03 | 2.86 | 2.87 | 2.91 | 2.98 | 2.96 | 3.61 | 1.18 | (15) |
| Cooch Behar | 2.02 | 2.01 | 2.41 | 2.20 | 2.25 | 2.13 | 2.54 | 2.64 | 2.61 | 3.13 | 4.01 | (3) |
| Darjeeling | 1.96 | 2.04 | 2.85 | 3.31 | 3.17 | 3.01 | 3.40 | 3.32 | 3.52 | 4.02 | 6.69 | (1) |
| Howrah | 2.80 | 2.58 | 2.84 | 2.92 | 2.77 | 2.65 | 3.09 | 3.11 | 3.06 | 3.85 | 2.84 | (10) |
| Hooghly | 2.91 | 2.86 | 3.25 | 2.89 | 2.79 | 2.77 | 2.83 | 2.93 | 2.88 | 3.98 | 1.36 | (14) |
| Jalpaiguri | 2.38 | 2.43 | 2.61 | 2.54 | 2.44 | 2.63 | 2.86 | 3.11 | 2.94 | 3.41 | 3.58 | (6) |
| Malda | 2.36 | 2.38 | 2.39 | 2.18 | 2.18 | 2.11 | 2.57 | 2.62 | 2.59 | 3.38 | 2.88 | (9) |
| Midnapore | 2.77 | 2.53 | 2.67 | 2.50 | 2.41 | 2.08 | 2.42 | 2.81 | 2.83 | 3.60 | 1.91 | (11) |
| Murshidabad | 2.36 | 2.35 | 2.34 | 2.30 | 2.29 | 2.22 | 2.79 | 2.83 | 2.74 | 3.50 | 3.72 | (5) |
| Nadia | 2.59 | 2.47 | 2.54 | 2.33 | 2.31 | 2.36 | 2.74 | 2.87 | 2.77 | 3.65 | 3.05 | (8) |
| North and South 24 Parganas | 3.02 | 2.75 | 3.51 | 3.11 | 2.97 | 2.65 | 2.95 | 3.24 | 3.13 | 3.91 | 1.54 | (13) |
| Purulia | 1.99 | 2.05 | 2.11 | 1.99 | 1.88 | 1.77 | 2.23 | 2.23 | 2.25 | 3.11 | 3.18 | (7) |

*(Contd.)*

**Table 3.53A** *(Contd.)*

| District | 1990-91 | 1991-92 | 1992-93 | 1993-94 | 1994-95 | 1995-96 | 1996-97 | 1997-98 | 1998-99 | 1999-00 | Annual Gr. Rate (%) | |
|---|---|---|---|---|---|---|---|---|---|---|---|---|
| Uttar and Dakshin Dinajpur | 1.40 | 1.45 | 1.71 | 1.79 | 1.99 | 1.84 | 1.72 | 1.79 | 2.17 | 2.74 | 5.38 | (2) |
| West Bengal | 2.59 | 2.45 | 2.72 | 2.54 | 2.49 | 2.35 | 2.65 | 2.81 | 2.80 | 3.54 | 2.42 | |
| **Coefficient of Variation** | 19.31 | 15.65 | 17.68 | 18.48 | 15.59 | 16.42 | 14.75 | 14.06 | 12.09 | 10.28 | | |
| **Real Wages (at 1960-61 Prices): Female Labourers** | | | | | | | | | | | | |
| Bankura | 2.55 | 2.30 | 2.08 | 1.91 | 1.87 | 1.82 | 2.15 | 2.32 | 2.38 | 2.88 | 1.33 | (11) |
| Birbhum | 1.96 | 1.87 | 1.97 | 1.77 | 1.72 | 1.67 | 2.06 | 2.34 | 2.19 | 2.75 | 3.31 | (6) |
| Burdwan | 2.78 | 2.33 | 2.42 | 2.13 | 2.05 | 2.10 | 2.28 | 2.44 | 2.45 | 3.08 | 0.93 | (14) |
| Cooch Behar | 1.59 | 1.62 | 1.72 | 1.58 | 1.69 | 1.70 | 2.06 | 2.14 | 2.12 | 2.59 | 4.95 | (3) |
| Darjeeling | 1.54 | 1.53 | 2.26 | 2.71 | 2.57 | 2.41 | 2.52 | 2.49 | 2.56 | 3.02 | 5.96 | (1) |
| Howrah | 1.89 | 1.74 | 2.01 | 2.02 | 2.10 | 2.09 | 2.38 | 2.45 | 2.42 | 2.99 | 4.78 | (4) |
| Hooghly | 2.54 | 2.49 | 2.60 | 2.21 | 2.18 | 2.20 | 2.26 | 2.36 | 2.35 | 3.36 | 1.03 | (13) |
| Jalpaiguri | 1.78 | 2.18 | 2.27 | 2.15 | 2.10 | 2.23 | 2.38 | 2.57 | 2.60 | 3.10 | 4.36 | (5) |
| Malda | 1.86 | 1.98 | 1.96 | 1.74 | 1.71 | 1.64 | 2.09 | 2.15 | 2.04 | 2.61 | 2.55 | (9) |
| Midnapore | 2.47 | 2.32 | 2.26 | 2.06 | 1.99 | 1.67 | 1.85 | 2.32 | 2.35 | 2.98 | 0.86 | (15) |
| Murshidabad | 2.03 | 2.00 | 2.21 | 2.02 | 1.80 | 1.76 | 2.13 | 2.20 | 2.25 | 2.97 | 2.62 | (8) |
| Nadia | 2.11 | 1.95 | 2.05 | 1.85 | 1.70 | 1.71 | 2.14 | 2.26 | 2.21 | 2.93 | 2.88 | (7) |
| North and South 24 Parganas | 2.29 | 2.21 | 2.69 | 2.34 | 2.14 | 2.07 | 2.33 | 2.54 | 2.41 | 3.04 | 1.71 | (10) |
| Purulia | 1.96 | 2.05 | 1.86 | 1.54 | 1.41 | 1.49 | 1.59 | 1.74 | 1.79 | 2.69 | 1.04 | (12) |
| Uttar and Dakshin Dinajpur | 1.16 | 1.15 | 1.27 | 1.33 | 1.40 | 1.33 | 1.42 | 1.40 | 1.72 | 2.26 | 5.75 | (2) |
| West Bengal | 2.18 | 2.08 | 2.11 | 1.90 | 1.84 | 1.77 | 2.00 | 2.19 | 2.21 | 2.85 | 1.89 | |
| **Coefficient of Variation** | 21.48 | 18.04 | 16.71 | 17.63 | 16.34 | 16.43 | 14.09 | 13.78 | 11.34 | 9.25 | | |

*Note*: Real wages have been computed by using consumer price index numbers for agricultural labourers for West Bengal. Figures in brackets are ranks.

*Source*: Government of India, *Agricultural Wages in India*, various years, Directorate of Economics and Statistics.

slightly higher than 9.10 per cent growth rate recorded for the female agricultural workers.[35] It is also interesting to note that, in the decade of 1990s, male agricultural wages grew at a higher rate in relatively backward districts of West Bengal (e.g. Darjeeling, Uttar and Dakshin Dinajpur, Cooch Behar, Birbhum, Murshidabad, Jalpaiguri and Purulia) as compared to the advanced ones (Burdwan, Hooghly, North and South 24 Parganas, Bankura, Midnapore and Howrah). Almost a similar picture is observable with regard to the growth of wages of female agricultural workers.

(5) It is also encouraging to note that real wages of both male and female agricultural workers registered positive growth in the state as well as all the districts in the decade of 1990s.[36] However, the growth of real wages for the male agricultural workers (2.42 per cent) was higher than the same for female agricultural workers (1.89 per cent). Once again, among the districts of West Bengal, the districts known to be agriculturally backward recorded relatively higher growth of real wages of agricultural workers (both male and female) as compared to the advanced ones.

It clearly emerges that not only both money and real wages of agricultural workers increased rather consistently in West Bengal and her districts in the decade of 1990s but there has been also a tendency of inter-district variation in terms of agricultural wages reducing.

### *Male-Female Differential in Wages*

We have noted above that the male agricultural workers receive higher wages as compared to their female counterparts, which is indicative of discrimination the female workers are confronted with in the agricultural labour market. This discrimination is visible in all the districts though at varying degrees. The issue we want to address further is: Is the wage gap between female and male agricultural workers declining in the state?

Table 3.53B presents information on the ratio of female agricultural workers' wages to that of males. It is found that for the state as a whole, while the ratio of female agricultural workers' wage to male agricultural workers' wage was 0.84 in 1990-91, the same

**Table 3.53B:** Ratio of Female Labourers' Wages (Money/Real) to Male Labourers' Wages

| *District* | *1990-91* | *1991-92* | *1992-93* | *1993-94* | *1994-95* | *1995-96* | *1996-97* | *1997-98* | *1998-99* | *1999-00* | *Trend* |
|---|---|---|---|---|---|---|---|---|---|---|---|
| Bankura | 0.89 | 0.87 | 0.79 | 0.79 | 0.78 | 0.79 | 0.82 | 0.85 | 0.80 | 0.83 | -ve, insig. |
| Birbhum | 0.88 | 0.87 | 0.93 | 0.91 | 0.84 | 0.86 | 0.86 | 0.90 | 0.85 | 0.86 | -ve, sig. |
| Burdwan | 0.92 | 0.85 | 0.80 | 0.70 | 0.72 | 0.73 | 0.79 | 0.82 | 0.83 | 0.85 | -ve, insig. |
| Cooch Behar | 0.79 | 0.81 | 0.71 | 0.72 | 0.75 | 0.80 | 0.81 | 0.81 | 0.81 | 0.83 | +ve, sig. |
| Darjeeling | 0.79 | 0.75 | 0.79 | 0.82 | 0.81 | 0.80 | 0.74 | 0.75 | 0.73 | 0.75 | -ve, sig. |
| Howrah | 0.68 | 0.67 | 0.71 | 0.69 | 0.76 | 0.79 | 0.77 | 0.79 | 0.79 | 0.78 | +ve, sig. |
| Hooghly | 0.87 | 0.87 | 0.80 | 0.76 | 0.78 | 0.79 | 0.80 | 0.81 | 0.82 | 0.84 | -ve, insig. |
| Jalpaiguri | 0.75 | 0.90 | 0.87 | 0.85 | 0.86 | 0.85 | 0.84 | 0.83 | 0.88 | 0.91 | +ve, sig. |
| Malda | 0.79 | 0.83 | 0.82 | 0.80 | 0.78 | 0.78 | 0.81 | 0.82 | 0.79 | 0.77 | -ve, insig. |
| Midnapore | 0.89 | 0.91 | 0.85 | 0.83 | 0.83 | 0.80 | 0.77 | 0.83 | 0.83 | 0.83 | -ve, sig. |
| Murshidabad | 0.86 | 0.85 | 0.95 | 0.88 | 0.79 | 0.79 | 0.76 | 0.78 | 0.82 | 0.85 | -ve, sig. |
| Nadia | 0.81 | 0.79 | 0.81 | 0.80 | 0.73 | 0.73 | 0.78 | 0.79 | 0.80 | 0.80 | -ve, insig. |
| North and South 24 Parganas | 0.76 | 0.80 | 0.77 | 0.75 | 0.72 | 0.78 | 0.79 | 0.78 | 0.77 | 0.78 | +ve, insig. |
| Purulia | 0.99 | 1.00 | 0.88 | 0.77 | 0.75 | 0.84 | 0.71 | 0.78 | 0.79 | 0.86 | -ve, sig. |
| Uttar and Dakshin Dinajpur | 0.83 | 0.79 | 0.74 | 0.74 | 0.70 | 0.72 | 0.82 | 0.79 | 0.79 | 0.82 | +ve, insig. |
| West Bengal | 0.84 | 0.85 | 0.78 | 0.75 | 0.74 | 0.75 | 0.75 | 0.78 | 0.79 | 0.80 | -ve, insig. |

reduced to 0.80 in 1999-2000. This is indicative of female-male wage gap widening in the state; the females getting increasingly lesser wages compared to the males. In order to know on a firmer basis whether such a tendency has been widespread in the state, we have fitted some regressions separately for each district.[37] We find that both in West Bengal as well as in 10 out of 15 districts, there has been a declining trend of the ratio of female wage to male wage in the decade of 1990s (though not always statistically significant). This implies that, in the agricultural labour market, there has been a tendency of female-male wage gap widening in the decade of 1990s. The other implication of this finding is that although both the male and female agricultural workers in the state gained through increase in their wages (money/real) in 1990s, the females have gained relatively less as compared to the males.

In the context of discussion on agricultural wages in West Bengal, it is also to be noted that not only the agricultural labourers have been able to enforce the minimum wages provisions but also they have been able to destroy the deleterious feudal/semi-feudal systems that propagate bondage of labour, extracting *begar* (free labour services) etc. This view gets echoed in almost all the village studies conducted by the LBSNAA in 1990s.

## ANTI-POVERTY AND RURAL DEVELOPMENT SCHEMES

This section concentrates on various anti-poverty and rural development schemes that are being implemented in the state and their implications towards reducing rural poverty. We begin by looking at the Anti-Poverty and Rural Development Schemes that are in vogue currently. We then examine the performance of the state towards implementation of the schemes, particularly the ones relating to self-employment and wage employment. Finally, we furnish the poverty profiles for the state to understand how the situation with regard to rural poverty has changed in West Bengal over the years.

### The Schemes

The various anti-poverty and rural development schemes could be classified under three broad headings: (1) Self-Employment Schemes, (2) Wage Employment Schemes, and (3) Other Schemes.

## *Self-Employment Schemes*

The Integrated Rural Development Programme (IRDP) was the first major self-employment programme under implementation in all blocks of the country from 2nd October 1980 and continued till 31st March 1999.[38] This programme aimed at providing assistance to the beneficiaries in the form of bank credit and Government subsidy to help them create income-generating assets. The beneficiaries were chosen from families below poverty line (BPL). In rural areas, they comprised the landless, marginal and small farmers, agricultural labourers, rural artisans and so on. With the objective of further strengthening the IRDP, few other programmes were initiated, namely the scheme for Training of Rural Youth for Self-Employment (TRYSEM) [started in August 1979], Development of Women and Children in Rural Areas (DWCRA) [started in 1982-83], Supply of Improved Toolkits to Rural Artisans (SITRA) [started in July 1992] and Ganga Kalyan Yojana (GKY) [started in 1996-97]. However, all these programmes have been amalgamated into a single self-employment programme, namely the Swarnajayanti Gram Swarozgar Yojana (SGSY) in April 1999. The SGSY is seen as a holistic self-employment programme with the objective of establishing a large number of micro-enterprises in rural areas.

## *Wage-Employment Schemes*[39]

Right from early 1960s several schemes have been conceived and implemented by the Governement in rural areas with the objective of providing additional employment opportunities to the rural poor. Among the early schemes are the Rural Manpower Programme (taken up from 1960-61), Crash Scheme for Rural Employment (CSRE) [for three years from April 1971], Rural Works Programme (RWP) [from 1970-71], Food for Work Programme (FWP) [from April 1977], National Rural Employment Programme (NREP) [from October 1980] and Rural Landless Employment Guarantee Programme (RLEGP) [from August 1983].

From April 1989, a new scheme is introduced by merging the NREP and RLEGP, which is named the Jawahar Rojgar Yojana (JRY). The primary objective of JRY was to "generate additional gainful employment for the unemployed and under-employed persons, both men and women, in the rural areas through creation of rural economic infrastructure, community and social assets particularly, in favour of rural poor and more so, with an aim at improving quality of life in rural areas" (Planning Commission, 2001, p. 16). The scheme was implemented with a funding pattern of 80 : 20 between the Centre and State. It is to be noted that two other programmes, namely the Indira Awas Yojana (IAY) and the Million Wells Scheme (MWS) were initially part of JRY. However, since January 1996, these have been made independent schemes. The JRY was restructured further w.e.f. April 1999 and is named as Jawahar Gram Samriddhi Yojana (JGSY). The aim of JGSY is "creation of demand-driven community infrastructure that would increase opportunities for sustained employment among the rural poor". While people below the poverty line constituted the target group under the JGSY, preference is given to members of Scheduled Castes and Scheduled Tribes. Another (supplementary) objective of this scheme has been to generate supplementary employment for the rural unemployed poor.

Another important wage-employment scheme is the Employment Assurance Scheme (EAS) that was launched in October 1993; by 1997-98, it was being implemented in all the rural blocks of the country. The main objectives of EAS are: (1) creation of additional wage employment opportunities for the rural poor living below the poverty line through manual work, during periods of acute shortage of wage employment and (2) creation of durable community, social and economic assets, to sustain future employment and development. Resources under the scheme are shared between the Centre and the States in the proportion 75 : 25. The Central assistance under the EAS is released directly to the District Rural Development Agencies (DRDAs)/Zilla Parishads. The DRDAs will release 30 per cent of the district allocation to the Zilla Parishad and 70 per cent to the Panchayat Samitis. It is to be noted that all works under EAS are to be executed by the respective 'Implementing Agencies' and in no case contractors can be engaged. The works under EAS have also to be labour-intensive having a wage-material ratio 60 : 40. As regards the works that would receive priority under this scheme are soil and moisture conservation, minor irrigation, rejuvenation of drinking water sources and augmentation of ground water, traditional water harvesting structures, works related to watershed schemes (not watershed development), construction of rural roads (linking villages with other villages/block headquarters) and roads linking the villages with agricultural fields, drainage works, forestry etc.

Finally, the Sampoorna Grameen Rojgar Yojana (SGRY) was launched in September 2001. The schemes of JGSY and EAS have been fully integrated with this scheme, w.e.f. 1-4-2002. The objective of SGRY is to provide additional wage employment along with food security, creation of durable community, social and economic assets and infrastructure development in the rural areas. The scheme envisages generation of 100 crore mandays of employment in a year in the country. The cost of the programme is to be shared between the Centre and the State on a cost sharing ratio 87.5:12.5 (including foodgrains component).

## *Other Schemes*

Among several other rural development schemes are:

- **The Indira Awas Yojana (IAY)**—As pointed out earlier, from January 1996 this has been conceived as an independent scheme. This scheme aims at providing dwelling units, free of cost to the poor families of the Scheduled Castes, Scheduled Tribes, freed bonded labourers, and also the non-SC/ST persons below the poverty line in rural areas. This scheme is funded on a cost-sharing basis of 75 : 25 between the Centre and the States.
- **Pradhan Mantri Gramodaya Yojana (PMGY)**—This is launched in 2000-01 to achieve the objective of sustainable human development at the village level. Initially, PMGY focused on village level development in five critical areas: primary health, primary education, rural drinking water and rural shelter and nutrition. Rural electrification has been added as an additional component from 2001-02.
- **Pradhan Mantri Gramodaya Yojana (Gramin Awas) (PMGY-GA)**—This scheme seeks to achieve the objective of sustainable habitat development at the village level.
- **Pradhan Mantri Gramodaya Yojana (Rural Drinking Water Project) (PMGY-RDWP)**—Under this programme, a minimum of 25 per cent of the total allocation is to be utilized by the respective States/UTs on projects/schemes for water conservation, water harvesting, water recharge and sustainability of the drinking water sources in respect of areas under Desert Development Programme/Drought Prone Areas Programme.

- **Pradhan Mantri Gram Sadak Yojana (PMGSY)**—This was launched on 25th December 2000 to provide road connectivity of every village with a population of over 1000 persons by 2003 and with a population of upto 500 by 2007. The present source of funding for PMGSY is the diesel cess, 50 per cent of which is earmarked for this programme. Efforts are underway to raise additional resources with financial assistance from the World Bank and the Asian Development Bank.
- **Antyodaya Anna Yojana (AAY)**—The Prime Minister launched this scheme on 25th December 2001. Under this scheme, 1 crore poorest families out of the BPL families covered under the Targetted Public Distribution System are identified. 25 kgs. of foodgrains were made available to each eligible family at a highly subsidized rate of Rs. 2 per kg. for wheat and Rs. 3 per kg. for rice. This quantity has been raised from 25 to 35 kgs. w.e.f. April 2002 for a period of one year.
- **Annapurna**—This scheme was launched on 1st April 2000 as a fully Centrally Sponsored Scheme. It aims at providing food security to meet the requirement of those senior citizens who though eligible for pension under the National Old Age Pension Scheme, are not getting the same. 10 kgs. of foodgrains per person per month are supplied free of cost. The scheme has been transferred to the State Plan from 2002-03.
- **Jai Prakash Rozgar Guarantee Yojana (JPRGY)**—The scheme seeks to provide guaranteed employment to the unemployed in the most distressed districts of the country. However, operational modalities for launcing of the scheme were still being worked out in March 2003.

## Implementation of Self-Employment and Wage Employment Schemes

We have noted above that various anti-poverty and rural development schemes are in operation in the state, as elsewhere. We have also noted that some of the earlier schemes have been re-modelled and new schemes introduced recently. However, it is not possible to assess the performance of all these schemes individually primarily because of paucity of detailed data. In this sub-section, we concentrate merely on the performance of the state with regard to implementation of two of the important schemes, those for self-employment and wage employment, during the decade of 1990s.[40]

As noted above, the most important self-employment scheme has been the IRDP, which after subsequent restructuring is renamed as SGSY. Table 3.54 presents data indicating performance of West Bengal as regards implementation of self-employment schemes in rural areas during past 10 years or so. It clearly emerges that after 1995-96, the number of rural families covered in this scheme drastically declined.[41] While in 1995-96 nearly 1.62 lakh families have been covered by the self-employment schemes, the number of families covered dropped to 7,351 only in 2001-01. The situation does not appear to have improved since then as in 2002-03 (upto November 2002) only 16,725 rural families in the state have benefited through self-employment schemes. The highly unsatisfactory performance towards implementation of self-employment schemes in West Bengal has been due, *inter alia*, to the banks' reluctance to supply credit for this purpose.

**Table 3.54:** Performance under Self-Employment Schemes in Rural West Bengal (IRDP/SGSY)

| *Year* | *Credit Disbursed (Rs. in lakh)* | *Subsidy Disbursed (Rs. in lakh)* | *Physical Achievements* | | *Cumulative Number of Families/ Swarojgaries Covered Since 1992-93* |
|---|---|---|---|---|---|
| | | | *No. of Families/ Swarojgaries Covered* | *Index (Base: 1992-93 = 100)* | |
| 1992-93 | 5788.00 | 104.49 | 154457 | 100 | 154457 |
| 1993-94 | 7542.00 | 42.99 | 73818 | 48 | 228275 |
| 1994-95 | 7478.00 | 82.86 | 159722 | 103 | 387997 |
| 1995-96 | 9472.64 | 5817.71 | 161724 | 105 | 549721 |
| 1996-97 | 8552.94 | 4485.75 | 110280 | 71 | 660001 |
| 1997-98 | 7480.25 | 3755.94 | 91733 | 59 | 751734 |
| 1998-99 | 6480.70 | 3141.78 | 71134 | 46 | 822868 |
| 1999-2000 | 7199.14 | 3466.73 | 75981 | 49 | 898849 |
| 2000-2001 | 766.66 | 380.68 | 7351 | 5 | 906200 |
| 2001-2002 | 2006.38 | 1016.68 | 15480 | 10 | 921680 |
| 2002-2003 (Upto November 2002) | 2406.77 | 1229.99 | 16725 | 11 | 938405 |

*Note*: IRDP (started in October 1980) has been renamed as SGSY from 1999-2000.

*Source*: Dept. of Panchayats and Rural Development, Govt. of West Bengal.

The performance of the state of West Bengal towards implementation of wage employment schemes in recent years could be understood in terms of data presented in Table 3.55. It is found that like self-employment schemes, the state suffered a down turn in the implementation of wage employment schemes in rural areas from 1995-96 onwards. Total employment generation (in mandays) under wage employment scheme has declined continuously during the period 1995-96 to 2001-02.[42] As a result, employment days available on average to an agricultural labourer (7.07 days in 1995-96), which was already very low, declined further to 2.48 days only in 2001-02.[43]

**Table 3.55:** Performance under Rural Wage Employment Schemes in West Bengal

| *Year* | *Expenditure (Rs. in lakh)* | *Total Employment Generation* | | *Estimated Number of Agrl. Labs.* | *Employment Days per Agrl. Labs* |
|---|---|---|---|---|---|
| | | *Mandays (in lakh)* | *Index (Base: 1991-92 = 100)* | | |
| 1991-92 | 19342.00 | 492.00 | 100 | 5383274 | 9.14 |
| 1992-93 | 21413.00 | 525.55 | 107 | 5454156 | 9.64 |
| 1993-94 | 27103.00 | 556.17 | 113 | 5628106 | 9.88 |
| 1994-95 | 30971.00 | 600.40 | 122 | 5807604 | 10.34 |
| 1995-96 | 31235.00 | 423.61 | 86 | 5992826 | 7.07 |
| 1996-97 | 25091.04 | 348.91 | 71 | 6183955 | 5.64 |
| 1997-98 | 24234.02 | 300.85 | 61 | 6381181 | 4.71 |
| 1998-99 | 22639.27 | 243.68 | 50 | 6584696 | 3.70 |
| 1999-2000 | 25951.52 | 241.55 | 49 | 6794702 | 3.55 |
| 2000-2001 | 29870.01 | 248.32 | 50 | 7011406 | 3.54 |
| 2001-2002 | 21145.87 | 179.18 | 36 | 7235021 | 2.48 |
| 2002-2003 (Up to November 2002) | 17347.67 | 250.73 | 51 | 7311133 | 3.43 |

*Note*: Since April 1989, the wage employment schemes are JRY, JGSY, EAS and SGRY.

*Source*: Dept. of Panchayats and Rural Development, Govt. of West Bengal.

The above discussion leads to the conclusion that as regards implementation of self-employment and wage employment schemes in rural area, the performance of West Bengal has been highly unsatisfactory, particularly since the middle of 1990s.

## Poverty in Rural West Bengal

In this sub-section, we focus our attention on changing poverty situation in rural West Bengal in recent years. There are two sources of data that we can utilise for this purpose. First, we have estimates of persons below poverty line in rural areas for the state as a whole that are computed by the Planning Commission for several years. We also have recent estimates of rural families that are lying 'below poverty line' (BPL) in West Bengal and her districts. These estimates have been based on recently conducted BPL surveys and are released by the Department of Panchayats and Rural Development (DPRD), Government of West Bengal, through its website. It is to be noted that the two sources adopted divergent methodologies for estimating poverty in the state and as such these data are not comparable. Nevertheless, we could rely on the Planning Commission estimates for obtaining some idea about temporal changes in poverty in rural areas of the state while the data from DPRD could be utilized for comparing poverty situations cross-sectionally, in different districts as well as among various classes/castes.

The Planning Commission's data on rural poverty in West Bengal are presented in Table 3.56. It is observed that the incidence of poverty in rural West Bengal has declined drastically during past 20 years or so, from 63.05 per cent in 1983 to 31.85 per cent in 1999-2000. It is also encouraging to note that the absolute number of rural persons living under poverty has also gone down over the years. However, it also needs to be noted that even in 1999-2000, 180.11 lakh persons in rural areas of West Bengal lived under poverty. Further, in spite of significant decline in the incidence of rural poverty in the state, in the year 1999-2000, the percentage of persons living under poverty (31.85 per cent) has been above the all-India figure of 27.09 per cent.

We now consider the DPRD data on poverty. It needs to be mentioned that the DPRD released data on number of families under the poverty line (called BPL families) for rural and urban areas together and also their distribution of poor persons between different caste/occupation groups. These data are available at the district level. Hence, these data could also be utilized to identify the most poverty-stricken districts of the state. The DPRD data on poverty are presented in Table 3.57. It is found that, as of 30-10-2002, 115.9 lakh families in the state are designated as the BPL families of which 86.67 lakh (nearly 75 per cent) belonged to the rural areas. It is also found that

**Table 3.56:** Number and Percentage of Population Below Poverty Line in West Bengal and All-India [Rural Areas only]

| *Year* | *Poverty Line (Rs.) ([per Capita, per Month)* | *No. of Persons Below Poverty Line (Lakh)* | *% of Persons* |
|---|---|---|---|
| *West Bengal* | | | |
| 1983 | 105.55 | 268.60 | 63.05 |
| 1993-94 | 220.74 | 209.90 | 40.80 |
| 1999-2000 | 350.17 | 180.11 | 31.85 |
| *All-India* | | | |
| 1983 | 89.50 | 2519.57 | 45.65 |
| 1993-94 | 205.84 | 2440.31 | 37.27 |
| 1999-2000 | 327.56 | 1932.43 | 27.09 |

*Source*: Planning Commission (2002), *National Human Development Report*, Govt. of India, pp. 164-166.

of the total BPL families (rural and urban combined) in the state, 34.26 per cent belonged to Scheduled Castes and 9.01 per cent to Scheduled Tribes. It is also to be noted nearly 54 per cent of BPL families are drawn from the category of agricultural labourers alone. Thus, the problem of poverty in West Bengal (as also in other states) has been relatively more prevalent among the families with inferior caste/class positions. If we look at the percentage of BPL families (rural and urban combined) for the districts, it appears that the most poverty-stricken districts (in descending order of percentage of BPL families) are Darjeeling, Cooch Behar, Birbhum, Murshidabad, Purulia, Dakshin Dinajpur, Bankura, Uttar Dinajpur, Malda, North 24 Parganas and South 24 Parganas. In all these districts, the percentage of BPL families has been above the state-average. Most of these districts (except North 24 Parganas) are known to be agriculturally backward. Further, as the percentage of BPL families has been the lowest in Burdwan which is one of the most agriculturally progressive districts of the state, it might be concluded that poverty in rural areas could reduce in the future with the advancement of agriculture further.

## SOCIAL STRUCTURE

In this section, we seek to examine social structures in rural West Bengal and her districts. This we do by using 1991 Census data on caste and region composition of rural population.[44] As regards the caste distribution, Table 3.58 shows that 27.56 per cent of rural

**Table 3.57:** Poverty in West Bengal by Districts According to BPL Survey (as on 30.10.02)

| District | BPL Families (Rural and Urban Combined) | | | Regionwise Distribution of BPL Families (%) | | | | Caste-wise Distribution of BPL Families (%) | | | Occupation-wise Distribution of BPL Families (%) | | | | |
|---|---|---|---|---|---|---|---|---|---|---|---|---|---|---|---|
| | No. (in lakh) | % to Total Families | | Rural | | Urban | | Sh. Castes | Sh. Tribes | General | Agrl. Labs. | Marginal Farmers | Small Farmers | Rural Artisans | Others |
| | | | | No. (in lakh) | % | No. (in lakh) | % | | | | | | | | |
| Bankura | 5.36 | 42.49 | (7) | 4.34 | 81.00 | 1.02 | 19.00 | 48.98 | 13.73 | 37.29 | 62.90 | 10.75 | 3.88 | 3.47 | 19.00 |
| Birbhum | 5.43 | 44.03 | (3) | 1.43 | 26.38 | 3.99 | 73.62 | 26.41 | 6.38 | 67.21 | 10.50 | 7.24 | 2.45 | 6.20 | 73.62 |
| Burdwan | 9.16 | 26.24 | (18) | 7.75 | 84.60 | 1.41 | 15.40 | 55.53 | 13.67 | 30.80 | 64.79 | 10.30 | 0.12 | 9.38 | 15.40 |
| Cooch Behar | 4.75 | 46.00 | (2) | 3.78 | 79.62 | 0.97 | 20.38 | 50.86 | 0.51 | 48.64 | 49.82 | 15.01 | 10.67 | 4.12 | 20.38 |
| Darjeeling* | 1.82 | 46.44 | (1) | 1.35 | 74.37 | 0.47 | 25.63 | 21.13 | 14.08 | 64.79 | 32.80 | 16.91 | 18.38 | 6.29 | 25.63 |
| Dakshin Dinajpur | 2.63 | 43.55 | (6) | 0.90 | 34.18 | 1.73 | 65.82 | 29.82 | 13.46 | 56.71 | 10.10 | 11.84 | 7.37 | 4.87 | 65.82 |
| Uttar Dinajpur | 4.27 | 40.98 | (8) | 2.34 | 54.87 | 1.93 | 45.13 | 30.00 | 10.00 | 60.00 | 22.79 | 11.84 | 7.37 | 12.87 | 45.13 |
| Hooghly | 6.73 | 29.08 | (16) | 4.02 | 59.74 | 2.71 | 40.26 | 50.15 | 8.16 | 41.69 | 55.28 | 1.69 | 0.26 | 2.52 | 40.26 |
| Howrah | 4.84 | 32.18 | (15) | 3.89 | 80.39 | 0.95 | 19.61 | 27.14 | 0.25 | 72.61 | 42.20 | 0.91 | 29.84 | 7.44 | 19.61 |
| Jalpaiguri | 6.02 | 35.88 | (12) | 4.59 | 76.24 | 1.43 | 23.76 | 44.49 | 22.27 | 33.25 | 45.08 | 28.91 | 0.64 | 1.61 | 23.76 |
| Maldah | 5.63 | 38.82 | (9) | 4.98 | 88.46 | 0.65 | 11.54 | 25.25 | 10.00 | 64.76 | 80.14 | 0.45 | 0.48 | 7.40 | 11.54 |
| Midnapore (East) | 7.02 | 26.89 | (17) | 6.42 | 91.40 | 0.60 | 8.60 | 20.71 | 0.97 | 78.32 | 74.03 | 12.65 | 0.43 | 4.30 | 8.60 |
| Midnapore (West) | 10.58 | 32.88 | (14) | 9.11 | 86.05 | 1.48 | 13.95 | 28.71 | 20.21 | 51.08 | 68.78 | 6.20 | 2.71 | 8.36 | 13.95 |
| Murshidabad | 10.68 | 43.71 | (4) | 8.49 | 79.55 | 2.18 | 20.45 | 15.86 | 2.09 | 82.06 | 61.04 | 12.05 | 1.70 | 4.75 | 20.45 |
| Nadia | 7.79 | 34.22 | (13) | 6.29 | 80.74 | 1.50 | 19.26 | 34.74 | 3.98 | 61.28 | 68.39 | 2.37 | 1.41 | 8.56 | 19.26 |
| North 24 Parganas | 8.25 | 37.71 | (10) | 6.94 | 84.10 | 1.31 | 15.90 | 44.03 | 7.42 | 48.55 | 75.65 | 3.71 | 0.23 | 4.51 | 15.90 |
| South 24 Parganas | 10.43 | 37.21 | (11) | 7.77 | 74.47 | 2.66 | 25.53 | 40.76 | 2.11 | 57.13 | 55.04 | 7.52 | 6.12 | 5.80 | 25.53 |
| Purulia | 4.52 | 43.66 | (5) | 3.62 | 80.17 | 0.90 | 19.83 | 20.59 | 24.15 | 55.26 | 38.15 | 21.65 | 14.65 | 5.73 | 19.83 |
| West Bengal | 115.90 | 36.69 | | 86.67 | 74.78 | 29.23 | 25.22 | 34.26 | 9.01 | 56.73 | 54.77 | 9.58 | 4.45 | 5.97 | 25.22 |

*Note*: * means Darjeeling including Siliguri Mahakuma Parishad.

*Source*: Dept. of Panchayats and Rural Development, Govt. of West Bengal.

**Table 3.58:** Distribution of Rural Population by Caste in West Bengal in 1991

| District | % of Rural Population as | | | | | Share of the District in Total SC Population of the State (Rural) | | Share of the District in Total ST Population of the State (Rural) | |
|---|---|---|---|---|---|---|---|---|---|
| | Scheduled Caste (SC) | | Scheduled Tribe (ST) | | Non-SC/ST | | | | |
| Bankura | 31.97 | (5) | 11.20 | (4) | 56.83 | 6.04 | (10) | 7.97 | (6) |
| Birbhum | 31.34 | (6) | 7.45 | (8) | 61.21 | 5.36 | (11) | 4.80 | (7) |
| Burdwan | 32.11 | (4) | 7.79 | (7) | 60.10 | 9.27 | (2) | 8.48 | (4) |
| Cooch Behar | 54.51 | (1) | 0.63 | (15) | 44.86 | 8.02 | (4) | 0.35 | (15) |
| Darjeeling | 18.14 | (14) | 17.56 | (3) | 64.30 | 1.21 | (16) | 4.39 | (10) |
| Hooghly | 29.14 | (10) | 5.58 | (10) | 65.28 | 6.42 | (8) | 4.63 | (9) |
| Howrah | 22.08 | (11) | 0.22 | (16) | 77.70 | 3.05 | (14) | 0.11 | (16) |
| Jalpaiguri | 39.33 | (2) | 24.76 | (1) | 35.91 | 6.77 | (6) | 16.06 | (2) |
| Malda | 18.46 | (13) | 6.93 | (9) | 74.61 | 3.32 | (13) | 4.70 | (8) |
| Midnapore (East + West) | 16.64 | (15) | 8.92 | (6) | 74.44 | 9.19 | (3) | 18.55 | (1) |
| Murshidabad | 13.01 | (16) | 1.41 | (13) | 85.58 | 4.06 | (12) | 1.66 | (14) |
| Nadia | 30.87 | (8) | 2.68 | (12) | 66.45 | 6.76 | (7) | 2.21 | (12) |
| North 24 Parganas | 30.63 | (9) | 4.23 | (11) | 65.14 | 8.00 | (5) | 4.16 | (11) |
| Purulia | 19.14 | (12) | 21.02 | (2) | 59.84 | 2.83 | (15) | 11.72 | (3) |
| South 24 Parganas | 37.04 | (3) | 1.37 | (14) | 61.59 | 13.49 | (1) | 1.88 | (13) |
| Uttar and Dakshin Dinajpur | 31.16 | (7) | 11.11 | (5) | 57.73 | 6.21 | (9) | 8.33 | (5) |
| West Bengal | 27.56 | | 7.32 | | 65.12 | | | | |

*Note*: Figures in brackets are ranks among 16 districts.

*Source*: Census of India (1991), Primary Census Abstract: General Population, West Bengal.

population in West Bengal belonged to the Scheduled Castes (SCs) and 7.32 per cent to the Scheduled Tribes (STs). Thus, nearly one-third of rural population of the state are members of SC/ST communities.

There are wide inter-district variations with regard to the concentration of SC/ST population in rural areas. The percentage of rural population belonging to the SCs has been the highest in Cooch Behar (54.41 per cent), the other districts where this has been higher than the state-average are Jalpaiguri (39.33 per cent), South 24 Parganas (37.04 per cent), Burdwan (32.11 per cent), Bankura (31.97 per cent), Birbhum (31.34 per cent), Uttar and Dakshin Dinajpur (31.16 per cent), Nadia (30.87 per cent), North 24 Parganas (30.63 per cent) and Hooghly (29.14 per cent).

As regards the percentage of STs to total population in rural areas, Jalpaiguri ranks first (24.76 per cent), which is followed by Purulia (21.02 per cent), Darjeeling (17.56 per cent), Bankura (11.20 per cent), Uttar and Dakshin Dinajpur (11.11 per cent), Midnapore (East+West) (8.92 per cent), Burdwan (7.79 per cent) and Birbhum (7.45 per cent). These are the districts where the percentages of STs have been higher than the state-average.

Table 3.58 further reveals that 80 per cent of rural SC population in West Bengal are concentrated in 10 districts only (out of a total of 16) that are South 24 Parganas, Burdwan, Midnapore, Cooch Behar, North 24 Parganas, Jalpaiguri, Nadia, Hooghly, Uttar and Dakshin Dinajpur and Bankura. On the other hand, only 6 districts accounting for 71 per cent of rural ST population of the state are Midnapore, Jalpaiguri, Purulia, Burdwan, Uttar and Dakshin Dinajpur and Bankura.

Let us now look at the composition of rural population in terms of religion. Table 3.59 presents data on composition of rural population by religion in 1991. It appears that the Hindus and Muslims are the two predominant categories in terms of religion in rural West Bengal. The Hindus and Muslims comprised 70.74 per cent and 27.44 per cent of rural population respectively in 1991. There are two districts in West Bengal where more than one-half of rural populations have been Muslims, which are Murshidabad (64.55 per cent) and Malda (50.24 per cent). The other districts with high percentage of Muslim population in rural areas are Uttar and Dakshin Dinajpur (41.69 per cent), North and South 24 Parganas (34.76 per cent), Birbhum

**Table 3.59:** Distribution of Rural Population by Religion in West Bengal in 1991

| *District* | *% of Rural Population as* | | | | *Share of the District in Total HINDU Population of the State (Rural)* | *Share of the District in Total MUSLIM Population of the State (Rural)* | |
|---|---|---|---|---|---|---|---|
| | *Hindu* | *Muslim* | | *Others* | | | |
| Bankura | 86.46 | 6.82 | (13) | 6.72 | 6.37 | 1.29 | (13) |
| Birbhum | 65.28 | 34.45 | (5) | 0.27 | 4.35 | 5.92 | (8) |
| Burdwan | 76.31 | 23.27 | (9) | 0.42 | 8.58 | 6.75 | (6) |
| Cooch Behar | 75.21 | 24.66 | (7) | 0.13 | 4.31 | 3.64 | (9) |
| Darjeeling | 75.49 | 4.59 | (15) | 19.91 | 1.95 | 0.31 | (15) |
| Hooghly | 82.85 | 16.46 | (10) | 0.68 | 7.11 | 3.64 | (10) |
| Howrah | 75.88 | 24.08 | (8) | 0.04 | 4.09 | 3.34 | (11) |
| Jalpaiguri | 82.88 | 11.23 | (11) | 5.90 | 5.56 | 1.94 | (12) |
| Malda | 49.49 | 50.24 | (2) | 0.27 | 3.47 | 9.09 | (3) |
| Midnapore | 86.72 | 10.82 | (12) | 2.46 | 18.65 | 6.00 | (7) |
| Murshidabad | 35.29 | 64.55 | (1) | 0.16 | 4.29 | 20.23 | (2) |
| Nadia | 68.34 | 30.95 | (6) | 0.71 | 5.83 | 6.81 | (5) |
| North and South 24 Parganas | 64.60 | 34.76 | (4) | 0.64 | 15.73 | 21.83 | (1) |
| Purulia | 90.90 | 5.83 | (14) | 3.28 | 5.24 | 0.87 | (14) |
| Uttar and Dakshin Dinajpur | 57.55 | 41.69 | (3) | 0.76 | 4.47 | 8.34 | (4) |
| West Bengal | 70.74 | 27.44 | | 1.82 | 100.00 | 100.00 | |

*Note*: Figures in brackets are ranks among 15 districts.
*Source*: Census of India (1991), West Bengal State: District Profile 1991.

(34.45 per cent) and Nadia (30.95 per cent). It is also to be noted that 3 districts of West Bengal (North and South 24 Parganas, Murshidabad and Malda) together accounted for one-half of rural Muslim population of the state.

It follows from the above discussion that the rural population in West Bengal has been far from being homogeneous in terms of their social composition as reflected by their caste/religion distribution. Not only the SC/ST and Muslims lived in sizeable numbers in rural areas but also the state is often credited for maintaining social harmony. There is rarely any conflict among the rural people that is related to their caste/region. This feature is also reported by the village level studies conducted by the LBSNAA towards the end of 1990s.

## GENDER EMPOWERMENT

Development of women has been receiving attention of the Government right from the very first Plan. However, at that time, this was treated as a subject of 'welfare' and clubbed with the welfare of other disadvantaged sections such as destitutes, disabled, aged etc. This approach continued till about the Fifth Plan. The shift in approach from 'welfare' to development of women took place in the Sixth Plan, which adopted a multi-disciplinary approach with a special thrust on the three core sectors of health, education and employment. In the Seventh Plan, the developmental programmes continued with the major objectives of raising women's economic and social status and bringing them into the mainstream of development.

The Ninth Plan made significant changes in the conceptual strategy of planning for women. 'Empowerment of Women' became one of the nine primary objectives of the Ninth Plan. Accordingly, the approach of the Plan was to create an enabling environment where women could freely exercise their rights both within and outside home, as equal partners along with men. The Ninth Plan also attempted convergence of existing services available in both women-specific and women-related sectors. To this end, it directed both the centre and the states to adopt a special strategy of 'Women's Component Plan' (WCP) through which not less than 30 per cent of funds/benefits flow to women from all the general development sectors. Apart from adopting WCP, there were several other initiatives during the Ninth Plan for the empowerment of women. Some of these are (see Planning Commission, 2002c, Ch. 2.11):

- Launching of '**Swa-Shakti**' to create an enabling environment for empowerment of women through setting up of self-reliant Self Help Groups (SHGs) and developing linkages with lending institutions to ensure women's access to credit facilities for income-generating activities (1998);
- '**Stree Shakti Puraskars**' instituted to honour 5 distinguished women annually for their outstanding contribution to the upliftment and empowerment of women (1999);
- Setting up of **Task Force on Women** (under the Chairmanship of K.C. Pant) to review the existing women-specific and women-related legislations and suggest

enactment of new legislations or amendments, wherever necessary (2000);

- Introduction of **Gender Budgeting** to attain more effective targeting of public expenditure and to offset any undesirable gender-specific consequences of previous budgetary measures (2000-01);
- Adoption of a **National Policy for Empowerment of Women** to eliminate all types of discrimination against women and to ensure gender justice, besides empowering women both socially and economically (2001);
- Celebration of the year 2001 as the '**Women's Empowerment Year**' for generation of awareness;
- Recasting of Indira Mahila Yojana (1995) as '**Swayamsidha**'—an integrated programme for empowerment of women through a major strategy of converging the services available in all the women-related programmes besides organizing women into SHGs for undertaking various entrepreurial ventures (2001);
- Launching of '**Swadhar**' to extend rehabilitation services for 'Women in Difficult Circumstances' (2001); and
- Introduction of a **Bill on Domestic Violence Against Women (Prevention)** to eliminate all forms of domestic violence against women and girl child (2002).

Finally, the Tenth Plan aims at empowering women through translating the National Policy for Empowerment of Women (2001) into action.

Having noted briefly the approaches adopted since the independence in general towards development and empowerment of women, it may be worthwhile to offer some brief comments on this in the context of rural West Bengal.[45] Our discussion above clearly reflected that the rural women in the state were discriminated against in the labour market that resulted in their having much lower worker-population ratio. We also found clear evidence of rural female workers getting engaged more in marginal economic activities as compared to male workers. The rate of illiteracy is also much higher among rural females in West Bengal as compared to their male counterparts. The rate of attendance by the rural girls at upper tiers of educational institutions has been abysmally low while their dropout rates being also much higher. Further, general health conditions for rural females have been worse in West Bengal as compared to all-India. The situation with regard to the level of empowerment of rural women in West Bengal provides some support to the general perception at the national level that "while the impact of various developmental policies, plans and programmes implemented over the last few decades have brought forth a perceptible improvement in the socio-economic status of women, problems like illiteracy, ignorance, discrimination and violence continue to persist even today" (Planning Commission, 2002c, p. 229).

However, it is also to be admitted that, in spite of the above weaknesses, women in rural West Bengal enjoy greater freedom in so far as their participation in outdoor and political activities are concerned. This has happened specifically with the reservation of one-third of panchayat seats for women from 1993. As regards the ever-married rural women in West Bengal, the NHFS-2 (1998-99) data clearly show that their degree of autonomy has been no less than their sisters at the all-India level (Table 3.60). Chattopadhyay and Seddon (2002) confirmed this observation in their study of a village in West Bengal. They found that women belonging to all communities, more surely, in the case of Scheduled Castes/Tribes, enjoyed fair degree of autonomy and freedom in the studied village. Finally, NHFS-2 data revealed that the percentage of rural women beaten and/or physically mistreated by their husbands and/or in-laws has been lower in rural West Bengal than the same for all-India.

The conclusion that follows here is that although rural women in West Bengal lagged far behind their male counterparts as regards their economic empowerment, they have surely progressed quite far from the point of view of political empowerment. This conclusion is also supported by some of the recently conducted village studies by the LBSNAA.

## SUMMARY AND CONCLUSIONS

The main purpose of this study has been to build profiles for understanding the social and economic structures in rural West Bengal in the decade of 1990s. In this process, this study also throws light on the socio-economic transformation processes that rural West Bengal

**Table 3.60:** Some Indicators of Autonomy of Ever-married Women in Rural Areas

| *Item* | *West Bengal* | *All India* |
|---|---|---|
| Per cent of cases where the decision is taken by women only: | | |
| (a) What items to cook | 70.6 | 71.7 |
| (b) Obtaining health care for herself | 16.0 | 25.7 |
| (c) Purchasing jewellery or other major household items | 14.4 | 9.7 |
| (d) Going and staying with her parents or siblings | 11.3 | 12.4 |
| (e) How the money she earns will be used | 46.5 | 36.5 |
| Per cent of women beaten or physically mistreated by husband and/or in-laws since age 15 | 19.6 | 22.5 |

*Source*: National Health and Family Welfare Survey 2 (1998-99), Reports for All India and West Bengal.

has been undergoing over past one decade or so. In order to build profiles for social and economic structures as also to capture the rural transformation processes, we focused specifically on aspects such as (1) Economic Activities; (2) Infrastructure; (3) Health; (4) Education; (5) Panchayati Raj System; (6) Agrarian Relations; (7) Anti-Poverty and Rural Development Schemes; (8) Social Structure; and (9) Gender Empowerment.

Some of the important findings of this study are the following:

(1) The employment structure in rural West Bengal has undergone significant restructuring in the decade of 1990s. There is clear indication of worsening of employment prospects for rural workers, both males and females. Our data show that whatever employment expansion has taken place in rural West Bengal during 1990s has been by and large of marginal types. The rate of marginalisation of rural employment has been very high in the decade of 1990s in West Bengal.

(2) Comparing between rural males and females, it is found that the employment situation has been worse for the latter as compared to the former. Both in terms of employment availability as well as employment quality, the rural females in West Bengal had to suffer. This conclusion follows from

the facts that worker-populations ratios for rural females have been much lower than the rural males and the rate of marginalisaion of employment for the females was also higher as compared to the males.

(3) We found clear evidence of wide inter-district variations both in terms of work-participation rates and the degree of marginalisation of employment. As regards work participation rates, our conclusion is that these are generally high for rural males in agriculturally progressive districts, for female workers these are high in the backward districts. On the other hand, marginalisation of employment has been generally high in the districts that are agriculturally backward. It is possible that owing to lack of stable employment opportunities as also their very poor economic conditions, a large section of rural workers in the backward districts of the state are rather compelled to accept employment that are of marginal character. In any case, this is indicative of the miseries of a large section of rural workers in West Bengal in recent years.

(4) The sectoral composition of rural workers has also undergone some important changes in West Bengal in recent years. Among the workers within the farm sector, there has been a tendency of the share of agricultural labourers increasing and that of cultivators declining in the decade of 1990s. The decline in the percentage of workers as cultivators is perhaps because of some of the erstwhile cultivating households and/ or some of their family members switching over to various kinds of non-farm activities. This seems plausible in so far as there has been a clear tendency towards greater absorption of rural labour in the non-farm sector during 1990s. This indicates diversification of employment by the rural workers in the state during 1990s. Analysing the degree of rural employment diversification in the districts, we found that, in the decade of 1990s, this has been related to the degree of advancement of agriculture. In other words, the districts of West Bengal displaying more diversified employment structure appear to be agriculturally developed (e.g. Howrah, Nadia and 24 Parganas) while some of the least diversified districts are also laggards in terms of agricultural

advancement (e.g. Uttar and Dakshin Dinajpur, Cooch Behar, Purulia, Bankura and Birbhum). Another point that needs mention here is that the incidence of non-farm employment has been relatively greater among the rural female workers in West Bengal as compared to the male workers.

(5) In spite of an observed tendency towards diversification of rural employment in the decade of 1990s, away from farm to the non-farm sectors, there is no denying the fact that the farm/agricultural sector still enjoys the status of most important sector in West Bengal. Currently, the farm sector absorbs nearly three-fifths of total workforce in rural areas and contributes about one-fourth of the Net State Domestic Product in West Bengal. The predominance of this sector in the rural economy of the state is also reiterated by the village studies conducted towards the end of 1990s by the LBSNAA.

(6) Recognising the importance of the agricultural sector in West Bengal, we attempted to understand its performance in recent years from various angles. We found that the state agriculture progressed well during 1990s from the perspective of expansion of cropping intensity. The cropping intensity for the state as a whole increased from 1.59 in 1990-91 to 1.74 in 1999-2000. However, there is wide inter-district variation in this regard. Among the districts, in the year 1999-2000, this has been the highest in Nadia (2.49) and lowest in Purulia (1.10). Our discussion on cropping pattern, however, clearly revealed the inadequacy of West Bengal agriculture to achieve high degree of crop-diversification even by the end of 1990s. The agriculture in the state as well as in most of the districts has been dominated by cultivation of foodgrains, more specifically Paddy. Our findings here on the basis of secondary data have been by and large corroborated by the LBSNAA village studies in West Bengal between 1995-2002.

(7) As regards adoption of modern agricultural technology, we found that, in 1990-2000, nearly one-half of net sown areas are irrigated in West Bengal. As expected, there are wide inter-district variations in this regard with Hooghly having the highest percentage of net sown areas under irrigation (90.74 per cent), the same being lowest in Darjeeling (13.87 per cent). The differences among the districts are also visible

with regard to application of fertilizers. While fertilizers used per hectare of gross cropped area in the state is found 129.04 kgs., this has been extremely high in two districts in particular, which are Howrah (346.25 kgs./hectare), and Hooghly (223.48 kgs./hectare). In terms of utilization of tractors and power tillers, Howrah, Hooghly and Burdwan occupy top three positions in the state. Overall, in terms of adoption of modern inputs and technology, the most progressive districts appear to be Hooghly, Burdwan, Howrah, Birbhum, North 24 Parganas, and Midnapore.

(8) The yield of Paddy, the most important crop of the state, has improved quite a bit during 1990s (from 1,800 kgs./hectare in 1990-91 to 2,237 kgs./hectare in 1999-2000). However, it also needs to be underlined that among the top 12 Paddy producing states of the country, West Bengal ranked sixth in this regard in 1999-2000. The state still lagged substantially from the yield levels of Paddy in Punjab (3,346 kgs./hectare), Tamil Nadu (3,278 kgs./hectare) and Andhra Pradesh (2,687 kgs./hectare). Another point that needs mention here is wide inter-district variation in terms of Paddy yield in West Bengal. In 1999-2000, while Burdwan comes first in terms of Paddy yield (2,740 kgs./hectare) this has been the lowest in Darjeeling (1,443 kgs./hectare). As regards yield levels of other commercial/cash crops such as Jute and Potato also there is some improvement in yield levels during 1990s. However, wide variations among the districts persist in this regard as well.

(9) In recent years, a great deal of discussion has taken place on the growth performance of agriculture in West Bengal particularly since early 1980s. Several recent studies show that the state agriculture has gained with impressive performance with regard to growth of foodgrains production in particular after the coming of the LFG. We looked afresh into the growth performance of agriculture in the state as well as districts by comparing growth rates of production during the decades of 1980s and 1990s. Our main finding here is that the annual growth of foodgrains production during 1980s was indeed spectacular (rising by 6.0 per cent per annum) while the same has slackened considerably in the

1990s (2.30 per cent per annum). As regards non-foodgrains, the yearly growth rates were 5.57 per cent and 3.72 per cent for the two decades respectively. It is clear that West Bengal agriculture has been entering, albeit slowly, into the phase of low production growth in the decade of 1990s. Our analysis also revealed that the deceleration in growth rates of foodgrains production in the state has been fairly widespread inasmuch as in all the districts the growth rates for the same were lower during 1990s as compared to 1980s.

(10) We have computed costs and returns (profit) from crop cultivation in West Bengal with reference to Aman Paddy—the most important crop of the state. We found that although the Paddy farmers in the state have not been incurring any loss, their margin of profit (Rs. 2,027 per hectare) has not been very high either when compared with other major Paddy growing states such as Tamil Nadu (Rs. 4,738 per hectare) and Punjab (Rs. 3,863 per hectare). The low returns from Paddy cultivation in West Bengal has been mainly due to application of much higher doses of human labour. For the sake of increasing average labour productivity as also profits from crop cultivation in the future, it is necessary to rationalise labour utilization in West Bengal agriculture by devising a more diversified cropping pattern, development of suitable technology for inter-cropping and creation of more employment opportunities in the rural non-farm sector.

(11) We looked into the status of rural infrastructures in West Bengal in terms of three important indicators, namely road connectivity in rural areas, rural electrification and banking network for rural areas. We found that for the state as a whole, the length of rural roads has been 57.35 km. per 100 sq. km. However, there is wide inter-district variation in this regard. While rural road per 100 sq. km. is the highest in Hooghly (241.30 km.), this is the lowest in Uttar Dinajpur (14.28 km. only). Apart from Hooghly, rural road connectivity has been impressive in Howrah and South 24 Parganas. As regards rural electrification, we found 78 per cent of villages in the state being officially declared electrified in 1999-2000. However, both in terms of road connectivity and availability of electricity, the actual situation appears to be worse than

what is reported through official documents. For example, it is found that among the villages having less than 1000 population in West Bengal, roads connected only 42.01 per cent in 1996-97. It is also found that only 19.2 per cent of rural households used electricity in 1998-99 in the villages. Some of the village studies by the LBSNAA also confirm this gap that exists in terms of road connectivity and availability of electricity at the household level in the villages in West Bengal.

(12) In terms of functioning of institutional credit agencies in rural areas, West Bengal presents a gloomy picture. Although the concentration of institutional credit agencies in rural areas appears to be quite impressive in some of the districts, in terms of supply of credit, they performed rather poorly. Our study clearly revealed that in all districts of the state, the rural credit-deposit ratios have declined during the period 1990-91 to 2000-01. Further, although the commercial banks are supposed to direct 18 per cent of total credit to the agricultural sector (as per the banking norm), in actuality, they have supplied much less, 4.47 per cent only in 2000-01. It, however, needs to be mentioned that the PACS have gradually emerged as the most important supplier of production credit to a vast majority of farmers in the villages in West Bengal. Nevertheless, the supply of institutional credit has been highly inadequate which encouraged emergence of various types of non-institutional lenders (e.g. village moneylenders, traders, inputs sellers, friends and relatives, big cultivators etc.) in the West Bengal countryside. This feature of rural credit markets in West Bengal is also reported by the LBSNAA conducted village studies in recent years. It also appears from some other micro studies that at present the non-institutional lenders fulfil nearly two-thirds of credit requirements of the rural borrowers in West Bengal.

(13) We also assessed the rural households' access to some other infrastructural facilities in West Bengal. It is clearly observed that, at present, in terms of availability of post office, telegraph office, STD telephone booth, co-operative societies of various types, fair price/PDS shop etc., the situation in West Bengal is worse as compared to all-India situation. This

finding also is corroborated by most of the village studies by the LBSNAA.

(14) As regards the availability of health care facilities in rural areas, West Bengal lags far behind the 'national norm' set for this purpose. For example, while the 'national norm' in plain area is to have 1 health sub-centre for every 5,000 population, 1 primary health centre for every 30,000 population and 1 community health centre/rural hospital for 1 to 1.2 lakh population, the availability of these institutions is highly inadequate. Compared to the 'national norm', the proportion of health sub-centre in rural West Bengal is 0.72, the same for primary health centre is 0.62 and rural hospital is 0.18. Apart from the inadequacy of public health care institutions in rural areas, there is also wide inter-district variation in this regard. Among the districts of West Bengal, rural health care facilities are worse than the state-average in Uttar Dinajpur, South 24 Parganas, Malda, Nadia, Jalpaiguri, North 24 Parganas, Cooch Behar, Murshidabad and Dakshin Dinajpur. The inadequacy/non-availability of public health care facilities at the village level has been highlighted by a number of village studies by the LBSNAA.

(15) In spite of inadequate availability of public health care institutions in rural areas, general health conditions of rural people in West Bengal do not appear to be much inferior, particularly when compared with all-India figures. On the basis of indicators such as the crude death rate for rural population and infant/child mortality rates, West Bengal appears to have a better situation than all-India. However, in terms of morbidity for rural population, the situation appears to be a mixed one. Compared with all-India, rural people in West Bengal are relatively more prone to the diseases such as asthama and jaundice; they are less affected by tuberculosis and malaria. It is also found that among various sections of rural population, the rate of ailment is higher among the non-SC/ST persons.

(16) Examining the NHFS-2 (1998-99) data, we found that the health conditions of rural children in West Bengal have been a matter for worry. The incidence of diseases such as anaemia, cough, respiratory infection, fever etc. has been high among

rural children in West Bengal (under age 3 years) than all-India levels. Further, among the rural children in the state, 18 per cent are 'severely under-nourished', 53 per cent 'under-nourished', 21 per cent 'severely stunted' and 45 per cent 'stunted'.

(17) The general health condition of the rural women in West Bengal has been no better either. We found that 64 per cent of ever-married women in rural areas suffered from anaemia (54 per cent at the all-India level) and nearly 50 per cent are nutritionally deficient (41 per cent for all-India). However, the pregnant women in rural West Bengal do receive better medical attention (through antenatal check-up, adoption of preventive measures etc.) than their sisters at the all-India level. Nevertheless, about three-fourths of rural women in the state reported their residences, rather than hospitals, as the place of childbirth.

(18) We also examined the performance of West Bengal in terms of implementation of health care programmes for rural children. We found that the performance of the state has been better than all-India with regards to programmes such as vaccination, Vitamin A supplementation etc. However, there still exists a wide gap towards achievement of complete vaccination/immunization of rural children in West Bengal. The available data show that by 1998-99, only 41 per cent of them were fully vaccinated (i.e. receiving BCG, all DTP, all Polio and measles vaccines).

(19) The level of health awareness has been generally high among the rural population in West Bengal than all-India. Nevertheless, some deficiencies still persist in this regard. For example, only about 4 per cent of rural people in the state use tap water for drinking which is the safest and 82 per cent use water from tubewells/hand pumps which, if not sunk deep, are likely to lift contaminated water. We also found that about 78 per cent of rural households did not have latrines for defecation in 1998-99. Further, 84 per cent of them lacked proper drainage facility. These are surely the means through which various kinds of diseases spread among the rural people in West Bengal. Some of these deficiencies are also highlighted by some of the village studies by LBSNAA.

(20) On the educational front, rural West Bengal is found to have made some progress over the decade of 1990s. This is visible particularly with regard to increase in rural literacy rate. In 2001, 74 per cent of rural males (aged more than 6 years) and 54 per cent of rural females are literates. However, there exists wide inter-district variation in this regard. It also appears that there exists caste/class/gender bias with regard to education in rural West Bengal. More specifically, the rate of illiteracy has been higher among the scheduled tribes/ castes, landless and sub-marginal landholders. The attainment of education beyond middle level has been also abysmally low among these categories along with the females in rural areas of the state. The fact that the females are lagging behind the males with regard to education is also borne out by low value of sex ratio (female : male) among the students in the state and most of the districts. This fact becomes more glaring as we move upto educational institutions of higher order.

(21) As regards the availability of educational institutions in rural areas, we found that the number of primary schools per 1,000 students in West Bengal is 5.82. There also exists wide variation among the districts in this regard. The districts that are better placed from the viewpoint of availability of primary schools are Bankura, Purulia, Darjeeling, Midnapore, Hooghly, Birbhum and Howrah. The numbers of high and higher secondary schools in the state and districts decline drastically, which indicate scarcity of such institutions in rural areas.

(22) In recent years, the Government launched Sishu Siksha Karmasuchi to promote the cause of elementary education. Accordingly, 14,699 Sishu Siksha Kendras (SSKs) have been formed and 33,670 *Sahayikas* recruited till September 2002. Our assessment regarding the SSKs is that they have less pressure of students and hence more favourable student-teacher ratio (24:1) as compared to traditional primary schools (61:1). Nevertheless, it also appears that there is lack of planning in opening the SSKs in the districts. This becomes clear from the fact that the concentration of students in SSKs varied widely among the districts. In particular, in the districts

of Drajeeling, Bankura, North 24 Parganas, Nadia, Midnapore, Cooch Behar, Dakshin Dinajpur, and Jalpaiguri, the number of students per SSK has been very thin (less than 50).

(23) Our study also provides some assessment of village-level availability of educational infrastructures in West Bengal. It is found that by early-1990s, 71 per cent of villages in the state were covered by primary schools, about 9 per cent by secondary schools and 2 per cent by higher secondary schools. Further, about 58 per cent of rural schools have dirking water facility, 15 per cent have urinal, 3 per cent have separate urinal for girls and 5 per cent have lavatory.

(24) The issue of incentive/disincentive towards pursuing education by the rural people is discussed in some detail in our study. It is found that in 1995-96, among the rural persons aged 5-24 years in West Bengal, nearly 31 per cent have never enrolled in any educational institution. Among the important reasons towards non-enrolment are financial constrains, lack of interest among the children/guardians, attending domestic civilities and so on. The percentage of dropouts from educational institutions by rural persons is also very high in West Bengal (nearly 65 per cent) and the vast majority (85 per cent) of those dropping out have done so at the primary/middle level of education. It also needs mention that, in 1995-96, although nearly two-thirds of rural persons pursuing education are found receiving free/subsidized books and/or stationary, only 6 per cent of them got scholarships and mid-day meals.

(25) We have discussed in considerable detail the evolution, structure and functioning of panchayati raj system in West Bengal. We noted that the present Left Front Government (LFG) displayed sustained interest in decentralization through the revival of the panchayati raj system since 1978. Apart from helping in the implementation of land reforms programme, the panchayats in West Bengal have been the most effective forum to organize the poorer sections to fight against the vested interests and exploiting classes in the villages. West Bengal has established a three-tier panchayati raj system comprising Zilla Parishads (ZP), Panchayat Samitis (PS), and Gram Panchayats (GP).

(26) As regards political composition of panchayat members in West Bengal, we found that the left parties, particularly the CPI (M), have dominated at each tier of panchayats all through the period 1978 to 2003. Following the latest panchayat election in 2003, the left parties together controlled 87 per cent of ZP seats, 74 per cent of PS seats and 66 per cent of GP seats. Among the opposition parties, Congress has a share of 10 per cent of ZP seats, 12 per cent of PS seats and 14 per cent of GP seats. The other opposition party, namely Trinamul Congress suffered some set back in the 2003 election. It now controls only about 2 per cent of ZP seats, 10 per cent of PS seats and 13 per cent of GP seats. Among the districts, the Congress has sizeable presence in the panchayats of Murshidabad, Malda and Uttar Dinajpur while the Trinamul Congress has some strength in North and South 24 Parganas, Nadia and Midnapore. In rest of the districts, the left parties have overwhelming dominance.

(27) In West Bengal, the panchayats have adequate representation by the members from Scheduled Castes/Tribes. Examining the caste backgrounds of GP members, we found that 44 per cent of them belonged to Scheduled Castes/Tribes in 1998. The discrimination against women as regards representation in panchayats has also been removed from 1993 with one-third of seats being reserved for them. As regards occupational background of GP members, we found that about one-third of them belonged to the category of cultivators/farmers in 1998. However, the class of agricultural labourers appears to be under-represented in the GPs in West Bengal. The school teachers shared about 15 per cent of the GP seats until 1993, but their share started declining thereafter. Over the years, there has been a tendency among all political parties to field their unemployed members in the panchayats. In 1998, about one-fourth of the GP seats have been captured by this category.

(28) We examined the structure of operational holdings in West Bengal and her districts using the Agricultural Census data for 1990-91 and 1995-96. It is found that the 'marginal' holdings constitute 76 per cent of all operational holdings in the state in 1995-96. These together with 'small' holdings

accounted for 93 per cent of all operational holdings. Clearly, West Bengal agriculture is now dominated very largely by the 'marginal and small' holdings. The average size of operational holding in the state has been reducing gradually over the years. In 1995-96, this stood at 0.85 hectare. However, it is encouraging to note that there has been a tendency of average size of operational holdings within the group of 'marginal' holdings increasing in recent years in the state and a majority of districts. Another important point to note is that over time the inequality in the distribution of operational holdings in the state and most of the districts have declined. This has possibly happened due to effective implementation of land reforms in West Bengal.

(29) As regards tenancy, the Agricultural Census data show that about 8 per cent of operated area in the state is under tenancy cultivation in 1995-96. This might be an under-estimate since the Census data are not considered fully reliable for this purpose. Among the districts, the incidence of tenancy cultivation in 1995-96 is found to be relatively high in the districts of Howrah, Birbhum, Dakshin Dinajpur, Malda, Jalpaiguri, Cooch Behar, Hooghly and Burdwan. As regards forms of tenancy, our study shows that crop-sharing has been the predominant form of tenancy in the state and all the districts. For the state as a whole, 86 per cent of tenanted area has been under crop-sharing arrangement in 1995-96.

(30) Our study specifically examined the performance of the state towards implementation of two most important land reforms programmes, namely 'Operation Barga' and land redistribution programme. We found that till September 2002, 15.08 lakh bargadars have been recorded in the state and they involved 11.09 lakh acres of land. On the other hand, till that date, 26.7 lakh persons benefited from land redistribution programme and 10.7 lakh acres of land were redistributed. These two programmes together involved 4.17 million people in rural areas (one-third of farm workers) and covered about 15 per cent of total cultivable land in West Bengal. Our computations further show that amount of land per bargadar is 0.74 acre while amount of land per beneficiary under land redistribution programme is 0.40 acre. It is also

encouraging to note that 42 per cent of bargadars and 56 per cent of beneficiaries under land redistribution programme are drawn from the Scheduled Castes/Tribes. The record of West Bengal with regard to implementation of land reforms measures appears quite impressive.

(31) Of course, the districts of West Bengal varied in terms of concentration of bargadars and beneficiaries under land re-distribution programme. The concentration of bargadars has been relatively high (above state-average) in Howrah, South Dinajpur, Birbhum, Hooghly, Midnapore, Cooch Behar, South 24 Parganas, Burdwan, Jalpaiguri, Malda and Bankura. On the other hand, the concentration of beneficiaries under land redistribution programme has been high in Darjeeling, Midnapore, Jalpaiguri, Malda, Uttar Dinajpur and Birbhum.

(32) The agricultural labour market in West Bengal has undergone some important changes in the decade of 1990s. The most important has been agricultural labourers being able to effect upward revision of their wages rather uninterruptedly. Both money wages and real wages of agricultural labourers in West Bengal and her districts registered positive growth rates during the decade of 1990s. It is, however, to be noted that there is inter-district variation with regard to the movements of wages of agricultural labourers (both males and females). However, in general, the wages of agricultural labourers are high in the districts that are agriculturally advanced. Nevertheless, a clear tendency is discernible in West Bengal towards inter-district variation in wages of agricultural labourers declining over time. Another important point to note is that in the market for agricultural labour in West Bengal, the females received lower wages than males and male-female wage differential has displayed a tendency of widening during the decade of 1990s. This negative feature notwithstanding, there has been no trace of feudal/semi-feudal bondage of agricultural labourers to their employers in the West Bengal countryside. This is specifically reported by most of the village studies conducted by the LBSNAA between 1995-2002.

(33) Our study examined the performance of West Bengal towards

implementation of two most important rural development schemes in the decade of 1990s that relate to self-employment and wage employment. Our observation here is that with regards to implementation of both these schemes, the performance of the state has been highly unsatisfactory, particularly after 1995-96. Thus, while 1.62 lakh rural families were benefited in West Bengal from the self-employment schemes in 1995-96, the corresponding figure in 2001-02 is 7,351 only. Similarly, while on average about 7 mandays were created per agricultural labourer under the wage employment scheme in 1995-96, this declined to only 2 mandays in 2001-02. It clearly appears from our study that West Bengal suffered a downturn with regards to implemetation of rural development schemes since mid-1990s. The same conclusion follows from some of the recently conducted village studies by the LBSNAA.

(34) Rural West Bengal witnessed significant reduction in the incidence of poverty over past two decades or so. Analysing the Planning Commission data, we found that the incidence of rural poverty in the state declined from 63 per cent in 1983 to about 32 per cent in 1999-2000. However, it needs to be noted that West Bengal has to achieve a lot more in this regard in as much as the incidence of rural poverty in the state is still above the national average (27 per cent) and nearly 180 lakh rural persons lived under poverty in West Bengal in 1999-2000.

(35) We attempted to form some idea about the poverty situation in the districts by analysing data on 'below poverty line' (BPL) families, compiled by the Department of Panchayats and Rural Development, West Bengal. We found that, as of October 30, 2002, there are nearly 87 lakh BPL families in rural areas of the state (75 per cent of total BPL families). The incidence of poverty among the families from Scheduled Castes/Tribes has been higher. Further, more than one-half of BPL families in West Bengal are drawn from the category of agricultural labour families alone. Among the districts, the most poverty-stricken are Darjeeling, Cooch Behar, Birbhum, Murshidabad, Purulia, Dakshin Dinajpur, Bankura, Uttar Dinajpur, Malda, North 24 Parganas and South 24

Parganas. The percentage of BPL families has been the lowest in Burdwan that is one of the most agriculturally progressive districts of the state. As most of the poverty-stricken districts (except North 24 Parganas) are agriculturally backward, poverty in rural areas could reduce in the future with the advancement of agriculture.

(36) In West Bengal, the social composition of rural population has been heterogeneous. The Scheduled Castes (SCs) represented nearly 28 per cent of rural population of the state while the share of Scheduled Tribes (STs) has been slightly above 7 per cent. Among the districts, more than one-third of rural population has been the SCs in Cooch Behar, Jalpaiguri and South 24 Parganas. On the other hand, the concentration of STs is particularly high in Jalpaiguri, Purulia and Darjeeling. The religion-wise break up of the rural population shows that Hindus and Muslims are the two most dominant groups, representing 71 per cent and 27 per cent of total rural population respectively. The concentration of Muslims is particularly high in the districts of Murshidabad, Malda and North and South 24 Parganas. In spite of so much heterogeneity of the population, there has been no major conflict in the rural areas along the caste/religion lines. The state deserves to be credited for maintaining social harmony.

(37) In recent years, the rural women in West Bengal achieved some degree of political empowerment. This has happened with the reservation of one-third of panchayat seats for them from 1993. It is also noted that the married women enjoyed higher degree of autonomy in their families and the incidence of their harassment by husbands and/or inlaws is much less in West Bengal as compared to all-India. However, with regard to economic empowerment, they lagged far behind their male counterparts. Not only the women have been discriminated against in terms of employment, but whatever employment were thrown on them were mostly of marginal types. Moreover, women in rural areas also lagged far behind the males in terms of education. Further, general health conditions of rural women in West Bengal are worse as compared to their sisters at the all-India level. The obvious conclusion here is that in spite of achieving greater degree

of political empowerment, women in rural West Bengal is yet to achieve economic empowerment in full. Some of the village studies by the LBSNAA supports this conclusion.

## The Postscript

Some of the above findings might change if more recent data are analysed. It also needs to be noted that since mid-2001, the LFG under the leadership of new Chief Minister Budhadeb Bhattacharjee, have been working vigously to change adverse scenarios in health and education. It is also very much under the knowledge of the Government that in view of high unemployment pressure in rural areas, the state would have to move to more labour-intensive and high-value agriculture. Thus, in recent years, the Government has been encouraging crop diversification and development of food processing sector. However, as agriculture alone cannot solve the unemployment problem in densely populated rural areas, efforts are being made to strengthen non-farm self-employment sector, through formation of self-help groups. Perhaps the most important aspect of the present Government has been its sincere efforts to improve industrial base of the state, particularly since 2003. Thanks to the initiative of the present LFG, West Bengal is being considered as a safe destination for investments, both by domestic and foreign investors. On its part, the Government has been trying to extend infrastructure facilities and disperse the industries across districts as much as possible. Several new industries have already come up while many others are in the process of commissioning, even in rural areas of the districts. The Government has been encouraging establishment of new growth centres in places away from Kolkata. How far West Bengal succeeds in improving quality of education, delivery of health services, expanding employment opportunities through further strengthening its agricultural base and industrial rejuvenation are important questions for future investigations.

## Appendix

### *List of LBSNAA Conducted Village Studies Consulted*

| *Sl. No.* | *Author* | *Village* | *District* | *Year* |
|---|---|---|---|---|
| (1) | Roshni Sen | Palasan | Burdwan | 1995 |
| (2) | Anoop Kumar Agarwal | Chandrapur | Birbhum | 1995 |
| (3) | Manish Jain | Lanka Bore | Cooch Behar | 1996 |
| (4) | Binod Kumar | Telota | Burdwan | 1998 |
| (5) | Onkar Singh Meena | Satghara | Hooghly | 1999 |
| (6) | Narayan Swaroop Nigam | Walipur | Midnapore | 2000 |
| (7) | Neelam Meena | Dharmadeb, Kharia-Berubari, Khaeya-2 and Araji-Marija-Kamala-Pukari | Jalpaiguri | 2000 |
| (8) | Parwez Ahmed Siddiqui | Bajuara | Midnapore | 2001 |
| (9) | Santanu Basu | Koimari | Cooch Behar | 2001-02 |
| (10) | Alakananda Dayal | Gotu | Hooghly | 2002 |
| (11) | Puneet Yadav | Silakota | Burdwan | N.A. |
| (12) | Ravinder Singh | Kharija-Berubari | Jalpaiguri | N.A. |
| (13) | Vandana Yadav | Shyamsunder | Burdwan | N.A. |

## NOTES

1. The village studies consulted for this paper are listed in the Appendix.
2. As per the census definition, the main worker is a person whose main activity is participation in any economically productive work and who has worked for 183 days or more in a year.
3. The same trend is also visible from the analysis of National Sample Survey data, as has been attempted by us elsewhere (see Bhaumik, 2002).
4. The marginal worker is the person who participates in any economically productive work but for less than 183 days in a year.
5. It is to be noted that we could not gather a detailed picture as regards sectoral distribution of workers, which becomes possible when more disaggregated data (for nine sectors) are available. Since Census 2001 has so far released data categorizing all workers into four sectors only, we have to restrict our discussion here. Nevertheless, we could still gather broad idea about farm-nonfarm break up of the workers using Census 2001 data.

6. Some researchers, using the NSS data, argue that rural non-farm employment have not expanded much during the decade of 1990s in India. Clearly, our observation in the context of West Bengal contradicts such a conclusion. See Bhalla (1997), Acharya and Mitra (2000).
7. This observation lends some support to the view that rural non-farm employment expands more in areas that characterize advanced agricultural systems. See, in particular, Mellor (1976), Papola (1987), Hazell and Ramasamy (1991), Chandrasekhar (1993), Chadha (1994).
8. In computing the 'combined rank', we have assigned the same weight to the three input items.
9. In order to counter such deceleration in agricultural production in the 1990s, Bandyopadhyay (2003a) calls for more serious efforts towards completion of agrarian reforms and improvement in rural infrastucture.
10. We have attempted to provide a systematic account of costs and profits from cultivation because a number of village studies by the LBSNAA have also attempted to do so, though in a rather casual manner.
11. Roads considered here include all types of roads (*pucca*, surfaced and un-surfaced).
12. The fact that rural West Bengal lacks in terms of road connectivity can also be justified by comparing data on percentage of its villages connected by roads with the same for all-India. It is found that in the year 1996-97, among the villages having population less than 1000, roads in West Bengal have connected 42.01 per cent of the villages; the corresponding figure at the all-India level has been 49.18 per cent. As regards villages having population 1000 to 1500, the corresponding figures have been 67.98 per cent and 74.58 per cent in West Bengal and all-India respectively. For the villages having more than 1500 population, these percentages are 64.50 and 78.04 respectively in West Bengal and all-India. See Planning Commission (2002a, p. 183).
13. Bhaumik and Rahim (2004) find that while average rate of interest on formal loan has been Rs. 12.45%, the same for informal loan has been Rs. 17.58% (including the loans from friends and relatives many of which bear zero interest).
14. The NSSO 52nd Round survey (1995-96) on *Morbidity and Treatment of Ailments* reports that among the rural persons in West Bengal only 15 per cent depended on government sources for treatment of their ailments, which for all-India is 19 per cent. The data available from National Family Health Survey-2 reveal that, in 1998-99, 27.4 per cent of rural households in West Bengal depended on public medical sector; the corresponding figure for all-India has been 30.6 per cent.

15. The same picture follows from the villages surveyed by the LBSNAA. While in some villages the incidence of various kinds of diseases is reported to be low, in others, people are reported to be suffering from various diseases.
16. In fact, this has been reported by some of the village studies by the LBSNAA. For example, the people in Palasan (Burdwan) are found to suffer from gastroenteritis due to absence of proper water supply in the village.
17. It has been reiterated recently by the President of West Bengal Board of Secondary Education that the primary schools should typically have a student-teacher ratio of 40:1. See the report published in *The Statesman*, August 19, 2003.
18. In a recent study Rana *et al.* (2003) observes that SSKs cover about eight per cent of primary school-going children in the state.
19. This finding is corroborated by some of the village studies of the LBSNAA.
20. This section draws heavily on Webster (1992), Institute of Social Sciences (2000) and Government of West Bengal (2002b).
21. Some scholars have expressed doubts as regards the rate of participation of villagers and also effectiveness with which gram sansad meetings are actually being performed. In a recent study covering 20 village constituencies, Ghatak and Ghatak (2002) observes that on average 15 to 16 per cent of voters remain present in the gram sansad meetings. They found lower participation rates specifically among the relatively affluent, people belonging to opposition parties, women and minority groups.
22. These data have been collected in the year 2000 in connection with a research project, entitled *West Bengal Panchayat Project*, carried out by us in collaboration with Professor Dilip Mookerjee of Department of Economics, Boston University, USA. There have been some attempts by several other scholars (e.g. Lieten, 1996) to understand the social and economic backgrounds of elected panchayat members by surveying a few selected villages in one or two districts. However, our survey, being comprehensive in nature, enables us to form a generalized view on this matter.
23. This finding does not fully support the observation of Lieten (1996, p. 135), which is based on survey of two blocks in Burdwan and Midnapore, that the agricultural labourers have come to the forefront of public arena through their representation in the panchayats.

24. According to Census 2001, among the rural workers (main+marginal) in West Bengal, 31 per cent belonged to the category of agricultural labourers.

25. It has been noted by the Eleventh Finance Commission that at the level of GPs in West Bengal, the percentage of own revenue to total revenue has been only 5.08 per cent in 1997-98, which for all-India is 10.43 per cent. See Planning Commission (2001, p. 292).

26. Bandyopadhyay (2003b) observes that even the recommendation of the First State Finance Commission (presided by Dr. Satyabrata Sen) to provide untied funds to panchayats and to transfer them local level functions of the line departments were put in cold storage.

    Some scholars find local organizations of the CPI (M) controlling panchayats whereby the real authority lies with the former while the elected panchayat representatives merely endorse and implement the party decisions. See Bandyopadhyay (2003b).

27. This experiment has been quite successful in Salboni block of Midnapore. See UNICEF (2000). For a discussion on the methodology of 'village-based decentralized district planning', one may refer to Majumdar (2002).

28. It is necessary to clarify the exact meanings of the terms 'decentralization' and 'devolution'. Simply speaking, decentralization means passing down some authority and decision-making powers to the local office. However, the higher-level government body retains the right to overturn local decisions and to take these powers back. On the other hand, devolution implies granting decision-making powers to local authorities and allowing them to take full responsibility without referring back to the higher-level government. Therefore, devolution encompasses a wider horizon of decentralization and often has statutory backing, accompanied by a functional, organizational and fiscal autonomy. See Oommen (1998) and Bhaumik (2000).

29. In a recent study of two villages in Bankura, Rawal (2001a) found evidence of 'landless' and 'poor' households acquiring land through 'net purchases'.

30. It is to be noted that the agricultural census data are not fully reliable to understand the tenancy system. Some scholars have argued that agricultural census in fact provides an under-estimate of tenancy (see Sharma, 1995, Ch. 4). This view gets supported from the LBSNAA-VSs, which report much higher incidences of tenancy than those reported in agricultural census reports. Among the secondary sources, the NSS data on tenancy are considered supeirior. However, we have to depend

upon the census data because of non-availability NSS data at the disaggregated (district) level.

31. As is well known, the 'Operation Barga' programme was launched for quick recording of the names of the bargadars (tenants) in order to provide them legal security against eviction by the landowners and enforcement of their crop-sharing rights. The programme was launched in 1978. Though the programme has been officially continuing even now, the pace of recording the bargadars' names has slowed down as the majority of them have been recorded in the initial years. For an early debate on the 'Operation Barga' programme, refer to the articles in *Economic and Political Weekly* (1981).

32. It is found that by September 2001, West Bengal alone accounted for 19.62 per cent of total beneficiaries in the country under this programme while its share in total distributed land has been 46.66 per cent. See Government of India (2002).

33. In a recent study entitled "Macro Level Study on the Socio-Economic Status of Pattadars and Bargadars" [commissioned by the State Institute of Panchayats and Rural Development (West Bengal)], A. K Chakraborty observed that these two land reforms programmes together have covered little over 40 per cent of West Bengal's rural population.

34. It is to be noted that the reports on *Agricultural Wages in India* provide operation-wise, month-wise and district-wise data on money wages of male, female and child labourers in agriculture. We have averaged these data to arrive at annual figures of wages. For getting wages for the state as a whole, we have averaged district level data on wages using number of agricultural labourers (male/female) in the districts as weights.

35. The growth rate of agricultural wages has been computed by fitting the semi-log function, which is Ln (W) = a + bT, where 'W' represents wage (money/real) and 'T' stands for time.

36. This is contrary to the situation prevailing before 1977, i.e. coming of LFG into power. In an early study, Jose (1984) noted that real wages for agricultural labourers in West Bengal started rising (particularly for males) from 1977-78 onwards.

37. We regressed 'the ratio of female wage to male wage' on 'time'.

38. It is to be noted that the IRDP was initially started in 20 blocks of the country in 1977 and was extended in 1978-79 to 2300 blocks.

39. The wage employment schemes referred to here are those launched till 2002. However, in November 2004, the Government launched National Food For Work Programme (NFFWP) in 150 most backward districts

to generate additional supplementary wage employment with food security.

More recently, the **National Rural Employment Guarantee Scheme** (NREGS) has been launched on 2nd February 2006. This scheme subsumes the on-going schemes of Sampoorna Grameen Rozgar Yojana (SGRY) and NFFWP. To begin with, this scheme is being implemented in 200 most backward districts of the country and it will be extended to all the districts within five years. The objective of this scheme is to enhance the livelihood security of the people in rural areas by generating wage employment through works that develop the infrastructure base of that area. It guarantees 100 days employment in a financial year to any rural household whose adult members are willing to do unskilled manual work. The cost of the scheme will be shared by the Central and State governments on 90:10 basis. Minimum wage has been fixed at not less than Rs. 60 per day. The ordinary people would play an active role in the implementation of employment guarantee scheme through *Gram Sabhas*, social audits, participatory planning and other means. Focus will be on creation durable assets. The activities to be preferred are: (i) water conservation and water harvesting, (ii) drought proofing, including afforestation and tree plantation, (iii) irrigation canals including micro and minor irrigation works, (iv) irrigation facilities for landowning households belonging to SC/ST, beneficiaries of land reforms, beneficiaries of Indira Awas Yojana etc., (v) renovation of traditional water bodies, including silting of tanks, (vi) land development, (vii) flood control and protection of works, including drainage in water logged areas, (viii) rural connectivity to provide all weather roads, and (ix) any other work, which may be notified by the Central Government in consultation with State Governments. This scheme is expected to transform the geography of poverty in rural areas.

40. The discussion here is confined to the state of West Bengal because of non-availability of systematic data at the district level from the published government reports.

41. The LBSNAA-VSs also confirm highly unsatisfactory implementation of self-employment schemes during 1995-2002.

42. This finding is also corroborated by most of the village studies by LBSNAA by the end of 1990s.

43. In a recent study, Corbridge *et al.* (2003) observed that the poor village people are not always fully aware of the presence of wage employment schemes. For example, this has happened in 1998-99 in the context of Employment Assurance Scheme in a sample block (Old Malda) in Malda.

44. We confine our discussion to the year 1991 because the Census data for 2001 on caste and religion-wise distribution of population were not available till the time of writing this paper.
45. It is to be noted that owing to non-availability of data, it is not possible to have a detailed view on the implementation of above-noted schemes in rural West Bengal. Perhaps future village studies to be undertaken by institutions such as the LBSNAA would throw useful light on this aspect.

## REFERENCES

Acharya, Poromesh (2002), 'Education: Panchayat and Decentralisation: Myths and Reality', *Economic and Political Weekly*, Vol. 37, No. 8, February 23.

Acharya, S. and A. Mitra (2000), *The Potential of Rural Industries and Trade to Provide Decent Work Conditions: A Data Reconnaissance in India*, ILO/SAAT Working Paper, New Delhi.

Bandyopadhyay, D. (2003a), 'Land Reforms and Agriculture: The West Bengal Experience', *Economic and Political Weekly*, Vol. 38, No. 9, March 1.

—— (2003b), 'Punchayat Puzzle', *The Statesman*, August 11 and 12.

Banerjee, Abhijit *et al.* (2002a), 'Industrial Revival in West Bengal' (mimeo.), Department of Economics, MIT/USA.

—— (2002b), 'Strategy for Economic Reform in West Bengal', *Economic and Political Weekly*, Vol. 37, No. 41, October 12.

—— (2002c), 'Empowerment and Efficiency: Tenancy Reform in West Bengal', *Journal of Political Economy*, Vol. 110, No. 2, April.

Bhalla, Sheila (1997), 'Trends in Poverty, Wages and Employment in India', *The Indian Journal of Labour Economics*, Vol. 40, No. 2.

Bhattacharjee, Dipankar (1993), 'New Challenges for Bengal Left: Panchayat Poll Pointers', *Economic and Political Weekly*, Vol. 28, Nos. 29-30.

Bhaumik, Alok (2000), *Political Economy of Panchayat Finances in West Bengal: An Analytical Study*, Research India Publications, Calcutta.

Bhaumik, S.K. (1993), *Tenancy Relations and Agrarian Development: A Study of West Bengal*, Sage Publications, New Delhi.

—— (2002), 'Emerging Employment and Unemployment Scenarios in West Bengal: Implications for Policy', *Journal of Indian School of Political Economy*, Vol. 14, No. 3.

—— (2003), 'Unemployment in India in the Post-Liberalisation Era', *The Indian Journal of Labour Economics*, Vol. 46, No. 1.

Bhaumik, S.K. and Abdur, Rahim (2004), 'Structure and Operation of Rural Credit Markets: Some Results Based on Field Surveys in West Bengal', *Journal of Rural Development*, Vol. 23, No. 1, January-March.

Boyce, James K. (1987), *Agrarian Impasse in Bengal*, Oxford University Press, Delhi.

Chadha, G.K. (1994), *Employment, Earnings and Poverty: A Study of Rural India and Indonesia*, Sage Publications, New Delhi.

—— (2001), 'Impact of Economic Reforms on Rural Employment: No Smooth Sailing Anticipated', *Indian Journal of Agricultural Economics*, Vol. 56, No. 3, July-September.

Chadha, G.K. and S.K. Bhaumik (1992), 'Changing Tenancy Relations in West Bengal: Popular Notions and Grassroot Realities', *Economic and Political Weekly*, Vol. 27, Nos. 19 and 20-21.

Chattopadhyay, Molly and David Seddon (2002), 'Life Histories and Long-Term Change: Rural Livelihoods and Gender Relations in a West Bengal Village', *Economic and Political Weekly*, Vol. 37, No. 49, December 7.

CMIE (2000), *Agriculture*, Mumbai, November.

Chandrasekher, C.P. (1993), 'Agrarian Change and Occupational Diversification: Non-agricultural Employment and Rural Development in West Bengal', *Journal of Peasant Studies*, Vol. 20, No. 2.

Corbridge, Stuart *et al.* (2003), 'Making Social Science Matter-I: How the Local State Works in Rural Bihar, Jharkhand and West Bengal', *Economic and Political Weekly*, Vol. 38, No. 24, June 14.

Deaton, Angus and Jean Dreze (2002), 'Poverty and Inequality in India: A Re-examination', *Economic and Political Weekly*, Vol. 37, No. 36, September 7.

Datta, Prabhat (1992), *The Second Generation Panchayats in India with Special Reference to West Bengal*, Calcutta Book House, Calcutta.

—— (1997), 'Panchayats in West Bengal' in *West Bengal: A Special Number on Two Decades of Left Front Rule in West Bengal*, Government of West Bengal, Calcutta.

*Economic and Political Weekly* (1981), Special Issue on Operation Barga in West Bengal, Vol. 16, Nos. 25-26, June 20-27.

Gazdar, Haris and Sunil Sengupta (1999), 'Agricultural Growth and Recent Trends of Well-Being in Rural West Bengal', in Ben Rogaly *et al.* (eds.),

*Sonar Bangla: Agricultural Growth and Agrarian Change in West Bengal and Bangladesh*, Sage Publications, New Delhi.

Ghatak, Maitreesh and Maitreya Ghatak (2002), 'Recent Reforms in the Panchayat System in West Bengal: Towards Greater Participatory Governance?', *Economic and Political Weekly*, Vol. 37, No. 1, January 5.

Government of India (2002), *Annual Report 2001-02*, Ministry of Rural Development, New Delhi.

Government of West Bengal (2002a), *Statistical Abstract 2001-2002*, Bureau of Applied Economics and Statistics (BAES), Calcutta.

—— (2002b), *Annual Report 2001-2002*, Panchayat and Rural Development Department, Calcutta.

—— (2002c), *Health on the March: West Bengal 2001-02*, State Bureau of Health Intelligence, Directorate of Health Services, Kolkata.

Harriss, John (1993), 'What is Happening in Rural West Bengal? Agraian Reform, Growth and Distribution', *Economic and Political Weekly*, Vol. 28, No. 24, June 12.

Hazell, Peter and C. Ramasamy (eds.) (1993), *The Green Revolution Reconsidered,* Oxford University Press, Delhi.

Institute of Social Sciences (2000), *Status of Panchayati Raj in the States and Union Territories of India*, Concept Publishing Company, New Delhi.

Jose, A.V. (1984), 'Poverty and Income Distribution: The Case of West Bengal' in Azizur Rahman Khan and Eddy Lee (eds.), *Poverty in Rural Asia*, ILO/ARTEP, Bangkok.

Khasnabis, Ratan (2003), 'Economic Consequences of Land Reforms: West Bengal Agriculture under the Left Rule', in A.K. Bagchi *et al.* (eds.), *Economy and the Quality of Life: Essays in Memory of Ashok Rudra*, Dasgupta & Co. (P) Ltd., Kolkata.

Kohli, Atul (1992), *Democracy and Discontent: India's Growing Crisis of Governability*, Cambridge University Press, Cambridge.

Lieten, G.K. (1992), *Continuity and Change in West Bengal*, Sage Publications, New Delhi.

—— (1996), *Development, Devolution and Democracy*, Sage Publications, New Delhi.

Mallick, Ross (1993), *Development Policy of a Communist Government: West Bengal Since 1977*, Cambridge University Press, Cambridge.

Majumder, Sankar (2002), *Methodological Issues in Village Based Decentralised District Planning*, Indian Institute of Advanced Study, Shimla.

Mellor, John W. (1976), *The Economics of Growth: A Strategy for India and The Developing World,* Cornell University Press, Ithaca.

Mishra, Surjya Kanta and Vikas Rawal (2002), 'Agrarian Relations in Contemporary West Bengal and Tasks for the Left', in Ramachandran, V.K. and Madhura Swaminathan (eds.), *Agrarian Studies: Essays on Agrarian Relations in Less-Developed Countries*, Tulika Books, New Delhi.

Mukarji, Nirmal and D. Bandyopadhyay (1993), *New Horizons for West Bengal's Panchayats: A Report for the Government of West Bengal*, Calcutta, February.

Mukherji, Badal and Swapna Mukhopadhyay (1996), 'Impact of Institutional Change on Productivity in a Small Farm Economy: The Case of Rural West Bengal', in Ajitava Raychaudhuri and Debjani Sarkar (eds.), *Economy of West Bengal: Problems and Prospects*, K.P. Bagchi & Co., Calcutta.

NCERT (1997), *Sixth All-India Educational Survey 1993*, Vols. I-VI, New Delhi.

Oommen, M.A. (1998), *Devolution of Resources to Rural Local Bodies*, Institute of Social Sciences Occasional Paper # 21, New Delhi.

Papola, T.S. (1987), 'Rural Industrialization and Agricultural Growth: A Case Study in India' in Rizwanul Islam (ed.), *Rural Industrialization and Employment in Asia,* ILO/ARTEP, New Delhi.

Planning Commission (2001), *Report of the Working Group on Poverty Alleviation Programmes for the Tenth Five Year Plan (2002-2007)*, Government of India, New Delhi, December 21.

—— (2002a), *National Human Development Report 2001*, Government of India, New Delhi, March.

—— (2002b), *Tenth Five Year Plan 2002-2007*, Vol. I, Government of India, New Delhi.

—— (2002c), *Tenth Five Year Plan 2002-2007*, Vol. II, Government of India, New Delhi.

—— (2002d), *India: Vision 2020* (Chairman: Dr. S.P. Gupta), Government of India, New Delhi.

Rajeev, M. and Sarmistha Deb (1998), 'Institutional and Non-Institutional Credit in Agriculture: Case Study of Hooghly District in West Bengal', *Economic and Political Weekly*, Vol. 33, Nos. 47-48, November 21.

Ramachandran, V.K. and Madhura Swaminathan (eds.) (2002), *Agrarian Studies: Essays on Agrarian Relations in Less-Developed Countries*, Tulika Books, New Delhi.

Rana, Kumar *et al.* (2002), *The Delivery of Primary Education: A Study in West Bengal*, The Pratichi (India) Trust, Santiniketan, West Bengal.

—— (2003), 'State of Primary Education in West Bengal', *Economic and Political Weekly*, Vol. 38, No. 22, May 31.

Rawal, Vikas (2001a), 'Agrarian Reform and Land Markets: A Study of Land Transactions in Two Villages of West Bengal', *Economic Development and Cultural Change*, Vol. 49, No. 3, April.

—— (2001b), 'Irrigation Statistics in West Bengal', *Economic and Political Weekly*, Vol. 36, No. 27, July 7.

Rawal, Vikas and Madhura Swaminathan (1998), 'Changing Trajectories: Agricultural Growth in West Bengal', *Economic and Political Weekly*, Vol. 33, No. 40.

Rogaly, Ben *et al.* (eds.) (1999), *Sonar Bangla: Agricultural Growth and Agrarian Change in West Bengal and Bangladesh*, Sage Publications, New Delhi.

Saha, Anamitra and Madhura Swaminathan (1994), 'Agricultural Growth in West Bengal in the 1980s: A Disaggregation by Districts and Crops', *Economic and Political Weekly*, Vol. 29, No. 13.

Sen, Abhijit and Ranja Sengupta (1995), 'The Recent Growth in Agricultural Output in Eastern India with Special Reference to the Case of West Bengal', Paper presented at the *Workshop on Agricultural Growth and Agrarian Structure in Contemporary West Bengal and Bangladesh*, Centre for Studies in Social Sciences, 9-12 January, Calcutta.

Sengupta, Sunil and Haris Gazdar (1997), 'Agrarian Politics and Rural Development in West Bengal', in Jean Dreze and Amartya Sen (eds.), *Indian Development: Selected Regional Perspectives*, Oxford University Press, Delhi.

Sharma, H.R. (1995), *Agrarian Relations in India: Patterns and Implications*, Har-Anand Publications, New Delhi.

Sundaram, K. and Suresh D. Tendulkar (2003), 'Poverty in India in the 1990s: An Analysis of Changes in 15 Major States', *Economic and Political Weekly*, Vol. 38, No. 14, April 5.

UNICEF (2000), *People First: People's Participation in Social Planning and Development*, Kolkata.

Webster, Neil (1992), *Panchayati Raj and the Decentralisation of Development Planning in West Bengal*, K.P. Bagchi & Co., Kolkata.

# 4

# Bihar

PRAVEEN JHA and ATUL K. SINGH*

## INTRODUCTION

Bihar is a study in paradoxes, a careful reading of which reveals dynamics of its underdevelopment along with latter's institutional and structural correlates. Bihar, on the eve of independence, had among the richest natural resource base in the country. While on the one hand is the fact of its huge mineral resource base, particularly that of iron and coal along with plentiful supply of water which endowed it with a potential of becoming pioneer state of industrial development, on the other, is the stark reality of its economic backwardness sixty years after independence. On the one hand is its assertive polity which saw a strong challenge thrown by the subaltern groups to the dominance by feudal elites, on the other is the stark reality of substantive unfreedoms which qualify the lives of masses struggling to eke out subsistence in an exceptionally weak economy of the state characterized by not only a distorted production structure, but also by poor infrastructural base.

Today, not only is Bihar home to a vast expanse of destitution and deprivation, the possibilities of negotiating this expanse seem rather bleak, in the background of a debilitated and further worsening social and physical infrastructure, and retreat of the state from its

* Praveen Jha is on the faculty of the Centre for Economic Studies and Planning, and Atul K. Singh is a research scholar at the same centre.

responsibility of arresting this decline. It is these contradictions, breach between proclamations of institutions and their actual realization, the dialectics between its state of underdevelopment and its potential of development that makes Bihar a very potent case study in any enterprise at understanding the dynamics of development.

In terms of most indicators of development, there are huge deficits in Bihar. The state witness second highest incidence of rural poverty in India. It not only has lowest per capita income in the country, the gulf between national and state's percapita income has been widening over time. While percapita income of Bihar, on the eve of independence, was around 81 per cent of the all India average, by 1960-61 it had declined to 70 per cent of the Indian average. This trend of widening inequity in income has particularly intensified since mid-eighties, as by 1993-94 state's per capita income had declined to 40 per cent, and further to 30 per cent of per capita national income by 2003-04. It is not only deprivation with respect to entitlements, but also with respect to capabilities that chains the development possibilities for the masses in Bihar. Bihar has poorest records of human development among the major states in India. As per the National Human Development Report prepared by the Planning Commision, 2001, Bihar is at the lowest position among the major states in India, and this has been so over last two and a half decades. While a majority of state's population (53 per cent) is illiterate, not even half of those in school have a chance to complete their education, as dropout rate in Bihar is about 52 per cent against the all-India average of 29 per cent.

The capabilities of the masses to successfully meet their deprivations are further compromised by a weak and stagnant economy with a distorted production structure. While agriculture contributes about 33 per cent of the state's domestic product, it provides employment to almost 74 per cent of its workforce. On the other hand, while tertiary sector produces more than 50 per cent of the state's domestic product, it employs a mere 17 per cent of the workforce (Table 4.1 and Table 4.2).

What is worse is that overtime income distribution across the sectors is increasingly getting skewed against agriculture. Over last decade, while share of agriculture in the GSDP has fallen by 12 per cent,

**Table 4.1:** Gross State Domestic Product (GSDP) at 1993-94 Prices (%)

| *Sectors* | *Bihar* | | *India* | |
|---|---|---|---|---|
| | 1993-94 | 2003-04 | 1993-94 | 2003-04 |
| Primary | 48.78 | 37.40 | 33.54 | 24.04 |
| of which Agr. | 45.27 | 33.15 | 28.39 | 19.73 |
| Secondary | 9.93 | 11.20 | 23.69 | 24.54 |
| Tertiary | 41.29 | 51.40 | 42.77 | 51.43 |
| Gross State Domestic Product | 100.00 | 100.00 | 100.00 | 100.00 |

*Source*: Sharma and Joddar, 2007, Table 2(a), p. 3.

**Table 4.2:** Employment Structure (% of UPSS Workforce)

| *Sectors* | *Bihar* | | *India* | |
|---|---|---|---|---|
| | 1993-94 | 2004-05 | 1993-94 | 2004-05 |
| Primary | 78.33 | 73.50 | 65.50 | 59.07 |
| of which Agr. | 77.57 | 73.40 | 64.75 | 58.50 |
| Secondary | 6.47 | 9.12 | 14.83 | 17.57 |
| of which Mnf. | 4.58 | 6.15 | 11.35 | 11.73 |
| Tertiary | 14 | 17.39 | 20.50 | 23.36 |
| All | 100.00 | 100.00 | 100.00 | 100.00 |

*Source*: Sharma and Joddar, 2007.

its share in total employment has fallen only by 4 per cent, thereby indicating a worsening of income distribution across the sectors. On the other hand, the services sector which sees its share increase in state's income by around 11 per cent, its share of total employment is seen to be increasing only by 3 per cent. This worsening of income distribution against agrarian Bihar, without any generation of adequate income and employment opportunities in other sectors of the economy is spelling doom for the rural masses.

With about 90 per cent of the state's population living in rural areas, and more than three-fourth deriving their sustenance from agricultural enterprise, worsening of income distribution against the sector essentially means worsening of position of an overwhelming majority of state's population in its production and distribution structure. And what is more alarming is that worsening of income distribution for this huge mass is taking place not from a standard of surplus but rather from a standard of subsistence. Agriculture in Bihar is predominantly subsistence agriculture. About 96 per cent of farmers in Bihar are marginal and small farmers, which forces their agricultural enterprise in subsistence mode. They cultivate essentially to provide for their own consumption. Condition of agricultural labourers and sub-tenants is even worse; they face an open existential question on almost a daily basis. This worsening of income distribution against these subsistence agricultuarlists is further confirmed by a drastic fall in foodgrain production in the state which is revealed by the official statistics (Bihar Economic Survey, 2006-07, 2007-08).

Backwardness of the economy, a distorted production structure, poor state of physical and social infrastructure, and substantive deprivations that this state of affairs entail for the masses is confirmed by a host of official statistics and a plethora of field studies done on the subject. Field reports of IAS probationers in Bihar submitted to LBS Academy, Mussoorie is one such source which not only reveals constraints faced by the rural-agrarian Bihar, but also their differential character across the state highlighting the fallacy of a uniform policy prescription for diagnosed ills of the state. The findings of these reports are useful pointers of capability of the masses to deal the given state of affairs, opportunities available to them to explore and expand their human potential, and effectiveness of the State in delivering these masses capacity and opportunity of escape from their poverty and destitution.

This paper in section one tries to read from these field reports of IAS probationers primarily positioning of the rural masses in terms of their assets and capabilities in the given socio-economic environment, and also reach and effectiveness of the welfare arm of the State. As land is a prerequisite of any agricultural enterprise, productive capacity of the masses, and the very character of agricultural production is largely determined by their access to land. The paper highlights broad findings of these field studies on the nature of land ownership and agricultural production in different parts of Bihar. Education is the most important asset as well as capacity at the hands of an individual to negotiate various challenges thrown up by her socio-economic and political environment. First section of the paper also tries to read the overall educational outcomes together with extant infrastructure, corroborated by the evidence generated by these field studies. Similarly, state of health infrastructure and access of the masses to which is one of the crucial determinants of well-being of the masses, is highlighted using the findings of the reports. Finally, this section takes a look at the reach and effectiveness of the poverty alleviation programmes which are indicative of not only efficiency of governance but also democratic credentials of the institutional construct of the state. A step towards negotiating the development challenges that the economy and the people of the state are faced with today involves a careful reading of the structuring of these deprivations. Second part of the paper tries to read the structuring the economic backwardness, and infrastructural and institutional poverty of the state.

## AN EVALUATION BASED ON FIELD REPORTS

### Access to Land

Land is a primary means of production in agriculture. However, in case of Bihar, as in any semi-feudal socio-economic environment where modern means of production and their concomitant relations of production have yet a very limited presence, land has a character larger than that of a production unit; it is more of a living unit. Here, relationship of man with land is not only a function of economic production, but also has as variables various social and cultural values which nevertheless are ideological constructs of a given system of power structure. Thus, demand on land is not merely fed by economic logic but a host of factors determined and in turn determining social and political dynamics. Such a socio-economic environment coupled with the fact that Bihar has highest population density in the country not only makes for an exceptionally high population pressure on land, but also gives a very complex character to the demand for land thereby making any effort at land management a herculean task.

There is a predominance of marginal and small holdings in Bihar, which together account for about 96 per cent of total number of holdings and 67.36 per cent of total owned area (Table 4.3). Despite population pressure on land, landownership has a clearly skewed distribution in the state as large landholdings account for only about 0.1 per cent of total number of holdings but 4.63 per cent of total owned area. In fact, while percentage of large landholdings has fallen in the nineties from 0.2 per cent in 1992 to 0.1 per cent in 2003, area

**Table 4.3:** Per cent Distribution of Households and Area Owned over Five Major Classes in Bihar

| Year | % of Land Holdings | | | | | | % of Area Owned | | | | | |
|---|---|---|---|---|---|---|---|---|---|---|---|---|
| | *Marginal (0<*<1ha)* | *Small (1<*<=2)* | *Semi-medium (2<*<=4)* | *Medium (4<*<=10)* | *Large (*>10)* | *All* | *Marginal (0<*<1ha)* | *Small (1<*<=2)* | *Semi-medium (2<*<=4)* | *Medium (4<*<=10)* | *Large (*>10)* | *All* |
| *Bihar* | | | | | | | | | | | | |
| 2003 | 89.40 | **7.10** | 2.70 | 0.70 | 0.10 | 100 | 42.07 | **25.29** | 18.53 | 9.56 | 4.63 | 100 |
| 1992 | 80.56 | **11.10** | 6.00 | 2.14 | 0.20 | 100 | 28.58 | **23.84** | 24.45 | 18.68 | 4.44 | 100 |
| 1982 | 76.55 | 12.42 | 7.79 | 2.82 | 0.31 | 100 | 23.96 | 22.91 | 27.02 | 20.22 | 5.90 | 100 |
| 1971-72 | 71.71 | 15.11 | 9.15 | 3.66 | 0.37 | 100 | 18.20 | 23.43 | 28.07 | 23.63 | 6.67 | 100 |
| *All India* | | | | | | | | | | | | |
| 2003 | 79.60 | 10.80 | 6.00 | 3.00 | 0.60 | 100 | 23.05 | 20.38 | 21.98 | 23.08 | 11.55 | 100 |
| 1992 | 71.88 | 13.42 | 9.28 | 4.54 | 0.88 | 100 | 16.93 | 18.59 | 24.58 | 26.07 | 13.83 | 100 |
| 1982 | 66.64 | 14.70 | 10.78 | 6.45 | 1.42 | 100 | 12.03 | 16.49 | 23.58 | 29.83 | 18.07 | 100 |
| 1971-72 | 62.62 | 15.49 | 11.94 | 7.83 | 2.12 | 100 | 9.76 | 14.68 | 21.92 | 30.73 | 22.91 | 100 |

*Source*: NSS Report 491: Household Ownership Holdings in India, 2003.

under such holdings has increased from 4.44 per cent to 4.63 per cent, thereby indicating a tendency towards further concentration at the top. At the lower end, there is a clear trend of increasing marginalization of land holdings over last three decades. Marginal holdings have increased from 71 per cent of the total in 1970 to almost 90 in 2003.

Predominance of small and marginal landholdings, and a tendency towards fragmentation is confirmed by the field reports of the IAS probationers. H.R. Srinivasa's report on Banaili village in Purnea notices the trend towards fragmentation propelled majorly by inheritance and sale of land. While absentee landowners are found to be selling out their land, distress sale by small and marginal farmers is also reported in the study. The latter observation is of crucial significance in the changed macro-economic environment in the country in the post-ninety era. Neo-liberal policy environment mandating retreat of state has not only meant rising costs of production in agriculture which has been linked extensively to the market on the input side, but also a highly constrained access to formal credit market. Consequently, it is commonplace to find a small/marginal farmer in debt trap of a local money lender and hence the distress sale.

Landownership among the households is found to closely correspond to their placement in social hierarchy. Field study of Dharampur village in Nalanda district done by Avinash Kumar clearly brings out this conformity between caste hierarchy and landownership as Kurmis (elites among the backward castes) were found to be the major landowning caste followed closely by the Yadavs. The SCs were at the worst position with very few owning land, and that too of very small plot sizes. Most of the landowning SC families are beneficiares of land reforms. Interestingly, the study also notes a trend of Kurmis selling out land with purchasers being mostly Yadavs. While Yadavs, Koeri and Kurmis are agriculturalist caste, Kurmis in this region have traditionally been the landlords. With time, it is their growing distance from cultivation and agriculture, following closely the trend of upper caste landlords, that gets reflected in the selling out of land.

Socially weak segments are also land poor, and this concordance between social and economic placement in the rural economy makes for sustenance of feudal/semi-feudal relations of production. Sharecropping and absentee landlordism is a classic example, where the landlord derives the maximum rent out of his ownership status without having to undertake any productive investment in land. The land-poor (share-croppers, agricultural labour) in most of the cases are barely able to derive their sustenance; faced with existential questions on almost regular basis, they are forced into a relationship of dependence on the patron/landlord/moneylender; since these existential questions are open ended, continual dependence propagates the exploitation which had in the first place had put survival open to question. This completes the trap of trinity, of exploitation, dependence and servility-exploitation forcing open question of survival, settlement of which leads to dependence on the exploiter, which in turn ensures continuance of exploitation.

So powerful is the trap, economically and even ideologically (laden with loaded social values and ethos), that even constitutional rights and probing of administration fails to solicit initiative on the part of the 'trapped' to get out of it. This is brought out very starkly in the field study of Mungauli village in Muzaffarpur district done by Jitendra Srivastava. He found that some of the sub-tenants were in tenancy arrangement for more than 12 years thereby were legally entitled to ownership rights. These sub-tenants very emphatically stated their unwillingness to move any petition for the same as suggested by the Assistant Collector himself because they thought it would spoil their 'peaceful relationship' with the landowners. This brings forth the limitations of legislative provisioning of 'rights' as a way of addressing such structural deformities so long as the capacity to claim and exercise the 'right' is missing.

Land reforms in Bihar have failed on this and many other counts. Bihar was the first state to have introduced the zamindari abolition bill, but was among the last to have passed it. Till date, only 3.85 lakh acres of land has been acquired as ceiling surplus. Against this, in 1973-74, the then revenue minister of Bihar had stated in the Legislative Assembly that the Amendment Act of 1972 would make available 18 lakhs of surplus land. A very similar figure for ceiling surplus land in the state was thrown up in a study done by IAS probationers for LBSNAA in 1989-90, which estimated ceiling surplus land in Bihar to be about 17.76 lakh acres.* These figures speak

* The basis of the estimate was Agricultural Census of 1970-71. They took a ceiling limit of 30 acres which was the ceiling limit of Class III land, and as number of holdings above 30 acre size was 135,105 and the average size of land above 30 acres was given to be 43.15 acres, the estimated ceiling surplus land came to be about 17.76 lakh acres.

volumes about the land reform exercise in Bihar. Worse still, till date only about 68 per cent of the land acquired has been distributed. Even that distribution has not resulted in effective control over the piece of land by the beneficiaries is brought to light by the field reports of Dewaria village in Gaya district by Arvind Kumar Choudhary, of Eraura Village in Bhojpur district by Prem Singh Meena and Kusmauth village in Begusarai district by Vandana Dedel. The parchas for the same piece of land are found with more than one person while the actual possession is found to be with third person. This peculiar phenomena of 'dual ownership' arises from the fact that the landlords in some cases had declared that piece of land ceiling surplus which they had already donated under *Bhoodan* and in some case also sold out to some third person. Thus while *Bhoodan Yajna* committee issued parcha to one beneficiary, parcha for the ceiling surplus was issued by the administration to someboly else. It was also found that absence of a well-thought out distribution plan has also resulted in distribution exercise becoming a farce. In cases where land distributed was located in villages other than that of beneficiary's, either he could not take possession of that land or was found to sell/mortgage it as reported in the study of Vandana Dedel. Furthermore, mere provision of land as an ownership right also does not seem to be helping the case of beneficiaries, as they lack the capacity to convert it into a production unit. As highlighted in the field studies, lack of infrastructural support such as irrigation, which otherwise is very expensive, adversely affect agricultural production of the weaker farmers. Thus any effect effort at reforming relations of production in agricultural sector has to see land as a productivity unit rather than a title in ownership.

## Education

The weak state of economy in Bihar is followed closely by acute poverty in both, social and physical infrastructure. Education is by far the most important social capital on which development of any society premised. While the state's literacy level (48 per cent) is the lowest in the country, with more than half of its population illiterate, its educational infrastructure too is in shambles reflected by a pupil-teacher ratio of 122:1 as against 40:1 for India as a whole (Bihar Development Report, 2004). The net primary enrolment rate for Bihar in 1999-2000 was 52 per cent, compared to 77 per cent nationally. In fact, Bihar has the distinction of being the only state in India where the primary enrolments have fallen in the nineties down 4 per cent for boys and 1 per cent for girls.

The poor educational outcomes in the state has a differential spread for different segments of the society, with the socio-economic status closely conforming to the literacy achievements. For example, in Munguali village of district Muzaffarpur, Jitendra Srivastava reports that while 52.8 per cent of Kurmi population was literate, literacy among the Muslims, Dhobi and Nuniya was 36.1 per cent, 34.21 per cent and 28.57 per cent respectively. Even within a given social group, a substantive gender divide is to be found in the literacy outcomes. While 61.3 per cent of Kurmi males were found to be illiterate, literacy among the women was only 38.3 per cent. Likewise while 34.21 per cent of Dhobi males were literate, their female literacy was only 21.43 per cent. Gender divide is found to be most significant among the Muslims, which had only 22.4 per cent of female literacy as against 50 per cent for their men. This highlights the need to take gender as a key classificatory category while defining underprivileged in the society.

The literacy outcomes themselves are not very good indicators of the capacity that the masses have to develop their lives and explore the opportunities that expanding economy and market present before them. For example, in Kusmauth village in Begusarai district, as reported by Vandana Dedel, while literacy rate was 85 per cent, not a single person was educated upto twelfth standard, and not a single female was found to be matriculate. What empowerment in terms of income opportunities outside agricultural sector would such an educational attainment provide is anybody's guess. High dropout rates is one of the most damaging ills plaguing educational arena in Bihar. Not only a substantive population of school going age children are found to be out of school, a majority of those who enter the school system are found to dropout. In 2000-2001 for the entire state, 24 per cent of primary school students transited to the upper primary level; 12 per cent from the upper primary level to the secondary level and 10 per cent from secondary level to the higher secondary level.

While low enrolment ratio is due to a variety of factors, poor educational infrastructure—both physical and human, along with poverty and absence of adequate employment opportunities is what is driving children out of school. It is worth noting that none of the twelve villages for which field report was done by IAS probationers had a high school, only 4 had a middle school. And even the schools that were there were found to be terribly lacking in both physical and human infrastructure. For example, in Eruaura village of Bhojpur district, pupil-teacher ratio was found to 160:1. Many of the primary schools are reported to have neither teachers nor building. In some one or two teachers are left to attend five classes at one time. High dropout rate, therefore, is not a puzzle hard to solve.

## Health

Poor educational outcomes in the state are followed by equally poor health scenario in the state. Health outcomes in Bihar, with some exceptions, are below the national average. MMR in Bihar is 707 per 100,000 women of reproductive age, compared to the national average of 404. Antenatal care reaches only around 10 per cent of women in Bihar compared to 32 per cent for India. The percentage of deliveries attended to by skilled health staff was only 23 per cent for Bihar as against 42 per cent for the country in 1998-99. In terms of nutritional status of children, despite some progress, the proportion of underweight children is still among the highest in the country.

The health care infrastructure organized on the principles of referral system is virtually non-existent in the state. There is a serious shortfall of health sub-centres and primary health clinics compared to the existing national norms. More importantly, existing centres and clinics are beset by the endemic problems relating to quality standards: poor maintenance of facilities, idle equipment, and chronic short supply of medicines and vaccines, particularly in the rural areas. As a result, there is significant reliance by the households on the private health providers for critical health services. Banaili village in Purnea district, H.R. Srinivasa reports that nearest PHC was 5 km away, and as such people depended on private practioners. Even where health centres/sub-centres were there, they are found to be in pathetic conditions with most of them having no doctors. In fact, out of the twelve villages, 9 reported having no exposure to registered medical practioners. And the worst effected by this poor state of health infrastructure is again the underprivileged and disadvantaged sections of the society. As reported by N. Sarvan Kurmar in village Sahmora in Saharsa district, infant and maternal mortality was found to be highest among the weaker sections of the society, in particular the Mushahar community.

Thus, in face of a virtually non-existent public health care system, it is not surprising that the Private doctors and quacks contribute nearly 74 per cent of all medical consultations, with government doctors being consulted in only 15 per cent of cases. More than half of women rely on provision of pre-natal care by the private providers, compared to just one-fifth on government providers. Not surprisingly, therefore, the ratio of private spending on health care, relative to public spending is the second highest in Bihar, and is a major source of indebtedness and perpetual impoverishment of the rural folks. Public spending on health has declined from 8 per cent of total expenditure in mid-1980s to 4 per cent in 2000. In 1995-96, Bihar recorded the lowest public health spending per capita among the major states—Rs. 15 compared to Rs. 84 for the country as a whole. Out of this limited spending, the poorest 40 per cent received only around 20 per cent of total public health spending. Of the subsidies on health, only 6 per cent of rural subsidies and 6 per cent of urban subsidies go to respcetive bottom quintiles, the top most quintiles received 42 per cent and 31 per cent subsidies respectively. The high cost of treatment in such a scenario is a significant strain on the already impoverished population of Bihar.

Poor social infrastructure is complemented even more intensely by poverty of physical infrastructure. Road density per lakh of population is the lowest in Bihar (90.1 km), compared to the national average (256.7 km). For every 100 sq. km the state has only 77 km of road length as against 169 km in Orissa, 118 in Tamil Nadu and 97 km in UP. This disparity becomes even wider, when one takes into account the share of surfaced roads in total road length—37.4 per cent in Bihar and 56.5 per cent in India as a whole. During the nineties, the disparity between Bihar and India has widened *vis-à-vis* annual growth of road lengths. For India as a whole, this growth rate was 3.5 per cent, for Bihar it was a meagre 0.6 per cent. The disconnect between the rural Bihar and urban centres and centres of governance can be gauged from the fact that most of the village studies done by the IAS probationers found an average distance of three to four kms to the nearest bus stop. Even worse is the case of railway connectivity. Nearest railway station for most of the villages was found to be more than 25 kms. Railroute density per lakh of population in Bihar is anyway lowest in the country.

Similarly, the power scenario is not only poor but has shown worsening trend over the years. During early nineties, the per capita consumption level of electricity in Bihar was 110 kWh, less than half of the national average of 253 kWh. By the end of the decade, the disparity was even wider—460 kWh for India and only 143 kWh for Bihar. Today, only 10 per cent of rural households use electricity as a source of lighting, and only 47 per cent of the villages have been electrified. Among the twelve villages studies by the IAS probationers, only four were found to have been electrified. This poor state of physical infrastructure is not only a disability for the masses, but also makes the economy and governance high cost and contributes to their inefficiency.

**Table 4.4:** Basic Infrastructure in the Villages surveyed by the Officer Trainees of LBSNAA

| *Village* | *District* | *Distance of Bus Stop* | *Distance from Railway Station* | *Nearest Bank Branch* | *Nearest Post-Office* | *Nearest Market* | *Nearest PDS Shop* | *Electricity* |
|---|---|---|---|---|---|---|---|---|
| Dharampur | Nalanda | 5 | 30 | 10 | 10 | 10 | Na | Yes |
| Bealur | Bhojpur | 0 | 25 | 10 | 0 | 10 | 0 | No |
| Saradhi | Munger | 0 | 8 | 2 | 2 | 2 | 0 | No |
| Dewaria | Gaya | 3 | 80 | 2 | 2 | 2 | 2 | No |
| Sonaru | Patna | 1 | 1 | 1 | 1 | 1 | 0 | Yes |
| Lodhipur | Gaya | 8 | 35 | 3 | 10 | 12 | Na | Na |
| Eraura | Bhojpur | 5 | 14 | 3 | 2.5 | 6 | 3 | No |
| Gidha | Bhojpur | 1 | 3 | 3 | 0 | 3 | 0 | Yes |
| Lanka | Palamau | 0 | | 3 | 3 | 3 | 3 | Yes |
| Siswa | Begusarai | 0 | 10 | Na | Na | Na | 2 | No |
| Sarkarwara sawik | Muzaffarpur | Na | 3 | | 3 | 3 | 0.5 | No |
| Mugaili | Muzaffarpur | 0.1 | 33 | 1 | 2 | 1 | 1 | Yes |
| Banaili | Purnea | 3 | 3 | 3 | 3 | 3 | 0 | No |
| Kusmauth | Begusarai | 4 | 5 | 5 | 0 | 5 | 0 | Na |
| Sahmora | Saharsa | Na | 28 | Na | Na | Na | 4 | Na |

## Poverty Alleviation Programmes

Work to hands, good health and education are three basic premises of human existence, on which the rural masses in Bihar suffer substantive disabilities. In such a scenario, welfare reach of a democratic State is not only a marker of its legitimacy but also a bulwark of political stability itself. It is through poverty alleviation programmes that the state tries to directly reach out with a helping hand in the existential struggle of the impoverished masses. Today, going by the official statistics (based on 61st round NSS report), Bihar has third highest incidence of rural poverty in India, with about 43 per cent of its rural population living below poverty line.

Poverty alleviation programmes in Bihar have been plagued by a plethora of problems ranging from problem in identification, to creation of asset, payment of due benefit to the targeted beneficiaries, and political economy of plunder of funds meant for the programme. As reported for the Eraura village in Bhojpur, which holds true in most of the cases, there is a collusion of the dominant sections of the society/polity with the block officials in preparation of the list of beneficiaries. This collusion at the identification stage is facilitated by inadequacy of awareness campaigns regarding BPL survey which is the duty of local administration. In the NREG programmes, it is common place to find that panchayat functionaries in collusion with block official preparing list of job-card holders who themselves are unaware of their inclusion. Nevertheless, work is sanctioned under the programme, number of employment days are shown on paper and funds withdrawn with hardly any real work being done. And this loot is facilitated by the fact that most of the works sanctioned are mud works, which thanks to annual flooding in Bihar are 'washed out' in official records, ready for the next harvest of floods.

Likewise there is a problem with rural banks, which are far from cooperative with the needy segments in granting loans. Even where they ultimately get financed, underfinancing is their next problem which is aptly reported in case of village Mungauli in district Muzaffarpur by Jitendra Srivastava. He reports that this underfinancing of their projects forced the beneficiaries, swarojgaris to take recourse to informal money market at very high interest rates to complete their projects. To further worsen the matter, it was found that banks do not give the loan amount directly to the beneficiary (whereas they required to do so) but instead gives him a delivery order. The delivery order entitles him to procure the asset required directly from the supplier and the beneficiary has no say in the choice of the supplier or the quality of the asset procured. The bank manager in turn takes a commission from the supplier also from favouring him over the others. Reeling under high cost put on their enterprise by the debt from informal money market, most of the swarojgaris eventually fail and turn broke.

To make things worse, none of the assests of swarojgaris were insured in Mungauli. None had training, and BDO revealed he had no fund for their training. There was no capacity build-up under either the infrastructure or training components of SGSY—and not only was it not there in the village, it is not even there in the block.

Problems with poverty alleviation programmes were very aptly highlighted in the study of Eraura village in Bhojpur. It was aptly pointed out that the very conceptualization of various schemes under the programme was flawed, primarily because of centralized and remote planning done at Delhi, which abstracts from the local specifics and hence is not only effective in impact but also misplaced in terms of local needs. Further, it was pointed out that effective monitoring in form of ground level inspection was hardly done to ensure compliance of the aims and objectives of the programmes. Thus, BDO and his staff became all powerful in this situation and the statistics prepared by them goes to the Central Government without much scrutiny. Further at the implementation stage, multiplicity of agencies involved in implementation of programme was cause for inordinate delay and inefficient and ineffective outcomes. It is ironical to note that the programmes directed at alleviating poverty are also found to eventually feed the socio-economic dominance of the powerful. For example, study of Gidha village in Bhojpur by Vinay Kumar reveals that assets created under these programmes are mostly privilege of the upper castes. Impact of PAPs on the rural Bihar is summed up in the observation of Arvind Kumar Choudhary who while reporting on Dewaria village in Gaya observed 'almost no impact of poverty alleviation programmes' although the mukhiya belonged to a backward caste.

## A BRIEF EXPLORATION INTO POLITICAL ECONOMY OF BIHAR'S BACKWARDNESS

Thus underdevelopment of Bihar is marked by a backward economy, substantive deprivations among the masses in terms basic abilities and opportunities needed to have a human existence, and stark poverty of infrastructure—not only physical but also that of governance. However, this state of affair is not a new phenomena, and has a historical precedent. On the eve of colonial subjugation, Patna was arguably the largest city in the country which is testimony to the economic vibrancy of the region not very long ago. The role of colonial revenue administration in structuring of the relations of exploitation in the rural economy through which agricultural surplus was expropriated by the colonial rulers and their local allies played a major role in structuring of underdevelopment in the state. The historical setting of permanent settlement ensured backwardness of the region as it made a system of primitive accumulation without making productive investment a necessary condition of continuation of the accumulation. The extent of plunder of the agrarian economy can be gauged by the fact that in general more than 50 layers of intermediaries were found between the rent paying tenant farmer and the state. As revenue of the state was fixed in perpetuity in these areas, there was no incentive for the state to undertake productive investments in the region, or to create institutional/administrative infrastructure other than the absolute minimal required to maintain its imperial hold on the region. This gets confirmed in the observation made in the Memorandum for the Indian Statutory Commission on the Working of the Reforms in Bihar and Orissa. The memorandum noted that the standard expenditure of Bihar and Orissa, worked out on the basis of actual expenditure prior to 1912, came to 8 lakhs per million of the population against 13 lakhs per million of the population in Bengal, though the cost of the administration in Bengal was the lowest in India.

In fact, state's imperial designs were very effectively carried out in collaboration with the local allies, who made fortunes from the sheer plunder of their fellow natives. A very descriptive account of this mechanism is given by Anand Yang in his book, *The Limited Raj*. Such was the degree of plunder that leakages from it created huge zamindari estates such as Shikarpur in West Champaran whose founder was the accountant of the Bettiah Raj, Kursela estate whose founder was the under-raiyat of the Darbhanga Maharaj, and a host of others. As this plunder was basically a rental accrual arising from monopoly over land, and various legal and illegal exactions associated with it in an agrarian economy, this surplus invariably went into either profligacy or into acquiring further rights into land, rather than into any kind of productive investment in land.

The extension of Permanent Settlement of 1873 to mineral rights in 1880 ensured that whatever opportunity the state had of developing on its huge mineral resource base was effectively scuttled. The opportunity was scuttled on two counts, one as the provincial government was denied any right to tax mining activities of the companies in the state. And, secondly, as companies having rights over these mineral deposits invariably were registered outside the state, the provincial government practically had no means of taxing the income of these companies generated from the mineral wealth of the state. Thus the mineral wealth of the poorest of the regions went into enriching and developing other states of India with favourable industrial and income environment, thereby creating a strange situation of the poorest of the regions subsidizing the prosperity and development of the richer regions of the colonial state.

This does not complete the story. Permanent settlement and its extension to mineral rights together with a near absence of industrial base in the region meant a financially poor provincial government with neither the resources, nor the incentive of making investment in both, physical and institutional infrastructure in the state. As noted above, in comparison with the population served, the administration of Bihar and Orissa costed less than that of any other province. This was only the necessary corollary of its inadequate revenue. This obviously constrained state spending which meant a significant backwardness of the state in institutional/infrastructural terms too.

Thus development potential of Bihar was chained during the colonial period. However, one must note that it was the colonial state together with its plundering local allies that was working true to its agenda of colonial exploitation. An important question that poses itself at this point is that what preventing unchaining and nurturing of the development potential of the state in the post-independence period. What fettered development of a state having richest of natural endowments that could have given it a geographical advantage in any enterprise of industrial development? The state given its mineral resource base had a natural advantage in setting up of a heavy industrial base together with its forward and backward linkages. However, a host of policy decisions such as freight equalization not only negated this geographical advantage of the region, but ensured that this already backward state subsidized consumption of items such as steel and coal by the developed industrial centres/regions of the country. This not only was a charge on backwardness of Bihar, but also seriously distorted the comparative cost advantage of locations for industries using these freight equalized commodities as inputs.

and induced inefficient locations of industries in terms of true domestic resource cost of production and supply. What could have stimulated such policy initiatives by a democratically elected government with an explicit mandate of developing the underdeveloped, deprived and the weak?

Post-Independence State is found not only culpable on count of fettering opportunities of industrial development in the region, it faltered even in delivering the agenda of agricultural transformation which the planners had very sacredly borrowed from western path of modern economic development, implicitly assuming that the path could be replicated in different spatial and temporal frameworks without any problem. According to this official perception of development trajectory for the country, structural constraints in transformation of agriculture had to be overcome. While one aspect of structural constraint was the infrastructural/institutional poverty of the sector, the other aspect was primitive relations of production prevalent in agriculture which thwarted forces of production. State had, therefore, a mandate to intervene on both these counts if any plan of agrarian transformation was to take off.

Thus reforming relations in land, and creation of adequate infrastructure in agricultural sector were the two most important mandates for the independent state. While state intervened on the first count through land reforms, these were largely limited to zamindari abolition. It hardly made a dent on iniquitous land holding pattern and therefore, relations of production, and whatever transfer that did take place was compensated which in turn meant that the transfer was in effect limited among the upper strata of the landholding class. In case of Bihar, as noted above, though these reforms were very limited in their redistributive design, nevertheless resistance to even this limited land reform agenda was manifold. Content and character of land reforms were limited not only by the resistance of the landed elites in the state, but also by the very character of peasant movement demanding it. Zamindari rights in these permanent settlement areas not only meant a host of legal execution from the peasantry, but also a slew of illegal executions and demands of labour which effected a vice like grip of these landed elites on the agrarian economy. These legal and illegal executions on the peasantry and the demands on the labour of the region were the prime movers of peasant agitation in Bihar, which was invariably led by middle peasantry.

Thus agenda of peasant movement was not so much redistribution of land as abolition of zamindari which would end legal and institutional backing of the grip of zamindars on the rural economy (Jannuzi, 1973). Thus while land reforms were executed in Bihar, they invariably failed to correct the institutional bottlenecks in land relations which were holding back forces of production.

On the other front, agricultural sector as a whole was treated as the bargain sector in the initial phases of Indian planning process. It was the food crisis of mid-sixties that forced a review of the strategy. The focus was now on betting on the strong, targeting subsidy and policy measures towards provisioning and incentivizing use of input package of HYV technology by the individuals and regions which already had the basic capacity to do so. Focus shifted from major and medium irrigation schemes to minor irrigation schemes. This again meant that the infrastructure which was to be provided to a subsistence agriculture could not be put in place, instead there was a public provisioning of private goods. Bihar, which hardly had any agricultural/rural infrastructure worth its name, given its historical neglect thanks to the Permanent settlement in the colonial period, was thus by policy design excluded from the green revolution flush in India. There was practically no public provisioning of agricultural infrastructure in Bihar, which would complement/facilitate any significant move towards an effective agrarian transformation.

## A CONCLUDING REMARK

Thus, while apathy of colonial state, dominance by feudal elites channelising primitive accumulation back into land, and lack of adequate infrastructure may be few of the explanatory variables for lack of industrial development in Bihar in the pre-independence era, even an independent democratic state with a welfare mandate requiring development of the weak and deprived could not make much difference to the state of economic backwardness of Bihar in post-independence period. Lives and work potential of an overwhelming majority of the population in the state is trapped in a vicious subsistence, sub-human existence underlined by both, inadequate capacity and lack of opportunities to break free. Not only are the capabilities of the masses are severely handicapped, capacity of the state governance machinery to deliver the same is also severely compromised by a long history of institutional neglect. Empathy for the backwardness of Bihar, abolishing dominance of the feudal elites and channelising the surplus towards productive investments in state's economy, and provisioning/creation of requisite infrastructure, were all as much within the reach of the free state as they were its responsibility. The state, however, has had very limited success on all these counts. This of course, emerges from the well-known large scale data systems and the same has also been captured very well by the field reports on which the first section was of this chapter based.

## REFERENCES

**A. LBS National Academy of Administration, Centre for Rural Studies, Socio-Economic Survey Reports of Rural India**

Choudhary Arvind Kumar, *Report on Socio-Economic Survey of Dewaria Village,* Gaya.

Dedel, Vandana, *A Socio-Economic Survey of Village Kusmauth*, Begusarai, Bihar.

Hans, Sanjeev, *Case Study of Sakarwara Sawik,* Muzaffarpur, Bihar.

Kumar, Avinash, *Socio-Economic Study of Dharampur Village,* Nalanda, Bihar.

Kumar, N. Saravana, *A Report on Socio-Economic Status and Land Reforms,* Sahmora, Saharsa.

Kumar, Rahul, *Socio-Economic Profile of Village Siswa,* Barauni, Bihar.

Kumar, Vinay, *Socio-Economic Survey of Village Gidha,* Bhojpur, Bihar.

Meena, Prem Singh, *Socio-Economic Study of Village Eraura,* Bhojpur, Bihar.

Rajendra, B., *Socio-Economic Survey of Village Saradhi,* Munger, Bihar.

Singh, Ajay Kumar, *A Report on Socio-Economic Survey of Lanka Village,* Palamu, Bihar.

Srinivasa, H.R., *Socio-Economic Study of Banaili Village*, Purnea, Bihar.

Srivastava, Jitendra, *Socio-Economic Report of Village Mungauli,* Muzaffarpur.

**B. Other Literature**

A Development Vision of Bihar; An IHD Report.

Acemoglou, D. and J. Robinson: *Why did the West Extend the Franchise?*

*Democracy, Inequality and Growth in Historical Perspective*, Working Paper, MIT, Economics Department,1998.

Alesina, A.: Macroeconomic Policy in a Two-Party System Repeated Game, *Quarterly Journal of Economics*, 1997.

Bagchi, A.K. (ed.): *Democracy and Development*.

Banerjee, A. and R. Somanathan: 'Caste, Community and Collective Action: The Political Economy of Public Goods Provision in India', mimeo, MIT Economics Department, 2001.

Bardhan, P.K.: *Political Economy and Governance Issues in India*.

Besley, T. and R. Burgess, 2000: 'Land Reform, Poverty Reduction and Growth: Evidence from India', *Quarterly Journal of Economics*.

Besley, T. and R. Burgess, 2001: The Political Economy of Government Responsiveness: Theory and Evidence from India', *Quarterly Journal of Economics*.

Betancourt, R. and S. Gleason: The Allocation of Publicly Provided Goods to Rural Households in India: On some consequences of Caste, Religion and Democracy, *World Development*, 2000.

Beteille, Andre, June 2000: 'The Scheduled Castes: An Inter-Regional Perspective', *Journal of Indian School of Political Science*, EPW.

World Bank, *Bihar—Towards a development strategy*: a World Bank Report.

Blair, Harry, W. Jan 1980: 'Rising Kulaks and Backward Classes in Bihar: Social Change in the Late 1970s', *EPW*.

Bose, Pradip Kumar, 1985: 'Mobility and Conflict: Social Roots of Caste Violence in Bihar' in *Caste, Caste Conflict and Reservations*, Ajanta Publications, Delhi.

Bourguignon, F. and T. Verdier, 2000: 'Oligarchy, Democracy, Inequality and Growth', *Journal of Development Economics*.

Collier, P., 1998: 'The Political Economy of Ethnicity', paper presented at the Annual World Bank Conference on Development Economics, Washington DC.

Corbridge, Stuart, Williams, Glyn. Srivastava, Manoj, Veron, Rene, June 2003: 'Making Social Sciences Matter-1: How the Local State Works in Rural Bihar, Jharkhand and West Bengal', *EPW*.

Dandekar, V.M., Jan. 1980: 'Bourgeois Politics of the Working Class', *EPW*.

Das, A.N., 1983: *Agrarian Unrest and Socio-Economic Change in Bihar, 1900-1980*, Manohar, New Delhi.

Das, A.N., 1992: *The Republic of Bihar*, Penguin Books, Delhi.

Drèze, J. and A. Sen,1995: *India: Economic Development and Social Opportunity,* Oxford University Press, Oxford.

Fox, Richard G., 1989: *Gandhian Utopia: Experiments with Culture*, Beacon Press, Boston.

Ghosh, Sugato and Pal, Sharmistha, *The Political Economy of Elite Dominance and Ethnic Heterogeneity: An Analysis of Disparate Social Development in the Indian States.*

Gupta, Dipankar, 2000: *Interrogating Caste: Understanding Hierarchy and Difference in Indian Society*, Penguin Books, New Delhi.

Jannuzi, F. Tomasson, 1974: *Agrarian Crisis in India: The Case of Bihar*, University of Texas Press, Austin.

Jha, Hetukar, April-June 2000: 'Promises and Lapses: Understanding the Experience of Scheduled Castes in Bihar in Historical Perspective', *Journal of Indian School of Political Science.*

Jha, Praveen, 2003: 'Causes of Poverty in Developing Countries: Stating A Longue Duree and Unfashionable Perspective', *Working Paper Number 17 for Institute for Human Development,* New Delhi.

Khemani, Stuti, *Partisan Politics and Intergovernmental transfers in India.*

Kothari, Rajni: *Caste in Indian Politics.*

Kumar Pankaj, Ashok and Singh, Mahendra Prasad, March 2005: 'The changing sociopolitical profile of local political elites (mukhias) in Bihar: a study of the 1978 and 2001 panchayat elections', *Indian Sociology.*

Louis, Prakash, 2003: 'Backward Caste Assertion' in *Backward Bihar*, Vikalp, Vol. 11.

Ozler, Berk, Gaurav Datt, and Martin Ravallion: "A Database on Poverty and Growth in India," Policy Research Department, The World Bank, 1996.

Prasad, Pradhan H., 1986: ' Land-Reforms in Bihar'. *EPW,* June, 30.

Prasad, Pradhan H., 1987: ' Agrarian Violence in Bihar', *EPW*, May.

Prasad, Pradhan H., 1991: 'Rise of Kulak Power and Caste Struggle in North India', *EPW.*

Sen, Amartya, 2000: *Development as Freedom*, Oxford University Press, New Delhi.

Sengupta, Nirmal, 1982: 'Agrarian Movements in Bihar' *in Agrarian Movements in India: Studies on 20th Century Bihar* (ed.), A.N. Das 1982, Frank Cassl, London.

Sharma, A.N., 1995: 'Political Economy of Poverty in Bihar', *Economic and Political Weekly,* October.

Sharma, A.N., 2005: 'Agrarian Relations and Socio-Economic Change in Bihar', *EPW*, March.

Singh, Shashi Bhusan, 2005: 'Limits to Power: Naxalism and Caste Relations in a South Bihar Village', *EPW*, June.

Srininvas, M.N. 1957: 'Caste in Modern India," *Journal of Asian Studies*, August.

Srininvas, M.N., 1996: *Studying One's Own Culture: Some Thoughts in Village, Caste, Gender and Method, Essays in Indian Social Anthropology*. Oxford University Press. Delhi.

Thelen, Kathleen and Steinmo, Sven: 'Historical Institutionalism in Comparative Politics' in *Structuring Politics* edited by Steinmo, Thelen and Longstrem,1957.

Yadav, Yogendra, 2000: 'Understanding the Second Democratic Upsurge: Trends in Electoral Politics in the 1990s' in F. Frankel, Zoya Hasan, R. Bhargava and B. Arora (Eds.), *Transforming India*, Oxford University Press, New Delhi.

Yang, Anand: *The Limited Raj*.

# 5

# Uttar Pradesh

BIMAL KUMAR

This report is based on survey conducted by IAS probationers. In all 14 villages were covered under the survey. These villages are spread in all economic regions. To that extent it could be said that the report present a representative view of socio-economic profile of rural Uttar Pradesh. However, since their selection is not based on strict sample selection, criteria, we treat them as case studies as well. Hence the format of the report consists of generalization of findings as well as village specific situations on selected topics.

The villages covered under this study are as follows:

**Eastern Region**

1. Village Avarata (District Allahabad)
2. Village Ranipur (District Azamgarh)
3. Village Parikhara (District Ballia)
4. Village Gulariha (District Gorakhpur)
5. Village Khirora Mohan (District Gonda)

**Bundelkhand Region**

6. Village Tikamau (District Mahoba)

**Western Region**

7. Village Himmatnagar Bhajhera (District Etah)

8. Village Jeesukhpur (District Etah)
9. Village Koyala Alipur (District Mathura)
10. Village Chirodi (District Meerut)
11. Village Shahpur Kalan (District Buland Shahr)
12. Village Jiraunia (District Pilibhit)

**Central Region**

13. Village Jaffarpur (District Barabanki)
14. Village Aloonagar Diguria (District Lucknow)

The study was sponsored by Lal Bahadur Shastri National Academy of Administration, Government of India, Mussoorie.

As this report is based on village level studies, it gives insights as to why the progress on socio-economic front as well as in respect of delivery mechanism and peoples participation has been so slow and why the efforts have not yielded desired result. The study also in the process focuses on the nature of micro level interventions and how they could be made more effective.

## INTRODUCTION

When India became independent, there was a vision that the development of nation would not only lead to higher economic growth with distributive justice but it would also mean eradication of poverty, universal education and good health for all.

Development planners hoped that in the long run, the growth of economy will take care of all other factors, it was only in the short run, that state needed to intervene for and provide facilities to those who were expected to be by passed in the process of development.

There were two inherent flaws in this approach. One, growth of economy should have been structurally linked to the structure of working population. This implies that there should have been synchronization of human development planning and economic resource planning. Despite five decades of planned development, the state of Uttar Pradesh (U.P.) lags behind in terms of almost all socio-economic indicators. The state plans had focused on development of both economic sector and social sector facilities. The economic sector facilities includes facilities for irrigation, power, transportation, communication, banking institutions and other economic infrastructural facilities. The priorities in the social sector included education, health drinking water etc.

The slow pace of development of U.P. in respect of economic and social indicators of U.P. not only kept U.P. as one of the slowest progressing states of India, but it also pulled down the rate of progress of India as a whole.

The information about dismal performance of U.P. in respect of socio-economic indicators is well documented, but villages level studies of the socio-economic profile will give important insights as to why the progress had been so slow and halting and why the efforts have not yielded desired results.

There are two aspects which need to be probed in this respect. One why per capita expenditure on economic infrastructural facilities and social infrastructural facilities have been lower in U.P. as compared to other states. Secondly, why the plan expenditure has not been properly balanced between economic infrastructural and social infrastructural.

Why Per Capita Expenditure has been Lower?

(i) Gap in per capital income of U.P. and that of all India has been increasing. In 1951 the per capita income of Uttar Pradesh was Rs. 259 against Rs. 269 of all India, i.e. the gap was in order of 8 per cent only. The gap increased to 35.3 per cent at the end of the Eighth Plan and to 41 per cent at the end of year 2000-01. The situation is likely to worsen in coming years because of slow growth rate of the economy of U.P. as compared to the country as a whole. The lower income lead to lower savings and lower per capita expenditure (Tenth Five Year Plan).

(ii) Gap in per capita state tax revenue has been still larger than the gap in per capita income. This shows that efforts to mobilize internal resources had either been tax or yielded poorer results in U.P. "If U.P. could achieve the same taxation level as that of Tamil Nadu, it could increase its tax revenue by Rs. 2200 crore more, i.e. almost double its tax revenue. Even it could raise its tax level to that of Rajasthan, it could generate tax revenue of the order of Rs. 6000 crore or about 25 per cent of its existing tax revenue" (Kripa Shanker).

(iii) Trends in planned expenditure on economic infrastructural (which includes power, irrigation and transport) shows that it was in the range of 41 per cent to 44 per cent of total plan expenditure during First, Second and Third Five Year Plans. The share on economic infrastructure was raised to 61 per cent in Fourth Five Year Plan, 66 per cent in Fifth Five Year Plan but thereafter its share started declining 60 per cent in Sixth Five Year Plan, 52 per cent in Seventh Five Year Plan, 49 per cent in Eighth Five Year Plan and 45 per cent in Ninth Five Year Plan.

The trend of planned expenditure on social infrastructure (which includes education, medical and public health and water supply and sanitation) shows that it was 21 per cent in the First Five Year Plan, 13 per cent in Second Five Year Plan and 16 per cent in the Third Five Year Plan. Then its share hovered around 10 per cent to 12 per cent during Fourth to Seventh Five Year Plans and remained around 15 per cent during the Ninth Five Year Plan.

## Economic vs. Social Infrastructure

Low per capita income puts the government in a state of dilemma, especially when there is resource crunch and per capita plan expenditure has to be kept at a lower rate. Because of the low per capita income, people have little capacity to invest. They cannot pay higher user charges for availing either the facilities of economic or social infrastructure. If private investments are made in economic or social infrastructure, then user charges would be high and only few would be able to pay such high charges. If, facilities of economic infrastructure (such as power, irrigation and transport) and social infrastructure (such as education, medical and public health, water supply and sanitation etc.) are required to be made available to the poorer strata also, then it becomes imperative for the state to invest in these sectors and provide facilities at affordable price.

And here lies the dilemma. The state itself if forced to keep the level of per capita expenditure on economic and social infrastructures. In order to attain a reasonable growth rate to keep parity at all India level, a minimum critical level of investment in the economic infrastructure is necessary. And if the per capita income increases, then in due course people would be able to pay higher user charges. That is, if investment on economic infrastructure could gradually become self-sustaining rather than subsidized base. However, if income does not increase to a sufficient level then services of economic infrastructure could be maintained only by subsidizing it. Not only this, if income of general population increases, it will also be able to spend more for availing social sector facilities.

On the other hand if facilities of the social sector are not adequate, the intergenerational disparity among different strata of population will increase in terms of their competencies, skills and freedom of choice.

The government of Uttar Pradesh had been facing this dilemma since the Eighth Five Year Plan. Due to worsening of financial position and increase in fiscal deficit, the government has been forced to reduce plan expenditure on economic and social infrastructure facilities.

This has been partly due to increase in expenditure on General Services and partly due to resource crunch.

Because of the reduction on plan expenditure on economic and social infrastructure, the government had chosen to cut sharply on economic infrastructure rather than on social infrastructure. Expenditure on social infrastructure could be sustained only if plan expenditure on economic infrastructure does not fall below a thresh hold point. The main reason for slower rate of growth of agricultural sector and very slow pace of diversification of agricultural economy had been reduction in plan expenditure on economic infrastructural facilities in the rural areas.

Furthermore, there is need to open up alternative channels for public investment and rural development. The areas could cover water and soil conservation, processing and preservation of local products and regeneration of internal markets.

## CONDITIONS IN SOCIAL DEVELOPMENT

### Education

The NSS 55th round survey shows that literacy ratio in U.P. was only 52.2 per cent as compared to 62.5 per cent for the nation as a whole. As per the census 2001, the literacy rate of U.P. [including Uttaranchal (now Uttarakhand)] was 58.1 per cent.

Another important aspect of literacy is revealed from the NSS 55th round data of the state. It shows that during 1999-2000 the literacy among females in rural areas was only 36 per cent as compared to 65.1 per cent among males (PMS report[1], 2002, p. 22). It also shows that there exists a positive correlation between literacy rate and monthly per capita expenditure (MPCE) in different classes. The lowest MPCE class of the 0 to 225 showed lowest literacy 34.5 per cent as against 69.8 per cent in the highest MPCE class of Rs. 950 and above in the rural areas of Uttar Pradesh.

The study further shows that "in view of mass literacy and poverty, family educational level and awareness but about educational institution, both play an important role in the promotion of enrolment rate". The study found a consistent increase in enrolment rate in each successive higher MPCE class. Girls were fond to be lagging behind the boys in terms of enrolment in rural as well as urban areas (*Ibid.*, p. 23).

The dropout rate and school completion rate were also found to be correlated to MPCE. A marked reduction in dropout rates in each of the successive higher MPCE class was found. As regards school completion rate, the highest completion rate was estimated at middle school level (*Ibid.*, p. 24).

Another study showed that enrolment ratio in 1995-96 was 90.8 per cent in age group of 6-11 years but came down to 55.7 per cent in the age group of 11-14 years. Enrolment ratios for girls are even lower 78.3 per cent at primary level and 39.4 per cent at secondary level. Girls constitute 40.5 per cent of total enrolment at primary level, but the figure goes down to 33.5 per cent at the secondary level (Singh[2], 2001, p. 19).

One reason for low literacy of girls has been attributed to the gender division of labour, which relegates most adult women (including those with relatively good education) to domestic work, and in turn diminishes the perceived 'returns' of investment in female education (Dreze and Sen[3], 1996, p. 84).

Dreze views poor performance in the field of education as a part of overall dismal functioning of public services in Uttar Pradesh. He observed that the comprehensive failure of public services, and of development-oriented interventions in general, can be seen to have two mutually reinforcing roots: (i) the states' low commitment to broad based development and social equity, and (ii) the failure of civil society to challenge that apathy, and more generally to promote social needs and the interests of disadvantaged groups (Dreze, 1996, p. 92).

The PROBE survey has found two types of situations. In the more deprived areas a vicious circle of neglect was found, where different flaws of the schooling system feed on each other. School facilities are minimal—classrooms are over crowded, school buildings are falling apart, teaching aids are a rare sight. Teachers feel trapped in a hopeless work environment, lack respect for local community, and yearn for better postings. Inspectors do not want to know. Parents themselves illiterate in many cases, are powerless. Hence nothing improves. Lacking faith in the system, parents are half hearted in their efforts to send their children to school. This further demotivates the teachers. Everyone's hopelessness feeds on everyone else. The children are the victims.

> "At the other end of spectrum, however, are villages where the spread of education has become self-sustained process .... There, parents often have a modicum of education, and they have high expectations of the schooling system. Also being batter off, they are not as powerless as the parents in more deprived villages: they are able to establish a rapport with the teachers, even to put some pressure on them, if needed, through local leaders or the school administration. This helps to keep the teachers on their toes. The teachers for their part, find their work facilitated by the keen interest of the parents, and face a less demotivating environment than in more deprived villages."[4] (p. 129).

The PROBE report, however, is not sure whether the teaching standard in public schools have declined or not.

The study of Dreze as well as PROBE report lament inertia on the part of the state.

The findings of the village survey conducted by IAS probationers was even more revealing.

The difference in the functioning of government schools and private schools (imparting teaching upto primary level) was very clear.

In **Avarata** village of Allahabad district the number of children enrolled in government school was 130 which was much higher than in private school, where only 50 students were enrolled.

But the attendance on the day of survey showed that only 50 per cent of students were present in the government school wheres 96 per cent students were reported present in the private school.

Another interesting finding was that despite the fact that mid-day meal programme was in operation in the government school, it has only partially helped in reducing dropouts.

Free text books and/or uniform was not being provided to students in any school. However, scholarship was being given to Scheduled Caste girl students in the government school, while such facility was not being provided by the private school.

The government school was better in providing other facilities also. Both government and private schools have their own building, play ground and drinking water facility. But there was no toilet facility in private school, while such a facility was available in the government school. Similarly, there was less rooms in private school than in the government school.

Private school was, however, better in terms of teacher pupil ratio. Whereas there were 3 teachers for 130 students in the government school, there were 3 teachers for only 50 students in the private school.

Hence what seemed to be crucial was (i) regularity of teachers and (ii) teacher-pupil ratio. And possibly these two factors help in raising the quality of teaching also.

**Avarata** village of Allahabad district has access to reasonably good educational facilities. However, around 44 per cent children were not availing these facilities.

This shows that even after facilities are made available at village level, the effective participation in education would be around 55 per cent to 60 per cent only.

If we want to increase participation beyond 60 per cent then some more efforts will have to be made at village level. Secondly, we will have to look in to factors other than 'school facility' to improve participation rate.

In **Ranipur** village (block Koilsa) of Azamgarh district, 53 per cent persons were reported literate according 2001 census. A literacy rate of 53 per cent for a village with no primary school within a radius of one kilometre could be termed as significant. The nearest government primary school is at a distance of one and a half kilometres. There are three private schools in the range of a distance of two kilometres.

Majority of children walk their way to school. Moreover, majority of school going children are enrolled in private schools. Villagers complained that the government primary school did not have proper building and teachers were mostly preoccupied with duties such as elections, census, etc. They preferred to send their children to private schools by paying fees ranging from Rs. 15.00 to Rs. 60.00 per month.

In the age group (5-14) years, more than 60 per cent children were either never enrolled in school or have dropped out subsequently. Even among those going to school, many are irregular. There were not significant gender differences in enrolment and dropouts.

Around one-fifth of those who were above the age group of 14 years had studied beyond high school level. There were 16 graduates, 7 postgraduates and two technical graduates in the village.

In **Gulariha** village of Gorakhpur district the literacy rate was found to be very low, a meagre 26.15 per cent as per the 1991 census. The literacy rate among males and females was reported to be 39 per cent and 11 per cent respectively.

As regards educational facilities, there were two primary schools, one general junior high school and one junior higher school for girls and a private nursery school in the village. There were two Inter Colleges within the radius of two kilometres. For higher studies students go to Gorakhpur which is at a distance of only 12-14 kilometres from the village.

The low rate of literacy in the village could be attributed to such factors as: (i) lack of interest on the part of the government teachers, and also parents; and (ii) ignorance on the part of villagers regarding the importance of education. Most of the primary schools are in dearth of teachers. One teacher was usually found struggling to manage children of three to four classes and also trying to teach all classes at a time. Another problem was that hardly one or two teachers out of three teachers for a school were found on any day. Lack of regularity on the part of teachers and lack of sincerity on the part of students were found to be the main causes for dismal performance in the field of primary education in the village.

In **Tikamau** village of Mahoba district, literacy rate of males 45 per cent, while that of females was 30 per cent (rough estimate) only.

One interesting feature about the children going to school is that the dropout rate was almost negligible. Parents who sent their children to school once have persuaded them to continue. Others had not sent their children to school at all.

More than 50 per cent of parents were of the opinion that it was useless to send their daughters to the school.

In Himmat Nagar Bajera of Etah district, only 27.5 per cent population is literate. Literacy rate among females was found to be a dismal 11.22 per cent.

There is no school in the main village. Though the government has sanctioned one school for the village, but due to caste struggle the place of school has not yet been decided. Location of school building is perceived to be of vantage point and linked with further possibility for capturing polling booth instead of suitability for their children.

In **Jeesukhpur** of Etah district there were 266 members above the age of 14 years out of which 42.11 per cent were illiterate and 12.78 per cent were educated upto primary level.

Out of 144 members in the age group (0-14) years, 63 were never enrolled, and 17 dropped out after enrolment. 18 are enrolled but irregular. 40 of them are enrolled in government school. Thus drop out ratio is quite high. One out of every four enrolled in primary school drops out.

In the village there is only one government school, and it is upto primary level. Hence students have to travel to Shivpur, around two kilometres away to attend high school. Besides that, there is one private school, upto primary level. It is not approved by the government. People prefer to send their children to private school, as standard/quality in the private school is higher than the government.

In the government school, there are six teachers—three of them are lady teachers. According to villagers, most of the students go to government school because wheat (in the name of mid-day meal) is distributed there. But those who can afford prefer to send their children to private school.

In **Koyala Alipur** of Mathura district there were two primary schools in the village—one was government run and the other private. 138 students were enrolled in the government primary school out of which 85 were boys and 53 were girls. 121 students were present on the day of survey of the school, i.e. only around 12 per cent students were absent while in the private school 5 students (i.e. around 14 per cent) were found absent out of 36 enrolled students. The proportion of girls in the private school was small as compared to the government school. It was so because fees in the private school was high. It seems, quality education was considered less important for girls.

There were 5 teachers for 138 students in the government school while two teachers were working in the private school having 36 students.

The private school was charging higher fees, but villagers preferred it for quality education. While salary of government school teachers was much higher than the teachers of the private school.

Neither study material nor uniform was being provided to students in any school. But in the government school, Scheduled Caste students were awarded scholarship.

The 'mid-day meal' programme was operational for students in the government schools during the past financial year (1999-2000). However, since the programme could not achieve the success and even the number of dropouts did not decrease, therefore, the scheme has been discontinued.

In the **Chirodi** village of Meerut district out of 1665 males 1154 (i.e. 69 per cent) were literate and out of 1363 females 812 (60 per cent) were literate. Village has good facility of primary schools, but there was no middle or high school in the village. The nearest such schools were 4 kilometres away.

There were two government primary schools and one private school in the village. The total number of students in government primary schools was 200 and there were only 3 teachers. Thus students teacher ratio was 67. Private school has 168 students and 5 teachers, i.e. the students-teacher ratio is around 34. Villagers were satisfied with the attendance of teachers in the private school.

Schools in the village have reasonably good infrastructure facilities. Drinking water facility and toilets were available in each school. Government school has also a playground. Blackboards are also available. Schools have their own buildings. However, furniture was not available and students used to sit on ground on mats. The infrastructure of government primary schools has improved after the implementation of District Primary Education Programme. Though government schools have reasonably good infrastructure facilities, the quality of education was poor. Even class-II students could barely read a sentence.

In the government schools, free text books were being provided to all students while scholarship was being awarded to students of Scheduled Caste and minority categories.

The difference in the number of students in class-I and class-V, could be seen to be larger in government schools. The number of students in class-I and class-V was 51 and 36 respectively in government schools while it was 39 and 35 respectively in private school. In the government primary school, the difference in numbers was larger because of sharper decline in the number of girls students. In case of boys, the number of 19 and 16 for class-I and class-V respectively. While in case of girls, the figures were 32 and 20 respectively.

**Table 5.1:** Mid-day Meal Scheme was Operational in the Village and had helped in reducing Dropout rates

| *Class* | *Government School* | | | *Private School* | | |
|---|---|---|---|---|---|---|
| | *Boys* | *Girls* | *Total* | *Boys* | *Girls* | *Total* |
| All Classes | 96 | 104 | 200 | 82 | 86 | 168 |
| Class-I | 19 | 32 | 51 | 18 | 21 | 39 |
| Class-V | 16 | 20 | 36 | 13 | 22 | 35 |

In **Shahpur Kalan** of Buland Shahr district there is a government primary school with 155 enrolled children—93 boys and 62 girls. At the time of survey, 130 students were present. There were four teachers in the school—all of them being males.

The mid-day meal scheme was in operation. Each school child got 3 kgs. of foodgrains at the end of the month. No free textbooks or uniforms were provided.

The school has drinking water facilities, a blackboard, a toilet and a playground. The school has only two classrooms. Villagers did not express dissatisfaction regarding the facilities of the primary school. The school was considered adequate in view of the population of the village. However, the building was considered inadequate—more classrooms, an office and a storeroom for the foodgrains etc. was also required. Villagers expressed the need for a junior high school and a girls primary school. An adult literacy centre was also sought to be introduced.

In **Jaffarpur** village of Barabanki district, there is one primary school, which was in a terrible condition. Cracks had appeared along the walls and ceiling. During the course of the survey the IAS probationer persuaded Basic Education Officer and the CDO to release funds for a new school. However, it is interesting to note that because of petty village politics and infighting between present Pradhan and former Pradhan (since they reside in different hamlets and hence could not decide on whose hamlet the school should be built in—an issue which divided the entire village) the new school building is yet to be built.

The IAS probationer also tried to motivate villagers to build the school by contributing material and labour. Villagers, particularly parents of school going children enthusiastically started to chalk out plans. It was decided that every able-bodied adult would contribute two days of labour, but finally, they could not agree as to where the school should be located. Petty politics once again prevented work from being carried out.

However, a good number of the children from the village were going to the private school in Satrikh, which is located around a distance of 3 kilometres from the village.

**Aloonagar Diguria** of Lucknow district is only at a distance of 15 kilometres from Lucknow, however, villagers do not want to send their children to school because of lack of money. Also they do not see any relevance in sending their children to school. There is a primary school in the village.

Villages in close proximity of the towns, serve as suppliers of labour—like a slum of the township.

Those who can afford and motivate generally prefer to send their children to private primary level schools. Those who cannot afford or less motivated to send their children (especially girl child) remain contented by sending their children to government primary school. But they are indifferent to the teaching or progress of their ward, as they are not sure, how much this teaching will help their ward in future.

## Health

The performance of U.P. in the area of health has been very poor. The average life expectancy at birth for women (54.5 years) in Uttar Pradesh is lower than the male expectation of life (56.8 years) whereas at national level this figure is slightly higher for females (59.4 years) than the males (59 years) [Tenth Five Year Plan—Vol. 1, part III, p. 285].

The plan document further records that

- The National Family Health Survey (1998-99) shows that 52 per cent of children below three years of age are under weight and 56 per cent are short for their age or stunted. This compares infavourably with the national level estimates of 47 and 46 per cent respectively.
- The proportion of fully vaccinated children is higher in urban than in rural area. Immunization against TB (BCG) was highest at 57.5 per cent, followed by Polio (42.3 per cent), measles (34.6 per cent) and DPT (33.9 per cent). In the case of both polio and DPT, immunization is fairly higher for the first dose but subsequently drops sharply till the final dose. Thus only a small proportion of population completes the full course of vaccination. Only 16 per cent of the children were fully vaccinated by the age of 12 months, which means that a fourth of the fully vaccinated children did not receive their vaccination within the given time frame of 12 months from birth. Female children with 19 per cent full

immunization received lower priority in vaccination as compared to male children (24 per cent).

- The number of maternal deaths is very high in Central, Western and Eastern U.P. The regional variation is in the line with the social status of women in these regions (RCHS 1998-99).

The poor performance in health sector is largely caused due to poor access to health services in the state. Nearly three-fourths of villages in U.P. are without any health facility whatsoever and in one-fifth villages there is no health facility within 5 kms. of the village (Singh, A.K., 2001, p. 20).

The gap in requirement and actual position is available from the *Bulletin on Rural Health Statistics in India, 1999*. The statement showing sub-centres, PHCs and CHCs required as per 2002 population and in position as on 31.12.1998 for Uttar Pradesh gives following figures.

**Table 5.2:** Required Health Centres and Shortfall

| *Health Centres* | *Required* | *In Position* | *Shortfall* |
|---|---|---|---|
| Sub-Centres | 27492 | 20153 | 7339 |
| Primary Health Centres | 4582 | 3808 | 774 |
| Community Health Centres | 1146 | 310 | 836 |

**Table 5.3 :** Health Manpower Required and Shortfall

| *Health Manpower* | *Required* | *In position* | *Shortfall* |
|---|---|---|---|
| ANMs/Health Workers (Female) (as on 31.12.97) | 23961 | 22629 | 1332 |
| Health Workers (Male) (as on 31.12.97) | 20153 | 8947 | 11206 |
| Doctors at PHCs (as on 31.12.97) | 3808 | 2263 | 1545 |
| Nurse/Midwife (as on 31.12.97) | 5978 | 803 | 5175 |

Out of 3808 PHCs functioning in U.P., 289 were without any doctor as on 31 December, 1992.

The studies of villages show that villagers largely depend on PHCs or Sub-Centres for immunization and vaccination.

As regards delivery, the large number of delivery still take place at home. Among those who could afford hospital, the deliveries were reported to have taken place both in PHCs and private hospitals.

Presence of PHCs or sub-centres do not stop proliferation of private practitioners or private hospitals. People also take help of Quacks and Rural Health Practitioners.

The village-wise details of health status as reported from some villages is as follows:

In **Avarata** village of Allahabad district PHC is 3 kms. away. PHC is first point of contact in case of emergency. People are aware about maternity care and immunization. The reason for this awareness is proximity of villages to towns and high literacy rate Private hospitals are in Handia.

Various vaccines are available in PHC. Out of 175 eligible couples for family planning 25 males and 50 females were using family planning devices. Out of 31 births which took place during the last one year, 19 deliveries took place at home and only 12 took place in government or private hospitals.

In **Ranipur** village of Azamgarh district, PHC and sub-centre are in villages. This has improved health status of villagers.

Out of 11 births last year--8 were in PHC or private hospital and only 3 by untrained persons. The level of immunization was found to be high. No impact of PHC was found on family planning programme. Of 90 eligible candidates, 72 per cent did not employ any method. Females adopted sterilization—76 per cent (among those who adopted any method). Temporary methods were not popular.

High income group people of the village and prefer to go to the nearby private hospital.

**Parikhara** village of Ballia district is only at a distance of 2 km. from district headquarter, therefore, villagers visit district hospital to avail medical facilities.

Out of 40 households covered under survey, delivery during the last one year as reported from 6 families only. Five pregnant women had undergone minimum three check ups and T.T. immunizations during last pregnancy. 4 children had been vaccinated for immunization of different diseases while two had received no immunization. The place of delivery in 4 cases was home, and in two cases it was hospital. Delivery was conducted by untrained person in case of home deliveries.

Three deaths were reported during last one year.

As regards family planning, out of 49 eligible couples (of 40 households), 10 females have been sterilized—4 of them belonged to S.C. category and 6 to general category.

A case study of quacks in the village **Khirora Mohan** of Gonda district is quite revealing. Three quacks were operating in the village. One of them, Mr. Devanand is aged 33 years and lives in Gonda. He has been running his clinic for the past twelve years, and claims to have received a degree of "Ayurved Ratna" from Hindi Sahitya Sammelan, Prayag. But he prescribes only allopathic medicines. On average, 7 or 8 persons come to him for treatment everyday. He also attends delivery cases for which he charges Rs. 60.00. He treats patients on credit basis too. Patients have also facility to pay in two or three installments. That is why, he is more popular than other two quacks.

In **Tikamau** village of Mahoba district, the nearest PHC is 12 kms. away from the village. Out of the 9 deliveries reported during the last one year, 4 were conducted at home and 5 at some hospital. Out of these 9 deliveries, 6 were conducted by trained person. As regards maternity coverage, 6 pregnant mothers received minimum ANC checkups and 7 received full TT doses. As regards immunization all except one was reported to have not received immunization vaccination.

In **Koyala Alipur** village of Mathura district there was no PHC. 33 deliveries took place during last one year. Total deaths during the same period were 18, out of these 5 were newly born children. ANM/ MPW never came to villages.

There were some Rural Health Practitioners in the village, whose help was taken by villagers whenever such need arises.

In **Chirodi** village of Meerut district there is a sub-PHC. PHC is around 4.5 kms. away. It has well qualified doctors. Besides providing regular services, PHC organizes various camps and also offers treatments of diseases like TB, leprosy, etc.

Sub-PHC caters the need of family planning and immunization. However, people were not very happy with the working of ANM. In case of minor illness and other problems people prefer to go to local unqualified doctors.

Situation of maternity and childcare was found to be good. Of the 53 births during the last one year, 30 were male and 23 female.

No case of infant mortality or maternal mortality was reported. This shows high level of awareness.

Out of 53 deliveries, only 5 took place in hospital and the rest were conducted at home either with the help of ANM or local midwife.

Awareness about family planning methods was there, but response was found to be mixed. About 50 per cent couples—mostly women, use such methods. Vasectomy is the most preferred method and tubectomy is next one.

Birth rate is 1.7 per cent. Death rate is very low—one death during last one year.

Immunization programme was running well in the village and is widely accepted by people—PHC is the model agency and ANM the grassroots worker for this programme.

In **Jaffarpur** village of Barabanki district, it was found that the nearest health centre is situated 3 kms. away from the village at Satrikh. Villagers complained that no ANM visited the village. In any case, villagers preferred to go to private doctors in Satrikh.

Villagers also made extensive use of government veterinary services available at Satrikh.

The PHC centre is situated in the hamlet Diguria in **Aloonagar Diguria** village of Lucknow district. But in case of emergency, people go to private medical facilities.

The above findings show that immunization programme was running well, but fell much short of achieving full success.

There was complaint against ANM in all villages. There was awareness about family planning, but the response was found to be mixed.

In case of deliveries, a good percentage was reported to be conducted by untrained persons.

In case of minor illness and less serious problems, people preferred to go to unqualified health practitioners.

There was a tendency to go to private hospital in cases of emergency or serious illness.

## Water Supply

Rural water supply has two aspects. One is to provide safe drinking water to each of the rural habitation. This covers both quality and quality of water. The other aspect is harnessing of available water at village level. This would include conservation and optional use of both surface water and ground water. Thus quality and sustainability are the two fundamental aspects on which rural water supply programme needed to be developed.

The village studies however show that there had been emphasis on only one aspect. Generally no problem of drinking water supply was reported from any village. At the same time report from each village showed that it was mainly due to installation of India Mark-II hand pumps.

There was no report on the aspect of harnessing of available water at village level and dovetailing of ground water use, ground water recharge with the watershed development programmes. This lopsided approach in water supply programme is not sustainable.

## Drainage and Sanitation

The supply of safe drinking water is crucially linked with drainage and sanitary facilities for creating conducive environment for providing sustainable health and hygiene benefits. Though supply of drinking water is essential, it cannot be deemed to be environment friendly unless drainage and sanitary facilities are simultaneously provided with it.

Reports from villages show dismal performance in this regard. Drainage facility was reported from one village only, while sanitary facilities were reported from 4 villages only. But the coverage of households even in these villages, in no case exceeded 20 per cent households of the village.

## Road Connectivity

Almost all the villages were connected by all weather roads.

The village-wise condition of water supply, drainage and road connectivity was found to be as follows:

**Avarata** village has brick roads called *Kharanja*. There are also drainages for waste water disposal. Village roads and drainages are maintained by Gram Panchayat. There had been no watershed development work in the village.

There is no problem of drinking water in **Ranipur** village. Hand pumps are the main source. Public hand pumps sanctioned through JRY supplemented the private ones.

The village has an all weather approach road. But lacks community latrines.

There is all weather road in the **Parikhara** village, facility for bus-stop.

Out of 40 sampled households, 35 have their own hand pumps. Three households (all being SC) use government hand pump. Two households use masonery well for drinking water. Out of 40, 7 households have their own latrines. Members of other households go outside for defecation.

In the village **Gulariha**, there is provision of pure drinking water through India Mark-II hand pump. The village is well connected by all weather roads.

There were sufficient number of hand pumps to take care or drinking water requirement of the villagers of **Khirora Mohan** village. 30 per cent households had their own hand pumps. Only 4 out of 40 people interviewed told that they depended on unprotected dug well for drinking water.

In **Himmatnagar Bhajhera** village of Etah district the number of own hand pump/TW was found to be 11 while the number of Public hand pump/TW was 29.

There was a dispute on taking water from a hand pump installed in the Mohalla of Chamars. Chamars did not allow Mehtars to take water from this hand pump just because of their being untouchables. When I, the probationer, asked them to let the Mehtars also take water from this hand pump, they argued that these people wash pig flesh at this hand pump.

In village **Jeesukhpur**, out of 80 families, only 18 use pit latrine as a place of defecation, and rest use open field. Majority of them, have their own hand pumps as a source of drinking water. Bus stop facility is available at the village.

Main sources of drinking water in the village **Koyala Alipur** of Mathura district are—hand pumps installed by the government and wells.

The village **Shahpur Kalan** of Buland Shahr district has facilities of an all weather approach road, a bus stop and government based safe drinking water sources.

There is a defunct community latrine in the **Jiraunia** village of Pilibhit district. Out of 80 households—2 have modern latrine, 24 pit latrine and 54 go to open field. There are a number of government as well as private hand pumps in the village for safe drinking water. Out of 80 households, 70 own hand pumps, and 10 use public hand pumps.

In **Jaffarpur** village of Barabanki district, out of 40 households interviewed, 4 households got their supply of water from their own private hand pumps, 3 from a protected public well and the rest from unprotected public wells. Villagers told that medicine was put into the public wells as a preventive measure. A few hand pumps had been installed in each of the hamlets and drinking water was made available to villagers through these. All villagers had access to these sources of drinking water without any discrimination.

No family out of 40 households constructed toilets—all went for open defecation. Pradhan claimed that he was able to bring funds from Zila Parishad to construct toilets, but he was apprehensive about the response of villagers in this regard.

## Other Aspects of Conditions of Living

Another important aspect of the study has been to capture as to how much development processes have affected conditions of life of an average villagers. Generally we have the data showing what facilities are available in the village. This does not reveal as to how many people have access to those facilities or availing those facilities. Village studies have gathered information about dwellings, electricity facilities, fuel, sanitation etc.

### *(a) Poverty Level*

It was found that number of persons living below poverty line varied vastly among the sampled households of villages from where such data was available. For example, in **Ranipur** (Azamgarh) 19.3 per cent households were identified as being below poverty line. Proportion of such households in other reporting villages was as follows: Parikhara (Ballia)—27 per cent, Gulariha (Gorakhpur)—85 per cent, Khirora Mohan (Gonda)—62.5 per cent and Tikamau (Mahoba)—45.79 per cent.

These variations could be due to difference in sample size or nature of sample. It is obvious that a sizeable number of households in villages are still living below poverty line. They do not have access to various facilities, or do not have the capacity to avail the facilities.

Secondly, even though, poverty alleviation programmes have covered a large number of them, many of them continue to remain below poverty line. A new strategy needs to be envisaged in which a group of socially cohesive families below poverty line be identified for group target oriented programme, rather than individual target oriented programme.

### (b) Public Distribution System

The information about functioning of Public Distribution System (PDS) was reported from three villages only, namely Ranipur (Azamgarh), Tikamau (Mahoba) and Aloonagar Diguria (Lucknow).

It was reported that even PDS has not improved the standard of living of people living below poverty line. Wheat and rice were not in great demand because difference in prices of these commodities in open market and PDS shops was very small. Kerosene was the most demanded commodity. Villagers also purchased sugar from PDS shop.

People had a lot of complaints against *Kotedars* such as not providing adequate quantity and not opening of shops regularly. Another fact which came to notice was that margin for the shop owner was very small and hardly enough to make him take pains of fetching and distributing the supply.

### (c) Housing Condition

The report about housing condition was available from 8 villages. More than 50 per cent houses were *kuchcha* houses. The villages where *pucca* houses were in sizeable number were Parikhara (62.5 per cent), Tikamau (30 per cent), Himmatnagar (45 per cent) and Jeesukhpur (50 per cent).

Most of the Scheduled Caste people lived in *kuchcha* houses or huts.

The impact of Indira Awas Yojana had not affected the housing conditions in any significant way in the villages.

### *(d) Electricity*

Rural electrification is an essential condition for accelerating growth in rural areas. The information about electrification of a village indicates that power connection is available in the village. It does not give any indication about coverage of households. The electrification can give real fillip to growth process only if coverage of households is also sizeable.

It was found that power connection was available in all the villages where study was conducted. However, coverage was found to be very poor. Among the reporting villages less than 25 per cent households had electricity facility. The number of households among the sampled households without electricity facility in reporting villages was as follows: Ranipur—74 per cent, Parikhara—50 per cent, Tikamau—85 per cent, Himmatnagar—100 per cent, Jeesukhpur—75 per cent, Jiraunia—88.75 per cent and Jaffarpur—92.5 per cent.

### *(e) Fuel*

Most commonly used fuel for cooking was found to be wood. Cow dung cake and agricultural wastes. Very few households reportedly used LPG or kerosene oil as cooking fuel. People normally collected wood/agricultural waste from nearby areas. The number of households purchasing fuel, except during crisis periods, was very small. In one village gobar gas plants were also in operation.

### *(f) Sanitation*

Sanitary toilets were reported from only 2 villages. In Jiraunia (Pilibhit) facility for toilet was as follows: modern latrine 24, open field 54. In Parikhara only 17.5 per cent households used clean toilet.

Construction of latrines depended more on cultural habits and less on capacity to invest on it. But once the attitude changes, at least 50 per cent houses would go for it in a short span of time. Another factor which deterred villagers from constructing modern latrines was inadequate availability of water at doorstep.

### *(g) Drinking Water*

India Mark-II hand pumps have been installed in all the villages. Though they are not in sufficient numbers to cover all the households.

Some private hand pumps were found to have been in operation also. Drinking water was public hand pump. The use of wells was found to be declining.

Village-wise situation of other aspects of conditions of living is as follows:

In village **Ranipur** as per the BPL survey conducted in 1999-2000, 32 households out of a total of 165, i.e. 39 per cent households were identified as being below poverty line. Excepting 2 all the BPL households belonged to S.C. and had income less than Rs. 12,000.00 per annum.

Most of the current BPL households have benefited from poverty alleviation programmes, yet they continue to remain below poverty line. Those above 60 years of age constituted 9 per cent of sample population implying high life expectancy.

The public distribution system (PDS) has not improved their standard of living either. As the difference between price of wheat and rice in open market and PDS shops is very small, people prefer to purchase them from open market as they get better quality at same price. Their income level is too little to purchase sugar. Each household however gets 3-5 litres of kerosene per month from PDS shop.

About 50 per cent of sampled households live in huts or *kuchcha* houses. Only 30 per cent live in *pucca* houses.

Though the village is electrified, 74 per cent of sample households did not have access to electricity. Even those who have connection, get power for less than 8 hours a day.

In village **Parikhara**, out of 40 sampled households, 11 (27 per cent) were found to be below poverty line. Caste-wise situation showed that 5 out of 9 SCs, 2 out of 12 BC and 4 out of other categories were below poverty line.

Out of 40 sampled households 25 (62.5 per cent) had *pucca* houses and only 5 (12.5 per cent) were living in huts. All the 40 households had houses on their own land.

Twenty houses (50 per cent) had electricity but no SC house was electrified, 7 (17.5 per cent) used clean toilet.

As regards fuel, 29 families (72.5 per cent) used wood, 3 (7.5 per cent) used LPG and 3 used cow dung cake and 3 used leafs as fuel.

In village **Gulariha** about 200 families (85 per cent) live below poverty line. Women, specially of *harijan basti* go out to earn some income.

Most of the villagers live in *kuchcha* houses with tiled roofs—some have built *pucca* houses under Indira Awas Yojana.

There is no community or private latrine in the village. People go out into the open field and to the canal for bathing.

Most of the households use *chulha* with agricultural waste as fuel for cooking purposes.

In village **Khirora Mohan**, of the 40 sampled households an alarming 62.5 per cent people lived in straw-thatched huts and 84 per cent of them belonged to Scheduled Caste.

As regards power consumption, only 15 per cent of the households were electrified. Even these households got power supply only for a few hours (normally 2-3 hours) in a day.

All the sampled households had their own houses.

No house in the village had sanitary toilet. Wood was the most common source of fuel. People normally collected wood from nearby areas—very few households purchased fuel wood from Gonda.

In village **Tikamau** 98 families out of a total of 214 families (i.e. 45.79 per cent) in the village were listed as below poverty line. The list had been prepared recently in connection with the distribution of cheaper foodgrains to the families having annual income less than Rs. 11,000.00. Almost all the families listed BPL were either from SC or OBC category. Most of these were landless labourers and marginal farmers.

Though the village is settled in one hamlet, house of Basor caste people are located at one common place, which could be distinguished easily as they are the community who are involved in pig rearing. Nearly 30 per cent of villagers live in *pucca* brick houses and the rest of them live in mixed type houses. Houses are located mostly on the private land. Some gram samaj land has also been allotted to members of SC community for residential purposes. The new *pucca* houses are being constructed at the outskirts of the village as more and more people want to gain access to the roads as far as possible.

In village **Himmatnagar Bhajhera** out of 40 selected households, 11 owned hand pump and 29 depended on public hand pump/tube well. Housing type—all the 40 had their own houses. Two had straw-thatched hut, 15 owned *kuchcha* bricks type, 18 owned *pucca* houses and 5 had *kuchcha-pucca* mix. Electricity was available to none of the 40 households. There was no community toilet. As regards fuel—25 used lay/leaves and 15 used gobar gas.

In village **Jeesukhpur** there were 493 persons below poverty line as per the data available in the block. Unemployment during lean seasons was widespread in this village.

Out of 80 families surveyed, only 18 used pit latrines as a place for defecation and the rest used open field.

Most of them used wood as source of fuel.

Majority of them have their own hand pumps.

The main source of light is "*dhibri*" followed by kerosene oil lantern. Only 25 per cent of the households were electrified.

Most of them have their own houses on inherited own land. 50 per cent of houses are *pucca* houses. Only a minority of them had straw-thatched hut. 25 per cent of houses were *kuchcha* houses.

The information about village **Jiraunia** showed that according to the list available with the block, the BPL population in the village **Jiraunia** is 547. The caste-wise breakup is as follows: SC—227, OBC—300, General—20.

The status of housing condition among selected 80 households was as follows: straw-thatched—11, *kuchcha*—23, *pucca*—22, *kuchcha-pucca*—24.

Out of these 80 houses only 9 had electricity.

The details of homestead land among selected 80 households is as follows: inherited own land—53, purchased land—4, government land with *purcha*—10, government land without *purcha*—11, landlords land—2.

The details of facilities for defecation is as follows: modern latrine—2, pit latrine—24, open field—54.

Source of drinking water—own hand pump—70, public hand pump—10.

Main source of light—Dhibri—65, kerosene oil/lantern—27, electricity—10.

Source of fuel—wood—8, kerosene oil—2, hay leaves—23, cow dung cake—47, agricultural waste—68, LPG—4.

**Table 5.4:** Basic Amenities in the Village

| District | Village | No. of Hamlets | Distance of Village from | | | | | | | | | |
|---|---|---|---|---|---|---|---|---|---|---|---|---|
| | | | District Headquarter | Block Headquarter | Nearest Bus Stop | Nearest Railway Station | Nearest Town | Nearest Market | Nearest Bank | Nearest P.O. | PHC/ Sub-centre | Grain Storage Facility |
| Allahabad | Avarata | 6 | 33 | 3 | 3 | 3 | 3 | 3 | 3 | 1 | 3/0 | 3 |
| Azamgarh | Ranipur | 2 | 28 | 2 | 1 | — | 1 | 1 | 2 | 2 | 0/0 | 2 |
| Ballia | Parikhara | 3 | 2 | 4 | 0 | 3 | 1 | 1 | 0 | 0 | — | 1 |
| Gorakhpur | Gulariha | 3 | 14 | 7 | 0 | 14 | 14 | 1 | 0 | 0 | 5/0 | 1 |
| Gonda | Khirora Mohan | — | 8 | — | 5 | 8 | 8 | 8 | 8 | 8 | 8 | — |
| Mahoba | Tikamau | 1 | 12 | 12 | 4 | 1 | 12 | 12 | 12 | 0 | 12 | 8 |
| Etah | Himmatnagar Bhajhera | 4 | 10 | 14 | 3 | 10 | 10 | 10 | 10 | — | 10 | — |
| Etah | Jeesukhpur | 1 | 11 | 11 | 0 | 11 | 11 | 11 | 5 | 0 | 3 | 11 |
| Mathura | Koyala Alipur | 3 | 5 | 5 | 0 | 5 | 5 | 5 | 5 | 5 | 5 | 5 |
| Meerut | Chirodi | — | 16 | 4 | 4 | 4 | 4 | 4 | 4 | 4 | 4/0 | — |
| Buland Shahr | Shahpur Kalan | — | — | 10 | 0 | 8 | 10 | 3 | 3 | 5 | 3 | 10 |
| Pilibhit | Jiraunia | — | 10 | 17 | 1 | 2 | — | — | 2 | 2 | 4/0 | — |
| Barabanki | Jaffarpur | 4 | 12 | — | 3 | — | 3 | 3 | 3 | 3 | 3 | 3 |
| Lucknow | Aloonagar Diguria | 5 | 15 | 8 | 16 | 6 | 3 | 3 | 0 | 0 | 0 | 7 |

**Table 5.5:** Basic Amenities in the Village

| *District* | *Village* | *Basic Amenities* | | | | | | | | |
|---|---|---|---|---|---|---|---|---|---|---|
| | | *Veterinary Dispensary* | *Electric Fiction* | *All Weather Approach Road* | *PDS Shop* | *Community Latrine* | *Safe Drinking Water Sources* | *ICDS Centre* | *Panchayat Bhawan* | *Street Light* |
| Allahabad | Avarata | No | Yes | Yes | Yes | No | Yes | No | Yes | Yes |
| Azamgarh | Ranipur | No | Yes | Yes | — | No | Yes | — | No | No |
| Ballia | Parikhara | No | Yes | Yes | Yes | — | Yes | — | Yes | — |
| Gorakhpur | Gulariha | No | Yes | Yes | Yes | No | Yes | Yes | Yes | No |
| Gonda | Khirora Mohan | No | Yes | Yes | No | No | Yes | No | No | No |
| Mahoba | Tikamau | No | Yes | Yes | Yes | No | Yes | No | Yes | Yes |
| Etah | Himmatnagar Bhajhera | No | Yes | Yes | Yes | No | Yes | — | Yes | — |
| Etah | Jeesukhpur | — | Yes | Yes | Yes | No | Yes | — | Yes | — |
| Mathura | Koyala Alipur | No | Yes | Yes | No | No | Yes | No | Yes | No |
| Meerut | Chirodi | — | Yes | Yes | Yes | — | Yes | Yes | Yes | — |
| Buland Shahr | Shahpur Kalan | No | Yes | Yes | Yes | No | Yes | No | No | No |
| Pilibhit | Jiraunia | — | Yes | Yes | Yes | Yes | Yes | Yes | Yes | Yes |
| Barabanki | Jaffarpur | No | Yes | No | Yes | No | Yes | No | — | — |
| Lucknow | Aloonagar Diguria | — | — | — | Yes | No | Yes | — | — | — |

In village **Jaffarpur** houses in all the hamlets were *kuchcha* apart from the few *pucca* houses. Although one finds a common doorway into the house, several families were found to be living together but cooking separately.

Of the 40 households interviewed, only 3 had electricity. Many others could not have electricity connection because some said they could not afford to pay electricity bills while some others said that electricity was not part of village life as they would start work early and finish their work and eat meals long before darkness fell.

Of the 40 households interviewed, 4 households had own private hand pumps, 3 got water from a protected public well and the rest from unprotected public wells. A few hand pumps had been installed in each of the hamlets and drinking water was made available to villagers through these. No households had constructed toilets.

## RESOURCE BASE OF VILLAGES

The study of resource base of villages showed that land continues to be the main resource for economic activities in the villages.

The land use classification of villages also reveals that except in village **Parikhara,** more than 70 per cent land was suitable for cultivation in all other villages. The land under forest cover was less than 4 per cent in all villages.

The area under community land was found to be very small in villages. Only in three villages its proportion was somewhat sizeable. They include Gulariha, Khirora Mohan and Shahpur Kalan.

### Common Property Resources

Common Property Resources in general were found to be declining. There were three main reasons for it. One was allotment of gram samaj land as patta under land distribution programme. The other reason is encroachment of gram samaj land by powerful and influential people of the village. The third reason is non-maintenance of such resources, specially tanks and ponds, chak roads, tree plantation on gram samaj land (which is under other community uses) and water logging due to unplanned constructions which restrict natural course of drainage.

Two pronged action could be taken to protect CPR. One is to initiate eviction proceeding against encroachers. The other step is to undertake afforestation, repair and other maintenance activities under JRY and other such programmes and ensure poor people's access to use CPR more frequently. CPR protection committees comprising landless and women be formed as these are the groups which suffer mostly when CPR declines.

The main CPR are pond, hand pump, panchayat bhawan and primary school in the village **Avarata**.

In village **Ranipur** the common property resources of the village include: Navin Parti (5.93 acres), Banjar (3.246 acres), Forest (2.484 acres), Pokhri (0.683 acres), Village road (1.426 acres), and Drains (0.426 acres).

The CPRs also include two ponds over an area of 0.251 acres. After the consolidation operations 0.175 acres of land has been reserved for *Khalihan* (a place for keeping crops after harvest). Provisions have been made for place of worship and chak-roads (0.777 acres) etc. Though the consolidation report claims to have made provisions for play ground, place for potters mud, no land exists under these heads. Also no provision has been made for grazing land, school and panchayat ghar.

An important reason for the reduction of CPRs is the distribution/allotment of Gram Sabha land. Out of the limited resources, 3 acres of land was distributed as agriculture pattas and 0.4 acres was distributed as housing pattas. The panchayat has passed a resolution allotting land for school and panchayat ghar.

The other reason for reduction of CPRs is encroachment. The main chak road of the village, which is supposed to be two metres wide is hardly half a metre wide. In another instance of encroachment, eviction proceedings under Section 115 (C) of ZALR Act has been initiated. In the last two years, encroachment of drain and a chak road were removed at the initiative of Gram Panchayat and they have been repaired under JRY. The forest land is also encroached and many private persons have planted trees in government land. It was difficult to ascertain encroachment due to lack of clear demarcation. There are no encroachments on land reserved for place of worship, *khalihan* and pond. And these are used by all sections of the village.

The common property resources in village **Gulariha** are slowly on decline due to allotment of land and also encroachment on these lands and water resources. Area under different use of Common Property Resources in the village is as follows:

Pasture—0.218 ha; Barren land—0.533 ha; Pond—3.940 ha; Nali—0.273 ha; Vacant land—0.098 ha; Drain—0.742 ha; Playground—0.150 ha; Plantation—0.146 ha; Main road—0.834 ha; Village road—1.255 ha; Chak road—4.619 ha; Panchayat Bhawan—0.081 ha; Place of worship—0.16 ha; Primary school—0.186 ha; Junior Girls High School—0.069 ha; Junior High School—0.777 ha; PWD road—3.157 ha; Khanta (Patri)—2.094 ha; Khall—Godha—0.080 ha; Shaur area—0.166 ha; Dhobi ka Ghat—0.028 ha; Shamshan—0.109 ha; Kabristan—0.214 ha and khal sthan—0.028 ha.

In village **Tikamau** the most important Common Property Resources is the area under the cover of bushes and some forest. This supplies the fuel wood needed by villagers. Other CPRs include 19 acres of pastures and grazing land. The concept of CPR is fast depleting as more and more villagers now-a-days use their own land for these resources. Moreover, the community land has been given on patta to landless labourers, resulting in shrinking of community land. But most of the drinking water needs are met by community wells. In some cases, ever irrigation needs are fulfilled by public wells.

Common Property Resource of the village **Jeesukhpur** includes pond, village settlement, panchayat ghar, playground, path ways and fertilizer pit. There are three ponds in the village. Largest of them is in the middle of the village. Its recorded area is 1.05 acre. Since there is *jalkumbhi* (water grass) in the pond, its water cannot be consumed by cattle. Around half acre of land has been encroached upon by villagers residing along side pond. They belong to Scheduled Caste and Backward Caste community.

The second pond was constructed by minor irrigation department. It is in the middle of fields of the Thakur community and therefore, others face difficulty in approaching to the pond.

The third pond has an area of 0.35 acres and is used for washing cloths.

The land earmarked for Panchayat Ghar is at present under private control, as it has been encroached upon by two persons. Last year the village *lekhpal* conducted a survey of the village and put stones as a sign and demarcated chak-roads. But in course of time they were dug up by adjacent field owners.

Nobody knows in the village about the area which has been left out for play field. There are some houses on the spot earmarked as play ground.

There are 4 compost pits in records with an area of 0.34 acres. Only one of them is lying vacant, rest three of them have been encroached upon.

The village has no grave yard. Earlier villagers used to bury children in field number 31/0.56 acre. Patta for this field had been given to Jagdish Jatav. There were two other grave yards on field number 16/0.54 acre and 37/0.6 acre. People have also encroached upon these plots. At present people bury or cremate dead bodies in their own field. But even this option is not available to landless households.

In village **Koyala Alipur** about 20-22 hectares of land was of gram sabha land, out of which 17 hectares was handed over to forest department for afforestation. About 12-13 hectares of land is used as grazing land. There are two small ponds in the village which are leased out to villagers on priority basis for fishery purposes.

Common Property Resources are almost negligible in the village **Chirodi.** There is no forest in the village, no pasture or grazing land. There are only three small ponds in the village with a total area of 0.819 hectare. These ponds are also not well maintained.

The common property resources of village **Shahpur Kalan** include grazing and pasture land of 1.5 ha, a part of which has been encroached upon, the rest is not maintained. Community forest land is of 0.02 ha. Forest under the forest department is 0.09 ha. 0.01 ha land is reserved for panchayat ghar which is under construction. Some land is also reserved for the temple and community meeting place. No land is reserved for the water tank, fishing pond, *ahars*, pynes or Kisan Sewa Kendra.

In village **Jiraunia** ponds, pastures, land used for compost pit and manure pit, land unfit for cultivation, graveyard and cremation place constitute CPR of the village. But due to extreme pressure of ever increasing population, these are ever under threat of encroachment. The village *lekhpal* is aware of this but he conveniently looks the other way when suitably rewarded.

**Table 5.6:** Land-Use Classification of Selected Villages

| *Districts* | *Villages* | *Total Area of Village* | *Land for Cultivation* | *Land under Forest Cover* | *Fallow Land* | *Pasture and Grazing* | *Waste Land* | *Land for Homestead* | *Net Sown Area* | *Community Land* | *Miscellaneous Land* |
|---|---|---|---|---|---|---|---|---|---|---|---|
| Allahabad | Avarata | 155.1 (100.0) | 150.6 (97.10) | – | – | – | – | 2 (1.29) | 150.6 (97.10) | 2.5 (1.61) | – |
| Azamgarh | Ranipur | 192.75 (100.0) | 152.65 (79.20) | 6.34 (3.29) | 9.15 (4.75) | – | – | 14.652 (7.60) | 149.38 (77.5) | 0.40 (0.21) | – |
| Ballia | Parikhara | 459.0 (100.0) | 306.00 (66.67) | 15.0 (3.27) | 14.0 (3.05) | – | 26.0 (5.66) | 46.0 (10.02) | 245.0 (53.38) | 4.0 (0.87) | 48.0 (10.46) |
| Gorakhpur | Gulariha | 461.1 (100.0) | 365.0 (79.16) | – | 5.0 (1.08) | – | – | 13.01 (2.82) | – | 70.98 (15.39) | – |
| Gonda | Khirora Mohan | 291.33 (100.0) | 269.16 (92.39) | – | 21.05 (7.23) | – | – | 4.7 (1.61) | 248.11 (85.16) | 17.5 (6.01) | – |
| Mahoba | Tikamau | 2335.0 (100.0) | 1734.0 (74.26) | 178.0 (7.62) | 74.0 (3.17) | 19.0 (0.81) | 439.0 (18.80) | 14.0 (0.60) | 1686 (72.21) | 32 (1.37) | 17 (0.73) |
| Etah | Himantnagar Bhikhera | 1167.5 (100.0) | 1069.17 (91.58) | 46.9 (4.02) | 26.8 (2.30) | – | – | 21.8 (1.87) | 1006.6 (86.22) | – | – |
| Etah | Jeesukhpur | 312.0 (100.0) | 275.16 (88.19) | – | – | – | – | – | – | – | – |

*(Contd.)*

**Table 5.6** (*Contd.*)

| *Districts* | *Villages* | *Total Area of Village* | *Land for Cultivation* | *Land under Forest Cover* | *Fallow Land* | *Pasture and Grazing* | *Waste Land* | *Land for Homestead* | *Net Sown Area* | *Community Land* | *Miscellaneous Land* |
|---|---|---|---|---|---|---|---|---|---|---|---|
| Mathura | Koyala Alipur | 1555.0 (100.0) | 1337.5 (73.15) | 42.5 (2.73) | 25.0 (1.61) | 30.0 (1.93) | – | – | 937.5 (7.29) | 12.5 (0.80) | 12.5 (0.80) |
| Meerut | Chirodi | 1134.91 (100.0) | 989.56 (87.19) | – | – | – | – | 66.25 (5.84) | – | – | – |
| Bulandsahar | Shahpur Kalan | 524.0 (100.0) | 455.0 (86.83) | 0.1 (0.02) | 8.75 (1.67) | 3.75 (0.72) | 23.0 (4.39) | – | 447.5 (85.40) | 19.25 (3.67) | 33.63 (6.42) |
| Pilibhit | Jiraunia | 950.0 (100.0) | 850.0 (89.47) | – | 10.0 (1.05) | 70.0 (7.37) | 20.0 (2.1) | – | – | – | |
| Barabanki | Jaffarpur | 73.45 (100.0) | | | | | | | | | |
| Lucknow | Aloonagar Diguria | 922.0 (100.0) | 880.0 (95.44) | | | | | | | | |

There are four very old ponds in the village. One of them is quite deep and is full of water even in summer. There is no major problem of soil erosion as such, neither is there any problem of water logging.

Common Property Resource available in village **Aloonagar Diguria** are *Khalihan*, school, chak-roads, grave yard and cremation ground, compost pit, for potters earth etc. Out of these, chak roads are being encroached upon and ploughed by landholders of adjacent fields leading to narrowing of chak road. Though some initiatives were taken, the government has failed to remove encroachments. Most of the CPR are being used by the influential people of the village as their personal property. Even the panchayat ghar is being used by the Pradhan for his personal use and was keeping his grains in it. The problem of the village has worsened because the Pradhan is a women and her husband is deputy Pradhan who interferes a lot.

## Soil and Crops of Selected Villages

In village **Avarata** the soil is of Balua type which is generally found near rivers. Chikni soil also known as *Chanchar* locally, is found in lower areas and is heavier. *Domat* or *matiar* soil, which is mixture of *Balua* and *Chikni* soils is also found here. It is fertile and black.

Paddy is the main kharif crop. Productivity is 2500 kg/ha in the village which is highest in the district. Crop-residue is used as fodder. Other important kharif crops are millets and maize.

Wheat is the main crop of rabi season sown by almost everyone. The average productivity is around 2200 kg/ha in the village. It is also sown with barley, gram and peas and is called *Gujai, Guchani* and *Bejhar* respectively.

There is very little area under *jayad* (summer crops). Muskmelon, watermelon, vegetables and spices are main crops of *jayad.*

In village **Ranipur** the soil is very fertile and is classified as "Doras Soyam" in the consolidation records. The soil is mostly alluvial. Out of 152.65 acres of cultivable land 30 acres is single cropped, 104 acres double cropped and the rest is three cropped.

Paddy and wheat are main crops in kharif and rabi seasons respectively. Other important crops are sugarcane, *arhar* and potato. The area under paddy, wheat and sugarcane cultivation is 92.5, 84.3 and 21.3 acres respectively. The field is generally low.

In village **Parikhara** main crops of kharif are paddy, *jawar, bajra* and maize. In 1995-96, area under different kharif crops was paddy—90.9 acres, maize—129.6 acres, *jawar*—13.7 acres, sugarcane—7.2 acres and *arhar*—4 acres.

Main crops of rabi seasons were wheat (179.1 acres), gram (1.4 acres) and peas (1.3 acres). Potato was also sown.

No crops were grown in *jayad.*

The soil in the village of **Gulariha** is quite fertile and good for cultivation. Sandy loam soil is mainly found here.

The major crops grown by villagers are paddy, wheat oilseeds, potato and peas. There are under cultivation of these crops are as follows:

Paddy—(143.025 ha), *chara*—(0.238 ha) in the kharif and wheat—(141.130 ha), pulse—(0.131 ha), carrot—(0.345 ha), potato—(0.908 ha), peas—(0.260 ha), *gobhi*—(0.307 ha), *chara*—(0.080 ha) in the rabi season.

The village **Khirora Mohan** is endowed with fertile sandy loan type of soil. The average rainfall is 1025 mm., around 70 per cent of which is received from south west monsoon.

The main crops are paddy, red gram, sugarcane and maize during kharif and wheat, *masur, lahi* and Bengali gram in rabi seasons.

Area under cultivation of different crops was as follows: Paddy—94.9 acres, Red gram—42.9 acres, Sugarcane—7.5 acres, Maize—6.00 acres are the main crops of kharif and Wheat—129.9 acres, *Masur*—12.9 acres, *Lahi*—21.6 acres, Bengali gram—4.3 acres are the main crops of rabi.

The soil composition in the village **Tikamau** includes black and laterite soils. The rocky strata also dominates most parts.

The main crops are as follows: *Jawar*—152 acres, Rapeseed—71 acres, Groundnut—21 acres, *Moong*—14 acres are the main crops of kharif and Wheat—315 acres, Gram—24 acres, Mustard—134 acres are the main crops of rabi.

In village **Himmatnagar Bhajhera,** present distribution of area under different crops are: Paddy—769.4 acres, Maize—65.0 acres, *Bajra*—181.2 acres are main crops of Kharif and Wheat—809.6 acres, Mustard—107.0 acres, Barley—43.0 acres, *Dal*—47.0 acres as main crops of rabi.

Farmers of the village were found reluctant to grow more cash crops like sunflower, mustard oil seeds, toliaceo, sugarcane etc. despite good irrigation facility. There was also no craze to grow vegetables, summer crops like watermelon etc. They preferred only wheat and paddy.

Land of this village is fertile. It is *domat* type of land.

Land of village **Jeesukhpur** is fertile. The village has two types of land—*Kachiyana* and *Domat*.

Maize and paddy are main Kharif crops while wheat, garlic barley are main crops of rabi.

In village **Koyala Alipur** the soil is blackish. Mainly Rabi and Jayad crops are grown in the village. Wheat is the main crop, and they use HYV seeds.

Some farmers also grow vegetables, which are sold in Mathura.

In village **Chirodi** out of total land under cultivation, 68 per cent is double cropped. No land is lying fallow.

Sugarcane is the main crop in rabi, farmers grow wheat on the area which becomes vacant by then as a result of cane cutting. Fodder is also grown in some land.

No farmer takes three crops. Cane is preferred because once sown, it gives crops for at least two years. HYV seeds are in use.

The village **Shahpur Kalan** comprises red, black, acidic and alkaline soils. Black soil is particularly fertile for sugarcane and wheat, which are major crops of the village. Average rainfall is 580 mm.

Wheat is the major rabi crop sown is 52 hectares. The productivity is 2080 qt. per ha. Paddy, is the major kharif crop and is sown in 49 hectares with productivity 1960 Qt./ha.

Pulses are cultivated in rabi and kharif and the area under pulses cultivation is 12 hectares.

Sugarcane is cultivated in 41 hectares with productivity 16,400 Qt./ha. Maize is sown in 25 hectares with productivity 700 Qt./ha. There was no land under horticulture.

In village **Jiraunia** there were mainly three types of soil, they are—*Domat Auwal, Domat Doyam and Matiyar*. While *domat* is considered good for sugarcane, *matiyar* is considered good for paddy. In the village about 70 per cent soil is *domat auwal*, about 20 per cent is *domat doyam* and the rest is *matiyar*.

About 60 per cent agricultural land is under wheat and paddy cropping, 35 per cent land is under sugarcane cultivation and the rest is under other crops such as *masur, lahi, bhindi*, potato and *gobhi.*

In village **Jaffarpur** the soil is very rich and the main crops are potatoes, wheat, sugarcane and vegetables.

The soil in the village **Aloonagar Diguria** is *domat* and sandy type. It is good for growing potato and wheat. There is no problem of soil erosion and water logging in the village.

The crops grown in this village are wheat, rice, potato, *bajra, jawar*, peas and gram. The village is neither flood prone nor drought prone.

Following facts are discernible from the above discussion:

Paddy is generally the main kharif crop in the selected villages. Maize was found to be an important kharif crop in Ballia district, while *jowar* and *arhar* were main kharif crops in Mahoba district.

Wheat is the main rabi crop in almost all villages.

Sugarcane was found to be major commercial crop in Meerut and Buland Shahr district. In Pilibhit 35 per cent land was under sugarcane cultivation.

This gives a very disturbing picture as most of the sown area is covered under wheat, paddy and sugarcane cultivation. There is need to diversify cropping pattern. This could be done by providing credit facility and price incentive for other crops, specially coarse grains pulses and oil seeds.

The other area for diversification is to support cultivation of vegetables, spices and also use some land for horticultural development.

## Irrigation

The rural economy is predominantly agriculture centred. Growth of all other activities are crucially dependent on the growth of agriculture. But the growth of agriculture itself is dependent on irrigation, adoption of new technology and land control system.

There has been sea-change in the area under irrigation as well as source of irrigation. More and more land is being brought under irrigation, which leads to double cropping and also provides incentives for growing commercial crops. This has led to shift from cultivation for personal consumption to cultivation for market also. Similarly, the source of irrigation has also changed from traditional sources to canals and tubewells.

In village **Avarata** canals and tubewells are main sources of irrigation. Out of 47 farmers covered under the sample study, 26 (i.e. 55.32 per cent) were using canal, 6 (i.e. 12.77 per cent) were using public tubewells and 15 (i.e. 31.91 per cent) had private tubewells.

In village **Ranipur** there is no canal irrigation and no government tubewell. Though there are small ponds, they are not used for irrigation. The main source of irrigation is tubewell—almost 90 per cent irrigation is mainly done by 18 private tubewells. The cost or irrigation is about Rs. 35 per hour. Almost all the plots in the village are irrigated.

In village **Parikhara** there is a state tubewell, with irrigation capacity of 250 acres. Besides this, there are also private electric/ diesel pumps in the village.

In village **Gulariha** the main source of irrigation are canals and private tube wells. There are eight private tube wells in the village, but no government tubewell. Some villagers have pump sets. Most of the villagers depend on rain as there is no government irrigation project in the village.

In village **Khirora Mohan,** while 99.4 per cent of area under wheat is irrigated, only 42.59 per cent of paddy is grown under irrigated conditions. This low area of paddy under irrigation is not due to lack of irrigation facilities, but it is due to people's non-preference for paddy cultivation under submerged conditions. Moreover, since south-west monsoon takes care of much of the irrigation requirements of paddy crop, there is no further need to use pump sets.

In village **Tikamau** the facilities for irrigation include a canal, wells and tanks. There are no watersheds in the village. The only government irrigation project is a canal taken out from Bija Sagar, which has a command area of nearly 300 acres in the village. The water rate till last year used to be Rs. 52.00 per acre, but recently it has been revised upwards by state government to Rs. 72.00 per acre. Private irrigation facilities cost Rs. 40.00 per hour and it takes nearly 10 hours for one acre, thus amounting to Rs. 400.00 per acre. The canal is functional at present.

In village **Himmatnagar Bhajhera** crops are irrigated by canal as well as by private tubewells. Total land are irrigated is 963 acres which is around 90 per cent of total land available for cultivation.

In village **Jeesukhpur** people use pump set for irrigation. Rs. 40.00 per hour is charged as rent for providing water to others.

In village **Koyala Alipur** tubewell is the main source of irrigation. Those who do not own tubewells, take water from others at the rate of Rs. 30.00 per hour. There were 182 private hand pumps in the village to irrigate 455 hectares of land, i.e. on average 1 pump set per 2.5 hectares of land.

The village **Shahpur Kalan** has no state irrigation sources like canal or tubewell, nor there was any watershed.

The major source of irrigation comprises private tubewells. 172 hectares is irrigated by this source. The water charge for this is Rs. 10 per hour. Seven hectares of land is irrigated by private pumping sets and the water charge is Rs. 15.00 per hour. Dependence of private owners' whims leads to tension, conflict and difficulty for poorer formers.

In village **Jiraunia** all the agricultural and is irrigated. The main source of irrigation is private boring well operated with the help of a 10-12 H.P. diesel engine. The engine consumes approximately 0.75 to 1 litre diesel in an hour and it takes 6 hours to irrigate on acre of land. Those who do not have their own boring engines hire it from others at Rs. 50.00 per hour. There is also a government tube well in the village. The irrigation capacity of this tube-well is 50 hectares per cropping season. But this tubewell is non-operational because the underground drains which carry water to different fields were damaged some time back and have not been repaired due to lack of funds. The present government rare for irrigation is Rs. 15.60 per hour. The government tubewell takes about 3 hours to irrigate one acre.

In village **Aloonagar Diguria** the main source of irrigation are tubewells—both private and government. The total irrigated area is 408 acres and 247 *khatedars* are dependent on government irrigation project for irrigation. The government irrigation projects provide irrigation facility to 245 acres of land. The water rate for the government irrigation project is Rs. 90.00 per acre, and the water rate or private irrigation sources is Rs. 25.00—Rs. 35.00 per hour.

The main problem with the government irrigation project is that they remain on-functional for a very long period. The operator of government tubewells also creates lost of problems.

Study of villages show two major trends in regard to irrigation. One, use of irrigation through Canals and Tubewells is increasing. Secondly, those who do not own tubewells or pumping sets take water from others at mutually negotiated rate. Taking water from private tubewells owners is increasing because supply of water from government owned sources is not assured at periods of critical needs.

## Agricultural Practices

The increase in agricultural productivity could be achieved only by improving agricultural practices and adoption of new techniques. Two types of techniques are being harnessed. One is land saving: These include adoption of HYV seeds. Use of fertilizers, pesticides/ insecticides etc. and finally, increasing cropping intensity. The other are labour saving, which are broadly related to mechanization and improvement in machines and tools used in different agriculture related operations.

Usually it is assumed that land saving inputs are divisible and therefore, their adoption will not depend on size of holding, except in cases where savings are too low to invest on these. But the assumption that labcur saving techniques are not size neutral needs some serious probing. As we find that hiring of their services has added a new dimension to this debate. We analyze it in the context of findings of the selected villages.

In village **Avarata** out of 57 farmers in sample, 18 do not use HYV seeds. The reason was attributed to lack of money and credit facilities to farmers.

Out of 52 farmers having means of ploughing, 26 were using tractors. It was also observed that mostly villagers hire tractor on rent.

In village **Ranipur** due to low size of holdings and low income levels, use of agricultural technology is relatively low. About 80 per cent of households surveyed used tractors for ploughing their fields. Though the number of tractors in the village is low, many use tractors of others for ploughing by paying user charges at the rate of Rs. 200.00 per hour. The use of HYV seeds has not taken off and more than 50 per cent of farmers do not use them—either because they are costly or they do not have knowledge about them. The seeds and fertilizers are purchased from the nearby cooperatives or open market.

Most of the farmers prefer to cultivate their own land and less than 10 per cent of the households engage casual labour in agriculture.

The agriculture is mainly subsistence type and productivity is not high. As the family size is generally large, most of the produce is generally consumed and no surplus is generally left to be marketed. Even those with marketable surplus cannot manage to sell the produce at government procurement centres. With these constraints, farmers are forced to sell their produce in the open market at lower prices.

In village **Parikha** out of the 40 selected households, only 18 owned land. Most of them plough through hired tractors as they were unable to keep bullocks because of very small holdings. Only one farmer owned bullocks, 8 had wooden plough and two had chaff cutter, i.e. fodder cutting machine.

In village **Gulariha** there is no tractor in the village. People plough their own fields with the help of bullocks or sometimes hire tractors for ploughing purpose.

Since farmers of the village have very small landholding, they do not resort to high technology methods. They hardly use HYV seeds. They were used to the old traditional methods of farming, and were satisfied. HYV seeds and supportive inputs were quite expensive, and furthermore were not available from the Cooperative Society (which could provide at subsidized rates) in time. They felt that purchasing from market was possible for big land owners only.

Bio-fertilizers and other modern methods were unknown to be common villager. The average amount of fertilizer used by the farmer was as follows:

For paddy DAP 40 kg., Urea 50 kg. and MOP 15-20 kg.

For wheat DAP 40 kg., Urea 50 kg. and MOP 15-20 kg.

In village **Khirora Mohan** latest agricultural techniques were not adopted, though fertilizer use was widely prevalent, though not in required quantities.

The village **Tikamau** has not yet taken up the advanced technological methods. The main reason behind this is the scarcity of water for irrigation, which results in only a single crop for most of the area and no one wants to invest a lot of money in the better technological implements for the land which is not very productive. Other rural artisans were also using old methods for their products.

In village **Himmatnagar Bhajhera** farmers do not use much scientific methods of farming. Summer crops are not grown. Only four households owned draught animals.

In village **Jeesukhpur** people use tractor for ploughing and thresher for threshing in this village. Out of 75 selected farmers only 3 used bullock plough while 72 used tractor. However, only 2 reportedly used HYV seeds.

In village **Chirodi** HYV seeds are used. Every farmer uses tractors. Some of them own tractors, while others hire them.

In village **Jiraukia** a survey of selected households showed that out of 55 reporting respondents, 49 used tractors while only 6 used bullock ploughs. But in case of use of HYV seeds, only 17 were found to use HYV seeds while 38 did not use it.

In village **Jaffarpur** the tools used for cultivation were found to be outmoded, and villagers were yet to exploit full potential of their land.

We had earlier discussed that seeds, fertilizers, pesticides and such other inputs are divisible. Therefore, they ought to be size neutral, which means, even small and marginal farmers should be in position to use them. However, it has been found that some farmers whose number vary from village to village were unable to use HYV seeds due to lack of money and credit facilities.

As regards use of tractors, it was found that though the number of tractor owners per village was very small, its services were utilized by even poor farmers, as they could hire it at affordable price. Secondly, with the practice of hiring tractors for ploughing, the need to keep bullocks and maintain them has considerably reduced. Contrary to popular belief this suits marginal farmers as they are unable to keep and feed bullocks or other draught animals throughout the year due to very small holdings.

Mechanisation was also found to be dependent on cropping intensity. For example, in village **Tikamau** of Mahoba district, improved technological methods were not adopted because only a single crop was grown in most of the area sown.

## Marketing of Agricultural Produce

In **Ranipur** as the average family size is large, most of the produce is consumed and no surplus is generally left to be marked. Even those with marketable surplus cannot manage to sell the produce at government procurement centres. As a result of this farmers are forced to sell their produce in the open market at a lower rate.

In **Partikhara** out of 40 sampled households, only 13 old their agricultural produce. They sold through traders at the door step and immediately after the harvest. Items sold were maize, wheat and potato.

In village **Gulariha** villagers hardly sell their produce as they had little surplus. However, there is no problem as Gulariha market is just adjacent to the village. Surplus producers sell their produce in this market.

In village **Khirora Mohan** people either sell their grains to middlemen or take the crop produce to Mandi Samiti just after harvesting. This was partly due to need for money and partly due to lack of storage facility.

In village **Tikamau** out of 37 households interviewed, 31 sold their agricultural produce just after harvest. While 6 reported that they sold during 3 to 6 months after harvesting. 33 of them sold in the local big market, 3 at the nearest *hatt* and 1 at the doorstep. 23 households sold through the middleman while 14 households sold directly to the trader.

In village **Koyala Alipur** inputs like seeds, fertilizers etc. are purchased from Mathura which is located at a distance of only 5 km. from the village. Agricultural produce including vegetables is also sold in Mathura.

In village **Chirodi** sugarcane is old to sugar mills. Daurala sugar mill is the nearest one and almost all farmers sell it there at the gate of mill.

In the case of wheat, almost half of the produce is kept for domestic consumption, while the rest is sold at the wheat purchase centre situated at Daurala.

In village **Shahpur Kalan** various agricultural inputs like urea, DAP, NPK, seed of wheat and paddy are purchased from cooperative society as well as open market. Sugarcane seed and pesticides are procured from open market.

Wheat, paddy and sugarcane are sold in the sub-divisional market of Sikandarabad. Farmers informed that they also sold in the village hat and to local people.

Despite the fact that the farmers in the village **Jaffarpur** sell their surplus produce, the economy is still a subsistence one. This is because of the absence of organized marketing which would have ensured that farmers get a profitable return for their produce. Potatoes grown by villagers are sold at throw away prices and middlemen often come to the village to pickup to produce.

The level of marketing of agricultural produce shows how far the agriculture has moved ahead from subsistence farming to marked oriented farming. This growth depends on two factors. One is the amount of marketable surplus. The other factor is institutions through which this marketing takes place.

In the selected villages, it was found that the marketable surplus with the majority of farmers was low. Therefore, majority of them were not very particular about institutions through which they sold. This factor was, largely, also responsible for not fetching them the remunerative price for their produce.

Most of them sold to traders, some of them to those who come to their village to purchase the agricultural produce immediately after the harvesting. This shows that they have not benefited from purchase centres of Mandi Samitis. Secondly, most of them have not been able to hold back the selling for few months after harvesting, when they could expect higher prices. This was partly due to lack of storage facilities and partly due to their immediate need for cash money.

Farmers of villages from only two district, namely Meerut and Bulandshahr which are more commercial oriented were found to sell their produce in markets where they got good prices.

## Credit Market

Credit is an important source for raising investment and/or start a new enterprise. In fact one of the main reasons for very slow pace of growth in rural areas could be attributed to low level of credit input in organization of their economic activities.

The information about the credit market in selected villages showed that loan was taken from institutional sources mainly as part of poverty alleviation schemes such as IRDP. Besides these, Primary Agricultural Credit Societies (PACS) provided load for agricultural purposes. Credit from both these sources had a set pattern.

Loan for poverty alleviation programmes was mainly provided to targeted population belonging to poorer weaker sections. Many micro level entrepreneurs, who were not below the poverty line, would not avail this facility to start or expand their non-agricultural enterprise.

Similarly, PACS restricted its credit to agricultural inputs.

The supply side constraints was not the only problem. There were even demand side constraints. Village studies reported that villagers felt that procedures for borrowing from institutional sources were cumbersome, would not get money in time and collateral guarantee has to be offered. There was also a tendency to expect waiver of loans or deferment of repayment.

The above mentioned factors/tendencies were obstacles in smooth functioning of the institutional credit market in rural areas.

The need of villagers to depend on informal credit sources were manifold. One was the anonymity factor. Other would not know that the person needed money and incurred debt. The other was freedom from cumbersome procedures. And most importantly institutional sources would not provide loan when it was required for various purposes such as consumption, illness, ceremonies etc.

There was no bank in the village **Ranipur.** In majority of cases of bank loans in the village, it was taken as part of poverty alleviation schemes such as IRDP, etc. Majority of bank loanees belonged to weaker sections.

There is no institution of money lender in the village. People in general borrow from informal sources—from within village or from neighbouring villages. The rates of interest charged by these informal sources are exorbitant—at times as high as 6 per cent per month.

Villagers preferred to take loans from informal sources rather than from banks because they felt that procedures for borrowing from banks were cumbersome, they would not get money in time and it also cost them a get one. They also did not need collateral guarantee for obtaining credit from informal sources. Another important factor was the anonymity factor in borrowing from informal sources. A mode of credit known as "*rehan*", in which the loan giver gets rights over loanee's land for carrying out farming till the clearance of debt, was also observed in the village.

In village **Parikhara** out of 7 families (among 40 sampled) were loanees, 5 had taken loan under IRDP, one from bank and 1 from friend.

In village **Gulariha** the Gorakhpur Kshetriya Gramin Bank provided loans to farmers for agricultural and allied activities. The Kisan Seva Sahkaro Samiti also provided loans for agricultural purposes.

Yet the village money lender was very active and popular. Villagers depended on Sahukars for emergency purposes—such as for daughters marriage, etc. Moneylender could be easily contacted while there were no many formalities in the Gramin Bank. Moreover there was no guarantee that loan would be made available.

In village **Khirora Mohan** people took loan from banks, moneylender, relatives and friends. Among these sources, moneylender was the most important.

The purpose of loan varied from meeting farming expenses, medical expenses, to social functions, however, consumption expenditure was the main reason for taking loan.

It came to light that a moneylender used to come to village from Lucknow on 17th of every month and he charged an exorbitant interest rate of 60 per cent per annum.

In village **Tikamau** out of 10 reporting cases of indebtedness, 2 had taken loan from Primary Agricultural Credit Society, 7 from bank and only one from other sources. Thus formal intuitional sources were the main sources of credit.

The purpose wise distribution of loanees showed that one had taken loan for cropping, one for out-migration, four for agricultural implements, one to purchase cattle and 3 for other purposes.

In village **Jiraunia** the main sources of credit were: (i) Moneylenders/petty traders in the village, (ii) Traders/Merchants in the city, (iii) Commercial banks, (iv) Primary Agricultural Credits Societies.

Approximately 70 per cent of villagers had need for credit. The rate of interest charged by traders/merchants was 3 per cent per month, i.e. 36 per cent per annum with the arrangement that the crop will be sold to them only. No collateral was required by them. Moneylenders also gave loans at 36 per cent interest rate, but they required collateral.

The rate of moneylenders within village was as high as 5 per cent per month, i.e. 60 per cent per annum.

PACS provided fertilizers on loan 10 per cent rate of interest. Since the fertilizer was never supplied in time by PACS, farmers had to purchase it from open market for their crops. But, even then, farmers took the fertilizer supplied by PACS. Then they sold this fertilizer to the fertilizer shops at a discount and utilized the cash thus received, for other purposes. Through this mechanism they were able to get credit at a cheaper rate than that available in the market.

Farmers also got credit from the sugarcane cooperative society. Commercial banks gave crop loans at 12 per cent rate of interest.

The sources of loan in the village **Aloonagar Diguria** were cooperative society, commercial banks and local moneylenders. The loan from cooperative society was available at the interest rate of 12.5 per cent per annum. But people generally took loan from local moneylenders whose rate of interest was around 50 per cent, because of its easy accessibility and hassle free nature.

People felt that the lending system of cooperative society was quite troublesome and complicated. The mentality of villagers was that they considered interest as the burden on the borrower. In fact they never wanted to pay back the money once they got it as IRDP loan etc. They through that the government would waive their interest and loan money. In Aloonagar, 75 per cent beneficiaries ware defaulters. They did not want to take the benefits of new IRDP schemes, because they were afraid that they would have to pay back the past loans.

## SOURCES OF LIVELIHOOD

In this section we deal with landholdings and occupational distribution.

### Land Holdings

There were only two types of villages in respect of distribution of landholdings: Villages where landless or near landless households constituted the vast majority. The other type of villages were those where majority of holdings were marginal or small holdings. There were only 3 villages where farmers owning more than 5 acres was also sizable. The average size of holdings was found to be declining because of divisions in family and consequent increase in number of marginal farmers.

This has a serious implication for future of farming. Because of uneconomic holdings, occupational multiplicity is increasing. An owner of small parcel of land works as a farmer, as an agricultural labour, as casual labour and may also engage in some other activity. Small period migrations also take place among them.

Secondly, if they could find some other remunerative work, then they also tend to lease out land to other fellow farmers.

The other factor which is creating conditions for increasing tendency of leasing out land by these farmers is their inability to keep draught animals for the whole year or invest on machines or equipments. Possession of mere labour power is not enough to sustain farming.

Hence there is a need to develop institutional framework and infrastructural support so that the interest of marginal farmers could be protected in both cases. That is whether they lease out land or cultivate it themselves.

In village **Avarata** farmers of higher caste generally have more than 1 acre of land.

Agricultural labourers were paid Rs. 50.00 per day. This rate was same for men and women. The distribution of landholdings in the village was as follows: landless—15, less than 1 acre—59, 1-3 acres—14, 3-5 acres—2, 5-10 acres—1.

In village **Ranipur**, among the sampled households, it was found, that more than 90 per cent of Scheduled Castes and 75 per cent of OBCs owned less than 1 acre while none of the general category households own less than one acre. All the landless belonged to SC/OBC categories. Some of the SCs and OBCs who were earlier landless became landowners after benefiting under the programme of distribution of government land. Generally landholdings in the village were small and uneconomical. The number of households in different landholding group was as follows: landless—6, less than 1 acre—47, 1-3 acres—10, 3-5 acres—13, 5-10 acres—3, above 10 acres—1.

In village **Parikhara** out of 40 sampled households, 9 were from Scheduled Castes and all of them were landless. Out of 12 households from OBC category 7 were landless, 3 owned less than 0.5 acres and one each belonged to holding group of 0.5-1 acre and 1-2 acres. Among the 19 households of category of others 6 were landless, 4 owned less than 0.5 acres, 2 owned 0.5-1 acre, and 3 each owned 1-2 acres and 2-3 acres respectively.

This shows that average size of landholding was very small in general but in case of OBC, most of them owned even less than 0.5 acre.

In the village the distribution of households by land ownership category was as follows: Landless—62, less than one acre—248, 1-3 acres—57, 3-5 acres—16, 5-10 acres—11, 10-20 acres—1, above 20 acres—1, all size groups—396.

In village **Gulariha** most of the land holders had less than one acre of land. The number of households in different landholding groups is as follows: landless—3, less than one acre—319, 1-2 acres—98 and above 2 acres—1 (who actually owned more than 10 acres).

In village **Khirora Mohan**, out of 40 sampled households 11 were landless and 26 owned less than 1 acre of land. Nine persons had been allotted Gaon Sabha land.

In village **Tikamau** the number of households in different landholding groups was found to be as follows: landless—17, less than one acre—27, 1-3 acres—98, 3-5 acres—19, 5-10 acres—32, 10-20 acres—11.

In village **Himmatnagar Bhajhera** the distribution of landholdings was found to be as follows: landless—96, less than one acre—115, 1-3 acres—435, 3-5 acres—33, 5-10 acres—63, 10-20 acres—6.

This shows that even though the number of small and marginal farmers was quite large, the number of medium size holdings was also quite sizable.

In village **Jeesukhpur** out of 80 households surveyed, 22 were landless, 43 owned less than 1 acre of land and 15 owned between 1-2 acres. Out of 43 owning less than one acre, 26 were Scheduled Castes and 16 were from backward caste. Among those who owned 1-2 acres, two belonged to SC and 13 to backward castes. The only households of general caste have sold their land.

Among the surveyed households, a total of 7.25 acre of land had been purchased. 19.3 per cent of this land had been purchased by SC and 66.91 per cent of it was purchased by the backward caste and the rest by general caste.

The reason given for selling land was repayment of debt. The distribution of landholdings in the village was as follows: landless—58 per cent, less than 1 acre—33 per cent, 1-3 acres—43.5 per cent, 3-5 acres—14.5 per cent, above 5 acres—3.2 per cent.

In village **Koyala Alipur** landowners had divided their land in such a way that they do not fall in the purview of Land Ceiling Act. Out of the 12 landless households, 7 were SC. The distribution of households was as follows: landless—12, less than 1 hectare—82, 1-2 hectare—112, 2-4 hectare—62 and 4-10 hectare—2.

In village **Chirodi** though SC are the largest community (56 per cent) in the village, they owned only 32 per cent of the land, while backward community with 58 per cent of population share owned 67 per cent of land. The upper caste, which constituted 6 per cent of population owned only 1 per cent of land.

Class-wise, top 5 per cent farmers owned about 20 per cent land and top 10 per cent owned about 30 per cent land, whereas bottom 20 per cent owned only 4 per cent of land.

In village **Shahpur Kalan** 80 per cent of the landholders held less than 1 hectare of land. This had fragmented the available land into often uneconomic holdings. The prevailing fragmentation is due to the internal familial partitions. 44 owned between (1-2) hectares of land while 13 landholdings were in the category of (2-4) hectares. 91 households were landless of which 72 belonged to Scheduled Caste.

In village **Jiraunia** caste-wise distribution of landholdings among selected households was as Table 5.7:

In village **Aloonagar Diguria**, there were 338 accounts as Bhumidhar with transferable right entered in *Khatauni* (record of right) and 93 accounts as bhumidhar with non-transferable right. There were 97 landless households in the village.

The pressure of population on the land had resulted in the gradual deduction or final elimination of land for other purposes like groves, grassland etc. and had resulted in fragmentation of land.

**Table 5.7:** Landholdings and Occupational Distribution

| Size Class | SC | BC | Others | Total |
|---|---|---|---|---|
| Less than 1 acre | 23 (67.7) (82.14) | 4(12.12) (25.0) | 6(18.18) (50.0) | 33 (100.0) |
| 1-2 acres | 4 (33.33) (14.29) | 7(58.33) (43.75) | 1(8.33) (8.33) | 12 (100.0) |
| 2-4 acres | 1 (14.29) (3.37) | 3(42.86) (18.75) | 3(42.86) (25.0) | 7 (100.0) |
| 4-10 acres | — | 2(66.67) (12.5) | 1(33.33) (8.33) | 3 (100.0) |
| Above 10 acres | — | — | 1(100.0) (8.33) | 1 (100.0) |
| All size groups | 28 (100.0) | 16 (100.0) | 12 (100.0) | 56 (100.0) |
| Landless | 16 | 8 | — | 24 |
| Total | 44 | 24 | 12 | 80 |

There were very small landholdings which affected the productivity of agricultural produce and led to poor savings. There were only three households in the village who owned land above 20 acres.

## Occupations

We have already mentioned about increase in occupational multiplicity due to increase in landless or near landless households.

The number of casual labourers was larger than agricultural labourers.

Secondly, there was seasonal migration of males, while women workers mostly sought work in the village or worked in houses.

Thirdly, there were very few opportunities of employment of educated youth in the village. They had to go to urban areas for their livelihood.

Fourthly, traditional skill based activities such as carpentry, black smithy etc. were waning.

Animal husbandry was found to be an important subsidiary occupation. But it was not large enough to make them prosperous.

In village **Avarata** main occupation of villagers was farming. Dairy was the most popular non-farming activity. Seasonal unemployment among agricultural labour and marginal farmers during summer was also reported.

At that time they go to nearby towns for daily wage work. Women mostly worked in houses. Women of BPL families/marginal farmers worked as labourers or worked in their own fields.

There were no opportunities of employment for educated youth in the village. They had to go to urban areas for their livelihood.

In village **Ranipur** most of the people depend primarily on agriculture for their livelihood. Some villagers worked in the nearby towns as unskilled labourers. Some peasants worked as tenants.

In village **Parikhara** out of 40 sampled households, the main occupation of 47 was cultivation, 3 were agricultural labourers, 14 households were engaged in non-agricultural labour work, 4 were engaged in trade and commerce, 7 households were in service and 3 were retired pensioners. Occupation of 5 households was reported as 'other occupation'.

In village **Gulariha** agriculture was the prime occupation of villagers. But since most of the households had very small landholdings, they were also engaged in labour and construction work. Some of them also went to Gorakhpur city to work as daily wage labourers or as rickshaw pullers or even as auto-rickshaw drivers. Some others were also engaged as vegetable sellers and fruit vendors in local market.

There were very few families which reared cattle or pig. Some families also possessed goats which were used for milk and meat. Some had cows which provided milk while a few families also possessed fowls for eggs and meat.

In village **Khirora Mohan** there were 158 workers out of a village population of 492. Occupation-wise distribution was as follows: Agriculture (75.95%), Tea-stall (3.16%), Provision store (0.63%), Rickshaw pullers (2.53%), Government service (2.53%), Other services (7.59%).

Majority of villagers had their own milk animals and three of them had draught animals also. Pigs were reared by members of SC community only. No surveyed household had goats or sheep.

In village **Tikamau** cultivation was the most important activity of villagers. The other important activity in which most of the workers were engaged was agricultural and non-agricultural labour. The nearby granite stone mines at Kabrai provided the opportunity for non-agricultural wage work. Very few villagers were engaged in traditional activities like carpentry, black smithy etc. Another important occupation was brick making.

Trade, commerce and service related occupations were not frequent. Only a few families had their members employed in service. Trade and commerce was restricted to the small shops or general merchants selling items of daily needs. Pig rearing was limited to members of Basor community only.

Other activities like cottage industry, food processing, poultry, fishery, sericulture, horticulture etc. were missing in the village. The village did not have any household enterprise or cottage industry. Absence of any market for such products was the biggest hindrance in this respect.

In village **Himmatnagar Bhajhera**, the distribution of workers was as follows: Cultivators (24.86%), Agricultural labour (2.45%), Forestry/Fishing (0.04%), Servicing/Repairs (0.11%), Construction (0.26%), Trade and Commerce (0.19%), Transport/Storage (0.93%), Others (4.23%), Non-workers (66.86%).

Non-workers were children, disabled, old or women. As regards non-farm activities, most of the villagers who were either landless or possessed little land, were engaged in non-farm activities such as artisan, mason, milk selling, tailoring, labour work, shopkeeper, barber, washer men etc. A very large number of them were engaged in milk selling. Milk selling was an allied activity for most of them followed by those who were engaged in labour work. Most of them had got work in JRY or EAS works. There were 23 artisans, 5 masons, 8 tailors, 9 shopkeepers, 6 barbers and 3 washer men in the village.

In village **Jeesukhpur** out of 410 persons in 80 selected households, 26 per cent were self-cultivator, 28.54 per cent were engaged in domestic work only, 20.98 per cent were doing no work whole 17.56 per cent were students. The number of persons in other occupations was as follows:

Engaged in self business—2, small business—5, retired—2, tenant—6, disable—1, class IV job—5, casual labour in agriculture—2, self-employed mechanic—2 and engaged in traditional occupation—3.

In village **Chirodi** agriculture was the main occupation of villagers. There were 369 farmers and 390 labourers in the village. Among the labourers—240 were males and 150 were females. During lean season they went to nearby town or villages to worked as construction worker.

Twenty families of the village were engaged in animal husbandry work. There were five small units which made milk product, and some local workers were engaged in them as labourers. Other occupations were vending, petty trade and few families were engaged in traditional trades.

The normal wage rate was Rs. 70.00-Rs. 80.00 per day for agriculture labourers.

In village **Shahpur Kalan** agriculture was the main occupation of villagers. Among non-farming activities vending and traditional trade and craft were the major ones. 10 households depended upon vending for livelihood. Their technology was traditional knowledge and source of finance was own sources. The place of marketing was village, block and district.

Traditional trade and craft provided livelihood to 8 households—for them moneylenders and self-finance were the main source of finance. The place of marketing was village, block and district. These crafts included weaving, knitting, cobbling and pottery.

In village **Jiraunia** out of 463 members in 80 selected households, 287 were non-workers. These included—underage (61), students (81), only domestic work (105), retired (13), disabled (3) and doing non-work (24).

The number of workers was 176. Their occupational distribution was as follows: self-cultivator—70, small business—6, casual labour in agriculture—21, tenant—16, attached agricultural labour—25, casual labour in rural non-farm—23, industrial casual labour—4, industrial regular labour—2, engaged in traditional work—3, class IV job—2, others—4.

Besides agriculture, the village had three mini rice plants/flour mills, one gur making plant and about three grocery shops. One doctor also practiced from a shop. The village also had some potters, carpenters and tailors.

Illicit liquor was also prepared in the village. Some *kisan* families were engaged in it.

In village **Jaffarpur** apart from agriculture, the village had good potential for dairy as every family kept a cow or two. The cattle population of village was very high.

To supplement households income, a good number of men in the village sought casual labour work in the brick kilns located nearby or in Barabanki or Lucknow. The daily wages varied from Rs. 20.00 to Rs. 60.00 per day. Villagers were not aware of the minimum wages.

In large families, some members of households were engaged in agricultural work while others went to nearby places in search of work to supplement income.

A few Muslim families who had no land, kept a large number of goats. The mutton was sold in Barabanki.

In village **Aloonagar Diguria** the main occupation of the village was agriculture. More than 80 per cent people were surviving on agriculture. But since the landholdings were getting smaller and smaller because of pressure of population on land and increase in number of families, it had become very difficult for the people to survive on agriculture alone. There were not much economic activities in the village to provide employment to people. Very few people were employed anywhere on regular basis.

Because of shrinking of job opportunities in the village, more and more people were seeking jobs in the cities.

In the name of non-farm activities in the village, animal husbandry and poultry farming were the main activities. There were 115 units of animal husbandry with 245 people engaged in the activity and there were 3 poultry units which involved 40 persons of the village.

Those who had no land were working as agricultural or factory worker. Wages in agriculture varied for different types of work. The wages were Rs. 25.00—Rs. 30.00 at the time of sowing and harvesting. Labourers in construction got Rs. 40.00 or Rs. 45.00 per day.

Some persons were engaged in self-employment such as electrician, mechanics, plumber, tea-shop owner etc.

Many persons were also involved in embroidery work, i.e. *chiken* and *zardoji* work. Raw material was provided to them by some women's organization and other individual businessmen. Such workers were paid on the basis of amount of output.

People also got work under JRY and SRY schemes, but in this genuine people were hardly benefited.

## IMPACT OF LAND REFORMS

The following major land reform measures were adopted after attaining independence:

(i) Abolition of Zamindari, i.e. abolition of intermediary tenures between the state and the cultivator. This included restriction on leasing barring some exceptions.
(ii) Conferment of ownership on tenure holders.
(iii) Ceiling on ownership of agricultural holdings.
(iv) Distribution of surplus land and gram samaj land to the landless poor.
(v) Modernization and updation of land records systems.
(vi) Tenancy.

The study of land reform measures in villages showed that even though conferment of ownership on land had been successfully completed in all the villages long back in the sense that there were no official intermediaries now, the practice of leasing out land had been detected even though it operates illegally and is unrecorded.

These tenants are not recorded tenants because it is prohibited under law. The revenue functionary would not enter the cases of leasing because there is no provision for recording such information in the format of *khatauni* or *khasara*—record of ownership and record of land use. But more importantly, even tenants do not make a claim to get recorded as tenant due to fear of getting evicted immediately. Two types of leasing was reported from villages covered under study. These included share-cropping and cash rent leasing. Under share cropping the proportion of sharing of input costs and the produce varied from village to village.

The popular form of share-cropping tenancy known as *adhiya* (half-half) was prevalent in most of the villages.

In **Avarata** village, under the *adhiya* system, all expenditures were born by tenant, and half of the produce was given to landowners.

In some other villages, the proportion of both input and output was found to be shared by tenant and landowner equally, i.e. fifty per cent by each.

Another form of sharecropping was reported from **Ranipur** village, namely Tirahi, i.e. one-third. Under this arrangement, input costs of seed, fertilizer, irrigation and ploughing are provided by the landowner. The owner also provides the cost of machinery (or rent for use) for ploughing, harvesting and threshing. The tenant contributes labour at all stages. The owner gets two-third share of the produce and by-products. The tenant gets one-third of the produce as well as that of the by-products.

The lease is generally on annual basis and renewable. Though there is no security of tenure on record, tenants enjoyed certain degree of security, if personal equations and share arrangements worked well. The land revenue is paid by landowners in all the cases.

Even though share cropping is the traditional mode of leasing after imposition of ban on tenancy, a new trend was found to be emerging on a wider scale. This is fixed cash rent leasing. In case of sharecropping, the landowner bears risk—the proportion of risk may vary in different types of crop sharing and cost sharing arrangements. But in case of fixed rent leasing, the landowner bears no risk. Such cases were reported from Koyala Alipur, Chirodi, Shahpur Kalan and Jiraunia villages.

The main reason for increasing trend in fixed rent leasing, is that, landowners (mostly belonging to new generation) are becoming non-resident villagers and are engaged in other professionals. Secondly, they have found that no body had been penalized for leasing out the land. The entries in the revenue records would continue to be made in his favour by bribing the *lekhpal* (revenue record keeper at the village level). Hence even the pretence of managing farm or bearing risk has been shed by new generation landowners.

## Distribution of Land

Another major land reform measure which was supposed to help poor landless peasants was land distribution. The land for distribution among poor was available from two sources—Ceiling surplus and Gram Samaj.

As regards ceiling surplus land, no land was declared as surplus land, under the Ceiling Act from five selected villages from where such information was collected. These included Avarata, Ranipur, Gulariha, Jeesukhpur and Jiraunia.

Land was acquired in four villages. In **Koyala Alipur**, where 24 acres of land was acquired, the land been distributed among landless agricultural workers.

In **Chirodi** village 57.914 hectares of land was declared surplus under Ceiling Act. This land was allotted to 24 persons.

Only 0.271 hectare of land was declared surplus in village **Shahpur Kalan**, which was allotted to one beneficiary.

In **Jaffarpur** 257 bighas of land was declared surplus, out of which 117 bighas were distributed to landless households while the rest was vested with the gaon sabha.

The land from gaon sabha land was allotted in Ranipur, Jeesukhpur, Chirodi, Shahpur Kalan and Jiraunia.

In **Ranipur** the land allotted was between 0.1 to 0.2 acres per beneficiary of land. The study of 10 selected allottees showed that all except one were in possession of land and cultivating it. Allottees felt that the size of land allotted was very small. Almost all of them said that allotment of land had not transformed their life but has helped meeting a portion of food requirement.

In **Jeesukhpur** and **Chirodi** also, allottees were in possession of their land and cultivating them. There was no provision of providing assistance to government land allottees. In **Chirodi**, out of 78 allottees 74 were Scheduled Caste. Even ten female beneficiaries were allotted government land.

Similarly in **Shahpur Kalan**, out of 30 allottees of government land 20 were Scheduled Caste and 9 of these allottees were women.

In **Jiraunia** village, all the *pattedars* of government land belonged to Scheduled Caste. Out of ten such *pattedars* from whom data was collected, only three were cultivating the land, four have leased out land on fixed rent and remaining three had sold their land to others. Each allottee was given around one acre of land. The land of three allottees was of medium quality, while that of other seven was of superior quality.

The general problems of allottees were:

(i) Uneconomic size of landholdings,

(ii) Low investible capacity, and

(iii) No assistance from the government.

## Consolidation of Holdings

The consolidation work had been completed in the following villages covered under the study: Ranipur, Koyala Alipur, Shahpur Kalan and Jiraunia.

The major achievement was in regard to reduction in plots. The number of plots reduced in reported villages were as follows: In **Ranipur** from 1202 plots before consolidation to 306 plots after consolidation, in **Jiraunia** the number of plots reduced from 1412 to 680. In **Shahpur Kalan** the number of plots increased from 530 to 563 because during the consolidation period, a landowner was generally succeeded by more than one successor.

In Ranipur, besides consolidating the holdings, it provided for chak roads, drainage and other common property resources such as *Khalihan* (place to keep harvested crop, place from potters mud). However, no land exists for playground (for which provision was made), for grazing and pasture land, school and Panchayat bhawan (for these no provision was made).

Except reduction in holdings, the land management had not improved in any of the reporting villages.

## Land Records

One of the weakest factors responsible for poor land management was poor up keep of land records.

The process of computerization has been started in some tehsils, yet due to error in maps proper demarcation of common property resources is hanging in the air as a result of which its encroachment continues. The record of rights (*khatauni*) and the annual survey register (*khasra*) are maintained by the *lekhpal*. But regular updation of records in computer must be ensured at all levels.

Village-wise information about land reform measures are discussed below:

## Village Avarata (District Allahabad)

No incidence of *begar*, *nazrana*, etc. is found in the village. There was no ceiling surplus land. There were 10 tenants in the village. These tenants were not recorded tenants because it is prohibited under law. Most popular form of tenancy in the region is *adhiya*, where all expenditures are born and half of the produce is given to landowner. Landowners are mainly businessmen or government servants. Tenants are mostly landless and marginal farmers.

Land records in Uttar Pradesh are computerized at present. Computers have been given at tehsil level. Now, copy of *khatas* can be obtained by computer. Zamindari abolition areas have two documents as land records, first is *khatauni* and second is *khasra*. *Khatauni* is record of rights and admissible in court as evidence. *Khasra* contains data about type of soil, crops, trees and actual possession of land. Now zamindari abolition areas have *khevat* in place of *khatauni*. *Khevat* is same as *khatauni* but has one more column.

## Village Ranipur (District Azamgarh)

Three acres of land was distributed among twenty-one persons in 1976. The beneficiaries included 5 SC landless, 8 OBC and 4 SCs who owned less than 3 acres. Each of the beneficiaries was allotted land varying between 0.1 to 0.2 acres. At the time of allotment, the beneficiaries were conferred with Sirdari Rights. Later on they were converted to Bhumidhars with Non-transferable Rights. As a result of an amendment to Zamindari Abolition and Land Reforms Act in 1955, every Bhumidhar with Non-transferable Rights, upon completion of 10 years acquired Bhumidhar with Transferable Rights. Entries to this effect have been made in the Records of Rights in 1997.

Of the allottees, ten cases were taken up for study. All of them were in possession of the land except one who had sold his land. All of them were cultivating the allotted land. They had not paid any money to Pradhan or Lekhpal to get land allotted. The guidelines for allotment were also adhered to.

The beneficiaries felt that the land allotted was very small in size. In one case 0.1 acre was allotted which was further subdivided among his five sons. Most of them had other sources of income either as sharecropper or as wage labourer. Almost all of them said that allotment of land had not transformed their lives. But it had helped them to cater to a portion of their foodgrain requirement.

Nine Harijans were allotted land for '*Abadi*'. Each was given 0.039 acres for housing along with 0.029 acres for development purposes. All of them were in possession of the allotted land and houses have also been constructed. Only those belonging to preferential categories (u/s 122C of ZALR Act) were allotted land.

Though the ZALR Act prohibits letting and subletting of land, the actual situation was entirely different. Concealed and unrecorded tenancy based on sharecropping is widely prevalent. There were about 28 tenants in the village, of which 15 belonged to OBCs, 11 belonged to SC and two belonged to forward castes.

Most of the tenants owned less than 0.25 acres of land. None of them had studied beyond high school and half of them were illiterate. About 20 acres of land was under tenancy in the village. This was about 15 per cent of the total land fit for cultivation in the village. Out of 28 tenants ten tenants were sampled for detailed study. The landowners mostly belonged to the forward castes especially Kshatriya. There was only one Kurmi (OBC) landowner and none from the Scheduled Castes.

The forms of tenancy that was prevalent were *Batai* (*Adhiya*) and *Tirahi*. The common form of tenancy or sharecropping was *Tirahi*, in which, input costs of seed, fertilizer, irrigation and ploughing, were provided by the landowner. The owner also provided the cost of machinery (rent for use) for ploughing, harvesting and threshing. The tenant contributed the labour at all stages. The land revenue was paid by the landowner. The owner got a two-thirds share of the produce and the by-products.

The other form of tenancy was *Batai*, a variant of sharecropping, in which the input cost of seeds, fertilizers, pesticides, irrigation, ploughing, sowing and harvesting was born by the tenant. The tenant contributes input cost and labour whereas the owner paid the land revenue (because proof of this can be used for proving lease of land). The owner and the tenant shared the produce as well as the by-products equally.

The lease was generally on seasonal or annual basis and is renewable. If the landowner was unsatisfied with the performance or otherwise with the tenant he could evict the tenant. The dissatisfaction may either be due to the landowner not being satisfied with the amount of labour and fertilizer put in by the tenant or when he felt that he could have earned better if some other crops or vegetables were planted by the tenant. Some landowners changed the tenant to preclude the eventuality of a tenant making a claim over the land. On the other hand the tenant was also free to leave if he was not willing to work. But generally the lease was renewed. Though there was no security of tenure on record, the tenants did enjoy certain degree of security. There were few cases where the lease had continued for more than 12 years; the period after which the tenant can claim transferable Bhumidhar Rights on the ground of adverse possession, but none had claimed so far.

The main reasons for which the landowners were leasing out land were that either they were engaged in other professions or that the plot given out on lease was a distant plot (not contiguous with their other plots) and its cultivation was uneconomical. It also provided labour when required (as it has now become difficult to find agricultural labourers as and when required).

There was no case of indebtedness among tenants. In two instances land was given out on *Rehan* (land is mortgaged with possession till repayment of loan). Though mortgage with possession is deemed to be a transfer, no action was taken under the U.P. ZALR Act.

The present record of rights (*khatauni*) pertains to 1407 *fasli* year (1999) and is due for updation in 2004. The process of computerization of land records of the village has not yet begun. The *lekhpal* regularly visits the village and the villagers do not have any problem in obtaining copies of land records. Due to certain errors in map, proper demarcation of a chak road was not possible and its encroachment continues. The *lekhpal* has done partals and the *khasra* (field book) is update.

The consolidation process in the village started in September 1970 and final publication was done in 1978. The number of plots before consolidation was 1202 and was reduced to 306 after the consolidation. Besides consolidating the holdings it provided for chak roads, *nalis* (drains) and other common property resources such as *khalihan* (a place for keeping the crop after the harvest), place for potter's mud. Though the consolidation report claimed to have made provisions for playground, no land existed under this head. No provision was made for grazing and pasture land, school and panchayat bhawan.

The problem with consolidation in the village was that few people were allotted chaks, which turned out to be *abadi* of others. Later on all such disputes were amicably settled. The villagers also complained of few errors in consolidation map, which have led to disputes regarding the location of chak roads and *nalis*. The villagers benefited from consolidation, as it paved way for use of better agricultural practices and thus increased agricultural production.

No land was declared as surplus under the Ceiling Act and hence none of the villagers gained any benefit from this land reform measure. There was no beneficiary under the distribution of *bhoodan* land too.

## Village Gulariha (District Gorakhpur)

Land reforms have been implemented in the village. The village has already been brought under consolidation and has been covered under the Zamindari Abolition and Land Reforms Act. There is no ceiling land in the village as most of the land holdings are small. Tenancy is not prevalent in the village and there is no Bhoodan Land in the village.

## Village Jeesukhpur (District Etah)

There are no allottees of Bhoodan land. Out of 10 households surveyed of Government land allottees. 5 belonged to Shakya caste and one belonged to Teli caste. They fall under backward caste. About 1.82 hectare of land was allocated to them. Rest of them were from Kori caste and had 1.22 hectare of land allocated to them. None of them were dispossessed from their land. None of the beneficiary had leased out his land. All the beneficiaries are growing wheat as rabi crop and paddy and coarse grains as kharif crop. There is no provision of providing assistance to government land allottees. Land, which was allotted, was of good condition and was doubly cropped.

No ceiling surplus land was distributed in this village. Of the 10 households, which were surveyed, one was from *thakur* (general caste) two were from Kori caste (Scheduled Caste) and seven were Shakya (other backward caste). All the land, which was operated by tenant, was irrigated. From the tenant household which were surveyed,

50 per cent were under Fixed Cash Rent, paying Rs. 12,500 per hectare and others were on share in input and produce basis. None of them provided free service to landlord. The condition of tenancy was similar over whole of the area and thus there was not much bargaining for fixing the condition of tenancy. It was fixed mutually among landlord and tenant. The reason for which tenant was changed by landlord was mainly the fear of loosing land. No serious conflict existed between tenant and landlord. No view was expressed by tenant, showing discontentment from the condition. Out of ten surveyed households, only one had taken loan from commercial bank. The share in input and produce in this type of tenancy, was on 50-50 per cent basis. Most of the tenants were landless farmers. They belonged to same village. Literacy rate among tenants surveyed, was about 50 per cent.

Land reforms related to ceiling have been implemented properly in the village. According to information gathered from village elders and village Patwari no one in the village held land more than the ceiling limit. According to them there was no Benami land holding in the village. 57.914 hectare land was declared surplus in the village as a result of ceiling. This land was allotted to 24 people. These people included former soldiers or their dependants. These people were generally from backward and general castes.

Letting of land by an able person is prohibited in UP ZALR Act. Only persons who are not able to cultivate on their own are allowed subletting their land. According to survey 20-25 farmers had sublet their land under this provision but even in those cases the terms and conditions were not written and everything was informal. Apart from them, there were 25-30 other farmers who had sublet their land against the provisions of the Act. The form of tenancy prevalent was fixed cash tenancy.

All the government land available in the village had been distributed to the landless villagers. In all there were 78 allottees of government land. Out of them 74 belonged to SC and 4 to other backward community. Among these 78, 10 were women. Total land allotted was 13.215 hec out of which 12.690 hec was held by SC and 0.525 hec by OBC. Women had been allotted 1.338 hec land.

Land records of the village were in good condition. Latest records were available with *lekhpal* who kept with him three main records:

(i) *Khatauni*.

(ii) *Khasra.*

(iii) *Shijra.*

*Khatauni* is the most important land record. Names of all landholders and land held by them is recorded alphabetically in it. *Khasra* shows who is in actual possession of each plot of land, what is being growing on it, what is the mode of irrigation etc. *Shijra* is the map of village showing every field and each field is numbered. It is open for villagers to obtain copy of any land record on payment of nominal fees. Previous records are available in tehsil and all older records are available in the district record room. Copy of these records can also be obtained. Record of all revenue cases are also preserved in the district record room.

## Village Shahpur Kalan (District Bulandshahr)

Only 0.271 hectare land in the village was surplus. The state took possession of the entire land. The entire land was allotted to only one beneficiary who is in possession of the land. The actual possession was given on 16.6.1993, the transfer was recorded in the revenue on 17.4.1993. The beneficiary had improved his status due to the allotment. The beneficiary was a member of the Scheduled Caste. His income had improved by Rs. 3000.00 per annum.

The total area available for cultivation was 182 hectares. Of which area leased-in by tenants was 8.40 hectares. This had been given to 12 tenants. The major forms of tenancy in the village included fixed cash rent and sharecropping, 6 of the tenants were marginal farmers, 1 was a small farmer, 3 were landless. All the tenants were residents of the village. Four were illiterate, three had education upto primary school level, one had studied upto higher secondary level, one was a class XII pass out. The total land under tenancy was irrigated. Of the 15 landowners involved, 8 lived outside the village. The general period of lease was 1 year. Seven of the tenants also cultivated their own holdings. 4 tenants out of 10 were in the fixed produce tenancy agreement, 3 belonged to the tenancy system which has a share in input and produce, 2 were fixed cash rent tenancies. One was an usufructuary mortgage. Paddy and wheat were the major crops produced in these leased in farms. Land revenue was paid by the landholder. Generally, tenancy in **Shahpur Kalan** is known by the term *lagaan.* Two tenants paid cash rent of Rs. 8000.00 per hec per annum. Only one of the tenants had taken a loan of Rs. 9000.00 from a commercial bank at an interest rate of 12.5 per cent for the leased-in farm. The amount outstanding was Rs. 3000.00. Tenants did not provide any free service to the landowners. Custom determined the tenancy agreement. Tenants were changed to get better terms of tenancy. The survey revealed that most tenants were relatively satisfied with the terms and conditions of the tenancy since the agreement was a mutually arrived upon one. Conflicts between the tenants and landlord were not revealed.

There were thirty allottees of government land, out of which 20 were Scheduled Caste members, 9 of these allottees were women. 1.05 hec had been given to female allottees. The total land allotted was 6.5 hec. Apart from the land allotted to women, 3 hec had been allotted to Scheduled Caste members and 2.45 hec had been given to other castes. There was no tribal land available in the village.

On 10.7.1982 consolidation was notified in **Shahpur Kalan**. It was finalized on 31.12.1986. The number of plots at the time of consolidation were 530. The number of consolidated plots were 563. This was due to the fact that during the consolidation period a landowner was generally succeeded by more than one successor. The new record of rights was operation *Kisan Bahis* had been distributed. Land records had not been computerized. The process of computerization was under way.

## Village Jiraunia (District Pilibhit)

No land was declared surplus in the village under ceiling. There was also no Bhoodan land in the village.

In **Jiraunia**, all the land distributed was government land and *pattedars* of government land were from Scheduled Castes. Data was collected from 10 *pattedars*. All of them had initially taken possession of the land allotted to them. The problem of dispossession from land was not reported in this village. The names of *pattedars* were also entered in revenue records, but only three of them were cultivating the land allotted to them. Four of them had given their land on contract to others for one year. Remaining three had sold their land to others.

Each allottee was given around one acre of land. Three persons were allotted land of medium quality, i.e. *Matiyar Doyam* and seven were allotted land of superior soil, i.e. *Dumat Awwal*. No assistance apart from the land, such as financial support, fertilizers, pesticides etc. was provided to the beneficiaries.

The problems faced by the *pattedars* were: the uneconomic land holdings, the reluctance of the persons cultivating the land to leave the land when the *pattedar* wanted to give his land to someone else on contract.

There was also a tendency, in this region to sell the government land in order to become eligible again for land allotment. There is a provision in law, which prohibits it, but somehow it is often ignored by the authorities.

The main form of tenancy prevalent in this village was fixed rent system. A tenant had to pay around Rs. 900.00—1000.00 per bigha, that is Rs. 5650.00—6250.00 per acre depending upon the quality of soil and the situation of the plot. The other form, though less prevalent, was that of share cropping in which tenant shared 50 per cent share of inputs as well as that of produce.

## Area Operated by the Tenants

**Table 5.8:** Category of Land Operated (hectares) out of Total Land Operated Area

| *Caste* | *Total* | *Owned* | *Leased-in* | *Mortgaged* | *Encroached* |
|---|---|---|---|---|---|
| General | 39.60 | 30 | 6 | 1.35 | 2.25 |
| OBC | 38.05 | 32 | 4.50 | 0.80 | 0.75 |
| SC | 25.75 | 19.25 | 5.00 | 1.00 | 0.50 |
| **Total** | **103.40** | **81.25** | **15.50** | **3.15** | **3.50** |

And important thing to note is that SCs also leased-in land. They had also got land mortgaged with them. As far as encroachment goes they have their share of encroached Gram Sabha land, also.

**Table 5.9:** Socio-Economic Status of Tenants

| *Land Ownership* | *SC* | *OBC* | *General* | *Total* |
|---|---|---|---|---|
| Landless | 1 | 1 | – | 2 |
| Marginal Farmer | 4 | 1 | 3 | 8 |
| Small Farmer | -- | – | – | – |
| Medium Farmer | – | – | – | – |
| Large Farmer | – | – | – | – |
| Total | 5 | 2 | 3 | 10 |

**Table 5.10:** Educational Status of Tenants

| *Education* | *SC* | *OBC* | *General* | *Total* |
|---|---|---|---|---|
| Literate | 5 | 1 | 2 | 7 |
| Illiterate* | — | 1 | 2 | 3 |

*Literate includes Primary, Middle, Secondary, Intermediate, Graduates

**Table 5.11:** Residential Status of Tenants

| *Place of Residence* | *SC* | *OBC* | *General* | *Total* |
|---|---|---|---|---|
| Same Village | 3 | 1 | 3 | 7 |
| | 42.86% | 14.29% | 42.86% | 100.0% |
| Outside Village* | 2 | 1 | – | 3 |
| | 66.67% | 33.33% | | 100.0% |

* Outside village includes Adjoining Village, Block HQ, Tehsil Headquarter

It is clear from above table that most tenants were landless and farmers with marginal landholdings. Almost three-fourth of the tenants were literate. Almost three-fourth of the tenants belong to the same village as land holder:

**Table 5.12:** Main Occupation of Tenant

| *Caste* | *Main* | *Number* |
|---|---|---|
| General | Self-cultivator | 1 |
| | Tenant | 2 |
| OBC | Self-cultivator | 1 |
| | Tenant | 1 |
| SC | Tenant | 5 |
| **Total** | | **10** |

It is noteworthy that all the SC tenants had tenancy as their main occupation but this was not the case with OBCs and upper castes.

## Indebtedness of Tenants

All the 10 tenants who were interviewed had incurred loan.

Trader/merchant is the most common source of loans as 7 tenants had taken loan from them. The moneylender gives loan on hypothecation. The trader gives loan at the same rate of interest but without hypothecation with the arrangement that the farmer will sell his produce to him only. Two had taken loan from moneylender or landowner, 2 from commercial bank and 3 from PACCs.

Most of the loan is taken for the duration of a crop or two only.

The main reason for changing the tenant was reported to be fear of loss of land. This was suggested by 6 tenants, while two suggested that landlord could change if unsatisfied with tenants labour. Only two tenants suggested that landowner could change tenant to keep terms of tenancy in his favour.

The reason of conflict between the tenant and landholder was generally on duration of tenancy. When the landholder wants to change the tenant there is some friction. When the tenancy is of such type in which the landholder and the tenant share the inputs and the produce, then the conflict is on the amount of labour put in by the tenant.

Consolidation was notified in the village in the year 1964. There were 219 *khatas* and 1412 plots before consolidation. After consolidation the number of *khatas* became 315 and the total number of consolidation plots became 680. The date of final publication was 8th August, 1966.

The basic record (*Zild Bandobast*) of village is present in the tehsil. The record of rights (*khatauni*), and the annual survey register (*khasra*) are maintained regularly. Land records of all the villages in the district have been computerized. But the regular updation of *khatauni* in computer is not taking place. A computerized copy of *khatauni* is available on nominal charges of Rs. 2 per *khata*.

## Village Jaffarpur (District Barabanki)

Land reforms in the village resulted in 257 bighas of land being declared surplus in the village. Of this 257 bighas 117 bighas were distributed and taken possession of and of these 9 SCs were given 15 bighas of land whereas 102 bighas were distributed to the OBCs and the Muslims. The rest were vested in the Gaon Sabha and was given for the school building too. Of the land vested in the Gaon Sabha the land falls in the *Ussar*, *Banjar* and *Khalihan* categories. A case was also going on against the former Pradhan as he had been accused of giving away land to some powerful people for setting up a brick kiln near the village.

Of the 40 households interviewed only one did not own any plot of land. He said that he had not been given any plot of land despite repeatedly asking for land from the LMC. Apart from the 40 who were surveyed, there were a few others who did not own land and the LMC had promised to given them land for which the proposal was to be prepared during the general meeting of the Gaon Sabha.

Land reform in Uttar Pradesh are at the crossroads. Over the past five decades, efforts to achieve allocative efficiency and equity through land reforms have largely failed, despite the adoption of a substantial amount of land reform legislation. The four broad components of land reform have included abolition of intermediary interests (tenures) in land; ceilings on land holdings; regulation of tenancy and land consolidation.

Following important issues need to be addressed in the process of land reform:

- Laws on land ceilings remain to be implemented effectively due to loopholes in and/or deliberative circumvention of the law;
- While tenancy has been abolished, there have emerged illegal, insecure and clandestine tenancies or leasing of land;
- There are constraints to land consolidation such as the existence of lands of varying qualities, with and without irrigation; absence of land valuation procedures; and land of institutional support to complete the processes expeditiously;
- Government land and common property resources, some of which might potentially provide an important source of subsistence to the rural poor, either remain to be distributed or where distributed are in a poor state of management;
- Land reforms have not addressed the issue of gender inequalities in land inheritance laws and ceiling laws;
- Updating of land records, through surveys and settlement of rights, remains a neglected or slow process due to the lack of institutional support in terms of trained staff, equipment, and working capital; and

- Computerization of land records has begun but the progress has been very slow due to lack of capital, trained staff, and the resistance of local officials to using computers.

## IMPACT OF POVERTY ALLEVIATION PROGRAMMES

### IRDP and Swarn Jayanti Gram Swarojgar Yojana (SGSY)

Main findings in regard to those programmes are as follows:

(i) Sometimes people who are not below poverty line are selected by gram panchayat.

(ii) Loan application are not timely processed.

(iii) The concept of Self Help Groups (SHGs) is new to villagers and it becomes very difficult to form a cohesive SHG. SHGs are assigned some activities and their produce has to be marketed. Due to lack of proper marketing facilities, their produce does not fetch good price and the groups are discouraged.

(iv) Except those who received assistance for running small business, sustenance of activity by IRDP beneficiaries was generally found to be very poor. The main reason for maintaining asset for only short duration is more interest in getting subsidy amount rather than creating an income generating asset. It was reported in **Ranipur** that out of loan subsidy, beneficiaries were net gainer of about Rs. 4000.00 after paying bribers etc. Other reason for selling assets were—low income, costly maintenance etc.

(v) No training was imported to beneficiaries to run the scheme.

(vi) The number of beneficiaries not paying their dues was also quite sizable.

### Jawahar Rozgar Yojana (JRY) and Sunischit Rozgar Yojana (SRY)

Studies in regard to these schemes showed that

(i) The total number of man days of employment created was generally small. Therefore, the impact of JRY or SRY in providing employment was not very significant.

(ii) Wages were generally paid as per the prescribed rate.

(iii) The quality of infrastructure created was generally not good as it would not last even one or two years. Earth work and *Kharanja* work would get damaged after one severe rain. the repair of these infrastructures took much longer time. The quality was found to be good in **Jeesukhpur** where gaon sabha took the decision about the work to be undertaken and in **Koyala Alipur** where school and panchayat buildings were constructed.

## Indira Awas Yojana (IAY), Million Wells Scheme (MWS) and Improved Tool Kit Scheme (ITS)

The number of beneficiaries under IAY was noticeable in selected villages but beneficiaries of schemes such as MWS and ITS were found to be very limited.

IAY beneficiaries were selected by gram sabha. Sometimes even non-eligible persons were selected. Misuse of funds which was transferred to the account of beneficiaries was also reported. Houses were generally constructed on gram sabha land.

In many cases inputs/materials provided were not sufficient for completion of the house. Beneficiaries had to invest their own money to complete the house.

The following observations about status of IAY in **Gulariha** village is symptomatic of conditions in all the villages:

(i) Only five out of the twelve beneficiaries had made latrine, but were not using it. The rest had utilized the place for constructing kitchen or had used the money to complete the house. This has defeated the purpose of providing latrine for every IAY house.

(ii) House built was being used by the family of beneficiaries.

(iii) Selection of beneficiaries was not made properly.

(iv) One beneficiary was using the room built under IAY as cowshed.

## Other Social Welfare Schemes

Other social welfare schemes like Maternity Benefit Scheme, Family Benefit Scheme and Old Age Pension Scheme were also being implemented in some of the village.

Information about Impact of Poverty Alleviation Programmes in different selected villages was as follows:

## Village Avarata (District Allahabad)

### *Swarna Jayanti Gram Swarozgar Yojana (SGSY)*

There are two kinds of beneficiary under this scheme: individuals and members of the self help groups. Individual beneficiaries are given one-time financial loans from banks with subsidy. Individual beneficiaries are selected by gram panchayat. Sometimes people who are not below poverty line are selected by gram panchayat. That has resulted in neglect of poor villagers who really need government assistance. The second problem is that loan applications are not timely processed by banks. Poor villages do not have anything worthy of being given as security for loans, so banks are not very enthusiastic about giving loans to them.

Self help groups (SHGs) are also formed under this scheme. In each group, there are around 15-20 people. The concept of SHG is new to villagers and it is very difficult to form a cohesive SHG. SHGs go through a long process of grading and the given financial assistance, so the results are not observed soon. SHGs are assigned some activities and their produce has to be marketed. Due to lack of proper marketing facilities, their produce does not fetch good price and the groups are discouraged. Banks are also not very enthusiastic about group loaning because they consist of members of BPL families. It was observed that to achieve the targets, SHGs are formed without motivating members. These kinds of groups are short lived and break soon. There are two SHGs in the village. Their bank accounts are not opened till date.

### *Sunischit Rozgar Yojana (SRY)*

Under this programme, funds are given to Zila Panchayat and Kshetra Panchayats to create rural infrastructure while providing wage employment. This scheme gets the largest funds. Funds are given to blocks for utilization. Generally, members of kshetra panchayats get roads, etc. built either by themselves or their relatives and force block development officer to pay them. BDO does not have any security and has to pay according to wishes of members of *kshetra* panchayat. Labourers are also paid at Rs. 50.00, which is lower than statutory minimum wage rate. The quality of material used and construction is aiso not very good. For example, bricks are purchased at Rs. 1575 per 1000 at the scheduled rate of PWD while bricks are available at Rs. 1200.00-1300.00 per 1000 in market. Moreover, rates are paid for No. 1 bricks but supplied bricks are of No. 2 and No. 3 standard.

### *Jawahar Gram Smridhi Yojana (JGSY)*

Under this scheme, funds are given to Gram Panchayats to create and maintain intra-village infrastructure and to provide wage employment. Funds are used at sweet will of gram pradhan. This has resulted in inferior quality of construction. Rates paid to villagers were also lower than market rate.

Other Social Welfare Programmes Implemented in the village are Indira Awas Yojana (IAY), Unnat Chulha Programme, PM Peyajal Yojana, maternity benefit scheme, family benefit scheme, scholarships for poor students in which cheques are dispatched from district office and if there is some mistake, it has to be returned back and issue of new cheque from district takes lot of time.

## Village Ranipur (District Azamgarh)

### *Integrated Rural Development Programme (IRDP)*

From the year 1993-94 only ten households were covered under IRDP. The eligible beneficiaries submitted their applications to BDO through Gram Pradhan who in turn forwarded to concerned banks. Of the ten households assisted under IRDP of which six belonged to the Scheduled Castes.

All the beneficiaries were provided loan in the form of loan subsidy. The purposes for which loan was taken are piggery, goat rearing, cycle repair shop, hotel/tea shop, photo framing etc. The performance of IRDP beneficiaries is unimpressive. Except Ramdular and Ramkumar who took loans for photo framing and electric tube well, all other beneficiaries have either sold off their assets or do not continue the enterprise for which loan was taken.

The main reason for failure is that most of beneficiaries were only interested in getting the subsidy amount rather than creating an income-generating asset. Majority of them admitted to payment of about Rs. 2000 as commission for obtaining loan. When asked they frankly answered that selling it off can cover the cost of asset purchased. Out of the loan subsidy, after paying commission, they are left with benefit of about Rs. 4000. Only two out of ten beneficiaries have defaulted on repayment of loan.

No training was provided to any of the beneficiaries to run the scheme and none of them got supplementary assistance provided in the form of repeat loan.

## Jawahar Rojgar Yojana (JRY)

In the year 1999-2000, Rs. 21,469 were utilized under the scheme. Under JRD, 19 metre *Kharanja* (brick road) was laid down. In other works such as construction of link road of 0.450 metre length, *Kharanja* of 0.108 km length and installation of 15 hand pumps, labour component was provided by JRY. For the year 1999-2000, the ratio of wage to material component of JRY works was about 80 per cent, much above the prescribed 60 per cent norm.

In all 330 man-days were generated during the year. The main beneficiaries under the wage employment of JRY are landless labourers belonging to the Scheduled Castes. No women got employed for even a single day. Non-residents of the village accounted for about 15 man-days. The wages paid to the workers were at the prescribed minimum wage of Rs. 47 per day per person. The wages were paid in cash and all the entries were made in the muster rolls. The beneficiaries paid no commission.

The quality of works executed under JRY is good and the assets generated were in use. A small percentage of low quality bricks instead of first class bricks were also used. Incidentally, the bricks used for works executed under various schemes were from the brick kiln owned by the Gram Pradhan. The impact of JRY in providing employment was negligible.

## Indira Awas Yojana, MWS and EAS

Under IAY, four houses were constructed in the village in 1986-87. The beneficiaries were earlier allotted government land for housing. The grant amount as drawn by the Gram Pradhan and the beneficiaries were given for building material. Two of the beneficiaries Munna and Sriram received 6,000 bricks, 7 bags of cement (of 50 kg. each), 80 kg. Iron rods and half trolley of sand each while other beneficiaries received 10,000 bricks, one quintal of iron rods and a wooden door.

As these inputs were not sufficient for completion of the house, the beneficiaries had put their own money to the tune of Rs 5,000.00 to complete it.

The beneficiaries were not aware of the grant amount sanctioned to them under the scheme. They were not aware if any commission/ cuts were involved. They expressed faith in the then Pradhan. All the houses were constructed and are in good condition. There was no beneficiary from the village under IAY since 1986-87.

Under Million Wells Schemes (MWS) only one person belonging to general category benefited from the village during 1999-2000. No work was taken up in the village under Employment Assurance Scheme (EAS). The Kshetra Panchayat (middle tier panchayat) does the selection of works under EAS. As the member of Kshetra Panchayat (BDO) from the village belonged to the rival group of Pramukh (Chairman: Kshetra Panchayat), no funds were allotted to the village.

## Village Gulariha (District Gorakhpur)

The village, **Gulariha,** is one of the poorest villages in the block with more than 70 per cent living below the poverty line. More than 80 per cent of the land holders have less than 0.5 acres of land. Due to its abject poverty and backwardness, the village was also selected as Ambedkar village in 1998-99 and a number of poverty alleviation programmes were implemented with a view to improve the condition of the villagers, under the Ambedkar Gram Vikas Yojana. Houses were constructed under the Indira Awas Yojana and loans distributed to IRDP beneficiaries, a group of 15 women were also trained in Masala Packing under the DWACRA scheme and the rural youth were also trained under the TRYSEM. Ration is being supplied to about 200 BPL families in the village and sugar and kerosene to about 500 APL families.

The following facts were revealed in the course of the socio-economic survey of the village.

### *Integrated Rural Development Programme*

The IRDP is one of the major poverty alleviation programmes being implemented in the village.

The last household survey in this village was conducted in April 1997. The selection of the beneficiaries was done as per government norms. The total number of IRDP beneficiaries in the year 1998-99 were 19 out of which 5 belonged to the Scheduled Caste and 5 of them were women beneficiaries. The total credit disbursement was Rs. 2.75 lakhs out of which Rs. 0.7 lakh was disbursed to the SC, Rs. 1.17 lakhs to the women beneficiaries and Rs. 2.05 lakhs to others. Sixteen of the total beneficiaries were marginal farmers while the rest three were non-agricultural labourers. The number of beneficiaries, sectorwise was: Primary Sector (Animal Husbandry)—5, Secondary Sector—2, Tertiary Sector—12.

All the beneficiaries received loan from the Gulariha Gramin Bank, Gulariha. Most of the beneficiaries were happy that they had started earning some money out of the business. All of them were repaying the loan amount in installments. Their life seems to have improved after starting the business. But none of them was really flourishing in the business. In fact, one beneficiary had sold his pigs to get money which he has used for some family work.

### *Indira Awas Yojana*

Under the IAY scheme, a total of 12 beneficiaries were provided loans in 1998-99. Ten out of twelve such beneficiaries were selected at random and were interviewed.

The following observations were made:

(i) Only five out of the twelve beneficiaries had made the latrine but were not using it. The rest had utilised the place for kitchen purpose or had used the money for completing the house itself, thereby defeating the very purpose of providing latrines for every IAY house.

(ii) The house built under the IAY was being used by the beneficiary and his family.

(iii) The major complaint was that the beneficiaries were not being selected properly. Only those on good terms with the village pradhan were able to reap the benefits, while the very poor and needy were left out.

(iv) Further, a lot of persuasion had to be done to construct the latrine. None of the villagers were interested in wasting the money for latrine as they were used to the open field and pond or canal system.

(v) One beneficiary was found using the room built under the IAY as cow shed.

### *Jawahar Rojgar Yojana*

The village, **Gulariha** was covered under the JRY in the year 1989-90. A total of Rs. 59,372 was released and utilised in 1998-99. Out of this, Rs. 12,448 was released for the Scheduled Caste. A total of 742 mandays were generated and Rs. 24,498 spent on labour and Rs. 34,874 on materials.

Most of the work done under the JRY was satisfactory. But people agreed that most of the work is done by the Pradhan Pati at his own discretion. Even selection of work to be done under the same is decided by him. But people do not have any complaints in general. Some part of the earthwork and *Kharanja* work done had got damaged. The Pradhan Pati promised to get them repaired in the next financial year.

### *TRYSEM*

Under the TRYSEM, a total of four unemployed youths had been imparted training in **Gulariha** village in the year 1998-99. Two of them belonged to the OBC. Two of them had been trained in carpentry while two others in electric works. They had also been provided a loan of Rs. 20,000 each, with a subsidy of Rs. 7,500, for starting some business. But, they had not started any business by the time of survey as the money had not been transferred to their respective accounts by then.

### *DWACRA*

A DWACRA group of 16 members had been formed at **Gulariha** in 1998-99. The group was imparted training in Masala Work (Packeting) for about three months by the Training Centre for Women at Sudiakuan in the month of April 1999. But they had not started any business till the date of survey as the revolving fund had not been released by the bank. They were keen and looking forward to start the business.

### *Pensions*

Various pensions being made available in the village are the Old Age Pension, Widow Pension and the Pension for the Handicapped. An amount of Rs. 750 in six months is given to the pensioners. There were about seven old age pensioners, and two disabled pensioners. There was no widow pensioner in the village.

### *Other Programmes*

Various other poverty alleviation programmes like the Smokeless *Chulha*, Bio-Gas, Swachcha Sauchalaya, Special Component Plan etc. were operational in the village Two big gas plants have been constructed under the Bio-Gas Scheme. Smokeless *chulhas* have also been provided to a few families.

## Village Khirora Mohan (District Gonda)

The study revealed that only 38.46 cent beneficiaries had their assets intact and were continuing the activity for which the loan was availed. It is disheartening to note that 46.15 per cent of the IRDP beneficiaries had sold off their assets due to various reasons like low income. Costly maintenance to meet consumption expenses etc. The perplexing point is that around 70 per cent of them said that the assets provided were of good quality and their choice prevailed in acquiring the assets. More than 90 per cent of the IRDP beneficiaries pointed towards Gram Sevak when they were asked who actually selected them for IRDP loan. The number of defaulters of the loan was high and it puts a question mark over the sustainability of the scheme itself. There was no DWACRA group in the village. Perhaps group loaning under DWACRA could be more viable as there would be constant pressure from fellow group members to repay the loan. None of the IRDP beneficiary had received training under TRYSEM.

Data on Jawahar Rozgar Yojana reveals that in the year 1996-97, Rs. 10,833 was allotted and that was utilised for tree plantation and for construction of a culvert. Expenditure on non-wage component was as high as 82.9 per cent which was clearly in violation of the guidelines prescribed by the Government of India. Forty-six mandays of employment was generated and five people were employed. Many people surveyed alleged that people not belonging to the village were also employed. The reason as quoted by them was that since the

Pradhan belonged to Narora Arjun, people of his village were given preference. There is one more problem. The funds of JRY is transferred to the bank account operated jointly by the Pradhan and Village Panchayat Officer. The schemes/projects for implementation are identified and selected by the gram panchayat. The people of Khirora Mohan expressed their unhappiness over disproportionately higher allocation of fund to Narora Arjun. For example, an amount of Rs. 47,859 was allotted to the gram panchayat during the financial year 1996-97 of which only Rs. 10,833 was spent on Khirora Mohan. The survey revealed that all those who were employed under JRY scheme preferred cash over food as wage. None of them was aware of the minimum wage under JRY (it is Rs. 43) and they got Rs. 30 per day as wage. No women labourer was employed. An overwhelming 37 out of 40 persons surveyed were of the opinion that there was no corruption in JRY and 34 of them felt that Jawahar Rozgar Yojana had helped improve their standard of living.

## Village Tikamau (District Mahoba)

### *IRDP and JRY Beneficiaries*

The various aspects related to the beneficiaries of poverty alleviation programmes of the government can be understood from the tables generated from the households data as given below:

**Table 5.13:** Distribution of Beneficiaries by Income from IRDP

| *Sl. No.* | *Income through IRDP programme (Per annum)* | *Number* |
|---|---|---|
| 1. | Nothing | 35 |
| 2. | Upto 4800 | 0 |
| 3. | 4800-6000 | 3 |
| 4. | Above 6000 | 2 |

**Table 5.14:** Distribution of IRDP Beneficiaries by Total Annual Income

| *Sl. No.* | *Income Category* | *Number* |
|---|---|---|
| 1. | Less than 3500 | 31 |
| 2. | Rs. 3500-8000 | 2 |
| 3. | Rs. 8000-12000 | 2 |
| 4. | Rs. 12000 and Above | 5 |

**Table 5.15:** Distribution of IRDP Beneficiaries by their performance

| Sl. No. | Physical Performance | Number |
|---|---|---|
| A. | Scheme Continuing at present | 5 |
| B. | Status of Assets | |
| | 1. Intact in Good Condition | 5 |
| | 2. Died | 2 |
| | 3. Sold Off | 1 |
| | 4. Others | 5 |
| C. | Reasons for assets not existing | |
| | 1. Low Income | 1 |
| | 2. Sold to Re-pay the loan | 1 |
| | 3. Died | 2 |
| | 4. Others | 9 |
| D. | Beneficiaries found defaulter for not paying back the loan | 5 |

**Table 5.16:** Beneficiary's Perception

| Sl. No. | Beneficiary's Perception | Number |
|---|---|---|
| A. | About Quality of Assets Provided | |
| | 1. Good | 6 |
| | 2. Poor | 1 |
| | 3. Can't say | 4 |
| B. | About the value of Assets Provided | |
| | 1. More than Market Price | 2 |
| | 2. Same to the Market Price | 4 |
| | 3. Cannot say | 5 |

**Table 5.17:** Process of Selection of Beneficiary and Acquisition of Assets

| Sl. No. | Process | Number |
|---|---|---|
| A. | Who Actually selected beneficiaries under IRDP | |
| | 1. Gram Sabha | 1 |
| | 2. VLM | 4 |
| | 3. Block Officials | 5 |
| | 4. Don't Know | 3 |
| B. | Whose choice prevailed in acquiring of assets | |
| | 1. Mukhiya | 1 |
| | 2. Beneficiary | 4 |
| | 3. Block Level Officials | 2 |
| | 4. Others | 4 |

## Village Himmatnagar Bhajhera (District Etah)

### *Coverage of IRDP*

In all 57 persons were benefited in different ways under Integrated Rural Development Programme. Out of this 44 beneficiaries belong to SC community (77.19 per cent), 5 to others (8.78 per cent) and 8 women (14.03 per cent). No one was benefited from handicapped persons, freed bonded labour and assignees of ceiling surplus land.

As per the record available at Block, a total amount of Rs. 4,31,200 was disbursed to the beneficiaries. Large amount of it went to the beneficiaries belonging to SC community. They got 74.42 per cent of total money disbursed. Women beneficiaries got Rupees 81,600 (18.92 per cent) while others got Rupees 28,700 (6.66 per cent).

Most of the IRDP beneficiaries were selected for milk-selling activity. In Primary Sector, 44 beneficiaries adopted animal husbandry activity and 8 adopted other activities, like purchase of pump sets and other agriculture implements. In Secondary sector only 5 beneficiaries took up activities like cloth vendors, bullock carts, general grocery shop. No one was benefited in handicraft, handloom, sericulture, bee-keeping and village industries.

Among the 44 beneficiaries who adopted animal husbandry activity, 34 were marginal farmers, 3 were small farmers, 7 agricultural labourers and 1 was non-agricultural labourer. Out of 8 beneficiaries who were selected for other activities like pump sets, 5 were small farmers, one was agricultural labourer and two were non-agricultural labourers, 4 beneficiaries were benefited with bullock carts and one with horse cart. This distribution indicates that the villagers preferred animal husbandry the most, and it has provided them a very good means of income also. It was found during my survey that such beneficiaries used to generate near about Rs. 3,000.00 per month from milk selling. The assets were also found mostly, in good condition. But in cases of other activities this was not so. Most of such beneficiaries were found defaulters. Reasons for default was reported to be either they did not invest the money disbursed to them or they could not maintain it. Some of the beneficiaries spent the money on social ceremonies, on meeting their liabilities or misutilised it in disposing of old loans. Another important fact in regard to selection of IRDP beneficiaries was that the village Pradhan selected them. The selection of beneficiaries used to be done arbitrarily and people had to pay some money either to the pradhan or to some local touts.

### *TRYSEM and DWACRA Trainees*

Though these schemes are undergoing in the district but in this village no one was benefited from TRYSEM or DWACRA Scheme.

### *Wage and Non-wage Component under JRY*

No work has been taken up by the village panchayat due to seal on panchayat's bank account during the last two years. The BDO has taken up some projects in one hamlet of this panchayat when this survey was being conducted. Before that, under JRY, the panchayat spent some money on constructing *kharanjas* and some on earth work. Mostly people got job in Earth and Brick works. As per the records of this village available at Block, expenditure on wage component was Rs. 32,820 and on non-wage component it was Rs. 21,886 during financial year 1996-97. Government wage rate is Rs. 49.00 per day that a labourer gets under the scheme.

## Village Jeesukhpur (District Etah)

Under Integrated Rural Development Programme, the last survey was conducted in February 1999. At that time, Gram Sabha selected 20 beneficiaries. Out of 20 selected beneficiaries, 6 were from Scheduled Caste and 5 of them were women. They were given Rs. 15,000 as credit. All of them were in Marginal farmer category. 10 of them bought Buffalo, 8 bought goat, 1 bought bullock, 1 chose bee-keeping as occupation. But in village nobody is doing bee-keeping.

Under JRY Rs. 38,691 was allocated in 1998-99 to the village and whole of it was spent. Work was not entrusted to contractor. Work which were undertaken were *Kharanja* construction, *Kharanja* repairing and earthwork. For each of them 96, 18 and 19 mandays of work respectively was generated. The work done was in good condition and locality-wise also it was not restricted to particular caste group. Labour was from the same village and all of them got Rs. 49.00 per day as wages which is the prescribed wage. Gaon Sabha took the decision for *Kharanja* construction.

Ten beneficiaries of Integrated Rural Development Programme were surveyed. Beneficiary's perception was found to be positive about the assets created. Also according to them the asset value was same as the market price. Out of ten households, four selected the assets themselves and six selected their assets on the choice of block level officials.

Five of them told that Gram Sabha selected them. Whereas according to four, village level workers selected them and one was selected by block level officials. On being asked whether they paid any cut, five of them responded in affirmative and out of these five, three paid to mediators. Most of them were not given any training.

Ten beneficiary households, which were surveyed for Jawahar Rojgar Yojana, benefited because of the wages they earned. All of them were Scheduled Caste. They were aware of the minimum wages, fixed by the government. Seven of them replied that they were given less wages. There was no disparity between the wages received by male and female. Wage was given in the form of cash.

## Village Koyala Alipur (District Mathura)

### *Rural Development Programmes*

Five beneficiaries were selected during the year preceding survey years out of which 4 were self-employed. Among the beneficiaries 4 were males and one beneficiary was female. Their literacy level was poor. As reported, their economic condition had improved after receiving assistance under IRDP. Two of them are now above poverty line. One beneficiary purchased buffalo while 3 others purchased goats and one used the assistance to improve his grocery shop. Those who purchased goat were given fifteen days training at Goat Research Centre, Mathura under TRYSEM. They were disbursed amounts ranging from Rs. 10,000.00 to Rs. 18,000.00 in which subsidy component ranged from Rs. 2,000.00 to Rs. 6,000.00. No one had given any bribe to get the money. Beneficiaries were not aware about the amount of installment or duration for repayment.

Under JRY two beneficiaries got employment for around 50 days during the past two years. While 3 other beneficiaries got employment for only 22 days. Some villagers questioned about the quality of material used, though our survey revealed that it was of an average standard. Works done under JRY included construction of *Kharanja* road, *Kuchcha* road, school and panchayat buildings.

Six beneficiaries got assistance under IAY. All the beneficiaries were BPL families and five of them belonged to Scheduled Caste category. Three of them were landless. All houses were constructed on gram sabha land. There was provision of latrines in all the houses. Beneficiaries were given freedom to design their houses. Only two beneficiaries, complained that they had given commission to gram pradhan and block level functionary, but did not name them. Beneficiaries were given Rs. 17,500.00 under the scheme and had to invest Rs. 6,000.00 from their own sources.

## Village Chirodi (District Meerut)

There were 47 families living below poverty line. Two main poverty alleviation programmes which were being implemented were SGSY and JGSY. There was one SGSY group in village which had 10 members. As a policy matter no individual help is given in villages where there are groups so there were no individual beneficiaries. The group was doing well and had got revolving fund also. The group was engaged in the production of milk related products. As a result of help under this scheme the group had increased its production and profit. Because of this success, another group had also been formed recently. NGO was involved in the implementation of this scheme. Though the NGO was working for the sake of money and not for social service, even than it had a positive impact on the working of the scheme.

JSGY was also being undertaken in the village and was being implemented through Panchayat. Village got Rs. 1,28,638.00 under this scheme in 2001-02 and Rs. 93,025.00 in 2000-01. This amount was unutilized in various construction works such as construction of drainage channel, brick street etc., as a result wage component has been less. In 2000-01 Rs. 25000 were spent on construction of drainage channel and Rs. 65,000 on construction of brick street. Selection of beneficiaries was not done carefully. Since prevalent wage rates were Rs. 10.00 to Rs. 20.00 higher than minimum wages, documents such as muster rolls were manipulated. Implementation of this programme leaves much to be desired.

Among other social welfare programmes: 3 people were getting handicap pension, 8 old age pension and 5 widow pension. Old age pension is Rs. 125.00 per month and it is directly transferred to beneficiaries account. Other pensions are given by checks. There is practically no person available in these categories that had been left uncovered. This social intervention had proved successful here.

In all 13 Indira Awas have been constructed out of which 5 belonged to SC community. In Indira Awas Yojana Rs. 20,000.00 are given to beneficiaries for construction of new house and Rs. 10,000 for upgradation of existing house. The money is transferred directly to the beneficiaries account. All the houses constructed in the village could be verified on the spot.

## Village Shahpur Kalan (District Bulandshahr)

The major development programmes being implemented in the village include the Integrated Rural Development Programme, JRY, Indira Awas Yojana.

Under the IRDP, the last household survey for the identification of beneficiaries was conducted in the current year. The beneficiaries, this survey revealed, were by and large selected as per norms. Roads were among the infrastructure developed. The total amount earmarked for infrastructure was Rs. 9,000.00. The amount utilised was Rs. 8,254.00. The percentage of work done was 100 per cent. The unspent amount was Rs. 746.00. The number of beneficiaries assisted for the previous year was 11. Among these 8 were Scheduled Caste members. 10 were women. The total credit disbursement for the previous year was Rs. 2,20,000.00. The total subsidy was Rs. 60,000.00. Rs. 48,000.00 was given to Scheduled Castes and Rs. 54,000.00 to women. The only item of benefit given was a milch animal. Among the beneficiaries, 1 was a marginal farmer, 8 agricultural labourers, 2 non-agricultural labourers.

There were many problems that were revealed by the survey in the IRDP. The sustainability of the asset given was a major problem. In the case of a milch animal, the insurance of the animal was often not paid after the demise of the animal. Most of the beneficiaries could not repay the loan in time and recovery notices were issued against them. But some of the beneficiaries stated that the asset had improved their financial status.

Jawahar Rozgar Yojana is the other major programme being implemented in the village. Schemes under the programme had been formulated at the village level. There was one scheme pending. All schemes were approved by the Gram Sabha. The assets included rural roads, and school building. They had been executed by local people, and had been completed. The number of mandays created was about 350. 18 people had benefited out of which 16 were SCs. The estimate for rural roads was Rs. 8,000.00 and Rs. 8,152.00 was spent, out of which Rs. 3,002.00 was spent on labour; and Rs. 5,150.00 was spent on materials. The maintenance of the school building was done by the State. Rs. 6,840.00 was spent on this. Maintenance of rural roads was done by the Panchayat and the expenditure was Rs. 21,702.00. The notified minimum wages for unskilled agricultural worker was Rs. 49.00. The survey revealed no disparity between the notified wage and the muster roll.

The survey revealed many weaknesses in implementation of JRY. First the assets created were of a limited nature and not always suitable to the needs of the village. The material was often substandard. The cost was over-estimated. It was not possible to give the proportional sum as wages.

25 houses were built under Indira Awas Yojana, out of which 24 belonged to the SCs. The total cost of the houses was Rs. 10,500.00.

A surprising feature of the Indira Awas Scheme in Shahpur Kalan was that of all the houses, none was inhabited. The survey revealed that most of them had alternate accommodation. During the DM's inspection, there were many complaints pertaining to this feature, and the DM on the spot ordered recoveries from the beneficiaries and a fresh allotment to homeless beneficiaries.

This scheme suffers, in the village from cuts that have to be paid to the Pradhan and the panchayat Secretary. As in Shahpur Kalan, the beneficiaries are often not eligible for the grant. Moreover, it fosters a sense of dependence in the beneficiaries.

## Village Jiraunia (District Pilibhit)

### *Integrated Rural Development Programme*

The last household survey for identification of beneficiaries was conducted in 1998. A list of all the BPL families of the village was prepared. Since 1993-94, a total of 34 beneficiaries had been provided loans under IRDP. There was no beneficiary last year. The various schemes under which loan was provided were as follows: bullock cart, pump set, horse cart, flour mill, and buffalo rearing. The break-up of beneficiaries is as follows: SC—19, Women—9, Others—5, Total—34.

Scheme-wise breakup of beneficiaries is as follows: Bullock Cart—15, Pump set—13, Horse Cart—3, Buffalo—2, Flour Mill—1, Total—34.

### *TRYSEM*

Nine beneficiaries had received training from 1996 onwards. Six men and three women had received training under this scheme. All the three ladies were trained as midwives. Three men received training to repair India Mark-2 hand-pumps that are installed in the village by the government for providing safe drinking water. One each was trained to repair TV and Radio while one was trained as a welder.

### *Improved Tool Kit Scheme*

Eleven persons were supplied improved toolkits. Five of them were those who had received training under TRYSEM. Three masons, two carpenters and one potter made the rest six.

### *DWCRA*

The scheme was operational in the block but there was no group formed in the village.

### *Jawahar Rozgar Yojana*

The village was covered under JRY in 1989. At that time the work undertaken was tree plantation. The grant received that year was Rs. 20,000. The village received Rs. 40,000 last year and the full amount was utilised. The works undertaken under JRY were village brick-road called *Kharanja* in local parlance and drains along side those roads. Since this kind of work is considered tough, therefore, the women are generally not employed under JRY. The work was undertaken by the Pradhan himself. Last year, about 225 metres of road along with drains was constructed.

Notified minimum wages for unskilled agricultural workers is Rs. 49 per day. The Minimum Wages Act is violated during lean seasons when the labourers are paid as low as Rs. 30-35. The wages shown in the muster roll are always equal to statutory minimum. The wage and non-wage component during last year was 25 per cent for unskilled labour and 75 per cent for non-wage component. The assets created under JRY were not of bad quality.

## Village Jaffarpur (District Barabanki)

There was no programme going on in the village. There was also a certain amount of apathy on the part of the villagers to governmental programmes. A good majority of the villagers were IRDP defaulters and they were not keen to pay back. On being persuaded to do so they simply stayed away from the village when they were sought to be querried. JRY funds were being used to make a *Kharanja* and extend a *nali* (drainage). The villagers interviewed had never heard of the OWACRA programme and some even thought it was the name of a person!

During the short period of village study, the IAS probationer tried to motivate the women in the village to form a DWACRA group and it was planned that the women would learn to make *aggarbatis* and sell them to supplement their household income but it did not materialize. The reasons were:

(i) It was not need-based as women did not really feel the need to do something to supplement the household income.

(ii) Men were reluctant to let women take part in the training.

(iii) Some women who had initially refused to join the group managed to influence and dissuade others from forming the group.

(iv) People expect a lot from the government but they expect it to be free ride. When they anticipate any kind of contribution and sacrifice on their part they would rather be satisfied with their lot.

The Public Distribution System in the village was a big farce and it was amazing that no inspection had been carried out here before. It was informed by the villagers that since the suspension of the Kotedar, a kotedar from the adjoining village had been attached to supply their ration. Ration supply was erratic. It was told that earlier a meeting had been held to select a person from the village to distribute ration and a few had given their names but finally all of them had withdrawn their names as they were reluctant to make the initial deposit which was necessary. When villagers were asked as to what should be made available to them through the PDS a good majority of them said that clothes and food grains could be made available to them through the PDS.

Programmes like the Pulse Polio immunisation were however carried out in the village there were not many health related problems.

In **Jaffarpur,** of the 40 households surveyed 10 had taken IRDP loans. All of them had taken loans under the individual scheme and they all had taken Rs. 8000 out of which the subsidy component was 50 per cent and the loan component was 50 per cent. All of them had bought buffalos with the loan and generally, they had to pay an additional Rs. 500 to Rs. 1000 from their own pocket as the loans were sometimes not adequate. None of them had repaid the loan which had been taken 2 to 4 years back. On being asked as to why they had not repaid they claimed that they faced problems as their crops had failed.

One of the beneficiaries even claimed that the Gram panchayat Adhikari had taken Rs. 1100 as "bribe" for getting him the loan. Most of the assets provided under the IRDP were not insured or the beneficiary was unaware of insurance. The IRDP scheme is more or less a failure in the village as far as the loan component is concerned. People tend to view this as an act of charity on the part of the government and many do not intend to pay back. As far as the selection of beneficiaries in Jaffarpur is concerned, the poorest of the poor were left out. Some of those who had not taken IRDP loans but had answered the questionnaire were of the view that the IRDP was not meant for the poorest as they cannot afford to pay back the loan. They had hesitated to take the loan because they did not want to be caught in the vicious circle of debts. This makes us question the very purpose for which these programmes are implemented. Are they really meant to empower the poor so that they can rise above their poor living conditions, or do they simply make the poor even more dependent on the system or are we encouraging free riders in society who do not feel any sense of responsibility to the State?

As far as JRY is concerned, a sum of Rs. 60,000 was allocated for the current financial year which had not been utilized. As mentioned before because of the intense rivalry between the present

Pradhan and the Former Pradhan developmental work had almost come to a standstill. Allegations were flying around that the former Pradhan had misutilised the JRY funds and the rival group was also making counter-allegations. In the end, it is the villager who suffers on account of the irresponsible actions of these grassroots level politicians. The villagers themselves do not make a collective effort to make their leaders more accountable to them.

## Village Aloonagar Diguria (District Lucknow)

There were many schemes running in the village to alleviate poverty and improve the condition of people like IRDP, SRY, JRY, IAY, MWS, smokeless *chulha* scheme, gobar gas plant, DWACRA, TRYSEM, etc. The performance of these schemes was found to be far from satisfactory. The benefit had not reached to the genuine people. The IRDP scheme is very good and is most popular one also but there were lot of flaws involved. First of all the selection of beneficiary was not done properly. Many times those people were selected who were closer to panchayat members and pradhans.

The most misused scheme was Indira Awas Yojana, because of lot of political interference. BDO also did not do physical verification to see that the scheme benefited the genuine people who had no house to live.

It was seen that the Indira Awas was given to people who already had house. One more thing was observed that none of the Indira Awas had toilets made, in spite of the money (about Rs. 3000) being sanctioned and released. The gram panchayat adhikari does not fill the work completion certificate with the help of pradhan so the estimate of actual work done in a year is difficult to make out. In Aloonagar Diguria, even the work completion certificate (*karya purti pramanpatra*) of work done in JRY of the year 1996-97 was incomplete. In fact the development was shown on the papers, targets were shown to be achieved at the end of financial year whereas lot of work was pending and some of the projects had not even started.

## PANCHAYATI RAJ AND PEOPLE'S PARTICIPATION

Even though gram panchayat is now a constitutional entity, and a number of works have been transferred to it, it has yet to become an effective form for peoples participation in their routine public work. Some of the findings of village studies are as follows:

- Panchayats were dominated by few people.
- Funds were not spent according to local needs, as pradhan decided about it.
- Enmity among panchayat members also hampered development work.
- Meeting of gram panchayat and gram sabha were not held regularly.
- Women members were generally not aware about meetings. They were generally represented by male members of the family.
- In some villages, people were divided in two (or there) groups. The rivalry was hampering development work.

Village-wise findings of functioning of panchayats are discussed below:

**Village Avarata (District Allahabad)**

The gram panchayat has one pradhan and 11 other members. Gram pradhan is from Scheduled Caste. There are 4 SC, 5 OBC and 2 general members. Among these four were women. The following works are transferred to gram panchayats:

- Maintenance of primary school, upper primary school and works of informal education.
- Maintenance and operation of public tube wells.
- Maintenance and operation of hand pumps.
- Yuvak Mangal Dal sports related works.
- Control of Mother and Child Welfare Centre.
- Control of ICDS centres.
- Control of group D hospitals.
- Power to supervise distribution of essential commodities.
- Distribution of HYV seeds, pesticides and other facilities.

- Funds are directly provided to gram panchayats for rural development works.

Panchayats were dominated by few people and beneficiaries were selected on caste basis. Funds were not spent according to local needs but pradhan decided it. Enmity among panchayat members also hampers development works.

## Village Ranipur (District Azamgarh)

The gram panchayat was constituted in 1950s. The present panchayat is the second one in the post 73rd Constitutional Amendment scenario. Elections were last held in June 2000. Unique feature of the Gram Panchayat is that ten out of eleven members of Gram Panchayat were elected unopposed. The panchayat is young in composition with 7 out of 12 members being below 35 years of age. All the members of the Gram Panchayat accept that they were nominees of the Pradhan.

The gram pradhan belonged to an affluent family of the village. He owned about 6 acres of land. He owned a brick kiln of one-lakh capacity, two trucks, a tractor, and a jeep and owned buildings that earn rents of about Rs. 25,000.00 per month. The Gram Pradhan is an engineering graduate. He took up the pradhanship and family business after his father's demise a couple of years ago. Most of the members were not economically powerful as 10 out of 11 members owned less than 2.5 acre of land. Three of the members were illiterate and the remaining had passed high school.

Though the panchayat is to meet twice in a month and the gram sabha is to meet twice a year, the meetings of gram panchayat and gram sabha were not held regularly. The meetings were held only when some work has to be taken up. There was no panchayat bhavan in the village. The meetings were held at Gram Pradhan's house. The women members were not aware of the meetings. A male member of the family generally represented them. They sign the minutes at a later date.

Though the meetings were not regular it did not affect the progress. In a meeting in August 1999, an annual plan identifying six works was prepared. Some works could not be taken up in that year due to paucity of funds and they were taken up in the year 2000-01. Only one work was pending because it needed Rs. 2 lakh much beyond the financial resources of the panchayat.

On constitution of new panchayats in August 2000, a meeting of gram panchayat was held and six mandatory committees relating to planning, education, construction, health and welfare, administration and water supply were formed. But in practice the Gram Panchayat did not function in the prescribed committee format. The gram panchayat took all the decisions itself.

Most of the members and particularly women members of panchayat were not aware of their duties. No training was imparted to the members of Gram Panchayat. Many villagers felt that the main responsibility of the panchayat was to settle disputes while it had no legal power to adjudicate any dispute. Most of the villagers were not aware of the amount of money allotted to the village.

About Rs. 80,000.00 was allotted annually to Gram Panchayat under the heads of JGSY, 10th FC and SFC. The gram panchayat got considerably fewer funds than other panchayats of similar size because of its low SC/ST population. The panchayat does not generate any internal resources. People in general expressed faith in the Pradhan. Most of them appreciated the quality of works executed and felt that there was no mismanagement of funds.

### Village Gulariha (District Gorakhpur)

The village, **Gulariha** has a gram sabha and gram panchayat too. All the adults in the village are members of the gram sabha. The present gram panchayat was elected in April 1995 during the Three-Tier Panchayat Election. Smt. Chandravati Devi is the Pradhan of the village. Surprising enough, she is literate. The Up-Pradhan is also a lady, Smt. Guddi Devi who belongs to the Scheduled Caste. There were a total of 14 members in the Gram Panchayat.

Thus, there were six women members in the gram panchayat and seven members belonged to the SC. There were two gram panchayat Vikas Adhikaris (Multipurpose worker) in the village, one of them is also the Secretary of the gram panchayat.

The gram panchayat, comprising elected representatives of the villagers, is the main executive body of the gram sabha. The panchayat looks after the needs and problems of the people. All the developmental activities in the village are carried out by the gram panchayat. Disputes in the village were also settled by the gram panchayat. All funds released under the Jawahar Rozgar Yojana, the

State Finance Commission and the Tenth Finance Commission etc. were utilized by the Gram Panchayat and the works to be undertaken under the same was also decided by the same. Selection of beneficiaries under various schemes is also to be decided by the Panchayat after holding a general body meeting.

Most of the villagers were not able to recollect when the last general body meeting was held in the village. The Pradhan's husband, was more active and decided most of the course of action. But the Pradhan was also aware of all these activities. But none of the villagers had any complaint against the village pradhan or her husband.

### *Public Participation*

The people did not seem to be very much interested in political life. However, everyone agreed that they went to cast their votes. Women acknowledged they cast their votes as per their husbands' wishes. They remembered that they had cast their votes in September 1999 but do not remember what was it for. People seemed to be satisfied with the present Pradhan. They agreed that they hardly went to general body meetings. No one remembered having approached the Pradhan for any work. People directly went to the Block to tell their problems regarding ration cards, pensions, IAY benefit, etc.

People had been casting their votes regularly in the general elections. But most of them were unaware of the political frenzy. Most of them could hardly recollect the name of the present Prime Minister of India. Before the elections, people came to their homes to advise them to cast vote in their favour. Women cast votes to the persons of their husbands' choice. But all of them were aware of their right to vote and that each vote is important. Perhaps, this is because of the propaganda by the contesting parties themselves before the elections.

## Village Khirora Mohan (District Gonda)

Though 'yes' was rarely the answer to the question 'Have you ever participated in gram sabha meeting during 1995-96', an overwhelming 95 per cent of those interviewed had cast their votes during the last general elections. This clearly shows that the people have confidence in democracy and democratic institutions. Then how could one explain their non-participation in gram sabha meetings? It could have been mainly due to the fact that since 1995 Khirora Mohan comes under Narora Arjun gram panchayat (prior to that Khirora Mohan itself a gram panchayat). The gram panchayat meetings used to take place in Narora Arjun which is situated 4 km. away and hence people of Khirora Mohan could not get timely information about these meetings and also they were reluctant to go to Narora Arjun.

## Village Himmatnagar Bhajhera (District Etah)

The village has its own gram panchayat. The head of this panchayat did not live in the village, instead he lived in Etah, the district headquarter. He was 58 years old and belonged to SC community. He possessed over 1.5 acre of land in this village. There were 13 members of the Panchayat apart from the Pradhan. Out of which 9 were male and 4 were female. Caste-wise break up showed that 4 belong to SC and 9 to OBC. Not a single member belonged to upper castes. The village panchayat had its own panchayat bhavan in the main village Himmatnagar Bhajhera. Election to the panchayat was held in 1995. The panchayat was not found working properly as there were lots of differences between the members. The Pradhan was non-resident villager. He did some irregularities in utilizing JRY money. That is why his account was sealed. His economic powers were taken away and vested in the Block Development Officer. For the last two years, no work had been undertaken under any government scheme.

## Village Jeesukhpur (District Etah)

The last election of the panchayat was held in 1995. The pradhan was 35 years old and belonged to Jatav community which falls under Scheduled Caste category. He owned total of 0.40 acre of land. There were 7 other members in panchayat. One of them belonged to Scheduled Caste and the rest were from backward caste.

Everybody was aware of Panchayat in the village. Less than 10 per cent of them had ever approached the panchayat for any work. Almost all of them had casted vote in the general election. Around 65 per cent of them had participated in gram sabha meetings, held in last one year. For those who had not participated in the meeting, the reason according to them was either they were not asked to attend the meeting or they felt that there was no use of attending meeting.

## Village Chirodi (District Meerut)

The gram panchayat consists of only one village that is Chirodi, Gram pradhna is a belonged to SC community. In all there, were 13 members including pradhan. All members were young and were between 30-40 years of age. Out of 12 other members, 5 were female all of whom were from SC community. Total number of members from SC community was 9. One belonged to general caste and two were from OBC. This shows dominance of Scheduled Caste community in village. Participation of women representatives was poor and they were generally represented by their male relatives.

Gram sabha meetings took place regularly. The trend was that most of meetings were cancelled because of lack of quorum and they had to be called again and they proceeded without quorum. Agenda of the Gram Sabha meetings was generally limited either to selection of beneficiaries of various poverty alleviation programmes, or decisions on various works related to physical infrastructure to be taken up by the Gram Panchayat.

Various pensions and scholarships were also distributed through the Panchayat.

On financial front panchayat did not have internal resources. It depended solely on government grants. Though it had got power to impose taxes but because of fear of unpopularity no tax had been imposed. Last year it got Rs. 15,662.00 by 11th Finance Commission, Rs. 65,220.00 from State Finance Commission and Rs. 1,28,638.00 under JGSY. Though this amount was less as compared to village's requirement but still it was a good amount.

Panchayat found it difficult to interact with functionaries such as teachers, ANM and patwari and co-ordination was based on informal relations. Panchayat members were happy with working of teachers and patwari but not with ANM.

## Village Shahpur Kalan (District Bulandshahr)

The gram panchayat was constituted in 1995. The total number of wards was 6. The seat for the panchayat was reserved for a Scheduled Caste candidate. Including the Gram Pradhan, there were 12 members in the panchayat. Out of these 4 were women and 7 belonged to SC. 8 were landless and the rest were marginal and small farmers. No member held any political office. The last meeting was held in August 1998. This was attended by 11 members. The gram panchayat had completed two major works in the previous years, first roads construction and second, maintenance of the school building. The internal resource mobilization within the last one year from various taxes was Rs. 1,050.00. External resource mobilization was from two sources, Central sector schemes and grant-in-aid. During 1997, the total income of the panchayat was Rs. 1,935.00. Grant-in-aid was Rs. 35,819.00. The total was Rs. 37,754.00. The expenditure for 1997 was Rs. 28,440.00 on maintenance of assets. Rs. 8,254.00 was spent on the creation of new assets. The total expenditure was Rs. 36,694.00 rupees.

During 1997, the judicial functions of the panchayat were related to settlement of minor family conflicts. The number of cases decided was 5. In this village the judicial functions fulfilled by the members was not significant.

Record maintenance and Gram Sabha functions are two areas in which members were trained. All the members had received this training in the village.

People's perception about the panchayat functioning was not optimistic in the village. People in general thought that the developmental work being carried out by the panchayat was inadequate and often corruption marred it. The panchayat secretary of the Block interfered too much. And that the whole system had got politicised. They also reacted against the hegemony of the Pradhan.

## Village Jiraunia (District Pilibhit)

The elections to the panchayat were held in June last year. The seat of the pradhan was reserved for an SC woman and a young woman of Dhobi community was elected as the new pradhan. The earlier pradhan was from Kisan community (OBC) and he had been the pradhan continuously for past 10 years. The panchayat had 13 members out of which 5 were women. The caste-wise distribution of the members was as follows: SC—5 and OBC—8. All the members had land holdings between 0.5 to 2.5 acres.

## Village Jaffarpur (District Barabanki)

Politics in **Jaffarpur** is caste based. Villagers were found to take immense interest in politics and since the general elections were around the corner of the time of survey, a lot of speculations were going on. The pradhan of the village was actively campaigning for his party and would often gather the villagers and take them to the political rallies. The perception of people of the village was very vague about the role of the panchayats and at the most, when questioned, would answer and say that the role of the panchayats was that of building *Kharanjas* and *Nalis*. Villagers were divided in their loyalty to two groups. One was that of the present pradhan and the other was that of the former pradhan. The rivalry was to such an extent that it was actually preventing the village development.

If the pradhan wanted to carry out some developmental work (invariably, in his hamlet) the other leader would oppose and try and wrest the programme for his hamlet. The result being that no work would eventually be carried out and the other two hamlets were often neglected. Because of the intense rivalry the gram sabha rarely had an open meeting and the registers were missing. The pradhan said that he had taken it for some work and had misplaced it whereas the former pradhan claimed that no open meetings were ever held. The villagers were also divided in their opinions. The pradhan claimed that open meetings were held but that the former pradhan kept the people away from the meeting. The Gram Panchayat Adhikari was of very little help too as he was also new to the circle.

Of the 12 gram panchayat members two were women who had very little to say. In fact, they came out after much persuasion and when they eventually did, it was their husbands who did most of the talking. They were basically included as members to give the appropriate representation to the womenfolk in the village but they were not being given any active role to play and they were also not being given an opportunity to voice their opinions.

A genuine problem that the pradhan of the village faced was the lack of programmes being implemented in his village. Because his village did not fall under the category of the Ambedkar village or the Gandhi Jayanti village not a single programme from the Block had been given to his village. Except the JRY funds, nothing had been allotted to this village. In the ongoing financial year not a single person had taken IRDP loan. Some of the villagers were rather bitter saying that just because they did not belong to the Scheduled Caste community, it does not mean that they did not need government help in building houses and improving their living conditions. The pradhan saw the problem more from the point of losing the votes and confidence of the villagers if he was not able to bring any concrete developmental projects to the village. The pradhan had, of course, every reason to fear losing his seat as he played an all powerful role in the village polity. In a way he now acts as a middleman between the block and the villagers and the villagers rely on him to get their block work done. Pradhan of the village could have put in more efforts to get more efforts to get more benefits for the village from the Block and the Zila Parishad but he spent more time running around for his political party.

## CONCLUSION

The state of U.P. is a typical example of having enlightened political elite, good planners but that of poor governance and poor work culture.

The problems had well identified in each five year plan since the inception of planning era. Even new policies were formulated and new institutions were built to combat those problems. But U.P. went on sliding down in respect of all socio-economic indicators.

The policies which were formulated for the poorest ended up in helping the powerful and influential people at the grassroots level. This could happen because the institutions which were built up for delivering goods could be manipulated by the influential people at the grassroots level. This was done by three methods. First, through recruitment or election of functionaries for these institutions who could support their case. For example, influential people could manage to get elected their proteges in school management, Panchayat, cooperatives and even as village level government functionaries. The obvious result is that they collaborate with the influential and powerful and even bend rules to favour them.

The other method is bribing of officials and sharing of funds allotted for development. Bribing is obvious. Sharing of funds takes place through collaboration of government functionaries and representatives in school management, collaboration or panchayats.

The third method is bribing mixed with terrorizing the government functionary at grassroots level. The method is simple-favour and get the share as briber or else be prepared to face consequences. The consequences range from physical assault to inflicting damages to property to transfer through pressure from higher ups and through various other means.

Corruption and criminalization have gone up together and engulfed within its oven government functionaries at the grassroots level, so called peoples representatives, functionaries of other institutions and local influential people.

Lately, a new dimension has been added to it, in the name of peoples involvement, Non Government Organizations (NGOs) are being involved as partners in development works. Suddenly many new NGOs have sprouted up who are getting responsibility to implement development works. Though studies have not focused on the impact of their role, NGOs, with dubious character have also come up and instead to clearing the stable, they are becoming part of network of vested interests at the grassroots level.

The question is how to combat such network of vested interests. Following measures could help in overcoming the dilemma.

(i) Increase the role of stakeholders. That is, in addition to government functionaries and elected bodies, beneficiaries/ users should also be involved in planning and implementation.

(ii) Ensure aggressive targeting and accountability. This means that target must be identified properly and achieved in time. And instead of the system, individuals should be held responsible for lapses and misdeeds. A system of providing reward and inventive should be introduced for achievers and punishment for non-achiever.

(iii) Instead of panchayat village, make the hamlet the unit to measure the level of development achieved. The information about village hides the conditions of hamlets in which socially deprived people live.

## Conditions in Social Development

If we look at the findings of village studies in respect of education we find that there was a tendency to enroll the wards in private schools if parents could afford it. Even if the facilities are made for education, effective participation in primary education would be in the range of 50 per cent to 60 per cent only. If we want to increase participation rate beyond 60 per cent, then some efforts will have to be made at hamlet level. Secondly, we will have to look to factors other than school facility to improve participation rate specially in case of girls.

It needs to be made friendly to the deprived. Teacher should be made motivator, facility be provide at hamlet level and teacher be made accountable if enrolment rate is less than 90 per cent or if drop out rate is higher than 10 per cent.

Similarly in case of health services, it was found that immunisation programme was running well, but fell much short of achieving full success. Generally, there was complaint against ANM, the health worker at the grassroots level. Though people were aware of family planning, their response was found to be mixed. As regards deliveries, a good percentage was reported to be conducted by untrained persons. Another aspect of health services was that in case of minor illness and less serious problems, people preferred to go to unqualified health practitioners. There was tendency to go to private hospitals in case of emergency of serious illness.

Another important area under social sector is supply of safe drinking water generally no problem of drinking water supply was reported from any village. But, it was mainly due to installation of India Mark II hand pumps. There was no report on the aspect of harnessing of available water at village level and need for development of micro-watershed management. This lopsided approach in water supply programme is not sustainable.

Secondly, though supply of drinking water is essential, it cannot be deemed to be environment friendly unless drainage and sanitary facilities are simultaneously provide with it. Report from villages showed dismal performance in this regard.

## Other Aspects of Conditions of Living

Another important aspect of the study has been to capture as to how much development processes have affected conditions of life of an average villages. Generally, we have the data showing what facilities are available in the village. This does not reveal as to how many people have access to those facilities or availing those facilities. Village studies have gathered information about dwellings, electricity facilities, fuel, sanitation etc.

## Poverty Level

It was found that number of persons living below poverty line varied among the sampled households of villages from where such data was available. For example, in Ranipur (Azamgarh) 19.3 per cent households were identified as being below poverty line. Proportion of such households in other reporting villages was as follows: Parikhara (Ballia) —27 per cent, Gulariha (Gorakhpur) —85 per cent, Khirora Mohan (Gonda)—62.5 per cent and Tikamau (Mahoba)—45.79 per cent.

These variations could be due to difference in sample size or nature of sample. It is obvious that a sizeable number of households in villages are still living below poverty line. They do not have access to various facilities or do not have the capacity to avail the facilities.

Secondly, even though, poverty alleviation programmes have covered a large number of them, many of them continue to remain below poverty line. A new strategy needs to be envisaged in which a group of socially cohesive families below poverty line be identified for group target oriented programme, rather than individual target oriented programme.

## Public Distribution System

The information about functioning of Public Distribution System (PDS) was reported from three villages only, namely Ranipur (Azamgarh), Tikamau (Mahoba) and Aloonagar Diguria (Lucknow).

It was reported that even PDS has not improved the standard of people living below poverty line. Wheat and rice was not in great demand because difference in prices of these commodities in open market and PDS shops was very small. Kerosene was the most demanded commodity. Villagers also purchased sugar from PDS shop.

People had a lot of complaints against Kotedars such as not providing adequate quantity and not opening of shops regularly. Another fact which came to notice was that margin for the shop owner was very small and hardly enough to make him take pains of fetching and distributing the supply.

## Housing Condition

The report about housing condition was available from 8 villages. More than 50 per cent houses were *kuchcha* houses. The villages where *pucca* houses were in sizeable number were Parikhara

(62.5 per cent), Tikamau (30 per cent), Himmatnagar (45 per cent) and Jeesukhpur (50 per cent).

Most of the Scheduled Caste people lived in *kuchcha* houses or huts.

The impact of Indira Awas Yojana had not affected the housing conditions in any significant way in the villages.

## Electricity

Rural electrification is an essential condition for accelerating growth in rural areas. The information about electrification of a village indicates that power connection is available in the village. It does not given any indication about coverage of households. The electrification can given real fillip to growth process only if coverage of households is also sizable.

It was found that power connection was available in all the villages where study was conducted. However, coverage was found to be very poor. Among the reporting villages less than 25 per cent households had electricity facility. The number of households among the sampled households without electricity facility in reporting villages was as follows: Ranipur—74 per cent, Parkhara—50 per cent, Tikamau—85 per cent, Himmatnagar—100 per cent Jeesukhpur—75 per cent, Jiraunia—88.75 per cent and Jaffarpur—92.5 per cent.

## Fuel

Most commonly used fuel for cooking was found to be wood, cow dung cake and agricultural wastes. Very few households reportedly used LPG or kerosene oil as cooking fuel. People normally collected wood/agricultural waste from nearby areas. The number of households purchasing fuel, except during crisis periods, was very small. In one village gobar gas plants were also in operation.

## Sanitation

Sanitary toilets were reported from only 2 villages. In Jiraunia (Pilibhit) facility for toilet was as follows: modern latrine—24, open field—54. In Parikhara only 17.5 per cent households used clean toilet.

Construction of latrines depended more on cultural habits and less on capacity to invest on it. But once the attitude changes, at least 50 per cent houses would go for it in a short span of time. Another factor which deterred villagers from constructing modern latrines was inadequate availability of water at doorstep.

## Drinking Water

India mark-II hand pumps have been installed in all the villages. Though they are not in sufficient numbers to cover all the households. Some private hand pumps were found to have been in operation also. Drinking water was public hand-pump. The use of wells was found to be declining.

## Resource-Base of Villages

The study of resource base of villages showed that land continues to be the main resource for economic activities in the villages. Except one village, more than 70 per cent land was cultivable land. The land under forest cover was less than 4 per cent in all the villages with some villages having only nominal area under forest coverage. The area under community land was also found to be very small.

Moreover, Common Property Resources in general were found to be declining. There were three main reasons for it. One was allotment of gram samaj land as patta under land distribution programme. The other reasons encroachment of gram samaj land by powerful and influential people of the village. The third reason is non-maintenance of such resources, specially tanks and ponds, chak roads, trace plantation on gram samaj land (which is under other community uses) and water logging due to unplanned constructions which restrict natural course of drainage.

As regards soils and crops, it was found that soil were generally of good quality for crop production. Paddy was generally the main kharif crop in the selected villages. Maize was found to be an important kharif crop in Ballia district, while *jowar* and *arhar* were main kharif crops in the Mahoba District. Wheat was the main rabi crop in almost all villages. Sugarcane was found to be the major commercial crop in Meerut and Bulandshahr Districts. In Pilibhit district, 35 per cent land was under sugarcane cultivation.

This gives a very disturbing picture as most of the sown area is covered under wheat, paddy and sugarcane cultivation. There is need to diversify cropping pattern. This could be done by providing credit facility and price incentive for other crops, specially coarse grains, pulses and oilseeds. The other area for diversification is to support cultivation of vegetables, spices and also use some land for horticultural development.

Study of villages in regard to irrigation showed two major trends. One is that use of irrigation through canals and tube wells is increasing. Secondly, those who do not own tube wells or pumping sets, take water from others at mutually negotiated rates. Taking water from private tube well owners is increasing because supply of water from government owned sources is not assured at periods of critical needs.

## Agricultural Practices

The increase in agricultural productivity could be achieved only be improving agricultural practices and adoption of new techniques. Two types of techniques are being harnessed. One is land saving: These include adoption of HYV seeds, use of fertilizers, pesticides/ insecticides etc. and finally, increasing cropping intensity. The other are labour saving, which are broadly related to mechanization and improvement in machines and tools used in different agriculture related operations.

Usually it is assumed that land saving inputs are divisible and, therefore, their adoption will not depend on size of holding, except in cases where saving are too low to invest on these. But the assumption that labour saving techniques are not size neutral needs some serious probing. As we find that hiring of their services has added a new dimension to this debate.

Assumption that since seeds, fertilizers, pesticides and such other inputs are divisible, therefore even small and marginal farmers should be in a position to use them was found to have only restricted validity. It was found from village studies that some farmers whose number vary from village to village are unable to use HYV seeds due to lack of money and credit facilities.

As regards use of tractors, it was found that though the number of tractor owners per village was very small, its services were utilized even by poor farmers as they could hire it at affordable price. Secondly, with the practice of hiring tractors for ploughing, the need to keep bullocks and maintain them has considerably reduced. Contrary to popular belief this suits marginal farmers as they are unable to keep and feed bullocks or other draught animals throughout they year due to small holdings. Mechanization was also found to be dependent on cropping intensity. For example, in village Tikamau of Mahoba District, improved technological methods were not adopted because only a single crop was grown in most of the area sown.

## Marketing of Agricultural Produce

The level of marketing of agricultural produce shows how far the agriculture has moved ahead from subsistence farming to market oriented farming. This growth depends on two factors. One is the amount of marketable surplus. The other factor is institutions through which this marketing takes place.

In the selected villages, it was found that the marketable surplus with the majority of farmers was low. Therefore, majority of them were not very particular about institutions through which they sold. This factor was, largely, also responsible for not fetching them the remunerative price or their produce.

Most of them sold to traders, some of them to those who came to their village to purchase the agricultural produce immediately after the harvesting. This shows that they have not benefited from purchase centres of Mandi Samitis. Secondly, most of them have not been able to hold back the selling for few months after harvesting, when they could expect higher prices. This was partly due to lack of storage facilities and partly due to their immediate need for cash money.

Farmers of villages from only two districts, namely Meerut and Bulandshahr which are more commercial oriented were found to sell their produce in markets where they got good prices.

## Credit Market

Credit is an important source for raising investment and/or start a new enterprise. In fact one of the main reasons for very slow pace of growth in rural areas could be attributed to low level of credit input in organization of their economic activities.

The information about the credit market in selected villages showed that loan was taken from institutional sources mainly as part of poverty alleviation schemes such as IRDP. Besides these, Primary Agricultural Credit Societies (PACS) provided loan for agricultural purposes. Credit from both these sources had a set pattern.

Loan for poverty alleviation programmes was mainly provided to targeted population belonging to poorer weaker sections. Many micro level entrepreneurs, who were not below the poverty line, would not avail this facility to start or expand their non-agricultural enterprise. Similarly, PACS restricted its credit to agricultural inputs.

The supply side constricted was not the only problem. There were even demand side constraints. Village studies reported that villages felt that procedures for borrowing from institutional sources were cumbersome, would not get money in time and collateral guarantee has to be offered. There was also a tendency to expect waiver of loans or deferment of repayment.

The above mentioned factors/tendencies were obstacles in smooth fencing of the institutional credit market in rural areas.

The need of villagers to depend on informal credit sources were manifold. One was the anonymity factor. Others would not know that the person needed money and incurred debt. The other was freedom from cumbersome procedures. And most, importantly, institutional sources would not provide loan when it was required for various purposes such as consumption, illness, ceremonies etc.

## Source of Livelihood

The major source of livelihood of people is land, though some people are also engaged in other activities.

### *Land Holdings*

There were only two types of village in respect of distribution of landholdings—villages where landless or near landless households constituted the vast majority. The other type of villages were those where majority of holdings were marginal or small holdings. There were only 3 villages where farmers owning more than 5 acres was also sizeable. The average size of holdings was found to be declining because of divisions in family and consequent increase in number of marginal farmers.

This has a serious implication for future of farming. Because of uneconomic holdings, occupational multiplicity is increasing. An owner of small parcel of land works as a former, as an agricultural labour, as casual labour and may also engage in some other activities. Small period migrations also take place among them.

Secondly, if they could find some other remunerative work, then they also tend to lease out land to other fellow farmers.

The other factor which is creating conditions for increasing tendency of leasing out land by these farmers is their inability to keep draught animals for the whole year or invest on machines or equipments. Possession of mere labour power is not enough to sustain farming.

Hence, there is a need to develop institutional framework and infrastructural support so that the interest of marginal farmers could be protected in both cases. That is whether they lease out land or cultivate it themselves.

## *Occupation*

We have already mentioned about increase in occupational multiplicity due to increase in landless or near landless households.

The number of casual labourers was larger than agricultural labourers.

Secondly, there was seasonal migration of males, while women workers mostly sought work in the village or worked in houses.

Thirdly, there were very few opportunities of employment of educated youth in the village. They had to go to urban areas for their livelihood.

Fourthly, traditional skill based activities such as carpentry, black smithy etc. were waning.

Animal husbandry was found to be an important subsidiary occupation. But it was not large enough to make them prosperous.

It was also found that only those non-farm activities provided sustainable opportunities where input-output linkages were strong. For example, a large number of persons were engaged in *chiken* and *zardori* work in Aloonagar Diguria of Lucknow district. In this work, raw material was provided to them by some women's organisation and other individual businessmen.

## Impact of Land Reforms

The study of land reform measures in villages showed that even though conferment of ownership on land had been successfully completed in all the villages long back in the sense that there were no official intermediaries now, the practice of leasing out land had been detected even though it operates illegally and is unrecorded.

These tenants are not recorded tenants because it is prohibited under law. The revenue functionary would not enter the cases of leasing because there is no provision for recording such information in the format of *khatauni* or *khasara*—record of ownership and record of land use. But more importantly, even tenants do not make a claim to get recorded as tenant due to fear getting evicted immediately. Two types of leasing was reported from villages covered under study. These included share-cropping and cash rent leasing. Under share-cropping the proportion of sharing of input costs and the produce varied from village to village.

The lease is generally on annual basis and renewable. Though there is no security of tenure on record, tenants enjoyed certain degree of security, if personal equations and sharing arrangements worked well. The land revenue is paid by landowners in all the cases.

Even though share-cropping is the traditional mode of leasing after imposition of ban on tenancy, a new trend was found to be emerging on a wider scale. This is fixed cash rent leasing. In case of sharecropping, the landowner bears risk—the proportion of risk may vary in different types of crop-sharing and cost-sharing arrangements. But in case of fixed rent leasing, the landowner bears no risk. Such cases were reported from Koyala Alipur, Chirodi, Shahpur Kalan and Jiraunia villages.

The main reason for increasing trend in fixed rent leasing, is that, landowners (mostly belonging to new generation) are becoming non-resident villagers and are engaged in other professionals. Secondly, they have found that no body had been penalized for leasing out the land. The entries in the revenue records would continue to be made in his favour by bribing the Lekhpal (revenue record keeper at the village level). Hence even the pretence of managing farm or bearing risk has been shed by new generation landowners.

As regards impact of land distribution, it was found that only few landless families have benefited from it. The problem of landlessness continues to be severe, but not enough land was available for distribution to them

The general problem of allottees was:

(i) Uneconomic size of landholdings,
(ii) Low invisible capability, and
(iii) No assistance from the Government.

The major achievement under the consolidation of holdings was in regard to reduction in plots. Except reduction in holdings, the land management had not improved in any of the reporting villages.

One of the weakest factors responsible for poor land management was poor up keep of land records.

The process of computerization has been started in some tehsils, yet due to error in maps proper demarcation of common property resources is hanging in the air as a result of which its encroachment continues. The record of rights (*Khatauni*) and the annual survey register (*Khasra*) are maintained by the Lekhpal. But regular updation of records in computer must the ensured at all levels.

Land reform in Uttar Pradesh are at the crossroads. Over the past five decades, efforts to achieve allocative efficiency and equity through land reforms have largely failed despite the adoption of a substantial amount of land reform legislation. The four broad components of land reform have included abolition of intermediary interests (tenures) in land; ceilings on land holdings; regulation of tenancy and land consolidation.

Following important issues to be addressed in the process of land reform:

- Laws on land ceilings remain to be implemented effectively due to loopholes in and/or deliberate circumvention of the law;
- While tenancy has been abolished, there have emerged illegal, insecure and clandestine tenancies or leasing of land;
- There are constraints to land consolidation such as the existence of lands of varying qualities, with and without irrigation; absence of land valuation procedures; and land of institutional support to complete the processes expeditiously;
- Government land and common property resources, some of which might potentially provide an important source of

subsistence to the rural poor, either remain to be distributed or where distributed are in a poor state of management;

- Land reforms have not addressed the issue of gender inequalities in land inheritance laws and ceiling laws;
- Updating of land records, through surveys and settlement of rights, remains a neglected or slow process due to the lack of institution support in terms of trained staff, equipment, and working capital; and
- Computerization of land records has begun but the progress has been very slow due to lack of capital, trained staff, and the resistance of local officials to using computers.

## Impact of Poverty Alleviation Programmes

### *IRDP and SwarnJayanti Gram Swarojgar Yojana (SGSY)*

Main findings in regard to these programmes are as follows:

(i) Sometimes people who are not below poverty line are selected by Gram Panchayat.

(ii) Loan application are not timely processed.

(iii) The concept of Self Help Groups (SHGs) is new to villagers and it becomes very difficult to form a cohesive SHG. SHGs are assigned some activities and their produce has to be marketed. Due to lack of proper marketing facilities, their produce does not fetch good price and the groups are discouraged.

(iv) Except those who received assistance for running small business, sustenance of activity by IRDP beneficiaries was generally found to be very poor. The reason for maintaining asset for only short duration is more interest in getting subsidy amount rather than creating an income generating asset. it was reported in Ranipur that out of loan subsidy, beneficiaries were net gainers of about Rs. 4,000.00 after paying bribes etc. Other reasons for selling assets were—low income, costly maintenance etc.

(v) No training was imported to beneficiaries to run the scheme.

(vi) The number of beneficiaries not paying their dues was also quite sizeable.

### *Jawahar Rozgar Yojana (JRY) and Sunischit Rozgar Yojana*

Studies in regard to these schemes showed that:

(i) The total number of mandays of employment created was generally small. Therefore, the impact of JRY or SRY in providing employment was not very significant.

(ii) Wages were generally paid as per the prescribed rate.

(iii) The quality of infrastructure created was generally not good as it would not last even one or two years. Earth work and *Kharanja* work would get damaged after one severe rain the repair of these infrastructures took much longer time. The quality was found to be good in Jeesukhpur where gaon sabha took the decision about the work to be undertaken and in Koyala Alipur where school and panchayat buildings were constructed.

### Indira Awas Yojana (IAY), Million Wells Scheme (MWS) and Improved Tool Kit Scheme (ITS)

The number of beneficiaries under IAY was noticeable in selected villages but beneficiaries of schemes such as MWS and ITS was found to be very limited.

IAY beneficiaries were selected by gram sabha. Sometimes even non-eligible persons were selected. Misuse of funds which was transferred to the account of beneficiaries was also reported. Houses were generally constructed on gram sabha land.

In many cases inputs/materials provided were not sufficient for completion of the house. Beneficiaries had to invest their own money to complete the house.

The following observations about status of IAY in Gulariha village is symptomatic of conditions in all the villages:

(i) Only five out of the twelve beneficiaries had made latrine, but were not using it. The rest had utilized the place for constructing kitchen or had used the money to complete the house. This has defeated the purpose of providing latrine for every IAY house.

(ii) House built was being used by the family of beneficiaries.

(iii) Selection of beneficiaries was not made properly.

(iv) One beneficiary was using the room built under IAY as cow-shed.

## Other Social Welfare Schemes

Other social welfare schemes like Maternity Benefit Scheme, Family Benefit Scheme and Old Age Pension Scheme were also being implemented in some of the villages.

## Panchayati Raj and People's Participation

Even though gram panchayat is now a constitutional entity, and a number of works have been transferred to it, it has yet to become an effective form for peoples participation in their routine public work. Some of the findings of village studies are as follows:

- Panchayats were dominated by few people.
- Funds were not spent according to local needs, as pradhan decided about it.
- Enmity among panchayat members also hampered development work.
- Meetings of gram panchayat and gram sabha were not held regularly.
- Women members were generally not aware about meetings. They were generally represented by male members of the family.
- In some villages, people were divided in two (or three) groups. The rivalry was hampering development work.

## NOTES

1. *Poverty and Social Monitoring in Uttar Pradesh – A Base Line Report 1999-2000*, Division of Economics and Statistics, State Planning Institute, U.P. (Lucknow), 2002.
2. Singh A.K. (2001), *Uttar Pradesh Development Report 2000*, New Royal Book Company, Lucknow.
3. Dreze, Jean and Sen, Amartya (1996), *Indian Development: Selected Regional Perspectives*, Oxford University Press, Delhi.
4. *Public Report on Basic Education in India (Probe)* (1999), Oxford University Press, New Delhi.

# Summing Up

## AGRICULTURAL REVIVAL

The increasing world population is spurring greater demand for food. According to a report drafted for ministers of G-8 nations, the world faces "a permanent food crisis and global instability unless countries act now to feed a surging population by doubling agricultural output."

On the supply side, great challenges are posed by the impact of climate change on agriculture, land degradation, growing uncertainty on crop yields and intensification of floods and droughts in tropical areas. This will worsen the volatility in food prices.

Studies by the Food and Agricultural Policy Research Institute (FAPRI), the International Food Policy Research Institute (IFPRI), the Organisation for Economic Co-operation and Development (OECD) and the Food and Agriculture Organisation (FAO) have projected an increase in the volatility of food and commodity prices for the next 10-15 years.

In India, during 2004-2009, the agricultural growth at 4.3 per cent per annum has been the highest since 1980. While farm-input prices have been subsidised, the price realisations for crop output have increased in line with the global prices.

The Government has now sharpened its focus on the Indian farmer, placing greater emphasis on the economic well-being of farmers and rural development rather than merely on agricultural production.

Improvement of rural infrastructure, expansion of irrigation area, improved water management, support for rural roads, housing, electrification, telecommunication and research have all been given high priority.[1] India was once at the apex of international achievement in agricultural innovation. Drawing on a wide variety of international grain types, pioneers of high yielding hybrid seeds, notably M.S. Swaminathan, were able to achieve in the 1960s and 1970s a real "green revolution" in India, boosting agricultural productivity impressively and making the country fully self-sufficient in its main food requirements for the first time in modern history. Scientific innovation was supported by energetic policies at the Union and State levels to achieve one of the world's most striking agricultural successes of the 20th century. But then, as so often with success, a purposeful policy dissolved into politicking and piecemeal implementation.

Unsupported by rigorous policy, excess use of fertilizers, unsustainable use of water resources encouraged by free or subsidised electricity for farm pumps led to soil degradation and depletion of sub-surface aquifers.

This occurred at a time when an expanding population, the first hint of the consequences of climate change and a sudden spike in agricultural commodity prices in 2007-08 linked to lower international grain stocks and a sharp rise in commodity prices, notably oil, provided an unwelcome reminder to Indians that all was not well with the agricultural policy. What ensued was impulse buying on international markets at the same time as export of some items was prohibited (hurting mainly other developing countries, the industrialised world having cornered all the food it needed). One salutary measure offered by Delhi was the lowering of tariffs on some necessary international food imports but by November 2008, the Government was again raising tariffs on some products (soya) in order to protect domestic producers.[2]

The negotiations on agricultural trade are at present at a crucial stage in WTO. The Government spokesmen never let an opportunity to escape to reiterate the resolve that the livelihood of millions of farmers will not be allowed to be jeopardised in these negotiations. It is common knowledge that the giant exporters of agricultural commodities and trade majors like the United States and European Union are bent on securing substantially greater access for their subsidised agricultural exports in our market. And they are doing their best to dilute and emasculate the defence mechanisms like

Special Produces and Special Safeguards Mechanism that developing countries are seeking to incorporate in the international discipline under negotiation. It would be a legitimate expectation that at this crucial juncture the Policy would indicate a clear guideline on how the oft-stated objective of protecting the livelihood and interests of millions of farmers would be achieved.[3] Several technological advances in bio-technology, scientific farming and marketing of agricultural produce demonstrated elsewhere in the world could be leveraged, customizing them for the Indian scenario.

Opportunities for technology deployment in the farming cycle involves three stages, namely crop production, post-harvest management, and marketing from a farmer's perspective.

## PRODUCTION TECHNOLOGIES

Crop planning plays a very significant role. At this stage besides finances, the most important decision of selecting the crop for cultivation is taken.

Standard crop rotation practices, expected market price, crop cycle time, soil and season are analyzed. Collectively these deci-information and communication technologies (ICT) like statistical modelling, forecasting and data analytic technologies for market supply/demand analysis, weather modelling and crop yield predictions can be developed at a macro level.

Moving on to cultivation, appropriate seed selection plays a major role in determining productivity. Bio-technology offers much promise in terms of high yielding seed varieties and new pest resistant seeds.

Through scientific farming practices it is possible to ascertain, the effects of weather, pest infestation on yield and the optimal amount of nutrients required.

Drip irrigation, as a farming practice has been gaining popularity. Drip irrigation provides the right amount of water at the right location—at the plant root zone and has many advantages over conventional flow method of irrigation, like higher yield, water/energy savings, lesser weeds, etc.

Most drip irrigation solutions require a water source and pump and quality water, availability of power and maintenance and agriculture knowledge.

Though subsidies are provided by the Government on initial investments, there is the additional cost of system maintenance, and the challenges of having the necessary infrastructure and technical support within a community to maintain these systems effectively.

Information dissemination and management is another area where technology platforms based on social networking such as Web 2.0 can help to inculcate scientific farming practices. Post harvest management, though a crucial phase, has been ignored for quite some time and has been gaining significant attention in recent years. Post harvest technologies can help in minimising wastage and improve the shelf life while maintaining the quality of the produce.

These technologies include automatic grading and sorting of produce, sensors for checking produce quality, packing and cold chain infrastructure for improving the shelf life of perishables and effective energy management and maintenance of the cold chain infrastructure, efficient logistics for transporting the agriculture produce, etc. Various sensors coupled with RFID technology are being mandated through international standards to track and establish traceability in the food supply chain. These standards will become mandatory in coming years and Indian exporters are expected to adhere to these standards.[4]

Water problems will not go away by themselves. On the contrary, they will worsen unless we, as a global community, respond. A series of recent studies shows how fragile the water balance is for many impoverished and unstable parts of the world. The UNESCO recently issued *The UN World Water Development Report 2009;* the World Bank issued powerful studies on India (*India's Water Economy: Bracing for a Turbulent Future*) and Pakistan (*Pakistan's Water Economy: Running Dry*); and the Asia Society issued an overview of Asia's water crises (*Asia's Next Challenge: Securing the Region's Water Future*).

These reports tell a similar story. Water supplies are increasingly under stress in large parts of the world, especially in the world's arid regions. Rapidly intensifying water scarcity reflects bulging populations, depletion of groundwater, waste and pollution and the enormous and increasingly dire effects of man-made climate change.

The consequences are harrowing: drought and famine, loss of livelihood, the spread of water-borne diseases, forced migrations, and even open conflict. Practical solutions will include many components, including better water management, improved technologies to increase the efficiency of water use, and new investments undertaken jointly by the Governments, the business sector, and civic organisations.

Solutions will have to be found at all "scales", meaning that we will need water solutions within individual communities (as in the piped-water project in Senegal), along the length of a river (even as it crosses national boundaries), and globally, for example, to head off the worst effects of global climate change. Lasting solutions will require partnerships between the Government, business, and civil society, which can be hard to negotiate and manage, since these different sectors of society often have little or no experience in dealing with each other and may mistrust each other considerably.[5]

## RURAL GOVERNANCE REFORMS

Villages cannot be dynamised until we reform the public sector, which includes health, nutrition, education, banking, watershed, irrigation, NREGA and the Forest Rights Act, embracing almost every element of rural life. Both NREGA and the Forest Rights Act are potentially revolutionary initiatives but have remained transformative only on paper, much like the land reforms legislation of the 1950s. They have opened up a space that demands unprecedented boldness of action, badly lacking on the ground so far. On the Forest Rights Act, which calls for a full democratisation of our forest bureaucracy, and is the key to addressing Naxalism, nothing at all has moved. On NREGA, what we expect from our gram panchayats to deliver has absolutely no correlation with what we have provided them in terms of human resource. How have we enabled them to dismantle the contractor raj? Where is the comprehensive cadre of functionaries fully accountable to them, which is the alternative implementation mechanism they require? The administrative allocation under NREGA has been raised to 6 per cent of its total outlay. But what to say of where this money will go? Why do we not stipulate that specific proportions be spent on professional support cost and on building capacities of those running NREGA? Without such specifications, it is difficult to see NREGA become the multiplier-accelerator propelling investment it needs to metamorphose into.

Trickling down of growth in which people are not partners is both an affront to their dignity and a tragic neglect of their enormous potential.

Livelihoods, education and health are not polio drops to be mechanically administered to the people. They represent complex outcomes that demand participatory processes and imaginative solutions. Merely throwing money at the people through direct cash transfers is not only insulting, it does not work. What ensures translation of outlays into outcomes is the software we put into place. This includes deployment of high quality human resource and systems that ensure accountability and stakeholder participation.

Democracy is the best insurance against abuse of power. It will be real for people only when they become partners in shaping the destiny of the nation, as a dynamic hub of compassionate and sustainable growth.[6]

The challenge is to achieve an attitudinal transformation within the system and to ensure that whatever is framed as policy, is implemented with a sense of commitment. A drastic change in work culture is prerequisite. That is the key for implementing quality enriched initiatives in education.[7]

Alongside investment, good governance is critical. In addition to schemes and adequate budgets, identification of target beneficiaries, timeliness for programme implementation as also monitoring and evaluation of policies is crucial. This is precisely where India falls short. Investments are inadequate and poor governance often means lack of accountability for sub-standard performance. While economic growth is most desirable, growth without equity could prove counter-productive, as it will widen income disparities among people, with the potential to set off socio-political upheavals. India has the capacity to make a substantial contribution to reducing poverty and hunger in the world; yet, the economic growth in recent years has been lop-sided, with concomitant problems of agrarian distress, migration to urban areas and, in extreme cases, suicides. The Eleventh Plan has inclusive growth as its central theme, but little to clearly indicate its magnitude. It goes without saying that there is need for a demonstrable commitment to investment and governance.[8]

## INCLUSIVE AND RAPID GROWTH

If the nation has to make any significant headway in the fight against poverty, the way out is not more subsidies and handouts but executing a concerted plan of action to improve the productivity, profitability and sustainability of the small farmer. Access to water and irrigation is the key determinant of land productivity given that the productivity of irrigated land is at least twice that of rain-fed land. Several cross-country studies have established that GDP growth originating from agriculture is at least twice as effective in reducing poverty as growth in non-agricultural GDP. The lack of adequate progress in addressing the issue of agricultural productivity has the potential to derail the long-term India growth story.

The sloth in governance is not restricted to the agricultural sphere alone. The state of urban infrastructure—weather roads, power, affordable housing and office space, drinking water and other municipal services—continues to be dismal despite the 40 per cent + growth in tax revenues. Several parts of the national highways network are in such a state of disrepair for years that inter-city long distance buses and trucks take long detours to save on high vehicle maintenance costs.[9]

A major reason why the impact of Government spending in the villages may not be clearly visible is that most of the increase in rural spending is through allocations by the Centre while the contribution of the States, which could make a difference, is declining on account of its preoccupation to meet the fiscal deficit targets. This is borne out from the fact that the States' expenditure, which accounted for nearly 95 per cent of total rural spending in the nineties has dropped to around 60 per cent at present, while the Centre's share has gone up from 0.5 per cent to 2-5 per cent during this period. However, the centrally sponsored schemes have proved unequal to ameliorate the plight of the rural populace. The leakages in delivery mechanism and poor accountability at the State level have prevented funds from reaching the targeted beneficiary.

Secondly, not only is rural funding inadequate but the amount disbursed is also spent inefficiently. For example, around 75 per cent of the amount allocated for agriculture is spent on subsidies with only 25 per cent made available for productive investments despite the latter providing higher returns. Besides, not much is being done to promote rural industrialisation. More than 50 per cent of the villages are yet to be covered by the Khadi and Village Industries Commission and the paucity of basic infrastructure like transport, communications and electricity is a major deterrent to the growth of rural SME clusters.

Additional funds are desperately required for improving

connectivity in the countryside. Connectivity enhances the value of every other rural investment since it empowers people through improved mobility and access. The green revolution in Punjab hinged not only on R & D but on rural roads too. And the inadequacy of incremental funds for further development and maintenance would erode the advantage so far enjoyed by the State. Perhaps, infrastructure development in rural India—notably irrigation, cold chains, roads, mandis, etc.—could be contemplated through annuity-based public-private-partnership model. Priority should also be given to enhance public spending on social infrastructure.[10]

The big question is how to foster accountability. The problems with public project executions are higher administrative cost in terms of implementation and corruption. Both can be minimised through a carrot and stick based strategy where the performers: Non-Governmental Organisations (NGOs) or panchayats—can be rewarded/penalised in terms of fund allocation for the next budgetary period. Some of the State Governments have started getting results in partnering with some NGOs—Pratham (in the area of education), Seva Mandir (health), Arghyam (water supply), ICICI Foundation (inclusive growth)—to name a few.[11]

Growth and reducing poverty are the major objectives of economic policy. Economic development and social development need to go hand in hand. It is like walking on two legs. Ignoring any one of them will make the country limp along. Therefore, the focus of economic policy must be to simultaneously accelerate economic growth and ensure that the basic minimum requirements are provided to everyone. The major challenge before the country is to come out of the impact of the economic crisis, which had originated abroad. We should be able to move to a higher trajectory of economic growth soon. We have, in the past, demonstrated our potential for high growth. The challenge before us is to realise this potential.

Over the medium term, there are mainly two areas that require focused attention on the real side. These are agriculture and infrastructure. Within infrastructure, power sector is very important. A substantially large segment of our population depends on agriculture for their livelihood. Improving farm productivity is important to raise their income levels as well as to ensure food security. Foodgrain production should exceed the population growth rate. Agricultural growth is a prerequisite for bringing about significant reduction in poverty.

Growth in infrastructure is fundamental for maintaining a sustained overall growth. Infrastructure sector needs to grow at a rate higher than the overall growth rate in the economy. The Eleventh Five Year Plan has set high targets for capacity creation in infrastructure. It is important that we achieve this. In the social sector, the most important area that requires attention, is health. Making available basic health facilities to everyone is an important way by which we can reduce the impact of poverty. The National Rural Health Mission (NRHM) needs to be strengthened and implemented efficiently.

India's financial sector has shown great resilience in the current period of global financial meltdown. The twin problems faced by financial institutions abroad were of liquidity and solvency. India's financial system, on the other hand, does not suffer from a solvency problem. It should become more efficient and should reach out to all productive sectors of the economy. Some reforms in this area are pending in the form of legislation.

We need to get the pending pieces of legislation in the insurance and banking sectors passed. Another important aspect of reform is that the regulatory framework should encompass all segments of the financial system. The biggest failure in the development world in the recent years has been regulatory failure. We, in India, have succeeded in putting in place a good regulatory framework. We must ensure that the regulations are followed in letter and in spirit by all financial institutions. The reform process is a continuous one. Its objective is to improve efficiency in the system. Therefore, the process should continue. But it is important to recognise that the emphasis on efficiency does not mean that we ignore considerations of equity. Efficiency and equity must be taken together and weaved into a coherent pattern of growth.

The first set of financial sector changes was injected gradually over a decade of low growth. Then, the main concern was capital adequacy in foreign exchange reserves and in the banking system. Now the reference point has to be capital efficiency. Banks have to move from mere compliance to a return-on-equity strategy. That objective is apt for the entire gamut of reforms required at this stage, be they in the delivery systems or in the use of foreign exchange reserves. Reforms need a context and the economy has provided it by outperforming official forecasts. The Government has been caught napping by its consequences: surfeit of riches in some regions and the lack of prosperity in others. Creating the framework to deal with both is the need of the hour.[12]

Obviously, without further opening of the economy to foreign direct investment and to import competition, investment in social (education and health) and economic (e.g. power, transportation) infrastructure, not only the growth of employment in manufacturing will be stunted, but also the recent growth of the service sector cannot be sustained.

Citing the National Rural Employment Guarantee Scheme (NREG) as an example, Mr. Montek Singh Ahluwalia said that "the XI Plan has a lot for those people living below the poverty line, including farmers and labourers. We are confident that the growth process we are witnessing today is more inclusive and will do more for the poor than in the past." (*The Hindu*, September 23, 2007)

Inclusive and rapid growth has always been the objective of India's pre- and post-Independence planners. What was lacking until the systemic reforms of 1991 and limited reforms of the 1980s was a strategy and a policy framework for realising the vision. But for the reforms India's growth acceleration and the associated reduction in poverty would not have come about.

What is needed now, among other changes, is to shed India's present dubious distinction as the most protected economy among developing countries and integrate it far more with the world economy. A well-executed NREG, while it would certainly help alleviate poverty, is not designed to lift the poor out of poverty once and for all. Our agricultural policies do not address the issue of the non-viability of millions of small and marginal farmers. We need to enable them to leave their non-viable farms to engage in more productive off-farm activities in rural and urban areas.

India has not abandoned vestiges of central planning. Unlike China which no longer has one, our Planning Commission lives on.[13]

On the macro economic front, the situation appears satisfactory with benign inflation and interest rates, better tax compliance and an improving fiscal situation. Foreign portfolio investors have been directing increasingly larger inflows into the Indian market and the surfeit of liquidity thus created is bolstering all asset prices including stocks and real estate. An appreciating rupee has added to the general sense of confidence in the economy and it appears that the "India Shining" montage is back with renewed vigour. However, it is essential to dig a bit deeper to analyse the undercurrents that are at the root of long-term bull markets that frequently escape the cursory examination.

One of the biggest challenges is the surge in capital flows that is turning into a major management problem; the Reserve Bank of India is attempting not only to maintain price stability but also exchange rate stability without affecting capital mobility. That "Impossible Trinity" is currently being managed by an expensive operation of liquidity sterilisation that will cost the Government dear through interest payments on the bonds issued to mop up the excess liquidity. Barely a few years into growth, the country's financial administration seems ill-equipped to deal with inflows in a more efficient manner. The second challenge is the institutional one because existing laws or structures appear incapable of permitting the deployment of investible capital for more profitable returns or for infrastructure growth. The poor in India are predominantly rural; and poverty and hunger reduction has been slowest among the poorest. Agriculture and related activities provide livelihood to the rural population which must enjoy enhanced access to assets, infrastructure and markets to improve their living standards. It follows that rural growth cannot take place without sustained investment in the creation and maintenance of assets (land, irrigation inputs), infrastructure (warehouses, rural roads) and markets (both input and output markets). Simultaneously, accelerated flow of investments is necessary in health, nutrition and education, particularly for women and children.[14]

## NREGS

The NREGS accords crucial role to the elected leaders of the gram panchayats. That party politics is an integral part of the panchayats is a truth that cannot be glossed over.

The NREGS without doubt is structured in a way that the traditional means by which some politicians employ to siphon funds—engaging machines and contractors—are not allowed. It also contains the provision that the funds allotted and the number of person-days are displayed at the work site and also that the specific projects are discussed in the gram sabha. These mechanisms and the aspect of social audit are certainly significant measures that will help the scheme work.

The gram sabha, for instance, should ensure democracy in the perfect sense of the term. But then, given the caste-based hierarchy that is still the reality in rural India, there is very little in the NREGS that will ensure daily wage employment to the members of the Scheduled Castes as much as it will to the equally poor but more assertive members from the Other Backward Castes. This is bound to defeat the purpose of the scheme.

Such an apprehension is inevitable given the fact that there is zero awareness among the rural people that they are entitled for work on demand and in the event there is no work, the State is bound to pay them unemployment allowance. It is a fact that there has hardly been an instance, hitherto, of unemployment allowance being disbursed in any district where the NREGS has been implemented since February 2006. This is to say that the NREGS has miles to go before it becomes what it is meant to be.

These are some issues that have come up out of the experience of the scheme in the course of its implementation. And it will make sense only when the civil administration and its political masters address these concerns that are bound to come up, before pushing it for implementation across the country.

An employment guarantee programme is capable of addressing some of the major concerns of the Indian economy. It can develop economic and social infrastructure; promote agricultural growth by constructing minor irrigation facilities, watershed development, maintenance of dams and check dams, farm ponds etc., it can prevent environmental degradation and regenerate natural resources and natural capital; and it can strengthen assets of the poor by giving them collective ownership of new assets or private assets like farm ponds and land development.[15]

What needs to be ensured, therefore, is that the planning under the EGS is sound. Sound planning does not mean listing works based on the demand for assets by people. It means a sound long-term plan prepared on the basis of long-term needs of the local economy, in consultation with experts at the village and district level; multi-level planning as and when necessary; and dovetailing of works with ongoing programmes to pool and use all available resources to supplement and complement each other. Such an approach will also give a push to aggregate demand in the economy, which, in turn, will give a big push to an inclusive economic growth, and enhance commitment of policy-makers to the NREGA.[16]

The NREGS has been one of the biggest programmes to combat rural poverty. Its legal guarantees have radically altered the relationship of the poor with the State.

The suggestions of improvement are based largely on a detailed set of operational guidelines issued by the Ministry of Rural Development, but not adhered to in large parts of the country. The most important challenge is to put into place a management structure that ensures an accountable administration at the level of implementation. Since the Act relies heavily on implementation through panchayats, it does not really require a huge new bureaucracy. Focusing on support structures at the panchayat and block level can actually help a working system that can allow panchayats to become an effective tier of local self-governance.

The size and scale of the NREGS does present a huge organisational challenge. But this is not insurmountable. The operational guidelines mandate a dedicated hierarchy of administrative and technical support, which many States have failed to put in place.

Meagre as these are, for the severely understaffed panchayats it is many steps forward. Several district programme coordinators have launched a number of innovations that can be emulated as best practices. The District Collector of Jhalore in Rajasthan, along with peoples' organisations, has upgraded the skills of the 'Mates' (work site supervisors), upgrading their capacity to micro-manage every work site. The Rajasthan Government plans to put this system into place across the State. Workers will get better wages, durable assets are built, other facilities provided, transparency measures ensured.

Kerala has established that citizen participation can be harnessed for development planning. The NREGS makes such resources available. Orissa NREGA information is online. In Andhra Pradesh, any expenditure can be tracked. It has institutionalised social audits in public meetings, corrective action is taken immediately, and money has been recovered.[17]

## EDUCATIONAL ENDEAVOURS

Expanding education at every stage is necessary. In fact, the expansion that has taken place till date is still inadequate. Millions of children are outside the pale of school education, and only around eight per cent of youngsters in the appropriate age group are in higher education. Dilution in quality does take place in such situations, but the system and the implementers should be able to anticipate the problems and put in place the necessary checks and balances.

Enhancing resource allocation is certainly a welcome step, but it has to be supplemented by greater school-university-society interaction, which is not taking place. If this takes place, it would increase confidence among people and bring credibility to the system.

Further private enterprise in education has to be accepted as a necessity, and therefore, should be encouraged to enter education to extend its outreach and inculcate values among the products. Those running private enterprises in education are fed up of the hurdles created by the education departments and the regulatory bodies. The existing system makes everyone sweat profusely before permitting them to open a school, a college or a professional institution, in particular. It may sound like a cliché, but is a hard fact that the Indian education system needs to take an incisive look on the functioning of its regulatory bodies. It must be professionally ascertained whether these are bringing in any value addition to the system or eroding its credibility. India needs big expansion in practically every sector of education, but the legacy of quota-permit-licence raj still persists in Government offices. The common man, unable to afford the high fee-charging "public" schools, laments about the neglect of schools and the institutions funded out of public money, but to no avail.

Public-private partnership in education is not only desirable but a necessity at this juncture. Private initiatives deserve encouragement, but with clear indications that education shall never be treated as a purely commercial enterprise. It shall always have a pronounced socio-cultural angle within the values associated with education that will prepare young persons for progress ahead. The Government has to ensure that there is a reasonable regional spread of such initiatives.

For an economy growing at eight per cent, the need for a skilled workforce increases immeasurably and enough concern has been voiced by industry and global analysts that if there is one field in which India has to do some rapid catching up, it is education. But the need for education enhancement opportunities is not simply rooted in the contingent needs of the economy. It is also a way to make growth more inclusive. Despite decades of planning and the existence of world-class institutions of higher learning, a large section of the people does not have access to basic education.

The Government appears to have taken some steps in the right direction. Plan allocations for education have been stepped up fivefold since the Tenth Plan, so that the share of education in the total Plan will increase from 7 per cent to 20 per cent. In budgetary terms, such allocations are nearing the targeted 6 per cent of GDP. But this should be just the beginning of an outreach process, not the end, as has been the case so far, when most Governments were content to simply allocate funds without ensuring timely delivery schedules. Accountability for tardy implementation would also need to be addressed at every stage and suitable remedial actions suggested.[18]

## HEALTHCARE

Every healthcare system around the world is constantly working with three objectives: equitable access, high quality and low cost. For care providers, these are often competing objectives, with the tradeoffs among these goals usually ridden with economic, social and political implications.

The inherent challenge in reconciling the three objectives is common to every healthcare system, and not unique to any particular country. For instance, many countries have learnt that higher spending does not correlate with higher quality or better outcomes, as is usually perceived by consumers. In fact, the first of the measures that we need to adopt to reduce healthcare costs focuses on reducing higher spendings.

Looking at the history of the evolution of healthcare systems around the world, we can surmise that throughout, it has been our emphasis on the curative approach, rather than adopting a preventive one, that has been responsible for boosting healthcare costs. Traditionally, for healthcare systems, health and wellness are personal matters, while access to care and its financing are more political ones. This view has to be modified considerably to help build an infrastructure to support basic levels of hygiene, and to encourage healthy lifestyles among individuals.[19]

What we need today is a sound public private partnership to put into place regulatory, fiscal and reform policies that will promote creation of capacity for labour, infrastructure and innovation on the one hand and institute sustainable financing mechanisms to collect and distribute funds on the other, thereby ensuring affordable quality healthcare to all.[20]

The key challenges that India must address to make healthcare affordable and accessible are: liberalising health insurance, digitisation of healthcare, create awareness about early health as a concept amongst the masses, and increasing the level of integration between the Government, hospitals and equipment manufacturers to improve the healthcare system. With insurance covering just 3 per cent of the total population, India remains one of the most under-insured countries in the world. A strong effort must be made to communicate who is covered, how to access benifits, and what screening and other preventive care is available under the Government and private pay policies. All consumers of healthcare will benefit from an increased understanding of what coverage insurance plans can offer.

Public-private partnerships are the way to revolutionize healthcare system and make it affordable to the masses. We need to develop healthcare infrastructure to cater to the projected demand for healthcare services. Private providers have already made substantial in-roads and have set up facilities both in India and overseas. The Government can help this through targeted incentives that can reduce the cost of creation of facilities upto 30 per cent.[21]

One of the most sinister aspects of the country's current state of affairs is pervasive malnutrition and under-nutrition, especially among women and children. As important as food security is nutrition security. The country is slowly turning nutrition insecure. This is because a significant number of people have inadequate access to adequate quantities of food. There has been a decline in per capita food grains availability.

It is the question of access and affordability. Access to food is restricted as the public distribution system does not cover the entire universe of poor or financially vulnerable people. Rising food prices of recent years—due to shortages, market distortions, high international prices—further reduce the quantum of food intake. Those in whose hands incomes are rising—about a third of the population—

are in a position to consume more because they enjoy both access and affordability. It is not the case with poor people.[22]

To make improvements in the delivery of health services, at least three reforms are urgently required. First, it is time to accept the fact that the Government has at best limited capability to deliver health services and that a radical shift in strategy that gives the poor greater opportunity to choose between private and public providers is needed. This can be best accomplished by providing the poor cash transfers for out-patient care and insurance for in-patient care. Once this is done, a competitive price must be charged for services provided at public facilities as well. The Government should invest in public facilities only in regions where private providers may not emerge.

Second, the Government must introduce upto one-year long training courses for practitioners engaged in treating routine illness. This would be in line with the National Health Policy, 2002, which envisages a role for paramedics along the lines of nurse practitioners in the United States. The existing RMPs (Rural Medical Practitioners) may be given priority in the provision of such training with the goal being replacement of all RMPs by qualified rural practitioners.[23]

## NOTES

1. Gopalakrishnan, R., "Golden years ahead for agriculture", *The Business Line* (New Delhi: 13.5.2009) p. 7.
2. Malone, David M., "India: challenges in agriculture", *The Hindu* (New Delhi: 7.2.2009) p. 10.
3. Shukla, S.P., "Policy for farmers defies logic", *The Asian Age* (New Delhi: 26.1.2008) p. 7.
4. Brahmajosyula, Jagadeesh, "Technologies seeding change in farm sector", *The Business Line* (New Delhi: 6.2.2008) p. 9.
5. Sachs, Jeffrey D., "Water scarcity and development", *The Economic Times* (Kolkata: 26.5.2009) p. 6.
6. Shah, Mihir, "UPA's challenge: rural governance reform", *The Hindu* (New Delhi: 28.5.2009) p. 10.
7. Rajput, J.S., "Programmes initiated, not implemented", *The Asian Age* (New Delhi: 2.1.2008) p. 6.
8. Editorial, "Poverty's rural dimension", *The Business Line* (New Delhi: 5.12.2007) p. 8.

9. Bhat, U.R., "Sustaining the growth momentum", *The Economic Times* (Kolkata: 10.12.2007) p. 16.
10. Ahuja, Shobha, "Declining rural funding by states", *The Economic Times* (Kolkata: 25.5.2009) p. 6.
11. Banik, Nilanjan, "Inclusive growth: an unfinished story", *The Business Line* (New Delhi: 7.2.2008) p. 8.
12. Editorial, "Pondering over reforms", *The Business Line* (New Delhi: 4.12.2007) p. 8.
13. Srinivasan, T.N., "Break the bureaucratic stranglehold", *The Business Line* (New Delhi: 21.11.2007) p. 9.
14. Editorial, "Poverty's rural dimension", *The Business Line* (New Delhi: 5.12.2007) p. 8
15. Ananth, Krishna V. "Problems in rural employment", *The Indian Express* (Chennai: 1.2.2008) p. 10
16. Hirway, Indira, "Plan for long term", *The Indian Express* (New Delhi: 2.2.2008) p. 13.
17. Roy, Aruna, "Act on the apathy", *The Indian Express* (New Delhi: 2.2.2008) p. 13.
18. Editorial, "Education and inclusiveness", *The Business Line* (New Delhi: 26.1.2008) p. 8.
19. Reddy, Sangita, "Debate: How can healthcare be made affordable", *The Economic Times* (Kolkata: 13.11.2007) p. 7.
20. Singh, Shubnum, "Debate: How can healthcare be made affordable", *The Economic Times* (Kolkata: 13.11.2007) p. 9.
21. Raja, V., "Debate: How can healthcare be made affordable", *The Economic Times* (Kolkata: 13.11.2007) p. 9.
22. Chandrashekhar, G., "Investment in health, education, a must", *The Business Line* (New Delhi: 21.12.2007) p. 9.
23. Panagariya, Arvind, "The crisis in rural health care", *The Economic Times* (Kolkata: 24.1.2008) p. 8.

# Index

Afforestation, 447, 449
*Aghani* rice, 38
Agrarian economy, 80, 410, 412
Agrarian reforms programmes, 324
Agri-Business Centres (ABCs), 43
Agricultural development, 7–8, 42, 129, 245
Agricultural enterprises, 397–98
Agro-based industries, 44
Agro-climatic zones, 2, 54–55, 62, 75
Agro-forestry, 43
Alcohol, 183–85, 214
Aman paddy, 30, 247, 257, 372
Ambedkar Gram Vikas Yojana, 494
Ambedkar village, 494, 517
Anaemia, 97, 275, 277, 374–75
Anganwadi workers, 160
Animal husbandry, 1, 26, 41, 43, 62–63, 469, 473, 495, 527
Annual Survey of Industries (ASI), 44
Anti-Poverty and Rural Development Schemes, 233, 352, 368
Anti-poverty programmes, 149, 151, 153, 163
Antyodaya Anna Yojana (AAY), 356
Antyodaya beneficiaries, 168
Asian Development Bank, 356
Asoka Mehta Committee, 307
Autonomy, 331, 367–68, 382
Avarata Village, 418, 433, 447, 452, 458, 470, 474, 478, 491, 510
Ayurved Ratna, 434
Azamgarh district, 418, 478, 492, 511, 521

Baburamdih Panchayat, 188
BAES, 250, 253
Bahal land, 110
Balasore plain, 72
Bamboo cultivation, 23
Bamboo Mission and Jatropha cultivation, 23
Banaras Silk and Brocade, 65
Banspal village, 94
Barabanki District, 419, 487, 507, 516
Bargadars, 342, 379–80
Barwatoli, 183–84, 196–98, 202, 207, 214–15, 220–21
Basic amenities, 85–89
Batane Waterbody, 39
Bay of Bengal, 68, 71–72, 74, 117
Below poverty line (BPL), 159, 162, 223, 353, 359, 381
Benami land, 482
Bengal Village Chowkidari Act, 305
Bengal Village Self-Government Act, 306
Bengali gram, 453

Bhoodan land, 481, 484
Bhumidhar, 468, 478
Bihar Economic Survey, 398
Bihar Rajya Beej Nigam, 42
Bihar State Seed Certification Agency (BSSCA), 42
Bio-Gas Scheme, 497
Birbhum, 234, 237–38, 244–47, 249–52, 261–62, 266–67, 282, 286, 291, 293, 295, 303, 338, 363, 370–71, 379–81
Bishnupur village, 96, 130, 141
Black soil, 75, 107, 109, 454
Blacksmithy, 213–14
Block primary health centres (BPHC), 35–36, 272
Bokaro, 226
Boro Paddy cultivation, 247
BPL category, 162
BPL families, 149, 151, 164, 167, 221, 356, 359–60, 382, 470, 491, 494, 503, 505
BPL survey, 221, 408, 441
Brahmani and Mahanadi rivers, 72
Bribing, 475, 518, 528
Buddhism, 70
Budhabalanga rivers, 72
Bundelkhand zone, 54–55
Bureau of Applied Economics and Statistics, 246, 248
Bushy forest patches, 85

Cash crops, 15–16, 62, 106–7, 110, 193, 247, 249, 371, 454
 cultivation of, 62
Cattle grazing, 225
Ceiling Act, 130, 135–36, 476, 481
Ceiling surplus land, 119, 135–36, 342, 344, 402, 476, 478, 481, 500
Centrally Sponsored Scheme, 356
Cereal crops, 16, 60
Chak roads, 446–48, 452, 477, 480–81, 523
Charai village, 186, 194, 206, 209–12
Chhamunda village, 89
Child Education Centres, 295
Chilika Lake, 72
Chirodi village, 428, 434, 476
Christianity, 183, 185
Coastal belt, 74–75, 141
Colonial state, 411, 413
Commercial banks, 40–41, 224–25, 262, 264, 266–68, 373, 464–65, 482, 484, 487
Commercial crops, 23
Common property resources (CPRs), 105, 198–99, 446–49, 452, 477, 480, 488, 523, 529
Community forest land, 449
Community lands, 104, 114, 446, 448, 523
Computerization of land records, 489, 530
Contaminated water, 280, 375
Cooch Behar, 234, 237–38, 244–47, 249–50, 252, 255, 261, 267, 272, 282, 286, 293, 295, 338, 363, 379–81
Co-operative banks, 28, 41, 262, 264, 266
Co-operative societies, 47, 61, 77, 203, 205, 269, 373, 459, 461, 465
Crash Scheme for Rural Employment (CSRE), 353
Credit-cum-subsidy programmes, 165
Credit-deposit ratio, 266
 rural, 264, 373
Crop cultivation, 372
Crop loans, 56, 205, 211, 224, 465
Crop losses, prevention of, 42
Cropped area, 16, 117, 247, 256
Cropping intensity, 24, 30, 103, 246, 249, 370, 460, 525
Cultivable Command Area (CCA), 34
Cultivable land, 15, 33, 103, 105, 126–27, 191, 202, 452, 523
Cultivation, 15, 24, 39–40, 46, 85, 101–4, 106–8, 132, 181, 196, 247, 256–57, 453–54, 456–57, 479–80, 535

Dadan Shramik, 156
Dakshin Dinajpur, 262, 282, 286, 291, 293, 338, 344, 360, 377, 379, 381
Darjeeling Gorkha Hill Council Act, 32–33
Darjeeling, 32, 237–38, 245–46, 249–52, 262, 266–67, 282, 286, 291, 293, 295, 303, 338, 346, 370–71, 380–82
Debt waiver schemes, 47
Degradation, 69–70
Department of Panchayats and Rural Development (DPRD), 359, 381
Dependency ratios, 81–82
Deprivations, 395–96, 399
Desert Development Programme, 355
Development of Women and Children in Rural Areas (DWCRA), 149–50, 153, 217,353, 506
Directive Principles of State Policy, 119, 179
District Administrative Committee, 306
District Central Cooperative Banks (DCCB), 28
District Primary Education Programme, 429
District Rural Development Agencies (DRDAs), 164, 169, 354
Drainage, 169, 280, 436, 446, 477, 507, 520, 523
Drinking water
  facility, 85–88, 90, 297, 425, 429–30
  problem, 156
  sources, 77, 85, 89–90, 169, 280, 354–55, 437–38, 443
  safe potable, 22
Drip irrigation, 535
Dropouts, 91, 94–95, 161, 302–4, 377, 404, 426, 428
Drought Prone Areas Programme, 355
Dumerpani village, 84, 89, 94–95, 99, 105–6, 125, 168–71
Dumka District, 184, 189, 204–5, 223–25
Durgawati Waterbody, 39

Eastern Ghats, 72–73
Electricity connections, 86–91, 446
Electrification, 440, 522, 534
Emergency feeding programmes, 13
Employment Assurance Scheme (EAS), 150, 153, 158, 169, 172–73, 209, 217, 219–20, 354–55, 493–94
Employment generation schemes, 77, 87, 324
Employment Guarantee Scheme (EGS), 158, 544
Eraura village, 408–9
Etah district, 418–19, 481, 500–501, 514
European vegetables, 60

Fair price shops, 89, 159
Family benefit schemes, 492
Farm women, 24
Farm workers, 10, 244, 342, 344, 379
Female education, 95, 424
Female farm workers, 244–45
Female literacy, 48, 91–92, 404
Female workers, 4, 137, 237, 244–45, 346, 350, 369
Female-male wage gap, 352
Fertile lands, 36, 69, 143
Fertilizer consumption, 40, 115, 117, 249–50
Fibre crops, 23, 37
Fisheries Development, 44
Five Year Plan
  First, 56, 365, 421
  Second, 421
  Third, 421
  Fourth, 421
  Sixth, 421
  Seventh, 421
  Eighth, 421–22

Ninth, 421
Eleventh, 22, 25, 29–30, 34, 56, 541
Tenth, 8, 23, 28, 61, 259, 420, 431, 547
Flood plains, 73
Flooding, 75
Food and Agricultural Policy Research Institute (FAPRI), 533
Food and Agriculture Organisation (FAO), 533
Food crops, 15, 62, 247
Food for Work Programme (FWP), 353
Food processing industry, 45
Foodgrains production, 254–55, 371
Forest bureaucracy, 537
Forest ecology, 179
Forest land, 104, 447
Forest Rights Act, 537
Fruit cultivation, 201
Fruit plants, 25
Fruit vendors, 470
Fund utilization, 52, 151–52

Gandhi Jayanti, 517
Ganga Kalyan Yojana (GKY), 150, 353
Gaon Sabha, 476, 487–88, 490, 501, 531
Gender gap, 48, 92, 94
Giridih District, 189, 198, 203, 221, 223
Gochar land, 85, 105
Gorakhpur Kshetriya Gramin Bank, 464
Government functionaries, 160, 518–19
Government land allottees, 476, 481–82, 484
Gram panchayat adhikari, 508–9, 517
Gram panchayat, 36, 157–58, 164, 306, 308, 317, 322, 377, 436, 447, 489, 491–92, 498, 509–15, 530, 532
Gram Pradhans, 492–93, 503, 510–11, 515
Gram Sabha, 164, 166, 169, 221, 306, 311, 490, 501–2, 505, 510–12, 517, 531–32, 544
Gram Samaj land, 442, 446, 474, 523
allotment of, 446, 523
encroachment of, 446, 523
Gram Sansad, 311
Gram Sevak, 497
Gramin Awas, 168, 355
Gramin Banks, 262, 264, 266, 464
Grazing goats, 181
Grazing land, 102, 105, 196, 205, 447–49
Ground water, 34, 69, 200, 354, 436
recharge, 436
Groundnut Farmer's Co-operative, 109
Gulariha Gramin Bank, 495
Gulariha village, 426, 453, 490, 496, 531

Hand pumps, 85, 87, 90, 210–11, 280, 375, 437–38, 441–43, 447, 493, 510
Handloom Cluster Scheme, 47
Harijans, 479
Health Care for Women, 276
Health facilities, 97, 270, 432
Health sub-centres (HSC), 210–11, 272, 374, 405
Healthcare systems, 547–48
Horticultural crops, 25, 60
Human Development Index (HDI), 2
HYV seeds, 38, 111–12, 193, 454, 458–60, 510, 524

IAS probationers, 1, 181, 226, 398, 401, 404, 406–7, 418, 425, 430, 507
Immunization programmes, 99, 435
Immunization, 22, 42, 211, 375, 431–34
Indian Council of Agricultural Research (ICAR), 43
Indira Awas Yojana (IAY), 52, 150–53, 163, 166–168, 219, 221, 354–55, 439, 442, 490, 492–96, 504–5, 509, 522, 531

Indira Mahila Yojana, Recasting of, 366
Industrial development, 395, 411–13
Information Act, 31
Institutional credit agencies, 264, 373
Integrated Child Development Scheme (ICDS), 88–89, 160, 172–73
Integrated Crop Management, 24
Integrated Rural Development Programme (IRDP), 149–50, 153, 197, 206, 219, 223, 353, 357, 463–64, 492, 494, 498, 500–502, 504–5, 508–9, 526
beneficiaries, 204, 489, 492, 494–95, 497–500, 530
loans, 217, 465, 497, 508, 517
Inter-cropping, 257, 372
International Food Policy Research Institute (IFPRI), 533
Irrigation facilities, 11, 24, 38, 75, 103, 107, 109, 113, 192, 195–96, 204, 221, 456–57
Irrigation schemes, 33–34
minor, 34, 413
Irrigation source, 39, 190, 193, 195, 197, 221, 455–56

Jaffarpur Village, 419, 430, 435, 438, 455, 460, 462, 473, 487, 507, 516
Jai Prakash Rozgar Guarantee Yojana (JPRGY), 356
Jainism, 70
Jalpaiguri, 234, 237–38, 245–46, 249–52, 255, 261, 267, 272, 282, 286, 291, 338, 342, 363, 379–80, 382
Janata Personal Accident Insurance Scheme, 56
Jawahar Gram Samriddhi Yojana (JGSY), 150, 164, 169, 354–55, 492, 503, 512, 515
Jawahar Rojgar Yojana (JRY), 149, 153, 163, 217–21, 223, 353–54, 437, 447, 471, 489, 493, 496–98, 501–2, 504–9, 512, 531
Jayad crops, 454
Jetropha cultivation, 62–63
Jiraunia Village, 419, 438, 443, 454, 457, 460, 464, 468, 472, 484, 505, 516
Joint families, 187
Jowar, 453, 455, 523

Kalahandi, 12, 71, 76–77, 83, 138, 153
Keonjhar district, 96, 130
Khadi and Village Industries Commission, 539
Kharif crops, 39, 56, 58–59, 75, 110, 113, 201, 256, 452–54, 481
Khunt-Katti village, 188
Kisan Credit Card (KCC), 28, 56
Kshetra panchayat, 491, 494
Kuchcha houses, 439, 441–43, 521–22
Kurmis, 189, 401, 479

Land alienation, 119, 225–26
Land Ceiling Act, 468
Land degradation, 102, 533
Land fragmentation, 126, 468
Land management, poor, 477, 529
Land ownership pattern, 125, 127
Land redistribution, 117, 121, 324, 344, 380, 413
Land Reforms Act, 478, 481
Land reforms, 29–30, 117–18, 120, 122, 194, 197, 223, 232, 255, 342, 379, 401, 412–13, 481–82, 487–88, 528–30
impact of, 474, 528
legislation, 488, 529
Land revenue, 475, 479, 483, 528
Land use pattern, 103–6, 109, 189, 194, 204
Landholdings distribution of, 465–68, 526
Landless agricultural labourers (LAL), 30, 134–35, 156–57
Landless families, 104, 125–26
Landless households, 124, 135, 197, 205, 449, 465, 468–69, 476, 526–27

Landlessness, 50, 182, 194, 528
Land-man ratio, 16, 30
Landownership, 123, 399, 401
Lateritic zones, 24
Left Front Government (LFG), 231–32, 342, 344, 371, 377, 383
Lekhpal, 475, 477–78, 480, 482, 528–29
Literacy gap, 91–92

Mahanadi rivers, 68, 140
Mahoba district, 455, 460, 523, 525
Maize, 37–39, 108–9, 180, 192, 202–3, 205, 452–55, 461, 523
*Makhana* cultivation, 45
Malhan Bhuiadih village, 188, 199, 209–11, 213, 215, 220
Malnutrition, 96–97, 210, 215, 219
Marginal economic activities, 237–38, 366
Marginal farmers, 16, 25–26, 28, 34, 50, 57, 60–62, 101, 121, 126–27, 147–49, 401, 460, 466–67, 470, 524–26
Marginal workers, 138, 234, 237–39
Marginalisation of employment, 238–39, 369
Marketable surplus, 114, 459, 461–62, 525
Maternity benefit scheme, 490, 492, 532
Mathura district, 434, 437
Mayurbhanj district, 71, 74
Meat, 26, 141, 470
Mechanised Agricultural Farms (MAF), 42
Medium irrigation schemes, 33, 413
Mid-day meal schemes, 94–95, 160–62, 299, 302, 377, 425, 428–30
Midnapore, 234, 237–38, 244, 246–47, 249–52, 255, 262, 266, 273, 282, 338, 342, 346, 363, 376–78, 380
Milch animals, 140, 206, 217, 504
Million Wells Scheme (MWS), 135, 150, 153, 220, 222, 354, 490, 493–94, 509, 531
Minimum Wages Act, 506
Mining activities, 411
Mixed cropping, 110
Model Terminal Markets (MTMs), 43
Mohandi villages, 76
Money wages, 346, 380
Moneylenders, 112, 114, 178, 181, 224–26, 402, 464–65, 472, 487
Mono-cropping, 74, 107–8
Monsoon, 16, 19, 38, 74–75, 112–13, 191, 198, 203, 205, 210
Monthly per capita expenditure (MPCE), 423
Mukhya Mantri Balika Cycle Yojana, 49
Murshidabad, 234, 237–38, 244–47, 249, 251–52, 267, 272, 282, 286, 291, 303, 314, 338, 342, 346, 363–64
Mushroom cultivation, 60
Muslim women, 216

Nabarangpur district, 76, 84, 89
Nakti village, 184, 189, 204–5, 223–25
National Policy for Empowerment of Women, 366
National Rural Employment Guarantee Act (NREGA), 29, 52, 537, 545
National Rural Employment Guarantee Scheme (NREGS), 29, 51, 408, 542–45
National Rural Employment Programme (NREP), 353
National Rural Health Mission (NRHM), 36, 541
Natural calamities, 8, 10, 12, 23, 77
Nichitpur Village, 185–86, 189–90, 192–93, 208–10, 217
Non Government Organizations (NGOs), 169, 171, 183, 503, 519, 540

Non-agricultural labourers, 148, 495, 500, 504
Non-farm activities, 77, 86–87, 203–4, 207, 245, 369, 471, 473, 527
Non-institutional lenders, 268, 373
Non-tribal women, 215
North Koel Waterbody, 39
Nuapada District, 84, 99

Oilseeds, 15, 23, 37, 55, 75, 193, 247, 524
Old Age Pension Scheme, 490, 532
Operation Barga, 324, 328, 342, 344, 379
Operational holdings, 8, 121–23, 126–27, 129, 191, 332, 378–79
Organisation for Economic Co-operation and Development (OECD), 533
Orissa Estates Abolition Act, 118
Orissa Government Land Settlement Act, 134
Orissa Land Reform Act, 118–19, 123, 127
Orissa Land Reforms, 131–32
Orissa Tenancy Act, 119
Orissa Tenants Protection Act, 118
Orissa Tenants Relief Act, 118–19
Ownership cultivation, 104, 114, 125–26

Paddy, 8, 39, 58, 74–75, 105–14, 193, 200, 202–3, 247, 249, 251–52, 256, 370–71, 452–56, 461–62, 523–24
  crop, 105, 108, 198, 205, 456
  cultivation, 8, 75, 106, 110, 201–2, 247, 257, 456
  farmers, 257, 372
Panchayat Act, 310, 331
Panchayat bodies, 29, 31, 34, 36, 308–9, 311
Panchayat functionaries, 31–32, 408
Panchayat ghar, 199, 447–49, 452
Panchayat Samiti, 165, 306, 308–11, 314, 317, 324, 327–28, 354, 377
Panchayat Sewak, 221
Panchayat villages, 519
Panchayati Raj Institutions (PRIs), 2, 164, 310, 324, 327
Panchayati raj system, 232–33, 305, 324, 328, 331, 346, 368, 377
Pani Panchayats, 7, 13
Pasture land, 198, 449, 477, 481
Patrabasa village, 104, 108, 114, 124
Patwari, 515
PDS shops, 269, 373, 439, 441, 521
Pesticides, 59, 61, 111, 136, 203, 458, 460–61, 479, 484, 510, 524
Peyajal Yojana, 492
Planning Commission, 34, 69, 128, 146, 259, 354, 359, 365, 367, 542
Plant root zones, 535
Plantation crops, 132
Ploughing, 111, 141, 207, 458, 460, 475, 479, 525
Potable water supply, 100
Poverty alleviation programmes, 142, 149, 151–52, 172, 217, 399, 407, 409, 439, 441, 463, 489, 491, 494, 497–98, 526
  impact of, 489, 491, 530
  physical performances of, 152
  sponsored, 150
Poverty alleviation strategies, 63
Poverty gap, 145–46
Poverty line, 12, 29, 52, 69, 145–49, 153, 162, 168–69, 216, 220, 353–55, 359–60, 438–39, 441–43, 502–3, 520–21
Poverty reduction, 11, 143, 153
Pradhan Mantri Gram Sadak Yojana (PMGSY), 356
Pradhan Mantri Gramodaya Yojana (PMGY), 355
Pratap Pur village, 189, 198, 221, 223
Primary Agricultural Credit Societies (PACS), 28–29, 225, 262, 373, 463–65, 526
Primary Health Centres (PHCs), 35–36, 49, 64, 98–99, 210, 272–73, 432–35

Public Distribution System (PDS), 63, 158–59, 166, 172–73, 269, 439, 441, 507–8, 521, 548
*Pucca* houses, 439, 441–43, 521
Pulses, 15, 22–23, 33, 37–38, 55, 58, 75, 100, 109–10, 193, 202–3, 205, 453–54, 524
Pump sets, 113, 456–57, 500, 506
Purulia, 234, 237–39, 244–47, 249–52, 260, 262, 267, 282, 286, 291, 293, 295, 303, 363, 370, 381–82

Rabi crops, 39, 59, 113, 180, 205, 249, 453–54, 481
Rabi season, 38, 40, 58–59, 109, 114, 202, 452–53
Rain shadow pockets, 100
Rainwater, 108, 181, 220
Raiyats, 118–19, 130–31, 135
Ram Krishna Mission, 183
Regional rural banks, 40–41
Reserve Bank of India, 543
Reserve forest, 33, 85
Revamped Public Distribution System (RPDS), 158
Revised Long Term Action Plan (RLTAP), 12
Rice beer, 182
Rice puff, 208
Rice-based cropping system, 23
River basins, 18–19, 39, 69
River valleys, 102
Rural development, 2, 29, 32, 172–73, 216, 219, 259, 307, 381, 422, 533, 545
Rural Drinking Water Project, 355
Rural electrification, 259–61, 355, 372, 440, 522
Rural hospitals, 272, 374
Rural Landless Employment Guarantee Programme (RLEGP ), 353
Rural literacy rate, 281–82, 376
Rural Manpower Programme, 353
Rural Wage Employment Schemes, 358
Rural Works Programme (RWP), 353
Rushikulya River, 71–72

Salebidi village, 76, 103, 109, 124, 135
Sampoorna Gramin Rozgar Yojana (SGRY), 13, 29, 150–52, 169, 355
Sanitary facilities, 436, 520
Sanitation, 2, 21, 96–97, 99, 210, 421, 436, 438, 440, 520, 522
Sapmundi Village, 125
Sarada lands, 75
Seed Multiplication Farms (SMF), 40, 42
Seed Replacement Rate (SRR), 39, 42, 58
Seledi village, 105, 140, 166–67
Self Help Groups (SHGs), 6, 13, 27–29, 36, 51, 53, 62–63, 150, 164–65, 167, 170–71, 365–66, 383, 489, 491, 530
Self-cultivation, 135, 141, 197
Self-employment schemes, 352–53, 357–58, 381
Share cropping, 128, 130, 136, 191, 197, 224, 401, 474–75, 479, 483, 485, 528
Shifting cultivation, 102, 104, 110
Sishu Siksha Kendra (SSK), 295, 297, 304, 376–77
Smokeless chulha schemes, 509
Social assistance schemes, 149
Social forestry, 30, 219
Social welfare schemes, 490, 503, 532
Sodic Land Reclamation Project, 63
Sonepur district, 90, 105
Special Area Development Programmes, 12
Special Area Programmes, 32
Special nutrition programmes, 13
Special Programmes for Rural Development, 29

Staple crops, 213
State Finance Commission, 513, 515
Sterilisation, 41–42
Sthayee Samitis, 308–9
Student-teacher ratio, 93, 291, 293, 295, 376
Subarnarekha river, 71
Sugarcane cultivation, 452, 455, 523–24
Sunischit Rozgar Yojana (SRY), 489, 491, 509, 531
Supply of Improved Tool-kit to Rural Artisans (SITRA), 149–50, 153, 353
Surplus lands, 119, 130, 133–36, 194, 402, 474, 476
Swarnajayanti Grameen Swarozgar Yojana (SGSY), 13, 51, 62–63, 142, 150–51, 153, 164–65, 169–70, 353, 357, 409, 489, 491, 503, 530
Swarnarekha river, 197
Swarozgaris, 150, 153, 164–65, 408–9

Taljhiri village, 84, 90, 94, 98–99, 109, 127
Task Force on Women, 365
Tax revenue, 421, 539
Tenancy
    agreement, 483–84
    cultivation, 125, 338, 379
    practice, 126–28, 130
    reforms, 117–18
Tikamau village, 418, 442, 448, 453, 456, 459–61, 464, 467, 498, 525
Tomato cultivation, 213
Tool Kit Scheme, 490, 506, 531
Training Centre for Women, 496
Training of Rural Youth for Self-Employment (TRYSEM), 149–50, 153, 219, 353, 494, 496–97, 501–2, 506, 509
Tribal
    communities, 27, 130, 140, 177, 179, 187, 216
    economy, 176–77, 179, 226
    land, 198, 225–26, 484
    societies, 84, 177–78, 184, 215
    villages, 98, 202
    women, 94, 96, 215–16
Trinamul Congress (TMC), 314, 378
Tube wells, 87, 90, 280, 524
Tuffed rice, 208

UN World Water Development Report, 536
Under-employment, 4, 10, 33
Unnat Chulha Programme, 492
Unnayan scheme, 49
Uthan Kendra scheme, 48

Vaccination, 276, 375, 431–32
Vana Samrakshana Samitis (VSS), 13
Vegetable crops, 192–93
Vegetable seeds, 25
Vegetable sellers, 470
Vested Land, 344
Village Development Committees (VDCs), 331
Village economy, 103–4
Village industries, 208, 500
Village lekhpal, 448–49
Village Level Worker, 157, 502
Village panchayats, 306, 501, 514

Wage employment, 30, 63, 156–57, 168–69, 219, 352, 354, 357, 381, 492–93
Water Conservations, 30, 43, 355
Water drainage, 39
Water logging, 102, 446, 452, 455, 523
Water resources Schemes, 34
Water stagnation, 90
Water table, 190–91
Watersheds, 13, 73, 354, 456, 544
Welfare schemes, 47, 162
West Bengal Panchayat Act, 34, 306–8

West Bengal State Co-operative Bank Ltd. 27
West Bengal Zilla Parishads Act, 306
Women beneficiaries, 495, 500
Women labourers, 219, 498
Women's Empowerment Year, 366
Work Participation Ratio (WPR), 50
Worker-population ratio, 234, 237–38
World Bank, 173–74, 356, 536
World Development Report, 173

Yadavs, 401
Yuvak Mangal Dal, 510

Zamindari Abolition and Land Reforms Act, 447, 478–82
Zamindari abolition bill, 402
Zari-zardosi, 65
Zila Swasthya Samitis, 100
Zilla Parishads, 165, 259, 306, 308–11, 354, 377